Contracts

MELVIN A. EISENBERG
University of California, Berkeley

SHAWN BAYERN
Florida State University

Fifteenth Edition

The publisher is not engaged in rendering legal or other professional advice, and this publication is not a substitute for the advice of an attorney. If you require legal or other expert advice, you should seek the services of a competent attorney or other professional.

Gilbert Law Summaries is a trademark registered in the U.S. Patent and Trademark Office

Copyright © 2002 by Thomson/West
© 2021 LEG, Inc. d/b/a West Academic
    444 Cedar Street, Suite 700
    St. Paul, MN 55101
    1-877-888-1330

West, West Academic Publishing, and West Academic are trademarks of West Publishing Corporation, used under license.

Printed in the United States of America

ISBN: 978-0-314-27619-3

Summary of Contents

CAPSULE SUMMARY V

APPROACH TO EXAMS LXIII

ISSUE SPOTTING IN CONTRACTS LXVII

INTRODUCTION—SOURCES OF CONTRACT LAW LXIX

Chapter One. Consideration 1
- A. Introduction 3
- B. Bargain Promises 5
- C. Accord and Satisfaction 38
- D. Waiver 42
- E. Unrelied-Upon Donative Promises 43
- F. Relied-Upon Donative Promises—Doctrine of Promissory Estoppel 46
- G. Moral or Past Consideration 48

Chapter Two. Mutual Assent—Offer and Acceptance 53
- A. Mutual Assent 55
- B. Offers 58
- C. Acceptance 89
- D. Time at Which Communications Between Offeror and Offeree Become Effective 104
- E. Interpretation 114
- F. The Parol Evidence Rule 118
- G. "Shrinkwrap" Contracts 129
- H. Online Contracting 130

Chapter Three. Defenses 133
- A. Indefiniteness 135
- B. Mistake 147
- C. Contracts Induced by Misrepresentation, Nondisclosure, Duress, or Undue Influence 154
- D. Unconscionability 157
- E. Statute of Frauds 162
- F. Lack of Contractual Capacity 172
- G. Illegal Contracts 174

Chapter Four. Third-Party Rights and Obligations 177
- A. Third-Party Beneficiaries 178
- B. Assignment of Rights and Delegation of Duties 191

Chapter Five. Performance and Breach 213
- A. Obligation to Perform in Good Faith 214
- B. Express Conditions 216
- C. Implied Conditions 226
- D. Order of Performance 227
- E. Doctrine of Substantial Performance 231
- F. Divisible Contracts 234
- G. Material vs. Minor Breach 235
- H. Anticipatory Breach 238
- I. Changed Circumstances—Impossibility, Impracticability, and Frustration 241
- J. Discharge 245

Chapter Six. Remedies 249
    A. Introduction 251
    B. Basic Measures of Damages.. 251
    C. Expectation Damages—General Limitations... 252
    D. Specific Performance—General Principles 256
    E. Expectation Damages and Specific Performance—Applied to Factual Contexts 256
    F. Nominal Damages 265
    G. Liquidated Damages 265
    H. Punitive Damages 267
    I. Damages for Emotional Distress 267
    J. Restitutionary Damages.. 268

EXAM QUESTIONS AND ANSWERS 271

REVIEW QUESTIONS AND ANSWERS 285

TABLE OF CASES 331

TABLE OF U.C.C. SECTIONS 335

TABLE OF RESTATEMENTS 337

INDEX 339

Capsule Summary

I. CONSIDERATION

A. INTRODUCTION

Generally, a promise is not enforceable unless it is supported by consideration. Early theories described consideration as a benefit received by the promisor or a detriment incurred by the promisee. Today, most authorities treat consideration as equivalent to *"bargain"* (*i.e.*, an exchange of promises, acts, or both, in which each party views what they give as the *price* for what they get). However, the bargain approach does not explain all situations where promises are enforceable (*e.g.*, detrimental reliance), and so some authorities treat as consideration *any factor* that will make a promise or contract enforceable.

B. BARGAIN PROMISES

1. General Rule—Bargain Constitutes Consideration

As a general rule, a bargain constitutes consideration. The law usually does not require bargained-for promises to be of equal value, but gross disparity may be used as *evidence* of defenses such as unconscionability, incapacity, fraud, and duress. Also, adequacy of consideration may be reviewed if an *equitable remedy* such as specific performance is sought.

2. Exceptions—Bargains That Are Not Consideration

a. Nominal consideration

A contract based on nominal consideration will fail for lack of consideration. A transaction involves nominal consideration if it has the *form* of a bargain but *lacks the substance* of a bargain; *i.e.*, no real bargain exists. For example, a promise to pay $1 for a house worth $100,000 is likely to be nominal consideration.

(1) Exception—options and guaranties

Under the majority view, nominal consideration will make an *option* enforceable if the option is *in writing and proposes fair terms*. Similarly, under the majority view, nominal consideration makes a *written guaranty* binding. These transactions are usually enforceable because they serve an important commercial purpose and are likely to be relied on.

b. Promises to surrender or forbear from asserting a legal claim

The modern rule is that a bargained-for promise to surrender or forbear from asserting a legal claim (or the actual surrender or forbearance) is deemed consideration if the promisor's belief in the claim's validity is *honest or reasonable*. Some authorities hold that a *written release* may constitute consideration even *without* an honest or reasonable belief in the claim.

c. Illusory promises

(1) General rule for bargains

A *bilateral contract* is a bargain contract in which the parties exchange a *promise for a promise* (*e.g.*, A promises to wash B's car in exchange for B's promise to pay $10).

(a) Effect of illusory promise

Under the traditional rule, if one party makes an *illusory* promise (a statement in the form but not the substance of a promise) in exchange for the other party's *real* promise, the illusory promise does not constitute consideration and *neither party is bound*. For example, a promise coupled with the power to terminate the obligation at will and without notice is illusory. This rule is disfavored (because it often puts form over substance) and has many exceptions.

(2) Exceptions to the mutuality rule

(a) Unilateral contracts

The rule of mutuality is *not* applicable to a unilateral contract (a contract in which a promise is given in exchange for an act).

(b) Slight consideration found

Promises that limit the promisor's options in *any way*—no matter how slight—are real and are consideration. For example, a promise coupled with the power to terminate the obligation at will with 2 days' notice is not illusory, because the promisor must give advance notice of termination and is bound at least until then.

(c) Voidable promises

An otherwise real promise is not illusory merely because it is voidable by one party *as a matter of law* (*e.g.*, a promise by a minor).

(d) Conditional promises

A promise that the promisor need only perform if a specified condition occurs is *not* illusory, because the promisor has limited their future options.

(e) Alternative promises

If the promisor reserves the right to discharge their obligation by choosing between two or more alternatives, there is consideration only if *each* alternative would be sufficient consideration if bargained for alone. If the *promisee* can choose one of several alternative promises from the promisor, consideration exists if *any* of the alternatives would be sufficient consideration if bargained for alone.

(f) Agreements allowing one party to supply a material term

At *common law,* such a promise is *illusory.* However, where one party has the power to *alter or modify* contract terms, many authorities hold that the promise is *not* illusory because the power is subject to the obligation to *perform in good faith*. Note that even the power to *supply* (rather than vary) a material term is not illusory if the term must be fixed in relation to an *objective measure* (*e.g.*, market price).

1) U.C.C. provisions

U.C.C. section 1–203 imposes a general obligation of *good faith* on all parties to a contract for the sale of goods. Thus, a contract for the sale of goods that gives one party the right to set a term contains consideration because the party must set the term in good faith. Furthermore, U.C.C. section 2–305(1) explicitly provides that the right to *set a price* in such a contract is enforceable if the parties so intend.

(g) Implied promises

A promise is real rather than illusory if it contains an implied promise, in fact or in law, that constitutes a real promise. A common type of implied promise involves a promise to use ***reasonable or best efforts*** to perform (rule of *Wood v. Lucy, Lady Duff-Gordon*).

1) U.C.C. in accord

The U.C.C. codifies the rule in *Wood* by providing that, unless otherwise agreed, a lawful agreement for exclusive dealing in ***goods*** imposes an implied obligation by the seller to use best efforts to supply the goods and by the buyer to use best efforts to promote their sale.

(h) Requirements and output contracts

Modern courts and the U.C.C. usually enforce these contracts because the party who determines quantity has limited their choice and thus made a real promise: if they ***buy or sell at all***, they must buy from or sell to the other party. Under the U.C.C., the quantity of the output or requirements must be provided in good faith and must not be unreasonably disproportionate to any stated estimate.

d. Legal duty rule—promise to perform act promisor already obliged to perform

The promise or performance of an act that the promisor has a preexisting legal duty to perform does not constitute consideration. This is commonly known as the ***legal duty rule***.

(1) Preexisting public duties

If an ***official's*** promised performance is ***within the scope of official duties***, neither the promise nor the performance thereof is legally sufficient consideration. Performance of a ***public duty required by law*** other than an official duty (*e.g.*, jury service) is treated similarly.

(2) Preexisting contractual duties

Generally, ***neither*** a promise to perform a preexisting contractual duty ***nor*** the performance of the duty is consideration. This rule covers the two following types of cases.

(a) Performance of preexisting contractual duty for increased payment

Where *A* and *B* have a contract and *A* refuses to perform unless *B* pays more than originally promised, *A*'s new promise to perform (or *A*'s performance) does not constitute consideration for *B*'s promise to pay a greater amount than originally promised. However, courts do not favor this rule, and the following ***exceptions*** have emerged.

1) Promise of different performance

Consideration exists if a party promises to perform an act similar to, but different from, the action they were contractually obliged to perform. Even a ***slight difference*** will be sufficient.

2) Preexisting duty owed to third party

Most authorities recognize the existence of consideration if a party owes a preexisting contractual duty to someone other than the party who makes the new promise. And nearly all authorities recognize an exception where a third party's promise runs to the two original contracting parties *jointly*.

3) Defense under original contract

If a party had a valid defense to performing under the original contract, the new promise to perform is sufficient consideration.

4) Modification—unanticipated circumstances

Under modern law, a new promise to pay is enforceable if unanticipated circumstances arise that make modification of the original contract terms *fair and equitable*.

5) Modification—sale of goods

The U.C.C. *does not require consideration* to make binding modifications to contracts for the sale of goods. However, the modifications must be sought in *good faith*.

6) Writing as substitute for consideration

A few state statutes provide that a contract may be modified by a subsequent *written* contract with *no new consideration*.

7) Mutual rescission

A few courts get around the legal duty rule by applying the fiction that the parties *mutually rescinded* the original contract and formed a new one.

8) Effect of performance

The legal duty rule is a defense to an action to enforce a contract; if the contract has been fully performed, neither party can use the legal duty rule to recover what it paid unless the party seeking to recover performed under *economic duress* (an *improper* threat leaving no reasonable alternative can constitute economic duress).

(b) Payment of lesser amount as discharge of debtor's full obligation

Generally, a promise by a debtor to pay less than the full amount owed to a creditor in exchange for the creditor's agreement to accept the lesser amount in full satisfaction or discharge of the entire debt is *not* consideration, and the creditor's promise to accept the lesser amount is not enforceable. *Exceptions* to this rule follow.

1) Different performance

The general rule is inapplicable if the debtor does something different from what they were obliged to do (*e.g.*, makes early payment).

2) Honest dispute

If there is an honest dispute as to whether a lesser amount is owed, payment of the lesser amount is consideration for the creditor's discharge in full.

3) Unliquidated obligations

If the amount owed is unliquidated (uncertain), a debtor's payment of the lesser amount is consideration for a creditor's discharge in full even if the debtor pays no more than they *admittedly* owe. However, if the debtor owes the creditor two *separate debts*, one liquidated and one not, payment of the liquidated obligation will not serve as consideration for the creditor's agreement to discharge the unliquidated obligation.

4) Composition of creditors

When a composition of creditors releases a debtor in full in exchange for part payment to each creditor, consideration may be found in the *creditors' mutual agreement* to accept lesser sums. The debtor may be able to enforce the composition agreement as a third-party beneficiary.

5) Agreement not to file for bankruptcy

If a creditor's purpose in discharging a debt in exchange for a lesser sum is to induce the debtor not to file for bankruptcy, consideration exists.

6) Written release

Statutes in several states provide that a written release by a creditor extinguishes the original debt.

7) Executory contracts

Some authorities hold that an agreement to accept lesser payments in a contract involving periodic payments is enforceable to the extent that the agreement is *executed, i.e.*, as to those periodic payments already made and accepted. Other authorities *permit* recovery of the shortfalls of prior periodic payments.

8) Full-payment checks

At *common law*, cashing a full-payment check (*i.e.*, a check that claims to be tendered in full payment of the creditor's obligation but that is for an amount less than the creditor claims is owed) constituted an accord and satisfaction that discharged the entire debt. Under U.C.C. section 3–311, cashing a full-payment check generally discharges a creditor's entire claim provided: (i) the check is tendered to the creditor *in good faith*, (ii) the check or an accompanying writing contains a *conspicuous statement* concerning full payment, and (iii) either a *bona fide dispute* exists as to the amount owed or the claim is *unliquidated*.

C. ACCORD AND SATISFACTION

1. Accord Defined

An accord is an agreement in which one party to an existing contract agrees to accept some performance other than the one to which the other party originally agreed.

2. "Satisfaction" Defined

A satisfaction is the performance of the accord by the promisor, the *effect* of which is to discharge both the accord and the original contractual duty.

3. "Executory Accord" Defined

An accord that has not yet been satisfied is an executory accord. Under the traditional rule, an executory accord is *not enforceable*. However, the traditional rule is usually ineffective in *modern practice* due to many *distinctions and exceptions*:

a. Substituted contract

An executory accord may be treated as a substituted contract that immediately discharges the original contract if the parties so intend. Such intent is most easily found if the duty under the original contract was *disputed,* was *unliquidated,* had not *matured,* and did not involve the *payment of money*.

b. Where executory accord is not a substituted contract

Even if an executory accord is not treated as a substituted contract and thus does not *discharge* the original contract, the executory accord still has three important effects:

(1) It *suspends the promisee's rights under the original contract* during the period in which the promisor is to perform the accord;

(2) If the promisor fails to perform the executory accord, the *promisee can sue under either the original contract or the accord*; and

(3) If the promisor *tenders performance* of an executory accord and the promisee *refuses* to accept the performance, under some authorities the promisor can either *enjoin* the promisee from bringing suit or can *sue* the promisee for damages for breach of the executory accord.

D. WAIVER

1. Definition

A waiver occurs when a party to an existing contract promises to perform even though some contractual *condition* to their obligation to perform has not occurred.

2. Enforceability

A waiver is enforceable if it is given for *separate consideration or* if (i) the waived condition was *not a material part* of the agreed upon exchange *and* (ii) the uncertainty of the occurrence of the condition was *not a risk assumed* by the party who gave the waiver.

3. Retraction

An otherwise enforceable waiver can be retracted if: (i) the waiver was *not given for separate consideration*; (ii) the other party has not changed position in *reliance* on the waiver; (iii) the waiver relates to a condition to be fulfilled by the *other contracting party* (not by a third party); *and* (iv) the retraction occurs *before* the time that the waived condition was supposed to occur, and *notice* of the intention to retract was given within a reasonable time for performance (or a *reasonable extension of time* was given).

E. UNRELIED-UPON DONATIVE PROMISES

1. General Rule

A donative promise to make a gift is generally *unenforceable* for lack of consideration *unless:* (i) it is *relied upon*, (ii) it is *compensation* for a previously conferred material benefit that created a moral obligation (under the modern rule), or (iii) in some states, it is under seal.

a. Exception

Charitable subscriptions (*i.e.*, pledges to support a *charity*) are often binding without consideration on the theory that reliance is *presumed*. "Marriage settlements" may also be enforceable without consideration.

2. Effect of a Seal

At common law, a seal made a donative promise enforceable. However, today most states have *statutorily abolished* the binding effect of the seal.

3. Effect of Writing

A writing does *not* make a donative promise enforceable at common law. However, a few state statutes provide that a donative promise in writing is *presumed* to have been given for consideration.

4. Nominal Consideration

Although not unanimous, the prevailing modern view is that nominal consideration (*i.e.*, where the parties falsely put their agreement in the form of a bargain) will *not* make a donative promise enforceable.

5. Conditional Donative Promise

A conditional donative promise exists when some condition must be met before the gift is made (*e.g.*, "If you come to my house, I will give you my old television set"). It is no more enforceable than any other donative promise, even if the condition has been satisfied.

a. Conditional donative promise vs. bargain promise

The test for which of these categories a promise falls into is the manner in which the *parties view* the condition. If the condition is viewed as a *technical requirement for making the gift*, the promise is donative. However, if performance of the condition is viewed as the *price* of the promise, there is a bargain.

F. RELIED-UPON DONATIVE PROMISES—DOCTRINE OF PROMISSORY ESTOPPEL

1. Modern Rule

If a donative promise *induces reliance* by the promisee in a manner the promisor should reasonably have expected, the promise is *enforceable*—at least to the extent of the reliance. This is known as the principle of *promissory estoppel*.

2. Reliance as Consideration

Some authorities (*e.g.*, Rest. 2d) treat "consideration" as equivalent to "bargain"; thus, a relied-upon promise is enforceable *despite* the lack of consideration. However, others view promissory estoppel as simply a type of consideration. The *result* is the same under either view.

G. MORAL OR PAST CONSIDERATION

1. Definition

A promise is given for moral or past consideration when the promisor seeks to discharge a *moral* (but not *legal*) obligation owed to the promisee and created by some *past event*.

2. Traditional Rule

Under the traditional rule, a promise based on moral or past consideration is *unenforceable*.

3. **Core Exceptions**

   a. **Promise to pay debt barred by the statute of limitations**

   Such a promise is enforceable despite the absence of new consideration. However, it is the *new* promise, not the old debt, that is enforceable.

   (1) **Effect of acknowledgment or part payment**

   Generally, a promise will be *implied* from an unqualified acknowledgment of the debt or from a part payment of it.

   (2) **Requirement of a writing**

   Most state statutes require such a promise either to be in writing *or* to be partially performed (part payment) to be enforceable.

   (3) **New promise made before statute runs**

   The above rules also generally apply if a new promise, acknowledgment, or part payment is made before the statute of limitations has run; the limitations period on the new promise will run from the date of the *new promise*.

   b. **Promise to perform a voidable obligation**

   A new promise to perform an obligation that is voidable (*e.g.*, by reason of fraud or infancy) is enforceable despite the absence of new consideration as long as the *new* promise is not subject to the same defense as the original obligation.

   c. **Promise to pay a debt discharged by bankruptcy**

   This was generally treated under contract law like a promise to pay a debt barred by the statute of limitations. However, today the ***Bankruptcy Code*** places a number of conditions on such promises.

4. **Modern Rule—Promise to Pay Moral Obligation Arising out of Past Economic Benefit to Promisor**

   The emerging rule is that, even if a core exception to the traditional rule does not apply, such a promise is ***enforceable***, at least up to the value of the benefit conferred, *if* the promise is based on a ***benefit*** (usually economic) previously conferred on the promisor that gave rise to an obligation (even if only moral) to make compensation.

   a. **Gratuitous benefits**

   If the past benefit was conferred as a gift, even the modern authorities would not enforce the promise because a *gift* does not create a moral obligation to repay.

   b. **Promise based on expense incurred by promisee**

   Even under the modern view, such promises generally are unenforceable if the promisor did *not* receive a *material* (*i.e.*, economic) *benefit*—even if the promisee incurred expenses.

5. **Promise to Pay Fixed Amount in Liquidation of a Legal Obligation**

   A promise to pay a fixed amount in liquidation of an unliquidated *legal* obligation is consideration if the *promisee accepts* the promise.

II. MUTUAL ASSENT—OFFER AND ACCEPTANCE

A. MUTUAL ASSENT

1. **Objective Theory of Contracts**

   A contract is formed by *mutual assent* of the parties. In determining whether the parties have mutually assented to a contract, one should generally use the *objective* theory of contracts (*i.e.*, determine what a ***reasonable person*** to whom an expression has been addressed would understand the expression to mean). The objective theory operates to ***protect the parties' reasonable expectations*** by permitting each party to rely on the other's ***manifested*** intentions. However, subjective intent is still part of the interpretive inquiry in some cases (*see infra*, pp. 114–115).

2. **Express and Implied Contracts**

   a. **Express contracts**

   In an express contract, mutual assent is manifested in ***words of agreement***, oral or written.

   b. **Implied contracts**

   (1) **Implied-in-fact contracts**

   If the promises of the parties are inferred from their acts or conduct, or from words that are not explicit words of agreement, the contract is implied in fact.

   (2) **Implied-in-law contracts**

   These are cases where a court ***fictionally*** implies a promise to pay for benefits or services to avoid inequities and unjust enrichment (also known as ***quasi-contracts***).

B. **OFFERS**

1. **Legal Significance of an Offer**

   An offer creates a ***power of acceptance*** in the offeree (*i.e.*, the power to ***conclude a bargain*** and ***bind*** the offeror by giving assent).

2. **What Constitutes an Offer**

   An offer is a manifestation of ***present willingness to enter into a bargain***, made in such a way that a reasonable person in the position of the person to whom it is addressed would believe that they could ***conclude the bargain*** merely by giving their assent—*i.e.*, by accepting the offer.

   a. **Essential elements**

   (1) **Intent to enter into a bargain**

   Offers must be distinguished from invitations to begin or continue negotiations. An intent to make an offer is reflected by language and the surrounding circumstances of the statement.

   (2) **Definiteness of terms**

   A statement usually will ***not*** be considered an offer ***unless*** it makes clear the ***subject matter*** of the proposed bargain, the ***quantity*** involved, and the ***price***.

   (a) **Intent determinative**

   Even if an important term is omitted, a statement can still be construed as an offer if (i) the statement otherwise evidences an intent to conclude a bargain, (ii) the omission does not indicate a lack of intent to conclude a bargain, ***and*** (iii) the court can fill in the missing term by implication.

   b. **Special rules**

   (1) **Advertisements**

   Advertisements are generally deemed to be ***invitations to deal*** rather than offers. However, a ***particular*** advertisement may be construed as an offer if it is definite in its terms and either (i) the circumstances clearly indicate an intention to make a bargain, (ii) the advertisement invites those to whom it is addressed to take specific action without further communication, or (iii) overacceptance is unlikely.

(a) Rewards

An advertisement for a reward is normally construed as an offer.

(2) Offering circulars

These are normally construed as *invitations to deal* rather than offers. However, they may be interpreted as offers if a reasonable person in the position of the addressee would think the communication had been addressed to them *individually* rather than as one of a *number of recipients*.

(3) Auctions

(a) Auction with reserve

An auctioneer's call for bids (putting an item *"on the block"*) is considered an invitation to make offers. A *bid* by a member of the audience is an *offer,* which can be accepted by the auctioneer's "hammering it down" or discharged by a new bid. The auctioneer can withdraw the goods at any time prior to having "hammered down" a particular bid.

(b) Auction without reserve

Same as an auction with reserve, except that once the auctioneer calls for bids, the goods *cannot* be withdrawn unless no bid is made within a reasonable time.

(c) Determining whether auction is with or without reserve

An auction is deemed to be with reserve unless otherwise stated.

(4) Putting contracts out for bid

Putting a contract out for bid usually is not deemed to be an offer, but the responding bids usually are considered offers. However, the language and circumstances may result in different interpretations; *e.g.*, a bid might be interpreted as only an invitation to deal.

3. Termination of Power of Acceptance

The termination of the offeree's power of acceptance may result from any of the following causes:

a. Expiration or lapse

This is the most common means of terminating an offer.

(1) If time for acceptance is fixed in the offer

In this situation (*e.g.*, "Acceptance must be in 10 days"), the offeree's power of acceptance lapses at the end of the stated period without any further action by the offeror. Usually, the stated period runs from the time the offer was *received*.

(2) If no time for acceptance is fixed in the offer

In this situation, the offeree's power of acceptance lapses after the expiration of a *reasonable time,* which depends on the circumstances (*e.g.*, subject matter of offer, medium through which made, etc.). When the parties bargain *face to face or by telephone*, the time for acceptance ordinarily does not extend beyond the conversation unless otherwise indicated. Acceptance of an offer sent *by mail* is timely if mailed by midnight on the day of receipt, or within a reasonable time depending on the circumstances.

b. Rejection by the offeree

The offeree's rejection of the offer terminates the offeree's power of acceptance even though the power of acceptance would not *otherwise* have lapsed.

(1) Exception for options

Some courts hold that an offeree's rejection during the option period does not terminate their power of acceptance because they has a *contractual right* to have the offer held open during its term. However, this rule does not apply if the offeror *relies* on the rejection.

c. Counteroffer

A counteroffer by the offeree (*i.e.*, an offer by the offeree concerning the same subject matter but containing different terms than the original offer) terminates the power of acceptance. However, because a counteroffer is also an offer, it creates a new power of acceptance in the original *offeror*.

(1) Distinguish—inquiries and requests

The offeree's power of acceptance is *not* terminated by an inquiry regarding the offer or by a request for different terms. The *test* for distinguishing between a counteroffer and an inquiry or a request is whether a reasonable person would believe the offeree's communication was *itself an offer* inviting acceptance.

(2) Exception for options

A counteroffer made during the option period does *not* terminate the offeree's power of acceptance under an option because the offeree has a *contractual right* to have the offer held open during the term of the option.

d. Conditional or qualified acceptance

This is a purported acceptance that *adds to or changes* the terms of the offer.

(1) Legal effect—general rule

Except in sale-of-goods contracts (*infra*, p. 71 *et seq.*), a conditional or qualified acceptance is deemed to be a counteroffer. Therefore, it (i) *terminates* the offeree's power of acceptance and (ii) is *itself* treated as an offer that the original offeror can accept.

(2) Exceptions to general rule

(a) Requests accompanying acceptance

An unconditional acceptance coupled with a *request* does not terminate an offeree's power of acceptance and instead *forms a contract*.

(b) "Grumbling" acceptances

A grumbling acceptance does not constitute a rejection and instead *forms a contract* if the expression of dissatisfaction or protest *stops short of actual dissent*.

(c) Implied terms

An acceptance that is conditional or qualified in *form*, but that in *substance* merely spells out an implied term of the offer, does not terminate the offeree's power of acceptance; a contract is formed.

(3) Common law mirror image rule

At common law, an acceptance had to mirror the terms of the offer exactly; any deviation made the putative acceptance a *counteroffer*.

(a) Last shot rule and form contracts

Typically, merchant sellers and merchant buyers use preprinted form contracts with individualized (*e.g.*, typed-in) terms. While the individualized terms may agree, the preprinted terms may not. Under the mirror image rule, if the parties' preprinted forms did not match, so that no contract was thereby formed, but the parties performed anyway, the courts would treat the last form sent as a *counteroffer* and the other party's *performance* as an *acceptance* of the counteroffer. Thus, the terms of the counteroffer would govern the contract. This was known as "the last shot rule."

(4) U.C.C. rule

The U.C.C. changes the mirror image rule concerning *sale-of-goods* contracts so that "a definite and seasonable expression of acceptance or a written confirmation that is sent within a reasonable time operates as an acceptance *even though it states terms additional to or different from those offered or agreed upon,* unless acceptance is *expressly* made conditional on *assent* to the additional or different terms."

(a) Acceptance "expressly made conditional"

If acceptance is expressly made conditional on the offeror's assent to additional or different terms, *no contract arises*. However, if the goods are delivered and accepted, the *parties' performance establishes a contract*. The terms of the contract would then consist of the written terms on which the parties agreed, plus any supplemental terms provided by the U.C.C. Courts are reluctant to find a conditional assent unless it tracks the language of the U.C.C.

(b) Effect of additional terms

Unless both parties to a contract are *merchants* (*i.e.*, persons who deal in the kind of goods sold or who otherwise hold themselves out as having knowledge or skill peculiar to the practices or goods involved in the transaction), additional terms in the acceptance are construed as *proposals* for additions to the contract that the offeror may agree to or ignore. However, if the parties are *both merchants*, the proposed terms *become part of the contract unless* (i) the offer *expressly limits* acceptance to the terms of the offer; (ii) the additional terms would *materially alter* the contract; or (iii) the offeror notifies the offeree within a reasonable time that they *object* to the additional terms.

(c) Effect of different terms

Different terms (*i.e.*, terms that contradict rather than add to the terms of the offer) do *not* automatically become part of the contract.

1) Knockout rule

Under the majority knockout rule, conflicting terms in both the offer and the acceptance drop out, and the contract consists of the *agreed-upon terms* plus terms supplied by the U.C.C. to replace the conflicting terms.

2) **Minority views**

One minority view treats different terms *like additional terms*; under another minority view, different terms in the acceptance always drop out, and thus the *terms of the offer govern*.

e. **Termination by revocation**

A revocation (*i.e.*, an offeror's retraction of an offer) normally terminates the offeree's power of acceptance, provided that the offer has not already been accepted.

(1) **Communication of revocation**

To be effective, a revocation must normally be *communicated* by the offeror to the offeree.

(a) **Exceptions**

1) **Offer to the public**

An offer made to the *public at large* can normally be revoked by publishing the revocation in the same medium as that in which the offer was made. The publication terminates the power of acceptance even of persons who saw the offer but not the revocation.

2) **Indirect revocation**

An offer is also deemed revoked, despite the lack of *direct* communication between the offeror and offeree, if the offeree obtains reliable information that the offeror has taken action showing that the offeror changed their mind.

(2) **Revocability of "firm offers"**

An offer that by its terms is to remain open until a fixed date can generally be revoked prior to the expiration of its term.

(a) **Exceptions**

1) **Options**

An option is irrevocable for the stated period because the offeree has given *consideration* for the promise to hold the offer open.

2) **Nominal consideration**

A firm offer is irrevocable if it *recites a purported or nominal* consideration, at least if it is in *writing* and proposes an exchange on fair terms within a reasonable time.

3) **Foreseeable reliance**

A firm offer is irrevocable if there is reasonably foreseeable reliance by the offeree prior to acceptance.

4) **U.C.C. provision**

A signed written offer by a *merchant* to buy or sell *goods,* which gives assurance that it will be held open, is not revocable for lack of consideration during the time stated (or if no time is stated, for a *reasonable* time); the period of irrevocability cannot exceed three months.

(3) Revocability of offers for unilateral contracts

Under the old rule, offers that were to be accepted by *performance of an act* remained revocable until performance was complete. However, modern courts *do not permit revocation once performance has begun*.

(a) Modern rule

1) Offer open for a reasonable time

Under Rest. 2d section 45, the offeror impliedly promises that once performance has begun, they will hold the offer open for the time stated in the offer, or, if none, for a reasonable time.

2) Preparation vs. performance

Under Rest. 2d section 45, *preparation,* as opposed to beginning performance, is *not* sufficient to make an offer for a unilateral contract irrevocable. However, if the offeree's preparation constitutes *reliance*, the reliance may prevent revocation under Rest. 2d section 87 and entitle the offeree to recover reliance or expectation damages, as appropriate.

f. Termination by operation of law

(1) Death or incapacity of offeror

This terminates the offeree's power of acceptance *whether or not* the offeree *knows* of the death or incapacity. However, this rule does not apply to *options,* at least when the individual performance of the decedent was not an essential part of the proposed contract. Also, the offeree's power to accept an offer to form a *unilateral contract* is not terminated by death or incapacity of the offeror once the offeree has *begun performance*.

(2) Changed circumstances

Changed circumstances, such as supervening illegality of the proposed contract or destruction of its subject matter, can also terminate the offeree's power of acceptance.

C. ACCEPTANCE

1. Is Offer for Unilateral or Bilateral Contract?

a. Acceptance of offer for a bilateral contract

An offer that calls for acceptance by a *promise* is an offer for a bilateral contract.

(1) General rule—promise mandatory

Ordinarily, such an offer can be accepted *only* by a promise, not by an act. (But the offeree's conduct might imply a promise.) There is a possible *exception* where the offeree tenders *full performance* prior to expiration of the offer.

(2) Modes of promissory acceptance

These include a *verbal* promise, a promise *implied in fact by the promisee's conduct*, an act designated by the offeror to *signify a promise*, and, *in some situations, silence*.

(3) Communication of acceptance

Generally, an offer to enter into a bilateral contract can be accepted only by a *communicated* promise. However, there are several *exceptions:*

(a) Mailbox rule

If the mail (or a similar mode of transmission) is a reasonable method of communicating an acceptance, the acceptance is usually effective when *dispatched* (sent). This is true even if the acceptance does not actually *reach* the offeror because it is lost in the mail.

(b) Waiver of communication

When the offer provides that the offeree must "accept" or "approve" the offer but waives notice of such acceptance or approval, a contract is formed when the offeree accepts or approves, even if the offeree does not notify the offeror. However, although such a contract is *formed* without notice, there may be an *implied condition* of notice of acceptance before the contract is *enforceable*.

b. Acceptance of offer for a unilateral contract

(1) Performance mandatory

A *unilateral contract* is a contract in which the parties exchange a *promise for an act*. Generally, an offer for a unilateral contract can be accepted only by performance, not by a promise.

(2) Notice of acceptance

A unilateral contract is formed by the offeree's beginning or completing performance, even if the offeror does not know at the time that the performance has occurred. However, if *notice of the completed performance* is not given to the offeror within a reasonable time, the contract will be discharged unless notice is waived.

(a) Sale-of-goods contracts

The U.C.C. provides that in sale-of-goods contracts, if the beginning of a requested performance is a reasonable mode of acceptance, an offeror who is not notified of the offeree's beginning of performance within a reasonable time may treat the offer as having *lapsed* before acceptance.

(3) Subjective intent of offeree

(a) Performance without knowledge of offer

The general rule is that if the actor has *no knowledge* of the offer for a unilateral contract at the time they perform the requested act, *no contract* is formed. A few cases have made an exception to the general rule for reward offers.

(b) Offer not the principal motive for performance

Generally, if the actor knows of the offer for a unilateral contract at the time they perform the requested act, a *contract is formed* even if the offer was not the principal motive for performance. However, *no contract* is formed if the act is done *involuntarily* (*e.g.*, under duress).

(4) Obligation of offeree

An offeree's acceptance of a *bilateral* contract binds the offeree as well as the offeror. However, if the offer is for a *unilateral* contract, the offeree is ordinarily *not bound*, because they never promised anything.

(a) Exception

If an offeree who has begun to perform should know that their performance is likely to come to the offeror's notice and that the offeror may treat the beginning of performance as an *implied promise* not to abandon performance, the offeror's *reliance* on the offeree's conduct may make the implied promise enforceable.

(5) Subcontractor's bid

If a contractor uses a specific subcontractor's sub-bid in determining its own bid, as a matter of contract law the contractor's use of the sub-bid does not constitute acceptance of the sub-bid, because the contemplated mode of acceptance in such cases is *communicated assent*, not the act of using the sub-bid.

c. Consequences of unilateral vs. bilateral offer

Whether a contract is bilateral or unilateral is important when considering (i) if the *mode of acceptance* used by an offeree was proper and (ii) if an offeree who has begun performance without having made a promise is protected against *revocation* by the offeror. An offeree is protected in this situation if the offer was for a unilateral contract.

d. Offers calling for acceptance by either a promise or an act

(1) Rule of Restatement Second

Where ambiguity exists, an offer is interpreted as inviting acceptance by *either a promise or performance*. The *U.C.C.* is in accord.

(2) Orders for prompt shipment

Under the U.C.C., an offer to buy goods for prompt or current shipment is construed as inviting acceptance by either a promise to ship or prompt and current shipment. Moreover, shipment of *nonconforming goods* is both an acceptance and a breach unless the seller seasonably notifies the buyer that the shipment is intended only as an *accommodation*.

2. Silence as Acceptance

a. General rule

As a general rule, silence (*i.e.*, inaction) of an offeree does *not* constitute acceptance.

b. Exceptions—silence constituting acceptance

(1) Implied-in-fact contracts

In the context of the general rule that silence does not constitute acceptance, "silence" means *inaction.* Thus, *communicated action* (*e.g.*, nodding one's head) does not constitute silence for purposes of this rule. In some cases, *both* the offer and the acceptance may be implied in fact from nonverbal actions.

(2) Offeree's behavior

Silence will constitute acceptance if the offeree, by their own prior words or conduct, has given the offeror reason to interpret their silence as acceptance. Similarly, if prior dealings or trade usage make it reasonable for the offeree to know that they should reply with a rejection if they do not intend to accept, their silence may constitute acceptance.

(3) Solicitation of offers

Acceptance by silence may also occur when (i) the offeree solicited the offer and drafted its terms, (ii) the offer is so worded that a reasonable offeror would deem it accepted unless notified of its rejection, and (iii) the offeror relies or is likely to have relied on the belief that silence constituted an acceptance (*e.g.*, solicitation of orders for goods by traveling salespersons).

(4) Subjective intent to accept

Silence can be acceptance if the offeror has said that silence will constitute acceptance and the offeree remains silent, subjectively intending to accept.

(5) Exercise of dominion

Silence constitutes acceptance if the offeree improperly exercises dominion over property sent for approval, inspection, etc. The offeree is contractually bound to purchase the property at the proffered price (unless manifestly unreasonable), even if they do *not* have the subjective intent to accept.

(a) Statutory exceptions

Several statutes (state and federal) have created an exception to this rule in the case of the exercise of dominion over *unordered merchandise*.

(6) Benefit from offered services

The offeree's inaction also can operate as an acceptance if the offeree (i) receives a benefit from offered services, (ii) has a reasonable opportunity to reject them, and (iii) has reason to know that they were offered with the expectation of compensation.

(7) Quasi-contract

Similarly, liability may be imposed on a person who silently receives benefits from the plaintiff if the plaintiff can show that (i) they have conferred a benefit on the defendant; (ii) they conferred the benefit with the expectation that they would be paid its value; (iii) the defendant knew or should have known of the plaintiff's expectation; and (iv) the defendant would be *unjustly enriched* if allowed to retain the benefit without paying its value.

(8) Late acceptance

A late acceptance has the legal effect of a counteroffer; *i.e.*, it is an offer that may be accepted by the original offeror. Moreover, if an offeree sends acceptance after a reasonable time for acceptance has elapsed, but within a period that the offeree might plausibly regard as reasonable, courts may require the original offeror to notify the original offeree that the acceptance was too late; otherwise, the late acceptance/counteroffer will be deemed accepted by the original offeror's silence.

D. TIME AT WHICH COMMUNICATIONS BETWEEN OFFEROR AND OFFEREE BECOME EFFECTIVE

1. In General

Normally, an acceptance is effective on *dispatch* and all other communications are effective on *receipt*. Delivering a communication so that it comes into the possession of the recipient counts as receipt, even if the letter is not actually read.

2. **Acceptance—"Mailbox Rule"**

An acceptance is effective on *dispatch* (except for *options*, for which many courts hold that acceptance takes effect on *receipt*).

a. **Requirements of mailbox rule**

(1) **Timely dispatch**

If no time period is specified in the offer, the offeree must accept within a *reasonable time*. If a time period is specified in the offer, unless otherwise specified, the time period *begins running* when the offer is *received,* and the acceptance must be dispatched within that time period.

(a) **Consequence of late dispatch**

If an acceptance is not dispatched in a timely manner and arrives too late, it is ineffective as an acceptance. However, it serves as a new offer and thus creates a power of acceptance in the *original offeror*.

(2) **Proper manner**

The acceptance must be dispatched with *appropriate care*—*e.g.*, correctly addressed. Unless otherwise specified by the offeror, under the modern rule an offer is deemed to invite acceptance by any medium of communication that is *reasonable* in the circumstances.

(a) **Reasonable medium**

A medium of communication is reasonable if (i) it is the one used by the offeror (unless specified otherwise) or (ii) it is customarily used in similar transactions at the time and place the offer is received. If the medium does not meet one of these two tests, it may still be reasonable, depending on circumstances such as the speed and reliability of the medium, the prior course of dealing between the parties, and usage of trade.

(b) **Consequence of unreasonable medium or lack of reasonable care**

If an acceptance was received, the offeree's failure to use a reasonable medium or reasonable care will not itself prevent contract formation, unless there was a failure to use a *required* medium. If the medium used was unreasonable or if reasonable care was not used in dispatching the acceptance, generally the acceptance will be effective *when it is received*, unless the acceptance was sent on time and received on time; such an acceptance is effective on *dispatch*.

b. **Significance of mailbox rule**

(1) **Crossed acceptance and revocation**

Because an acceptance is effective on dispatch and most states hold that a revocation is effective on receipt (*supra*, p. 104), if an acceptance is dispatched *before* a revocation is received, a contract generally is formed.

(2) **Lost or delayed acceptance**

A properly dispatched acceptance that is lost or delayed en route to the offeror is still effective under the mailbox rule; risk of loss or delay is on the *offeror*.

(3) **Effective date of obligation to perform**

Under the mailbox rule, the obligation to perform becomes effective when the acceptance is *dispatched*.

c. Offeror's power to negate rule

The offeror may negate the mailbox rule by providing in the offer that the acceptance will be effective only upon receipt, but normally only *clear language* will have that effect.

3. Revocation

The general rule is that a revocation by the offeror is effective only upon *receipt*, although a few states have statutorily changed the rule to make the revocation effective on dispatch.

4. Rejection

Generally, a rejection of the offer by the offeree is effective only upon *receipt*.

a. Where offeree sends both rejection and acceptance

(1) Acceptance mailed before rejection

In this case, a *contract* arises on dispatch of the acceptance, regardless of which communication is received first by the offeror, *unless* the offeror *detrimentally relies* on a rejection that they receive before the acceptance.

(2) Rejection mailed before acceptance

(i) If the *rejection arrives first, no contract* is formed; the *mailbox rule does not apply* and the "acceptance" becomes a *counteroffer*. (ii) If the *acceptance arrives first,* a contract *is* formed. However, if the offeror regards the *later-arriving rejection* as a *repudiation* of the contract and relies thereon, the offeree is estopped from enforcing the contract.

5. Repudiation of Acceptance

A repudiation of an acceptance is a communication dispatched by an offeree who has already dispatched an acceptance, stating that they *do not intend to be bound* by the acceptance. A repudiation differs from a rejection in that in a rejection, the offeree turns down the offer, whereas in a repudiation the offeree "turns down" their own earlier acceptance.

a. Acceptance arrives first

In this situation, a *contract is formed* because the later-arriving repudiation does not relieve the offeree of liability under the contract. However, if the offeror regards the offeree's repudiation of the acceptance as a repudiation of the contract and *relies* upon it, the offeree will be *estopped* from enforcing the contract.

b. Repudiation arrives first

Under the Rest. 2d, a contract is formed in this situation (although the cases are split). However, if the offeror regards the repudiation as a rejection and relies on it, the offeree will be estopped from asserting that a contract was formed.

6. Withdrawal of Acceptance

This occurs when the offeree dispatches an acceptance and then manages to *retrieve* it before it reaches the offeror. Under the Rest. 2d, a contract is formed when the acceptance is *dispatched*, and a withdrawal is ineffective.

7. Crossed Offers

Under the conventional view, a contract is *not* formed by crossed offers, on the theory that an offer is not effective until received and cannot be accepted until it is effective. However, the result may differ where the parties had *previously agreed* on all but one minor point, and in crossed letters they each propose identical terms as to that point.

E. INTERPRETATION

1. General Rule

Expressions used by the parties usually are to be given an *objective* interpretation; *i.e.*, words or acts are given the meanings a reasonable person in the addressee's position would attach to them. In applying this test, one should ask what interpretation would be given by a reasonable person *knowing all that the addressee knew*.

a. Application to contract interpretation

Interpretation is not purely objective, however. Under the Rest. 2d, objective reasonableness is used to *select* between the parties' two competing interpretation, if those interpretations differ. That is, the objective approach is not meant to impose on the parties a meaning that *neither* of them adopted. Instead, the *more reasonable* party's interpretation should prevail.

2. Exceptions

a. The *Peerless* rule

When an expression is susceptible of two *equally reasonable* meanings and each party understands the term differently, no contract is formed.

b. Both parties have same subjective interpretation

If both parties subjectively attach the same meaning to a term, that meaning will govern even if it is not the reasonable meaning of the term.

c. One party knows of the other's different interpretation

If two parties attach different meanings to a term and only one party knows of the meaning that the other party attached to the term, the meaning that the party without knowledge attached to the term prevails, even if that party's meaning is less reasonable.

3. Extrinsic Evidence

The traditional rule was that if there was no ambiguity in a written contract on its face, and no special meaning attached to the words of a written contract by custom or usage, extrinsic evidence was inadmissible. Today, however, extrinsic evidence is increasingly allowed to show what the parties intended by their words.

4. Course of Performance, Course of Dealing, Usage, and Usage of Trade

Course of performance (*i.e.*, the parties' repeated, unobjected-to performance during the course of the contract), *course of dealing* (*i.e.*, conduct between the parties prior to the contract), *usage* (*i.e.*, habitual or customary practice), and *usage of trade* (*i.e.*, usage regularly observed in a vocation or trade) may be helpful in interpreting what was meant by the contracting parties.

F. THE PAROL EVIDENCE RULE

1. The Rule

Parol evidence will not be admitted to *vary, add to, or contradict* a written contract that constitutes an integration.

a. What constitutes an "integration"

For the rule to apply, it must appear that the parties *intended* the writing to be the final expression of at least some part of their agreement.

(1) Formal intent test

The traditional view is that the parties' intent must be determined from the face of the instrument itself (Williston view).

(2) Actual intent test

Today, many courts consider a writing to be an integration only if the parties *actually intended* it to be so. These courts will consider *any* relevant evidence when determining the parties' intent (Corbin view).

(3) Application of competing views

The actual intent test results in a more frequent admission of parol evidence than the formal intent test.

(4) Merger clauses

Under the traditional approach, merger clauses (*e.g.*, a clause stating, "this contract is the entire contract between the parties") are *determinative* of whether a writing is an integration, *unless* there is a defense to the clause's effectiveness (*e.g.*, mistake). Some modern courts have held that a merger clause is only *one factor* in determining whether a writing was an integration.

b. What constitutes parol evidence?

If there is a writing that is an integration, evidence of an alleged *prior oral or written agreement* that is within the scope of the writing, or evidence of an alleged *contemporaneous oral agreement* that is within the scope of the writing, constitutes "parol evidence." The alleged agreements that such evidence concerns may be called "parol agreements." The parol evidence rule renders these agreements unenforceable as a matter of law.

2. Exceptions to the Rule

a. Separate consideration

If the written agreement and the alleged parol agreement are each supported by *separate consideration*, courts permit the admission of the parol agreement.

b. Collateral agreement

Parol evidence may be admissible if the alleged parol agreement is collateral to (*i.e.*, related to the subject matter but not part of the primary promise of), and does not conflict with, the written integration.

c. "Naturally omitted" consistent terms

Under the Restatement, a term that would be *naturally omitted* from the writing is admissible. A term will be treated as naturally omitted if it *does not conflict* with the written integration *and* if it concerns a subject that similarly situated parties would *not* be expected to include in the written agreement.

(1) Williston formal approach

Under the traditional approach, courts determine whether an *abstract reasonable person* would naturally have omitted the term from the writing.

(2) Corbin individualized approach

Under the modern approach, courts determine whether the *actual parties* under the particular circumstances of their case might have naturally omitted the term from the writing.

(3) Application of competing approaches

More terms are found to be naturally omitted under the Corbin individualized approach. Therefore, parol evidence is admitted more frequently under that approach than under the Williston formal approach.

(4) U.C.C. test

The U.C.C. is even more permissive than the Restatement, as parol evidence is admissible in contracts for the sale of goods unless the parol agreement would *"certainly have been included"* in the writing.

(5) Inconsistent terms

Parol evidence that is inconsistent with a written agreement is *not* within the parameters of the "might naturally be omitted test" and thus will be excluded.

d. "Partial" integration

A partial integration is an integration of the *subjects actually covered* in the writing, but parol evidence is admissible on subjects not covered.

e. Lack of consideration

Parol evidence is admissible to show a lack of consideration.

f. Fraud, duress, or mistake

Parol evidence is admissible to show fraud, duress, or mistake.

g. Existence of a condition precedent

Under the traditional rule, parol evidence is admissible to prove there was an oral or written condition precedent to the *legal effectiveness* of a written agreement but normally is *not* admissible to *add* a condition under a *legally effective* written contract.

h. Evidence to explain or interpret terms of the written agreement

Such evidence may be used to show what the *parties meant* by the words in the written agreement.

(1) Plain meaning rule

This rule will *bar* explanatory or interpretive evidence if there is *no ambiguity* on the face of the writing and *no special meaning* attached to the words by custom or usage. However, under the *modern approach*, there is an increasing tendency to *allow* such evidence. Nevertheless, even under the modern approach, the process of interpretation cannot be used to *contradict* the written terms.

(2) Course of performance, course of dealing, and usage

Extrinsic evidence is admissible to show special meanings of words derived from course of performance, course of dealing, and usage, sometimes even if the meaning is contradictory.

(3) Filling in gaps

If a contract term is missing, extrinsic evidence is admissible to show what a *reasonable term* would be and, under the *modern approach*, what the parties *actually agreed to* concerning the term (as long as the agreement *does not contradict* the written contract).

i. Modifications

A *later* oral agreement modifying an existing written contract does not fall under the parol evidence rule because it is a *subsequent* writing. However, to be enforceable, the agreement needs *consideration* (except in contracts for the sale of goods) and must comply with any applicable provision of the Statute of Frauds (*infra*, p. 162 *et seq.*).

(1) Contractual requirements—"No oral modification" clauses

Under the traditional rule, a provision *in a contract* requiring all modifications to be in writing will normally *not be enforced*. This rule does not apply to modifications of sale of goods contracts under the U.C.C. (and some other state statutes). If a contract for the sale of goods includes such a provision, modifications must be in a signed writing.

(a) Waiver

However, the U.C.C. also provides that an oral modification of a sale of goods contract can operate as a waiver of a writing requirement.

G. "SHRINKWRAP" CONTRACTS

1. In General

Customers often buy a wrapped box that contains, along with a product, proposed contract terms; they can review the terms only after a contract is formed. Enforcement of such terms is more likely if (i) the customer is reasonably on notice that the terms exist and (ii) the customer has a reasonable opportunity to return the product and rescind the sale.

2. Form Terms—Unconscionability and Unfair Surprise

Even if the form terms generally become part of the contract, the customer may have a defense if the terms are unconscionable or unfairly surprising. (*See infra*, p. 158.)

H. ONLINE CONTRACTING

1. Electronic Agents

Under the U.E.T.A., contracts can be (and routinely are) formed electronically, even between two computers. Any electronic records can count as a writing or a signature for the purposes of contract law.

2. "Clickwrap" Agreements

One way a contract can be formed online is for a customer to click a button labeled "I Agree" (or something similar) on a website or in an app. Clicking such a button has the same legal effect as signing a form. As with other form contracts, if particular terms of the contract are unconscionable or unfairly surprising, the customer may have a defense against those terms. (*See infra*, p. 158.)

3. "Browsewrap" Agreements

It is more controversial whether contract law will enforce the terms on a webpage labelled "Terms and Conditions" (or something similar) even if the visitor to the website does *not* expressly acknowledge those terms. One question that has been important to courts in deciding whether these terms create a contract is whether a reasonable website visitor is on notice that they were agreeing to a contract. The precise placement of links and the design of the website, not just the content of the terms, can be legally significant.

III. DEFENSES

A. INDEFINITENESS

1. General Rule—Certainty of Terms Required

An apparent agreement will *not* be enforced if (i) the court finds that the incomplete terms indicate that the *parties* did not regard the contract as being completed or (ii) the *court* cannot determine the terms of a contract with reasonable certainty or fashion an appropriate *remedy for breach*.

a. Filling gaps by implication

A court can fill in gaps in an agreement through the process of implication. However, there must be a *basis* for the implication. (For example, a court will hold that there is an implied promise to convey marketable title in a simple promise to convey title, based on community practice and reasonable expectations, but it will probably hold that a promise to erect a "house" is too indefinite without any plans.) Note that a court may enforce an otherwise indefinite contract if the contract has been *partly performed*.

2. Examples of Recurring Types of Omissions

a. Price

Many modern cases and the U.C.C. hold that if a contract is *totally silent* as to the price, a reasonable price can be implied provided the court is satisfied the parties *intended to conclude* a contract and there is some *objective standard* for determining a reasonable price.

(1) Indefinite standard

If the parties attempt to define the price through an *indefinite standard*, such as the parties' further agreement, traditionally the courts refused enforcement because it could not be inferred that the parties intended a "reasonable price." Today the U.C.C. (and some courts in non-U.C.C. cases) would probably enforce such an agreement using the standard of "a *reasonable price* at the time of delivery."

b. Time for performance

Generally, the courts will fill a gap as to time of performance by holding that a *reasonable time* was implied. What is considered a reasonable time will depend on the nature of the contract, custom and usage in the community, and prior dealings between the parties.

(1) Special cases

####### (a) Employment contracts—"at will" doctrine

In an employment contract with no specified duration, the usual rule is that the contract is *terminable at will* by either party, even if the contract describes a pay period. Even an agreement for *permanent employment* (*e.g.*, "for life") is usually terminable at will by either party, unless the agreement *specifically limits* the employer's power to terminate (*e.g.*, "only for good cause") or the circumstances *clearly indicate* permanent employment was intended by the parties. The *majority* of courts *enforce* an employer's promises contained in an *employee handbook* (*e.g.*, no discharge without good cause). Furthermore, evidence of *express* oral promises or *implications* from other factors (*e.g.*, longevity of service) may be used to overcome the at will doctrine.

(b) Distributorship and franchise contracts

If the duration is left open, the law implies that such contracts will last a ***reasonable*** time (*e.g.*, the time it will take the distributor to recover its investment).

3. U.C.C. Provisions

"Even though one or more terms are left open, a contract for [the sale of goods] does not fail for indefiniteness if the parties have intended to make a contract and there is a reasonably certain basis for giving an appropriate remedy." [U.C.C. § 2–204(3)]

a. Gap fillers

Gap filler provisions of the U.C.C. provide designated terms in various circumstances (*i.e.*, reasonable price; delivery at seller's place of business; reasonable time for delivery and shipment; and payment when and where buyer receives goods). Thus a bargain may be ***enforceable*** under the U.C.C. despite the omission of such terms. *Note:* The U.C.C. does ***not*** contain a gap filler for ***quantity***.

4. Modern Trend Toward Increased Enforcement of Indefinite Contracts

Modern authorities have begun to apply the U.C.C. approach to contracts generally, rather than only to sale-of-goods contracts. Thus, if a court is convinced that the parties ***intended to make a contract,*** it is more willing to supply reasonable terms to fill in gaps.

5. Indefiniteness Cured by Part Performance

An agreement otherwise unenforceable as too indefinite may be enforceable if the parties have ***begun performance***.

6. Bargains Capable of Being Made Certain

A bargain lacking an essential term is nevertheless enforceable if it makes reference to an ***objective standard*** to be used to fill in the missing term (*e.g.*, output and requirements contracts, custom or usage).

7. "Agreements to Agree"

Agreements to agree are bargains in which the parties explicitly reserve some term to be agreed on in the ***future***. Such agreements traditionally were unenforceable, but the modern trend (U.C.C., Rest. 2d) is to ***enforce*** them if the parties manifested an intent to conclude a contract. Under modern law, an agreement to agree may also give rise to an enforceable obligation to negotiate in ***good faith***. Moreover, under the U.C.C., even if the parties fail to reach an agreement as to price, the price is the ***reasonable price*** at the time of delivery.

8. Bargains Subject to Power of One Party Concerning Performance

a. Unrestricted option

(1) Common law rule

If either party retains an unlimited option or right to decide the nature or extent of their performance, their promise is too indefinite to be enforced.

(2) U.C.C. and Restatement Second rule

Under the U.C.C., as long as the parties intended to be bound, an agreement for the sale of goods at a ***price to be fixed*** by the seller or buyer ***is enforceable*** if done in ***good faith***. The Rest. 2d takes the same position as the U.C.C.

b. **Alternative promises**

   A bargain is not too indefinite because it reserves to the *promisor* the right to choose which of two or more performances will be rendered, provided *each* performance constitutes consideration. A bargain reserving to the *promisee* the right to choose between performances is enforceable if *any* of the performances constitutes consideration.

c. **Promise dependent on ability to pay**

   A bargain in which a party agrees to pay "as soon as they are *able*" is enforceable because the party's ability to pay is capable of objective determination.

9. **Bargains Where Future Written Contract Contemplated**

   Where parties enter into a bargain on the understanding that a formal contract will be executed and such execution does not occur, the issue then arises as to what function the parties intended the writing to serve.

   a. **Writing as evidentiary memorial**

      If it appears that the parties intended the writing only as an evidentiary memorial of the terms of their agreement, and the agreement was complete, the *oral agreement is enforceable*.

   b. **Writing as consummation of agreement**

      The oral agreement is *not enforceable* if it appears that the parties intended not to be bound unless and until a writing was executed.

   c. **Determining intent**

      Important factors for determining the parties' intent include: (i) whether the contract is of a type usually put in writing; (ii) whether there are few or many details; (iii) whether the amount involved is large or small; and (iv) whether a formal writing is necessary for full expression.

10. **Preliminary Agreements**

    Courts distinguish between two kinds of agreements made in contemplation of a future final contract.

    a. **Agreement contemplating formalization**

       If the parties reach agreement on the negotiated issues but intend to later *formalize* the agreement as an *evidentiary memorial,* their agreement is *binding as a contract* at the time it is made.

    b. **Agreement contemplating further good faith negotiations**

       This is a preliminary agreement that expresses a mutual commitment to a contract on agreed major terms while recognizing the existence of open terms that will be *negotiated in good faith in the future* (*e.g.*, letter of intent containing general terms and demonstrating an intent to negotiate further). Modern cases recognize that an *express* agreement to negotiate in good faith is *enforceable*. Even *without* an express agreement, courts may find an *implied* mutual commitment to negotiate in good faith so that a final agreement can be executed.

11. **Reliance on Indefinite Contract**

    Even when an agreement is too indefinite to enforce, if (i) the agreement was one on which the promisor should have realized the promisee would rely, (ii) the agreement induced such reliance, (iii) the promisee suffered a loss, and (iv) injustice could be avoided only by compensating the promisee, the promisee may recover *reliance damages* on the basis of promissory estoppel (*Red Owl* case). *Note:* If the promisee has **begun to perform**, rather than merely preparing to perform, the court may allow recovery of **expectation** damages instead of reliance damages.

  a. **Alternative doctrine**

  The **duty of good faith negotiation** (*supra*, p. 146) may be a better alternative to handle cases in this situation.

B. MISTAKE

1. **Mutual Mistake**

   The modern rule is that when parties enter into a contract under a mutual mistake as to a **basic assumption of fact** and the mistake has a material effect on the agreed exchange, the contract is **voidable** by the adversely affected party.

   a. **When a party bears risk of mistake**

   Mutual mistake is not a defense if the adversely affected party **bore the risk** that the assumption was mistaken (*e.g.*, the parties **knew** their assumption was **doubtful**).

   b. **Mistake in judgment no defense**

   Mutual mistake is also **not** a defense if the mistake concerns **prediction or judgment**.

2. **Unilateral Mistake**

   In contract law, a unilateral mistake refers to a **mechanical** error of computation, perception, etc., concerning a **basic assumption** on which the contract was made, that is made by only **one** of the parties to a contract.

   a. **Nonmistaken party aware of error**

   If the nonmistaken party **knows or should know** that the other party has made a unilateral mistake, the mistake is known as a **palpable unilateral mistake**. A palpable unilateral mistake makes the contract **voidable** by the mistaken party.

   (1) **Errors in judgment**

   The rule of palpable mistake applies only to mechanical errors. It does **not** apply to errors in judgment as to the value or quality of the work done or goods contracted for.

   b. **Nonmistaken party reasonably unaware of error**

   If the nonmistaken party neither knew nor had reason to know of the error, the **traditional** rule is that there is a **binding contract**. If the mistaken party refuses to perform, that party is liable for **expectation damages**.

   (1) **Modern trend**

   Under the modern trend, if the mistaken party notifies the other party of a unilateral mistake before the other party has changed its position in reliance, the mistaken party can **rescind** the contract. Some cases hold that even if the nonmistaken party **has** changed its position, recovery is limited to **reliance** damages.

3. **Mistranscription**

   Mistranscription occurs where, because of a mechanical mistake, the written agreement does not correctly embody the oral agreement. The aggrieved party is entitled to the equitable remedy of **reformation** (correction of the writing) if they prove their case by "clear and convincing" evidence.

4. **Misunderstanding**

   This occurs where the parties' expressions are susceptible of two different but equally reasonable interpretations and each party subjectively intends a different meaning (*see supra*, p. 114). In such a case, there is *no contract*. But if one meaning is *more reasonable* than the other, a contract is formed on the more reasonable interpretation.

5. **Mistakes in Transmission by Intermediary**

   These are cases where an intermediary used by the offeror to transmit the offer makes a mistake in transmitting it to the offeree (in theory, such cases could also involve an acceptance).

   a. **Offeree aware of mistake**

      If the offeree *knew or should have known* of the mistake (*e.g.*, because of a large discrepancy between the market price and the offer), there is *no contract*.

   b. **Offeree unaware of mistake**

      If the offeree *neither knows nor should have known* of the mistake, the authorities are split. The *majority* view is that a *contract* is formed on the terms conveyed by the *intermediary*. The *minority* view holds that there is *no contract*.

C. **CONTRACTS INDUCED BY MISREPRESENTATION, NONDISCLOSURE, DURESS, OR UNDUE INFLUENCE**

   1. **Fraudulent Misrepresentation**

      A misrepresentation (*i.e.*, a statement that is not in accord with the facts) is *fraudulent* if a party makes it with the *intent* to induce the other party to enter an agreement *and* they either (i) know or believe the assertion is untrue; (ii) lack confidence in the truth of the assertion but present it as fact; or (iii) say or imply that there is a basis for the assertion when there is not. Contracts based on fraudulent misrepresentations are *voidable* by the innocent party.

   2. **Material Misrepresentation**

      Whether or not it is fraudulent, a contract based on a *material* misrepresentation is *voidable* by the innocent party. A misrepresentation is material if it will induce a *reasonable* person to agree to a contract *or* the misrepresenting party knows that the assertion probably will make a *particular* person agree.

   3. **Nondisclosure**

      The general rule is that a party who proposes a contract does *not* have an obligation to affirmatively disclose material facts concerning the subject matter of the contract.

      a. **Exceptions**

         Disclosure may be required in the following circumstances: (i) to avoid *misleading half-truths* or to *correct* a previous statement, even if it was true at the time; (ii) if the prospective parties are in a relationship of *trust or confidence*, such as a fiduciary relationship; (iii) if one party knows of another party's mistake as to the meaning or content of a *writing*; or (iv) if one party knows material facts by virtue of their *special position* (*e.g.*, seller of home). Rest. 2d would require disclosure when needed to "correct a mistake of the other party as to a basic assumption on which that party is making the contract . . . if non-disclosure of the fact amounts to a failure to act in good faith and in accordance with reasonable standards of fair dealing."

   4. **Duress**

      If consent was induced by *wrongful* threats, the contract is *voidable* on grounds of duress.

- a. **Economic duress**

    Economic duress is a defense only where (i) one party ***threatens (or commits) a wrongful act*** that seriously threatens the other party's property or finances, and (ii) ***no adequate means are available to prevent the loss*** other than entering the contract.

5. **Undue Influence**

    Undue influence is unfair persuasion of a party, *A*, who is under the domination of the person exercising the persuasion, *B*, or who by virtue of the relation between them is justified in assuming that *B* will not act in a manner inconsistent with *A*'s welfare. The contract is ***voidable*** by the victim.

D. **UNCONSCIONABILITY**

1. **Development of Doctrine—U.C.C.**

    U.C.C. section 2–302 provides that "[i]f the court as a matter of law finds the contract or any clause of the contract to have been unconscionable at the time it was made the court may refuse to enforce the contract, or it may enforce the remainder of the contract without the unconscionable clause, or it may so limit the application of any unconscionable clause as to avoid any unconscionable result." This principle also applies to non-sale-of-goods contracts and is embodied in Rest. 2d section 208.

2. **Meaning and Scope of Doctrine**

    The scope of the doctrine of unconscionability is still uncertain. Even the U.C.C. does not define the term. Analyses of unconscionability often divide the concept into "procedural" unconscionability (*i.e.*, a defect in the bargaining ***process***) and "substantive" unconscionability (*i.e.*, lopsided or oppressive ***terms***).

    a. **Procedural unconscionability—unfair surprise**

        Many cases of unconscionability involve unfair surprise—*i.e.*, the disputed term is not one that a reasonable person would expect to find in the type of contract in question, and the drafting party, who has reason to know this, nevertheless fails to call it to the other party's attention.

        (1) **Adhesion contracts**

            Unfair surprise is particularly prevalent in standardized form contracts, sometimes called "adhesion" contracts—*i.e.*, agreements in which one party is in an inferior bargaining position and is forced to "accept" the preset terms dictated by the other party (*e.g.*, life insurance policies, loan agreements, clickwrap agreements [*infra*, p. 130]).

        (2) **Party's lack of knowledge of provisions in contract**

            Modern cases hold that in standardized form contracts, a party is bound only by provisions that are not unfairly surprising. The harsher the provision, the more scrupulous the courts usually are in making certain that the weaker party had knowledge.

    b. **Substantive unconscionability**

        The extent to which courts will invalidate a contract or its terms solely because of substantive unconscionability is still unresolved. The U.C.C. suggests that unconscionability is limited to prevention of oppression and unfair surprise; the Rest. 2d says substantive unconscionability ***is*** possible but ordinarily involves other factors. Some cases have invalidated unconscionable price terms. Substantive unconscionability may also provide evidence of procedural unconscionability.

3. **Types of Unconscionable Provisions**

   a. **Exculpatory clauses**

   An exculpatory clause releases a party from liability for injury caused by their actions. Clauses relieving a party of liability for their own ***intentional or reckless wrongs*** causing personal injuries are ***not*** upheld. Clauses relieving a party of liability for personal injuries caused by their ***negligence*** are controversial.

   b. **Disclaimers and limitations of warranty liability**

      (1) **Disclaimers**

      Under the U.C.C., a seller of goods may disclaim (*i.e.*, negate) an implied warranty. To disclaim an ***implied warranty of merchantability*** (*i.e.*, a warranty by a merchant that goods are fit for their ***ordinary*** purposes), the word "merchantability" must be mentioned and the disclaimer must be conspicuous. Disclaimer of the ***implied warranty of fitness*** (*i.e.*, a warranty by a seller who knows the buyer is relying on its skill or judgment that goods are fit for the ***particular*** purpose the buyer has for the goods) must be in writing and conspicuous.

      (2) **Limitation of remedies**

      The U.C.C. provides that agreements for the sale of goods ***may*** limit damages (*e.g.*, limiting the buyer's remedies to repair and replacement). There are two major ***exceptions*** to this rule.

         (a) **Where exclusive remedy fails of its purpose**

         Where circumstances cause the limited remedy to fail of its essential purpose, other appropriate U.C.C. remedies may be applied. This provision is frequently invoked when the remedy is limited to repair and replacement and the seller does not comply within a reasonable time.

         (b) **Where there is personal injury**

         The U.C.C. provides that a limitation on consequential damages for injury ***to the person*** resulting from consumer goods is prima facie unconscionable. Limitation of damages for ***commercial*** losses is not prima facie unconscionable.

E. **STATUTE OF FRAUDS**

1. **In General**

   The Statute of Frauds requires that certain types of contracts be evidenced by a signed writing containing essential terms.

2. **Purpose**

   The basic purpose of the Statute is to prevent fraud and perjury.

3. **Types of Contracts that Must Be Memorialized in Writing**

   a. **Contracts for the sale of land**

   A contract for the sale of an interest in land must be memorialized in writing.

      (1) **Part performance doctrine**

      A ***seller*** who conveys an interest in land to the purchaser can recover the contract price from the purchaser even if the contract is oral. Certain kinds of part performance by the ***purchaser*** of an interest in land may take the contract out of the Statute where ***equitable relief*** (*i.e.*, specific performance) is sought.

(a) Reliance doctrine

Traditionally, only certain types of part performance by a purchaser would take a contract for the sale of land out of the Statute of Frauds. Under *modern law*, part performance that does not meet the traditional test but that constitutes *reliance* may estop the other party from pleading the Statute of Frauds.

b. Contracts for the sale of goods

Contracts for the sale of goods priced at *$500 or more* must be memorialized in writing.

(2) Exceptions

An oral contract for the sale of goods priced at $500 or more *will* be enforced if:

(a) *The buyer accepts and receives* all or part of the goods (whereupon the contract becomes enforceable as to the goods accepted and received);

(b) *The buyer makes part payment* for the goods (in which case the contract is enforceable as to the goods for which payment has been made);

(c) *The contract calls for manufacture of special goods* for the buyer, and the goods are not suitable for sale to others in the ordinary course of the seller's business. The seller must also have made a *substantial beginning* in the manufacture of the goods or *commitments* for their procurement;

(d) *The contract is between merchants* and within a reasonable time a *written confirmation* (which satisfies the Statute as to the sender) is sent and the receiving party does not dispatch a written *objection* within 10 days; or

(e) *The contract is admitted* by the party against whom enforcement is sought "in his pleadings or testimony in court."

(3) Modifications

A modification of a contract for the sale of goods is within the Statute if the contract *as modified* is within the Statute.

(4) Sale of goods vs. contract for services

When a contract requires both the supplying of goods and the rendering of services (*e.g.*, providing parts to repair a television), the *predominant factor* of the contract determines whether it falls within the U.C.C. Statute of Frauds.

(a) Minority rule

An alternative approach is to split the contract into its component parts, effectively treating it as two contracts (one for goods and one for something else, like services).

c. Contracts in consideration of marriage

Contracts in consideration of marriage (but not contracts *to marry*) must be memorialized in writing. This includes marriage settlements (which are increasingly uncommon) and prenuptial financial agreements.

d. Contracts that cannot be performed within one year of making

Contracts that *by their terms cannot be performed within one year* of making must be memorialized in writing.

(1) Performance possible but unlikely

Even if it is unlikely that a contract will be performed within a year, if the contract is *capable* of being performed within the year, it is not within the Statute and is enforceable even if it is oral. For example, a contract to take care of another person until they die is capable of being performed within a year because the person *could* die within a year.

(2) Exception for performance

If a contract is impossible to perform within one year but is *fully executed on one side,* most courts hold that the contract is taken out of the Statute and is enforceable even if it is oral.

e. Suretyship contracts

Promises made to *another person's* creditor to "answer for" (be responsible for) that person's debt must be memorialized in writing. However, if an oral suretyship promise is made *to the debtor,* it is enforceable.

(1) Primary debt by promisor

The Statute applies only to promises to be *secondarily* liable for a third party's obligation (*e.g.*, "I will pay for the vacuum John is buying from you if John doesn't pay for it"), not to promises to be *primarily* liable (*e.g.*, "Send a vacuum cleaner to John and bill it to me").

(2) Main purpose rule

A suretyship promise is enforceable, even if oral, if it appears that the promisor's *main purpose* in guaranteeing the obligation of another was to secure an advantage or pecuniary benefit *for themselves* (*e.g.*, Homeowner prevents unpaid Subcontractor from walking off its building project by guaranteeing General Contractor's payment of Subcontractor).

4. Type of Writing Required

a. Memorandum of essential terms

A writing will satisfy the Statute if it is *signed* by the party to be charged and contains: (i) the identity of the contracting *parties;* (ii) a description of the contractual *subject matter;* (iii) the *terms and conditions* of the agreement; and (iv) *in many states*, a recital of the *consideration*. The writing need not be "the contract" to satisfy the Statute; it can be a memorandum that follows the oral formation of a contract. Electronic records count.

b. U.C.C. provisions

In the sale of goods, the writing need only be "sufficient to indicate that a contract for sale has been made" and specify the *quantity* term. Written confirmations sent by one merchant to another merchant in a form sufficient to bind the sender bind the recipient absent an objection.

c. Signatures

Signatures may be handwritten, typed, printed, or electronic. What counts as a signature is interpreted very broadly.

(1) Agent's signature

Under the original Statute of Frauds, a memorandum was sufficient if signed by an authorized agent of the party to be charged. However, some states have *equal dignity statutes* requiring the agent's authority to be in writing to bind the principal if the underlying contract is required to be in writing.

(2) Party to be charged must sign

Only the signature of the party sought to be held liable must appear. Normally, the signature can appear anywhere on the writing or record.

d. Consolidation of several documents

The required writing may consist of several documents or records.

e. Auction sales

In auction sales, the auctioneer's memorandum of terms of sale, signed only by the auctioneer, is a sufficient writing to bind both parties.

5. Effect of Noncompliance with the Statute of Frauds

a. Majority view—contract voidable

Failure to comply with the Statute renders the contract *voidable* (*i.e.*, unenforceable against a party who has not signed the requisite writing) but *not void*.

(1) Effect

Although suit cannot be brought on an oral contract that is within the Statute, the contract is valid for all other purposes. For example, if an oral contract is confirmed in a later writing, the contract becomes enforceable against the signing party even though no new consideration is given. Similarly, once a contract has been performed on both sides, neither party is entitled to recover what they have given based merely on the fact that the Statute of Frauds was not satisfied.

(2) No third party defense

Generally, the Statute may be raised only by a party to the contract, not by a third party.

b. Minority view—contract void

In a few states, failure to comply with the Statute renders a contract void.

6. Recovery in Restitution

Normally, courts grant restitution for benefits conferred pursuant to a contract that is unenforceable under the Statute, even where such a contract is deemed to be "void."

7. Reliance on Contracts Within the Statute of Frauds

In increasing numbers, modern courts will estop one party from asserting the Statute as a defense if the other party has detrimentally relied on the contract.

F. LACK OF CONTRACTUAL CAPACITY

1. Minors

A minor's contracts are *voidable* at the option of the minor, although the minor may enforce the contract against the adult. However, a minor is liable in restitution for the reasonable value of any *necessaries* (*e.g.*, food, shelter) furnished to them.

2. Mental Incapacity

Under the *traditional* (and *majority*) view, mental incapacity to contract exists *only if* a person's mental processes are so deficient that they *lack understanding* of the nature, purpose, and effect of the transaction. The *Rest. 2d* adds a rule that *expands* the mental-incapacity doctrine: a party lacks capacity if they are unable to act in a *reasonable manner* and the other party *has reason to know* of this condition.

a. Effect of incapacity

The contract is *voidable* by the incompetent party or a guardian acting on their behalf, but not by the other contracting party. However, if the person has been *adjudicated* insane or incompetent, their contracts are entirely void in many states.

b. Restitutional liability for necessaries

Whether the contract is void or voidable, the estate of an incompetent party is still liable in restitution for the value of any *necessaries* furnished to that party.

3. Drunken or Drugged Persons

The main test for this *temporary incapacity* defense is whether the person was so intoxicated as to be *unable* to understand the nature, purpose, and effect of what they were doing.

G. ILLEGAL CONTRACTS

1. In General

If the subject matter of a contract was legal when the offer was made but became illegal *before* acceptance, the offer is *terminated* as a matter of law. If the contract was legal at the time it was made but became illegal afterwards, the contract is *discharged* (*see infra*, p. 241).

2. What Constitutes "Illegality"

If the contract's *consideration or object* is illegal, the contract is treated as illegal. An otherwise valid contract is *not* illegal merely because its performance will *indirectly aid* the accomplishment of an illegal object, provided it does not involve a serious crime or great moral turpitude.

3. Effects of Illegality

The general rule is that if a contract is illegal, the courts *will not intercede* (even by restitution) to aid either wrongdoer. However, there are several important *exceptions* to this rule:

a. Severable portion may be enforced

To be severable, an agreement must expressly require performance in distinct installments or portions, and a *separable consideration* must be given for each portion. In such cases, where the illegal portion does not go to the "essence of the bargain," the legal portion may be enforced.

b. "Locus penitentiae" doctrine

Some decisions hold that where one party to an illegal contract repents and repudiates the contract, that party may obtain restitutionary recovery for the value they gave in performance.

c. Not "in pari delicto" ("in equal fault")

A party who is not guilty of serious moral turpitude and is not as blameworthy as the other party may be able to bring a suit in restitution for the value of the benefit conferred. However, this exception is *inapplicable* if the contract is *malum in se* ("evil in itself").

(1) Member of a protected class

If one party is a member of a class for whose benefit a statute is enacted, they are usually not considered in pari delicto and may recover in restitution.

d. Malum prohibitum

If the contract is only malum prohibitum (*i.e.*, contrary to statute or regulation but not *malum in se*), restitutionary recovery may be available to the relatively innocent party.

e. Licensing requirements

If an unlicensed person contracts to perform services, whether the contract is enforceable depends upon whether the licensing statute's purpose is for *protection of the public* (contract unenforceable) or for *fiscal regulation* or *taxation* (contract enforceable).

IV. THIRD-PARTY RIGHTS AND OBLIGATIONS

A. THIRD-PARTY BENEFICIARIES

1. In General

A third-party beneficiary contract exists when two parties (the *promisor* and the *promisee*) contract for a performance that will benefit a third party (the *third-party beneficiary*).

a. Common law rule—promise unenforceable

The common law required a person to give consideration to, and be in privity of contract with, the party to be charged in order to enforce the contract. Thus, a third-party beneficiary *could not enforce* the contract.

b. Modern law

Under modern law, a third-party beneficiary may sue and recover in appropriate cases.

2. Traditional Modern Law Test—Third Party Must Be Donee or Creditor Beneficiary

Under the traditional modern law test, popularized by *Rest. 1st*, "creditor" and "donee" beneficiaries can sue under the contract; "incidental" beneficiaries cannot.

a. Creditor beneficiary

If the promisee's primary intent was *to discharge a duty owed to the third party,* the third party is a creditor beneficiary and can directly *sue* the promisor under the contract. It is *not* necessary that the promisee owe an actual duty to the third party, but only that they *believe* they owe such a duty.

b. Donee beneficiary

If the promisee's primary intent in contracting was to *confer a gift* or to *confer a right to performance* against the promisor upon the third party, the third party is a donee beneficiary and can *sue* the promisor.

c. Incidental beneficiary

This is a third-party beneficiary who is neither a creditor nor a donee beneficiary. An incidental beneficiary *cannot bring suit* under the contract.

3. **Restatement Second Terminology**

   Rest. 2d substitutes the term "intended beneficiary" for Rest. 1st's terms "creditor" and "donee" beneficiary, and it retains the term "incidental beneficiary." Although the terminology is different, the tests are largely the same. A party is an ***intended beneficiary*** if recognition to a right to performance in the beneficiary is appropriate to ***effectuate the intention*** of the parties ***and either*** (i) performance of the promise will fulfill an obligation of the promisee to ***pay*** the beneficiary or (ii) circumstances indicate that the promisee intends to ***give*** the beneficiary the benefit of the promised performance. An ***incidental beneficiary*** is a party who is not an intended beneficiary.

4. **Recurring Third-Party Beneficiary Cases**

   a. **Assumption of a mortgage**

      An assumption agreement occurs when the promisor undertakes to perform the duties already owed by the promisee to a third person. The third person in an assumption agreement is a ***creditor beneficiary.*** A common type of assumption agreement involves mortgages. A person who sells property that is subject to a mortgage often requires the purchaser to ***assume*** (promise to pay) the mortgage debt.

      (1) **Purchaser "assumes" mortgage debt**

          If the purchaser assumes the mortgage, the mortgagee (creditor) becomes a third-party beneficiary. As such, the mortgagee has an additional remedy in the event of default. They can foreclose on the property and, in most states, can sue not only the ***original*** mortgagor (debtor) but also all ***subsequent*** purchasers who have ***assumed*** the mortgage for any deficiency owing after the property is sold.

      (2) **Purchaser takes "subject to" mortgage**

          In this case, there is no assumption agreement and the mortgagee has no direct action against the purchaser. Their remedy is to foreclose and then sue the ***original*** mortgagor for any deficit.

   b. **Would-be legatees**

      When a party takes nothing under a will because an attorney failed to properly draft a will or to draft it in accordance with the decedent's wishes, most courts hold that the party has a right to sue the attorney as an ***intended third-party beneficiary*** of the attorney-client contract. Some courts reach the same result by allowing a ***negligence*** action.

   c. **Government contracts**

      As a general rule, a member of the public who would benefit, directly or indirectly, from a promise to render performance to a governmental entity ***cannot*** sue to enforce the promise.

      (1) **Restatement First exception**

          Under Rest. 1st, members of the public can sue the promisor if an ***intention*** to compensate the public is manifested in the contract.

      (2) **Restatement Second exception**

          Under Rest. 2d, members of the public can sue the promisor if either (i) the ***contract terms*** provide for public liability or (ii) the ***government*** is subject to ***damages liability*** to the members of the public and a direct action against the promisor is consistent with the contract and with public policy.

- d. **Subcontractor suits against sureties of prime contractors**

    Prime contractors often are required to post (i) a *performance bond*, under which a surety guarantees the owner that the contractor will perform its contract; (ii) a *payment bond*, under which the surety specifically guarantees the owner that subcontractors' claims will be paid; or (iii) both.

    (1) Payment bonds

    Traditionally, subcontractors could recover against sureties as third-party beneficiaries of payment bonds running to public owners but not private owners. *Modern courts* usually allow recovery against sureties under payment bonds running to *either public or private owners*.

    (2) Performance bonds

    If an owner requires only a *performance bond*, unpaid subcontractors *cannot recover* against the sureties as third-party beneficiaries.

5. **Defenses Assertable by the Promisor Against the Beneficiary**

    The promisor can assert against a third-party beneficiary any of the *defenses* that they could have *asserted against the promisee* in connection with *formation or performance* of the contract.

    a. **Defenses promisee could have asserted against beneficiary**

        These defenses are likely to arise only in a *creditor beneficiary* context. If the promisor's promise is interpreted to be a promise to *pay whatever liability the promisee was under to the beneficiary*, the promisor *can* raise any defense the promisee could raise. However, if the promisor's promise is interpreted to be a promise to *pay a given amount of money to the beneficiary*, the promisor *cannot* raise any of the promisee's defenses.

    b. **Rights of beneficiary against promisee and promisee's rights against promisor**

        (1) Donee beneficiary

        A donee beneficiary *cannot sue* the promisee because the promisee owes the beneficiary no obligation. Such a promisee also has *no cause of action* against the *promisor* for breach of contract or any other action at law, because they have no damages. However, the modern trend is that the promisee can seek equitable relief (*i.e.*, *specific performance* of the promisor's promise).

        (2) Creditor beneficiary

        If the promisor fails to pay a creditor beneficiary, the *beneficiary can sue the promisee* on the original (preexisting) obligation. Also, the *promisee can sue the promisor* for failure to perform because the promisee's obligation to the beneficiary remains outstanding because of the promisor's failure to perform.

6. **Termination or Variation of Third-Party Beneficiary Rights**

    Until a donee or creditor beneficiary's rights *vest*, they can be cut off or varied by mutual agreement of the promisor and promisee. Once the third party's rights vest, no agreement between the contracting parties can impair or vary these rights.

    a. **Restatement First view**

        A *donee beneficiary's* rights vest automatically upon the *making* of the contract. A *creditor beneficiary's* rights vest only when they have *detrimentally relied* or brought suit on the contract.

b. Restatement Second view

The rights of *any intended beneficiary* (creditor or donee) vest only when the beneficiary *manifests assent* in the requested manner, *brings suit* to enforce the promise, or *materially changes position* in justifiable *reliance* on the contract. Most modern courts follow this approach.

B. ASSIGNMENT OF RIGHTS AND DELEGATION OF DUTIES

1. In General

a. Nature of an assignment

An assignment is the transfer of a right under an original contract. It operates to extinguish the right in the transferor (*assignor*) and to set it up exclusively in the transferee (*assignee*). The nonassigning party to the original contract is called the *obligor*.

(1) Effect of assignment

Under modern law, the *assignee* is the real owner of the transferred right, and *they alone* may enforce the contract against the obligor without joining the assignor, whose contractual right has been *extinguished*.

(2) Governing law

Today, *Article 9* of the U.C.C. is the most important source of law governing assignments. It applies to almost any transaction intended to create a *security interest* in *personal property*.

2. Rules Governing Assignability of Rights

a. General rule

The general rule is that all contract rights are assignable.

b. Exceptions—nonassignable rights

(1) Rights whose assignment would materially change the obligor's duty

Rights cannot be assigned where the obligor would be required to perform *personal services* to the assignee (*e.g.*, contract with artist to paint portrait). Similarly, *requirements and output contracts* generally cannot be assigned because the assignee's business circumstances could materially change the obligor's duty.

(2) Rights whose assignment would materially increase the burden or risk of the obligor

Assignments requiring the obligor to assume a materially increased burden or risk from that originally contemplated are also not permitted (*e.g.*, insurance policies, personal loans, purchase money mortgages).

(3) Assignments that would materially change contract terms

An assignment will not be allowed to alter the material terms of the contract.

3. Partial Assignments

Today, an assignor may transfer assignable rights to several assignees. Alternatively, the assignor may transfer *some rights* and retain the rest.

4. General Requirements for Effective Assignment

Any manifested intention by a party to a contract to make a *present* transfer of rights to another will constitute an assignment. The right assigned must be adequately described and *present words of assignment must be used* (*e.g.*, "I transfer" rather than "I will transfer"). Consideration is *not required* for an effective assignment.

a. Gratuitous assignments generally revocable

Gratuitous assignments are generally effective but *revocable*, subject to the following *exceptions*:

(1) Delivery of tangible token

If a chose (*i.e.*, claim or right) is represented by a tangible token (*e.g.*, a certificate), *delivery* of the token makes even a gratuitous assignment irrevocable.

(2) Writing

A gratuitous assignment is irrevocable if the assignment is made in a writing that is *delivered* to the assignee.

(3) Estoppel

If the assignee *detrimentally relies* on the gratuitous assignment, the assignor may be estopped from revoking.

(4) Novation

Irrevocability results if the assignee, assignor, and obligor *all mutually agree* that the assignor should be substituted for the assignee; such a three-way agreement is called a *novation*.

b. How revoked

A gratuitous assignment not made irrevocable by an exception is effectively revoked by:

(1) A *notice of revocation* given by the assignor to either the assignee or the obligor;

(2) The assignor's *later assignment of the same right* to someone else;

(3) The *assignor's death*;

(4) The *assignor's bankruptcy*; or

(5) An *acceptance by the assignor of payment or performance directly from the obligor*.

c. U.C.C. requirements

For an assignment to be effective under Article 9 of the U.C.C., the debtor must have either *signed or otherwise authenticated* a security agreement describing the assigned collateral, or the assigned collateral must already be in the assignee's *possession.*

5. Effectiveness of Assignments of Future Rights

At common law, future rights under an *existing* contract are generally freely assignable. Some common law authorities allow assignment of the right to payments expected from a *continuing business relationship*, even without an existing contract. Rights under a *future* contract or business relationship are *not* assignable at common law (but *equitable relief* may be possible if the assignment was given for consideration).

a. U.C.C.

Future rights covered by U.C.C. Article 9 are assignable whether or not they arise under an existing contract or business relationship.

6. **Effect of Contractual Provisions Prohibiting Assignment**

    At common law, provisions against assignment of contract rights in any kind of contract are in principle *valid*, both between the parties and as to any assignee with notice of the assignment. In practice, however, the courts narrowly construe such prohibitions so as to drastically limit their effectiveness.

    a. **Form of prohibition**

        A contract containing a *promise* not to assign destroys the *right*, but *not the power*, to make an assignment. However, if the prohibition is stated as a *condition*, it destroys the obligee's right *and power* to assign, so that an assignment is unenforceable.

    b. **Restatement approach**

        Under the Restatement, a contract provision that prohibits *assignment of the contract* is construed to bar only the *delegation* of the assignor's duties, not the assignment of their rights.

    c. **U.C.C. approach**

        Contractual prohibitions on assignments of most types of *rights to payment* that are covered by U.C.C. Article 9 are *ineffective.* Similarly, Article 2 provides that a right to *damages* for breach of a *sales* contract is *assignable,* even if the contract contains an express prohibition against assignment.

7. **Wage Assignments**

    An assignment of wages to be earned in the future under an existing contract of employment is *effective* under contract law, even where the employment contract is terminable at will. However, many states have statutory restrictions on the assignment of future wages.

8. **Rights, Liabilities, and Defenses After an Effective Assignment**

    An effective assignment extinguishes the assigned right in the assignor and sets it up in the assignee. Thereafter, the assignee alone is entitled to performance from the obligor.

    a. **Rights of assignee against obligor**

        An assignee can enforce their rights by direct action against the obligor. Once the obligor has *notice* of the assignment, they must render performance to or pay the assignee.

    b. **Defenses available to the obligor**

        Under U.C.C. Article 9 and the common law, defenses can be asserted *against the assignee* whether they arise before *or after* notice of the assignment is given *if* they (i) assert that the underlying contract was *not validly formed* or (ii) arise *under* the contract or the transaction that gave rise to the contract.

        (1) **Holder in due course and waiver of defenses**

            If a claim is embodied in a negotiable instrument (*e.g.*, a promissory note), the claim is assigned by transferring or assigning the instrument. If the instrument is transferred or assigned to an assignee who is a holder in due course (generally, a person who purchases the instrument for value, in good faith, and without notice of any defenses), the obligor *cannot assert* against the holder any *contract-related defenses* (except limited defenses, such as duress or incapacity). With nonnegotiable instruments, a similar result can be achieved with *waiver-of-defense clauses* (*i.e.*, clauses stating that the obligor will not assert against the assignee any defenses that they may have against the assignor).

- (a) **F.T.C. rule**

    The F.T.C. effectively limits both waiver-of-defense clauses and the holder in due course rule in consumer credit sales. Persons who sell consumer goods or services on credit are required to include a notice in consumer credit contracts or promissory notes that the assignee of the contract takes *subject to all claims or defenses* that the consumer debtor could assert against the seller.

- (b) **Consumer protection statutes**

    Many states have consumer protection statutes that also prohibit such waivers in retail installment contracts, so that no assignee can take free of defenses assertable against the seller.

(2) Modification after assignment

If the assignor and obligor in good faith modify the contract after the obligor has been given notice of the assignment, the traditional view is that the modification *does not affect* the rights of the assignee. (The U.C.C. is contra as to modifications of assignments of rights to payment that (i) are made in good faith and in accordance with reasonable commercial standards, and (ii) have not yet been earned by performance).

(3) Unrelated defenses

A defense unrelated to the contract can be asserted against the assignee *only if* it accrued *before* the assignee gave the obligor notice of the assignment.

c. Rights of assignee against assignor—warranties

The law reads into every assignment for consideration four implied warranties by the assignor:

(1) *That the right assigned actually exists and is subject to no limitations or defenses* other than those stated or apparent at the time of the assignment;

(2) *That any document or paper* regarding the assignment *is genuine* and what it purports to be;

(3) *That the assignor has the right to assign* (*i.e.*, no prior assignment of the same right); and

(4) *That the assignor will do nothing in the future* to defeat the assigned right (*i.e.*, will not attempt a *subsequent assignment* of the same right).

9. Priority of Competing Assignees

Successive assignments of the same right raise the question as to which assignee is entitled to the obligor's performance.

a. Common law

If the *first assignment is revocable*, any subsequent assignment revokes the first assignment and the subsequent assignee prevails. If the assigned claim is represented by a *tangible token* and the first assignee leaves the token in the assignor's possession, the subsequent assignee prevails.

(1) Other cases

Other cases are governed by three competing rules:

- (a) **"New York" rule**

    Under this rule, the first assignee in point of time prevails.

- (b) **"English" rule**

    Under this rule, the first assignee to give notice to the obligor prevails if they paid value for the assignment and did not have notice of the prior assignment.

- (c) **"Massachusetts" rule**

    Under this rule, the first assignee *prevails unless* the second assignee acquired the assignment in *good faith* and for *value*, and (i) took from the assignor a *tangible token*; or (ii) *collected* the claim from the obligor; or (iii) got a *judgment* against the obligor; or (iv) secured a *novation* from the obligor.

b. **U.C.C.**

U.C.C. section 9–322 provides for the public filing of a financing statement by any person claiming an assignment of a contract right in order to give all other persons constructive notice of the interest claimed. The basic rule is that assignments are protected in order of their filing or perfection.

10. **Delegation of Duties**

    a. **Nature of a delegation**

    A delegation of a contractual duty is an appointment, by a party to a contract (*delegor* or obligor), of another person (*delegee*) to perform the delegor's contractual duties. (*Note:* Distinguish this from a novation, which is a substitution of parties to the contract).

    b. **What duties are delegable**

    Any contractual duty may be delegated *unless* the obligee has a substantial interest in having the original obligor perform *personally* (*e.g.*, personal services contracts). Contractual restrictions on delegation are normally enforced.

    c. **Effect of valid delegation of duties**

    A valid delegation does not excuse the delegor from their own duty to perform but merely places *primary responsibility* to perform on the delegee (who becomes the principal debtor), and *secondary liability* (as surety) on the delegor.

    d. **Effect of attempt to delegate nondelegable duty**

    The mere attempt to delegate a nondelegable duty does not amount to a contract breach. However, if the original obligor indicates to the obligee that they will not perform personally, this may constitute an anticipatory breach of contract (*infra*, p. 238) or give the obligee a right to demand assurance of performance.

    e. **Rights of the obligee against the delegee**

    (1) **Promise to assume duties**

    This situation constitutes a typical *assumption agreement* (*supra*, p. 183). The obligee is a creditor beneficiary of the contract between the delegor and the delegee and thus may sue the delegee for nonperformance.

    (2) **Implied assumption of duties**

    In some cases, one party simply "assigns" a contract to another who does not expressly agree to perform the assignor's duties. *Traditionally*, the mere acceptance of contractual benefits was *not* sufficient to imply a promise to bear the contractual burdens. The *modern view*, however, is that when a contract that is wholly or partially executory on both sides is assigned, the assignment is construed as a *delegation*, and acceptance is construed as an acceptance of the delegation (with the possible exception of assignments of contracts for the sale of land).

(3) Effect of tender by delegee

If a delegee makes a satisfactory tender of performance to the obligee, the obligee must accept it or the duty is discharged.

V. PERFORMANCE AND BREACH

A. OBLIGATION TO PERFORM IN GOOD FAITH

Under modern contract law, *each party* has an obligation to perform in good faith.

B. EXPRESS CONDITIONS

1. In General

In contract law, the term *"express condition"* normally refers to an *explicit contractual provision* providing that either (i) a party to the contract is *not obliged to perform* duties unless some event or state of the world occurs (or fails to occur) or (ii) if some event or state of the world occurs or fails to occur, the performing party's obligation to perform is *suspended or terminated*.

2. Conditions and Promises Distinguished

a. In general

A *promise* is an undertaking to perform (or refrain from performing) some act. The fulfillment of a *condition* creates or extinguishes a duty to perform by the promisor.

b. Differences in legal effect of promises and conditions

An unexcused failure to perform a promise is *always* a breach of contract and *always* gives rise to liability; nonfulfillment of a condition is *not* a breach of contract and does *not* give rise to liability. Breach of a promise by one party *may or may not* excuse the other party's duty to perform under the contract; nonfulfillment of a condition normally *will* excuse a duty to perform that was subject to the condition.

3. Interpretation of a Provision as Condition or Promise

a. Parties' intent controls

If the contract language is ambiguous, the court construes the words used to determine whether the parties intended a provision to be a promise or a condition.

b. Where parties' intent unclear

Several factors are considered in determining the parties' intent. Words such as "provided," "if," etc. usually indicate a condition; the words "promises," "agrees," etc. generally indicate a promise. In case of doubt, contractual provisions ordinarily will be construed as *promises*.

4. Implication of a Promise from a Condition

In some cases, a contractual term that operates as a condition also gives rise to a promise by implication (*e.g.*, condition of third party's approval gives rise to promise to *seek* third party's approval).

5. **Provision Both Promise and Express Condition**

   In this situation, a party may promise to bring about a given state of events *and* the contract pertaining to that promise may also expressly state that the other party's duty to perform is conditioned on the occurrence of the state of events.

6. **Conditions Precedent and Conditions Subsequent**

   a. **Conditions precedent**

      A condition precedent is a condition under which some state of affairs must occur *before* a party has a duty to perform.

   b. **Conditions subsequent**

      A condition subsequent is a condition under which the occurrence or nonoccurrence of a state of affairs *extinguishes or terminates* a previously absolute duty to perform. True conditions subsequent are rare. Many provisions are *worded* as conditions subsequent in *form* but are conditions precedent in *substance*.

   c. **Procedural effect of condition subsequent**

      The burden of proof as to the occurrence of conditions precedent is generally on the plaintiff in a breach-of-contract action. However, the burden of proof of the occurrence of a condition subsequent is generally on the *defendant*.

7. **Conditions of Satisfaction**

   a. **Performance to satisfaction of promisor as condition precedent to promisor's duty to perform**

      When "personal satisfaction" is not expressly specified, modern courts construe a provision requiring the promisor's satisfaction as described below.

      (1) **Subject matter involves mechanical fitness, utility, or marketability**

          When the subject matter involves mechanical fitness, utility, or marketability, "satisfaction" means performance that would satisfy a *reasonable person*.

      (2) **Subject matter personal**

          When the contract involves personal taste or personal judgment, the condition of satisfaction is fulfilled only if the promisor is *personally* satisfied. However, the *dissatisfaction must be honest and in good faith*, or the condition of satisfaction will be *excused*.

   b. **Performance to the satisfaction of a third party**

      If the contract requires satisfaction of a third party, most courts hold that the third party must *personally* be satisfied. However, the *dissatisfaction must be honest and in good faith*, or the condition of satisfaction will be *excused*.

8. **Conditions Relating to Time of Payment**

   If a court interprets a provision as a promise to pay *only if a condition has occurred*, the promise to pay is *unenforceable* unless the condition occurs. However, if a court interprets a provision as an *unconditional* promise to pay with payment *postponed* until the stated condition occurs, the payment *must* occur within a *reasonable time*, even if the condition does not occur.

9. **Excuse of Conditions**

   Generally, no duty to perform arises until all conditions have been *fulfilled*. However, a duty may arise in some cases where the condition has been *excused*.

a. Excuse by prevention or hindrance

A condition will be excused if the party favored by the condition *wrongfully* prevents or hinders its fulfillment. Wrongfulness means that under the circumstances, the other party *would not reasonably have anticipated* the type of prevention or hindrance that occurred (*e.g.*, termination of a seller's business in an output contract).

b. Waiver

Fulfillment of a condition may be waived (*see supra*, p. 42 *et seq.*).

c. Impossibility

Impossibility or impracticability may excuse performance of a condition if it is not a material part of the agreement and forfeiture would otherwise result (*see infra*, p. 241 *et seq.*).

d. Forfeiture

If nonfulfillment of a condition would result in a disproportionate forfeiture, the condition may be excused *unless* fulfillment was a material factor.

C. IMPLIED CONDITIONS

1. In General

Often, even though a condition is *not expressed* in a contract, it is nevertheless clear that the obligation to perform is subject to a condition. In such cases, the condition is said to be an "implied" or "constructive" condition.

2. Implied Conditions of Performance

The most important type of implied condition to the duty of each party to perform is the performance (or tender of performance) of the other party.

3. Implied Conditions of Cooperation and Notice

A party's duty to perform may be conditional on the other party's cooperation or giving of notice that performance is due.

D. ORDER OF PERFORMANCE

1. Protracted Performance Is Condition to Performance of Single Act

If one party's performance will take some period of time, while the other's may be performed in a moment, completion of the performance that will take time is an implied condition to the duty to render the momentary performance.

2. Earlier Performance Is Condition to Later Performance

If one party promises to perform *prior* to the time the other party promises to perform, the first party's performance is an implied condition to the other's later duty to perform.

3. Simultaneous Performances Are Conditions Concurrent

If a contract *fixes the same time* for the performance of both promises, and both are capable of simultaneous or nearly simultaneous performance, each party's performance is an *implied condition concurrent* to the other's performance; *i.e.*, each must tender their performance as a condition to the other party's duty to perform.

4. No Time Set for Either Performance

Conditions concurrent will also be implied if no time is set for performance and the promises are capable of nearly *simultaneous performance*.

5. **Time Set for One Performance But Not Other**

   In this situation, *conditions concurrent* will be implied if both promises are capable of nearly *simultaneous performance*.

6. **Anticipatory Repudiation**

   A performance or tender that normally would be an implied condition to the other party's performance or tender will be excused if the other party *repudiates* the contract prior to the time when performance was to occur. In addition to being excused from holding themselves ready to perform and from tendering performance, the nonrepudiating party can normally *sue* the repudiating party for *breach* even before the scheduled time for performance.

7. **Prospective Inability to Perform**

   This occurs when circumstances make it appear that one party will be unable to perform (*e.g.*, a *seller's encumbrance* of property after they contract to sell it to another). Prospective inability to perform excuses the other party's duty to perform. If prospective inability to perform arises from *voluntary conduct*, it may also constitute anticipatory breach.

   a. **U.C.C.**

      Under the U.C.C., either party can demand assurances if reasonable grounds for insecurity exist and may suspend performance until assurances are given. Unjustified failure to give assurances within 30 days constitutes a repudiation.

E. **DOCTRINE OF SUBSTANTIAL PERFORMANCE**

When one party's performance is an implied condition to the other party's duty of counterperformance, the implied condition will normally be satisfied by *substantial* performance. Thus, if the doctrine of substantial performance is applicable and one party renders substantial performance, the other party comes under a duty of counterperformance, but they can deduct any damages suffered because the first party's performance was less than complete.

1. **What Constitutes "Substantial" Performance**

   This is a question of fact, to be governed by the circumstances of each case. The test used is whether the performance meets the *essential purpose* of the contract.

2. **Application**

   The doctrine is applied primarily to *construction contracts*, where it would be unjust to allow an owner to retain the value of a building free of charge just because the builder deviated somewhat from the agreed specifications.

   a. **U.C.C.**

      In theory, the U.C.C. adopts the "perfect tender" rule, thus not recognizing the doctrine of substantial performance in *sale of goods* contracts. In practice, *exceptions* to the rule (*e.g.*, seller's right to cure a defect) have left little of the general rule.

3. **Damages**

   A party receiving substantial performance may deduct from the payment due any damages suffered from the defective performance. The usual measure of damages is the *cost of completion.* However, *diminution in value* is sometimes used as an alternative measure of damages.

4. Remedy in Restitution

Even if substantial performance is *not* found, a party still may recover in restitution for the reasonable value of benefits they conferred. In practice, the measure of recovery when performance is incomplete but readily remedial is usually the ***unpaid contract price less the cost of completion,*** up to the value of the benefit received by the defendant.

F. DIVISIBLE CONTRACTS

A contract is said to be divisible if the parties' performances can be apportioned into pairs of matching or corresponding parts that the parties treat as equivalents.

1. Significance

If a contract is divisible, a party who has performed one or more parts is entitled to collect the contract price for ***those parts*** even though they are in breach as to the other parts. However, because there is still one contract, the right to collect is subject to an ***offset*** for damages resulting from breach of the other parts.

2. "Entire" Contract

A contract that is ***not divisible*** is said to be "entire."

3. Employment Contracts

If an employment contract (or state law) requires ***periodic salary payments*** (*e.g.*, $1,000 per month), courts usually hold the contract to be divisible.

G. MATERIAL VS. MINOR BREACH

An actual breach of contract ***at the time performance is due*** gives rise to an immediate cause of action for damages. Whether a breach also ***excuses the duty of counterperformance*** depends on whether it is ***material*** or ***minor***.

1. Distinguishing Material from Minor Breach

The following six factors are relevant in determining whether a breach is material or minor:

(i) ***The extent to which the breaching party has already performed*** (a breach at the outset is more likely to be material);

(ii) ***Whether the breach was willful,*** negligent, or the result of purely innocent behavior;

(iii) ***The extent of uncertainty*** that the breaching party ***will perform*** the remainder of the contract;

(iv) ***The extent to which the nonbreaching party will obtain*** (or has obtained) the substantial ***benefit*** they bargained for;

(v) ***The extent to which the nonbreaching party can be adequately compensated*** for the defective or incomplete performance; and

(vi) ***The degree of hardship*** imposed on the breaching party by holding the breach material and terminating all their contractual rights.

a. Repudiation

A repudiation consists of words or conduct by a party that a reasonable person would interpret as an expression of ***refusal to perform further***. An act considered to be a minor breach will be treated as a material breach if accompanied by an express repudiation.

b. Effect of parties' agreement

The contract, either expressly or impliedly, may make the time, manner, or other details of performance *material*, in which case the specified deviations would traditionally be considered material (*e.g.*, "time is of the essence" clauses, although today courts may apply such clauses less strictly).

2. Effect of Material Breach

A material breach always gives rise to an *immediate* cause of action for breach of the entire contract. It also *excuses* further performance by the innocent party.

3. Effect of Minor Breach

A minor breach gives rise to an immediate cause of action for whatever damages were caused by the breach but *not* a cause of action on the entire contract. The minor breach may *suspend, but does not excuse*, the duty of counterperformance.

4. Response to Breach

If the breach is *material*, the innocent party may sue for damages and let the contract *continue*, or *terminate* the contract and sue for total breach. A *minor* breach permits a suit for damages but *not termination*.

5. Material Breach vs. Substantial Performance

Material breach and substantial performance are similar in that both distinguish between major or important breaches and minor or less important breaches. But the two are used differently. *Substantial performance* usually is invoked by a party *who has breached* but seeks the contract price minus a setoff for damages, whereas *material breach* usually is invoked when one party has breached in a minor way, the other party terminates the contract as a result, and the first party wants to argue that there was *no right to terminate* because the breach was not material.

a. Substantial performance

This doctrine involves the question: When can a party who has breached bring suit for *damages* rather than *unjust enrichment*?

b. Material breach

This doctrine involves the question whether a victim of a breach can terminate the contract and be entitled to damages for the *whole contract*, or cannot terminate the contract and is entitled only to damages for *partial breach*.

H. ANTICIPATORY BREACH

If either party to a contract *repudiates* the contract prior to the time set for performance, the other party may treat the anticipatory repudiation as a *present, material breach* of contract and bring an *immediate* action for the entire value of the promised performance.

1. Acts Sufficient

The repudiation can be by *words* or by a *voluntary act* that disables the promisor from performing.

2. Insistence on Terms Not Part of the Contract

This type of insistence constitutes an anticipatory breach.

3. Requirement of Unequivocal Repudiation

An anticipatory repudiation requires a *positive, unconditional refusal* to perform as promised in the contract. Ambiguous expressions (*e.g.*, "I doubt") are insufficient. They may, however, constitute a prospective inability to perform whereupon the other party may suspend counterperformance.

4. **Exception Where Nonrepudiating Party Has Completed Performance**

    The doctrine of anticipatory repudiation does *not* apply where the only remaining duty of performance is a unilateral duty of the repudiating party, especially a duty to pay money in installments. Usually, in such a case the innocent party must wait to sue until an *actual breach* occurs at the time set for the other party's performance.

5. **Retraction**

    Generally, the repudiator may retract a repudiation at any time prior to the date set for their performance, unless the innocent party has either *accepted* the repudiation or has changed position in *detrimental reliance* thereon.

6. **Determining Damages**

    Generally, the injured party must act promptly to mitigate damages after learning of the repudiation.

    a. **U.C.C.**

        Under the U.C.C., the measure of damages for a *buyer's* anticipatory repudiation of a contract for the sale of goods is the difference between the contract price and the market price at the *time and place for tender*. If the *seller* anticipatorily repudiates, the buyer may either *cover* or recover *damages* equal to the difference between the market price at the *time the buyer learned of the breach* and the contract price.

7. **Mitigation of Damages**

    The *innocent party owes a duty to mitigate* (*e.g.*, to stop performance), and if they fail to do so, they are not entitled to recover damages they otherwise could have avoided.

8. **Prospective Inability to Perform**

    If the prospective inability is caused by *voluntary conduct*, it may constitute an anticipatory breach (*see supra*, p. 238 *et seq.*).

I. **CHANGED CIRCUMSTANCES—IMPOSSIBILITY, IMPRACTICABILITY, AND FRUSTRATION**

1. **General Rule**

    Performance of a contract will normally be excused when it has been made *impossible*—more accurately, *impracticable*—by the occurrence of an event the nonoccurrence of which was a *basic assumption* on which the contract was made, *unless* the adversely affected party has *assumed* (expressly or impliedly) the risk that the event might occur.

2. **Recurring Types of Impracticability Cases**

    a. **Supervening illegality**

        If performance of a contract has become illegal due to *changes in the law* or through some other *act of government* after the time of contracting (*e.g.*, new zoning ordinances are enacted), performance is *excused*.

    b. **Supervening destruction or nonexistence of subject matter**

        If this situation occurs through no fault of the promisor (*e.g.*, a concert hall in which a singer was to perform is destroyed), the promisor's duty is *excused*.

- c. **Specific source of supply contemplated**

    The seller's duty to furnish goods under a contract of sale may be excused on the failure of a particular source of supply specified or contemplated by both parties (*e.g.*, failure of a particular crop specified by the parties).

- d. **Construction contracts**

    Generally, a contractor's duty to construct a building is *not excused* by *destruction of the work in progress* because the building can be rebuilt.

- e. **Repair contracts**

    However, a contractor's duty to repair or renovate an *existing building* is *excused* if the building is accidentally destroyed without fault by either party. The contractor may recover in quasi-contract the reasonable value of work done prior to the destruction.

- f. **Land sale contracts**

    Traditionally, the purchaser, as the equitable owner from the time of contracting, bears the risk of loss from *destruction of improvements*. However, the *modern trend*, absent a contrary agreement, is to place the *risk on the seller* until closing or a change in possession so that destruction of improvements excuses payment by the buyer.

- g. **Sale of goods**

    Under the U.C.C., if contracted-for goods are identified when the contract was made and are destroyed without the fault of either party before the risk of loss passes, the contract is *avoided*. If goods are to be *shipped* to the buyer, the risk of loss passes to the buyer when the seller delivers them to the carrier, *unless* the contract requires delivery to a particular destination, in which case the risk of loss passes when the goods are tendered at the destination. If *no shipment* is involved, the risk of loss passes to the buyer upon their receipt of the goods if the seller is a merchant; if seller is not a merchant, the risk of loss passes on tender.

- h. **Death or illness**

    Death or incapacitating illness of a specific person *necessary* for the performance of a promise (*personal service contract*) *excuses* the duty to perform. A service is "personal" if the right to command the services cannot be validly assigned or the duty to perform cannot be validly delegated.

3. **Temporary Impracticability**

    Temporary impracticability (*e.g.*, being drafted into the Army while performing a personal services contract) merely *suspends* (rather than excuses) the promisor's duty. After the impracticability ceases, the duty reattaches, but *only if* performance thereafter would not substantially increase or make different the burden on either party.

4. **Partial Impracticability**

    If there is partial impracticability, the promisor is still bound to perform the practicable remainder of performance if they are able to render substantial performance and the remainder is not made materially more difficult or disadvantageous. The promisee is bound to accept the modified performance with an appropriate offset.

5. **Recovery in Restitution for Part Performance**

   Either party may recover in restitution for the ***reasonable value*** of their performance prior to a contract's being discharged for changed circumstances. A few cases allow recovery for ***reliance*** damages.

6. **Frustration**

   Even if a bargained-for performance is still possible, a contract is discharged under the doctrine of ***frustration*** if the ***purpose or value*** of the contract has been destroyed by some supervening event that was not reasonably foreseeable at the time of contracting.

J. DISCHARGE

1. **Discharge by Mutual Rescission**

   A contract still executory on ***both*** sides may be discharged by an ***express agreement between the parties*** to rescind or call off their deal. Such an agreement is itself a binding contract; *i.e.*, each party is giving up the right to performance by the other, so no other consideration is necessary.

   a. **Formalities**

   The rescission may be oral, unless it would cause a transfer of an interest in land or a sale of goods within the Statute of Frauds.

2. **Release**

   A contract may be discharged by the execution and delivery of a release in which the maker expresses an intention to extinguish contractual rights existing in their favor, provided there is ***consideration*** for the release. A number of states and the U.C.C. have ***abolished*** the consideration requirement if the release is in ***writing***.

3. **Accord and Satisfaction**

   A contract may be discharged by an accord and satisfaction or a substituted contract (*see supra*, p. 38 *et seq.*).

4. **Payment-in-Full Check**

   A contract may be discharged by such a check, even if for less than the amount claimed due, if the payee cashes it, provided certain conditions are met (*see supra*, p. 36).

VI. REMEDIES

A. BASIC MEASURES OF DAMAGES

1. **Damage Measures**

   a. **Expectation damages**

   These have the purpose of putting the promisee in the position they would have been in if the promise had been performed; *i.e.*, they give the promisee the ***benefit of the bargain***. Expectation damages are the usual remedy for breach of contract.

   (1) **Incidental damages**

   These include expenses such as the seller's costs of shipping goods to and from a buyer who has breached or a buyer's costs of finding substitute goods after a seller breaches. Incidental damages are normally ***added*** to the general damage award.

b. Reliance damages

These are based on the nonbreaching party's *costs* and have the purpose of putting the promisee in the position they would have been in *had the promise not been made*. Reliance damages are the usual remedy for promissory estoppel.

c. Restitutionary (or quasi-contract) damages

These are based on the reasonable value of a *benefit conferred* by the promisee on the promisor and are available in a variety of circumstances—for example, where:

(1) The benefit was *conferred under a contract that turned out to be unenforceable*;

(2) The promisor is in *material breach*; or

(3) *No contract was formed but a benefit was conferred in a precontractual stage* when the parties believed they had concluded or would conclude a contract.

B. LIMITATIONS ON EXPECTATION DAMAGES

1. Principle of *Hadley v. Baxendale*

A party injured by breach can recover only those damages that (i) should reasonably be considered as arising naturally (*i.e.*, in the usual course of things) from the breach or (ii) might reasonably have been contemplated by the parties at the time the contract was made.

a. General damages

These are damages that flow from a given type of breach regardless of the breach victim's particular circumstances and are *always recoverable*. For example, if a seller breaches by not delivering contracted-for goods, the buyer may recover either the market price minus the contract price or the cost of substitute goods minus the contract price.

b. Consequential damages

These are damages above and beyond general damages that result from the buyer's particular circumstances (*e.g.*, a factory's loss of profits if a needed assembly-line part is not delivered on time). They are recoverable only if the seller had *reason to foresee* the damages *as a probable result* of the breach. Today "probable" is often interpreted as a *"significant likelihood"* that the damages would result.

2. Certainty

Only damages that are *reasonably certain* of computation are recoverable; *speculative* damages *cannot* be recovered. Thus, *lost profits* from an *existing business* can be awarded, but lost profits from a new business were historically regarded more skeptically. However, even lost profits from a new business may be awarded today based on the profits of similar existing businesses. The modern trend is not to cut off remedies unless the uncertainty is *severe*.

a. Reliance as a substitute for uncertain expectation damages

If expectation damages are uncertain, the promisee may seek reliance damages (*i.e.*, the promisee's *costs*) instead.

3. Duty to Mitigate

An injured party cannot recover damages that could have been *avoided* by reasonable efforts.

a. Contracts for the sale of goods

If a buyer fails to cover (buy substitute goods) when they could have, they will not be permitted to recover consequential damages that could have been avoided by covering. Similarly, if the buyer repudiates, the seller cannot run up charges by packing, shipping, etc. and must cease manufacturing goods contracted for unless the completion would facilitate resale and thereby reduce damages.

b. Employment contracts

If an employer wrongfully terminates employment, the employee must look for a *comparable* job (*see infra*, p. 262).

c. Construction contracts

A contractor cannot continue to work after the owner breaches but generally is *not* under a duty to find an alternative construction job during the period they would have been working on the canceled contract.

d. Expenses recoverable

The nonbreaching party may recover the reasonable costs of mitigation efforts, even if the efforts are unsuccessful.

C. SPECIFIC PERFORMANCE

Specific performance (*i.e.*, an order from a court to a contracting party to perform as promised) is an equitable remedy that is available only if the *remedy at law is inadequate*. This includes cases where the subject matter is *unique*, including all contracts for interests in land and contracts for the sale of unique goods. Specific performance will *not* be awarded to force someone to work under an employment contract, even if the employee's services are unique, but courts might issue an *injunction* against the breaching party to prevent them from working for competitors.

D. EXPECTATION DAMAGES AND SPECIFIC PERFORMANCE IN CERTAIN CONTEXTS

1. Contracts for the Sale of Goods

a. Breach by seller

(1) General damages for breach as to accepted goods

If the buyer accepted goods that do not conform to the contract (usually giving rise to a breach of warranty action), the buyer's general damages normally are measured by the value the goods *would have had had they been conforming* minus the value of the *accepted goods*. This difference in value may be measured by the cost of repairing the goods.

(2) General damages where seller fails to deliver or buyer rightfully rejects or revokes acceptance

The buyer can recover either (i) the *market price* at the time they learned of the breach minus the *contract price* or (ii) the *cost of cover* (*i.e.*, the cost of substitute goods) minus the *contract price*.

(3) Specific performance and replevin

The U.C.C. permits a buyer to get specific performance "where the goods are unique or in other proper circumstances."

(4) Buyer's incidental and consequential damages

Incidental damages generally include *reasonable expenses* incident to the seller's delay or other breach, such as inspection costs, expenses relating to cover, etc. Consequential damages include any loss resulting from the requirements of the buyer of which the seller was aware at the time the contract was made and that could not have been prevented by cover.

(5) Damages for late performance

If the seller breaches by late performance and knew or had reason to know that the goods would be resold by the buyer, the buyer can recover the reduction in market value of the goods between the time performance was due and the time performance was rendered.

b. Breach by buyer

(1) General damage measures

(a) Market damages

If a buyer refuses to purchase the goods, the seller can recover the *contract price* minus the *market price* at the time and place for tender.

(b) Lost profits

If the market price formula above will not put the seller in as good a position as performance would have (*e.g.*, cases where the seller has lost the volume of sales it otherwise could have made but for the breach), the seller can recover lost profits—*i.e.*, the contract price minus either the seller's cost of purchasing the goods (if the seller is a *dealer*) or the costs of manufacture (if the seller is a *manufacturer*).

(c) Resale

Alternatively, the seller can resell the goods in good faith and in a commercially reasonable manner and recover the *contract price* minus the *resale price*.

(2) Action for price

A seller can maintain an action for the full price (an equivalent to specific performance) if the buyer refuses goods that have been *identified to the contract* and the seller is *unable to resell* the goods after reasonable efforts or such efforts would be unavailing (*e.g.*, where the seller has specially manufactured goods for the buyer that are unsuitable for sale to others, such as calendars imprinted with the buyer's name).

(3) Incidental damages

In a proper case, the seller may also be able to recover *expenses* incurred as a result of buyer's breach, such as extra transportation, sales, and commission costs.

2. Contracts for the Sale of Realty

a. Breach by seller

(1) Damages

Many states limit a buyer's damages for a seller's refusal to convey real property to the buyer's *out-of-pocket expenses*, *unless* the breach is in *bad faith*, in which case the buyer can recover the *market price* minus the *contract price*.

(2) Specific performance

Alternatively, the buyer is entitled to specific performance in the form of a decree ordering the seller to convey.

b. Breach by buyer

(1) Damages

If the buyer refuses to purchase, the seller is entitled to recover the *contract price* minus the *fair market value* of the land.

(2) Specific performance

Alternatively, the seller can obtain a decree of specific performance, which will usually provide that if the buyer does not pay by a specified date, the seller can resell and collect any deficiency between the resale price and the contract price from the buyer.

3. Employment Contracts

a. Breach by employer

The employee is entitled to the *remainder of their wages* minus *wages actually received* from substitute employment or that *would have been received* had substitute employment been sought. Note that the *duty to mitigate* is only to find work of the *same type and in the same locale*.

b. Breach by employee

The employer is entitled to recover the wages that *must be paid to a replacement* minus the *employee's wages*.

c. Specific performance

This remedy is not available, but a court may issue an *injunction* barring the employee from working for a competitor.

4. Construction Contracts and Other Contracts for Services

a. Breach by owner

The contractor is entitled to recover the *contract price* minus *costs saved by the breach* (*i.e.*, costs remaining to be incurred by the contractor for the part of the contract that no longer needs to be completed because of the breach), with an *offset* for amounts already paid by the owner. *Alternatively*, the contractor can recover *lost profits* plus *out-of-pocket costs incurred* prior to breach, with an *offset* for amounts already paid by the owner.

b. Breach by contractor

(1) Cost of completion

If the contractor breaches, the owner normally is entitled to recover the difference between the contract price and the cost of completing the contract by hiring a substitute contractor.

(2) Diminished value damages

If completion would lead to waste or the cost-of-completion measure would be unreasonably disproportionate to the owner's gain, the owner's damages may be limited to the value of what they *received* minus the value of what they *would have received* had the contract been performed in full.

c. Specific performance

Generally, a contract for construction will *not* be specifically enforced.

5. Contracts for Carriage

If the subject matter of a contract for carriage consists of goods to be sold by the shipper (and this was reasonably foreseeable), the shipper can recover for the reduction in market value between the time performance was due and the time it was rendered. Alternatively, the shipper's damages are often measured by the reasonable daily rental value of the shipped goods during the delay.

E. NOMINAL DAMAGES

If a victim of breach cannot prove a loss, they are entitled to at least nominal damages (normally $1).

F. LIQUIDATED DAMAGES

A liquidated damages provision will *not* be enforceable if the court determines the provision is a *penalty*. The name the parties give to the provision is *not controlling*.

1. Requirements

For a liquidated damages provision to be *enforceable*, the amount of damages fixed must be a *reasonable estimate* of the damages that would result from breach. The ease of estimating damages may be taken into account in making this determination.

2. Subsequent Events

The traditional rule was that whether a clause was a reasonable estimate of damages was to be determined at the time the contract was made. The modern rule is that a court can also evaluate events subsequent to contract formation to determine the reasonableness of a clause's estimate of damages (and thus its enforceability). The Rest. 2d and the U.C.C. both adopt this modern rule.

3. Deposits

Deposits may serve the same purpose as liquidated damages provisions, and a deposit that was made by a party in breach often may be recovered to the extent that it exceeds the innocent party's actual damages *unless* the deposit is also a valid liquidated damages provision.

G. PUNITIVE DAMAGES

It is widely stated that punitive damages are not available for breach of contract alone.

1. Tort and Other Egregious Cases

However, punitive damages may be available if the breach also constitutes a tort, has tortious elements, or (sometimes) is fraudulent, willful, oppressive, outrageous, or the like.

2. Good Faith

Punitive damages may also be available if there is a breach of the duty of good faith, particularly by insurers against their insureds.

H. DAMAGES FOR EMOTIONAL DISTRESS

Contract damages may be awarded for emotional distress if the distress accompanies *bodily injury* or the contract involved *personal*, rather than strictly financial, interests. Being foreseeable is not enough for emotional harms to be recoverable; the harms need to be *particularly likely* based on the nature of the contract or the breach.

I. RESTITUTIONARY DAMAGES

1. Unenforceable Contracts

Restitutionary damages are available to recover the value of a benefit conferred under a contract that is unenforceable because of the Statute of Frauds, impossibility, etc.

2. Breach of Contract

Restitutionary damages may also be awarded as an alternative to expectation damages against a party who has *materially* breached. This remedy usually is sought when the nonbreaching party has no expectation damages.

3. Plaintiff in Default

Even a party who has *materially breached* may be able to bring an action for restitution, such as where a deposit exceeds the innocent party's damages.

4. Disgorgement

Under modern law, a promisee may be able to recover the *promisor's gains from breach*. Disgorgement has long been recognized as a remedy in cases of conversion of property or breach of fiduciary duty, but there is a modern trend for courts to hold that it is available independently for breach of contract in appropriate cases.

Approach to Exams

Just about any Contracts exam question can be answered by analyzing five basic issues. Of course, not all Contracts questions will require a thorough discussion of all five issues, but you should consider each of them at least briefly before writing your answer.

1. *Was a contract made* between the parties? (Formation problems—offer and acceptance, consideration.)

2. Are there any reasons *the contract should not be enforced* as agreed? (Defenses to formation—indefiniteness, mistake, Statute of Frauds, etc.)

3. *Who has enforceable rights and/or duties* under the contract? (Problems of third-party beneficiaries, assignees, and delegees.)

4. Is there an *absolute duty to perform*? (Problems of conditions, changed circumstances, discharge.)

5. *If the contract has been broken, what remedies* are available to the innocent party?

These issues are analyzed more fully below. For study purposes, be sure to review the more detailed approaches to specific topics in the *chapter approach sections* at the beginning of each chapter.

A. **Has a Valid Contract Been Formed?**

   To establish an enforceable contract there must be a showing of (i) *consideration*, and (ii) mutual assent, usually manifested by an *offer* and an *acceptance*.

   1. **Was There Consideration?**

      Look for a bargain or other basis for enforceability.

      a. **Bargain**

         Did the parties make a bargain? (p. 5)

         (1) Is the promised consideration more than *nominal*? (pp. 7–9)

         (2) If the agreement was based on a promise to forbear from asserting a legal right, did the promisor have an *honest or reasonable belief* in the validity of his claim? (pp. 9–11)

         (3) Did the agreement involve an *illusory promise*? If the promisor has reserved some right, option, or alternative limiting his obligation, consider whether this right is unqualified (if so, the promise may be illusory). (pp. 11–22)

         (4) Did the agreement involve a promise merely to perform some act that the promisor is *already obliged* to do? (pp. 24–37)

         (5) Was the agreement an *accord*? (pp. 38–41)

      b. **Other bases for enforceability**

         If the parties did not make a bargain, was there some *other factor* that made their agreement enforceable?

         (1) Was there *foreseeable reliance* on the promise? (pp. 46–47)

         (2) Was there a *waiver* of some *nonmaterial* condition to the bargain? (pp. 42–43)

(3) Was there an enforceable promise to pay based on ***moral or past consideration*** (*e.g.*, a promise to pay a debt barred the statute of limitations, a promise to pay a voidable obligation)? (pp. 48–52)

(4) Was the promise in some ***special form*** (*e.g.*, under seal) that makes it enforceable? (p. 44)

2. **Was There an Effective Offer?**

   Consider the following:

   a. **Bargaining intent**

   Does it appear that the offeror intended to create ***present contractual rights and duties***, or were they merely negotiating or inviting the other party to make an offer? (pp. 58–59)

   b. **Definiteness**

   Is the proposal sufficiently definite, expressly or impliedly, with regard to important terms? (p. 59)

3. **Was There an Effective Acceptance?**

   Consider:

   a. **Intent and manner**

   Did the offeree apparently intend, by ***words or conduct*** in response to the offer, to create a contractual relationship? And, did the offeree manifest assent to the offeror's proposal in the ***manner*** required by the offer—*i.e.*, by the doing of an act or by the giving of a promise? (This raises the distinction between unilateral and bilateral contracts; p. 88 *et seq.*) Special problems arise when:

   (1) The offeree remains ***silent*** (pp. 99–103); and

   (2) The offeree purports to "accept" the offer in a ***manner different*** from that requested by the offeror. (pp. 106–108)

   b. **Timeliness**

   Did the acceptance become effective ***prior to the termination of the offer*** (termination may occur by revocation of the offer, lapse of time, rejection of the offer, or counteroffer)? (pp. 64–89)

   (1) Where the parties are ***dealing at a distance***, special rules (*e.g.*, the "mailbox rule") must be considered as to when an offer, acceptance, repudiation of acceptance, revocation, or rejection becomes effective. (pp. 104–113)

   (2) If the offeror has attempted to ***revoke***, special rules must be considered as to whether the offer was revocable. (pp. 80–88)

   c. **Unconditional**

   Has the offeree given ***unqualified assent*** to the proposal? If not, "acceptance" may operate as a rejection of the proposal and as a counteroffer. (pp. 68–79)

B. **Are There any Reasons Not to Enforce the Contract?**

Assuming that a contract has been formed, consider whether there are any defenses to the enforcement of the contract:

— ***Indefiniteness*** (pp. 135–147)

— ***Mistake*** (pp. 147–153)

— ***Misrepresentation, nondisclosure, duress, or undue influence*** (pp. 154–157)

- *Unconscionability* (pp. 157–161)
- *Lack of a writing* (in cases where the Statute of Frauds requires one) (pp. 162–172)
- *Lack of contractual capacity* (minors, mental incompetents) (pp. 172–173)
- *Illegality of contract purpose or consideration* (pp. 174–176)

C. **Do Any Third Parties Have Enforceable Rights and/or Obligations Under the Contract?**

1. **Third-Party Beneficiary**

    The "reasonable expectations" induced by the making of the contract may be those of some third party. If so, the third party (as well as the original promisee) may be *entitled to enforce* the bargain promise made in their favor. (p. 179) In determining the rights of such third parties, consider the following:

    a. **Status**

       Consider the distinction between *"intended beneficiaries"* (which include "donee" and "creditor" beneficiaries) and *"incidental beneficiaries."* (pp. 179–182)

    b. **Vesting**

       Have the rights of the third party vested, so that they *may not be terminated or varied* by an agreement between the promisor and the promisee? (p. 190)

    c. **Defenses**

       What defenses or offsets may be asserted against the third party? (pp. 188–189)

2. **Assignees and Delegees**

    Where, *subsequent* to the original contract, either party seeks to transfer to a third party some right and/or duty provided under the contract, several matters should be considered:

    a. **Assignment of rights**

       (1) Are the rights *assignable*? (pp. 194–197)

       (2) What is the *effect* of the assignment (what rights does the assignee have against the obligor, what rights does the obligor have against the assignor, and what defenses may be asserted by the obligor)? (pp. 202–205)

       (3) If the rights have been assigned successively to several assignees, which one of them has *priority*? (pp. 205–207)

    b. **Delegation of duties**

       (1) Is the duty *capable* of being delegated? (p. 209)

       (2) What is the *effect* of the delegation (what are the liabilities of the delegee to the obligee and the obligor)? (pp. 209–211)

D. **Is There a Duty to Perform?**

Once you have determined that a contract has been made, determine whether the reasonable expectations induced by the contract have been fulfilled. If not, think about whether performance has somehow been *excused* by events occurring after formation of the contract. Consider:

1. **Condition vs. Promise**

    Is the contractual provision a condition or a promise? (pp. 217–220) In addition to any *express* conditions, was there any *implied* condition? (pp. 226–227) If there is a condition (express or implied), ask:

    a. Has the condition been *met*?

- b. If the condition has not occurred, has it been *excused* so that there is a duty to perform despite the fact that the condition did not occur? (pp. 223–225)

2. **Present Duty to Perform**

    a. **Conditions precedent**

    Have all *conditions precedent* been performed or excused (*e.g.*, by anticipatory repudiation, prospective inability to perform, or substantial performance)? (pp. 227–241)

    b. **Changed circumstances**

    Did the circumstances change so that performance was *impossible* or highly *impracticable*? (pp. 241–244)

    c. **Frustration**

    Did the *purpose or value* of the contract become totally frustrated by a supervening event? (p. 244)

3. **Discharge of Contract**

    Has the contract been discharged by full performance or some other ground such as rescission, release, accord and satisfaction, or a payment-in-full check? (pp. 245–247)

E. **What Remedies Are Available to the Innocent Party?**

Which remedies are available for breach of contract?

1. **Damages**

    a. **In general**

    Remember that damages are the most common remedy. (p. 251)

    b. **Expectation damages**

    Expectation damages are the normal remedy for breach of a bargain contract. Applying this measure, what is required to put the injured party into the position they would have occupied had the promise been *performed*? (This depends on the nature of the contract and the position of the injured party.) (pp. 256–265)

    c. **Reliance damages**

    Reliance damages are the usual remedy for promissory estoppel. (pp. 46–47) They may also be available in some cases of bargain contracts. (pp. 254–255)

    d. **Liquidated damages**

    What is the effect of any *agreed measure* of damages or any *limitation* on the measure of damages? (pp. 265–266)

2. **Specific Performance**

    Is the legal remedy (*i.e.*, damages) adequate? If not, consider whether specific performance of the contract would better remedy the breach of contract. (p. 256)

3. **Restitution**

    Would this alternative to damages be a more appropriate remedy (*e.g.*, if the contract is a *losing one* or if it is *unenforceable*)? (Plaintiff may recover the reasonable value of the *benefit conferred*.) (pp. 268–270)

Many Contracts questions will also require that you consider matters of interpretation (pp. 114–117) and the special role of written contracts (*i.e.*, the parol evidence rule). (pp. 118–126)

Issue Spotting in Contracts

You may find that an effective way to study for Contracts exams is to learn to recognize which legal issues are raised by particular types of facts. Most Contracts exams present a fact pattern and require that you analyze it rather than simply asking you to explain rules of contract law in the abstract.

The following chart categorizes many of the major rules of contract law by the facts that commonly raise issues about them:

FACTS	LEGAL ISSUES THAT MAY BE RAISED
The contract is made **orally** (*e.g.*, face to face using spoken words, by phone) or on a document that is *not signed* by one of the parties.	• Statute of Frauds [pp. 162–172] • "No oral modification" clause [p. 127]
The contract is **written** (*e.g.*, concluded on paper or by mail or email).	• Parol evidence rule [pp. 118–126] • Plain meaning rule [pp. 115, 125]
One party may be making a **gift** rather than a self-interested bargain.	• Consideration [Chapter 1, specifically pp. 43–47]
The contract involves, or recites, a **small amount of money** (or an item of insignificant value) exchanged for something of significant value.	• Nominal consideration [p. 7] • Unconscionability [pp. 157–161] • Duress [p. 156] • Undue Influence [p. 157] • Misrepresentation [p. 154]
One party makes a promise that doesn't really **bind** them, or doesn't bind them to anything **new**.	• Illusory promise rule [pp. 11–22] • Legal duty rule [pp. 24–37]
One party **relies** on another's promise (even if there is no bargain).	• Promissory estoppel [pp. 46–47]
The contract involves the sale of **goods**.	• Does U.C.C. Article 2 differ from the common law? [see provisions throughout, and specifically p. 85]
The parties **modify** a contract.	• Legal duty rule [pp. 24–37]

	• Economic duress [pp. 31, 156] • "No oral modification" clauses [p. 127]
The parties use ***mail or email*** (or anything with a potential delay or problems with delivery) to communicate.	• Rules about when communications are effective [pp. 104–113]
The contract is formed ***online***.	• Clickwrap agreements [pp. 130–131] • Browsewrap agreements [pp. 131–132] • Unconscionability [pp. 157–161, specifically p. 158]
The offeror attempts to ***revoke*** an offer.	• Mailbox rule (to determine whether an acceptance is timely, in view of the revocation) [pp. 104–110] • Firm offer rule/Unilateral contracts [pp. 82–88]
The parties disagree about what ***words*** or ***conduct*** means.	• Interpretation [pp. 114–117] • Parol evidence rule [pp. 118–126] • Plain meaning rule [pp. 115, 125]
At least one party is ***wrong*** about a material fact.	• Mutual mistake [pp. 148–149] • Misrepresentation [p. 154] • Nondisclosure [p. 154]
At least one party has made a ***typo*** (or similar mechanical error).	• Unilateral mistake [pp. 149–150] • Mistranscription [p. 150]
The promisee loses ***profits*** as a result of the promisor's breach.	• Foreseeability (*Hadley v. Baxendale*) [pp. 252–254] • Certainty [p. 253] • Mitigation [pp. 255–256] • Lost-volume sellers [p. 259]
More than two parties have possible rights or duties under the same contract.	• Third party beneficiaries [p. 178–190] • Assignment [pp. 191–207] • Delegation [pp. 207–211]

Introduction—Sources of Contract Law

Common Law

Contracts is largely a common law subject. That is, the law of Contracts is largely caselaw made by judges. One of the advantages of judge-made law is that it is adaptable to the changing norms and changing needs of society.

Statutes

Certain statutes are relevant to contract law:

> **Uniform Commercial Code**—The major exception to the common law nature of Contracts is that contracts for the *sale of goods* (tangible movable property) are governed by Article 2 of the Uniform Commercial Code ("U.C.C."). The U.C.C. is a model statute that covers a variety of commercial subjects. The purpose of the U.C.C. is to make commercial law uniform among the states. The U.C.C. was drafted, and is periodically revised, by the National Conference of Commissioners on Uniform State Laws (also known as the Uniform Law Commission) and the American Law Institute ("A.L.I."). It has been adopted by every state except Louisiana (although Louisiana has adopted portions of the U.C.C.). Even in the case of contracts for the sale of goods, the common law remains important. Article 2 of the U.C.C. does not cover every contract law issue that may arise in such contracts (*e.g.*, Article 2 does not address the issue of mistake). When Article 2 does not cover a contract law issue, the common law governs that issue. [U.C.C. § 1–103] Although the major impact of the U.C.C. on contract law concerns Article 2, other Articles are also relevant, especially Article 1, which sets forth general provisions that apply to all of the U.C.C., and Article 9, which governs most assignments.

> **Statute of Frauds**—Another statute that is central to contract law and that is adopted by all the states is the Statute of Frauds, which governs the issue of whether a contract is enforceable if it was *made orally*.

> **State and Federal Statutes**—In addition to the U.C.C. and the Statute of Frauds, various state and federal statutes have been adopted that relate to isolated issues of contract law.

The Restatements

The A.L.I. issues "Restatements" of various areas of law, including Contracts. The Restatements of contract law are the Restatement of Contracts ("Restatement First") and its revision, the Restatement (Second) of Contracts ("Restatement Second"). Unlike statutes or caselaw, Restatements do *not have the force of law*. They are basically intended to set forth the law of the subjects they cover and to reconcile conflicting state rules by adopting the best of the rules. Often, however, the Restatements reach out somewhat to push the law in a desirable direction. Though they do not have the force of law, the Restatements have been very influential, particularly in contract law.

Contracts

Fifteenth Edition

Chapter One
Consideration

CONTENTS	PAGE
Chapter Approach	2
A. Introduction	3
B. Bargain Promises	5
C. Accord and Satisfaction	38
D. Waiver	42
E. Unrelied-Upon Donative Promises	43
F. Relied-Upon Donative Promises—Doctrine of Promissory Estoppel	46
G. Moral or Past Consideration	48

Chapter Approach

Not every promise is legally enforceable. Promises that are legally enforceable are called "contracts." Formation of a contract requires two basic elements: consideration and mutual assent. This chapter focuses on the element of *consideration*. The next chapter will discuss mutual assent.

The concept of consideration is one way that contract law distinguishes legally enforceable promises from legally unenforceable promises. The term "consideration" has two related but somewhat different meanings. Traditionally, the term was used only to refer to a "bargain"—an exchange of promises (*e.g.*, Tom promises to give Carina $500 if Carina promises to paint Tom's fence) or the exchange of a promise for performance (Tom promises to give Carina $500 for actually painting the fence). Today, however, the term "consideration" may also be used more broadly to refer to any factor that makes a promise enforceable (*e.g.*, justifiable reliance on the promise).

A typical Contracts examination question involves a broken promise, and your answer to the question should begin with an analysis of whether the promise that was broken was legally enforceable—in other words, whether there was consideration.

Because the basic kind of consideration is a bargain, you should begin your analysis by determining whether the broken promise was given as part of a bargain. The answer to that question determines how you should then proceed.

1. If the promise was apparently given **as part of a bargain,** you should ask yourself the following questions:

    a. Was the bargain merely *nominal* ("in name only")—*i.e.*, a bargain in form but not in substance? If so, the promise may be unenforceable because it is essentially a donative promise (*i.e.*, a promise to give a gift).

    b. Was the bargain based on a promise to *surrender* or *forbear from asserting* a legal claim? If so, usually it is enforceable only if the claim was reasonable or held in good faith.

    c. Did the bargain involve an *illusory promise*—*i.e.*, a statement that appeared to be a real promise, but in fact did not commit the promisor to any more than what they might later desire to do, or gave them a free way out of their apparent commitment? If so, the promise may be unenforceable for lack of mutuality.

    d. Did the bargain involve a promise merely to take an action that the promisor was already *legally obliged* to take, usually either because of statutory law (like criminal law) or because of a prior contract? If so, the bargain may be unenforceable under the legal duty rule.

2. If the promise was **not given as part of a bargain,** it is unenforceable unless there is some *other* factor that makes it enforceable. Possibilities include:

    a. *Reliance*—did the promisee (the person to whom a promise is made) reasonably rely on the promise?

    b. *Past or moral consideration*—was the promise given in recognition of a benefit previously conferred on the promisor by the promisee that gave rise to an obligation to compensate the promisee?

    c. *Waiver*—did the promise merely waive a nonmaterial condition under a bargain?

    d. *Form*—was the promise in some special legal form, such as under seal in a state that still recognizes the binding force of the seal?

If any of these factors is present, the promise may be enforceable even though there was no bargain.

A. Introduction

1. Importance of Consideration

The concept of "consideration" is very important in the law of contracts, because consideration is required to make a promise or contract enforceable.

2. What Is Consideration?

a. "Benefit/Detriment" Approach

At an early stage in contract law, consideration was defined as either a *benefit* received by the party promising to perform (the *promisor*) or a *detriment* incurred by the party to whom performance was promised (the *promisee*). (When there is a bargain, each party is both a promisor and a promisee. When focusing on a broken promise, courts frequently call the plaintiff the promisee and the defendant the promisor.)

Example: Hannah promises to pay Victoria $100 for her television set. Hannah as promisor will receive a benefit (*i.e.*, receiving the television set) and Victoria as promisee will incur a detriment (*i.e.*, delivering the television set). Conversely, Victoria as promisor will receive a benefit (*i.e.*, receiving money for the television set) and Hannah as promisee will incur a detriment (*i.e.*, paying $100 for the television set).

(1) Comment

In practice, the benefit/detriment definition of consideration was not very helpful. First, the definition is too broad, because some promises not generally found to constitute consideration fit the definition. For example, a promise to make a gift that imposes a condition (detriment) on the receiver of the gift (the promisee) would fit the definition, but conditional gifts are held to lack consideration (*see infra*, p. 45). Second, there are many cases where the definition does not really explain the results, because the law gives a special meaning to the terms "benefit" and "detriment." For example, if Uncle promises to pay Nephew $5,000 if he refrains from smoking, drinking, swearing, and gambling until he reaches the age of 21, although one might say Nephew received a moral or physical benefit from his abstinence, Nephew incurred a *legal* detriment because he gave up the *legal right* to drink, smoke, swear, or gamble. [**Hamer v. Sidway,** 124 N.Y. 538 (1891)]

b. "Bargain" Approach

Because of the weaknesses of the early approach to consideration, the next stage of development was to treat consideration as equivalent to bargain. A bargain is an exchange of promises, acts, or both, in which each party views what they give as the *price* of what they get. This bargained-for price may include not only promises and acts but also promises to forbear (refrain from doing something) and actual forbearance from performing acts one is legally entitled to perform. The concept that equates consideration and bargain is called the ***bargain theory of consideration***.

Example: Carina promises to paint Tom's fence in exchange for Tom's promise to pay her $500. Carina and Tom each have bargained for the other's promise as the price of the promise they made. This ***exchange of promises*** constitutes consideration.

cf. **Compare:** Carina paints Tom's fence with no expectation of payment. One year later, Tom tells Carina he will pay her $500 for the work she did. There is *no consideration* for Tom's promise because Tom did not bargain for Carina's painting the fence. When she painted the fence, Carina did not view Tom's payment as the price for her service.

e.g. **Example:** Hannah offers a reward of $50 to anyone who returns her lost dog. Joe sees the reward offer and then finds and returns Hannah's lost dog. The exchange of Hannah's *promise* to pay for Joe's *act* of returning the dog is a bargain and therefore constitutes consideration.

e.g. **Example:** Bob and Sara get into a car accident. Sara promises to pay Bob $500 if he promises not to sue her for damage to his car. There is consideration for this agreement. In giving up his right to sue, Bob gave up a legal right (*i.e.*, refrained from suing Sara) as a bargain for Sara's promise of payment.

c. "Enforceable Factor" Approach

The bargain theory of consideration has certain limits. First, not all bargain promises are enforceable (*see infra*, p. 7 *et seq.*). Second, some promises are enforceable even though they are not bargains. Therefore, some authorities treat consideration as equivalent to *any factor*—including but not limited to bargains—that will make a promise or contract enforceable. Factors other than bargain that make a promise enforceable include: reliance on a promise by the other party (*see infra*, p. 46 *et seq.*), certain promises given in return for nonbargained-for acts or promises (*i.e.*, past or moral consideration; *see infra*, p. 48 *et seq.*), waiver of nonmaterial conditions of the bargain (*see infra*, p. 42), and promises made in special legally recognized forms, such as promises under seal (*see infra*, p. 44).

e.g. **Example:** Lydia promises to give Kay $500,000 as a gift to buy a house. In reliance on Lydia's promise, Kay buys a house, intending to use the promised money to cover the purchase price. Later, Lydia refuses to give the money to Kay. While Lydia's promise to pay Kay $500,000 is not consideration under the bargain approach, Kay's reliance on the promise does constitute consideration under the enforceable factor approach.

3. Kinds of Promises That Raise Consideration Issues

With the above background in mind, this chapter will examine the kinds of promises that may raise problems of consideration or enforceability. For this purpose, promises can be divided into six broad categories:

a. Bargain promises;

b. Promises involving an accord and satisfaction;

c. Promises to waive conditions;

d. Unrelied-upon donative promises;

e. Relied-upon donative promises; and

f. Promises based on past or moral consideration.

B. Bargain Promises

1. General Rule—Bargain Constitutes Consideration

A bargain is an exchange in which each party views his promise or performance as the price of the other's promise or performance. As a general rule, a bargain constitutes consideration—*i.e.*, a bargained-for promise is enforceable.

a. Equal Value Not Required

In most cases, the law does not examine whether a bargained-for promise or performance is commensurate in value with the counterpromise or performance, as long as the contract is not "unconscionable" (*i.e.*, so unfair as to shock the court's conscience; *see infra*, pp. 157–161). [**Batsakis v. Demotsis,** 226 S.W.2d 673 (Tex. 1949); Restatement Second ("Rest. 2d") §§ 71, 72, 79] The theory is that the parties to a bargain are the best judges of its desirability for each of them. The traditional way in which this approach is formulated is that "adequacy of consideration will not be reviewed," and that "a bargain will be enforced according to its terms."

e.g. **Example:** Eric agrees to buy a used car from Priya for $22,000. Strong evidence shows that cars of this type, with similar age, mileage, and condition, ordinarily sell for no more than $11,000. The parties have a bargain, and their contract is enforceable unless some other defense (*e.g.*, incapacity, fraud, duress, etc., *see infra*, p. 154 *et seq.*) applies. There is consideration on both sides even though the "value" is not equal.

(1) Gross Disparity as Evidence

However, gross disparity between the value of what is done or to be done by each party may be used as *evidence* to support certain defenses—*e.g.*, incapacity, fraud, duress, etc. (*infra*, p. 154 *et seq.*). It also may be *evidence* that the parties did not intend a bargain but, instead, made a payment as nominal consideration (*infra*, p. 7).

(2) Unconscionability

Furthermore, under the modern doctrine of unconscionability, courts may directly examine a disparity in value to determine whether the disparity is so great as to be unconscionable. Normally this doctrine is applied to determine whether the *process* that led to the bargain was unconscionable—*e.g.*, because terms in a form contract were unfairly surprising, or because one party improperly exploited the other's ignorance. In some cases, however, the courts use the doctrine to overturn contracts that appear to be so imbalanced as to be oppressive without regard to defects in the bargaining process. (*See infra*, p. 159.)

(3) Equitable Remedies

Historically, courts were divided into law courts and equity courts, each with differing rules and remedies. Vestiges of this division remain today. While adequacy of consideration generally is not reviewed when a party sues at law for damages, adequacy of consideration may be reviewed by the courts when a party seeks an equitable remedy such as specific performance, under which a court orders a party to perform rather than merely to pay damages (*infra*, p. 256 *et seq.*). Unlike law, equity normally requires a showing of fairness and substantial equivalence in value as a condition to granting relief.

APPROACH TO ENFORCEABILITY OF PROMISES—CONSIDERATION

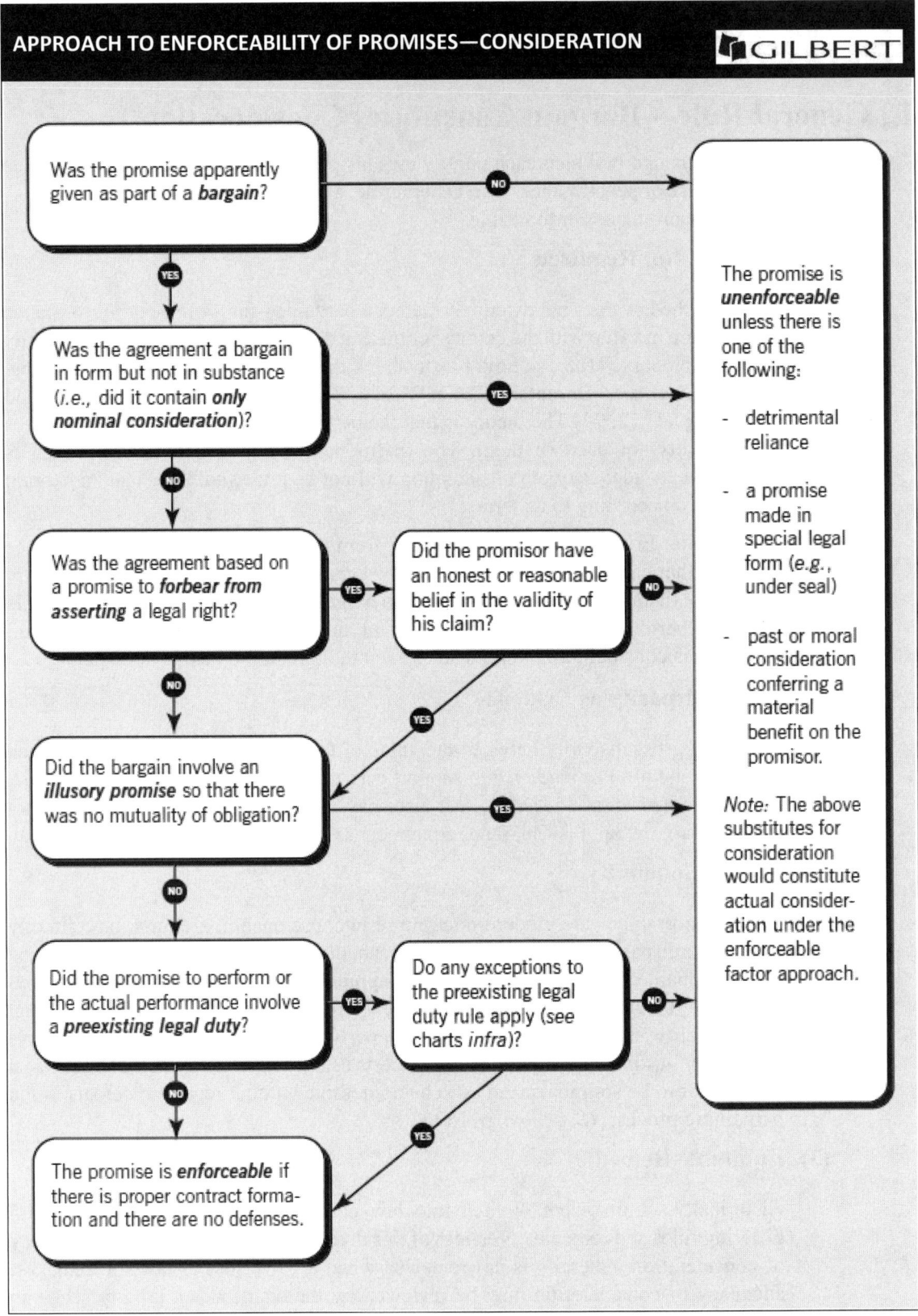

2. Exceptions—Bargains or Apparent Bargains That Are Not Consideration

Although bargains normally constitute consideration and are therefore legally enforceable, there are several types of cases in which bargains or apparent bargains do not constitute consideration (or "lack consideration") and are therefore unenforceable. These cases fall into four major categories:

(i) *Nominal consideration* (transactions that are bargains in form but not in substance);

(ii) Promises to *surrender or forbear from asserting a legal claim* that is unreasonable (or, under some authorities, that is neither reasonable nor held in good faith);

(iii) Apparent bargains involving an *illusory* promise; and

(iv) Bargains in which one party promises to do only what she is already *legally obliged* to do.

a. Nominal Consideration

A transaction is said to involve nominal consideration (*i.e.*, consideration in name only) when a promisor falsely casts her promise in the *form* of a bargain with the promisee in an attempt to make the promise enforceable, but the transaction lacks the *substance* of a bargain because neither party views each promised performance as the price of the other. To put this differently, nominal consideration exists when there is a *recital* of a bargain but *no real bargain*.

Example: Father promises to give Daughter a house in exchange for one dollar. It is clear that neither Father nor Daughter views the dollar as the price of the house. Rather, the transaction has only the form of a bargain—a form adopted for the obvious purpose of making Father's donative promise legally enforceable. The purported consideration—*i.e.*, the bargain—is not real; it is only nominal.

EXAM TIP

If the facts of a question indicate that the value of the parties' promises or performances differs greatly, be sure to consider the issue of nominal consideration. Remember that if the parties truly **intended to make a bargain** (*i.e.*, if each party views their performance as the price of the other party's performance), a court generally will find that there is consideration, no matter how disproportionate the two performances seem to be (although disproportion may be relevant to whether there is unconscionability, fraud, duress, or the like). However, if the parties never really intended to make a bargain, but instead tried to make a donative promise look like a bargain, the court will deem that the purported "bargain" lacks consideration.

Note that it is not the *value* of a promise alone, but the parties' intent, that distinguishes real bargains from nominal bargains. The question is not whether $10, or some service or action, is or is not nominal consideration in the abstract. There is not a specific threshold past which a service or item or amount of money converts from nominal consideration to actual consideration. The question is simply whether the parties saw the money or action in question as the price of their own promise or performance.

(1) Enforceability of Promises Given for Nominal Consideration

(a) Donative Promises

Although the authorities are not in complete accord, the prevailing modern view is that nominal consideration normally will not make a donative promise enforceable. [**Schnell v. Nell**, *supra*, p. 5; Rest. 2d § 71] That is, courts look to the substance of what the parties are doing (are they making a bargain or a gift?) rather than to its form.

In the past, it was more likely that courts would treat nominal consideration as consideration (based on its form alone) and therefore to enforce a promise that was, in substance, only a donative promise.

(b) Options and Guaranties

However, nominal consideration *can* make promises enforceable in two situations: *options* and *guaranties*.

1) Options

An option is a promise to hold an offer open for a fixed amount of time. Although the cases are split, most courts hold that nominal consideration makes an option binding, at least if the option is in writing and proposes an exchange on fair terms. [**Real Estate Co. of Pittsburgh v. Rudolph**, 153 A. 438 (Pa. 1930); Rest. 2d § 87; *and see infra*, p. 67] Some courts require that the nominal consideration actually be paid rather than just recited, but this view is less common today. [**1464-Eight, Ltd. v. Joppich**, 154 S.W.3d 101 (Tex. 2004)]

Example: A landowner emails a potential buyer: "You can buy my property at any time until March 31 for $200,000. In exchange for this right, I agree to accept $10 from you." The landowner's promise (to keep the offer open until March 31) is likely enforceable. Some courts require that the buyer actually pay the landowner $10, but this view has faded. Note that the underlying real-estate transaction (the property for $200,000) has consideration regardless, so if the buyer accepts the landowner's offer while it is still open, the parties have an enforceable contract. The issue is just whether the *option* (the landowner's promise to keep the offer open until March 31) is enforceable if, for example, the landowner choose to revoke the offer before March 31 and before the buyer has accepted it.

a) Distinguish—U.C.C. "Firm Offers"

The U.C.C., which governs contracts for the sale of goods, is even more lenient here. Under the U.C.C., a written "firm offer" by a merchant to buy or sell goods is irrevocable for the period of time stated in the offer (or if no time is stated, for a reasonable time) without the necessity of any consideration or even a recital of consideration. [U.C.C. § 2–205; *and see infra*, pp. 84–85]

2) Guaranties

A guaranty is a promise to answer for another party's debt or for her performance of a contractual obligation. As with options, most courts hold that nominal consideration will make a guaranty binding, at least if the promise is in writing. [Rest. 2d § 88]

3) Rationale—Serve Commercial Purposes

Most options and guaranties are given for commercial rather than purely donative reasons. That is, they are promises designed to facilitate or further a proposed bargain, not only to gift a gift. As a result, they are likely to be relied on.

Also, many options in the real world have low market values (*e.g.*, the option to buy a piece of real estate for $1 million over the next few weeks may well be worth only a few hundred dollars; the value will depend on the market value of the real estate and how quickly that value is expected to change), and courts may not want to mistake those low values for nominal consideration.

Therefore, it is not surprising that the law would be ready to enforce such promises even if they are not bargained for. Note, however, that if an option or a guaranty lacks both real *and* nominal consideration—*i.e.*, if it is neither a real bargain nor in the form of a bargain—it will normally be unenforceable unless either (i) it is relied upon or (ii) a statute, such as U.C.C. section 2–205, provides for its enforcement; *see infra*, pp. 84–85.

b. Promises to Surrender or Forbear from Asserting a Legal Claim

A bargained-for promise to surrender or forbear from asserting a legal claim that is reasonable and held in good faith constitutes consideration. (This rule covers ordinary settlements of legal claims.) A problem arises, however, when the underlying legal claim is (i) not reasonable, (ii) not held in good faith, or (iii) neither reasonable nor held in good faith.

(1) Former Rule—Honest *and* Reasonable Belief Required

At one time, the courts held that a bargained-for promise to surrender or forbear from asserting a legal claim would constitute consideration only if there was an honest *and* reasonable basis for believing the claim to be valid. [**Springstead v. Nees,** 125 App. Div. 230 (1908)] This rule was adopted in Restatement First section 76, which provided that "[t]he surrender of, or forbearance to assert, an invalid claim or defense by one who has not an honest *and* reasonable belief in its possible validity" is not consideration. (Emphasis added.) *Honesty* refers to the potential plaintiff's subjective view of the case, whereas *reasonableness* is objective.

e.g. **Example:** Kevin injures himself while running with scissors. He threatens to sue the scissors' manufacturer claiming there was a product defect, but the scissors were not defective and under state tort law he would, as a matter of law, have no case. The scissors' manufacturer offers to resolve the potential lawsuit for a small sum. Under the former rule, Kevin's promise not to sue is *not* consideration, even if he honestly believes his lawsuit has merit, because the lawsuit has no reasonable basis.

(2) Modern Rule—Honest *or* Reasonable Belief Suffices

The modern rule is that a promise to surrender or forbear from asserting a claim is consideration if the promisor's belief in the validity of the claim is *either* reasonable *or* held in good faith. [**Kossick v. United Fruit Co.,** 365 U.S. 731 (1961); **Dyer v. National By-Products, Inc.,** 380 N.W.2d 732 (Iowa 1986)]

(a) Restatement Second

This rule has been adopted in Restatement Second section 74, which changes the rule of Restatement First section 76 by providing that "forbearance to assert, or the surrender of, an invalid claim or defense is not consideration unless (i) the claim or defense is in fact doubtful because of uncertainty as to the facts or law, *or* (ii) the forbearing or surrendering party honestly believes that his claim or defense is just and may be determined to be valid." (Emphasis added.)

(b) Minimum Validity

Under a *pure* good faith test, forbearance to press a claim held in good faith could be consideration even if the claim is completely ill-founded. However, a claim that lacks any validity at all might not be treated as made in good faith under this rule. For example, in **Duncan v. Black,** 324 S.W.2d 483 (Mo. 1959), the court said that "if the claimant, in good faith, makes a mountain out of a mole hill, the claim is 'doubtful' [so that forbearance will constitute consideration]. But if there is no discernible mole hill in the beginning, then the claim has no substance" and forbearance to assert the claim will not be consideration.

Example: Landowner Lou's house, worth $250,000, is destroyed in a fire. He believes the fire was worsened by building materials that his homebuilder used several years earlier, and he asserts that their use was negligent. He has little evidence of this, and he consults with a lawyer who tells him that state tort law is not on his side. Nonetheless, he sends a demand letter to the homebuilder. Eager to settle the claim and sympathetic with Lou's plight, the builder offers to settle with Lou for $8,000. Lou accepts. There is likely consideration on both sides under the modern rule. But if Lou had sued a cell-phone company in an earnest but implausible belief that its cell-phone towers a mile away had caused his house to catch fire, some courts say that his promise not to sue would not amount to consideration, even if Lou's belief about the underlying tort lawsuit against the cell-phone company was held in subjective good faith, because it is objectively baseless.

(3) Actual Surrender or Forbearance

The rules that govern a bargained-for *promise* to surrender or forbear from asserting a claim also govern a bargained-for *act* of surrendering or forbearing to assert a claim. That is, a bargain for the actual surrender of or actual forbearance to assert a claim (as opposed to a bargain for a promise to surrender or forbear) will constitute consideration only when the claim is reasonable or held in good faith.

(4) Written Release

Some authorities take the position that execution of a written release may constitute consideration even if there is neither a reasonable basis for the claim released nor a good faith belief in its validity. [**Mullen v. Hawkins,** 40 N.E. 797 (Ind. 1895); Rest. 2d § 74] This rule applies most readily to situations where someone honestly believes and says they have no claim but the other party, to be sure of the matter, wants a written release anyway.

Example: Steven Surrender, while a passenger in Nora Negligent's car, is involved in a minor accident resulting from Negligent's lack of care. Surrender, believing he has suffered no injury, makes no claim against Negligent or

Negligent's insurer. However, Negligent's insurer is eager to close the file on the case. The insurer therefore approaches Surrender and offers him $200 if he will sign a release. Some authorities hold that Surrender's execution of the release constitutes consideration even though Surrender does not believe he has a claim.

(5) Forbearance Where No Specific Period Stated

Suppose a person agrees, as part of a bargain, to forbear from asserting a legal claim, but no specific period of time is stated during which she must forbear. In such cases, the court will interpret the promise as one to forbear for a *reasonable time.*

Example: Josh requests Heather to forbear from asserting a claim that she has against Miguel, and promises to pay her if she forbears and Miguel does not pay her. Heather agrees and forbears for 11 months. At the end of 11 months, Heather sues Miguel or otherwise asserts her claim. When Miguel does not pay, Heather sues Josh. Josh defends on the ground that because Heather asserted her claim against Miguel, she did not keep her part of the bargain. In such a situation, most courts hold that Heather's promise should not be interpreted as a promise to forbear *forever,* but only as a promise to forbear for a *reasonable* time. [*See* **Strong v. Sheffield,** 144 N.Y. 392 (1895)] Therefore, if 11 months was a reasonable time, Heather will prevail in her action against Josh.

c. Illusory Promises

(1) General Rule—Mutuality of Obligation Required in Bilateral Contract

A *bilateral contract* is a bargain contract in which the parties exchange a promise for a promise (*e.g.,* A promises to pay B $100 for B's used television set, to be delivered in one week, and B promises to deliver the set in one week for $100). A *unilateral contract* is a bargain contract in which the parties exchange a promise for an act (*e.g.,* A promises B that A will pay B $100 to paint A's fence, but makes clear that he does not want B's promise to paint the fence; only the act of painting the fence will do).

MEMORY TIP   **GILBERT**

This terminology may seem confusing, but the term *bilateral contract* simply refers to a contract with bilateral promises (that is, a promise on each side), whereas the term *unilateral contract* simply refers to a contract with a unilateral promise (that is, a promise on only one side).

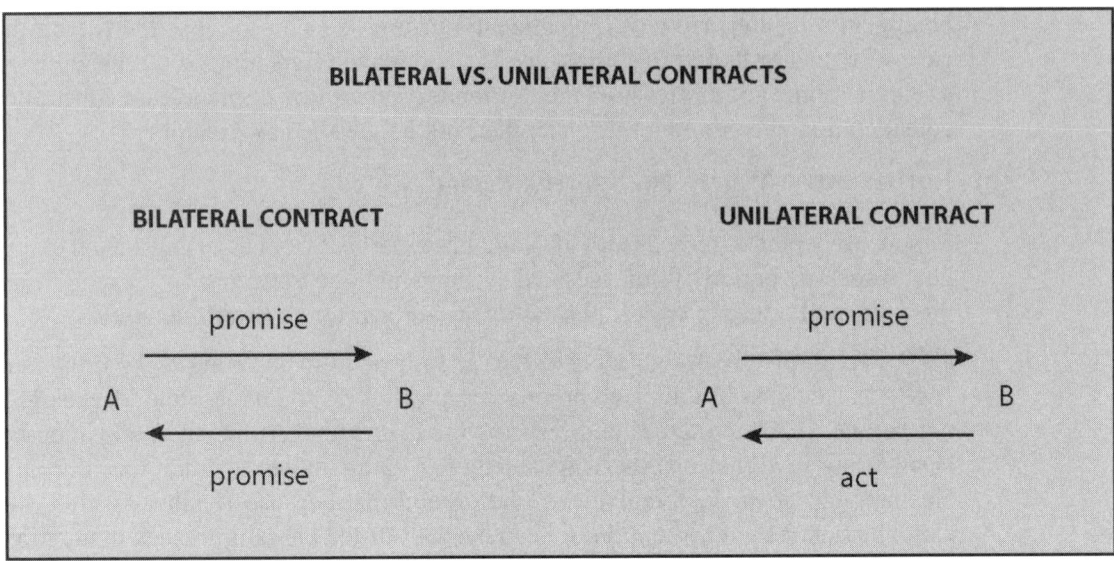

The general doctrinal rule is that for a bilateral contract to be enforceable, it must have *mutuality of obligation*—*i.e.*, both parties must be bound. If both parties to a bilateral contract are not bound, neither will be bound. The major impact of the mutuality rule is that an illusory promise is not consideration. Courts and commentators widely regard this rule as undesirable, however, and it has been significantly eroded. As one court has put it, "the mutuality doctrine has become a faltering rampart to which a litigant retreats at his own peril." [**Helle v. Landmark, Inc.,** 472 N.E.2d 765, 776 (Ohio. App. 1984)] The reason for this erosion is that the illusory promise rule serves no clear moral or economic goal.

EXAM TIP

Rules like the illusory-promise rule highlight significant changes in American contract law over the last hundred years. Professors teach this material differently. Some emphasize the older, doctrinal rule. Some use it as an opportunity to show how the law has changed or to emphasize the subtlety of the common law. Some use it as an opportunity to study policy arguments. The rule has many exceptions [*infra* p. 15 *et seq.*] that courts can apply generously to restrict the force of the rule.

(a) "Illusory Promise" Defined

An illusory promise is a statement that has the *form* of a promise but is not a real promise in *substance.* A *real promise* is a commitment that limits one's future options as compared to one's options immediately before the promise was made. An *illusory promise* does not limit one's future options. Rather, an illusory promise is an *apparent commitment* that actually leaves a "free way out" (*e.g.*, "I will buy wheat from you at $10/bushel *insofar as I want to buy* wheat from you at that price," or "I will buy all my requirements of wheat from you at $10/bushel but *I may terminate my obligation at any time*").

(2) Effect of Illusory Promise

Under the mutuality rule, if one party makes an illusory promise in exchange for another's real promise, neither party is bound. The first party is not bound simply because he has not made a real promise—nothing he has said limits his future options. The second party is not bound because all she received in exchange for her real promise was an illusory promise, which is not consideration, and a promise without consideration is unenforceable.

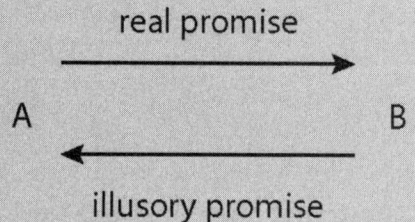

ILLUSORY PROMISE ILLUSTRATION

The force of the illusory promise rule is that if *B* gives an illusory promise to *A*, *A* is not bound—even though they gave a real promise to *B*—because *A* did not receive consideration for that promise. That is, *B*'s illusory promise does not count as consideration, so *A*'s promise is not enforceable.

B's promise is unenforceable regardless, simply because it is illusory. There is no way to enforce an illusory promise precisely because it is illusory.

(a) Common Types of Illusory Promises

1) Promise to Do an Act "if I Want to"

One common type of illusory promise is a promise to do a certain act "if I want to." The "promise" is illusory because after making the statement, the "promisor" has not limited their options. They are just as free to do whatever they want after they make the statement as they were before they made the statement. They have a free way out by simply deciding that they do not want to do the act. [**Office Pavilion S. Florida, Inc. v. ASAL Prods., Inc.,** 849 So.2d 367 (Fla. Dist. Ct. App. 2003)]

Example: On January 1, Seller agrees to sell to Buyer, at $100/ton, all the steel that Buyer orders from Seller until December 31. In exchange, Buyer agrees to buy from Seller, at $100/ton, "all the steel that she decides to order from Seller" until December 31. Seller then refuses to fill Buyer's orders, and Buyer sues. Under the illusory-promise rule, Seller wins. Buyer's "promise" is illusory. All Buyer has said is that she will buy from Seller as much steel *as she decides to order* from Seller. After making this statement, Buyer is just as free to buy (or refuse to buy) from Seller as she was before she made the statement; she can buy the steel she needs from Seller or anyone else. Because Buyer's promise is illusory, it is not consideration for Seller's promise, and therefore Seller's promise is unenforceable.

cf. Compare: In the example above, if Buyer had promised to buy from Seller "*all the steel she requires,*" rather than "all the steel she decides to order from Seller," she might be deemed to have made a real promise—a promise to purchase her steel requirements *from Seller.* (*See infra*, pp. 21–22.) In that case, Buyer would be bound because she would have made a commitment that did limit her future options. And if Buyer would be bound, Seller would be bound, because the agreement would not lack mutuality.

e.g. Example: Buyer says to Seller, "I promise to buy your house if I decide it suits my needs." Seller agrees to sell to Buyer at Buyer's option. Buyer's promise is probably illusory, and therefore, under the illusory promise rule, Buyer cannot enforce Seller's promise because Buyer provided no consideration for it.

cf. Compare: Buyer says to Renter, "If I buy that house by March 30, I promise to lease it to you for a year." Renter agrees that if Buyer buys the house, Renter will rent it for a year. Both promises are real promises, *not* illusory promises. It is true that Buyer's promise is subject to a condition that is entirely under Buyer's control, but the promise does shrink Buyer's options: after making the promise, Buyer is not free to buy the house and *not* rent it to Renter (*e.g.*, Buyer is not free to refuse to rent it at all or to rent it to a third party). Therefore, both promises are enforceable—but neither party will have an obligation to perform unless Buyer does in fact buy the house by March 30. [*Cf.* **Scott v. Moragues Lumber Co.,** 80 So. 394 (Ala. 1918); *infra* p. 17]

EXAM TIP   **GILBERT**

Closely analyze the wording of contract terms; language can make a big difference here. To determine whether a promise is illusory (and therefore not sufficient consideration), remember to ask yourself whether the promisor has ***limited his future options.*** For example, a contract term such as "Seller will sell Buyer *all the widgets that Seller produces*" limits Seller's future performance by requiring Seller to sell his total output of widgets to Buyer. However, a term such as "Seller will sell Buyer *all the widgets Seller wants to sell to Buyer*" does not limit Seller's future options because Seller can choose to sell the widgets to another buyer if he wishes. Therefore, the promise is illusory and the contract will fail for lack of consideration.

---

2) Right to Terminate at Will Without Notice

Another common type of illusory promise is a real promise that is coupled with a power to terminate the obligation under the promise at will and without notice. Such a power gives a free way out and therefore renders the promise illusory. [**Miami Coca-Cola Bottling Co. v. Orange Crush Co.,** 296 F. 693 (5th Cir. 1924); **Bernstein v. W.B. Manufacturing Co.,** 131 N.E. 200 (Mass. 1921)]

e.g. Example: Orange Crush, a soft-drink company, entered into an agreement with Miami Coca-Cola Bottling Co. ("Coke"), a soft-drink bottler. Under the agreement, Orange Crush granted Coke a license to manufacture the drink Orange Crush and use the Orange Crush trademark. In return, Coke agreed to buy a certain amount of Orange Crush concentrate, maintain a bottling plant, solicit orders, advertise the product, and increase the product's sales. This license was perpetual, but it allowed

Coke to cancel the agreement at any time. About one year later, Orange Crush asserted that it no longer wished to be bound by the agreement and Coke sued to enforce the contract. The court held that the contract was void for lack of mutuality because it could be terminated by Coke at any time. [**Miami Coca-Cola Bottling Co. v. Orange Crush Co.,** *supra*]

a) Exception: U.C.C. Section 2–309

U.C.C. section 2–309(3) provides that "termination of a contract by one party except on the happening of an agreed event requires that *reasonable notification* be received by the other party, and an agreement dispensing with notification *is invalid* if its operation would be unconscionable." (Emphasis added.) Under this section, a contractual provision that gives one party to a sale-of-goods contract the right to cancel or terminate may be held subject to an implied requirement of reasonable notification. Such a contract therefore might not be illusory, because the promise would be binding during the period between the time when notice was given and the reasonable time thereafter until the notice would be effective. Similarly, an agreement *dispensing* with the necessity of notice for termination may be held invalid under section 2–209(3) and therefore might not render the promise illusory. If a right to cancel at any time is in fact limited under section 2–209(3), and the promise that is subject to the right to cancel therefore is not illusory, the contract would have consideration and could be enforced by either party.

(b) General Exceptions and Variations to Mutuality Rule

1) Unilateral Contracts

The doctrine of mutuality is applicable only to *bilateral* contracts (*i.e.*, contracts in which a promise is given in exchange for a promise). It is not applicable to *unilateral* contracts. In a unilateral contract, *A* makes a *promise* in exchange for *B*'s *act*. *B* is not bound to perform the act, but if they do, *A*'s promise becomes enforceable. But *B* never bound: *B* is not bound before they do the act, because they did not promise to do anything. (*B* could simply have not accepted *A*'s offer and walked away.) *B* is not bound after doing the act, because the act is completed at that point and *B* made no promise to do anything further. Nevertheless, *A*'s promise is enforceable. *Rationale:* Unlike the bilateral contract case, where the person who makes the real promise does not get anything in return (except a "meaningless" illusory promise), in the unilateral contract case the promisee *does* get something in return—the act they bargained for.

e.g. Example: Vladimir promises to pay Bianca $200 if Bianca cuts down a tree in Vladimir's yard. Vladimir makes it clear that he wants Bianca's performance, not merely her promise. Bianca never promises to cut down the tree, but she does so. Vladimir must pay Bianca $200, even though Bianca was never bound.

> **EXAM TIP**   **GILBERT**
>
> In an exam question, if the parties form a *unilateral* contract, do not apply the rule of mutuality of obligation (*i.e.*, the illusory promise rule) in your answer. Mutuality is required only for bilateral contracts, not for unilateral contracts.

2) Limited Promises

If a real promise is made, lack of mutuality is not a defense, *no matter how limited the promise may be.* [**Lindner v. Mid-Continent Oil Corp.**, 252 S.W.2d 631 (Ark. 1952); **Gurfein v. Werbelovsky**, 118 A. 32 (Conn. 1922)] The smallest obligation is enough to convert an illusory promise into a real promise.

Example: Lindner leased a filling station to Mid-Continent for three years, also giving Mid-Continent an option to renew for two more years. Although Lindner was therefore bound for up to five years, Mid-Continent had the right to terminate the lease at any time on 10 days' notice. Lindner claimed the lease lacked mutuality. The court held for Mid-Continent. At the very least, Mid-Continent bound itself to pay rent for 10 days, and therefore Mid-Continent had made a real promise. [**Lindner v. Mid-Continent Oil Corp.**, *supra*]

Example: Buyer promises to buy 200 tons of steel per month from Seller at $500/ton, subject to cancellation by Buyer without notice at any time. As discussed above, Buyer's promise is illusory. However, if Buyer also had agreed to purchase a minimum of 2 tons in total, or to cancel only on at least 1 day's notice, Buyer would have limited their future options, and their promise therefore would constitute consideration.

3) Voidable Promises

A real promise is not rendered illusory merely because the contract is voidable by one party as a matter of law. [**Atwell v. Jenkins**, 40 N.E. 178 (Mass. 1895); Rest. 2d § 78]

Example: Teen, who is 17 years old, agrees to buy a two-carat diamond ring from Seller for $5,000, and Seller agrees to sell the ring to Teen for that price. The contract is voidable by Teen on the ground of infancy (*see infra*, p. 172) and is therefore unenforceable against Teen. Nevertheless, Seller is bound if Teen seeks to enforce the promise. Although the contract is not enforceable against Teen, Teen has made a real promise. The bargain can therefore be enforced *by Teen* despite the fact that it cannot be enforced *against Teen.* The same result would follow if the contract was voidable by Teen (and therefore unenforceable against them) for some other legal reason, such as the Statute of Frauds (*see infra*, p. 162 *et seq.*).

a) Distinguish—Void Promises

It is sometimes said that a promise that is unenforceable by reason of law *is* illusory if the promise is not merely voidable, but void. [*See* Rest. 2d § 75] However, this distinction between void and voidable promises is questionable, both in terms of the doctrine and the cases, and in any event very few contracts are completely void (*see infra*, pp. 173, 174).

4) Conditional Promises

A conditional promise is a promise that the promisor need only perform if a specified condition occurs. Such a promise can be a real commitment: the promisor has ordinarily limited their future options because if the condition does occur, the promisor must perform. Therefore, a conditional promise is ordinarily not illusory and constitutes valid consideration. This is true even if the condition is within the promisor's control. [**Scott v. Moragues Lumber Co.**, 80 So. 394 (Ala. 1918)]

Example: Rosanna and Jamie agree that if Rosanna acquires a Chevrolet dealership, she will hire Jamie as her sales manager for one year at a salary of $80,000, and Jamie will accept this employment. Although the occurrence of the condition is within Rosanna's control (because she need not acquire the dealership), Roseanne has nevertheless limited her options and her promise is a real promise (***not*** an illusory one). Before Rosanna made the agreement, she had the option of acquiring the dealership and hiring anyone she wanted as sales manager. After she made the agreement, if she acquires the dealership, she is bound to hire Jamie as her sales manager. Both parties' promises count as consideration and are enforceable.

Note that a promise that is conditional in form may still be an illusory promise. For example, "I promise to buy you dinner on Friday if I choose to buy you dinner on Friday" is conditional but is also illusory. The difference is that in this promise, the condition ensures that the promisor has not restricted their freedom in any way by making the promise: the promisor cannot be accused of breaking the promise because they can simply reply "I chose not to buy you dinner." In the example above, Rosanna's promise removes an opportunity from her scope of potential freedom (she cannot choose to buy the dealership and then refuse to employ Jamie).

5) Alternative Promises

An alternative promise is one in which the ***promisor*** can discharge their obligation by choosing between two or more alternatives (*e.g.*, *A* promises *B* that they will paint either *B*'s porch or *B*'s garage for $500).

a) General Rule—Each Alternative Must Constitute Consideration

A contract involving alternative promises will be enforceable ***only if each*** of the performances would have been consideration if bargained for alone. *Rationale*: If the promisor knows they can choose a path later that doesn't count as consideration, their promise is not a real promise because it doesn't really bind them to do anything new.

Example: Reader promises Bookseller that if Bookseller gives Reader $100, Reader will either give Bookseller a rare copy of *Tom Sawyer* or straighten out Bookseller's shelves for five hours, at Reader's choice. Reader's promise constitutes consideration because either performance would be consideration.

cf. **Compare:** Reader promises Bookseller that if Bookseller gives Reader a free paperback version of *Tom Sawyer*, Reader will either work for Bookseller for 30 minutes or buy any rare books from the store that Reader chooses to buy. Reader's promise does not constitute consideration because Reader is free to choose the latter option, which is an illusory promise. Not all of the options constitute consideration, so Reader's promise is not consideration.

b) Distinguish—Contracts Giving *Promisee* the Right to Choose Between Alternatives

If, on the other hand, the *promisee* has the right to demand one of several alternative performances from the promisor, a promise to render alternative performances is consideration if *any one* of the alternative performances would be consideration. *Rationale:* Because the promisor does not know which choice the promisee will make, the promise restricts the promisor's options at the time the promise is made. Therefore the promise is consideration.

e.g. **Example:** Reader promises Bookseller that if Bookseller gives Reader $100, Bookseller may choose to have Reader either give Bookseller a rare copy of *Tom Sawyer* or serve on a jury if called to do so. Because the promisee, Bookseller, could choose to receive the book, Reader's promise is consideration, even if serving on a jury when called to do so does not constitute consideration because it is a legal duty (see *infra*, pp. 24–26).

EXAM TIP   **GILBERT**

Be sure to note which party has the right to pick between alternative promises. If the *promisor* is entitled to choose, *all* alternatives must constitute consideration for the contract to be enforceable. If the *promisee* is entitled to choose, the contract is enforceable as long as *at least one* alternative constitutes consideration.

---

6) Agreements Allowing One Party to Supply or Determine a Material Term

An agreement may leave open a term (*e.g.*, price or quantity) and provide that one of the parties has the unilateral right to supply or determine the term in the future.

a) Common Law Rule—Promise Illusory

At historical common law, the general rule is that if the omitted term is *material,* the promise is illusory.

e.g. **Example:** Farmer agrees to sell Buyer wheat at a designated price, and the contract provides that Farmer can determine how much wheat he will sell. Under the common law rule, Farmer's promise is illusory, on the theory that Farmer has undertaken no more of an obligation than he might decide to impose on himself at some later date. As a result, under the doctrine of mutuality neither Farmer nor Buyer would be bound. [*See* **Washington Chocolate Co. v. Canterbury Candy Makers,** 138 P.2d 195 (Wash. 1943)]

b) Exceptions

1/ Power to Alter or Modify Terms

A number of decisions hold that if a term is fixed in the contract, but one party is given the power to *alter or modify* the term, the power does not make that party's promise illusory. These cases construe such a power as subject to the *obligation to perform in good faith.* Therefore, the party with the power to alter or modify the term does not have a free way out: their power to alter or modify the term is not completely free but must be exercised in good faith. [**Automatic Vending Co. v. Wisdom,** 182 Cal. App. 2d 354 (1960)]

2/ Objective Standard for Establishing Terms

Even the power to *set* (rather than merely to alter or modify) a term does not necessarily render illusory the promise of the party who has the power to set the term, if the term must be set in relation to an objective measure. For example, a power in a seller to set the price would not render the seller's promise illusory if (i) the same price must be charged by the seller to all other buyers or (ii) the contract price is "four cents less than the market price at Town *A*" or the "posted price charged by the seller" in a given area. [**Moore v. Shell Oil Co.,** 6 P.2d 216 (Or. 1931)]

3/ Material Term Omitted and Neither Party Given Power to Supply or Determine the Term

In the basic case (*supra*, p. 18) a material term is omitted and the contract gives one of the parties the power to supply or determine the term. Often, however, a material term is omitted, but neither party is given the power to supply it or determine it. In that case, the law will imply a reasonable term unless the contract is too indefinite to enforce. (*See infra*, pp. 135–147.) Because the implied term is imposed by law, not by the will of one of the parties, the parties' promises are not illusory and the contract will not present a problem of consideration—although, to repeat, it may present a problem of indefiniteness.

c) U.C.C. Provisions

The U.C.C. potentially affects the common law rule in several ways.

1/ General Obligation of Good Faith

U.C.C. section 1–304 imposes an obligation of good faith on every party with respect to their performance of contractual obligations. Thus, a party who has the right to set a term in a contract for the sale of goods is limited by the duty to act in good faith in setting the term. Although section 1–203 does not specifically provide that an agreement permitting a party to set a contract term satisfies the requirement of consideration, this result can be reached on the following theory: Because of the good faith requirement, a party with the right to set a term does not have unlimited discretion and therefore the party's promise is not illusory.

2/ Setting Price

The U.C.C. has a special rule—beyond section 1–304's general obligation of good faith—if a party is given the right to set the price term in a contract for the sale of goods. U.C.C. section 2–305(1) explicitly changes the common law rule by providing that such contracts are *enforceable* if the parties so intend. Under U.C.C. section 2–305(2), the party setting the price has a duty to exercise the power in good faith, whether or not the contract explicitly so provides.

7) Implied Promises

The principle of mutuality is satisfied when, although a party does not seem to have made a promise with their explicit words, a promise nevertheless is *implied* (in fact or in law) from the party's words or actions. In such cases, the implied promise serves as consideration just as if it were an explicit promise.

a) Implied Promise to Use Reasonable or Best Efforts

A common type of implied promise is an implied promise to use "reasonable efforts" or "best efforts." For example, suppose Designer promises to give Marketer an exclusive right to market Designer's products, but Marketer does not explicitly promise to market those products. Designer then claims that the contract is unenforceable because it lacks consideration, since Marketer made no promise (or just an illusory promise of the form "I will market your products if I choose to do so").

1/ Landmark Case

In the landmark case of **Wood v. Lucy, Lady Duff-Gordon,** 222 N.Y. 88 (1917), Judge Cardozo held that Marketer could enforce a contract of this sort, on the ground that Marketer had made an *implied* promise to use *reasonable efforts* to market Designer's services and products. In other words, Marketer's promise was not illusory, even though Marketer had made no explicit promise to market the goods, because Marketer made an implied promise to use reasonable efforts.

2/ U.C.C. Section 2–306(2)

In cases involving the sale of goods, U.C.C. section 2–306(2) codifies the rule in *Wood* by providing that unless the parties agree otherwise, a lawful agreement for exclusive dealing in goods imposes an obligation "by the seller to use best efforts to supply the goods and by the buyer to use best efforts to promote their sale."

a/ Note

Because the U.C.C. rule applies only to the sale of goods, *Wood* remains an important precedent in cases involving other types of contracts, such as contracts for services or real estate.

8) Requirements and Output Contracts

In a ***requirements*** contract, the buyer agrees to buy all of their requirements of a given commodity from the seller, and the seller agrees to sell that amount to the buyer. In an ***output*** contract, the seller agrees to sell all of their output of a commodity to the buyer, and the buyer agrees to buy that amount from the seller.

Example: A utility company agrees to buy all the natural gas it needs for the calendar year 2023 from a particular supplier of natural gas. This is a ***requirements contract***. A lithium mine agrees to sell all of the products of its mining in the calendar year 2024 to a particular chemical processor. This is an ***output contract***.

a) Former Rule—Agreement Illusory

At one time, some courts treated requirements and output contracts as illusory, on the ground that the buyer in a requirements contract was not obliged to have any requirements and the seller in an output contract was not obliged to produce any output. However, such contracts were enforceable if the promisor had an established business at the time the contract was made. [**Pessin v. Fox Head Waukesha Corp.,** 282 N.W. 582 (Wis. 1938)] The rule was probably misguided because a promise to, *e.g.*, sell all the lithium a company mines to a particular buyer does in fact restrict the mine's choice and is a real, not an illusory, promise: even though the mine might not mine any lithium, it is no longer free after making the promise to mine lithium and sell it to anyone else. (*Cf. supra* p. 17.)

b) Modern Rule

Today, courts normally enforce requirements and output contracts, regardless of whether the promisor had an established business at the time the contract was made, because the parties really have limited their options. If the buyer in a requirements contract wants to buy ***any*** of the commodity during the term of the contract, he must buy it all from the seller. If the seller in an output contract wants to produce ***any*** of the commodity during the term of the contract, he must sell it all to the buyer. [**McMichael v. Price,** 57 P.2d 549 (Okla. 1936)]

Example: Buyer promises to buy from Seller "all the coal that I will need" or "all the coal that I require in my business." Buyer's promise *is* consideration. Buyer's promise restricts its freedom of action because if Buyer needs any coal, it must buy the coal from Seller and no one else. (Buyer is not free to (1) choose to buy coal and then (2) buy it from a different seller.)

Compare: Buyer simply promises to buy from Seller "such coal as I may wish to order from you." Buyer has actually promised nothing because it is still free to buy from anyone else. Buyer's promise is illusory and does not constitute consideration. [**Wickham & Burton Coal Co. v. Farmers' Lumber Co.**, 179 N.W. 417 (Iowa 1920)]

c) U.C.C. Rule

A requirements or output contract that involves the sale of goods (as most such contracts do) is governed by U.C.C. section 2–306(1). This section *assumes* the enforceability of such contracts (*i.e.*, it treats them as not raising consideration problems) and goes on to provide rules governing the performance of such contracts.

1/ Obligation of Good Faith

The U.C.C. provides that "a term which measures the quantity by the output of the seller or the requirements of the buyer means such actual output or requirements as may occur *in good faith*." (Emphasis added.) Thus, the party who determines the quantity of requirements or output under such a contract must conduct business in good faith and according to commercial standards of fair dealing in the trade. Because the party whose requirements or outputs can influence the final quantity of goods sold has a real obligation—the obligation to act in good faith—their promise is *not* illusory. [U.C.C. § 2–306(1), comment 2]

Example: Buyer promises to buy from Seller "all the coal that I will need" or "all the coal that I require in my business." As noted *supra* [p. 21], this promise constitutes consideration anyway under modern principles. But if there were any doubt, it is definitely consideration under the U.C.C. because Buyer has an obligation to determine how much coal it needs *in good faith*.

2/ Limitations on Quantity

In addition to the limit imposed by the principle of good faith, U.C.C. section 2–306(1) provides an objective limit: The quantity tendered under an output contract or demanded under a requirements contract cannot be "unreasonably disproportionate to any stated estimate, or in the absence of a stated estimate to any normal or otherwise comparable prior output or requirement." The U.C.C.'s Official Comment adds that if an estimate of requirements or output is included in the agreement, it will be treated as "a center around which the parties intend [any] variation to occur." [U.C.C. § 2–306(1), comment 3]

3/ Implied Promise to Remain in Business

It might be thought that a seller could avoid the obligation of an output contract, and a buyer could avoid the obligation of a requirements contract, by going out of business, in which event the seller would have no output and the buyer would have no requirements. However, going out of business is itself detrimental. [**Brightwater Paper Co. v. Monadnock Paper**

Mills, 161 F.2d 869 (1st Cir. 1947); **McMichael v. Price,** *supra*] Furthermore, the freedom to go out of business may be limited by the obligation to perform in good faith. As a general rule, if a party to an output or requirements contract goes out of business for reasons ***other than*** the profitability of the contract in question, there is no breach of the duty to perform in good faith. However, a shutdown motivated by the unprofitability of the contract in question may violate the duty. Thus, a shutdown by a requirements buyer for lack of orders might be permissible, whereas a shutdown merely to curtail losses under the contract in question (*i.e.*, to eliminate requirements under a badly negotiated requirements contracts) might not be. [*See* U.C.C. § 2–306(1), comment 2]

EXAMPLES OF ILLUSORY AND NONILLUSORY PROMISES

PROBLEM LANGUAGE—NO CONSIDERATION:	VALID LANGUAGE—CONSIDERATION:
Promise to do an act "if I want to": "I will buy from you all of the chairs I desire [*or* I decide I want]."	***Requirements/output limitation:*** "I will buy from you all of the chairs I require [*or* all the chairs you produce in May]."
Right to terminate at will without notice: "I will perform lawn services for you once a week, terminable at will and without notice."	***Right to terminate at will with notice:*** "I will perform lawn services for you once a week, terminable at will upon 10 days' advance notice" *or* "I will perform lawn services for you once a week, for at least one week."
Void promise: "I promise to sell you one kilogram of cocaine."	***Voidable promise:*** "I promise to buy your motorcycle" (said by a 16 year old).
Conditional promise with no limitation: "If I get the job, and also if I decide to do so at the time, I will rent your apartment for one month."	***Conditional promise that is real commitment:*** "If I get the job, I will rent your apartment for one month." A more subtle case: "If I get the job and your apartment is still in satisfactory condition at the time, I will rent your apartment for one month." Courts may hold that because you must decide whether the apartment is satisfactory in good faith, your promise is not illusory. [**Mattei v. Hopper,** 51 Cal. 2d 119 (1958); *cf. infra* p. 222]

Alternative promises—one alternative not consideration:	*Both alternatives constitute consideration [promisor's option]:*
"I promise to sell you my car for $500 or pay you the money I owe you when the debt is due, at my option." (*cf.* legal duty rule, *infra*, p. 24 *et seq.*)	"I promise to sell you my car for $500 or my bicycle for $50, at my option."
	One alternative constitutes consideration [promisee's option]:
	"I promise to sell you my car for $500 or pay you the money I owe you when the debt is due, at *your* option."

d. Legal Duty Rule—Promise to Perform Act Promisor Already Obliged to Perform

(1) General Rule

Another exception to the principle that bargains are consideration is that a promise to perform an act that the promisor has a preexisting legal duty to perform (*i.e.*, a legal duty that existed before the new promise) does not constitute consideration, even if bargained for. This is often referred to as the ***legal duty rule*** or the ***preexisting duty rule***. The same rule applies to the actual performance of such a duty. [Rest. 2d § 73]

e.g. **Example:** Contractor agrees to construct a factory for Manufacturer for $5 million. When the factory is 75% completed, Contractor tells Manufacturer that he will not complete the job unless Manufacturer agrees to pay $6 million. At this point, getting a substitute contractor would be very time-consuming, and the resulting delay in the completion of the plant would cause a significant loss of profits to Manufacturer. Therefore Manufacturer agrees to pay $6 million rather than $5 million. Manufacturer's new promise for $6 million is unenforceable.

(a) Party Asserting the Rule

Usually the legal duty rule is asserted as a defense ***not*** by the person who has made the promise to perform the preexisting legal duty but rather by the party to whom the promise was made. Thus, in the example above, Manufacturer argues that his new promise is unenforceable because all that he received in exchange for the promise to pay $6 million was Contractor's promise to perform (or Contractor's actual performance of) a preexisting legal duty, and that because such a promise (or performance) is not consideration, Manufacturer's new promise is not enforceable. To put it differently, Manufacturer's new promise clearly constitutes consideration; the promise that fails to constitute consideration is Contractor's promise to do the same work that Contractor had already promised to do.

(2) Types of Preexisting Legal Duties

There are two principal types of preexisting legal duties: ***public duties*** (*e.g.*, the duty of a judge to preside fairly or the duty of a witness to testify truthfully) and ***contractual duties.*** Application of the legal duty rule differs somewhat between the two categories.

(a) **Public Duties**

  1) **Official Duties**

   Under the legal duty rule, the promise of an official to perform an act that falls within the scope of the official's duties is not consideration, and neither is the actual performance of such an act. [**Gray v. Martino,** 103 A. 24 (N.J. 1918)]

   Example: Andres, a police officer, promises Kairi, a merchant who owns a store within Andres's beat patrol, that he will keep an eye on Kairi's store during the week in exchange for Kairi's promise to pay him $50 a month. Kairi's promise is unenforceable because Andres's promised performance is within the scope of his official duties.

   a) **Scope Test**

   Note that the legal duty rule is applicable to a promise by an official whenever the action is within the *scope* of the official's duties, even though performance of the *specific* act is not legally required. For example, in the police-officer example above, Andres does not have the specific duty to watch Kairi's store: he may properly choose to walk his beat on some days down streets other than the one on which the store is located. However, the legal duty rule is applicable to Andres because watching Kairi's store is within the scope of Andres's duties as a police officer.

   b) **Action Not Within Scope of Official Duties**

   The legal duty rule is not applicable if the act promised or performed by an official is not within the scope of their official duties, even though it is similar to those duties. [**Denney v. Reppert,** 432 S.W.2d 647 (Ky. Ct. App. 1968); **Harris v. More,** 70 Cal. 502 (1886); Rest. 2d § 73]

   Example: Sarah, a San Francisco police officer, is on vacation in Arizona, staying at Owner's hotel. Sarah agrees with Owner to spend three hours a day watching the hotel lobby in exchange for a free room. Since the promised performance is not within the scope of Sarah's official duties (because those duties do not apply in Arizona), Sarah's promise is consideration and Owner's promise is enforceable.

   c) **Pretense of Bargain Not Sufficient**

   The legal duty rule cannot be avoided by a bargain that merely pretends to call for a performance outside the scope of an official's duties. The difference between the official duty and the promised performance must be real and material, not a slight difference contrived to make the contract enforceable. [Rest. 2d § 73]

   Example: In the first police-officer example above, if Andres promises that he will keep an eye on Kairi's store and also check the windows each night to make sure they are properly locked, the bargain will still not be enforceable as a result of the legal duty rule. Even though checking the window locks is not part of Andres's official duty, the slight deviation is not enough to make the contract enforceable.

2) Other Public Duties

Performance of a public duty required by law, other than an official duty, is treated in the same way as is performance of an official duty. [**Van Boskerck v. Aronson,** 197 N.Y.S. 809 (1923); Rest. 2d § 73, comment b]

Example: Witness and Plaintiff make an agreement under which Witness promises to tell the truth as a witness in a suit that Plaintiff has brought against Defendant, and Plaintiff promises to pay Witness $1,000 in exchange. Witness is subpoenaed and tells the truth on the witness stand, as she promised to do, but Plaintiff refuses to pay. Witness sues Plaintiff for the $1,000. Plaintiff prevails because every citizen has a public duty to tell the truth as a witness, and so Witness's promise to tell the truth is not consideration under the legal duty rule.

EXAMPLES OF LEGAL DUTY RULE—PUBLIC DUTIES — GILBERT

TYPES OF PREEXISTING LEGAL DUTIES	EXAMPLE OF NO CONSIDERATION	EXCEPTION— CONSIDERATION
PROMISE BY AN OFFICIAL TO PERFORM ACT *WITHIN SCOPE OF OFFICIAL DUTIES*	Police officer promises to watch store on his beat for $50 per month. Police officer cannot enforce store owner's promise to pay	Performance *outside scope* of official duties (*e.g.,* promise to watch store while off-duty)
PROMISE BY A PRIVATE CITIZEN TO PERFORM *PUBLIC DUTY REQUIRED BY LAW*	Witness promises Plaintiff to tell truth on stand for $1,000. Witness cannot enforce Plaintiff's promise to pay	Performance of public duty that is not required by law (*e.g.,* witness promises to travel outside of her state of residence to testify, in return for payment of her travel expenses)

(b) Contractual Duties

The general rule is that a promise to perform, or the actual performance of, a preexisting contractual (as compared to public) duty that is owed to the promisee is *not* consideration. The cases covered by this branch of the legal duty rule tend to fall into two patterns: (i) one party is under a contractual duty to render some performance to another and receives a promise to be *paid more* for the very same performance, or (ii) a debtor owes money to a creditor, and the creditor agrees to *accept less* than that amount in full discharge of the debtor's obligation to the creditor.

Cases of preexisting contractual duties normally involve *modifications* to contracts. The general background rule is that just like original contracts, modifications to contracts require consideration on both sides.

1) Performance of Preexisting Contractual Duty for Increased Payment—No Consideration

Assume two parties, Architect and Brewery, have a contract under which Architect is under a duty to design and supervise the building of a new plant for Brewery. Architect and Brewery then agree to a ***modification*** of the contract under which Architect promises only to render the same performance, but Brewery agrees to pay more than the amount it originally agreed to pay. Under the legal duty rule, Architect's new promise is ***not consideration*** for the promise by Brewery to pay a greater amount than was set out in the original contract, and Architect therefore cannot enforce the modification against Brewery. [**Lingenfelder v. Wainwright Brewery Co.,** 15 S.W. 844 (Mo. 1891)] The same rule would also apply to Architect's actual performance, as opposed to Architect's promise to perform. That is, under the legal duty rule, neither Architect's promise to perform a preexisting contractual duty to Brewery, nor Architect's actual performance of this duty, is consideration for Brewery's promise to pay more for the same performance.

Note that the legal duty rule is only a rule of consideration, so its only effect is on whether promises are enforceable. If Architect refuses to work unless Brewery pays Architect more than originally agreed and then Brewery actually makes this payment, the legal duty rule is not relevant because there is no promise to enforce; Architect has Brewery's money and has no need to enforce a contract for payment from Brewery. However, if the payment resulted from duress, Brewery may have a right to recover the payment. (*See infra* p. 30.)

a) Exceptions

The legal duty rule is often not in accord with generally accepted commercial practice, at least in cases where the preexisting duty is a contractual one. Therefore, the courts have recognized a number of exceptions to the rule when it applies to modifications of contracts. *Rationale:* Often parties—for example, parties in a long-term commercial relationship with each other—make legitimate modifications to their contracts in which only one side gives something up. If the modification is the result of duress, it is problematic, but the legal duty rule treats the modification as unenforceable on purely formal grounds rather than by examining whether the modification resulted from duress.

1/ Promise of Different Performance

If the modification involves the performance of an act that is similar to, but ***different from,*** the performance required under the preexisting contract, there is consideration; *i.e.*, the legal duty rule does not apply. Furthermore, because the courts do not favor the legal duty rule as it applies to preexisting contractual duties, even a relatively small difference between the performance required under the modification and the performance required under the original contract may suffice to constitute consideration.

> **Example:** Builder agrees to construct a house for Owner for $430,000. Under the contract, the house is to have pine doors. Builder and Owner then modify the contract so that the doors will be made of redwood, and Owner will pay $470,000. The modification is enforceable, even if the increased cost to Builder is only $15,000, rather than the $40,000 increased price to Owner, because the performance required by the modification differed from that required by the original contract. Each side has promised something new, so there is consideration on both sides.

2/ Preexisting Duty Owed to Third Party

The legal duty rule is also usually inapplicable if the preexisting contractual duty is owed to someone *other than the person who makes the new promise* to induce performance of the duty. [**Joseph Lande & Sons, Inc. v. Wellsco Realty, Inc.,** 34 A.2d 418 (N.J. 1943); Rest. 2d § 74]

> **Example:** Constructco contracts with Lessor to construct a commercial building by July 31. Toyco, a prospective tenant in the building, is eager to ensure that the building is completed on schedule. Accordingly, Toyco promises to pay Constructco $5,000 if it completes construction by July 31. Constructco completes the building by July 31, but Toyco refuses to pay. The contract is enforceable, because at the time Toyco made the promise to Constructco, Constructco was under a contractual duty to Lessor, not to Toyco.

a/ Minority Position

A few authorities do not recognize an exception to the legal duty rule in such a case, on the ground that when Constructco made the promise to Toyco, Constructco was under a preexisting legal duty to perform, even though the duty did not run to Toyco. [**De Cicco v. Schweizer,** 221 N.Y. 431 (1917)] However, even this minority view recognizes an exception to the legal duty rule where Toyco makes a contract with Constructco and Lessor *jointly*—i.e., where Toyco promises something to Constructco and Lessor in return for their joint promise to have the construction completed by July 31. [**De Cicco v. Schweizer,** *supra*] The rationale is that Constructco and Lessor originally had a legal right to mutually rescind their preexisting contract (as between themselves), but by jointly agreeing with Toyco to perform their contract, they promised to do something they were not previously obliged to do—*i.e.*, refrain from mutually rescinding their contract.

3/ Availability of a Defense Under Original Contract

The legal duty rule is also inapplicable if a party who promises to do no more than was required under the original contract had a ***valid defense*** under the original contract (*e.g.*, mutual mistake). In such a case, that party was not legally obliged to render any performance because of the defense. Therefore, their promise is enforceable because it is not simply a promise to perform a preexisting legal duty.

Example: Buyer and Seller enter into an oral agreement under which Seller agrees to sell Buyer a parcel of land for $450,000. The agreement is unenforceable against either party under the Statute of Frauds because a contract to sell land must be evidenced by a writing to be enforceable [*infra*, p. 162 *et seq*.]. Seller later states that she will not sell the parcel for $450,000, but she will sell it for $500,000. Buyer agrees, and the agreement is put into writing. Buyer's promise is enforceable because, as a result of the Statute of Frauds, Seller was not under a preexisting legal duty to sell the parcel.

4/ Fair and Equitable Modification in Light of Unanticipated Circumstances

Some courts now also hold that the legal duty rule is inapplicable to a modification of an ongoing contract if the modification is based on *unanticipated circumstances* and is *fair and equitable* in view of the circumstances. This exception is applicable even if the unanticipated circumstances would not provide a defense of "impossibility" or "changed circumstances" under the preexisting contract. [**Angel v. Murray**, 322 A.2d 630 (R.I. 1974); Rest. 2d § 89] Note that this approach essentially overturns the legal duty rule in many cases.

Example: Builder agrees to excavate a cellar for Owner for $6,000. Builder unexpectedly encounters subsoil hard-pan, and so notifies Owner. The unanticipated subsoil conditions do not give Builder a defense for nonperformance of the contract. (*See infra*, p. 241 *et seq*. for a discussion of the doctrine of impracticability.) Nevertheless, in view of the unanticipated circumstances, which significantly increase Builder's costs, Owner agrees to pay Builder an additional $2,000 for the excavation. This increase is fair and equitable in view of the unanticipated greater difficulty of performance. Owner's new promise is therefore enforceable.

EXAM TIP   **GILBERT**

If an exam question involves a promise to perform a preexisting contractual duty, check to see if the promisor's new obligation **varies** from the old one **in any way.** If the promisor gave new or different consideration, made her promise to a party who was not a party to the original contract, forfeited a valid defense when she made her new promise, or encountered unanticipated circumstances, the contract may contain consideration.

5/ Modification of Contract for the Sale of Goods

Under the U.C.C., an agreement modifying a contract for the *sale of goods* is binding *without consideration.* [U.C.C. § 2-209(1)] Thus, the legal duty rule (and the general rule that modifications require consideration) is inapplicable to contracts for the sale of goods because Article 2 of the U.C.C. overrules it in those cases.

Example: Under a contract lasting for two years, Manufacturer agrees to buy 50 tons of steel per month from Supplier for $700/ton. The price of steel dramatically increases, and Supplier requests a price modification from Manufacturer to $750/ton for future deliveries. Manufacturer agrees. No consideration is needed for this modification, and Manufacturer's new promise is enforceable under the U.C.C.

a/ Fairness Not Explicitly Required

Unlike the common law exception for modifications (*supra*, p. 29), U.C.C. section 2–209 is not explicitly limited to agreements that are fair and equitable in view of unanticipated circumstances. However, the modification must meet the general test of "good faith" under U.C.C. section 1–304 (*supra*, p. 19), so that a modification that is not fair and equitable would probably not be binding. [U.C.C. § 2–209, comment]

b/ Distinguish—Waivers

Although a *modification* of a contract is enforceable without consideration under U.C.C. section 2–209, a *waiver* of a right under a contract is enforceable without consideration only if the waiver is *not validly withdrawn*. (The distinction between a waiver and a modification, and the circumstances under which a waiver may be validly withdrawn, are discussed *infra*, p. 42.)

6/ Writing as Substitute for Consideration

In a few states, a contract may be enforceably modified by a writing even if no new consideration is given. [*See* Cal. Civ. Code § 1697]

7/ "Mutual Rescission"

A few courts have gotten around the legal duty rule by concluding that the new promise constitutes a mutual rescission of the preexisting contract and the formation of a new contract. [**Schwartzreich v. Bauman-Basch, Inc.,** 231 N.Y. 196 (1921); **Watkins & Son v. Carrig,** 21 A.2d 591 (N.H. 1941)] However, the finding of a mutual rescission is usually fictional. In effect, courts that adopt this reasoning simply undercut the legal duty rule.

8/ Effect of Performance

Because the legal duty rule is just a rule of consideration and affects only the enforceability of *promises*, the legal duty rule has no application once a contract has been fully performed and no promise remains to be enforced. For example, once a promisor makes a payment of extra money, the promisor cannot recover that payment under the legal duty rule even if the promise to make the payment would not have been enforceable. However, the promisor may recover the payment if it was made under duress (see below) or if there is some other separate claim for recovery (like a claim for fraud or for restitution of a mistaken payment).

a/ Preexisting Legal Duty Coupled with Economic Duress

If a party's new promise is made under economic duress, the party who was under duress usually *can* recover any payment in excess of that promised in the original contract. A contract is made under economic duress if a promisor's assent is induced by an *improper* threat by the promisee that leaves the promisor no reasonable alternative. Although a threat to break a contract is improper, such a threat does not constitute economic duress unless it leaves the promisor with no reasonable alternative.

EXAM TIP — GILBERT

There is no simple test for economic duress because the facts can vary sharply, but courts look at how much pressure the promisor was under when making the new promise (*i.e.*, whether it had any reasonable alternative choices), how much circumstances have changed since the original promise, and whether the promisee has requested the promise in good faith. For example, a company about to go bankrupt might truthfully tell a customer "If you don't pay us more, we're not going to be able to perform, so it's in both of our interest if we raise the price slightly to suit new market conditions." By contrast, an unscrupulous company might make a similar request in bad faith, just to extract more than they were able to negotiate in the original contract. [**Austin Instrument v. Loral Corp.,** 29 N.Y.2d 124 (N.Y. 1971), *reversing* 316 N.Y.S.2d 528 (N.Y. App. Div. 1970)]

Example: Builder has a contractual duty to construct an addition to Manufacturer's factory for $10,000. Before performance begins, Builder says that it will render the performance only if Manufacturer will pay Builder $12,000, citing increased costs of materials. At this point, there are other contractors who could take Builder's place without undue delay or loss to Manufacturer's profits. Manufacturer agrees to Builder's terms. Builder renders the performance, and Manufacturer pays Builder $12,000. Because other contractors were available at the time Manufacturer made the new agreement, and Builder had completed performance at the time Manufacturer paid, Manufacturer was not under economic duress either at the time she made the new agreement or at the time of the payment. Even after making the new agreement, Manufacturer could have refused to pay $12,000 under the legal duty rule unless an exception to the rule applied. However, after paying the $12,000, Manufacturer cannot recover the $2,000 difference in price.

cf. Compare: Same facts as above, but after performance has begun, Builder threatens to walk off the job unless it is paid $12,000 on the spot, knowing that Builder cannot be readily replaced by another contractor and that Manufacturer will lose a substantial amount of money if the addition to the factory is delayed. Under these circumstances, the new agreement and the payment are likely made under economic duress, and Manufacturer can likely recover the extra $2,000 it paid to Builder.

2) Payment of Lesser Amount as Discharge of Debtor's Full Obligation—No Consideration

The legal duty rule also applies when a debtor owes a certain amount of money to a creditor, and the creditor agrees to accept payment of a lesser amount in full satisfaction or discharge of the debt. The same general rule applies to this case as to the case in which one party promises to pay the other party more for rendering a performance that the other party is already contractually obliged to perform: Under the legal duty rule, the debtor's payment of the lesser amount is *not* consideration because the debtor is doing only what he has a preexisting legal duty to do. Therefore, the creditor's promise to accept the lesser amount as full payment is not enforceable. As a result, after the debtor has paid the lesser amount, the creditor can sue for the balance even though that the creditor agreed to accept the lesser amount in full discharge of the debtor's obligation. [**Foakes v. Beer,** 9 App. Cas. 605 (1884)]

e.g. Example: Debtor owes Creditor $100,000, which was due on January 1. On January 15, Debtor offers to pay Creditor $90,000 by January 20 if Creditor will agree to accept that amount in full satisfaction of the $100,000 debt. Creditor agrees, and Debtor pays $90,000 to Creditor. Creditor then sues Debtor for $10,000 (the difference between the $100,000 originally owed and the $90,000 paid). Debtor defends on the ground that the debt has been discharged. Creditor wins. Because Debtor owed Creditor $100,000, Debtor's payment of $90,000 did not constitute consideration for Creditor's promise to accept that amount in full satisfaction of Debtor's debt. The promise therefore is not binding.

a) Exceptions

As applied to this type of case, the legal duty rule would prevent routine settlements of debt, as in the example above. Parties may have many sound reasons for making such settlements. In the above example, Creditor may want to encourage a faster payment from Debtor, to avoid forcing Debtor into bankruptcy, to encourage Debtor to seek alternative financing to pay the obligation to Creditor, and so on. Sensitive to these possibilities, courts have developed a number of exceptions to the legal duty rule in cases where a creditor agrees to accept a lesser amount from a debtor in full satisfaction of a debt.

1/ Different Performance

The general rule is inapplicable if the debtor does something *different* from what they were obliged to do, *e.g.*, if the debtor pays a lesser sum *before* the full obligation is due or renders a service in lieu of paying money. [**Jaffray v. Davis,** 124 N.Y. 164 (1891)]

e.g. Example: Debtor and Creditor in the example above agree that Debtor will pay $85,000 and work for Creditor for a week to discharge Debtor's original $100,000 obligation. This modification to the agreement has consideration on both sides and is enforceable.

2/ Honest Dispute

If there is an honest dispute about whether the debtor owes the creditor an obligation, payment by the debtor of a lesser amount than that claimed by the creditor is consideration for a promise to discharge in full. [Rest. 2d § 73; *and see supra*, pp. 9–10]

e.g. Example: Carla completed a service contract for Damien and has maintained for months that Damien owes her $12,000 under that contract. Damien once admitted this debt but now disputes it, honestly claiming that he believes Carla's work fell short of what was agreed to under the service contract. Carla and Damien negotiate and reach an agreement that Damien will pay her $10,500 in full satisfaction of any claims Carla has against Damien. The new agreement is enforceable.

3/ Unliquidated Obligations

Furthermore, even when there is no honest dispute about whether the debtor owes the creditor an obligation, if the *amount* of the obligation is unliquidated (*i.e.*, unclear or uncertain), payment of an amount that is less than the creditor claims is consideration for a discharge of the debt in full. [Rest. 2d § 74]

a/ Payment of Amount Admittedly Due

When the full obligation is unliquidated, even if the debtor pays only the amount she *admits* she owes to the creditor, the payment is consideration for discharge of the full debt. [**Flambeau Products Corp. v. Honeywell Information Systems, Inc.,** 341 N.W.2d 655 (1984)]

e.g. Example: Plumber performs plumbing services for Customer. Customer requested Plumber to perform these services, but the parties did not discuss Plumber's charges in advance. Plumber claims that on the basis of her standard charges, Customer owes $500. Customer admits that he must pay for Plumber's services and that he should pay at least $200. Customer offers to pay $200 if Plumber will accept that amount in full satisfaction of her entire claim. Plumber resists but eventually accepts this offer, and

Customer pays the $200. Plumber then sues for the $300 balance that she claims is due. Customer wins. Since the debt was unliquidated, the payment of $200 was consideration for Plumber's agreement to accept that amount in full satisfaction of Customer's obligation, even though Customer did not dispute that he owed at least that much.

b/ **Separate Obligations**

If the debtor owes the creditor two *separate* obligations, one liquidated and one not, payment of the liquidated obligation will *not* serve as consideration for the creditor's agreement to discharge the unliquidated obligation. [Rest. 2d § 74]

EXAM TIP   GILBERT

In practice, it frequently is difficult to differentiate between cases involving two separate obligations and cases involving one obligation, part of which is admittedly due and part of which is contested. The best guideline is whether the two obligations arose out of one contract or transaction or more than one. If the two obligations arose out of one contract or transaction, they are likely not to be treated as separate; if they arose out of more than one contract or transaction, they are likely to be treated as separate. However, even separate transactions may be closely related (*e.g.*, a series of sales in the course of an ongoing relationship between a buyer and a seller). In such a case, the total debt arising out of the related transactions may be considered as one debt, rather than as separate debts, for purposes of applying the rule concerning the settlement of unliquidated obligations.

4/ **Composition of Creditors**

A composition of creditors is an agreement *among creditors* to settle with a debtor. Where a composition of creditors releases the debtor in full in exchange for part payment (*e.g.*, the creditors agree that each will accept 60% of the debt owed to them by the debtor), consideration may be found in the creditors' mutual agreement to accept lesser amounts than those actually due. Thus, the creditors have a separate contract among themselves in which each promises to sue the debtor only for the agreed amount. In this situation, even though the debtor is not a party to the composition agreement, she may be able to enforce the contract as a third-party beneficiary. [**Massey v. Del-Valley Corp.**, 134 A.2d 602 (N.J. 1957); *and see infra*, pp. 178–180]

5/ **Agreement Not to File a Bankruptcy Petition**

Payment by the debtor of a lesser amount than owed may constitute consideration for the creditor's promise to give a discharge in full if the creditor's purpose in agreeing to such a discharge is to induce the debtor not to declare bankruptcy. *Rationale:* The debtor has forgone the exercise of a legal right—the right to declare bankruptcy. [**Melroy v. Kemmerer**, 67 A. 699 (Pa. 1907)]

6/ Written Release

Statutes in several states provide that a written release by a creditor will operate to extinguish the original debt. [*See, e.g.,* Cal. Civ. Code §§ 1524, 1541]

7/ Executory Contracts

There is a split of authority concerning the effect of payment of a lesser amount than is due in the case of a contract that involves ongoing periodic payments (*e.g.,* reduced rent payments under an ongoing lease). Some authorities hold that in such cases, an agreement to accept lesser payments in full satisfaction of the payments already due is enforceable to the extent that it is *executed* (*i.e.,* the agreement is enforceable as to those periodic payments already made and accepted). [*See, e.g.,* **Julian v. Gold,** 214 Cal. 74 (1931)] Other authorities hold that because *performance* of a preexisting legal duty is no more consideration than a promise to perform, the shortfalls in payments already made can be recovered. [*See, e.g.,* **Levine v. Blumenthal,** 186 A. 457 (N.J. 1936)]

EXAMPLES OF LEGAL DUTY RULE—CONTRACTUAL DUTIES — GILBERT

TYPE OF LEGAL DUTY CASE	EXAMPLE OF NO CONSIDERATION	EXCEPTION— CONSIDERATION
PROMISE TO PERFORM PREEXISTING DUTY FOR EXTRA PAYMENT	Contractor asks for more money to complete house. Even if Owner agrees to pay extra money, Owner's promise is not enforceable	*Different promise* (*e.g.,* promise to build garage in addition to house) Promise **made to a different party** (*e.g.,* promise to Neighbor to complete house on schedule so Neighbor can have some peace) Promise **to perform despite defense** to performance in original contract (*e.g.,* promise to complete house even though contract was unenforceable under Statute of Frauds) *Fair and equitable modification of contract in light of unanticipated circumstances* (*e.g.,* foundation will be more expensive due to unforeseen subsoil conditions) *U.C.C. overruling of legal duty rule*—applies to sale-of-goods contracts only (good faith may be required)

PAYMENT OF LESSER AMOUNT AS DISCHARGE OF FULL OBLIGATION	Debtor offers to pay 90% of debt in full satisfaction of debt, and Creditor agrees. After accepting payment, Creditor can still sue for remaining 10%	***Different performance*** (*e.g.*, Debtor offers to pay 90% **before** debt is due or to pay 90% **and** give Creditor tickets to a sporting event)
		Honest dispute whether debt is owed (*e.g.*, Debtor pays Creditor $500 for a $1,000 debt that Debtor thinks was already paid in full)
		Amount of debt is unliquidated (uncertain) (*e.g.*, debt is for services rendered and the parties did not establish the cost of services in advance)
		Composition of creditors (*i.e.*, creditors agree among themselves to settle with Debtor for lesser amount)
		Debtor's agreement not to file bankruptcy (*e.g.*, Creditor accepts 90% as payment in full in exchange for that payment plus Debtor's promise not to file for bankruptcy)

8/ Full-Payment Checks

A special problem occurs when the debtor, who owes the creditor an unliquidated obligation, tenders a *check* to the creditor that purports to be in full payment of the debtor's obligation to the creditor but which is for an amount less than the creditor claims. For example, Camille may claim that Devin owes her $10,000 while Devin claims he owes only $8,000. Devin writes on a check that the check is in full payment of all obligations owed by Devin to Camille and then gives the check to Camille. Such checks are known as *full-payment checks*. Legal questions arise if Camille cashes the check but then sues to recover the balance of her claim ($2,000).

a/ Common Law

The common law rule was that cashing a full-payment check constituted an accord and satisfaction (*see infra*, pp. 38–41) that **discharged the entire debt,** provided there was a good faith dispute concerning the obligation and the creditor had reasonable notice that the check was a full-payment check. This was true even if the check was for no more than the amount the debtor admittedly owed. [*Cf. supra*, p. 33.]

b/ U.C.C. Rule

U.C.C. section 3–311 ("Accord and Satisfaction by Use of Instrument") explicitly deals with full-payment checks. The general rule of section 3–311 is that if a creditor cashes a full-payment check, the creditor's entire claim is discharged (*i.e.*, the creditor cannot sue for the balance of their claim) if certain conditions are met. These conditions are (i) the check is tendered ***in good faith*** as full satisfaction of a claim; (ii) the check or an accompanying writing contains a ***conspicuous statement*** to the effect that the check is so tendered; and (iii) the amount of the claim that the check concerns is unliquidated or the ***subject of a bona fide dispute.***

Note that U.C.C. section 3–311 is from Article 3 of the U.C.C. (governing checks and other negotiable instruments), not Article 2 (governing contracts for the sale of goods). Therefore, it applies generally, not just to contracts for the sale of goods.

1] Exception—Check Not Sent to Prescribed Person, Office, or Address

The general rule does not apply (and the cashing of a full-payment check therefore does not discharge the creditor's claim) if (i) the creditor is an organization; (ii) within a reasonable time before the check was tendered, the creditor sent a conspicuous statement to the debtor that checks tendered in full satisfaction of debts are to be sent to a designated person, office, or address; (iii) the check was not sent to that person, office, or address; and (iv) the creditor did not know, within a reasonable time before initiating collection of the check, that the check was tendered in full satisfaction of the creditor's claim.

a] Rationale

Because it would be difficult for a company receiving large amounts of checks to scrutinize each check for full-payment language, this rule allows the company to create a special department for dealing with full-payment checks, make its customers aware of that department, and have liability only to those customers who notify the special department that the check is a full payment of their debt.

2] Exception—Repayment Tendered

The general rule also does not apply (and the cashing of a full-payment check therefore does not discharge the creditor's claim) if (i) the creditor tenders a repayment of the amount of the check within 90 days after the check has been paid; (ii) the creditor (if it is an organization) did not send to the debtor, within a reasonable time before the debtor tendered her own check, a conspicuous statement that full-payment checks were to be sent to a designated person, office, or address; and (iii) the creditor did not know, within a reasonable time before initiating collection of the check, that the check was tendered in full satisfaction of the creditor's claim.

C. Accord and Satisfaction

1. "Accord" Defined

An "accord" is an agreement in which one party to an existing contract agrees to accept, in lieu of the performance that they are supposed to receive from the other party to the existing contract, some other, different performance.

Example: Mel owes Alicia $1,000 under a contract. Mel promises to give his car to Alicia in settlement of the debt, and Alicia agrees to accept the car in settlement of the debt. This agreement is an accord.

a. Type of Obligation

If the new performance promised under an accord is no more than what the promisor was already obliged to do under the original contract, the accord will be unenforceable under the legal duty rule unless it comes within some exception to that rule. Typically, however, as in the example above, both parties agree to do something that they were not obliged to do. (In the example above, Mel was not obliged to give Alicia his car, and Alicia was not obliged to accept the car in lieu of the $1,000 debt.)

2. "Satisfaction" Defined

A "satisfaction" is the performance of the accord by the promisor. That is, if an accord is performed (*i.e.*, if the promisor tenders the performance they promised to render under the accord and the promisee accepts the performance), there is said to be a "satisfaction" of the accord.

a. Effect of Satisfaction

The satisfaction of an accord discharges both the accord and the original contractual duty. In the example above, if Mel tenders his car to Alicia and Alicia accepts it, the accord is discharged and so is Mel's original duty to pay Alicia $1,000.

3. "Executory Accord" Defined

An accord that has not yet been performed (*i.e.*, one that has not yet been *executed* or "satisfied") is referred to as an "executory accord."

a. Effect of Executory Accord

It might be thought that even before satisfaction, an accord is a fully enforceable modification of the original contract, because if each party to a contract agrees to do something ***different*** from what they were obliged to do, the parties have made a (new) bargain and the legal duty rule normally would not apply. For purely historical reasons, however, the law is not so simple.

(1) Traditional Rule

The traditional rule is that an executory accord is ***unenforceable.*** This rule is inconsistent with the bargain principle, because an executory accord is a bargain, and bargains are normally enforceable.

(2) Modern Rules

Although in theory the traditional rule above is still the law, the rule has been eroded with a number of exceptions and distinctions, so that in practice it has little force today.

(a) "Substituted Contract"

In some cases, an executory accord is treated as a "substituted contract." If an accord is treated as a substituted contract, the accord immediately discharges the original contract. (To put this differently, a "substituted contract" is simultaneously an accord and a satisfaction.) Accordingly, if there is a substituted contract and it is breached by either party, the other party can bring suit for that breach, but neither party can bring suit for breach of the original contract because that contract has been discharged. Whether an accord is a substituted contract is a question of the parties' intent. The courts are likely to find that an accord is a substituted contract if the duty under the original contract was disputed, unliquidated, had not matured, and involved a performance other than the payment of money. Correspondingly, the courts are likely to find that an accord is not a substituted contract if the above factors are not met. [Rest. 2d § 281, comment e]

Example: Ethel agrees to perform agricultural services for Cyril in March, and Cyril agrees to pay Ethel on June 30. On June 1, the parties disagree over what payment is due. Ethel claims that Cyril is obliged to deliver three cows to her. Cyril claims that his obligation is to deliver one cow. Ethel and Cyril later agree that Cyril will deliver two sheep and that Ethel will accept the two sheep as full payment of Cyril's obligation. The accord is likely to be treated as a substituted contract, and therefore itself a satisfaction, because the duty under the original contract was not to pay money, was disputed, was unliquidated, and had not matured.

Compare: Same facts as above, except that Cyril's clear obligation under the original contract is to pay Ethel $900, and the new agreement (under which Cyril will deliver two sheep, in lieu of paying $900) is made on July 2. The accord (to deliver two sheep) is not likely to be treated as a substituted contract because the duty under the original contract was to pay money, was not disputed, was liquidated, and had matured.

(b) Where Executory Accord Is Not A Substituted Contract

Even when an executory accord is not a substituted contract, so that the original contract is not discharged, the accord nevertheless has several significant effects:

1) Suspension of Rights Under Original Contract

Under the modern rule, an executory accord operates to suspend the promisee's rights under the original contract (*i.e.*, the promisee cannot sue the promisor on the original contract) during the period in which the promisor is supposed to perform the accord.

2) Suit Against Promisor

If the promisor fails to tender performance under the executory accord, the promisee can sue the promisor under *either* the old contract or the accord. [Rest. 2d § 281]

3) Suit Against Promisee

Some authorities take the position that if the promisor tenders performance under an executory accord and the promisee refuses to accept the performance (*i.e.*, insists on performance under the original contract), the promisor can either permanently enjoin the promisee from bringing suit or can sue the promisee for damages for breach of the executory accord. [*See* Rest. 2d § 281, comment c] It is not clear that this position would be widely accepted, because under this position, almost nothing is left of the traditional rule concerning executory accords.

APPROACH TO ACCORD AND SATISFACTION

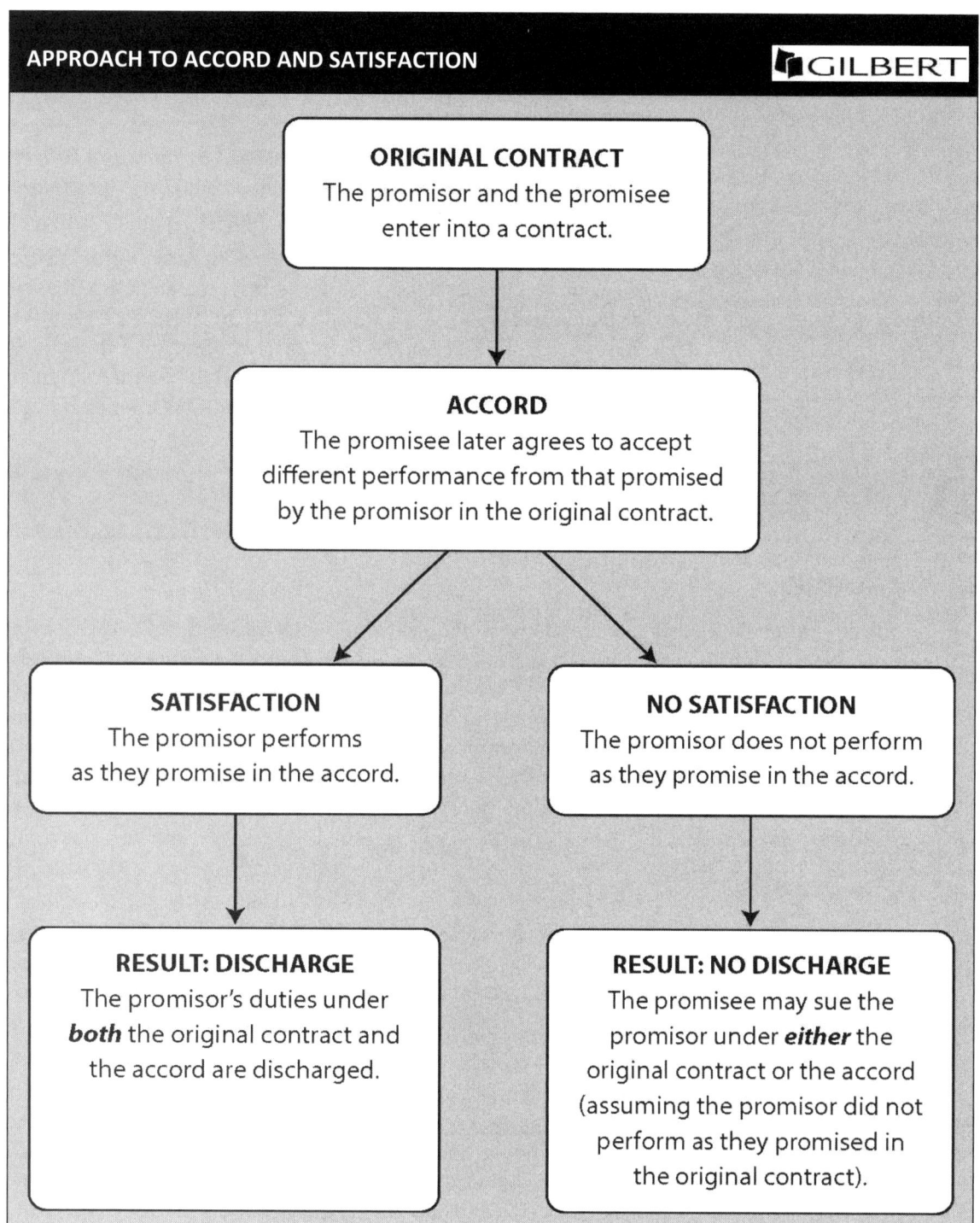

4) **Application**

Natasha owes Boris $1,000, payable on May 1. On May 5, the parties agree that in settlement of the $1,000 obligation, Natasha will give Boris her car on June 1. Because the original performance was an undisputed obligation to pay a fixed sum of money, the accord will probably not be treated as a substituted contract, and Natasha's duty to pay the $1,000 therefore will not be discharged unless there is evidence that the parties intended it to be. However, Natasha's duty is suspended until June 1. Thus:

a) ***If Boris breaches the executory accord by bringing an action to recover*** the $1,000 prior to June 1, Natasha may sue in equity to enjoin Boris's proceeding until June 1. [**Union Central Life Insurance Co. v. Imsland,** 91 F.2d 365 (8th Cir. 1937)]

b) ***If Natasha breaches the executory accord by failing to deliver the car,*** Boris may recover a judgment for the $1,000 or, at his option, may seek damages for the failure to deliver the car.

c) ***If Boris breaches the executory accord by refusing to accept the car*** when it is tendered on June 1 and bringing an action for the $1,000 thereafter, Natasha may also be able to bring an action for breach of the accord, or to sue for specific performance of the accord or an injunction to block Boris's suit on the ground that the original contract is suspended even after June 1. [**Dobias v. White,** 80 S.E.2d 23 (N.C. 1954)]

D. Waiver

1. Definition

A *waiver* is often defined as the intentional relinquishment of any known right. However, in contract law the term is more properly confined to cases where a party excuses (or promises to excuse) the nonoccurrence or delay in fulfillment of a *condition to that party's duty to perform under the contract*. (*See infra*, p. 216.) For example, a fire-insurance contract might provide that no insurance claim is to be processed or paid unless the claim is submitted in writing (*i.e.*, submitting a written claim is a condition for payment under the contract), but the insurer may choose to *waive* this condition by promising that it will process a claim that was submitted by phone instead.

2. Enforceability

A waiver is enforceable if it is given in exchange for separate consideration. It is also enforceable (subject to the possibility of retraction, *see infra*, p. 43) **without separate consideration** if (i) the waived condition was not a material part of the agreed-upon exchange, and (ii) uncertainty of the occurrence of the condition was not an element of the risk assumed by the party who gave the waiver. [Rest. 2d § 84(1)]

Example: Owner employs Builder to build a house by December 1 for $400,000, payable upon the production by December 10 of an architect's certificate, signed by Owner's architect, Álvaro, that the house has been completed according to contract specifications. Builder builds the house, but Álvaro rightfully refuses to give the certificate because the house is defective in several respects. Owner says to Builder, "My architect, Álvaro, rightfully refused to give you a certificate, but because the defects are not serious, I will pay you the full $400,000." Owner's waiver is enforceable (even though Builder gave no new consideration for it) because production of the architect's certificate was neither a material part of the agreed-upon exchange nor an element of the risk assumed by Owner.

Example: Acme Insurance Company insures Rachel for $100,000 against Rachel's becoming disabled while traveling. The policy is payable only if Rachel or her beneficiary gives Acme written notice of loss within 30 days after the loss occurs. Rachel is disabled in an auto accident but does not give Acme notice until 34 days after the accident. Acme informs Rachel that this notice is sufficient, thereby waiving the 30-day condition. Acme's waiver is enforceable, even though Rachel gave no consideration for the waiver, because the provision concerning notice was not a material part of the agreed-upon exchange, and uncertainty about the timing of the notice was not an element of the risk assumed by Acme.

cf. Compare: Same facts as in the example above, but Rachel is disabled while working at home. Acme waives the requirement that the accident occur while traveling. Acme's waiver is unenforceable, because the condition that the disablement occur while traveling was a significant element of the risk assumed by Acme in its insurance contract.

3. Retraction

Even though a waiver is otherwise enforceable, it can be *retracted* if each of four conditions is met:

(i) The *waiver was not given for separate consideration;*

(ii) The *other party has not changed position* in reliance on the waiver;

(iii) The *waiver relates to a condition to be fulfilled by the other party* to the contract, rather than by a third party; *and*

(iv) The *retraction occurs before* the time that the waived condition was supposed to occur *and* the party who gave the waiver either (a) gives notice of its intention to retract while there is still a reasonable time for fulfilling the condition, or (b) provides a reasonable extension of the time in which to perform.

[Rest. 2d § 84(2)]

e.g. Example: Assume that in the example concerning the architect's certificate (*supra*, p. 42), Owner attempts to retract the waiver. The retraction would be ineffective for two reasons: (i) the waiver did not relate to a condition that was to be fulfilled by the other party to the contract (Builder) but rather by a third person (Álvaro, Owner's architect); and (ii) at the time the waiver was given, the time for fulfilling the condition (*i.e.*, the time for producing the certificate) had already passed.

cf. Compare: Assume in the Acme insurance policy example (*supra*, p. 42) that Acme waived its 30-day-notice requirement *four* days after the accident and then attempted to retract that waiver the next day, before Rachel had changed her position in reliance on it. Here, the retraction is effective because: (i) the waiver was not given for separate consideration, (ii) the waiver was not relied upon, (iii) the waiver related to a condition to be fulfilled by Rachel, and (iv) the retraction occurred before the waived condition was supposed to occur (*i.e.*, before 30 days after the accident, the deadline for notice) and while there was still a reasonable time for Rachel to fulfill the condition (by submitting notice before the deadline).

E. Unrelied-Upon Donative Promises

1. General Rule

A *donative* (or *gratuitous*) promise is a promise to make a gift (*e.g.*, Aunt promises to give Nephew a car). The general rule is that a simple donative promise is *unenforceable* because there is a lack of consideration. [**Schnell v. Nell,** 17 Ind. 29 (1861)]

a. Exceptions

A donative promise may be enforceable if it is relied on (*see infra*, p. 46), or, at early common law and still in some states, if it is under seal (*see infra*, p. 44). In addition, under an emerging rule of modern contract law, a promise to compensate for a material benefit that was previously received by the promisor and that gave rise to a moral (although not a legal) obligation to make compensation is enforceable (*see infra*, p. 48 *et seq.*). For example, if Joey's horse escapes and Monica cares for the horse until it is returned to Joey, Joey's subsequent promise to pay Monica for the cost of the horse's care is enforceable under this emerging rule. [Rest. 2d § 86]

Moreover, charitable subscriptions (such as ongoing pledges to nonprofit universities) are usually binding without consideration, as are "marriage settlements," an increasingly uncommon practice. [Rest. 2d § 90(2)] Such promises are often ***presumed*** to have been relied on (*see infra* p. 46), even if in fact they weren't.

2. Effect of a Seal

A seal is a piece of wax (or a paper wafer or some other substance similar to a piece of wax) affixed to a written contract, or an indented impression resembling a seal (made with an embossing tool) on a written contract. By statute or decision in many states, a seal may also be written or printed, or may consist of the word "seal," or a pen scrawl (or "scroll"), or some other sign to represent a seal (including the letters "L.S.," which stands for "locus sigilli," meaning "place of the seal" in Latin). At common law, any promise under seal, even a donative promise, is legally enforceable. This rule still holds true where it hasn't been changed by statute.

a. Statutory Modification

A large number of states have enacted statutes that either abolish the binding effect of a seal or provide that a seal raises only a presumption of consideration. [*See, e.g.*, Wis. Stat. Ann. § 402.203]

(1) Presumption Statutes—Promisor Must Show Lack of Consideration

A statute providing that a seal raises only a presumption of consideration is usually interpreted to mean that if a promisee brings an action on a promise that is under seal, the ***promisor*** has the burden of proving the absence of consideration. (Normally, a ***promisee*** has the burden of proving the presence of consideration.)

3. Effect of Writing

Absent a statute to the contrary, a donative promise is ***not*** enforceable merely because it is in writing. [**Hill v. Corbett,** 204 P.2d 485 (Wash. 1949)]

a. Statutory Modifications

A few states have statutes providing that a promise in writing is presumed to have been given for consideration. [*See, e.g.*, NM Stat § 38–7–2; Cal. Civ. Code § 1614] However, this presumption may be rebuttable.

4. Nominal Consideration

Nominal consideration exists when a donative promise is falsely put by the parties into the ***form*** of a bargain (*e.g.*, *A*, who wants to promise to make a gift of a car to *B*, agrees to "sell" *B* a new car for $1; this is called "nominal" consideration because there is consideration—a bargain—in name only). Although the authorities are not in accord, the prevailing view today is that nominal consideration will *not* in general make a donative promise enforceable (*see supra*, pp. 7–9).

5. Conditional Donative Promise

A donative promise is conditional if the promisor intends to confer a gift on the promisee, but the nature of the gift is such that some condition must be fulfilled before the gift is made (*e.g.*, *A* tells *B* that she will give *B* her television if he comes over to her house to get it). A conditional donative promise is no more enforceable than any other donative promise. This is true even if the condition has been fulfilled, except to the extent that fulfillment of the condition constitutes foreseeable reliance (*see infra*, pp. 46–47).

a. Conditional Donative Promise vs. Bargain Promise

A conditional donative promise sometimes looks like a bargain. The difference between a conditional donative promise and a bargain is that in a conditional donative promise, fulfillment of the condition is not the ***price*** of the promisor's performance. Instead, it is just a technical or incidental requirement for executing the gift that the promisor has in mind. It is sometimes difficult to distinguish a conditional donative promise from a bargain promise. The test is how the ***parties view*** the condition. If the condition is viewed as simply a necessary part of making the gift, the promise is donative. But if the parties view performance of the condition as the price of the promise, there is a bargain, and the rules applicable to bargains apply. Note that the same condition could give rise to either a conditional donative promise or a bargain, depending on circumstances.

Example: Aunt says to Nephew, "I'd like to pay for your college tuition. Please send me your bank-account information, and I'll wire you $50,000." Nephew provides his bank-account information, but Aunt refuses to pay. This is a conditional donative promise, not a bargain. Aunt does not see Nephew's bank-account information as the ***price*** of $50,000. She just needs a way to transfer the money to Nephew.

Compare: Company sends out an email to all its employees that reads, "To save the company money, we would like to start paying you by direct deposit instead of by check. Any employee who signs up on our website for direct deposit and provides their bank-account details by Friday will receive a $100 bonus on their next paycheck." This is an offer for a bargain, and if employees provide their bank-account details on the website by Friday, doing so constitutes consideration. Here, the company sees the $100 "bonus" as the ***price*** of acquiring the bank-account details of its employees so that it can reduce the cost of its payroll system.

Example: Yen telephones Liora and says, "I have a gift for you. If you come over to my house, you can have it now." Liora comes over, but Yen does not give her the gift. Yen's promise is not enforceable because coming over to her house was not the price of the gift but simply the means of effectuating the gift.

Compare: Yen telephones Liora and says, "I'm lonely. If you come over to my house to keep me company this afternoon, I'll give you that bicycle you've always liked. It's valued at about $200, so it's worth a few hours of your time!" Liora comes over, but Yen refuses to let her keep the bicycle. Yen's promise is enforceable because coming over to her house was, as she expressed it, the price of the bicycle. (Note that parties frequently use words like "give" in bargain contexts, as when a customer at an art gallery says "I'll give you $3,000 for that painting.")

Example: Uncle promises to pay Nephew $5,000 if Nephew will abstain from smoking and drinking until he reaches age 21. Nephew agrees and abstains. Uncle must pay the $5,000. Even if Uncle's motive was altruistic, it was understood that $5,000 was the price Uncle was willing to pay for Nephew's abstinence. [**Hamer v. Sidway,** *supra*, p. 3]

CONDITIONAL DONATIVE PROMISE VS. BARGAIN PROMISE		**GILBERT**
	CONDITIONAL DONATIVE PROMISE	**BARGAIN PROMISE**
CONCEPT	Promisor intends to give a gift, but promisee needs to fulfill a condition that is incidentally necessary to effectuate the gift.	Promisor and promisee make a bargained-for exchange in which each party gives up something to receive something.
EXAMPLE	"I'll give you a watch if you come to my store and pick it up."	"I'll give you a watch if you mind my store for an hour."
CONSIDERATION?	No	Yes

F. Relied-Upon Donative Promises—Doctrine of Promissory Estoppel

1. Former Rule—Reliance Irrelevant

Often, a donative promise is relied upon by the promisee. The rule at one time was that reliance was irrelevant; a donative promise was unenforceable even if it was relied upon. [**Kirksey v. Kirksey,** 8 Ala. 131 (1845)]

2. Modern Rule

Today, however, the rule is that if a donative promise induces reliance by the promisee in a manner that the promisor should reasonably have expected, the promise will be *legally enforceable,* at least to the extent of the reliance. [**Feinberg v. Pfeiffer Co.,** 322 S.W.2d 163 (Mo. 1959)]

a. Restatement First Section 90

The modern rule stems from section 90 of the Restatement First, which provides that "a promise which the promisor should reasonably expect to induce action or forbearance of a definite and substantial character on the part of the promisee and which does induce such action or forbearance is binding if injustice can be avoided only by enforcement of the promise."

(1) Principle of "Promissory Estoppel"

The principle of section 90 is sometimes known as the principle of "promissory estoppel." This terminology reflects the idea that if a promisee has relied on a donative promise, for reasons of justice the promisor should be estopped (prevented) from pleading lack of consideration. Under modern law and practice, reliance is viewed as either a substitute for consideration (when the term "consideration" is used to mean a bargain) or as consideration itself (when the term "consideration" is used to mean any factor that makes a promise enforceable). The term "promissory estoppel" nevertheless remains in wide use as a description of the principle that reliance may make a promise enforceable.

b. Restatement Second Section 90

Section 90 of Restatement Second perpetuates Restatement First section 90, with certain changes:

(1) Remedy May Be Limited to Extent of Reliance

Under Restatement First, some authorities argued that if a relied-upon donative promise was enforceable at all, it was enforceable to its *full extent* (*i.e.*, the amount promised, or "expectation damages"). [Williston, Treatise on the Law of Contracts ("Williston") (3d ed. 1979) § 1338, n. 7] However, Restatement Second section 90 provides that damages may be limited *to the extent of the reliance* (*i.e.*, "reliance damages") by stating that "the remedy granted for breach may be limited as justice requires." [Rest. 2d § 90]

Example: Aunt promises to reimburse Nephew $1,000 for opera tickets that Nephew will purchase for his own use. Nephew purchases tickets for $500, and then Aunt communicates that she will refuse to pay Nephew. Under Williston's view, Nephew might have been entitled to the full extent of the promised sum—$1,000. Under Restatement Second section 90, however, Nephew would be entitled to enforce Aunt's promise only to the extent that the promise was relied upon—$500.

(2) Substantial Reliance Not Required

Restatement First section 90 required that the reliance be of "a definite and substantial character." Under Restatement Second section 90, it is enough that the promisor should have reasonably expected that the promise would induce reliance.

EXAM TIP GILBERT

Because courts following the Restatement Second may limit recovery under promissory estoppel to reliance damages, a bargain contract (remedied by expectation damages) is more valuable to a promisee than a promise that can be enforced only under the principle of promissory estoppel. Thus, when determining whether a party can prevail based on an agreement, always check first to see if there is a **bargain contract** before considering promissory estoppel.

---

3. Reliance as Consideration

Some authorities, including the Restatements, limit the term "consideration" to bargains. According to these authorities, a relied-upon donative promise is enforceable *despite* the absence of consideration—*i.e.*, despite the absence of bargain. However, other authorities treat promissory estoppel as simply a type of consideration. [**Feinberg v. Pfeiffer Co.**, *supra*, p. 46]

a. Comment

This difference in approach is mostly just a question of nomenclature. The result in any given case is the same under either view—the promise is enforceable.

G. Moral or Past Consideration

1. Definition

A promise is said to be given for "moral" or "past" consideration when the promisor's motivation for making the promise is a *past* benefit to the promisor or detriment to the promisee that gave rise to a *moral* obligation, but no *legal* obligation, to make compensation. Such a promise is similar to a pure donative promise (*supra*, p. 43) in that the promise is not bargained for and is altruistic. However, such a promise differs from other donative promises because it is rooted in the motive to pay for a past benefit that gave rise to a moral obligation to make compensation.

2. Traditional Rule

The traditional rule is that a promise based on moral or past consideration is simply a donative promise and is therefore *unenforceable.* [**Mills v. Wyman,** 3 Pick. 207 (Mass. 1825)]

3. Core Exceptions

There are three core exceptions to the traditional rule. These exceptions concern a promise to pay a debt barred by the statute of limitations, a promise to perform a voidable obligation, and a promise to pay a debt discharged by bankruptcy.

a. Promise to Pay Debt Barred by Statute of Limitations

A statute of limitations is a statute that sets a deadline for a particular type of lawsuit. In other words, after the statutory period is over, the lawsuit can no longer be brought. A promise to pay a debt barred by the statute of limitations is enforceable even if no new consideration is given by the promisee. [Rest. 2d § 82]

Example: Tony owes Maria a debt of $1,000, but the statute of limitations has run on the debt, so that Maria cannot sue to recover it. Nonetheless, Tony writes to Maria, "I realize I still owe you $1,000, and I will pay it because I take my debts seriously." Tony's new promise is enforceable.

(1) Action is on New Promise

In such cases, it is the *new promise,* not the old debt, that is enforceable. Therefore, if the debtor promises to pay less than the amount of the barred debt, or promises to repay the debt only in installments or only under stated conditions, then that is all the debtor is obliged to do. [**Brown v. Hebb,** 175 A. 602 (Md. 1934); Rest. 2d § 82]

Example: After the statute has run, Tony writes to Maria, "I realize I owe you $1,000, and I will pay it to you if I am promoted to a better job." The promise is enforceable, but Tony need perform only if he is promoted because it is the new promise, not the old debt, that is enforceable.

Example: After the statute has run, Tony writes to Maria, "I realize I owe you $1,000, and I will pay you $800." The promise is enforceable, but Maria can recover only $800 because it is the new promise, not the old debt, that is enforceable.

(2) Effect of Acknowledgment or Part Payment

The new promise need not be explicit. A promise to pay a debt barred by the statute of limitations will normally be implied from an unqualified acknowledgment that the debt is owing or from a part payment of the debt. [Rest. 2d § 82]

(a) Implication from Acknowledgment or Part Payment Not Determinative

In such a case, it is not the acknowledgment or part payment that is decisive, but the implication of a promise from the acknowledgment or part payment. Therefore, if such an implication cannot fairly be drawn, no action will lie.

Example: Margaret owes Brandy $5,000, but the debt is barred by the statute of limitations. Brandy asks Margaret to pay, and Margaret writes, "I acknowledge that I owe you that money, and I should pay it to you by all rights, but you'll never get a cent." Brandy has no cause of action, because even though Margaret acknowledged the debt, a promise to pay cannot be implied from the acknowledgment. [Rest. 2d § 82]

Compare: Same facts as above, except that Margaret writes, "I'm sorry I haven't paid, but I had no extra money last year." The court might treat this statement as an unqualified acknowledgment of the debt that will give rise to an implied promise. [**Buescher v. Lastar,** 61 Cal. App. 3d 73 (1976)]

(3) Requirement of a Writing

A promise to pay a debt barred by the statute of limitations does not fall within the Statute of Frauds as originally enacted. (The Statute of Frauds requires some contracts to be evidenced by a writing to be enforceable; *see infra*, p. 162 *et seq.*) However, most states have now adopted special Statute of Frauds provisions, known as "Lord Tenterden's Acts," which provide that a promise to pay a debt barred by the statute of limitations is not enforceable unless the promise is in writing or a part payment has been made. [*See, e.g.*, Mass. Gen. Laws ch. 260, §§ 13, 14]

(4) New Promise Made Before Statute of Limitations Has Run

The rules set forth above are also generally applicable to a new promise, an acknowledgment, or a part payment that is made *before* (rather than after) the statute of limitations has run on the old debt. In such a case, the statute of limitations on the new promise will begin to run from the date of the new promise, acknowledgment, or part payment.

b. Promise to Perform a Voidable Obligation

A promise to perform a voidable obligation (known as a *ratification*) is enforceable despite the absence of new consideration if the new promise is not subject to the same defense that made the original obligation voidable. [Rest. 2d § 85]

Example—infancy: Marta and Elizabeth reside in a state where the age of majority is 18. Just before Marta turns 18, she enters into a contract with Elizabeth. Two weeks after Marta turns 18, she promises Elizabeth that she will perform the contract. The contract is enforceable against Marta even though there is no consideration for Marta's new promise. [*See* Rest. 2d § 85]

Example—fraud: Ilana is defrauded by Ben into entering into a contract to purchase Redacre. Ilana learns of the fraud but still wants Redacre, so she promises Ben that she will perform. The contract is enforceable against Ilana even though there is no consideration for Ilana's new promise. [*See* Rest. 2d § 85]

c. Promise to Pay a Debt Discharged by Bankruptcy

(1) Under Contract Law

As a matter of *contract law,* a promise to pay a debt that has been discharged by bankruptcy is enforceable. Such a promise is given the same treatment as a promise to pay a debt barred by the statute of limitations, with certain exceptions:

(a) Acknowledgment and Part Payment

Although a promise to pay a debt barred by the statute of limitations may be implied from an acknowledgment or part payment, in most states a promise to pay a debt discharged by bankruptcy will *not* be implied from a mere acknowledgment or part payment. That is, a promise to pay a debt discharged by bankruptcy will be enforceable only if it is *express.* [Rest. 2d § 83]

(b) Requirement of a Writing

Although a promise to pay a debt barred by the statute of limitations normally must be in writing, as a matter of contract law most states do *not* require that a promise to pay a debt discharged by bankruptcy be in writing to be enforceable. [*See* **Zabella v. Pakel,** 242 F.2d 452 (7th Cir. 1957)] However, such a requirement is statutorily imposed in a few states.

(2) Under Bankruptcy Law

The U.S. Bankruptcy Code has sharply changed the rules concerning a promise to pay a debt discharged by bankruptcy. Under the Bankruptcy Code, a promise to pay a debt that has been discharged by bankruptcy is normally enforceable only if a number of very stringent conditions are met. These conditions are highly detailed. Generally speaking, they are intended to assure that the debtor is fully informed; that the new agreement does not impose an undue hardship on the debtor; and that either the debtor is represented by counsel, the court holds a hearing on whether the requirements of the Bankruptcy Code have been satisfied, or both. [*See* 11 U.S.C. § 524 (c), (d)] *Rationale:* These changes were motivated by the unequal bargaining position of debtors and creditors and creditors' superior experience in bankruptcy matters. The traditional common law rule allowed debts that were discharged under bankruptcy law to be revived. But if it is too easy for a bankrupt debtor to be maneuvered into reviving such debts, bankruptcy law would be undermined.

4. Modern Rule—Promise to Pay Moral Obligation Arising out of Past Economic Benefit to Promisor

a. In General

Beyond the three core cases listed above, the principles that govern past or moral consideration are still in the process of development. The emerging modern rule is that a promise based on a moral obligation *is* enforceable, even if it does not fall within one of the three core exceptions, *if* the promise is based on a *material benefit* (usually meaning an economic benefit) that was previously conferred by the promisee upon the promisor, provided the benefit gave rise to an obligation—even if only a moral obligation—to pay for it.

Example: Webb saves the life of McGowin but sustains serious injuries during the rescue. McGowin promises to pay Webb a bimonthly stipend for the rest of Webb's life. McGowin pays Webb the stipend for more than eight years, but on McGowin's death, his estate refuses to continue the payments to Webb. McGowin's promise is binding because the promise to pay was based on a material benefit to the promisor that constituted valid consideration. [**Webb v. McGowin,** 168 So. 196 (Ala. 1935)]

(1) Restatement Position

This position is adopted by Restatement Second, which provides that "a promise made in recognition of a benefit previously received by the promisor from the promisee is binding to the extent necessary to prevent injustice," but is not binding "to the extent that its value is disproportionate to the benefit." [Rest. 2d § 86]

(2) Status of Modern Rule

Because the modern rule adopted in the Restatement Second is still emerging, some courts may continue to follow the traditional rule and hold that a promise based on moral or past consideration is unenforceable unless it falls into one of the three traditional categories [*supra*, pp. 48–50].

(3) State Statutes

The issue of past or moral consideration is affected by statute in some states. For example, a New York statute provides that past consideration is valid to support a written promise if the consideration is expressed in writing, is proved to have been given or performed, and would have been valid consideration if it were present rather than past consideration. [N.Y. Gen. Oblig. Law § 5–1105] And a California statute provides that "a moral obligation originating in some benefit conferred upon the promisor . . . is . . . a good consideration for a promise, to an extent corresponding with the extent of the obligation, but no further or otherwise." [Cal. Civ. Code § 1606]

b. Benefits Conferred Gratuitously

Even under the modern view, a promise to make compensation for a past benefit conferred will not be enforceable if that benefit was conferred as a ***gift,*** because there is no moral obligation to repay the value of a gift. [Rest. 2d § 86]

Example: Juan's wealthy older sister, Julia, gives Juan a new car for his 21st birthday. Later, Juan promises to pay Julia the value of the car. Juan's promise is unenforceable.

c. Promise Based on Expense Incurred by Promisee

Even under the modern view, a promise based on a moral obligation will normally not be enforced if the promisor did not receive a material (*i.e.*, economic) benefit—even if the promisee incurred expenses. [**Old American Life Insurance Co. v. Biggers,** 172 F.2d 495 (10th Cir. 1949); **Mills v. Wyman,** *supra*, p. 48]

Example: Wyman's adult son, Levi, becomes ill while away from home. Without having been requested to do so by Wyman, Mills takes care of Levi, but Levi dies. Wyman then writes to Mills promising to pay the expenses for his son's care. Wyman's promise is unenforceable because he did not receive a "material" (*i.e.*, economic) benefit from Mills's action. *But note:* This is a borderline case. Contract law has given increasing recognition to the reliance interest (*i.e.*, compensating the promisee's costs) and may come to recognize it in this situation too. Also, in some cases an expense of the promisee may be treated as a benefit to the promisor so as to make the promise enforceable. And courts may go out of their way to classify essentially noneconomic benefits as "material" for the purposes of this rule. [*E.g.*, **Webb v. McGowan,** *supra*, p. 50]

5. Promise to Pay Fixed Amount in Liquidation of a Legal Obligation

If a promisor promises to pay a certain amount for a benefit she received in the past that gave rise to a *legal* obligation to pay (*e.g.*, "I promise to pay you $500 for painting my fence pursuant to our earlier enforceable contract in which the price term was undecided"), can the promisee sue for the amount promised or can they sue only for restitution?

a. Acceptance by Promisee Constitutes Bargain

If the promisee *accepts* the promisor's promise, there is a bargain between the parties to substitute a liquidated amount for an unliquidated obligation, and there is consideration.

b. Split of Authority Where No Acceptance

If, however, the promisee does not specifically accept the promisor's promise, the courts are divided:

(1) Some cases hold that the new promise is *merely evidence of what is reasonable compensation.* [**Old American Life Insurance Co. v. Biggers,** *supra;* **Conant v. Evans,** 88 N.E. 438 (Mass. 1909)]

(2) However, other cases hold that the *promise defines the extent of the promisor's implied-in-fact duty.* Under this view, the promise may be enforceable without regard to the actual value of the services rendered. [*In re* **Bradbury,** 105 App. Div. 250 (1905); **Estate of Hatten,** 288 N.W. 278 (Wis. 1940)]

Chapter Two
Mutual Assent—Offer and Acceptance

CONTENTS	PAGE
Chapter Approach	54
A. **Mutual Assent**	55
B. **Offers**	58
C. **Acceptance**	89
D. **Time at Which Communications Between Offeror and Offeree Become Effective**	104
E. **Interpretation**	114
F. **The Parol Evidence Rule**	118
G. **"Shrinkwrap" Contracts**	129
H. **Online Contracting**	130

Chapter Approach

Unless a Contracts question specifically states that the parties made a contract, the answer to the question should address whether a contract was formed. Usually this requires a determination of whether there was consideration (as discussed in Chapter 1) and whether there was an offer and acceptance. This chapter discusses offer and acceptance. You should watch for the following five situations:

1. **The question sets out the texts of two or more communications**

    In that case, consider whether each communication was an invitation to deal, an offer, a revocation, an acceptance, an inquiry, a conditional acceptance, a counteroffer, or a rejection. When considering the category of each communication, keep in mind that:

    a. Frequently there is ***ambiguity*** as to what legal category a communication falls into. If that is the case, you must explore the ambiguity in your answer.

    b. The interpretation of each item in a ***series of communications*** is related to the interpretation of ***earlier items*** in that series. For example, if you determine that the first communication in a series is an invitation to deal, the question you should ask about the second communication is whether it is an offer or another invitation to deal. But if you determine that the first communication in a series is an offer, the question you should ask about the second communication is whether it is an acceptance, a conditional acceptance, a counteroffer, an inquiry, or a rejection.

    c. A response to an offer that purports to be an ***acceptance*** must be examined to determine whether it (i) is ***timely;*** (ii) is in the ***proper form*** (*e.g.*, does the offer require acceptance by a promise or by an act?); and (iii) ***deviates*** from the offer in any way. If a response that purports to be an acceptance deviates from the offer in any way, it is normally not an acceptance unless (i) it simply spells out an implication of the offer or (ii) the transaction involves a contract for the sale of goods, in which case the response may be an acceptance, even though it differs from the offer, under U.C.C. section 2–207.

    d. After determining the category into which each communication falls, you should determine the ***legal effect of each communication.*** For example, an offer creates a power of acceptance in the offeree; a rejection terminates the power of acceptance; a conditional acceptance normally terminates the power of acceptance and operates as a counteroffer (except under the U.C.C); a counteroffer terminates the offeree's power of acceptance, but creates a new power of acceptance in the original offeror; and an acceptance concludes a bargain if the acceptance is timely and in the proper form.

2. **The question sets out the dates on which two or more communications were sent between the parties**

    In that case, be sure to consider (i) whether a purported acceptance was ***timely according to the period for acceptance,*** if any, expressly required under the offer, or (ii) if no period was expressly required under the offer, whether the acceptance was ***within a reasonable time.***

    Questions that set out the dates of individual communications also may raise questions of revocation, below.

3. **The question states that a party made an offer that was then revoked**

    In that case, the question will normally raise the issue of whether the revocation was effective:

    a. ***If the revocation crosses paths with an acceptance,*** you must determine whether the acceptance or the revocation takes effect first. Depending on the way an acceptance is sent, it may be effective on dispatch (*i.e.*, at the moment it is sent), but a revocation is effective only on receipt.

b. Alternatively, the problem may be whether the offeror has the ***right to revoke.*** The general rule is that an offer is revocable, but there are important exceptions:

(1) If the offer is for a ***unilateral contract,*** it is not revocable if the offeree began performance prior to the revocation.

(2) If the offer is for a ***bilateral contract***, it may not be revocable if (i) the offeree gave consideration for it; (ii) the offer is in writing and recites at least nominal consideration; (iii) the offeree has relied on the offer in a foreseeable way; or (iv) the offer is for the sale of goods and therefore falls within the U.C.C.

4. The question involves an offer by one party but no explicit acceptance by the other

In that case, be sure to consider (1) the issue of *silence* as acceptance and (2) the possibility of acceptance by *conduct.*

5. The question states that an offer or acceptance was lost or delayed in the mail

In that case, the question will normally raise the issue of the effect of the loss or delay. Generally, an acceptance is effective on dispatch (even if lost), but all other communications are effective only on receipt (and therefore are ineffective if lost).

Next, if you determine that a contract was formed, you might find that the contract raises problems of ***interpretation.*** Also, if the agreement has been reduced to a ***written*** form, watch for the effects of the parol evidence rule.

Finally, if a contract question involves one party who provides standard form terms, consider whether the other party has assented to a contract in the first place. Also, if the contract was made online, consider whether the case falls into several modern patterns (like "clickwrap" or "browsewrap" contracts).

A. Mutual Assent

1. Existence of Mutual Assent Determined Under Objective Theory of Contracts

For a contract to be formed, there must be mutual assent. In determining whether mutual assent has been achieved for contract law purposes, most cases apply an ***objective*** theory of contracts (*i.e.*, applying what a ***reasonable person*** to whom an expression—words or conduct—has been addressed would understand the expression to mean). An expression is ***not*** interpreted simply by asking what the person making the expression subjectively meant the expression to convey or what the person to whom the expression was addressed subjectively understood the expression to mean.

However, for two reasons, the parties' subjective understandings may still be relevant: (1) even in applying the objective theory of contracts, one approach that courts follow is to choose which of the parties' subjective interpretations is more reasonable, or at least to pick one that is reasonable over one that is unreasonable [Rest. 2d § 201(2)(b)]; and (2) in some particular types of cases, a court may enforce a party's subjective interpretation (*see infra*, pp. 114–115) in spite of the objective theory of contracts.

a. **Rationale—Protection of Parties' Reasonable Expectations**

At one time, contract theory seems to have required an actual "meeting of the minds" to form a contract. This term implies that there is a subjective element to contract formation—that two people's minds must share the same intent. Modern contract law has rejected the concept that an actual, subjective meeting of the minds is necessary to form a contract. Rather, the importance of protecting the parties' reasonable expectations in relying on a promise, and the need for security and certainty in business transactions, make it imperative that each contracting party be able to rely on the other party's *manifested* intentions, not their thoughts or mental reservations. [Rest. 2d § 18; **Brant v. California Dairies, Inc.,** 4 Cal. 2d 128 (1935)]

(1) Note

Notwithstanding the rise of the objective theory of contracts, courts often continue to speak of a "meeting of the minds." When modern courts use that term, however, it is simply a shorthand phrase for the formation of a contract and does not require an actual subjective meeting of the minds.

b. Application

There is a sufficient manifestation of assent whenever a party uses an expression that he knows, or has reason to know, the other party would reasonably interpret as an offer or acceptance, and the other party does so interpret it. [Rest. 2d § 19]

Example: Lucy offers to buy Zehmer's farm for $50,000 cash. Zehmer accepts the offer in jest, believing Lucy does not have the money. The two parties work out the terms of the contract, Zehmer writes out the contract on a restaurant check, and Zehmer and his wife sign it. Lucy takes the writing and attempts to enforce it. Even if Zehmer did not subjectively intend to sell the farm, the contract is binding because a reasonable person in Zehmer's position would have believed it to be a serious transaction. [**Lucy v. Zehmer,** 84 S.E.2d 516 (Va. 1954)]

c. Alternate Approaches

Some courts and authorities purport to apply an *entirely objective* to interpretation, holding that expressions mean whatever the court believes a reasonable person would understand them to mean. [**Hotchkiss v. Nat'l City Bank,** 200 F. 287 (S.D.N.Y. 1911)] This raises the possibility that a court will impose a meaning on the parties that neither one of them intended, just because the court believes that meaning is objectively reasonable. Restatement Second rejects this approach, instead using objective reasonableness as a way, at least in theory, to choose between the parties' actual, subjective interpretations. [Rest. 2d § 201; *see also infra*, p. 114 *et seq.*]

APPROACH TO OBJECTIVE AND SUBJECTIVE FACTORS IN CONTRACT INTERPRETATION

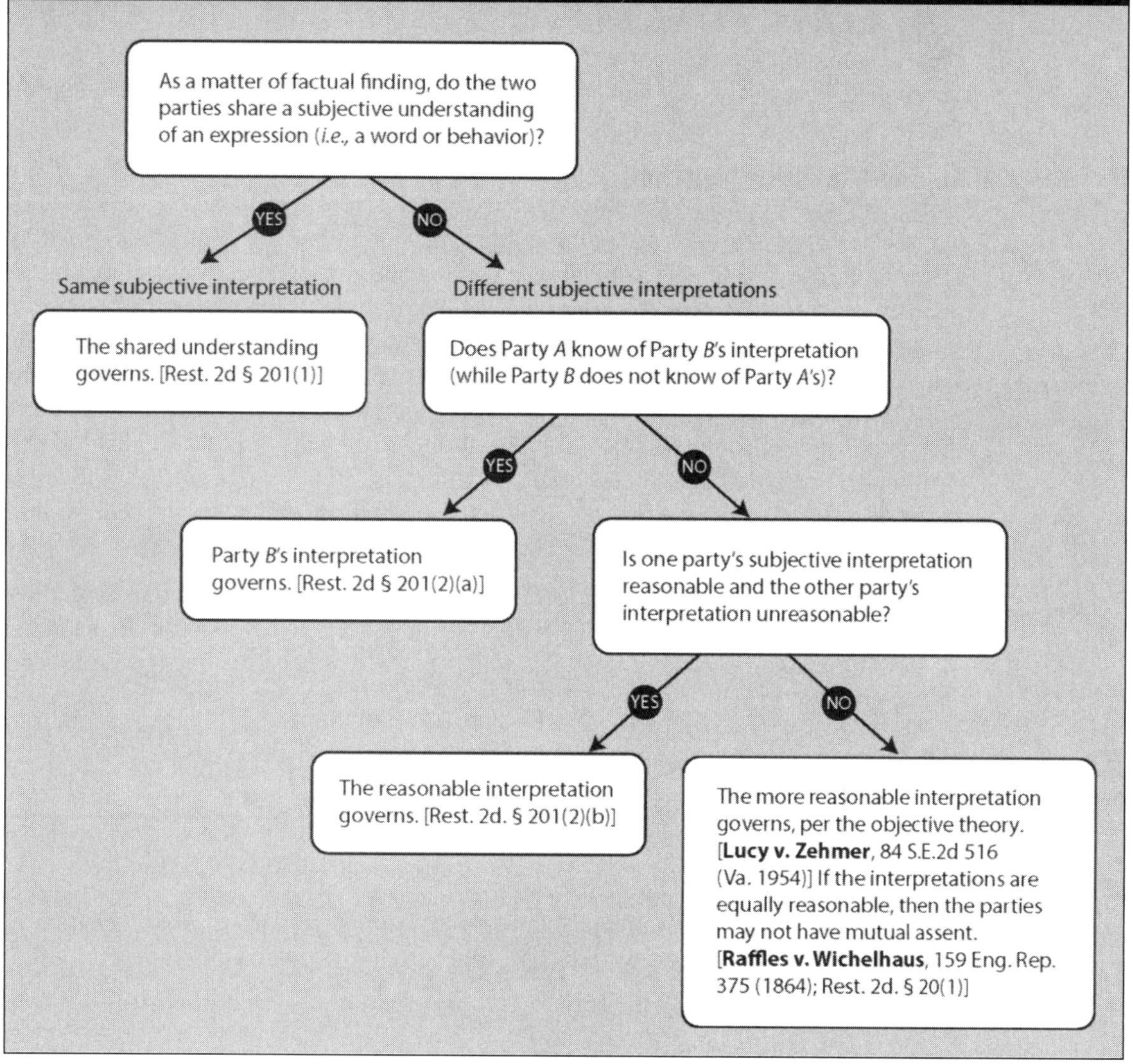

As a matter of factual finding, do the two parties share a subjective understanding of an expression (*i.e.*, a word or behavior)?

- **YES → Same subjective interpretation**
  - The shared understanding governs. [Rest. 2d § 201(1)]
- **NO → Different subjective interpretations**
  - **Does Party A know of Party B's interpretation (while Party B does not know of Party A's)?**
    - **YES** → Party B's interpretation governs. [Rest. 2d § 201(2)(a)]
    - **NO** → **Is one party's subjective interpretation reasonable and the other party's interpretation unreasonable?**
      - **YES** → The reasonable interpretation governs. [Rest. 2d. § 201(2)(b)]
      - **NO** → The more reasonable interpretation governs, per the objective theory. [**Lucy v. Zehmer**, 84 S.E.2d 516 (Va. 1954)] If the interpretations are equally reasonable, then the parties may not have mutual assent. [**Raffles v. Wichelhaus**, 159 Eng. Rep. 375 (1864); Rest. 2d. § 20(1)]

2. Express and Implied Contracts

a. Express Contracts

If mutual assent is explicitly manifested in oral or written words of agreement, the resulting contract is said to be *express.*

b. Implied Contracts

(1) Implied-in-Fact Contracts

If the promises of the parties are inferred from their acts or conduct, or from words that are not explicitly words of agreement, the contract is said to be *implied in fact.* Although implied, such contracts are true contracts. The mutual assent is inferred, but it is real, not fictional. [Rest. 2d § 4]

 Example: Auctioneer conducts a "Dutch auction" of a vase. (In a Dutch auction, the auctioneer starts with a high price, and reduces the price step-by-step until a member of the audience bids by raising a hand. That bidder "wins" the auction.) When the price for the vase falls to $190, Bidder raises her hand, and Auctioneer knocks down the hammer. Auctioneer and Bidder have an implied-in-fact contract for the sale of the vase at $190.

Example: Fred asks Barney, a plumber, to repair Fred's sink. Barney does so, without either party discussing any further contractual details. There is an implied-in-fact contract under which Fred must pay Barney his usual rates for such a job, provided the rates are reasonable.

(2) Implied-in-Law Contracts

To be carefully distinguished from contracts implied in fact are contracts *implied in law.* A contract is said to be implied in law when one party is required to compensate another for a benefit conferred in order *to avoid unjust enrichment,* rather than because there has been an actual or implied-in-fact promise to pay for the benefit. Unlike implied-in-fact contracts, implied-in-law contracts are not real contracts. The basis for implied-in-law contracts is unjust enrichment, not assent. The term "contract" is used only because, for purely technical reasons, the English courts historically classified these cases under a contract heading by *fictionally* implying a promise to pay for benefits or services rendered in order to prevent unjust enrichment. (*See infra*, p. 251.)

Example: Doctor sees Pedestrian lying in the street unconscious and renders medical services. When Pedestrian recovers, Doctor bills Pedestrian. Pedestrian is liable for the reasonable value of Doctor's services under an implied-in-law contract.

B. Offers

1. Introduction

Most contracts, particularly on contracts exams, are formed by *offer and acceptance.* Therefore, the first step in analyzing a contracts problem often is to determine whether an offer has been made.

2. Legal Significance of an Offer

The legal significance of determining that a particular expression (*i.e.*, word or other communication) is an offer is that an offer creates a *power of acceptance* in the person to whom the expression was addressed. That is, if an expression constitutes an offer, the addressee has the power to *conclude a bargain* (and thereby enter into a contract and *bind* the offeror) merely by giving assent in the appropriate manner (*see infra*, p. 89 *et seq.*).

3. What Constitutes an Offer?

An offer is an expression of present willingness to enter into a bargain, made in such a way that a reasonable person in the position of the person to whom the expression is addressed would believe that they can *conclude a bargain* merely by giving assent in the manner required by the expression. [Rest. 2d § 24] (Informally, an offer is a communication that an offeree can say "yes" to and reasonably believe that a contract has thereby been created.)

a. **Two Essential Elements**

To be sufficient as an offer, an expression must meet two criteria, each of which is discussed in detail below: (i) ***intent*** to enter into a bargain and (ii) ***definiteness*** of terms.

(1) intent to Enter into a Bargain

(a) Offer vs. Invitation to Deal

The fact that an expression moves toward a bargain does not make the expression an offer if it is clear from the language or circumstances that the expression reflects merely an intent to begin or continue negotiation. Such expressions are called *"preliminary negotiations"* or *"invitations to negotiate"* or *"invitations to deal,"* rather than offers.

1) Words Suggesting Negotiations

Typically, words such as "Are you interested ...?," "Would you give ...?," "I quote ...," or "I would consider ..." suggest only preliminary negotiations or invitations to deal. [**Elkhorn-Hazard Coal Co. v. Kentucky River Corp.**, 20 F.2d 67 (6th Cir. 1927)]

Example: Buyer asks Seller whether Seller would sell a certain store property for $30,000. This is not an offer. Seller replies, "I would not be selling for under $40,000." This is also not an offer, but merely an invitation to Buyer to continue to negotiate.

2) Words Suggesting an Offer

On the other hand, words such as "I will sell (or buy)" or "I offer" suggest that an offer is intended.

3) Words Not Conclusive

However, the words used in an expression are not conclusive by themselves. Depending on the circumstances, an expression that uses the word "offer" may still be construed as an invitation to deal, and an expression using the word "quote" could be an offer. (*See infra*, p. 61.)

EXAM TIP   GILBERT

Most offers are easy to spot, but watch out for language that sounds like an offer but is really an ***invitation to deal.*** For example, advertisements sound like offers, but usually are just invitations for people to come in and deal (*see infra*, pp. 60–61).

---

(2) Definiteness of Terms

Another index to whether an expression constitutes an offer is whether its terms are sufficiently ***definite.*** Although what constitutes sufficient definiteness varies considerably with the circumstances, and although an offer need not cover all possible contingencies, usually offers make reasonably clear: (i) the subject matter of the proposed bargain; (ii) the price; and (iii) the quantity involved.

(a) Intent Determinative

Even the omission of one of the above terms does not necessarily preclude an expression from being an offer if: (i) the expression otherwise evidences an intent to conclude a bargain, (ii) the omission does not indicate a lack of such intent, and (iii) the court can fill in the omitted term by implication. (*See* discussion on definiteness of terms, *infra*, p. 135 *et seq*.)

Example: Manufacturer proposes to sell Farmer a tractor for $3,000, with $1,000 down and the remainder to be paid in "regular installments." Farmer accepts. Although the size and timing of the installment payments is undecided, if the facts indicate that both parties intended to conclude a bargain, the court may enforce the contract. [Rest. 2d § 33, ill. 1]

EXAM TIP   GILBERT

If there has been a **series of communications** between the parties, pay attention to the legal significance, if any, of **each statement**. For example, if you determine that *A*'s first statement to *B* is not an offer because it is too indefinite, *B*'s response cannot be an acceptance (because there is nothing to accept). You must then consider whether *B*'s response is an offer or another indefinite expression. Keep checking until you find whether there is an offer and an acceptance.

---

b. Special Rules

Some types of statements are governed by special rules.

(1) Advertisements

The general rule is that advertisements are normally deemed to be invitations to deal rather than offers. [**Craft v. Elder & Johnston Co.,** 38 N.E.2d 416 (Ohio 1941)]

Example: Department Store advertised in a magazine that belts were on sale for $10 each. Customer went to Department Store to buy a belt, but all the belts were already sold. Customer has no power to accept an offer and demand damages, because this advertisement was a mere invitation to deal rather than an offer.

(a) Rationale

The general rule governing advertisements is usually based on one or more of the following three grounds:

1) *Advertisements are usually indefinite* as to quantity and other terms;

2) *Sellers ought to be able to choose* with whom they will deal; and

3) *Advertisements are typically addressed to the general public,* so that if an advertisement was considered to be an offer, a seller might find the offer "overaccepted"—*i.e.*, the number of people who try to accept might exceed the number of items that the advertiser had available for sale.

(b) Exceptions

Although the general rule is that advertisements are normally deemed to be only invitations to deal, a particular advertisement might be construed as an offer. This is most likely if the advertisement is definite in its terms, and either (i) the circumstances clearly indicate an intention to make a bargain, (ii) the advertisement invites those to whom it is addressed to take a specific action without further communication, or (iii) overacceptance is unlikely. [**Lefkowitz v. Great Minneapolis Surplus Store,** 86 N.W.2d 689 (Minn. 1957)]

Example: Rare Books, Inc., publishes the following advertisement in *The New York Times Book Review:* "Rare Books, Inc. will pay $100 for every copy of the first edition of Sinclair Lewis's *Main Street* sent to us by January 1, 2024." This advertisement is an offer. It is definite in its terms and invites those to whom it is addressed to take a specific action (sending in the book) without further communication. Since Rare Books has signified an intention to buy any and all of the (limited number of) first editions, there is no significant problem of overacceptance.

Example: A department store runs the following advertisement in the newspapers: "Saturday, 9 A.M. Sharp, 3 Brand New Fur Coats Worth Up to $1,000, $100 each, First Come, First Served." This is also an offer. Again, it is definite in its terms and invites those to whom it is addressed to take an action (being first in line) without further communication. Since the number of available coats is specified, there is no significant risk of overacceptance. [**Lefkowitz v. Great Minneapolis Surplus Store,** *supra*]

1) **Rewards**

   An advertisement that a reward will be paid (*e.g.*, a reward for the return of lost property or for the capture of a criminal) is normally construed as an offer. (*Compare infra*, p. 119.) The act is specified; there is a clear intention that those who see the advertisement will rely on it; and because only one person normally can claim a reward, there is no significant problem of overacceptance. (Offers for rewards are ordinarily offers for unilateral contracts, accepted by completing the terms of the offer.)

STATUS OF ADVERTISEMENTS — GILBERT

	STATUS	EXAMPLES
GENERAL RULE	Advertisement is not an offer but merely an ***invitation to deal***	"Shoes for sale, $20 each!" "25% off the entire store!"
EXCEPTION	It is an offer if ***definite terms*** and (i) circumstances indicate ***intention*** to make a bargain, (ii) ***specific action*** is invited without further communication, or (iii) ***overacceptance is unlikely***	"Arrive at our store at 10 a.m. on Saturday to buy the only table saw we have in stock for $20. First come, first served." "Will pay $10,000 for any of Hank Aaron's rookie baseball cards." "Lost cat. Answers to 'Smokey.' Return to 417 Grand Street for a $50 reward."

(2) **Offering Circulars**

"Offering circulars" are general mailings sent out by merchants to a number of potential customers, setting forth the terms on which a merchant is ready to deal. Offering circulars are treated like advertisements—*i.e.*, they are normally construed as invitations to deal, but they may be construed as offers in a given case. The usual test is whether a reasonable person in the position of the addressee would think the communication had been addressed to him ***individually*** (in which case it will be treated as an offer) or only as *one of a number* of recipients (in which case it will be treated as an invitation to deal). Use of the word "offer" usually, but not always, suggests an offer. Use of the word "quote" usually, but not always, suggests an invitation to deal.

> **e.g. Example:** Buyer receives a printed letter from Seller stating, "We are authorized to offer Michigan fine salt in full car load lots of 80 to 95 barrels, delivered at your city at 85 cents per barrel." Because the letter does not appear to be directed at Buyer individually, it is merely an invitation to deal, despite use of the word "offer." [**Moulton v. Kershaw,** 18 N.W. 172 (Wis. 1884)]

> **e.g. Example:** Buyer sends an inquiry to Seller asking Seller's price for Mason jars. Seller replies, "We quote you Mason fruit jars, pints $4.50, quarts $5.00, half gallons $6.50 per gross, for immediate acceptance." Because the response was directed to Buyer individually, it is an offer despite use of the word "quote." [**Fairmount Glass Works v. Grunden-Martin Woodenware Co.,** 51 S.W. 196 (Ky. 1899)]

(3) Auctions

(a) Auction with Reserve

The usual auction (sometimes called an auction "with reserve") is subject to the following rules:

1) Putting an Item on the Block

The act of an auctioneer in putting an item "on the block" (*i.e.*, calling for bids on the item) is not an offer. Rather, putting an item on the block is considered an invitation to make offers. Because putting an item on the block is not an offer, a bid by a member of the audience is not an acceptance; instead, it is an offer. Therefore, the auctioneer may withdraw the item even after the bidding has begun, unless and until the auctioneer has actually "hammered down" (*i.e.*, accepted) a particular bid. [U.C.C. § 2-328(3)]

2) Bids

A bid by a member of the audience is an offer, which is accepted if the auctioneer "hammers it down."

a) Because an offer is normally revocable (*see infra*, p. 80 *et seq.*), until a bid is accepted by being hammered down, the bid may be withdrawn (revoked).

b) Each new bid (offer) automatically terminates all earlier bids. [U.C.C. § 2-328(2), (3); **Payne v. Cave,** 3 Term R. (LB.) 148 (1789)] Thus, if a bid is withdrawn before it is hammered down, the auctioneer is not free to accept earlier bids.

(b) Auction Without Reserve

Certain different rules apply to an auction that is announced to be "without reserve." In such an auction, once the auctioneer puts an item on the block (*i.e.*, calls for bids on an item) the item cannot be withdrawn unless no bid is made within a reasonable time. [U.C.C. § 2-328(3)] However, *bids* in an auction "without reserve" are treated the same way as bids in a normal auction (*i.e.*, the bids can be withdrawn at any time before being hammered down).

(c) Determining Whether Auction Is "with" or "Without" Reserve

An auction is deemed to be "with reserve," and therefore subject to the normal rules, unless the terms of the auction state that it is to be without reserve. [U.C.C. § 2–328] Thus, the usual auction is with reserve, and the auctioneer may reject any and all bids, and withdraw any item from sale, at any time before the hammer has fallen.

(4) Putting Contracts out for Bid

A government agency or a private firm may put a contract "out for bid"—*i.e.*, the agency or firm may let it be known, by formal publication or otherwise, that it contemplates entering into a contract for a certain performance, such as building a warehouse or purchasing office equipment. The agency or firm typically publishes or otherwise makes available the contract specifications and asks potential contractors or suppliers to submit bids that state the price at which the contractor or supplier would render the performance. (Individuals may also put contracts out for bid, such as a contract to build a private residence.) Similarly, contractors who plan to submit bids may themselves request bids from subcontractors on defined portions of the work (*e.g.*, on the carpentry portion of a construction contract).

(a) Legal Status

Putting a contract out for bid usually is *not* deemed to be an offer. However, the bids submitted in response usually *are* considered offers.

Example: Builder, a general contractor who wants to make a bid on a school construction job, requests plumbing subcontractors to give her bids on the plumbing part of the job. This request is not an offer to the subcontractors. Builder is therefore free to decline all of the subcontractors' bids, or to accept a bid other than the lowest bid. However, bids by the subcontractors are offers to Builder. [**Drennan v. Star Paving Co.,** 51 Cal. 2d 409 (1958); *and see infra*, p. 83]

(b) Interpretation

As in the case of advertisements and offering circulars, the rules governing contract bidding involve matters of interpretation. Therefore, depending on the language and circumstances, putting a contract out for bid *might* be interpreted as an offer [*see, e.g.*, **Jenkins Towel Service, Inc. v. Fidelity-Philadelphia Trust Co.,** 161 A.2d 334 (Pa. 1960)], while a bid might be interpreted as only an invitation to deal [*see* **Leo F. Piazza Paving Co. v. Bebek & Brkich,** 141 Cal. App. 2d 226 (1956)]. However, such interpretations are very exceptional.

APPROACH TO INTERPRETING PARTIES' EXPRESSIONS

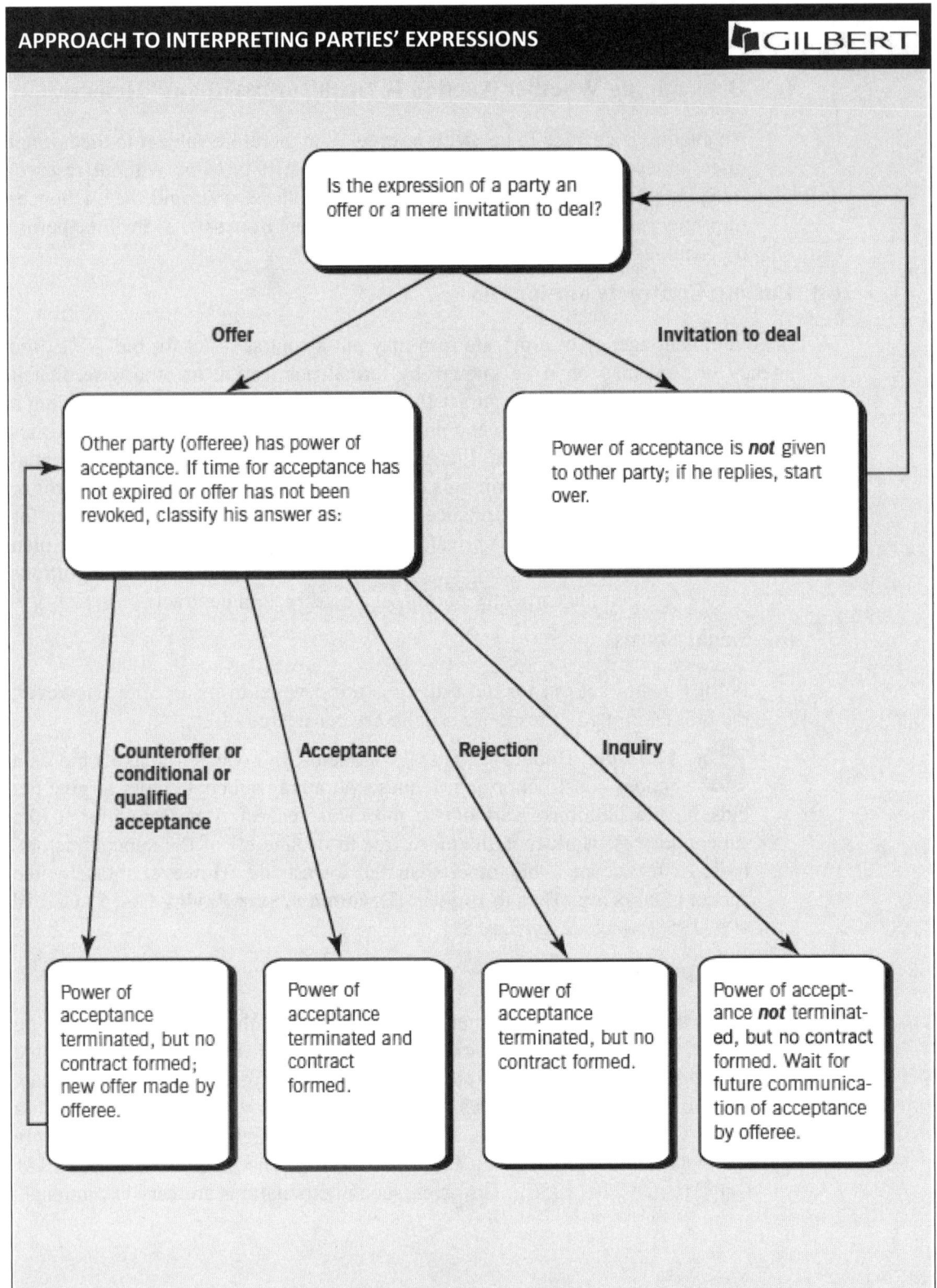

4. Termination of Power of Acceptance—in General

An offeree can conclude a bargain by giving assent only if his power of acceptance has not been terminated—*i.e.*, if the offer is still "open." Termination of the offeree's power of acceptance may result from any of the following causes:

(i) Expiration or lapse of the offer;

(ii) A rejection by the offeree;

(iii) A counteroffer by the offeree;

(iv) A qualified or conditional acceptance by the offeree;

(v) A valid revocation of the offer by the offeror; or

(vi) By operation of law.

a. Termination of Power of Acceptance by Expiration or Lapse of the Offer

Perhaps the most common manner in which the power of acceptance is terminated is through *expiration* or *lapse.* The rules governing this method of termination depend in part on whether a time period is fixed in the offer itself.

(1) Where Time for Acceptance Is Fixed in the Offer

If the offer states that it will be "held open," or "is good," or the like, for a certain period of time, the offeree's power of acceptance expires or lapses at the end of that period without any further action by the offeror. [Rest. 2d § 41]

(a) Interpretation of Stated Time Period

Suppose an offer sent through the mail states that it will be held open for 10 days. Does this mean 10 days after the offer was *sent,* or 10 days after it was *received?* There is sparse authority on this issue, but what little caselaw exists indicates that unless the offer otherwise provides, the time runs from the day of *receipt,* at least if the offer was not obviously delayed in transmission. **[Caldwell v. Cline,** 156 S.E. 55 (W. Va. 1930)]

1) Delay in Transmission

Suppose the offer was delayed in transmission. If the offeree had no reason to know of the delay, the same rule applies. However, if the offeree *knew or should have known* of the delay (as where an offer dated March 1 is received on March 19), the time period begins to run from the day on which the offeree *would have received* the offer if the delay had not occurred. [Rest. 2d § 49] This is true even if the delay in transmission was the offeror's fault (as where the offeror carelessly misaddressed the letter).

(2) Where No Time for Acceptance Is Fixed in Offer

If the offer does *not* state a period of time during which it will remain open, the offeree's power of acceptance expires or lapses after the expiration of a *reasonable time.* **[Loring v. City of Boston,** 48 Mass. (7 Metc.) 409 (1844)]

(a) What Constitutes a Reasonable Time?

What constitutes a reasonable time depends on the circumstances: *e.g.*, the nature of the subject matter of the offer, the rapidity of price fluctuation for that subject matter, the medium through which the offer is made (face-to-face, letter, telegram, and so forth), and business custom. [Rest. 2d § 41]

1) Face-to-Face and Telephonic Bargaining

When the parties bargain *face-to-face or by telephone,* the time for acceptance ordinarily does not extend beyond the end of the conversation,, unless a contrary intention is indicated (*e.g.*, if the offeror says, "Well, think it over . . ."). [Rest. 2d § 41]

2) Offer Sent by Mail

When an offer is sent *by mail,* an acceptance mailed by midnight on the day of receipt is timely, unless the circumstances indicate otherwise. [Rest. 2d § 41] However, an acceptance may be timely even if it is sent later, provided it is sent within a reasonable time under the circumstances and the offer does not restrict the time. But remember that a special rule might apply where the offer is delayed in transmission and the offeree knows or should know of the delay. (*See supra*, p. 65.)

b. Termination of Offer Through Rejection by Offeree

A rejection is a statement by an offeree that he does not intend to accept the offer. An offeree's power of acceptance is terminated by a rejection, even though the power of acceptance would not otherwise have lapsed. [**Goodwin v. Hidalgo County Water Control & Improvement District No. 1,** 58 S.W.2d 1092 (Tex. 1933)]

Example: On January 2, Leonardo offers to paint Lisa's portrait in February for $10,000, the offer to be held open until January 11. On January 5, Lisa *rejects* the offer. On January 7, Lisa changes her mind and accepts the offer. The acceptance is ineffective because Lisa's power of acceptance was terminated on January 5 by her rejection.

(1) Rationale—Protection of Offeror

When an offeree rejects the offer, the offeror is likely to believe the offeree is no longer interested and may therefore take actions that he would not have taken if he thought the offeree might accept. For instance, in the example above, after Lisa rejected the offer, Leonardo might have contracted to paint someone else's portrait in February.

(2) Exception for Options

Some authorities take the position that in the case of an *option,* a rejection during the option period does *not* terminate the offeree's power of acceptance, *i.e.*, his right to "exercise the option." [**Ryder v. Wescoat,** 535 S.W.2d 269 (Mo. 1976)] The rationale is that the offeree has a *contractual right* to have the offer held open during its term (*see infra*, p. 83). However, even under these authorities, the offeror would be protected if he *relied* on the rejection.

Example: On May 1, Retailer pays Supplier for an option to purchase up to 220,000 nitrile gloves at $0.04/glove at any time through May 25. On May 10, Retailer casually notifies Supplier that it is no longer interested in exercising the option, but then it puts in a formal order for gloves on May 12, purporting to be exercising the same option. Retailer's communication of May 10 may not count as a rejection or terminate Supplier's offer unless Supplier changed its position in response to that communication (*e.g.*, by exhausting its supply of gloves in a sale to a different buyer).

Compare: Suppose there were no option and, instead, Supplier had made a simple offer to Retailer on May 1: "We offer to sell you up to 220,000 nitrile gloves at $0.04/glove. This offer is good through May 25." On May 10, Retailer emails Supplier, saying, "Thanks for your offer, but we have all the gloves we need at this time. Please keep us in mind in the future." This email constitutes a rejection, and Retailer has no power to accept on May 12.

c. Termination of Power of Acceptance by Counteroffer

A counteroffer is an offer made by an offeree to an offeror that concerns the same subject matter as the original offer but differs in its terms. A counteroffer is deemed by law to operate as a rejection, so it terminates the offeree's power of acceptance. [**Livingston v. Evans,** [1925] 4 D.L.R. 769 (Can.); Rest. 2d § 39] *Rationale*: An offeree who receives a counteroffer is assumed to believe that the offeree is no longer interested in the original offer.

Example: Same facts as in the portrait example above, except that on January 5, Lisa responds, "I will give you $2,000." This is a counteroffer and terminates Lisa's power of acceptance.

(1) Status as Offer

As already mentioned, one legal effect of a counteroffer is that it terminates the offeree's power of acceptance. However, a counteroffer also has a second legal effect: because a counteroffer is an offer, it creates a new power of acceptance in the original offeror.

(2) Inquiries and Requests

The offeree's power of acceptance is *not* terminated by an *inquiry* concerning the offer or by a *request* for different terms. [**Stevenson, Jaques & Co. v. McLean,** 5 Q.B.D. 346 (1880)]

Example: Assume the same facts as in the portrait example above, except that on January 5, Lisa responds, "Does the price you quote include framing?" This is an inquiry, not a counteroffer, and does not terminate Lisa's power of acceptance.

(a) Test

A test for distinguishing between a counteroffer and an inquiry is whether a reasonable person in the offeror's position would think that the communication from the offeree was *itself an offer* that could be accepted. For example, Lisa's question about framing is obviously not itself an offer.

EXAM TIP GILBERT

If the facts in an exam question indicate that a party has made a counteroffer, remember that the counteroffer serves not only as a rejection but *also as an offer* to the original offeror. Therefore, you should carefully examine the original offeror's response to the counteroffer. If the original offeror accepts the counteroffer, a contract is formed according to the terms of the counteroffer. If the original offeror rejects the counteroffer or makes another counteroffer to the original offeree, no contract is formed and you must continue to analyze the parties' communications for a valid offer and acceptance.

---

(3) Exception for Options

In the case of an *option,* a counteroffer made during the option period does *not* terminate the offeree's power of acceptance—that is, the offeree's right to exercise the option. [**Humble Oil & Refining Co. v. Westside Investment Corp.**, 428 S.W.2d 92 (Tex. 1968)]

(a) Rationale

The offeree has a *contractual right* to have the offer held open during its term (*see infra*, p. 83).

Example: Assume the same facts as in the nitrile-gloves example above. If Retailer sends an order to Supplier while the option is open for 20,000 gloves at $0.03/glove instead of $0.04/glove, Supplier has the power to accept this offer, but the new communication does not terminate Retailer's rights under the original option.

d. Termination of Power of Acceptance by Conditional or Qualified Acceptance

A purported acceptance that adds to or changes the terms of the offer is known as a *conditional* or *qualified* acceptance.

(1) Legal Effect—General Rule

Except in the case of contracts for the sale of goods (*infra*, p. 71), a conditional or qualified acceptance generally constitutes a counteroffer, not an acceptance, even if the offeree labels it as an acceptance. Therefore, it terminates the offeree's power of acceptance. [**Minneapolis & St. Louis Railway v. Columbus Rolling-Mill**, 119 U.S. 149 (1886)]

Example: On January 8, Justin makes a written offer to Melissa to sell his house for $50,000, the offer to be held open until January 20. On January 12, Melissa replies in writing, "I accept your offer on the condition that you install a new front door." Melissa's reply constitutes a conditional or qualified acceptance and therefore terminates her power of acceptance.

(2) Status as offer

A conditional or qualified acceptance, like a counteroffer, is itself an offer, which can be accepted by the original offeror.

(3) Exceptions to General Rule

(a) Acceptance Coupled with Request

An unconditional acceptance coupled with a *request* is a valid acceptance and forms a contract. [**Culton v. Gilchrist,** 61 N.W. 384 (Iowa 1894)]

Example: Same facts as the home sale example, above, except that on January 12, Melissa replies, "I accept your offer gladly. I do hope that you will install a new front door before I take possession." Melissa's response is an acceptance because in this example the installation of a new front door is merely a request, not a condition.

(b) "Grumbling" Acceptances

A "grumbling" acceptance is an acceptance accompanied by an expression of dissatisfaction or a protest. (For example, "Send the goods, but I sure wish you could give us a better price" or "I accept the renewal of my yearly employment contract with serious reservations, because the terms are unfair, and I will consider all legal options that are available to me.") A grumbling acceptance is a valid acceptance and forms a contract as long as the expression of dissatisfaction stops short of actual dissent. [**Price v. Okla. Coll. of Osteopathic Med. & Surgery,** 733 P.2d 1357 (Okla. Ct. App 1986); **Johnson v. Federal Union Surety Co.,** 153 N.W. 788 (Mich. 1915)]

(c) Implied Terms

An offeree's power of acceptance is not terminated by an acceptance that is conditional or qualified in *form,* but in *substance* merely spells out an implied term of the offer. [Rest. 2d § 59; *see also* **State Dep't of Transp. v. Providence & Worcester R.R.,** 674 A.2d 1239 (R.I. 1996)]

Example: Same facts as the home sale example above, except that on January 12, Melissa replies, "I accept your offer on condition that you convey marketable title." Melissa's reply is not a conditional acceptance because in the absence of a disclaimer of title, a promise to convey marketable title is implied in a contract for the sale of land, and Melissa's reply merely spells out that implication.

(d) U.C.C. Rule

In the case of a contract for the sale of goods, U.C.C. section 2–207(1) changes the common law rule by providing that "a definite and seasonable expression of acceptance . . . operates as an acceptance *even though it states terms additional to or different from those offered or agreed upon,* unless acceptance is *expressly* made conditional on assent to the additional or different terms." (Emphasis added.) This section of the U.C.C. is discussed at length *infra*, p. 71 *et seq*.

(4) The Mirror Image Rule

At common law, an acceptance needed to be a perfect "mirror image" of the offer. In other words, if a purported acceptance deviated from the offer in any way—even in an immaterial way—it was deemed a qualified or conditional acceptance and did not form a contract; instead, it had the legal effect of a counteroffer. [**Poel v. Brunswick-Balke-Collender Co.,** 216 N.Y. 310 (1915); *see supra*, p. 68]

(a) Form Contracts and the Last Shot Rule

1) The Problem

The mirror image rule had a particularly strong bite in the case of form contracts. Typically, commercial sellers and buyers transact by exchanging preprinted forms, usually called Sales Orders, Purchase Orders, Confirmations, or Acknowledgments. The most important terms of a transaction—such as the description of the subject matter, the quantity, price, delivery date, and terms of payment—normally are negotiated, typically correspond with each other, and usually are individualized (*e.g.*, manually entered or handwritten) onto each form. However, other terms—such as warranties or disclaimers of warranties—will typically be preprinted on each form in fine print. Invariably, the printed terms of a seller's form will differ from the printed terms of the buyer's form because each form is drafted to favor the party who prepared it. Nevertheless, if the individualized terms on the forms agree, the seller will normally ship the goods described and the buyer will normally accept the goods, even though the preprinted terms of the forms differ.

2) Common Law Last Shot Rule

Under the common law mirror image rule, when a buyer and a seller exchange forms whose terms differ even slightly, no contract arises from the exchange of the forms even if the material and individualized terms on the two forms agree. If the buyer sends the first form (*e.g.*, a Purchase Order) and the seller responds by shipping goods and includes, with the goods, its own form (*e.g.*, an Acknowledgement) that contains any terms that do not perfectly match the buyer's form, the seller's form is deemed to be a conditional acceptance and therefore a counteroffer. The seller was under no obligation to ship any goods, and the buyer is under no obligation to accept the goods that were shipped. However, if the buyer does accept the goods, the buyer is deemed to have accepted them pursuant to the last form sent—here, the seller's outstanding counteroffer. This approach is known as the last shot rule because, under this approach, the terms of the contract are those set out in the last form sent, which could be either the seller's form (if the transaction was initiated by the buyer's form) or the buyer's form (if the transaction was initiated by the seller's form).

Example: Buyer sends Seller a Purchase Order for 1,000 desk chairs. Seller sends back a Sales Order. The manually entered terms of the Purchase Order and the Sales Order agree, but the preprinted form terms differ. Seller then ships the chairs, and Buyer accepts them. Under the common law mirror image rule, a contract was not formed by exchanging the Sales Order and Purchase Order because the Sales Order would be deemed a conditional acceptance. However, a conditional acceptance, like a counteroffer, creates a power of acceptance in the original offeror (here, Buyer). Therefore, if the chairs are shipped and accepted, Buyer, the original offeror, was deemed to have accepted Seller's conditional acceptance/counteroffer by Buyer's act of accepting the chairs. The terms of the contract would be those set out in the Sales Order (the last form sent) because Seller would be deemed to have shipped the goods on the terms of the Sales Order and Buyer would be deemed to have accepted the goods on those terms.

Compare: Same facts as in the example above, except that the transaction is initiated by a Sales Order sent by Seller, followed by a Purchase Order sent by Buyer. On these facts, under the last shot rule of the common law, the shipment and acceptance of the goods would form a contract on the basis of the terms in the Purchase Order.

Compare: Same facts as in either the example or the comparison above, except that Seller never sends the goods, or Seller sends the goods and Buyer rejects them. Under these facts, no contract is formed. The Sales Order in the example is an offer, but if the goods were not shipped, or if they were shipped and rejected, there is no acceptance. The parties are still free to "walk away" from the deal. The same is true of the Purchase Order offer in the comparison.

(5) U.C.C. Rule

The U.C.C. has changed the mirror image rule regarding contracts for the sale of goods, so that for such contracts "a definite and seasonable [*i.e.*, timely—*see supra*, pp. 64–66] expression of acceptance . . . operates as an acceptance **even though it states terms additional to or different from those offered or agreed upon,** unless acceptance is expressly made conditional on assent to the additional or different terms." [U.C.C. § 2–207(1)] *Rationale:* The mirror image rule often undercut the parties' expectations, because the rule applies even to expressions that purport to accept an offer, and it applies even if the parties both think they have a deal according to business customs. As a result, the U.C.C. effectively repeals the mirror image rule in many sales of goods cases.

(a) Sale of Goods

As indicated above, U.C.C. section 2–207 is applicable only to contracts for the sale of *goods* (although some courts might apply it to other contracts by analogy). [*See In re* **Doughboy Industries, Inc.,** 17 App. Div. 2d 216 (1962)]

(b) Form Contracts—"Battle of the Forms"

Although in theory U.C.C. section 2–207 is applicable to all contracts for the sale of goods, the section was really designed to deal with the problem raised by form contracts—in particular, situations where two parties exchange different forms, a scenario known as the "battle of the forms." Therefore, as a practical matter, in determining whether section 2–207 is applicable in a given case, the courts may take into account whether a form contract is involved. [**Columbia Hyundai, Inc. v. Carll Hyundai, Inc.,** 484 S.E.2d 468 (S.C. 1997)] (For cases of "shrinkwrap" contracts in which a seller includes terms inside a product's box—which are not "battle of the forms" cases because there is only one form—*see* p. 129, *infra*. For rules that govern form terms in general, *see* p. 158, *infra*.)

(c) "Definite" Expression of Acceptance

U.C.C. section 2–207(1) leaves open the issue of what constitutes a *definite* expression of acceptance, and the cases have not definitively settled the issue. It is clear that the offeree's response must *purport* to be an acceptance. It is also clear that because the very purpose of section 2–207 is to *change* the mirror image rule, divergences from the offer will not by themselves prevent a purported acceptance from counting as an acceptance under section 2–207. However, if an offeree's response diverges from the offer in its individualized terms—such as the description of the subject matter, price, or quantity—the response probably will not be considered a definite expression of acceptance within the meaning of section 2–207. The question is largely whether the parties appear to be continuing negotiations or whether, under business customs, it is reasonable for them to think they have a deal by means of the forms they have exchanged.

Example: On January 2, Buyer sends Seller a form Purchase Order for 1,000 barrels of nails at $20/barrel, delivery on February 1, payment in 30 days. Seller replies by sending Buyer a form Sales Order which confirms all the principal terms of Buyer's offer. However, on the reverse side of the Sales Order are various printed terms, one of which provides that "any claims arising under this Sales Order must be submitted to arbitration under the rules of the

American Arbitration Association." Buyer's Purchase Order did not include such a provision. Despite the fact that Seller's Sales Order varies from Buyer's offer in this way, there is a contract under U.C.C. section 2–207(1). (For the *effect* of the added provision, *see infra,* p. 160.)

cf. Compare: Same facts as in the example above, except that manually entered terms in large print on the face of Seller's Sales Order provide for delivery on April 1 (not February 1, as stated in the Purchase Order). No contract arises from the exchange of forms. Although Seller has purported to accept Buyer's offer, Seller's response cannot be fairly characterized as a "definite expression of acceptance."

1) "Written Confirmation"

Under U.C.C. section 2–207(1), the rules applicable to a definite expression of acceptance are also applicable to a written ***confirmation*** of a prior agreement.

e.g. Example: On August 1, Buyer sends a Purchase Order for 10,000 petri dishes to Seller at $0.09/petri dish to be delivered on August 24. The Purchase Order contains many standardized terms. On August 2, Seller calls Buyer and says, "The price, quantity, and date all look good—we have a deal, and you can expect us to fill this order." Seller emails Buyer a few days later, writing: "This confirms the deal we discussed by phone on August 2 for 10,000 petri dishes at $0.09 each for delivery on August 24." Seller's email contains an attachment labelled "Sales Order" that includes a number of standardized terms that differ from Buyer's terms. Seller's emailed confirmation operates as an acceptance under U.C.C. section 2–207(1), and the parties have a contract.

(d) Acceptance "Expressly Made Conditional"

U.C.C. section 2–207(1) is inapplicable by its terms if an acceptance is "expressly made conditional on the offeror's assent to the additional or different terms in the acceptance."

e.g. Example: Same facts as in the barrel-of-nails example above (*supra,* p. 71), except that Seller's Sales Order states, "This Sales Order is expressly made conditional on the buyer's assent to additional and different terms contained herein." There is no contract under U.C.C. section 2–207(1) unless Buyer gives such assent (which rarely happens).

1) Effect on Contract Formation

The effect of a conditional assent clause is dramatic. If a responsive form contains such a clause, *no contract* results from the offeree's sending the form to the offeror, even though under U.C.C. section 2–207(1) a contract would have resulted from sending the same form without a conditional assent clause.

2) Interpretation

Because the effects of a conditional assent clause are relatively drastic (and because finding many such clauses would serve mainly to restore the mirror-image rule of the common law), the courts have been reluctant to interpret language in a form as a conditional assent clause unless it closely tracks the language of the conditional assent exception in U.C.C. section 2–207(1). An example of such tracking is: "Metal-Matic, Inc.'s acceptance . . . is hereby expressly made conditional to purchaser's acceptance of the terms and provisions of the acknowledgment form." **[Diamond Fruit Growers, Inc. v. Krack Corp.,** 794 F.2d 1440 (9th Cir. 1986)] In contrast, a seller's acknowledgment form providing that acceptance of orders was subject to the terms and conditions of the seller's form has been held not to contain a conditional assent clause. It was not enough, the court said, to make acceptance expressly conditional on the offeree's *terms*. Instead, the acceptance must be made expressly conditional on the offeror's *assent to those terms*. **[Dorton v. Colins & Aikman Corp.,** 453 F.2d 1161 (6th Cir. 1972)]

EXAM TIP   **GILBERT**

The difference here, which may seem arbitrary, is between an offeree's preprinted reply that says "Our acceptance is subject to the terms included herein" and "Our acceptance is subject to *your assent* to the terms included herein." In some courts, the former language would *not* trigger the U.C.C.'s "expressly made conditional" rule, whereas the latter would. The rationale is simply that some courts are motivated to avoid triggering the "expressly made conditional" rule (which does, after all, require the condition on the offeror's assent to be "expressly made").

1/ Note

Although courts are reluctant to find that a provision is a conditional assent clause unless it tracks the language of U.C.C. section 2–207(1), in principle exact tracking is not required. (There need not be any "magic language.") One court has said that whether an acceptance is expressly conditional on the offeror's assent is dependent on the commercial context of the transaction—in particular, whether under commercial understanding a contract has or hasn't been formed. **[Gardner Zemke Co. v. Dunham Bush, Inc.,** 850 P.2d 319 (N.M. 1993)]

(e) Contract Formed by Conduct of the Parties

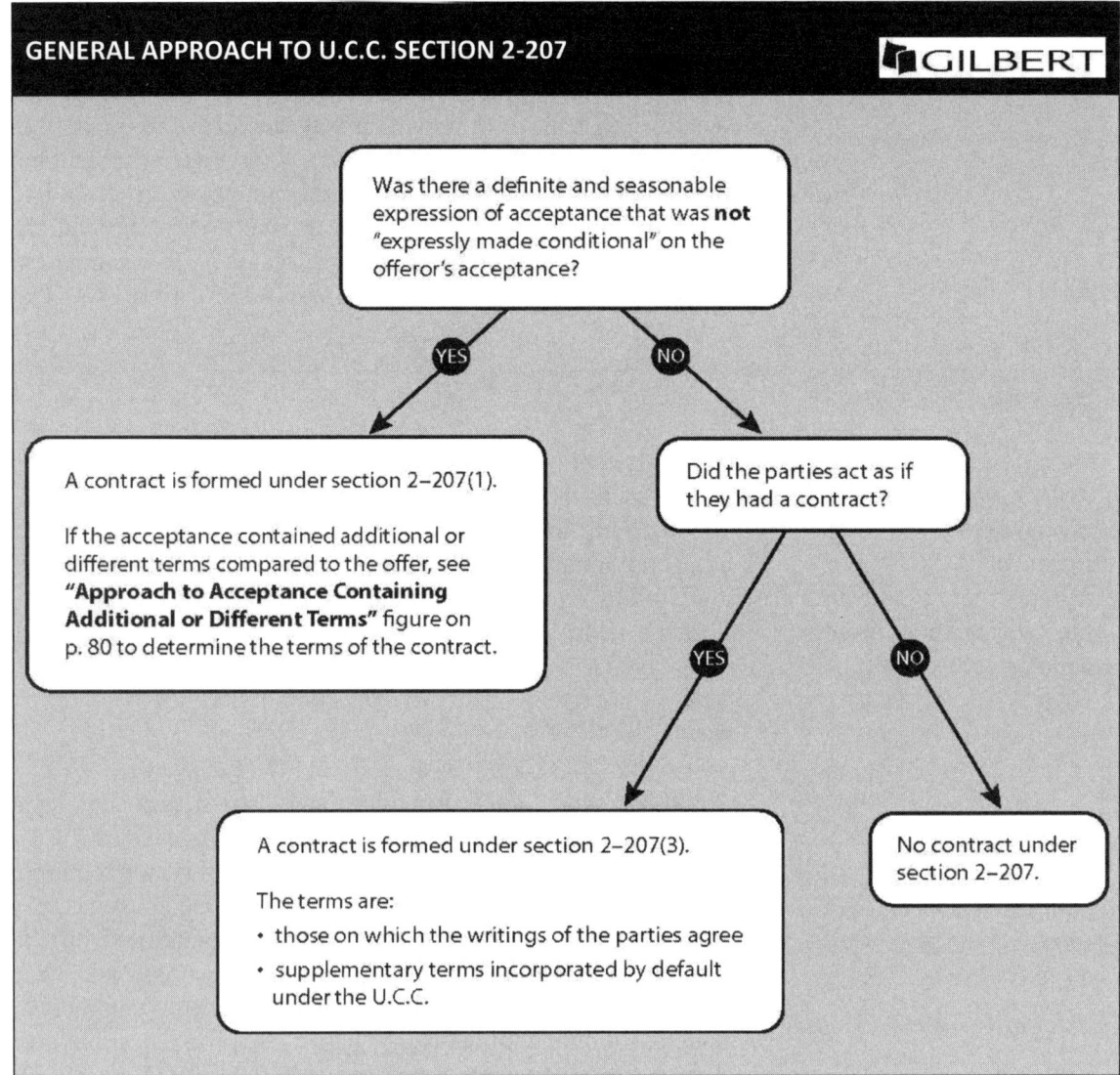

Even if a contract is not formed under U.C.C. section 2–207(1)—for example, because the offeree never sent a written reply to the buyer's form, or because the reply lacked a "definite" expression of acceptance, or because the acceptance was "expressly made conditional" on the offeror's acceptance to new terms—parties may still have a contract under section 2–207(3). Under that section, conduct by both parties that recognizes the existence of a contract is sufficient to establish a contract for sale even though the writings of the parties do not otherwise establish a contract. U.C.C. section 2–207(3) provides, "Conduct by both parties which recognizes the existence of a contract is sufficient to establish a contract for sale although the writings of the parties do not otherwise establish a contract."

| EXAM TIP | GILBERT |

When answering an exam question involving buyers and sellers of goods who exchange forms, first decide whether a contract was formed under section 2–207(1) by the exchange of forms. If it was not, then determine whether the parties performed (anyway) *as if a contract had been formed*. Such performance may create an enforceable contract under section 2–207(3).

1) Background and Rationale

In many or most cases, the parties pay little or no attention to the preprinted terms on forms, so they may still act as if they have a contract even when the law does not recognize one from their forms alone. For example, the parties may have no contract under section 2–207(1), but the seller may still send out goods and the buyer may still accept them. In circumstances like this, the parties have not paid much attention to which of their forms counts as an "offer" and which counts as an "acceptance," but it is nonetheless clear that the parties have formed a contract.

2) Contract Terms

When a contract is formed under U.C.C. section 2–207(3), the terms of the contract consist of the terms on which the parties' writings match, plus any supplementary terms (sometimes called *default rules*) incorporated under other provisions of the U.C.C. Typically, when the parties use preprinted forms, only the individualized provisions of each form will agree. As a result, most of the preprinted provisions of both forms are likely to drop out.

Example: Buyco sends Sellco a Purchase Order for 100 widgets to be delivered on April 1 at $5 per widget. Sellco then sends Buyco a Sales Order promising to deliver 100 widgets on April 1 at $5 per widget, but containing different warranty provisions than the Purchase Order. The Sales Order further states that Sellco's acceptance of the Purchase Order is conditional on Buyco's assent to any additional or different terms in the Sales Order. So far, there is no contract (under section 2–207(1)) because of the conditional acceptance clause, and neither party is bound to perform. However, if Sellco ships the widgets and Buyco accepts the widgets in spite of the lack of a binding contract, a contract is formed under U.C.C. section 2–207(3). The terms of the contract consist only of those terms on the Purchase Order and the Sales Order that agree (100 widgets to be delivered on April 1 at $5 per widget), and any terms that do not agree (the warranty provisions) will drop out.

(f) Additional or Different Terms in Writings

A contract may be formed under U.C.C. section 2–207(1) despite the presence of additional or different terms in the acceptance. If a contract is formed under U.C.C. section 2–207(1), the next question is the effect of such additional or different terms. In determining that effect, U.C.C. section 2–207 draws a distinction between "additional" terms (*i.e.*, terms that add to the offer but do not *contradict* it) and "different" terms (*i.e.*, terms that *contradict* the terms of the offer). [U.C.C. § 2–207(2)]

Example: In its preprinted terms, an offer sent by a buyer states: "The buyer will have 3 months to dispute the quality of any goods sold under this contract." In its own preprinted terms, the acceptance by the seller states: "Buyers must notify us of any defects in goods within 14 days after delivery, or else their right to remedy those defects terminates. Any disputes that arise under this contract must be arbitrated under the rules of the American Arbitration Association." The seller's term about arbitration is an ***additional*** term because the offer says nothing about arbitration; the seller's term about the buyer's deadline to dispute the quality of goods is a ***different*** term because it contradicts the duration specified in the buyer's offer.

1) Additional Terms as Proposals

Under U.C.C. section 2–207(2), ***additional*** terms contained in the acceptance are to be construed as proposals for additions to the contract. Proposals have no legal effect by themselves; they are simply offers to adjust the contract and might be accepted by the original offeror.

2) Additional Terms Added to Contract by Operation of Law

However, *if the parties are both merchants,* additional terms become part of the contract by operation of law, unless:

(i)   The offer ***expressly limits acceptance to the terms of the offer,***

(ii) The ***additional terms would materially alter the contract,*** or

(iii) The ***offeror either notifies the offeree within a reasonable time that he objects*** to the additional terms or has ***already notified*** the offeree of his objection.

Tip: Factors (i) and (iii) are very similar, because they both involve the offeror's express unwillingness to deal with the offeree's additional terms. In (i), the offeror has expressed this unwillingness in the offer itself. In (iii), the offeror either has expressed the unwillingness previously (in some form other than including it in the offer itself) or does so in a reasonable time after receiving the acceptance. You may find it easier to remember or apply these two factors by thinking of them simply as, "The offeror objects to additional terms."

a) Merchant

Under the U.C.C., a "merchant" is a person who deals in the kind of goods involved in the transaction or who otherwise holds themselves out as having knowledge or skill peculiar to the practices or goods involved in the transaction. [U.C.C. § 2–104(1)]

Example: Amy, a ***nonmerchant,*** sends an offer to Widgetco, a ***merchant,*** offering to buy a specific number of widgets at a specific price. Widgetco replies with a Sales Order agreeing to the terms of Amy's offer but adding, "Any complaints concerning the widgets must be made in writing within 12 months after the widgets have been received." A contract is formed, but because Amy is a nonmerchant, the terms of the contract are limited to those contained in Amy's offer. The Sales Order's additional terms are deemed to be proposals that Amy may accept or reject.

e.g. Example: Same facts as above, except Amy is a ***merchant.*** If Amy does not notify Widgetco that she objects to their term about the timing of complaints, that term would probably become part of the contract. Both Amy and Widgetco are merchants; Amy's offer did not expressly limit acceptance to the terms of the offer; and the additional term would probably not materially alter the contract.

cf. Compare: Same facts as in the example above, except that Widgetco's Sales Order contains a term on the reverse side disclaiming all warranties. There is a contract under section 2–207(1). However, the disclaimer does not become part of the contract under section 2–207(2) because it would materially alter the contract.

b) **Material Alteration**

Ordinarily, a *material* alteration is one that makes a noticeable economic difference (or one that would be likely to affect the offeror's willingness to assent to the deal). However, the Official Comment to U.C.C. section 2–207 suggests that "materially alter" in U.C.C. section 2–207(2) refers only to additional terms that would result in "surprise or hardship" to the offeror. Courts have followed this Comment. [**Aceros Prefabricados, S.A. v. TradeArbed, Inc.,** 282 F.3d 92 (2d Cir. 2002); **Dale R. Horning Co. v. Falconer Glass Indus., Inc.,** 730 F. Supp. 962 (S.D. Ind. 1990)]

3) **Different Terms**

As described above, U.C.C. section 2–207(1) permits acceptances to have terms "additional to or different from" the terms of the offer [*supra*, p. 69]. However, section 2–207(2) provides guidance only on how to handle "additional" terms [*supra*, p. 76]. U.C.C. section 2–207 says nothing about the effect of ***different*** (rather than additional) terms. In light of this omission in the statute, Courts and commentators have struggled to decide the legal effect of ***different*** terms in the acceptance. Three broad views have emerged:

a) **Knockout Rule**

The majority rule is that different terms do not become part of the agreement, but they negate—knock out—the terms in the offer from which they differ. This approach is similar to the U.C.C.'s approach to acceptance by the conduct of the parties [U.C.C. § 2–207(3); *supra*, p. 74], but it is not identical: when a contract is formed by the parties' conduct, the terms of the contract are ***those where the parties' terms match***, whereas the ***knockout rule*** applies only to terms that are ***different***. It does not knock out terms that appear in only one of the forms.

e.g. Example: Buyer's form includes preprinted terms about warranty provisions and the buyer's right to inspect the goods. Seller's form includes preprinted terms requiring arbitration and also includes warranty provisions that contradict those in the offer. Under U.C.C. section 2–207(3), for a contract formed by the parties' conduct rather than by exchange of forms, none of these terms would be included in the contract. Under the knockout rule, if a contract is formed under section 2–207(1), only the warranty terms would be excluded from the contract because they contradict one another. The buyer's term about inspection rights would be accepted by the seller's acceptance; the seller's term about arbitration would be included in the contract as an additional term if the parties are both merchants and the term is not considered to materially alter the contract (*see supra*, p. 75 *et seq.*).

1/ Rationale

This rule has some modest support in Comment 6 to U.C.C. section 2–207, which provides,

> Where clauses on confirming forms sent by both parties conflict each party must be assumed to object to a clause of the other conflicting with the one on the confirmation sent by himself. As a result the requirement that there be a notice of objection which is found in subsection (2) is satisfied and the conflicting terms do not become part of the contract. The contract then consists of the terms originally expressly agreed to, terms on which the confirmations agree, and terms supplied by this Act . . . .

However, Comment 6 refers only to "confirming forms," which seems to mean writings that follow up on an oral deal rather than the more common case of forms that cause a contract to be offered and accepted. Nevertheless, the knockout rule is supported very strongly by the *purpose* of section 2–207 because under this rule, neither party gets the unfair advantage of having its preprinted terms prevail if those terms are contradicted by the other party's form. **[Gardner Zemke Co. v. Dunham Bush, Inc.,** 850 P.2d 319 (N.M. 1993)]

b) Different Terms Treated Like Additional Terms

Standing in opposition to the knockout rule are two minority views. Under one minority view, different terms are treated like additional terms. [*See* **Steiner v. Mobil Oil Corp.,** 20 Cal. 3d 90 (1997)] This view finds support in Comment 3 to U.C.C. section 2–207, which states that "[w]hether or not *additional or different* terms will become part of the agreement depends upon the provisions of subsection (2)." (Emphasis added.) (Recall that subsection (2) to U.C.C. section 2–207 covers "additional," but not "different," terms.) In theory, under this view different terms may become part of the agreement under section 2–207(2) if (i) the offer has not expressly limited acceptance to the terms of the offer, (ii) the different terms do not materially alter the offer, (iii) the offeror has not given notice of objection to the different terms or does not object within a reasonable time, and (iv) the parties are both merchants. In practice, however, different terms will usually drop out under this view, because generally they will materially alter the terms of the offer.

c) Different Terms Always Drop out

Under another minority view, different terms in the acceptance always drop out. [Air **Products & Chemicals, Inc. v. Fairbanks Morse, Inc.,** 206 N.W.2d 414 (Wis. 1973)] This view finds support in the language of section 2–207(2), which provides that under defined circumstances "additional" terms become part of the contract but does not provide that "different" terms become part of the contract. Therefore, under this view, the contract will contain any additional terms in the acceptance that meet the section 2–207(2) test but not any different terms in the acceptance. However, the result under this view conflicts with the purpose of section 2–207, which is to get away from giving one party (here, the offeror) an unfair advantage by having their preprinted terms automatically control. To put it differently, this view would replace the arbitrary "last shot" with an arbitrary "first shot" rule.

APPROACH TO ACCEPTANCE CONTAINING ADDITIONAL OR DIFFERENT TERMS

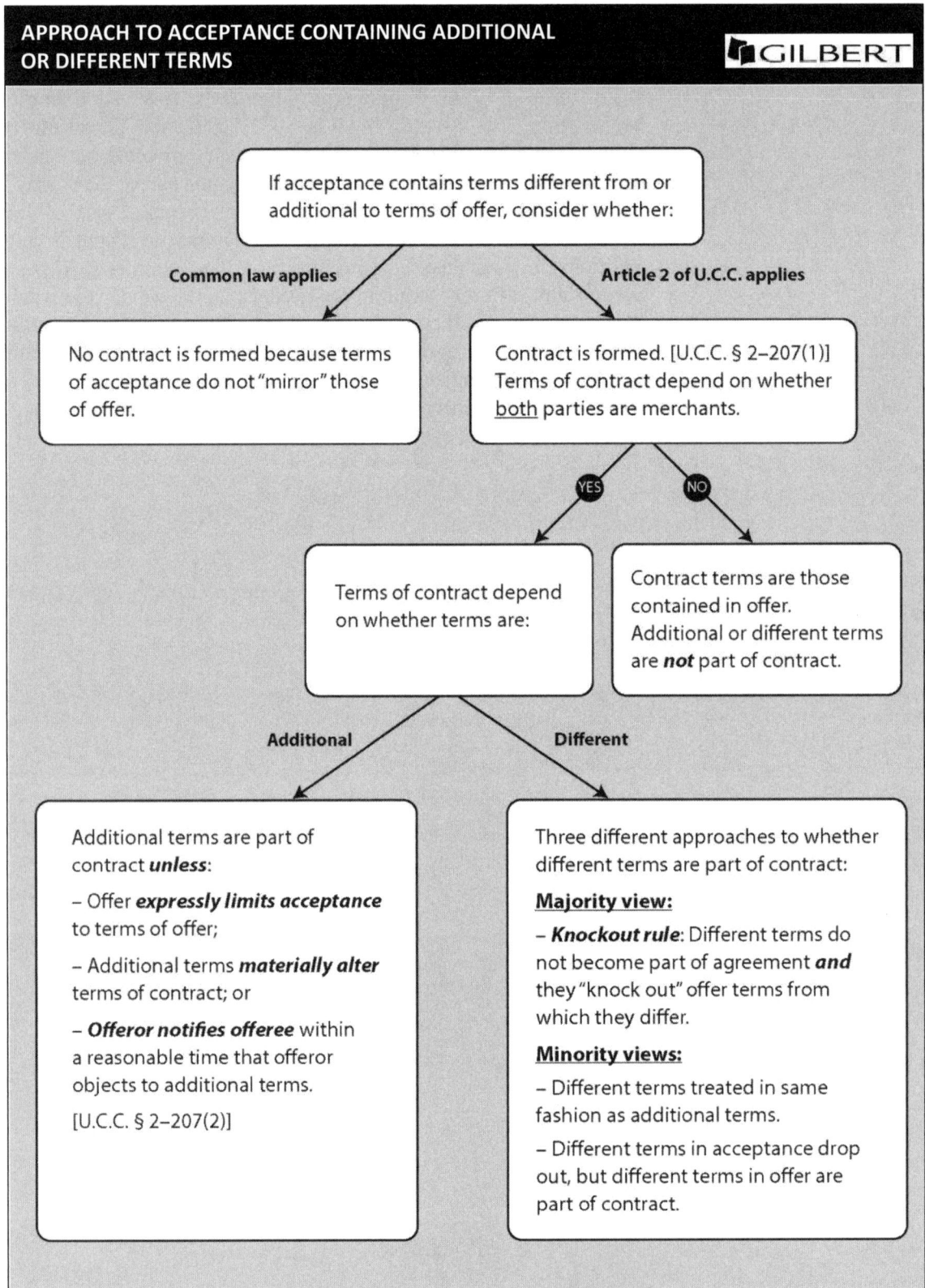

e. **Termination of Power of Acceptance by Revocation**

A *revocation* is a retraction of an offer by the offeror. The general rule is that a revocation terminates the offeree's power of acceptance, provided of course that the offer has not already been accepted.

(1) When Revocation Is Effective

Under the great weight of authority, a revocation is effective only when it is received by the offeree. [Rest. 2d § 42] (In contrast, an acceptance is usually effective when it is sent.)

(a) Minority View

By statute, California and a few other states follow a minority view under which a revocation is effective when it is sent (*i.e.*, on "dispatch").

(2) Communication of Revocation

To be effective, a revocation must normally be communicated by the offeror to the offeree (unless a statute, like that of California, provides otherwise).

(a) Exception—Offer to the Public

An offer made to the public at large, such as a reward, can normally be revoked by publishing the revocation in the same medium as that in which the offer was made. Such publication terminates the power of acceptance even of those persons who saw the offer but did not see the revocation. [**Shuey v. United States,** 92 U.S. 73 (1875)]

(b) Exception—Indirect Revocation

An offer is also deemed revoked, despite the absence of direct communication between the offeror and the offeree, if the offeree obtains reliable information that the offeror has taken action showing that they have changed their mind. (This is often known as an "indirect revocation," or "the rule of *Dickinson v. Dodds*.") [**Dickinson v. Dodds,** 2 Ch. D. 463 (1876)]

Example: On June 10, Dodds offers to sell real property to Dickinson for £800, the offer to be held open until June 12. On June 11, Dickinson learns from his own agent that Dodds has sold the property to a third party. On June 12, Dickinson hands Dodds a written acceptance of Dodds's offer. The acceptance is ineffective. The fact that Dickinson obtained reliable information that Dodds changed his mind has the same effect as a revocation. [**Dickinson v. Dodds,** *supra;* Rest. 2d § 43]

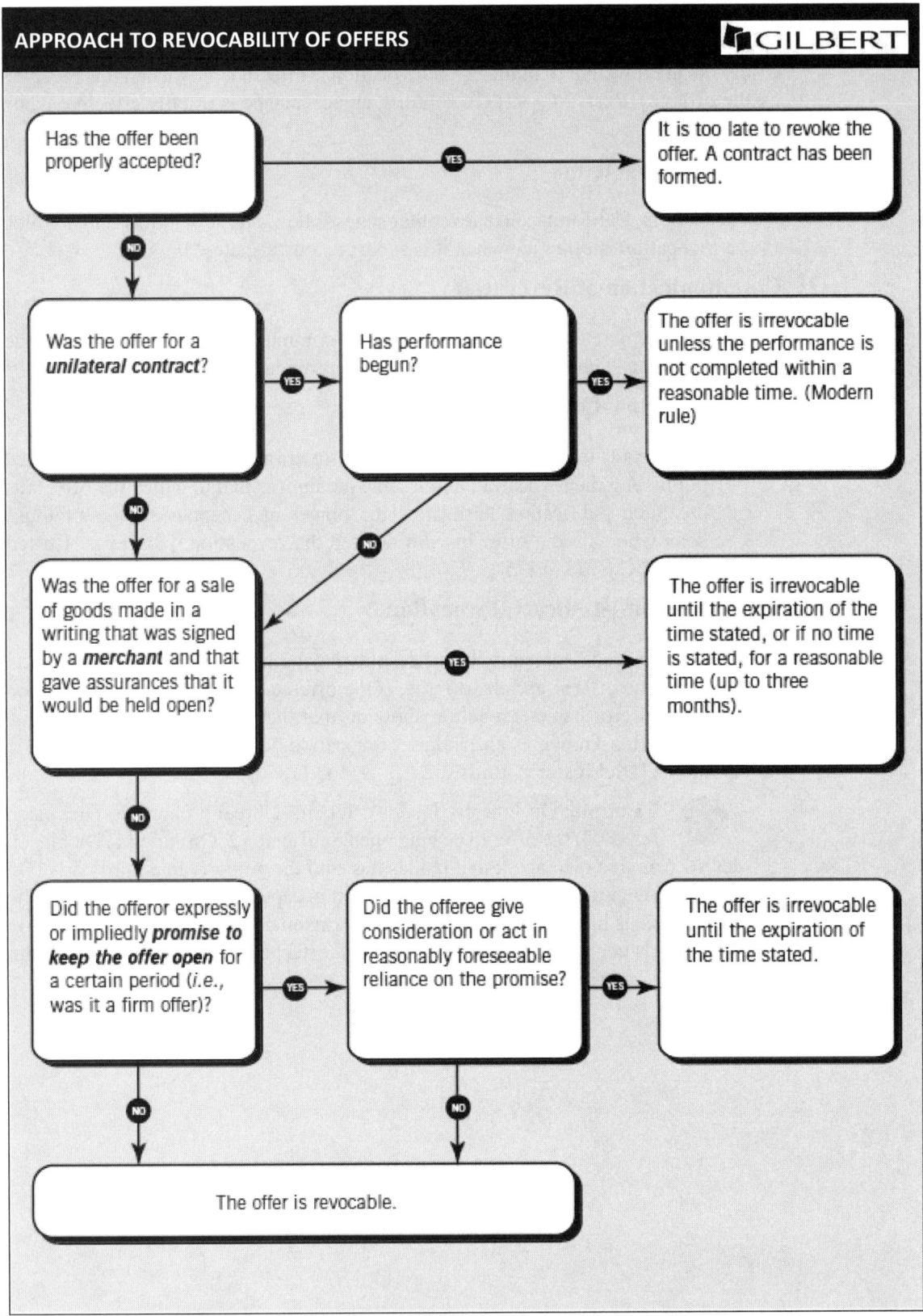

(3) **Revocability of "Firm offers"**

A firm offer is an offer that by its express or implied terms is to remain open for a certain period (*e.g.*, "This offer is good until November 17," or "You have two weeks to decide whether to accept"). The general rule is that a revocation of a firm offer, even within the period during which it was to remain open, has the same effect as the revocation of an ordinary offer—*i.e.*, it terminates the power of acceptance despite the fact that the offer by its terms was to remain open. [*See, e.g.*, **Dickinson v. Dodds**, *supra*] However, this rule is subject to some important exceptions.

Example: Under the facts of the example above (*supra*, p. 81), Dickinson's June 12 acceptance is ineffective, even though Dodds promised to hold his offer open until that date, because Dodds's earlier (indirect) revocation terminated Dickinson's power of acceptance.

(a) Rationale—No Consideration

The rationale of the firm offer rule is as follows: The term of the offer that states that the offer will be held open for a certain period is, in effect, a promise by the offeror to hold the offer open for the designated period. But a promise without consideration is normally not binding. (*See supra*, p. 3.) Therefore, the promise to hold the offer open for a fixed period is not binding, and the offer is just as revocable as it would have been if the offeror had not promised to hold it open for a certain period. Despite this logic, the revocability of firm offers frequently defeats reasonable commercial expectations, so courts and statutes have developed a variety of exceptions to it.

(b) Exceptions

1) Options

Because the firm offer rule is based on the rationale that there is no consideration for the offeror's promise to hold the offer open for a certain period, if the offeree *gives consideration* for the promise, the offer is *irrevocable* for the stated period. [**Humble Oil & Refining Co. v. Westside Investment Corp.,** 428 S.W.2d 92 (Tex. 1968)] When consideration has been given for the promise to hold the offer open for a certain period, the firm offer is called an *option.*

2) Nominal Consideration

Even if there is no true consideration for a firm offer, under the majority rule the offer is irrevocable if it *recites* a purported or *nominal* consideration—at least if the offer is in writing and proposes an exchange on fair terms within a reasonable time. [Rest. 2d § 87(1)(a); *see supra*, p. 8]

3) Reliance

A firm offer is also irrevocable if the offeror reasonably should have foreseen that the offer would induce reliance by the offeree prior to acceptance, and if such reliance in fact occurs. [**Drennan v. Star Paving Co.,** *supra*, p. 63]

Example: Contractor Camille plans to bid on a contract to construct a school building for School Board. Bids are to be submitted to School Board by 5:00 p.m. on February 1. Before determining her own bid, Camille asks various subcontractors, including Steve, to send her sub-bids for paving the schoolyard. On January 31, Steve gives Camille a written bid to do the paving for $24,000 and states that this bid will be held open for acceptance by Camille until February 3.

Camille uses Steve's paving bid in making up her own bid, and early on February 1, Camille submits her bid to School Board. When the bids are reviewed by School Board at 5:00 p.m. on February 1, Camille's bid is the lowest, and Camille is immediately awarded the contract by School Board. At 9:00 a.m. the next day, before Camille has accepted Steve's sub-bid, Steve calls Camille and attempts to revoke the sub-bid. The attempted revocation is ineffective. Steve reasonably should have foreseen that Camille would rely on Steve's paving bid in setting the terms of Camille's own bid. Therefore, Steve's promise to hold open his sub-bid until February 3 is enforceable, and the sub-bid is irrevocable until that date.

a) Implied Promise to Hold Offer Open

A promise to hold an offer open may be implied rather than express. Thus, in the above example, even if Steve had not explicitly promised to hold his paving bid open until February 3, there would be an implied promise to hold it open until a reasonable time after School Board awarded the contract.

b) One-Sided Effect of Rule

Note that under the foregoing rule, subcontractor Steve is bound to perform if general contractor Camille gets the contract, but normally Camille would not be bound to give the subcontract to Steve even if Camille uses Steve's bid in making her bid and is awarded the contract. This has been criticized as "commercial imbalance." [*See* 19 U. Chi. L. Rev. 237 (1952)]

1/ Note

In certain limited cases, however, Camille may be bound to Steve. (*See infra*, p. 97.)

c) Older View

Some cases have allowed an offeror to revoke a firm offer notwithstanding the offeree's reliance. However, most of these are older cases and probably would not be followed today. [*See, e.g.,* **James Baird Co. v. Gimbel Bros.,** 64 F.2d 344 (2d Cir. 1933)]

d) Restatement View

Restatement Second has explicitly adopted the rule that reliance on a firm offer makes the offer irrevocable, at least to the extent necessary to avoid injustice. Under Restatement Second section 87, "an offer which the offeror should reasonably expect to induce action or forbearance of a substantial character on the part of the offeree before acceptance and which does induce such action or forbearance is binding as an option contract to the extent necessary to avoid injustice." [Rest. 2d § 87]

4) Contracts for the Sale of Goods—U.C.C. Section 2–205

Under U.C.C. section 2–205, a signed, written offer by a *merchant* to buy or sell goods, which gives assurance that it will be held open, is not revocable for lack of consideration during the time stated (or if no time is stated, for a reasonable time). This period of irrevocability cannot exceed three months. Thus, the U.C.C. effectively overturns the firm offer rule in many cases for merchants in goods.

a) Operation of U.C.C. Section 2–205

For U.C.C. section 2–205 to be applicable, the following conditions must be satisfied:

1/ Written and Signed

The offer must be in writing and must be signed by the offeror. Furthermore, if the offer is on a form prepared by the offeree, the offeror must separately sign the provision to hold the offer open. (That is, a simple signature at the end of the whole document does not suffice under section 2–205 if the offeree has supplied the form. Instead, the offeror needs to separately sign or initial next to or near the language that states the firm offer.)

2/ Irrevocability

The offer must state that it is irrevocable. However, the offer need not state the time during which it is irrevocable. If no time is stated and all the other requirements of section 2–205 are met, the offer will be irrevocable for a reasonable time, not to exceed three months.

3/ Sale of Goods

Like all other provisions of U.C.C. Article 2, section 2–205 applies only to contracts for the sale of goods.

4/ Merchant Offeror

Unlike most provisions of Article 2, section 2–205 is limited to offers by *merchants.*

Example: On January 2, Liz, the owner of a textile company, makes a written and signed offer to sell her personal grand piano to Justin for $3,000. The offer provides that it will be held open until January 10. On January 4, Liz revokes her offer. The revocation is effective. In selling her personal piano, Liz is not a merchant within the meaning of section 2–104. (*See supra*, p. 76.) Therefore, section 2–205 is inapplicable and, assuming that Justin has not foreseeably relied on Liz's offer, the offer is revocable under the general common law rule.

(4) Revocability of Offers for Unilateral Contracts

An offer that is to be accepted by *performance of an act* is known as an offer for a *unilateral* contract. (In contrast, an offer that is to be accepted by a promise is known as an offer for a *bilateral* contract.) (*See supra*, p. 11.) Special problems arise when a person who has made an offer for a unilateral contract attempts to revoke the offer after performance has begun but before performance has been completed.

(a) Old Rule—Offer Revocable Until Performance Is Complete

Under the old rule, an offer for a unilateral contract was revocable until the offeree had completed performance of the act specified in the offer. As long as performance had not yet been completed, an offer for a unilateral contract was deemed revocable even if the offeree had begun performance of the act in reliance on the offer. [**Petterson v. Pattberg,** 248 N.Y. 86 (1928)]

Example: Under this rule, at least in theory, if *A* offered *B* $50 to cross the Brooklyn Bridge, *A* could revoke when *B* was halfway across. [26 Yale L.J. 136 (1916)] This was true even if *B* started to cross the Brooklyn Bridge in reliance on *A*'s offer.

1) Rationale

The rationale of the old rule was that an offer for a unilateral contract, by definition, can be accepted only by performance of an act. Because an offer is revocable until accepted, until the act was completed there was no acceptance, and therefore the offer was revocable.

2) Note

Not all courts followed this rule. [*See, e.g.,* **Brackenbury v. Hodgkin,** 102 A. 106 (Me. 1917)—once performance had begun, the offeror was not allowed to revoke her promise to leave her farm to her daughter and son-in-law if they would care for her during her life]

(b) Modern Rule—Offer for Unilateral Contract Not Revocable After Performance Has Begun

Modern courts reject the old rule. Under the modern rule, an offer for a unilateral contract cannot be revoked once performance has begun, unless the performance is not completed within a reasonable time.

1) Rationale

The rationale of the modern rule is as follows: An offer for a unilateral contract includes an implied promise to hold the offer open for a reasonable time if the offeree makes a substantial beginning of performance prior to revocation. The beginning of performance in reliance on this implied promise renders the offer irrevocable. The modern rule also comports with commercial expectations more than the old rule, because offerees probably expect to be able to rely on offers for unilateral contracts and offerors probably expect them to.

(c) Restatement Second Section 45

The modern rule is embodied in Restatement Second section 45, which provides:

(1) Where an offer invites an offeree to accept by rendering a performance and does not invite a promissory acceptance, an option contract is created when the offeree tenders or begins the invited performance or tenders a beginning of it.

(2) The offeror's duty of performance under any option contract so created is conditional on completion or tender of the invited performance in accordance with the terms of the offer.

> **Example:** Homeowner says to Landscaper, "If you plant three new red oak trees in my front yard, I'll pay you $4,000. I don't want your promise; I'll just pay you on completion of the work if you choose to do it." (This is an offer for a unilateral contract.) Landscaper plants one red oak tree. Homeowner then attempts to revoke the offer. Homeowner's attempted revocation is ineffective, and if Landscaper plants the remaining two red oak trees in a reasonable time, Landscaper has accepted the offer and has a right to payment under the contract.

Section 45 is widely followed by the courts. The following three aspects of the rule that it sets out are noteworthy:

1) Revocation Before Performance Begins

The offeror *can* revoke before the offeree begins performance, subject to a possible exception in case of reliance by the offeree *other* than performance (*see supra*, p. 84).

> **Example:** Same facts as above, but Homeowner revokes before Landscaper has acted or relied on the offer. Homeowner's revocation is effective.

2) Offer Open for Reasonable Time

Under section 45, the offeror impliedly promises that once the offeree begins to perform, the offeror will hold the offer open for the time stated in the offer—or, if no time is stated, for a reasonable time. So the offeror can revoke even *after* the offeree begins performance if the offeree does not complete performance within the time given or a reasonable time.

> **Example:** Same fact as above, except that Landscaper plants one tree and then does nothing further for a year. Homeowner's revocation at that point would likely be effective.

3) Preparation vs. Performance

A problem may arise when the offeror revokes after the offeree has begun *preparing* to perform but before the offeree has actually begun *performing*. For example, suppose the offer is for building a shed. If the offeree has only purchased lumber but has not begun to construct the shed, it might be said that the offeree has begun *preparing* to perform but has not begun to *perform*.

a) Restatement First

The Comment to Restatement First section 45 stated that preparation, as opposed to the beginning of performance, was *not* sufficient to make an offer for a unilateral contract irrevocable.

1/ Comment

The preparation/performance distinction is often simpler to state than it is to apply. Furthermore, it is not clear that courts will always make the distinction.

b) Restatement Second

Although the Comment to Restatement Second section 45 continues to draw a distinction between preparation and performance, the Comment also recognizes that the offeree's preparation may constitute *reliance* of a type that contract law should protect. Such reliance may prevent revocation under the principle reflected in Restatement Second section 87 (*see supra*, p. 84) even if section 45 is inapplicable because performance has not begun.

1/ Significance

Because preparation to perform is likely to constitute reliance that may make the offer irrevocable under section 87, why does Restatement Second draw a distinction between preparation and performance under section 45? The answer seems to be a difference in the measure for damages. Under Restatement Second, if a unilateral contract's offeree has begun *performance,* so that the rule embodied in section 45 is applicable, the offeree should normally be entitled to *expectation* damages if the offeror revokes. However, if the offeree has simply begun *preparation,* so that the case falls under the principle of Restatement Second section 87, the offeree may be entitled only to *reliance* damages. (On these two measures of damages, *see infra*, p. 251.)

EXAM TIP   GILBERT

Remember that the general rule is that an offer is **revocable** unless an exception applies. *Exceptions:* The offer (i) was supported by consideration (real or nominal), (ii) caused reasonably foreseeable reliance, (iii) was a U.C.C. firm offer, or (iv) was an offer for a unilateral contract in which performance already began.

---

f. Termination of Power of Acceptance by Operation of Law

An offeree's power of acceptance may also be terminated by operation of law through the death or incapacity of the offeror or as a result of changed circumstances.

(1) Death or Incapacity of Offeror

An offeree's power of acceptance is terminated by the offeror's death or incapacity, *whether or not* the offeree *knows* of the death or incapacity. [Rest. 2d § 48]

Example: On January 2, Luis sends Eva a written offer to buy Eva's property for $50,000, the offer to be held open until January 11. On January 5, Luis dies. On January 7, Eva, unaware of Luis's death, mails an acceptance of Luis's offer. The acceptance is ineffective because Eva's power of acceptance was terminated on January 5 by Luis's death.

Example: Same facts as in the example above, except that on January 5, Luis becomes incompetent by reason of a stroke. Again, Eva's acceptance is ineffective.

(a) Options

Note, however, that death or incapacity of the offeror does *not* terminate the offeree's power of acceptance under an *option* (*i.e.*, a situation where the offeree has given the offeror consideration to hold the offer open for a fixed period of time), at least when individual performance by the decedent was not an essential part of the proposed contract. So, for example, the grant of an option to purchase property is binding on a decedent's estate. [Rest. 2d § 37]

1) Unilateral Contracts

As to unilateral contracts, the rule embodied in Restatement Second section 45 is that the offeree's power of acceptance is not terminated by the offeror's death or incapacity once the offeree has begun performance.

Example: On January 2, Owner writes to Painter, "If you paint my country house dark green by January 15, I will pay you $5,000." On January 3, Painter begins painting the house. On January 4, Owner dies, unbeknownst to Painter. Painter's power of acceptance is not terminated by Owner's death. Owner's offer was for a unilateral contract, and when Painter began performance, the offer became irrevocable under the principle embodied in section 45.

Compare: Instead, Owner writes to Painter, "If you promise to paint my country house dark green by January 15, I will pay you $5,000. Let me know your answer by January 10." Again, on January 4, Owner dies, unbeknownst to Painter. On January 5, Painter sends a letter accepting Owner's offer. Painter's acceptance is not effective. Owner's offer was for a bilateral contract, and Painter's power of acceptance was therefore terminated by Owner's death.

a) Rationale

Restatement Second section 45 treats offers as options once the offeree has begun to perform, and options are not terminated by the offeror's death or incapacity.

(2) Changed Circumstances

The offeree's power of acceptance may also be terminated by operation of law as a result of certain very limited types of changed circumstances, such as supervening illegality of the proposed contract or destruction of its subject matter. (*See* the discussion of changed circumstances *infra*, pp. 241–244.)

C. Acceptance

1. Introduction

Assuming there is an offer and the offeree's power of acceptance is still open, the next question is whether the offer has been accepted. Three major issues arise in connection with this question:

(i) What *kind* of acceptance is required (promise or act);

(ii) When can *silence* operate as an acceptance; and

(iii) What is the effect of a purported acceptance that *deviates from the terms* of the offer?

2. Is Offer for Unilateral or Bilateral Contract?

An offer may specify whether the offer needs to be accepted by promise, by act, or by either. [Rest. 2d §§ 50, 53(1), 62]

ACCEPTANCE—BILATERAL VS. UNILATERAL CONTRACTS		**GILBERT**
	BILATERAL CONTRACT	**UNILATERAL CONTRACT**
MODES OF ACCEPTANCE	- Express promise - Promise implied from conduct - In appropriate cases, performance of an act designated by the offeror to signify a promise - In appropriate cases, silence (*e.g.*, when offeree leads offeror to believe silence will constitute acceptance or when offeror specifies that silence will constitute acceptance and offeree subjectively intends silence to constitute acceptance)	- Performance of the act requested in the offer
COMMUNICATION TO OFFEROR	Offeree must communicate acceptance to form a contract	Offeree does not need to give notice of performance to *form* a contract, but must diligently try to notify offeror in a reasonable time after completion of performance to *obligate* the offeror
OBLIGATION OF OFFEROR	On acceptance, both offeree and offeror are bound to perform	On acceptance, offeror is bound to perform; offeree has already completed performance

a. Acceptance of Offer for Bilateral Contract

An offer that requires acceptance by a promise is called an offer for a ***bilateral contract***.

(1) General Rule—Promissory Acceptance Required

The general rule is that an offer that requires acceptance by a promise can be accepted *only* by a promise, not by an act. [*See* **White v. Corlies,** 46 N.Y. 467 (1871)] (Note, however, that the required promise may be either express or implied, and in some cases a promise can be implied from an act (*see infra*, p. 92).)

Example: On January 2, Owner says to Painter, "I promise to pay you $500 if you promise to paint my garage dark green and to finish the job by January 10. I must have your promise by January 5." Painter makes no promise, but on January 4, while Owner is away for the weekend, Painter begins painting Owner's garage. On January 5, Owner (who is unaware that Painter has begun painting) calls Painter and revokes the offer. There is no contract even though Painter has begun to perform. Owner's offer was for a bilateral contract and could be accepted only by Painter's promise. Because Painter had made no promise prior to the revocation, the revocation was effective. (Painter's reliance does not limit Owner's power to revoke, because it was unreasonable for Painter to begin painting Owner's garage before accepting Owner's offer, and only reasonable reliance prevents an offeror from revoking.)

cf. Compare: While Owner and Painter are next to Owner's fence, Owner says to Painter, "I will give you $200 if you agree to paint this fence." Painter immediately picks up a paint brush and begins to paint the fence. A contract is formed. Owner's offer required an acceptance by promise, but under the circumstances a promise can be implied from Painter's act.

(a) Possible Exception—Tender of Full Performance

Despite the general rule that an offer for a bilateral contract can be accepted only by a promise, it is sometimes said that such an offer can be accepted, without a promise, by *full performance* prior to termination of the offeree's power of acceptance.

1) Two Views

a) Restatement First

The major support for this exception was Restatement First section 63, which provided that a contract was formed where an offer called for acceptance by a promise and the offeree (i) fully performed, or tendered full performance, before his power of acceptance had terminated; and (ii) notified the offeror of that fact within the time allowed for accepting by promise.

e.g. Example: Farmer writes to Worker, "I will pay you $100 for plowing Flodden Field if you will promise by the end of Monday to plow the field by a week from Monday." Worker makes no promise, but begins and completes plowing Flodden Field on Sunday and notifies Farmer on Monday that the plowing has been completed. Restatement First section 63 took the position that on these facts, a contract was formed.

1/ Rationale

In such a case, the offeror is not prejudiced by getting the "wrong" kind of acceptance: the offeror gets more than, or at least as much as, they bargained for. In the example above, the plowing of Flodden Field is completed early.

b) Restatement Second

Restatement Second has dropped Restatement First section 63 on the theory that the rule in section 63 involved a departure from the basic principle that the offeror may control the terms on which an offer is to be accepted. [Rest. 2d § 62] Therefore, the status of the rule embodied in Restatement First section 63 is now uncertain.

(2) Modes of Promissory Acceptance

Note that even though an offer for a bilateral contract can be accepted only by a promise, the promise need not be *verbal* or explicit.

(a) Promise Implied from Offeree's Conduct

As discussed above, in some cases a promise (and therefore an acceptance of an offer for a bilateral contract) may be implied in fact from the offeree's conduct (*see supra*, p. 57).

Example: Owner says to Painter, "I promise to pay you $500 if you promise to paint my garage dark green." Painter nods her head yes, and the parties walk away reasonably understanding that there is a deal. Under these circumstances, there is a contract. Painter's nodding of her head is a promise to perform the painting job and constitutes an acceptance of Owner's offer.

Example: Same facts as in the example above, except that when Owner makes his offer, Painter does not nod her head. Instead, she immediately (and in sight of Owner) picks up a paintbrush and begins painting Owner's garage dark green. Again, there is a contract. Under the circumstances, Painter's act of beginning to paint is equivalent to nodding her head yes. It constitutes a promise to perform the painting job and is therefore an acceptance of Owner's offer.

1) Contract Terms

When an offeree's conduct implies an acceptance by promise, a contract is formed There may, however, still be a dispute as to the contract's terms. Under the common law last shot rule (*see supra*, p. 70), the offeree is deemed to have accepted all the terms of the offeree's offer. For contracts for the sale of goods, the U.C.C. recognizes the formation of a contract by the parties' conduct, but it overturns the last shot rule, instead providing that the terms of the contract are terms on which the writings of the parties agree (plus background provisions supplied by law). (*See supra*, p. 74; U.C.C. § 2–207(3).)

Example: Factory emails DumpCo, proposing that DumpCo provide disposal services for waste chemicals that Factory produces. The email has an attachment that includes Factory's standard terms. DumpCo never replies to the email (instead confirming some details by phone) and then provides, for several years, the services that Factory requested in its offer. DumpCo's conduct is sufficient to imply an acceptance (by promise) of Factory's offer, including all its terms, under the common law rule. [*Cf.* **Polaroid Corp. v. Rollins Envtl. Servs.**, 624 N.E.2d 959 (1993)]

Compare: Similar facts as above, except Factory emails Supplier proposing a purchase of goods (along with an attachment including Factory's standardized terms). Without formally accepting this offer by email, Supplier delivers the goods, and Factory pays for them. Affixed to the shipping container for the goods was a "receipt" printed by Supplier that lists the price and quantity of the goods. The parties have a contract by their conduct under U.C.C. section 2–207(3), but the only terms incorporated into the contract from the parties' writings are the price and quantity of goods.

(b) Act Designated by Offer to Signify a Promise

A comparable case is that in which the offer provides that the offeree can do some act to *signify* their promise. In that case, performance of the act constitutes a *promissory* acceptance.

Example: Buyer sends Seller a written offer to buy Seller's car for $6,000. The offer states, "If you want to accept my offer, let me know by leaving your car in my driveway on Thursday." Seller can accept by leaving her car in Buyer's driveway on Thursday. If Seller does so, a bilateral contract is formed.

1) Note

In such cases, doing the act specified as a signal of acceptance is not the bargained-for consideration. It merely *signifies* the return promise (*e.g.*, in the example above, to sell the car for $6,000).

2) Limitation

The offer cannot designate an act to signify acceptance that is an act that the offeree might very well do anyway. Thus, in the example above, if Buyer had written, "If you want to accept my offer, let me know by parking your car in your own garage on Thursday," and Seller goes home Thursday evening and parks her car in her own garage with no intent to accept Buyer's offer, there is no contract.

(c) Silence as Acceptance

In some situations, a promissory acceptance may even be inferred from the offeree's silence (*see infra*, pp. 99–103).

(3) Communication of Acceptance of Offer for Bilateral Contract

The problem of whether an offeree must *communicate* acceptance normally does not arise in the case of an offer for a bilateral contract, because normally such an offer can be accepted only by a communicated promise. However, there are several instances in which this is not true:

(a) Mailbox Rule

Under the so-called mailbox rule (discussed *infra*, p. 104), where use of the mail is a reasonable method of communicating an acceptance, the acceptance normally is effective when *sent* ("dispatched"). This is true even if the acceptance does not actually *reach* the offeror because it is lost in the mail. [Rest. 2d § 56]

(b) Waiver of Communication

In some cases, the offer provides that the offeree must "accept" or "approve" the offer, but *expressly waives communication* of the acceptance or approval. In such cases, a contract is formed when the offeree accepts or approves, even before the offeree communicates acceptance. [**International Filter Co. v. Conroe Gin, Ice & Light Co.,** 277 S.W. 631 (Tex. 1925); Rest. 2d § 56]

1) Implied Condition of Notice

Even though a contract is formed in such cases when the offeree accepts, it may be an implied condition that *notice* of the acceptance be sent by the offeree within a reasonable time after the acceptance is effective, so that the offeror knows that the contract is on. If such a condition is implied, a contract would be *formed* when the offeree approves the offer, so that the offer would no longer be revocable. However, the contract would not be *enforceable* unless the offeree gave notice of the acceptance within a reasonable time thereafter.

2) Implied Waiver

Communication of an acceptance may be *impliedly* waived in cases where *silence* constitutes acceptance (*see infra*, pp. 99–103).

b. Acceptance of Offer for Unilateral Contract

An offer that calls for acceptance by performance of an act is known as an offer for a *unilateral contract.* Such an offer can be accepted only by performance—not by a promise.

Example: Owner emails Painter, "I am going away until next Friday. If you have painted my garage dark green by the time I return, I will pay you $500. Don't bother to promise or not promise that you will do it: I am just telling you that if you do it, I will pay." Painter replies, "It's no bother to promise—I promise to paint the garage." An hour later (and before Painter begins to paint), Owner revokes the offer. The revocation is effective. No contract was formed by Painter's promise, because Owner's offer could be accepted only by an act. Restatement Second sections 45 and 87 (*supra*, pp. 84, 86) do not prevent Owner from revoking because Painter had not begun to perform and had not otherwise relied on the offer.

(1) Notice of Acceptance

Recall that an offer for a bilateral contract normally requires a promissory acceptance—subject to the limited exceptions discussed *supra* (p. 91)—and the acceptance itself will therefore normally be a notice of acceptance. When there is an offer for a unilateral contract, however, a contract may be formed by beginning or completing performance, even though the offeror does not immediately know that performance has begun or been completed. Therefore, a problem of notice to the offeror may arise in unilateral contract cases.

(a) Notice of Completed Performance Required

The general rule is that a unilateral contract is *formed* when the offeree completes performance, but the offeror's *obligation* under the contract is subject to the implied condition that they receive notice of the offeree's performance within a reasonable time thereafter. Thus, if an offeree under a unilateral contract performs in full but fails to notify the offeror of this performance within a reasonable time, a contract will be formed by the performance but the offeror's obligation under the contract will be discharged by the offeree's failure to give notice. [**Bishop v. Eaton,** 37 N.E. 665 (Mass. 1894)]

Example: On February 1, Jenny writes to Sam as follows: "If you loan money to my brother Eric or cosign a loan to him from someone else,

I will reimburse you for any losses you suffer if he doesn't pay back his debt." On March 1, Sam cosigns for a loan that Eric gets from Megabank, thereby helping Eric qualify for the loan. On March 3, before Sam has given Jenny notice that he cosigned for Eric's loan application, Jenny telephones Sam and revokes the offer. The revocation is ineffective. A contract was formed when Sam completed performance by cosigning for the loan. Although Sam was obliged to notify Jenny that he had done this within a reasonable time after doing so, a reasonable time had not elapsed before Jenny tried to revoke.

Compare: Same facts as in the example above, except that Sam does not give Jenny notice that he cosigned for Eric's loan until he is sued by Megabank two years later. Jenny is not bound. A contract between Jenny and Sam was formed when Sam cosigned for the loan, but Jenny's obligation under the contract was discharged by Sam's failure to give notice within a reasonable time.

1) Diligence in Giving Notice

It is sufficient that the offeree uses reasonable diligence to give notice of completed performance. If the offeree uses such diligence, the offeror will be bound even though for some fortuitous reason (such as loss of a letter in the mail) the notice does not actually reach the offeror. [**Bishop v. Eaton,** *supra*]

2) Exceptions

An offeree under a unilateral contract who has completed performance is not required to give notice of that fact to the offeror if any of the following exceptions apply:

(i) The offeror expressly or impliedly has waived the need for notice;

(ii) The performance would come to the offeror's attention within a reasonable time in the normal course of things and the offeror has not explicitly required notice; *or*

(iii) The performance actually comes to the offeror's attention within a reasonable time.

[**Midland National Bank v. Security Elevator Co.,** 200 N.W. 851 (Minn. 1924); Rest. 2d § 54]

(b) Contracts for the Sale of Goods

In most cases, the offeree under a unilateral contract need only notify the offeror that performance has been ***completed***—not that performance has begun. However, in the case of a contract for the sale of goods, U.C.C. section 2-206(2) provides that "where the beginning of a requested performance is a reasonable mode of acceptance, an offeror who is not notified of [such beginning of performance] within a reasonable time may treat the offer as having lapsed before acceptance."

(2) Subjective Intent of Offeree

An offer for a unilateral contract contemplates acceptance by performance of an act. Suppose the act called for by an offer is performed by either (i) a person who has no ***knowledge*** of the offer or (ii) a person who knows of the offer but who is ***principally*** *motivated* to perform by some reason other than the offer. The two situations are treated differently.

(a) Performance Without Knowledge of Offer

1) General Rule

The general rule is that in the case of an offer for a unilateral contract, performance of the requested act by a person who had no knowledge of the offer at the time they performed the act ***does not form a contract.*** [**Broadnax v. Ledbetter,** 99 S.W. 1111 (Tex. 1907)]

> **Example:** *A* offers a reward of $50 for his lost wallet. Without knowing of the reward, *B* finds *A*'s wallet and returns it to *A*. *B* cannot collect the reward.

2) Minority Rule

A few cases have held that for an offer for a reward, a contract can be formed even though the offeree had no knowledge of the offer, on the theory that people should be encouraged to take virtuous action in hope of receiving a reward. [**Dawkins v. Sappington,** 26 Ind. 199 (1866)]

a) Statutory Rewards

Also, it is sometimes held that knowledge is not required in the case of a reward that is offered by statute, on the ground that liability in such a case is statutory rather than contractual. [**Choice v. Dallas,** 210 S.W. 753 (Tex. 1919)]

(b) Offer Not the Principal Motive for Performance

1) General Rule

If an actor knows of an offer for a unilateral contract at the time they perform the act called for by the offer, the general rule is that a contract is formed even if the offer was not the principal motive for performing the act. [**Klockner v. Green,** 254 A.2d 782 (N.J. 1969)]

> **Example:** Same facts as in the last example, except that *B* knew of the reward but returned the wallet principally because of ethical considerations. *B* is entitled to collect the reward.

2) Exception—Involuntary Acceptance

Performance of the act requested by an offer for a unilateral contract might not form a contract if the act is done ***involuntarily.*** [**Vitty v. Eley,** 51 App. Div. 44 (1900)]

> **Example:** Store Owner offers a reward for information leading to the arrest of the person who burglarized her store. Buddy, a friend of the criminal, knows of the reward and is interrogated by the police. During the interrogation, Buddy is forced by threat of prosecution into giving information that leads to the arrest of the true perpetrator. Buddy might not be able to collect the reward.

(3) Obligation of Offeree

An offeree's acceptance of an offer for a ***bilateral*** contract binds the ***offeree*** as well as the offeror. Such an acceptance involves making a promise (explicitly or implicitly), and that promise binds the offeree. However, if the offer is for a ***unilateral*** contract, the offeree's beginning of performance obliges the ***offeror*** to hold the offer open (*see supra*, p. 86) but does not ordinarily oblige the ***offeree*** to complete performance, because the offeree has never promised anything.

(a) Exception

In some cases, an offeree who has begun to perform under an offer for a unilateral contract should know that the beginning of performance is likely to come to the offeror's notice, and that the offeror is likely to treat the beginning of performance as an implied promise by the offeree to complete the performance. This is most likely to be true where the offeree's failure to complete performance will make the offeror worse off than they would have been if the offeree had not begun. For example, if the performance consists of transporting goods, and the offeree begins to transport the goods, there is an implied promise that he will not abandon the goods midway. Because the offer is for a unilateral contract and therefore can be accepted only by an act, an implied promise to complete once performance has begun will not create a bilateral contract. However, if the offeror relies on such an implied promise by the offeree, the reliance might make the implied promise enforceable under the reliance principle. [Rest. 2d § 90]

(4) Use of Subcontractor's Bid

Suppose a general contractor (*i.e.*, a contractor who is responsible for an entire construction project, like the construction of a new research facility for a university) uses a specific subcontractor's sub-bid in computing its main bid for the project. (The general contractor uses subcontractors to do parts of the work—*e.g.*, painting, drywall construction, and installation of the electrical system. The bid that the general contractor places on the project depends in part on the bids that the general contractor receives from subcontractors.) In this scenario, does the general contractor's conduct in using the sub-bid constitute an acceptance of the sub-bid, so that a contract is formed in which the general contractor must use the subcontractor's services if the overall project is awarded to the general contractor? As a matter of ***contract*** law, the answer is no, because the contemplated mode of accepting the sub-bid is assent by the general contractor, not the act of using the bid. [**Southern California Acoustics Co. v. C.V. Holder, Inc.,** 71 Cal. 2d 719 (1969); **Williams v. Favret,** 161 F.2d 822 (5th Cir. 1947)]

(a) Statutory Approaches

However, in some states, ***statutes*** provide that a general contractor who bids on a ***government*** job must include with its bid a list of all subcontractors whose sub-bids it has used, and that except under designated circumstances, the general contractor may not substitute any subcontractors for those it has listed. If the general contractor makes an impermissible substitution, the subcontractor whose sub-bid was used can bring suit against the general contractor ***under the statute***. [**Southern California Acoustics Co. v. C.V. Holder, Inc.,** *supra*]

EXAM TIP

The main consequence of whether an offer is for a bilateral or unilateral contract is whether acceptance is proper. For example, an offer may call for acceptance by an act, in which case it cannot be accepted by a promise. (But note that offers that call for acceptance by a promise *can* effectively be accepted by an act if the act is sufficient to *imply* a promise that constitutes valid acceptance.) An offeree's power to accept may be terminated by the offeror's revocation or death until the offeree makes a proper acceptance.

c. Offers Calling for Acceptance by Either a Promise or an Act

In many cases, an offer is ambiguous as to whether it requires acceptance by a promise or by an act.

Example: Owner says to Painter, "I will give you $500 to paint my house." This is an offer, but it is ambiguous whether it is an offer for a bilateral contract (to be accepted by a promise—*e.g.*, "I accept") or for a unilateral contract (to be accepted by performance—*e.g.*, painting the house).

(1) Restatement First Rule

Restatement First provided that in case of doubt about whether an offer called for acceptance by a promise or by an act, it was to be presumed that the offer invited the formation of a ***bilateral*** contract by a ***promissory*** acceptance. [**Davis v. Jacoby**, 1 Cal. 2d 370 (1934)]

(a) Criticism

The Restatement First rule created a problem when there was doubt about what kind of acceptance was required and the offeree interpreted the offer as calling for acceptance by an act and began performing. Under the Restatement First rule, the beginning of performance by the offeree had no legal significance, and the offeror would therefore be free to revoke even after performance had begun.

(2) Restatement Second Rule

Because of the unfairness of this result, Restatement Second adopts a different rule: in case of doubt, an offer is interpreted as inviting acceptance by ***either*** a promise ***or*** performance. Under this rule, if there is doubt about whether the offer requires acceptance by a promise or by performance, the offeree is protected no matter which interpretation they place upon the offer.

(a) U.C.C. in Accord

Similarly, in the case of contracts for the sale of goods, U.C.C. section 2-206(1)(a) provides that "unless otherwise unambiguously indicated by the language or circumstances . . . an offer to make a contract shall be construed as inviting acceptance in any manner . . . reasonable in the circumstances."

1) Orders for Prompt Shipment

The general rule of U.C.C. section 2-206(1)(a) is applied in section 2-206(1)(b) to the specific case of "an order or other offer to buy goods for prompt or current shipment." Under section 2-206(*l*)(b), such an order is construed as inviting acceptance ***either*** by the prompt or current shipment of the goods ***or*** by a prompt promise to ship. (However, if the offeree chooses to accept by shipping the goods and the offeror is not notified within a reasonable time that shipment has begun, the offeror may treat the offer as having lapsed before acceptance.) [U.C.C. § 2–206(1)(b); *see* Sale & Lease of Goods Summary]

a) Shipment of Nonconforming Goods

The seller's shipment of goods will be deemed an acceptance even if the goods shipped are "nonconforming" (*i.e.*, they do not meet the specifications set forth in the buyer's offer). In such a case, the shipment is simultaneously an acceptance of the buyer's offer and a breach of the resulting contract. However, if the shipper "seasonably notifies the buyer that the shipment is offered only as an *accommodation* to the buyer," then there is no breach if the goods are nonconforming. In such cases, the shipment of nonconforming goods is not construed as an acceptance but rather as a counteroffer. [U.C.C. § 2–206(*l*)(b); *see* Sale & Lease of Goods Summary]

3. Silence as Acceptance

a. General Rule

The general rule is that the silence of an offeree does not constitute acceptance. [**McGlone v. Lacey,** 288 F. Supp. 662 (D.S.D. 1968)]

(1) Rationale

The purpose of this rule is to prevent an offeror from placing an offeree involuntarily in a situation where the offeree must either take an affirmative action to reject the offer or else become liable on a contract.

b. Exceptions

There are a number of exceptions to the general rule. In most of these exceptions, the offeree is *not* involuntarily put into a situation where they must either take an affirmative action to reject the offer or else become liable on a contract.

(1) Implied-in-Fact Contracts

The rule about "silence as acceptance" doesn't refer to literal silence. Instead, it refers to *inaction*. Accordingly, the general rule does not apply to *communicated action*, even if the action is nonverbal and occurs in "silence." (*See supra*, p. 92.)

Example: Buyer bids $150 for a painting at an auction. After waiting a few seconds, the auctioneer says, "Do I hear more?" and then knocks the hammer down. Buyer's bid is an offer, and the auctioneer's action of knocking down the hammer (even without saying anything) is an implied-in-fact acceptance of that offer.

Example: Owner writes a note to Plumber, requesting Plumber to repair Owner's leaky faucet. Plumber comes the next day while Owner is home and proceeds to make the repair. Owner's request is an offer to pay Plumber's usual rates, provided they are not unreasonable. Plumber's action of making the repair is an implied-in-fact acceptance of that offer.

(a) Implied-in-Fact Offer and Acceptance

In some cases, both the offer and the acceptance may be implied in fact from nonverbal actions.

Example: Neighbor often mows Homeowner's lawn for $25. One week, as Homeowner is backing out of his driveway to leave for work, Neighbor arrives to mow Homeowner's lawn. Neighbor points to the lawn, and Homeowner nods as he is driving away. The conduct of Neighbor and Homeowner results in an implied-in-fact contract for Neighbor to mow Homeowner's lawn for $25.

1) U.C.C.

Likewise, under the U.C.C., conduct by both parties that recognizes the existence of a contract for the sale of goods is sufficient to establish a contract, even though the writings of the parties do not otherwise establish a contract. [U.C.C. § 2–207(3); *see supra*, p. 74]

(2) Offeree Leads Offeror to Believe That Silence Will Constitute Acceptance

Silence will constitute acceptance if the *offeree*, by their own prior words or conduct, has given the offeror reason to interpret their silence as an acceptance. [**Hobbs v. Massasoit Whip Co.,** 33 N.E. 495 (Mass. 1893); **National Union Fire Insurance Co. v. Ehrlich,** 122 Misc. 682 (1924); Rest. 2d § 69(1)(c)]

Example: Buyer, a rare book collector, tells Seller, a rare book dealer, "You know what kind of books interest me. If you run across any, send them to me with a proposed price. If I do not return the book promptly, you may deem it accepted at the price you state." Seller sends a book with a stated price of $300. Buyer receives it, does not return it promptly, and says nothing. As a result of her earlier statement, Buyer's inaction constitutes acceptance, and she is contractually bound to pay Seller $300.

(a) Implication from Prior Dealings and Trade Usage

Even without a specific communication by the offeree that addresses the offer, silence may constitute acceptance when the prior dealings of the parties or trade usage (*see infra*, p. 117) make it reasonable, in general, for the offeree to know that they should reply with a rejection if they do not intend to accept. (*See also infra* pp. 99–100.)

Example: Same facts as above, except that Buyer and Seller have had no specific prior communication with each other but are part of a local trade association that frequently adopts Seller's practice outlined above (sending a book with a proposed price for tacit approval or express rejection). If a merchant in the position of Buyer would reasonably be aware of this practice, Buyer's inaction will constitute acceptance.

(3) Solicitation of Offer on Form Drafted by Offeree

Similarly, silence may count as acceptance when (i) the *offeree* has solicited the offer and drafted its terms; (ii) the offer, as drafted by the offeree, is so worded that a reasonable person in the offeror's position would believe that the *offer was to be deemed accepted* unless the offeree notifies the offeror that the offer is rejected; and (iii) the *offeror relies* or is likely to have relied on the reasonable belief that lack of a prompt rejection constituted an acceptance. This pattern commonly arises in two situations:

(a) Solicitation of Orders for Goods

When a seller sends out traveling sales representatives to take "orders" by customers (which are technically offers by the customers) on order forms prepared by the seller, and the order is so worded that the customer would reasonably believe that they can deem the order accepted unless notified otherwise, the seller may be under a duty to fill the order unless it specifically rejects the offer within a reasonable time. [**Cole-McIntyre-Norfleet Co. v. Holloway,** 214 S.W. 817 (Tenn. 1919); **Ammons v. Wilson & Co.,** 170 So. 227 (Miss. 1936)]

(b) Applications for Insurance

The result is similar when an applicant applies for an insurance policy on a form provided by the insurer, the insurer holds the application for an unreasonably long time without making a decision, and the applicant suffers a loss while the insurer is holding the application. Here the applicant is technically the offeror, but many cases hold that the insurer is liable if it fails to reject the application in a timely manner—at least if the application was in good order and the loss occurred after the expiration of a reasonable time in which the insurer should have made a decision. [**Kukuska v. Home Mutual Hail-Tornado Insurance Co.,** 235 N.W. 403 (Wis. 1931)]

1) Rationale

The insurer should know that the applicant will rely on reasonably expeditious processing. While an applicant waits to hear from the insurer, as a practical matter they usually cannot make offers to other insurers because more than one insurer might accept.

(4) Silence Coupled with Subjective Intent to Accept

Silence will constitute acceptance where the offeror has said that silence will constitute acceptance *and* the offeree remains silent with a *subjective intent* to accept. [Rest. 2d § 69(1)(b); *see* **International Filter Co. v. Conroe Gin, Ice & Light Co.,** *supra,* p. 93]

Example: On January 2, Seller writes to Buyer, "I will send you lithographs by messenger from time to time, with a stated price. If I do not hear from you within five days, I will deem the lithographs accepted at that price." Buyer does not reply. On February 1, Seller sends Buyer a lithograph by messenger with a stated price of $300. Buyer inspects the lithograph and forms a subjective intent to accept Seller's offer in accordance with Seller's letter of January 2. Buyer's subjective intent constitutes acceptance of Seller's offer, and Buyer is contractually bound to pay Seller the stated price. If Buyer had not formed a subjective intent to accept, she would not be bound, provided she did not exercise dominion over the lithograph. (*See infra,* p. 102.)

EXAM TIP ■ GILBERT

Note that this rule is contrary to the objective theory of contracts (under which mutual assent is formed by the objective manifestations of the parties rather than the parties' subjective intent). (*See supra,* p. 55.) Under this rule, *both* an objective manifestation of assent (*i.e.,* an offer allowing acceptance by silence and the offeree's silence in response to the offer) ***and*** the offeree's subjective intent to accept are necessary to form a contract.

(5) Exercise of Dominion over Property

An offeree who improperly ***exercises dominion*** over goods sent to them for approval, inspection, or the like is contractually bound to purchase the goods at the proffered price, unless that price is manifestly unreasonable—even if the offeree does not have a subjective intent to accept. [**Louisville Tin & Stove Co. v. Lay,** 65 S.W.2d 1002 (Ky. 1933); **Indiana Manufacturing Co. v. Hayes,** 26 A. 6 (Pa. 1893); Rest. 2d § 69(2)]

Example: Same facts as in the lithograph example above, except that Buyer does not form a subjective intent to accept Seller's offer of the lithograph. Nevertheless, Buyer sends the lithograph to her son at college, telling him to hang it in his dormitory room. Buyer is contractually bound to pay Seller $300.

(a) Note

If goods are sent for inspection, ***mere inspection*** does not constitute an improper exercise of dominion.

(b) Statutory Exceptions

A federal statute now provides, "Except for (1) free samples clearly and conspicuously marked as such, and (2) merchandise mailed by a charitable organization soliciting contributions, the mailing of unordered merchandise . . . constitutes an unfair method of competition and an unfair trade practice." Any merchandise mailed in violation of this statute "may be treated as a gift by the recipient, who shall have the right to retain, use, discard, or dispose of it in any manner he sees fit without any obligation whatsoever to the sender." [39 U.S.C. § 3009] Similar statutes have been enacted in several states. [*See, e.g.*, Cal. Civ. Code § 1584.5] These statutes in effect overturn the "exercise of dominion" rule in the cases to which they apply.

(6) Benefit from Offered Services

The offeree's inaction also operates as acceptance if the offeree (1) receives a benefit from offered services, (2) has a reasonable opportunity to reject them, and (3) has reason to know that they were offered with the expectation of compensation. [Rest. 2d § 69(1)(a)] This situation is similar to one of an implied-in-fact contract [*supra*, p. 99] but does not require action or communication of any kind on the offeree's part.

Example: Homeowner has a contract with LawnCo under which LawnCo provides various lawnmowing services for Homeowner. Homeowner and LawnCo's representatives have discussed the possibility that LawnCo would provide pruning services for several large trees on Homeowner's property for $400, but the parties have not reached a formal agreement on the matter. Within Homeowner's sight, a LawnCo employee begins pruning Homeowner's trees, and Homeowner says nothing while this continues for several hours. Homeowner's inaction is sufficient to accept LawnCo's offer of services.

Compare: Niece is staying at Uncle's house on a vacation. Uncle sees Niece start washing his car but says nothing. Though Uncle benefits from this service, he has no reason to know that it is being offered with the expectation of compensation. (It could plausibly have been performed as a gift.) Even if Niece had subjectively intended to offer her car-washing services for money, Uncle's silence does not constitute acceptance.

(7) Unjust Enrichment or Quasi-Contract

Similarly, under the principle of ***unjust enrichment*** or ***quasi-contract,*** liability may be imposed on someone who receives a benefit even in the absence of a promise to pay for the benefit. A plaintiff can recover in restitution or quasi-contract if they can show that:

(i) They have conferred a ***benefit on the defendant;***

(ii) They conferred the benefit with the ***expectation that they would be paid*** its value;

(iii) The defendant ***knew or had reason to know*** of the plaintiff's expectation; *and*

(iv) The ***defendant would be unjustly enriched*** if allowed to retain the benefit without paying its value.

e.g. Example: Tom begins to build a party wall (*i.e.*, a wall that straddles the boundary between two properties) on the boundary between his property and Al's property. A reasonable person in Al's position would know that because Al will have legal ownership of half the wall (because the wall is partly on Al's side of the boundary line), Tom expects Al to pay for half the value of the wall. Al says nothing and lets Tom continue to work. Al is liable for half the value of the wall. [**Day v. Caton,** 119 Mass. 513 (1876)]

(a) Failed Express Contract

The four requirements discussed above need not be proved if a plaintiff seeks a quasi-contract remedy because an express contract has failed (*e.g.*, because of noncompliance with the Statute of Frauds). In that event, the plaintiff need only prove (1) the express contract and (2) the unjust enrichment that would result absent the quasi-contractual remedy.

(8) Late Acceptance

A late acceptance has the legal effect of a counteroffer—*i.e.*, a late acceptance does not conclude a bargain, but it is treated as an offer that can be accepted by the original offeror. (*See infra*, p. 106.) In addition, however, if an offeree sends an acceptance after a reasonable time for acceptance has elapsed (so that it is late), but within a period that the offeree might plausibly regard as reasonable, courts have held that good faith and fair dealing require the original offeror to notify the original offeree that the acceptance was too late. If the original offeror does not give such notice, the offeree's late acceptance/counteroffer will be deemed accepted by the original offeror's silence. [**Phillips v. Moor,** 71 Me. 78 (1880); Rest. 2d § 70]

D. Time at Which Communications Between Offeror and Offeree Become Effective

1. In General

When parties negotiate over a mode of communication (like mail) that involves potential delays in the receipt of communications, it often becomes important to determine when a communication, such as an acceptance, a revocation, or a rejection, takes effect. The rules vary according to what type of communication is involved. In general and subject to the exceptions described below, all communications except an acceptance are effective *on receipt*. An acceptance is effective when it is *sent*—i.e., *on dispatch*.

a. Receipt of Mail

When a communication is legally effective on receipt, a question may arise as to what counts as "receipt," particularly if the recipient is a business. The general rule is that any of the following constitute receipt of a letter: (1) the letter comes into the possession of the recipient; (2) the letter comes into the possession of the recipient's agent; (3) the letter is deposited in a place that the recipient has authorized for this communication or similar ones. [Rest. 2d § 68]

Example: Corporation *A* emails an offer to *B* on *A*'s corporate letterhead, which includes the address of *A*'s headquarters. *B* sends a rejection of the offer to that address on May 25. The postal service delivers the letter to the mailroom of *A*'s headquarters on May 28, but the letter is not opened until May 30. The rejection is effective on May 28.

b. Receipt of Email

Under the Uniform Electronic Transactions Act (U.E.T.A.), a statute that has been adopted by the vast majority of states, email is deemed to be received when it enters the recipient's computer systems (*i.e.*, the "information processing system[s] that the recipient has designated or uses for the purpose of receiving electronic records or information of the type sent and from which the recipient is able to retrieve the electronic record") in a format suitable for electronic processing, even if no human being has yet read it. [U.E.T.A. § 15]

2. Acceptance—"Mailbox Rule"

Although a promise normally must be communicated to be effective, for policy reasons the general rule is that an acceptance is effective when it is sent or "dispatched"—and thus even before it is received. This rule is known as the "mailbox rule," the "dispatch rule," or the rule of **Adams v. Lindsell**. [**Adams v. Lindsell,** 106 Eng. Rep. 250 (1818)]

a. Rationale

The mailbox rule creates a contract earlier than most alternative rules, thereby allowing at least one side (the offeree) to begin relying on and performing the contract. The main effect of the rule is to cause an acceptance to be effective even if the offeror had previously sent a revocation (which has not yet arrived), but revocations are relatively rare, so it would be wasteful to require that all offerees who accept a contract through the mail wait to see if the offer was revoked before performing or relying on the contract. The mailbox rule therefore gives a productive security or certainty to the offeree, which in turn encourages contracting over a distance. Moreover, the offeror was typically the party that originally chose to use the mail, in which case it is fair to place the risk of an unwanted acceptance on the offeror.

b. Scope

The mailbox rule developed in the 1800s and historically pertained to postal mail. Because email can involve similar delays and the possibility of missed communications, the rule may apply to email as well, though caselaw is sparse and the matter is unsettled. As communication has gotten faster, the role of the mailbox rule has diminished, but its policies still apply in principle to any mode of communication where delays are possible. (Email often seems instantaneous, but it is not necessarily so.)

c. Exception for Options

Some authorities, including the Restatement, take the position that in the case of an *option,* an acceptance (or "exercise" of the option) is not effective until *received*. **[Cities Service Oil Co. v. National Shawmut Bank,** 172 N.E.2d 104 (Mass. 1961); **Scott-Burr Stores Corp. v. Wilcox,** 194 F.2d 989 (5th Cir. 1952); Rest. 2d § 63] However, other courts apply the mailbox rule even to the exercise of options. **[Palo Alto Town & Country Village v. BBTC Co.,** 11 Cal. 3d 494 (1974); **Shubert Theatrical Co. v. Rath,** 271 F. 827 (2d Cir. 1921)]

d. Requirements Necessary to Satisfy the Mailbox Rule

To be effective upon dispatch, the acceptance must be dispatched in a ***timely*** and ***proper*** manner. [Rest. 2d § 63]

(1) Timely Dispatch

Whether dispatch is timely depends in part on whether the offer specifies a period of time for acceptance.

(a) No Time Specified for Acceptance

If no period of time for acceptance is specified in the offer, the offeree must accept within a ***reasonable time*** (*see supra*, p. 65).

(b) Specified Period for Acceptance

If a period of time is specified in the offer, then unless otherwise specified the time period begins running ***when the offer is received,*** and the acceptance must be dispatched within that time period. [**Caldwell v. Cline,** *supra*, p. 65]

(c) Time of Dispatch, Not Receipt, Significant

If the acceptance is dispatched within the appropriate time period, it is timely even if in the normal course of mail delivery it will be (and is) received by the offeree after the specified period. [**Falconer v. Mazess,** 168 A.2d 558 (Pa. 1961)]

 Example: *A* lives in Atlanta and *B* lives in New York. The course of post between Atlanta and New York is five days. On January 2, *A* mails a written offer to *B*. The offer states that it will remain open for 10 days. *A*'s letter arrives on January 4. The 10-day time period begins running on January 4. *B*'s acceptance will be timely if it is dispatched by mail on or prior to January 14.

(d) Consequences of Late Dispatch

If an acceptance is not dispatched in a timely manner and arrives too late, it is ineffective as an acceptance. However, it does serve as a counteroffer and therefore creates a power of acceptance in the original offeror.

1) Note

Under certain circumstances, the original offeror's failure to *reject* the late acceptance/counteroffer will operate as an acceptance by silence (*see supra*, p. 103).

(e) Options

Remember that some authorities do not apply the mailbox rule if the offer is an option. According to those authorities, if the offeree has a specified period of time in which to exercise the option, the acceptance must be ***received*** (not merely dispatched) within that period.

(2) Proper Manner

Assuming an acceptance has been dispatched in a timely fashion, the next question is whether it has been dispatched in a proper manner.

(a) Appropriate Care

To begin with, the acceptance must be dispatched with appropriate care—correctly addressed, stamped, and so forth. [Rest. 2d § 66; **Shubert Theatrical Co. v. Rath,** *supra*, p. 105]

(b) Medium of Communication

The offeree must also dispatch the acceptance using an appropriate medium of communication. What constitutes an appropriate medium depends in part on whether the offeror has suggested or prescribed a medium of acceptance.

1) Where Offeror Does Not Suggest or Prescribe Medium of Acceptance

a) Traditional Rule

The traditional rule was that when the offeror did not prescribe or suggest the medium of acceptance, an acceptance would be effective on dispatch only if the offeree used a medium of communication that the offeror had at least ***impliedly*** authorized. For example, the offeror was deemed to impliedly authorize the medium by which they sent the offer. [**Henthorn v. Fraser,** [1892] 2 Ch. 27]

b) Modern Rule

The modern rule is that unless otherwise specified an offer is deemed to invite acceptance by any medium ***"reasonable in the circumstances."*** [Rest. 2d § 30; U.C.C. § 2–206(*l*)(a)]

1/ "Reasonable" Medium

A medium of communication normally is reasonable if it is the one used by the offeror (unless the offer specifies otherwise) or if it is customary in similar transactions at the time and place the offer is received. [Rest. 2d § 65]

2/ Other Factors

Even if the medium does not meet one of these two tests, it may still be reasonable, depending on the speed and reliability of the medium, the prior course of dealing between the parties (*see infra*, p. 116), and usage of trade (*see infra*, p. 117). [Rest. 2d § 65]

3/ Use of Mail

Traditionally, acceptance by mail was ordinarily considered reasonable when the parties were negotiating at a distance, even if the offer was not made by mail, unless there was a special reason for speed, such as rapid price changes.

Example: Employer lives in Los Angeles and Applicant lives in San Francisco. Employer makes a face-to-face offer of employment to Applicant in Los Angeles, and gives Applicant two days to consider the offer. Applicant says he will go back to San Francisco and think about it. That evening, Applicant posts an acceptance by mail from San Francisco. The acceptance is effective on dispatch. Since the parties live in different cities, Employer should have contemplated that Applicant would use the mails. In any event, except in unusual situations, such as those involving a subject matter whose price fluctuates rapidly, the mails are a customary means of conducting business negotiations.

a/ Note

Today, acceptance by email would probably be deemed reasonable in the ordinary case—probably even more reasonable than postal mail in many cases.

2) Where Offeror Suggests Medium of Acceptance

If the offeror explicitly suggests a medium of acceptance, use of that medium is always appropriate. Failure to use a suggested medium may (but does not necessarily) mean that the medium that was used is unreasonable.

3) Consequence of Unreasonable Medium or Lack of Reasonable Care

Unless the offer prescribes the medium of communication (*see infra*, p. 108), a contract may be formed even if the offeree failed to use a reasonable medium or reasonable care in dispatching an acceptance. However, if the medium employed is not a reasonable one, or if reasonable care was not employed in dispatching the acceptance, the acceptance will not be effective unless it actually *arrives*. *Note:* If an acceptance is *dispatched on time* through an unreasonable medium or without reasonable care but it *arrives on time,* it is treated as operative on *dispatch,* just as if it were properly sent. [Rest. 2d § 67]

4) Where Offeror Prescribes Medium of Communication

If the offeror *prescribes* a medium of communication, no contract will be formed *unless* that medium is used.

Example: Seller offers to sell their land to Buyer on certain terms and states, "You must accept this offer, if at all, in person at my office at noon, tomorrow." Buyer's power of acceptance can be exercised *only* in the manner Seller has designated. Acceptance in any other manner is a mere counteroffer. [Rest. 2d § 60]

a) Interpretation

Language that appears to *prescribe* a medium of acceptance may be interpreted only to *suggest* that medium. In such cases, the offeree can use some other medium, but if that other medium is not reasonable under the circumstances, the acceptance will be effective only if it arrives no later than would an acceptance that had been sent through the suggested medium. [Rest. 2d § 60]

Example: *A* mails an offer to *B* in which *A* says, "Accept by return mail." Because there ordinarily is no reason why an offeror would insist on use of the mails to the exclusion of all other media, the offer would probably be interpreted: (i) to suggest rather than require use of the mails; (ii) to require that an acceptance by any other medium arrive as soon as a letter would have arrived; and (iii) to require that the acceptance be in writing. Therefore, a written acceptance sent on time by any other means would create a contract on dispatch if the means of communication was reasonable. If the means of communication was not reasonable, the acceptance would be effective if it arrived as soon as a letter sent by return mail would have arrived. [Rest. 2d § 60] Furthermore, if such an acceptance is sent on time and arrives on time, it will be deemed effective on dispatch.

EXAM TIP

Although the mailbox rule treats acceptances as effective when they are sent, remember that an acceptance must still be sent in a *timely and proper manner* for the rule to apply. Therefore, if the purported acceptance was sent too late or in an improper manner, it is not effective on dispatch, and it will not operate as an acceptance if it is received too late.

e. Significance of Mailbox Rule

If an acceptance is properly dispatched and the mailbox rule therefore applies, a number of consequences may follow:

(1) Crossed Acceptance and Revocation

In most states, a revocation is effective only on receipt. (*See infra*, p. 110.) Therefore, under the mailbox rule, if an *acceptance* is *dispatched* before a *revocation* is *received,* a contract is formed. This is true even if the acceptance is dispatched after the revocation is dispatched and received after the revocation is received.

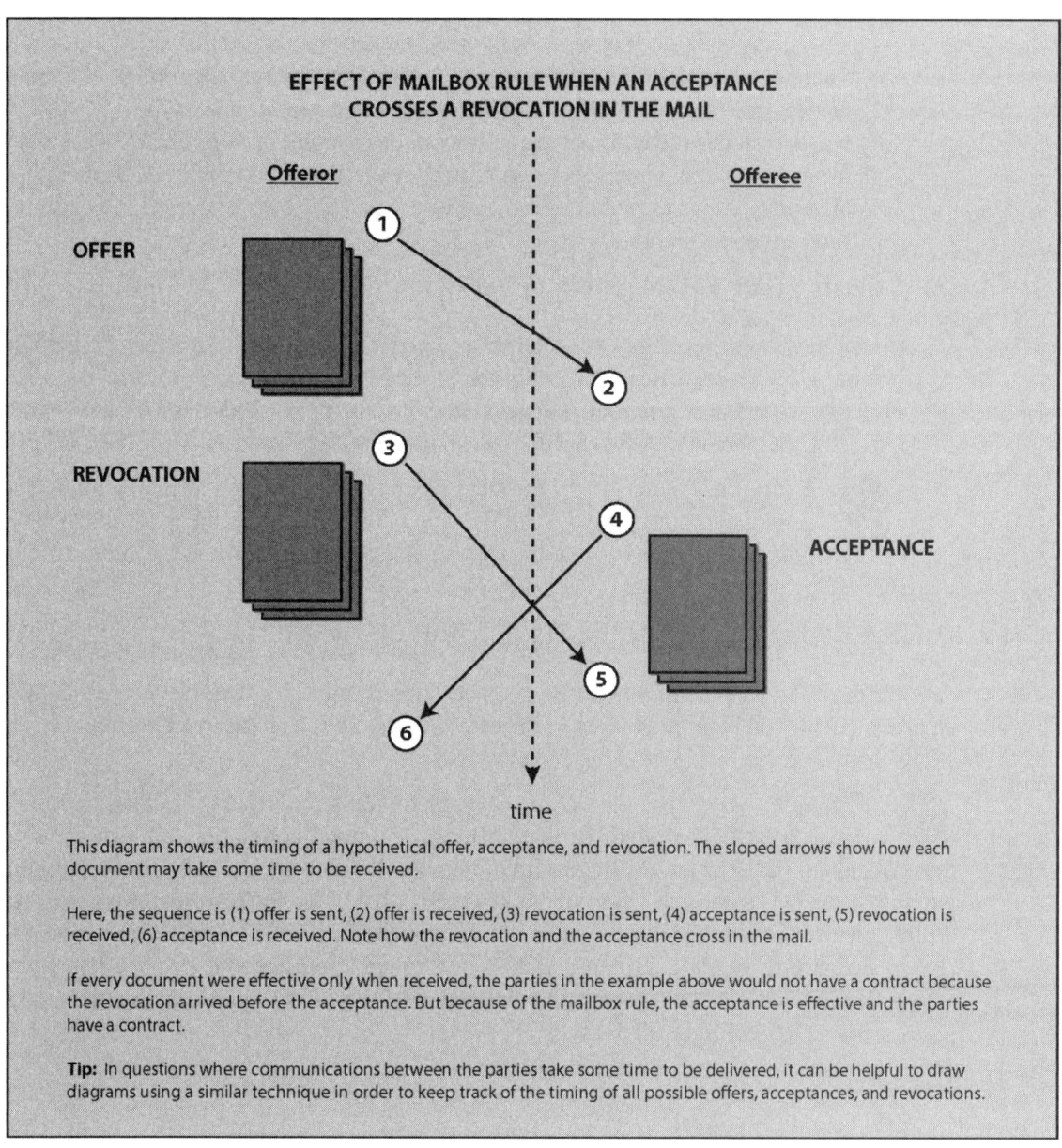

EFFECT OF MAILBOX RULE WHEN AN ACCEPTANCE CROSSES A REVOCATION IN THE MAIL

This diagram shows the timing of a hypothetical offer, acceptance, and revocation. The sloped arrows show how each document may take some time to be received.

Here, the sequence is (1) offer is sent, (2) offer is received, (3) revocation is sent, (4) acceptance is sent, (5) revocation is received, (6) acceptance is received. Note how the revocation and the acceptance cross in the mail.

If every document were effective only when received, the parties in the example above would not have a contract because the revocation arrived before the acceptance. But because of the mailbox rule, the acceptance is effective and the parties have a contract.

Tip: In questions where communications between the parties take some time to be delivered, it can be helpful to draw diagrams using a similar technique in order to keep track of the timing of all possible offers, acceptances, and revocations.

(a) Minority View

Statutes in a few states, including California, provide that a revocation is effective on *dispatch*. In such states, a contract is formed if the acceptance is dispatched first, but not if the revocation is dispatched first. [Cal. Civ. Code § 1587]

(2) Lost or Delayed Acceptance

Suppose a properly dispatched acceptance is lost or delayed by the carrier, so that it does not arrive at all or arrives late. Under the mailbox rule, the acceptance is nevertheless effective and a contract is formed. In other words, under the mailbox rule the *risk of loss or delay* in transmission of a properly dispatched acceptance is on the *offeror.*

(b) Note

There is authority for the proposition that even though a contract is formed despite the fact that the acceptance does not arrive, the *offeror's duty to perform* under the contract is conditional on the receipt of notice of acceptance from the offeree. Under these authorities, even though a contract is formed, the offeror's failure to perform will not be a breach unless and until they receive such a notice. [**Haas v. Myers,** 111 Ill. 421 (1884); Rest. 2d § 63]

(3) Effective Date of Obligation to Perform

Sometimes it is necessary to determine when the parties' obligation to perform becomes effective. Under the mailbox rule, the obligation to perform becomes effective when the acceptance is dispatched. [**Taylor v. Merchant's Fire Insurance Co.,** 50 U.S. (9 How.) 390 (1850)]

Example: Owner mails Builder an offer, and Builder accepts by mail. The signed agreement says, "Builder must complete the project within 21 days of when this contract was formed." That period begins running at the time Builder mailed the acceptance.

f. Offeror's Power to Negate the Mailbox Rule

An offeror can negate the mailbox rule by specifying in the offer that the acceptance will be effective only on receipt. However, the offeror must use clear language to achieve that result.

Example: Lewis lives in California and Browning lives in Massachusetts. Lewis makes a written offer to Browning by mail, which concludes, "If you agree to this offer and will telegraph me on receipt of this, I will order my agent in Boston to begin performance. Telegraph me 'Yes' or 'No.' If 'No,' I will go to Boston and make other arrangements. If a telegram from you is not in my hands within 12 days, I shall conclude 'No.'" Browning sends a properly dispatched telegraphic acceptance, but it fails to arrive. There is no contract, because the language of the offer negates the mailbox rule. [*See* **Lewis v. Browning,** 130 Mass. 173 (1881)]

3. Revocation

As noted above, the general rule is that a revocation is effective only *upon receipt,* subject to statutory exceptions in a few cases. [**Stevenson, Jaques & Co. v. McLean,** *supra*, p. 67]

a. Crossed Acceptance and Revocation

Because an acceptance is effective on *dispatch,* but a revocation is effective only on *receipt,* if an offeree dispatches an acceptance after the offeror dispatches a revocation but before the revocation arrives, a contract is formed. [**Stevenson, Jaques & Co. v. McLean,** *supra*; **Henthorn v. Fraser,** *supra*, p. **Error! Bookmark not defined.**; *and see supra*, p. 109]

4. Rejection

The general rule is that a rejection of an offer is effective only *upon receipt*. [Rest. 2d § 40]

a. Where Offeree Sends Both Rejection and Acceptance

Special problems arise when an offeree first sends a rejection and later changes their mind and sends an acceptance—or vice versa.

(1) Acceptance Mailed Before Rejection

Because an acceptance is effective on dispatch and a rejection is effective on receipt, if an acceptance is mailed before a rejection, a contract is formed on dispatch of the acceptance, regardless of whether the offeror receives the acceptance or the rejection first.

(a) Rationale

The rule prevents the offeree from sending an acceptance and then waiting to see if conditions change before sending a rejection, thereby speculating on those conditions (such as price) at the offeror's expense. For example, suppose an offeree receives a letter saying, "I propose to sell you two widgets at $1500 each." Without this rule, the offeree could send an acceptance and then, knowing that mail to the offeror takes three days to arrive, monitor the price of widgets in that time period. If the price increases, the offeree could let the acceptance stand. If the price declines, the offeree could send a rejection that overtakes the acceptance (and then buy widgets at the lower price under a different contract).

(b) Exception—Detrimental Reliance

If the offeror receives the offeree's rejection before the acceptance, and then the offeror detrimentally relies on the rejection, the offeree is *estopped* from enforcing the contract. [Rest. 2d § 63]

(2) Rejection Mailed Before Acceptance

When the offeree's rejection is mailed before their acceptance, the result depends partly on which communication was received first by the offeror.

(a) Rejection Arrives First

If the rejection arrives before the acceptance arrives, there is no contract, even if the acceptance was dispatched before the rejection arrives. In other words, the *mailbox rule does not apply* in this case. [Rest. 2d § 40]

1) Rationale

When the offeror receives a rejection without having yet received an acceptance, their expectation is that negotiations have terminated. That expectation should be protected, particularly because receiving both an acceptance and a rejection of the same offer is so rare.

2) Effect of Later-Arriving Acceptance

Although the later-arriving acceptance in such a case will not be effective as an acceptance, it will be effective as a *counteroffer,* creating a power of acceptance in the original offeror.

(b) Acceptance Arrives First

If the rejection arrives *after* the acceptance arrives, a contract *is* formed.

1) Rationale

When the offeror receives an acceptance without having yet received a rejection, their expectation is that a contract is formed. Again, that expectation should be protected.

2) Effect of Later-Arriving Rejection

The later-arriving rejection in such a case is not effective as a rejection and does not relieve the offeree of liability under the contract. However, the offeror may regard the rejection as a repudiation of the contract. If the offeror *does* so regard the rejection, and relies on the belief that the contract has been repudiated, the offeree will be estopped from enforcing the contract.

5. Repudiation of Acceptance

A repudiation of an acceptance is a communication by an offeree who has previously sent an acceptance, stating that the offeree does not intend to be bound by the acceptance. That is, the offeree first sends an acceptance and then changes their mind and sends a repudiation. A repudiation therefore differs from a rejection. In a rejection, the offeree turns down the offer. In a repudiation, the offeree "turns down" their own earlier acceptance. By its nature a repudiation can be sent only after an acceptance is sent, because before the acceptance is sent there is nothing to repudiate. When an offeree sends both a repudiation and an acceptance, the governing rules are comparable to the rules that govern the case in which an offeree sends both a rejection and an acceptance. In both cases, the result turns in large part on which communication arrives first.

a. Acceptance Arrives First

If an acceptance arrives before a repudiation of an acceptance arrives, a contract is formed.

(1) Rationale

When the acceptance arrives, the offeror's expectation is that a contract is formed. That expectation should be protected.

(2) Effect of Later-Arriving Repudiation

The later-arriving repudiation in such a case is not effective to relieve the *offeree* of liability under the contract. However, the *offeror* may regard the offeree's repudiation of the acceptance as a repudiation of the contract. If the offeror does so regard the repudiation, and relies on the belief that the contract has been repudiated, the offeree will be estopped from enforcing the contract.

b. Repudiation Arrives First

Suppose instead that the acceptance is *sent* first but the repudiation *arrives* first. Under a strict application of the mailbox rule, a contract would still be formed, because under the mailbox rule an acceptance is effective on dispatch, and the acceptance was dispatched before the repudiation arrived. The Restatement takes just this position. [Rest. 2d § 63] However, the cases are split. [*Compare* **Morrison v. Thoelke,** 155 So. 2d 889 (Fla.

1963)—contract formed, *with* **Dick v. United States,** 82 F. Supp. 326 (Ct. Cl. 1949)—contract not formed]

(1) Rationale of Restatement Rule

Because the offeror receives the repudiation first, the offeror's expectation is probably that no contract is formed. If that were the rule, however, an offeree could speculate at the offeror's expense by mailing an acceptance and then watching the market while the letter traveled through the mail. [*Cf. supra*, p. 111] If the market moved in the offeree's favor, they could let the acceptance stand so that a contract would be formed. If the market moved against them, they could send a repudiation by faster mode of communication so that the repudiation overtakes the acceptance. The Restatement rule, that a contract is formed even when the repudiation arrives first, is intended to prevent such speculation by binding the offeree as soon as they send an acceptance.

(2) Effect of Repudiation

At least under the Restatement rule, the earlier-arriving repudiation does not prevent formation of a contract. However, because the offeror receives the repudiation first, the offeror may regard it as a rejection and rely on it. If the offeror does this, the offeree will be estopped from asserting that a contract was formed.

6. Withdrawal of Acceptance

A withdrawal of an acceptance occurs when the offeree sends an acceptance and then manages to ***retrieve*** the acceptance before it reaches the offeror. For example, the offeree might retrieve a mailed letter of acceptance from the post office. There is very little law on this issue, but the Restatement takes the position that the mailbox rule is still applicable in such a case—*i.e.*, a contract is formed when the acceptance is dispatched, and the withdrawal is therefore ineffective. [Rest. 2d § 63; *see* **G.C. Casebolt Co. v. United States,** 421 F.2d 710 (Ct. Cl. 1970)]

a. Note

There is a practical problem in such cases: because the offeror never receives the acceptance, the offeror may never learn that the offeree had dispatched the offer and then withdrawn it.

7. Crossed Offers

Suppose *A* writes to *B* on January 2 that she will sell Orangeacre to *B* for $40,000, and coincidentally on the same day *B* writes to *A* that he will buy Orangeacre for $40,000. Is there a contract? This kind of situation is called "cross offers" or "crossed offers." The general rule is that a contract is ***not*** formed by crossed offers, on the theory that an offer is not effective until received, and cannot be accepted until it is effective. [**Tinn v. Hoffman,** 29 L.T.R. (n.s.) 271 (1873)]

a. Exception

There is very little authority for this rule. Moreover, a contrary result has been reached when the parties had previously agreed upon all but one minor point and then, in crossed letters, each propose identical terms on that point. [**Asinof v. Freudenthal,** 195 App. Div. 79 (1921)]

E. Interpretation

1. General Rule

A contract can be based on either words or conduct. Words or conduct that are addressed by one party (the addressor) to another (the addressee) can be called an "expression." The general rule of interpretation in contract law is that expressions should be given *objective* interpretations. This means that an expression should be given the interpretation that a reasonable person in the addressee's position would give it, rather than the interpretation that the addressor subjectively intends.

Example: Employee is employed by Employer under a 10-month contract expiring on December 31. On December 15, Employee asks Employer to renew the contract for another 10 months, stating that if Employer does not renew, Employee will immediately take steps to find a new job. Employer replies, "Don't worry, you're all right," and Employee says, "O.K." Employee subjectively interprets the conversation to be an agreement on a new contract. Employer does not. Employee's interpretation is more reasonable than Employer's; consequently, there is a contract. **[Embry v. Hargadine-McKittrick Dry Goods Co.,** 105 S.W. 777 (Mo. 1907)]

a. Application—Choice Between Addressor's and Addressee's Meaning

As in the example above, the modern approach [Rest. 2d § 201] is that objective reasonableness is used to *select* between the parties' two competing interpretations, not to impose an abstract interpretation that a reasonable third party might have chosen.

b. Application—Reasonable Person Knowing What Addressee Knows

Moreover, even under the objective theory, the question should be not simply how a *generalized* reasonable person in the addressee's shoes would interpret the relevant expression, but what interpretation would be given by a reasonable person knowing all that the addressee knew. Accordingly, if the parties are in a special trade, the interpretation must include the usages of the trade. Similarly, if the addressee knows special circumstances that would give the expression a different meaning than it would normally be given, those circumstances are relevant even to an objective interpretation.

2. Exceptions

There are several major exceptions to the normal rule of objective interpretation.

a. The *Peerless* Rule

When the parties understand an expression differently and these two understandings are *equally reasonable*, objective reasonableness cannot be used to break the tie between the parties' meanings. This occurred in the famous *Peerless* Case. In that case, both parties used the term "ex ship *Peerless*," each thinking there was only one ship named *Peerless*. Ironically, there were in fact two ships named *Peerless*, and each party subjectively intended a different *Peerless*. The rule in such cases is that if both parties subjectively attach different, equally reasonable, interpretations to their expressions, no contract is formed. [**Raffles v. Wichelhaus,** 159 Eng. Rep. 375 (1864) (the "*Peerless* Case"); **Oswald v. Allen,** 417 F.2d 43 (2d Cir. 1969); Rest. 2d § 20]

(1) Note

The *Peerless* rule is limited to cases where two or more meanings are *equally reasonable.* If an expression is susceptible of two or more meanings, but only one meaning is reasonable, or one meaning is more reasonable than the other, the objective theory of contracts prevails and the interpretation is based on the reasonable (or more reasonable) meaning, provided that that is the meaning one of the parties intended. [Rest. 2d § 201]

b. Both Parties Have Same Subjective Interpretation

If both parties subjectively attach the same meaning to a term, that meaning will govern even if it is not the reasonable meaning of the term. [Rest. 2d § 201(1)]

Example: Two parties, both understanding their actions to be part of a joke, go through the motions of selling an expensive watch for $15. The parties do not have a contract. [**Keller v. Holderman,** 11 Mich. 248 (1863)]

Note: This sort of case is rare and potentially abstract; it typically depends on good evidence of prior subjective intent that one of the parties later denies in court. Normally, when there is a dispute about interpretation, each party asserts that they adopted a *different* meaning, and the question is which of those different meanings is reasonable (or more reasonable). [Rest. 2d § 201(2)]

c. One Party Knows of the Other's Different Interpretation

If one party, *A*, knows or has reason to know that another party, *B*, attaches a certain meaning to an expression, and *B* does not know or have reason to know that *A* attaches a different meaning to the expression, the meaning that *B* attaches to the expression will prevail, even though under a strictly objective test *A*'s meaning is more reasonable. [Rest. 2d § 201(2)]

Example: Buyer and Seller have discussed the collectibles, worth about $400, in a fireproof safe in Seller's home. A day later, Seller says to Buyer, "I'll sell you all the contents of my safe deposit box for $400," and Buyer agrees. Seller currently has an empty safe deposit box in a bank. The term "safe deposit box" is not generally used to refer to residential safes (versus individual compartments in a bank vault), but Seller expects that under the circumstances Buyer will interpret the phrase "safe deposit box" to refer to Seller's residential fireproof safe. The parties have a contract to sell the contents of the residential safe for $400.

3. Extrinsic Evidence

In cases of a *written* agreement, questions often arise whether "extrinsic evidence"—*i.e.,* evidence outside the writing itself, such as conversations between the parties and surrounding circumstances—may be admitted in aid of interpretation.

a. Traditional Rule

The traditional rule was that if there was no ambiguity in a *written* contract on its face, and no special meaning attached to the words of a written contract by custom or usage, the terms of the contract were to be interpreted only according to their "plain meaning," and extrinsic evidence was inadmissible. [**Rowe v. Chesapeake Mineral Co.,** 156 F.2d 752 (6th Cir. 1946); *see infra,* p. 125] This is sometimes called the *plain meaning rule* or the *four corners rule.*

b. Modern Rule

Over the 1900s, courts tended to adopt a broader approach to contract interpretation and allow extrinsic evidence to show what the parties intended by their words, without regard to their "plain" meaning or a prior showing of ambiguity. (*See infra*, p. 125.)

(1) Rationale

No language is infallible; what is "plain" to the judge may not have been "plain" to the parties. Furthermore, whether a contract is ambiguous cannot be determined unless and until all the relevant circumstances have been considered. **[Pacific Gas & Electric Co. v. G.W. Thomas Drayage & Rigging Co., 69 Cal. 2d 33 (1968)]**

4. Course of Performance, Course of Dealing, Usage, and Usage of Trade

Course of performance, course of dealing, usage, and usage of trade are all relevant in interpreting contracts.

a. Course of Performance

Some contracts involve multiple opportunities for performance—*e.g.*, goods may be delivered every month, or a lawnmowing service may mow someone's lawn every two weeks. If the particular contract at issue is such a contract, and one party has performed its duties under the contract in a certain way in the past with the knowledge of and without objection by the other party, that *course of performance* is a very useful guide to interpretation because it strongly suggests what the parties intended their words and conduct to mean. [Rest. 2d § 202; U.C.C. § 1–303(a)]

b. Course of Dealing

A *course of dealing* is a sequence of conduct between the parties *prior to the contract* at issue (*e.g.*, a sequence of earlier contracts between the parties) that fairly influences what their words and conduct will mean to each other. This evidence, too, may inform the interpretation of the parties' words and conduct. [Rest. 2d § 223; U.C.C. § 1–303(b)]

(1) U.C.C. Limitation

The U.C.C.'s current definition of course of dealing includes only "conduct concerning previous transactions between the parties," [U.C.C. § 1–303(b)] whereas the Restatement (and an older U.C.C. definition) includes no such restriction.

c. Usage

A *usage* is a habitual or customary practice. An agreement is interpreted in accordance with, supplemented by, or qualified by a relevant usage if each party knew or had reason to know of the usage. [Rest. 2d §§ 219–221]

Example: In a particular locale, when a buyer and a seller agree to the sale of a home at a particular price, the seller is understood to promise to reimburse the buyer for a portion of the end-of-year property taxes that the buyer is projected to pay at the end of the year. (This portion corresponds to the portion of the year that the seller still possessed the home.) All local lawyers and real-estate agents who assist with property transactions are aware of this practice, even though it is not explicitly included in the standard written contract template used by the local realty association. Sam and Josie, who have both purchased and sold homes in the area before and are both represented by local real-estate professionals, sign a real-estate contract (using the standard local template contract) under which Josie will buy Sam's house. In accordance with the custom, Sam is legally required to reimburse part of Josie's projected property taxes.

d. Usage of Trade (Trade Usage)

A ***usage of trade*** or ***trade usage*** is a usage regularly observed in a vocation or trade. Unless otherwise agreed, a usage of trade in the vocation in which the parties are engaged gives meaning to, supplements, or qualifies their agreement. [Rest. 2d § 222; U.C.C. § 1–303(c)]

Example: Buyer and Seller contract for scraps of horse meat that contain "minimum 50% protein." Horse meat delivered under the contract contained 49.53 to 49.96% protein. Under a prevailing usage of trade, "more than 50% protein" in contracts like this one meant "at least 49.5% protein"—*i.e.*, the trade appeared to recognize only two significant digits, so that 49.5% was rounded to 50%. The delivered horse meat complies with the contract, even though 49.53 is less than 50 as a matter of general arithmetic. [**Hurst v. W. J. Lake & Co.**, 16 P.2d 627 (Or. 1932)]

e. Priorities

Restatement Second and the U.C.C. lay out the following order of priorities, from most important to least important, for different types of evidence: (1) express terms, (2) course of performance, (3) course of dealing, (4) trade usage. [Rest. 2d § 203(b); U.C.C. § 1–303(e)] The rationale for this ordering is that more specific evidence about the parties' intent for a contract at issue is more important than more general evidence. That said, the Restatement and the U.C.C. both require that whenever reasonable, these four forms of evidence be interpreted as consistent with each other, thereby directing courts to harmonize the various forms of evidence (*e.g.*, by using one to explain or give context to the other) when reasonably possible. [Rest. 2d § 202(5)] The U.C.C. also defines the parties' "agreement" specifically to *include* course of performance, course of dealing, and trade usage. [U.C.C. § 1–201(b)(3); *cf. infra*, p. 125]

EXPRESS TERMS, COURSE OF PERFORMANCE, COURSE OF DEALING, AND USAGE — GILBERT

Type of Evidence	Definition	Example
Express terms	Words or conduct of the parties	The written agreement says, "Delivery will be made to Buyer's dock."
Course of performance	Evidence about how *this contract* has been performed in the past, without objection by the other party	The contract calls for delivery every month, and delivery in past months has always been made to Buyer's dock, where Buyer has always accepted it without comment.
Course of dealing	Evidence about past contracts between the parties	Under prior contracts, goods have always been delivered to Buyer's dock.
Usage (or trade usage/usage of trade)	Custom or habitual practice (A *trade usage* is a custom or habitual practice regularly observed in a trade.)	In Buyer's and Seller's industry, shipped goods are routinely delivered to the buyer's dock.

Higher items in this chart take priority over lower items but should be interpreted as being consistent with each other whenever reasonable.

F. The Parol Evidence Rule

1. The Problem

Often, an agreement has been put in writing, but one party claims there was *also* an *earlier* oral or written agreement, or a *contemporaneous* oral agreement, that was not included in the writing but was intended to be part of the contract. In such cases, the admissibility of the alleged additional agreement turns on the applicability of the parol evidence rule.

2. The Rule

Stated simply, the parol evidence rule provides that parol evidence will not be admitted to *vary, add to, or contradict* a written contract that constitutes an integration. That formulation leaves open what constitutes an *integration* and what constitutes *parol evidence*. **[Hayden v. Hoadley,** 111 A. 343 (Vt. 1920)]

a. What Constitutes an "Integration"?

A written contract constitutes an "integration" if the parties to the contract intended the writing to be the final expression of at least some part of their agreement—*i.e.*, if the parties intended to integrate their agreement into the writing. There is substantial disagreement on how the courts should determine whether the parties had such an intention.

(1) Formal Intent Test

The traditional view was that a writing would be treated as an integration if, taken as a whole and *on its face*, the writing appears to be an instrument that expresses the parties' final agreement. "Intent" under this test is essentially a matter of form—*i.e.*, the question is whether the writing has the form of a final and comprehensive instrument. [70 A.L.R. 752; **Gianni v. R. Russel & Co.,** 126 A. 791 (Pa. 1924)] This view was associated with Professor Williston.

(2) Actual Intent Test

Today, many courts follow a competing test that is associated with Professor Corbin. Under this test, a writing is deemed to be an integration only if the parties actually *intended* it to be an integration. The court will consider *any* relevant evidence to determine the parties' intent. [**Masterson v. Sine,** 68 Cal. 2d 222 (1968); Rest. 2d § 209]

(3) Application of Competing Theories

The Williston "formal" test is a standardized and objective test based on the terms of the written contractual documents as understood by a reasonably intelligent person. This leads to a *broad* application of the parol evidence rule and consequently leads to the frequent exclusion of parol evidence. The Corbin "actual intent" test is an individualized test that requires the judge to determine the legal relations of the parties in accordance with their actual intentions, even when the forms—*i.e.*, writings—they employed suggest otherwise. This leads to a *narrower* application of the parol evidence rule and consequently leads to the more frequent admission of parol evidence. The tendency over the 1900s was for more courts to follow the Corbin view, but many cases still follow the Williston view.

EXAM TIP

In most courses, you need to be aware of both views of the parol evidence rule. As one court has put it, "It is unlikely that any jurisdiction will inflexibly adopt one approach to the exclusion of the other; each is likely to influence the conduct of judges and the disposition of cases." [**Interform Co. v. Mitchell,** 575 F.2d 1270, 1276 (9th Cir. 1978)]

(4) Merger Clauses

Many written contracts contain provisions stating that the written contract is the entire contract between the parties, or is the "final, complete, and exclusive statement of all the terms the parties have agreed upon," or the like. These kinds of provisions are known as "merger" clauses, because they say, in effect, that all agreements between the parties have been merged into the writing. In these cases, the written agreement itself purports to decide the question of whether it is an integration. The traditional approach, like the traditional (Williston) approach to the parol evidence rule itself, was that the presence of such a clause was determinative on the question of whether a writing was an integration—unless the clause was itself the result of fraud, mistake, or some comparable defense. This is probably still the majority rule, but modern courts sometimes say that a merger clause is only one factor in determining whether a writing was an integration.

b. What Constitutes Parol Evidence?

If there is a writing that is an integration, evidence of an alleged *earlier oral or written agreement* that is within the scope of the writing, or evidence of an alleged *contemporaneous oral agreement* that is within the scope of the writing, constitutes parol evidence. The alleged agreement that the parol evidence concerns may be referred to as the *parol agreement.* Parol evidence will be excluded if it would add to, vary, or contradict the written agreement.

EXAM TIP

Remember that a contract must be in **writing** for the parol evidence rule to apply. If the contract is oral, **any** prior or contemporaneous oral or written agreements may supplement or explain it.

---

(1) Definition of "Parol"

Parol simply means "oral." (It shares a root with "parable.") Note, however, that the parol evidence rule does not apply only to oral evidence. In the context of the parol evidence rule, "parol" refers to (1) oral or written agreements made prior to an integration and (2) oral agreements made at the same time (contemporaneously with) an integration.

(2) Admissibility of Evidence vs. Enforcement of Parol Agreement

The parol evidence rule does not just restrict the admission of evidence. Even if evidence of parol agreements is admitted into a trial for some other reason, the parol evidence rule may still render those agreements unenforceable as a matter of law.

3. Exceptions

The parol evidence rule is subject to a number of exceptions.

a. Separate Consideration

Even if a writing *is* determined to be an integration, parol evidence is admissible if the written integration and the alleged parol agreement are each supported by *separate consideration.*

b. Collateral Agreement

Parol evidence is often said to be admissible if the alleged parol agreement is *"collateral"* to (*i.e.,* related to the subject matter but not part of the primary promise of) the written integration and does not conflict with the integrated writing. This test is not very helpful, because a determination of whether the agreement was "collateral" is conclusory.

c. "Naturally Omitted" Consistent Terms

A widely accepted rule, adopted in the Restatement, is that parol evidence is admissible if it concerns a term that would *naturally be omitted* from the written agreement. Under the Restatement, a term will be treated as naturally omitted if:

(i) The term *does not conflict* with the written integration; *and*

(ii) Similarly situated parties would *not ordinarily be expected to include* the term in the written agreement.

[Rest. 1st § 240; *and see* Rest. 2d § 216]

(1) Two Approaches

The same approaches that are used to determine whether a writing is an integration (*see supra*, p. 119) are used to determine whether a parol agreement is one that would be naturally omitted from the writing.

(a) Williston Formal Approach

Under the Williston formal approach, the court does not give much weight to the individual circumstances of each particular case, but instead treats cases generically to determine whether an abstract reasonable person would naturally have omitted the term in question from the writing.

Example: The Mitchills and the Laths entered into a written agreement under which the Mitchills agreed to purchase the Laths' farm, which the Mitchills planned to make into a summer residence. The Laths also agreed, orally, that in connection with the purchase, and with no additional consideration, they would tear down an unsightly "ice house" across the road from the farm. The court took the Williston approach and held that evidence of the oral agreement was inadmissible because reasonable persons who made a written contract of the kind entered into by the Mitchills and the Laths, and who also made an oral agreement of the kind made by the Mitchills and the Laths, would not have naturally omitted the oral agreement from the writing. The court deemed it irrelevant that Mrs. Mitchill made the written contract while Mr. Mitchill made the oral agreement. [**Mitchill v. Lath,** 247 N.Y. 377 (1928)]

(b) Corbin Individualized Approach

Many modern courts follow the Corbin approach and give an expansive reading to the Restatement rule by taking into account all of the circumstances of the individual case to determine whether the ***actual parties*** (as opposed to abstract reasonable persons) might naturally have omitted the parol agreement from the writing.

Example: Dallas and Rebecca Masterson conveyed their ranch to Lu and Medora Sine by written deed. Medora was Dallas's sister. The deed provided that the Mastersons had an option to repurchase the ranch at a designated price. The parties orally agreed that the option was personal to the Mastersons (*i.e.*, the option could not be assigned or transferred to a third party). The court took the Corbin approach and held that evidence of this oral agreement was not barred by the parol evidence rule. In reaching this conclusion, the court took account of the particular circumstances of the case, rather than simply looking to what abstract reasonable persons would have done. For example, the court pointed to the difficulty of accommodating personal oral agreements on a formalized real-estate deed, and it noted that the transaction was between members of a family and that nothing indicated the parties were aware of the dangers of not putting the oral agreement into the deed. [**Masterson v. Sine,** *supra*, p. 119]

(c) Application of Competing Approaches

As with determining whether a written instrument constitutes an integration, application of the Williston approach to the question of whether terms might naturally be omitted leads to broad application of the parol evidence rule, and it consequently frequently leads to exclusion of parol evidence. Application of the Corbin approach leads to more frequent admission of parol evidence because the party who seeks to have the parol evidence admitted can often point to some special feature of their case that explains why, given all the particular circumstances, it was natural for the actual parties not to have included their separate parol agreement in their written agreement, even though abstract reasonable parties would have done so. Just as the tendency of modern courts is to focus on the parties' actual intent in determining whether a writing is an integration (*see supra*, p. 119), so too the tendency of modern courts is to take into account all the circumstances of a particular case to determine whether a parol agreement is one whose terms would naturally be omitted.

(2) Comment

The modern views concerning the "might naturally be omitted" test and the test to determine what constitutes an integrated contract result in courts being more ready to admit parol evidence than they were in the past. However, even under the modern Corbin approach, the rule still has a bite because, the judge, rather than the jury, determines (1) whether a writing is an integration and (2) if so, whether parties situated like the actual parties might naturally have made a separate parol agreement that was omitted from the integration. Furthermore, even though the long-run tendency may be toward weakening the parol evidence rule, the courts still regard the rule as important and apply it to bar parol evidence in many cases.

(3) U.C.C. Test—Consistent Additional Terms

The U.C.C. adopts an even more permissive view of parol evidence than the Restatement. Under the U.C.C., in contracts for the sale of goods, parol evidence of "additional consistent terms" is admissible unless the matter covered in the alleged parol agreement *"certainly would have been included"* in the written agreement. [U.C.C. § 2–202, comment 3 (emphasis added)]

(4) Inconsistent Terms

A parol agreement that is *inconsistent* with an integration does not fall within the "might naturally be omitted" test and therefore will be excluded. However, there are two views on what "inconsistent" means for these purposes.

(a) Logically Inconsistent Terms

Some courts essentially treat parol evidence as inconsistent only if it *logically contradicts* the integration. A way to test whether the parol agreement is logically inconsistent with the integration is to ask whether the integration would have been internally inconsistent if the parol agreement had been included in it. For example, if parties (1) enter into a written option agreement that does not specify any conditions on the exercise of the option, but (2) also make an oral agreement imposing a condition on the exercise of the option, the oral agreement would *not* be logically inconsistent with the writing, because if the condition had been specified in the writing, the writing would not have been internally inconsistent. [**Hunt Foods and Industries, Inc. v. Doliner,** 270 N.Y.S.2d 937 (1966)]

(b) Reasonably Harmonious Terms

Other courts, however, treat parol evidence as inconsistent with an integration if the parol evidence is not *reasonably harmonious* with the integration. For example, under this view, if a written contract gives a party a right of final approval of the price under the contract, and an oral agreement limits the party's right of approval, evidence of the oral agreement might be barred on the ground that it is not reasonably harmonious with the writing. [**Alaska Northern Development, Inc. v. Alyeska Pipeline Service Co.,** 666 P.2d 33 (Alaska 1983)]

d. **"Partial" (vs. "Complete") Integration**

A *complete* integration is a statement of the parties' *entire* agreement and bars parol evidence even of consistent, additional terms (on the premise that if the integration is the parties' *complete* agreement, there can be no further terms in the same contract). A merger clause [*supra*, p. 119] may lead a court to find that a document is a complete integration, but any other evidence of completeness (*e.g.*, how comprehensive the document appears to be) may be relevant. Even if a writing is not a *complete* integration, it may be a *partial* integration—*i.e.*, an integration of the **subjects actually covered** in the writing. A partial integration is controlling on those subjects that it covers, but it does not bar parol evidence on subjects that it does not cover. [Rest. 1st § 239; Rest. 2d §§ 210, 213, 216]

Example: *A* emails *B*, writing: "I'm glad we were able to come to an agreement by phone the other day. I look forward to working with you." *B* replies: "Likewise." This is a memorandum of an agreement but is not an integration because it does not serve as a final expression of the terms of the parties' deal. Neither reasonable persons nor the parties themselves would view those emails as intending to supplant the oral deal that the parties reached.

Compare: A 5-page agreement titled "Publication Agreement" is signed by both Author and Publisher. Its terms are somewhat detailed, but they all address printed copies of a particular book to be published. The document makes no mention of an electronic edition of the book, although the parties reached an oral agreement about such an electronic edition in the same meeting where they signed this agreement. The written agreement may be a partial integration. If so, it is sufficient to prevent terms that would contradict it (as to printed copies of Author's book) but not sufficient to prevent proof of additional, consistent terms about electronic editions (subject to the rules discussed *supra*, pp. 120–122).

Compare: The same agreement as above contains a merger clause, declares that the parties have no other agreements, and lists different terms for hardcover, paperback, and electronic editions of the book. The agreement is likely a complete integration.

(1) **Comment**

The distinction between partial and complete integrations is perhaps more theoretical than real. Even a complete integration is deemed to have a "scope," so there is a limit to the parol evidence it bars. [Rest. 2d § 213, comment c] As noted above, [*supra*, p. 120] even a complete integration does not rule out parol evidence of a separate or unrelated contract.

EXAM TIP

It may be easier to apply these rules if you focus on the parties' intent—either the objective intent under Williston's view or the actual intent under Corbin's view. Whether an integration is complete or partial, the main force of the parol evidence rule is to bar evidence of parol terms that the parties "intended" for the integration to bar.

e. Lack of Consideration

Parol evidence is always admissible to show a lack of consideration.

Example: Uncle and Nephew execute a written agreement stating that Uncle agrees to deliver his almost-new Toyota Camry to Nephew in exchange for $25,000, which Nephew has paid to Uncle. In fact, Nephew did not pay $25,000 to Uncle; the writing was only a way in which Uncle tried to make a binding donative promise to give Nephew the car. Uncle is allowed to show that the recital of consideration was false.

f. Fraud, Duress, or Mistake

Parol evidence is also admissible to show fraud, duress, or mistake. Furthermore, under the law of misrepresentation, a person who makes a promise that they have no intention of performing commits "promissory fraud." Applying this concept to the parol evidence rule, under the fraud exception it is usually permissible to introduce evidence that one of the parties entered into the parol agreement with no intention to perform it, as a means to induce the other party to enter into the written agreement.

g. Existence of a Condition Precedent to Legal Effectiveness of Written Agreement

The traditional rule has been that parol evidence is admissible to prove that there was a condition precedent (written or oral) to the *legal effectiveness* of a written agreement. **[Hicks v. Bush,** 10 N.Y.2d 488 (1962); **Pym v. Campbell,** 6 Ellis & Blackburn 370 (Q.B. 1856); Rest. 1st. § 241] Under this rule, however, that parol evidence was not admissible to prove that the parties previously added a condition to a promisor's obligation to render *performance* under a written contract whose legal effectiveness is not in question.

Example: Hicks and shareholders of Clinton G. Bush Co. ("Shareholders") sign a written instrument whereby they will merge their respective corporations into a single new holding company. The written instrument provides that Hicks will subscribe for 425,000 shares of stock in the new holding corporation, and Shareholders will subscribe for over 1 million shares. Shareholders do not perform, and Hicks brings suit. In response, Shareholders claim that the parties orally agreed that the written instrument was not to be legally effective as a contract until "equity expansion funds" of $675,000 had first been procured from third parties. The evidence is admissible because it concerns a condition to the legal effectiveness of the contract. **[Hicks v. Bush,** *supra*]

Compare: Same facts as in the last example, except that Shareholders do not allege that the instrument was not a legally effective contract, but instead allege only that the parties orally agreed that Shareholders' *duty to perform* under the contract was conditioned on third parties' contribution of $675,000 in new equity funds. This parol evidence is inadmissible. It does not fall within the "legal effectiveness" exception because the alleged parol agreement modifies an admitted legally effective contract by adding a condition to *performance* under the contract, rather than by showing that there was a condition to the writing becoming a *legally effective* contract.

(1) Criticism

The "legal effectiveness" exception has been inconsistently applied. [Rest. 2d § 217, comment b] As these two examples suggest, the exception is muddled because there is only a narrow and unclear line between (i) evidence of an agreement that a written instrument will not become *legally effective* unless a certain condition is fulfilled (which falls within the exception and is admissible) and (ii) evidence of an agreement that *performance under an admittedly effective contract* is subject to a condition (which does not fall within the exception and is not admissible).

h. Evidence to Explain or Interpret Terms of Written Agreement

The parol evidence rule does not bar admission of extrinsic evidence to show *what the parties meant* by the words used in their written agreement. The rationale of this exception is that such evidence *explains* the written agreement rather than adding to, varying, or contradicting it. To qualify under the exception, the evidence must not be in the form of a promise or agreement, but rather must be in the form of background discussion, surrounding circumstances, or the like.

(1) "Plain Meaning" Rule

Technically, extrinsic evidence concerning interpretation is not parol evidence at all, because it does not concern alleged parol *agreements,* but rather only extrinsic evidence *other than agreements*. However, such extrinsic evidence may be barred by the "plain meaning" rule (sometimes called the "four corners" rule). Under the plain meaning rule, if there is no ambiguity in a written contract on its face and no special meaning attached to the words of a written contract by custom or usage, the terms of the contract are to be interpreted only according to their "plain meaning," and extrinsic evidence is inadmissible either to interpret the contract or to establish that the contract is ambiguous so that extrinsic evidence should be admitted to clarify its meaning. The courts often lump together the plain meaning rule and the parol evidence rule, because both rules concern evidence that is outside a written agreement. (*See supra*, p. 120.)

(a) Modern Approach

Over the long run, there has been an increased tendency to allow extrinsic evidence to show what the parties intended by their words, even if the words apparently have a "plain meaning." *(See supra, p. 119.)*

Example: Repair Company agrees to "indemnify" Electric Company against "any injury to property" caused while Repair Company is repairing Electric Company's machinery. Extrinsic evidence is admissible to show that these words refer only to injury to the property of third persons, not injury to Electric Company's own property. [**Pacific Gas & Electric Co. v. G.W. Thomas Drayage & Rigging Co.,** *supra*, p. 116]

1) Limitation

The process of "interpretation" cannot be used to *contradict* the terms of the written instrument. Accordingly, parol evidence that bears on interpretation is admissible only if the interpretation does not contradict the words in the writing or, to put it differently, is an interpretation that the words in the writing *will bear*. However, what constitutes a contradiction is itself ambiguous. (*See supra*, p. 122.) Note also that with enough explanation and context, words can bear a wide range of meanings. (*Cf. supra*, p. 117.)

(2) Course of Performance, Course of Dealing, and Usage

Extrinsic evidence is also admissible to show any special meanings attached to words used in the written agreement deriving from course of performance, course of dealing, or usage. Over the long term, courts have been increasingly inclined to admit such evidence, even if it contradicts the *implications* that would otherwise be drawn from the writing, and sometimes even if the evidence seems to contradict the writing itself.

Example: Columbia and Royster formed a contract in which Royster agreed to sell phosphate to Columbia for fertilizer at a stated price and minimum quantity throughout the following three years. During that three-year period, phosphate prices plunged, and Columbia refused to buy the designated tonnage of phosphate from Royster. In a suit for breach, Columbia may introduce evidence of course of dealing and usage to show that the price and quantity terms were merely projections to be adjusted according to market forces. [**Columbia Nitrogen Corp. v. Royster Co.,** 451 F.2d 3 (4th Cir. 1971); *cf.* **Nanakuli Paving & Rock Co. v. Shell Oil Co.,** 664 F.2d 772 (9th Cir. 1981); *but see* **Southern Concrete Services, Inc. v. Mableton Contractors, Inc.,** 407 F. Supp. 581 (N.D. Ga. 1975)]

(a) Comment

Strictly speaking, evidence of course of dealing, course of performance, or trade usage is not parol evidence because it does not concern *agreements* between the parties. Furthermore, in contracts for the sale of goods, U.C.C. section 1-201(b)(3) defines "agreement" to mean "the bargain of the parties in fact, as found in their language or inferred from other circumstances, *including* course of performance, course of dealing, or usage of trade" (emphasis added). And U.C.C. section 1-303 requires courts to harmonize express terms with course of performance, course of dealing, and trade usage whenever reasonable. (*See supra*, p. 117) Literally, therefore, under the U.C.C. course of dealing, course of performance, and trade usage are not parol evidence outside the agreement but are *part* of the agreement. On this view, course of dealing, course of performance, and trade usage are admissible even if they *contradict* the writing. Courts have increasingly tended toward this view by admitting such evidence, at least if the evidence is not *logically inconsistent* with the explicit language of the agreement. However, some courts still view the admissibility of such evidence as an issue under the parol evidence rule and exclude such evidence on that ground if there is a lack of reasonable harmony between the course of dealing, course of performance, or trade usage (on one hand) and the writing (on the other).

(3) Filling in Gaps

(a) Traditional Approach

Under the traditional approach, if a written contract left a gap as to some term (*e.g.*, time of performance), evidence would be admitted on the issue of what was a *reasonable term* for the court to imply, but parol evidence was not admissible to show that the parties had *actually reached an agreement* concerning the subject matter of the gap. [**Hayden v. Hoadley,** *supra*, p. 118]

(b) Modern Approach

Modern courts are increasingly inclined to admit parol evidence of agreements concerning gaps under the "interpretation" exception to the parol evidence rule as long as the evidence does not squarely contradict the contract language. Some cases admit parol evidence even though the evidence contradicts the implication of law that would be drawn in the absence of the parol evidence. For example, in **Masterson v. Sine,** *supra*, p. 119, parol evidence was held admissible to show that the parties had made an agreement that an option was intended to be exercised only by the optionee, even though in the absence of such evidence the normal rule is that the right to exercise an option is freely assignable.

i. Modifications

A *later* oral agreement that modifies a ***previously existing*** written contract does ***not*** fall within the parol evidence rule, because the modification is subsequent to, rather than prior to or contemporaneous with, the written agreement. Therefore, the fact that a modification is oral does not make it unenforceable under the parol evidence rule.

(1) Consideration

Of course, such an agreement still needs consideration to be enforceable (except in contracts for the sale of goods; *see supra*, p. 29).

(2) Statute of Frauds

Furthermore, even if a modification is not invalid for lack of consideration, it must still comply with any applicable provision of the Statute of Frauds (*see infra*, p. 162 *et seq.*).

(3) Contractual Requirement of a Writing—"No Oral Modification" Clauses

In some cases, a written contract contains a provision requiring that any modification of the contract be in writing. This is sometimes called a "no oral modification clause." Under common law, such provisions are not normally given effect; that is, an oral modification of a contract containing such a provision is normally enforceable at common law if the modification is otherwise legally enforceable (*i.e.*, if the modification has consideration, need not be in writing under the Statute of Frauds, is not made under duress, etc.). [**Teer v. George A. Fuller Co.,** 30 F.2d 30 (4th Cir. 1929)]

(a) Rationale

The rationale for not giving effect to such a provision at common law is that if the modification has consideration, it is a new contract, and the new contract implicitly includes a mutual agreement to abandon the requirement of a writing set out in the old contract.

(b) U.C.C.

Under U.C.C. section 2–209(2), in the case of a contract for the sale of goods, if the original contract excludes modification or rescission other than by a signed writing, then a modification or rescission must be in writing.

1) Waiver

However, U.C.C. section 2–209(4) provides that an oral modification of a contract for the sale of goods that is unenforceable because it is required to be in writing, either under the Statute of Frauds or under a provision of the original contract, can still "operate as a ***waiver***."

2) Retraction of Waiver

The issue of whether the waiver can be *retracted* then arises. According to U.C.C. section 2–209(5), a party who has made a waiver affecting an *executory* (*i.e.*, not yet performed) portion of a contract may retract the waiver if they reasonably notify the other party that strict performance of the waived terms is once again required. However, the party may not retract their waiver if it would be unjust in view of a material change of position in reliance on the waiver by the other party. U.C.C. section 2–209(5) does not explicitly address whether a waiver that concerns an *executed* (*i.e.*, previously performed) portion of a contract can be retracted. The courts have divided on that issue. [*Compare* **Wisconsin Knife Works v. National Metal Crafters,** 781 F.2d 1280 (7th Cir. 1986)—a waiver can be retracted under U.C.C. section 2–209 unless it has been relied upon; *with* **Getty Terminals Corp. v. Coastal Oil New England, Inc.,** 995 F.2d 372 (2d Cir. 1993)—a waiver can be retracted under U.C.C. section 2–209 only insofar as the waiver affects the unperformed portion of a contract, and even then only on timely notice of retraction]

EXAM TIP

Remember that the parol evidence rule bars evidence only of agreements made ***prior to or contemporaneous with*** the final integration. If the facts in an exam question indicate that an agreement was made ***after*** the final integration, the agreement is a ***modification*** of the final integration and is ***not*** subject to the parol evidence rule. Instead, you should make sure that the modification is supported by consideration, that there are no Statute of Frauds defenses, etc.

(c) Other Statutes

Occasionally state statutes give effect to "no oral modification" clauses even in cases to which the U.C.C. does not apply. [*See* Cal. Civ. Code. § 1698(c); N.Y. Gen. Oblig. Law § 15–301]

SUMMARY OF PAROL EVIDENCE RULE

GENERAL RULE: PAROL EVIDENCE IS *NOT ALLOWED* IF:

☑ There is a ***written agreement*** that serves as an ***integration*** (a record that the parties intended to serve as a final expression of at least some part of their agreement);

AND:

☑ The offered parol evidence is of an ***earlier written or oral*** agreement ***or*** a ***contemporaneous oral*** agreement within the scope of the integration;

AND:

At least one of the following is true:

☑ The offered parol evidence would ***vary or contradict*** the terms of the integration.

OR:

☑ The integration is ***complete***.

OR:
☑ The offered parol agreement is one that the parties would *not* have *"naturally omitted"* from the integration.
EXCEPTIONS: PAROL EVIDENCE *MAY BE ADMISSIBLE* IF:
☑ Offered to show *lack of consideration*;   OR:
☑ Offered to show *fraud, duress, or mistake*;   OR:
☑ Offered to show a *condition precedent to effectiveness* of the final contract;   OR:
☑ Offered to *explain or interpret* terms of the contract;   OR:
☑ It concerns a *modification* of the contract (*i.e.*, later agreement);   OR:
☑ *Separate consideration* was given for the parol agreement.

G. "Shrinkwrap" Contracts

In modern commerce, a customer commonly buys a sealed box that contains not only a product but also some purported contract terms inside the box—usually terms that purport to limit the customer's rights. These contracts are often called "shrinkwrap" contracts because the purported contract terms are inside the product's plastic wrap and are unavailable until the customer opens the box, which they cannot ordinarily do until after making the purchase. A similar situation arises when a customer orders a product online and receives purported contractual terms later, along with the product. These situations are similar to the "battle of the forms" (*see supra*, p. 71 *et seq.*), except there is only one form: the seller's. Although contracts like this often involve sales of goods and are thus governed by Article 2 of the U.C.C., the U.C.C. does not specifically address this contracting pattern, so courts have needed to develop rules to address it.

1. Contract Terms Available Only After Initial Formation

The general question in shrinkwrap cases is whether the terms inside the box bind the customer—*i.e.*, are they part of the contract even though the customer had no chance to read them at the time of the purchase? In a controversial and widely discussed pair of cases, the Seventh Circuit held that terms inside the box bound the buyer, at least if the buyer had an opportunity to review the terms and to return the product if the buyer sought to reject the terms. [**Hill v. Gateway 2000**, 105 F.3d 1147 (7th Cir. 1997); **ProCD, Inc. v. Zeidenberg**, 86 F.3d 1447 (7th Cir. 1996)] Some courts have required that, for such proposed terms to be enforceable, the seller must put a reasonable buyer on notice of the proposed terms—and on notice that the proposed terms are contractual in the first place. [**Norcia v. Samsung Telecommunications America, LLC**, 845 F.3d 1279 (9th Cir. 2017)—a brochure inside a box titled "Product Safety & Warranty Information" was insufficient to make the contents of the brochure part of the contract]

2. Form Terms—Unconscionability and Unfair Surprise

Even if a buyer is deemed to assent to a collection of shrinkwrap terms in general, the buyer may have a defense to particular terms if those terms are unconscionable or unfairly surprising. (*See infra*, p. 158.)

Example: A consumer buys a cell phone online and receives in the mail a box that contains the phone, a power cord, and a 20-page brochure labeled "**IMPORTANT: Contract Terms—Please Read. Your use of this phone constitutes your acceptance to these terms.**" The consumer keeps the phone and doesn't read the terms. Most of the terms in the brochure are routine terms about warranty coverage, forum selection, etc. Those terms are probably enforceable. One of the terms, however, listed in fine print in the middle of the document, purports to require the consumer to buy their next two phones from the same manufacturer. This term is unenforceable (*see infra*, p. 158).

H. Online Contracting

1. Electronic Agents in General

Under the Uniform Electronic Transactions Act (U.E.T.A.), contracts may be formed online or by any other electronic means. Any electronic communication—an email or even a text message or a voicemail—can count as a writing (*e.g.*, for the purposes of the parol evidence rule, *supra*, p. 118 *et seq.*) or a signature (*e.g.*, for the purposes of the Statute of Frauds, *infra*, p. 168 *et seq.*). Assuming the other elements of contract formation have been met, contracts can be formed between a computer and a person (as when a customer visits a website) or even between two computers (as when companies arrange for goods, securities, etc., to be exchanged between them automatically).

Example: Two law students agree through text messages to sell a set of used 1L textbooks for $520. This is a valid contract and is capable of satisfying the requirement in the Statute of Frauds for a signed writing (*infra*, p. 168 *et seq.*).

Example: Businessperson, who runs a sole proprietorship, works toward selling all their business's assets to BuyCo by negotiating, over email, an "Acquisition Agreement." The final version of this document is 14 pages long and covers many details. BuyCo's CEO prints out the document, signs it with a pen, scans the paper using a scanner, and sends the result as a PDF file attached to an email to Businessperson. Businessperson adds an electronic image of their signature to the PDF and returns the modified file by email. The parties have a contract, and the electronic document can be an integration for the purposes of the parol evidence rule (*supra*, p. 118 *et seq*).

2. "Clickwrap" Agreements

A common way for contracts to be formed is for a person to click a button that reads "I Agree" (or something similar) on a website or mobile app. These cases are commonly called "clickwrap" contracts, by analogy to "shrinkwrap contracts" (*supra*, p. 129). Often, clicking "I Agree" or "Confirm" or a similar button is sufficient to manifest assent to a contract, because the website is set up to indicate that a contract is contemplated and gives the user an opportunity to review terms and decide whether to proceed. The user has made a contract even if—as is typical, of course—they have not read the terms. If particular terms of the contract are unconscionable or unfairly surprising, however, the user may have a defense against those terms. (*See infra*, p. 158.)

Example: Reader visits Newspaper's website and sees that Newspaper has an online crossword puzzle that is available only to users who pay for a subscription. Reader clicks a button labeled "Subscribe," and Newspaper's website presents a list of terms that the reader can scroll through. At the bottom of the terms, there is a checkbox labeled "I accept these terms and conditions," followed by a space for Reader to enter credit-card information. Reader checks the box and enters this information. Finally, Reader presses a button labeled "Pay Now." Newspaper has offered, and Reader has accepted, a contract. Legally, the situation is indistinguishable from one in which Reader is given a form contract to sign at a sales counter. As to the enforceability of any terms that are unconscionable or unfairly surprising, see *infra*, p. 158.

3. "Browsewrap" Agreements

a. In General

Contract formation is considerably more controversial when a website purports to bind a visitor just because (i) the website contains "Terms and Conditions" or similar information, perhaps linked from the bottom of the homepage or otherwise discoverable by the visitor, and (ii) the visitor has continued to use the website, made a purchase on it, or done something else that, according to the owner of the website, ***implicitly*** manifests assent to the terms. This situation is commonly called a "browsewrap agreement," by analogy to "shrinkwrap agreement" (*supra*, p. 129). These cases differ from clickwrap agreements (*supra*) because the visitor has ***not*** clicked an "I Agree" (or similar) button.

Example: Same facts as in the previous example, but the website does not show its proposed terms on the page where Reader makes a purchase. Instead, the terms are available through a link on the bottom of the website's homepage labeled "Terms and Conditions." When Reader clicks "Subscribe," Newspaper's website simply presents general information about subscription options (*e.g.*, "1 year for $12; 2 years for $20"), permits a general choice among these options, and provides an opportunity to enter credit-card information. The terms on the "Terms and Conditions" page are purported *browsewrap* terms, and their enforcement is controversial.

Example: Max visit Newspaper's website to read the local news. "Terms and Conditions" are available through a link on the bottom of the website. This is a purported *browsewrap contract*, and enforcement of the terms is controversial.

Compare: Max attempts to read the news on Newspaper's website, but the website does not permit him to read anything more than headlines until he creates a free account. Creating an account requires that he enter his name, email address, and age in several boxes. Under those boxes, there is a scrollable window that contains 20 paragraphs of "Terms and Conditions," followed by a button that says "Agree to Terms and Create Account." This is a *clickwrap agreement* and is likely enforceable, subject to the usual defenses against standardized form terms.

b. Notice and Contractual Context Required—Website Design May Be Significant

Caselaw is mixed on browsewrap agreements. One problem in these cases is that the visitor to a website may not know that a contract was even on the table. Accordingly, one question that has been important to some courts is whether a reasonable website visitor would have been put on notice that they were agreeing to contract terms. [*See* **Nguyen v. Barnes & Noble Inc.,** 763 F.3d 1171 (9th Cir. 2014); **Specht v. Netscape Communications Corp.,** 306 F.3d 17 (2d Cir. 2002)] Some authorities analogize these situations to older cases where purported contract terms were included on a token or ticket that did not put customers on notice that a contract was involved. [*Cf.* Rest. 2d § 211, comment d]

EXAM TIP	

For questions involving potential browsewrap contracts, pay attention to details about the precise placement and appearance of "Terms and Conditions" links and other purported contractual terms. Some court opinions literally include annotated screenshots of the website at issue in the case. [*E.g.*, **Vitacost.com, Inc. v. McCants,** 210 So. 3d 761 (Fla. Dist. Ct. App. 2017)] As a leading treatise puts it: "The cases suggest that . . . the website owner must involve legal counsel not just in drafting the terms of use but in advising about the design and content of the webpage to insure that the user will be on inquiry notice of the terms . . . ." [1 Corbin on Contracts § 2.12 (2019)]

c. Form Terms—Unconscionability and Unfair Surprise

As with shrinkwrap and clickwrap agreements, even if a contract is formed, the website visitor may have a defense to particular standardized terms if those terms are unconscionable or unfairly surprising. (*See infra*, p. 158.)

Chapter Three
Defenses

CONTENTS	PAGE
Chapter Approach	134
A. **Indefiniteness**	135
B. **Mistake**	147
C. **Contracts Induced by Misrepresentation, Nondisclosure, Duress, or Undue Influence**	154
D. **Unconscionability**	157
E. **Statute of Frauds**	162
F. **Lack of Contractual Capacity**	172
G. **Illegal Contracts**	174

Chapter Approach

After you determine that a contract has been formed, you must next determine whether the contract is unenforceable by reason of some *defense* related to the *formation* of the contract. (Defenses concerning the *performance* of the contract will be considered in Chapter 5.) The most important of these defenses are indefiniteness, mistake, misrepresentation, nondisclosure, duress, undue influence, unconscionability, the Statute of Frauds, lack of capacity, and illegality.

1. **Indefiniteness**

    For a bargain to be enforceable, its terms must be sufficiently definite to (i) evidence that the parties have concluded a deal (rather than that they merely engaged in preliminary negotiations) and (ii) enable the court to determine the terms of the bargain with sufficient certainty to fashion a remedy for breach. If you see a question that involves a bargain in which the parties have failed to specify price, quantity, or payment terms, or have stated that a formal contract will follow, you should always consider the defense of indefiniteness. You must also be aware, however, that often courts will fill in gaps in contracts, so a contract that has gaps will not necessarily fail on the ground that it is too indefinite. If the contract is for the sale of goods, it will fall within the U.C.C., which includes a number of "gap filler" provisions, including for such terms as price.

2. **Mistake**

    Whenever a question involves a promise that is made under some kind of false impression, other than one induced by misrepresentation or nondisclosure, there is likely to be an issue of mistake. These issues fall into five categories:

    a. A *mutual mistake* occurs when the parties made a contract under a *shared* mistake concerning a *basic assumption of fact* on which the contract was made. In such cases, the adversely affected party is normally entitled to rescission (*i.e.*, cancellation of the contract) *unless* they bore the risk of the mistake.

    b. A *unilateral mistake* occurs when something goes wrong with the mental machinery of *one* of the parties, as when one of them makes a typo or a mistake in computation (as distinct from a judgment about risk or value). Such a mistake is a ground for rescission by the mistaken party if the nonmistaken party *knew or should have known* of the mistake, so that the mistake was "palpable." Some courts hold that even if a unilateral mistake is *not* palpable, the mistaken party is liable only for reliance (rather than expectation) damages.

    c. A *mistranscription* occurs when an error was made in transcribing an oral agreement into writing. In such cases, either party is entitled to have the writing corrected through the remedy of *reformation.*

    d. A *misunderstanding* occurs when (i) the parties made a contract under the mistaken impression that their language was unambiguous, when in fact it was ambiguous; (ii) each party gave the language a different interpretation; and (iii) each party's interpretation was equally reasonable. (*See supra*, p. 114.) In such cases, the general rule is that neither party is liable.

    e. A *mistake in transmission* occurs where an intermediary, such as an interpreter, makes an error in transmitting an offer or acceptance. Normally, if the recipient *knew or should have known* of the error, there is no contract. If the recipient did not know of the error (and had no reason to know), under the majority rule a contract is formed using the intermediary's terms.

3. **Misrepresentation, Nondisclosure, Duress, Undue Influence**

   In some cases, a party acts under a mistaken impression as a result of the other party's fraud or nondisclosure. *Fraudulent or material misrepresentation* is *always* a defense. *Nondisclosure* is normally *not* a defense unless the parties were in a relation of trust or confidence or under certain other limited circumstances. A contract is voidable on the basis of *duress* if consent was induced by wrongful threats. *Undue influence* is unfair persuasion of a party who is under the domination of the person exercising the persuasion, or who by virtue of the relation between them is justified in assuming that that person will not act in a manner inconsistent with their welfare. If a party's assent is induced by the undue influence by the other party, the contract is voidable by the victim.

4. **Unconscionability**

   A contract may also be unenforceable on the ground of unconscionability. Although a contract may be deemed unconscionable because it is grossly lopsided, most unconscionability problems involve *unfairness in the bargaining process,* such as the use of a form contract that contains unfairly surprising terms (terms that a reasonable person would not expect, or that are not written clearly). Be especially aware of unconscionability issues in any question that involves a standard form contract.

5. **Statute of Frauds**

   Always note whether the contract in question is in writing. If the contract *is* in writing, the question may raise a parol evidence rule problem. (*See supra*, p. 118 *et seq.*) If the contract is *not* in writing, you must ask yourself whether the contract falls within the Statute of Frauds. In particular:

   a. Is the contract for the sale of an *interest in land*?

   b. Is the contract for the *sale of goods* at a price of *$500 or more*?

   c. Is the contract in c*onsideration of marriage*?

   d. By its terms, can the contract *not be performed within one year* of the making of the contract?

   e. Is the contract one of *suretyship*?

   If the contract falls into one of these categories and is not in writing, it is unenforceable unless (i) there is a written memorandum signed by the party against whom enforcement of the contract is sought or (ii) it is "taken out" of the Statute of Frauds by an appropriate exception, like part performance or reliance.

6. **Lack of Capacity**

   If a party to an agreement lacks capacity to contract, the resulting agreement may be voidable. Capacity issues may arise in contracts with either a minor or a person who is suffering from a permanent or temporary mental incapacity.

7. **Illegality**

   A contract is unenforceable if it is illegal.

A. Indefiniteness

1. General Rule

An apparent bargain will *not* be enforced if it is found to be too indefinite. An apparent bargain will be found to be too indefinite if either (i) its terms are so incomplete or uncertain that they show that the *parties* did not regard themselves as having completed a contract or (ii) even if it seems that the parties regarded themselves as having completed a contract, it is so indefinite that a *court* cannot determine its material terms with reasonable certainty or fashion an appropriate remedy for breach.

a. Implication of Terms

The mere fact that an agreement leaves gaps does not render it fatally indefinite; almost all contracts leave some gaps that the court can fill through the process of ***implication.***

Example: An agreement to convey title to a specific parcel of land is not too indefinite, even though the agreement makes no mention of the *quality* of title to be conveyed. The courts will hold that there was an implied promise to convey "marketable" title.

Example: Similarly, an agreement to paint a house usually will not be rendered too indefinite merely because it sets no time for completion. A "reasonable time" for completion is implied.

Compare: However, an agreement to build "a house," where no plans or specifications are given, normally would be too indefinite to be enforced: "Reasonable" plans cannot be implied. [*See* **Stanton v. Dennis,** 116 P. 650 (Wash. 1911)] Therefore, the courts normally would not have a sound basis for determining what constitutes a "house" for purposes of a given contract.

(Even here, however, the result might be different if there *were* a basis for such a determination—*e.g.*, if the house was to be one of a number of tract houses that are all virtually identical.) [*See* **City Stores Co. v. Ammerman,** 266 F. Supp. 766 (D.D.C. 1967), *aff'd,* 394 F.2d 950 (D.C. Cir. 1968)]

b. Part Performance

As a practical matter, what constitutes sufficient definiteness is a question of judgment. One factor that often affects this judgment is whether the contract has been partly performed. Generally speaking, a court might enforce a contract that has been partly performed even though the court might have held the same contract too indefinite if the contract had not been partly performed. (*See infra*, p. 141.)

2. Examples of Recurring Types of Omissions

a. Price

(1) Omission of Price

Under the older cases, a gap as to price was usually fatal, on the theory that courts could not infer what price the parties intended. However, under many modern cases and the U.C.C. (*see infra*, p. 139), if the contract is ***totally silent*** as to price, a reasonable price can be supplied by the court *if* the court is satisfied that the parties intended to conclude a contract and there is some objective standard (*e.g.*, fair market value) for determining a reasonable price. [**Bendalin v. Delgado,** 406 S.W.2d 897 (Tex. 1966); *see infra*, p. 142 *et seq.*]

(a) Intent to Conclude a Contract

Even under the modern trend, a court will not enforce the bargain unless the court determines that the parties ***intended*** to conclude a contract. The omission of price may be deemed evidence that the parties were still in preliminary negotiation. [**Western Homes, Inc. v. Herbert Ketell, Inc.,** 236 Cal, App. 2d 142 (1965)]

(2) Indefinite Standard Provided by Parties

If the parties attempt to define the price through a standard that is itself indefinite, the traditional approach is to refuse enforcement on the ground that in such cases it cannot be inferred that the parties intended a "reasonable price." [**Walker v. Keith,** 382 S.W.2d 198 (Ky. 1964)]

Example: A proposal to furnish services at cost "plus a fair profit" would be unenforceable for indefiniteness under the traditional approach, because a court cannot determine either what is an objectively fair profit or what profit the parties would have intended as fair. [**Gaines & Sea v. R.J. Reynolds Tobacco Co.,** 174 S.W. 482 (Ky. 1915)]

(a) Modern Trend

Under the U.C.C., such an agreement would probably be enforced using the standard of "a reasonable price at the time of delivery." [U.C.C. § 2–305(1); *see infra* p. 139, 143] Furthermore, at least some modern courts might be willing to enforce such an agreement, even if it does not fall under the U.C.C., if the parties had intended to conclude a contract (*see infra*, p. 143).

b. Time for Performance

(1) General Rule—Reasonable Time Implied

A gap as to time of performance is rarely fatal. Instead, the courts will usually fill the gap by holding that performance of the contract within a *reasonable time* was implied. [**Automatic Sprinkler Co. v. Sherman,** 294 F. 533 (5th Cir. 1923)]

(a) Test of Reasonableness

What is a reasonable time will depend on the nature of the contract, custom and usage in the community, and prior dealings between the parties.

(2) Special Cases

(a) Employment Contracts—"at Will" Doctrine

In an employment contract whose duration is not specified, the usual rule (perhaps more accurately, the presumption) is that the contract is ***terminable at will*** by either party. [**Atchison, Topeka & Santa Fe Railway v. Andrews,** 211 F.2d 264 (10th Cir. 1954)]

1) Rationale

Employment involves personal relationships, and it may be objectionable to treat either party as bound to continue in such a relationship against their will unless the parties have so provided.

2) Stated Pay Period Not Controlling

A statement of a pay period does not change the usual rule; *i.e.*, the fact that the employee's salary or other compensation is payable weekly, monthly, or annually does not mean that the employment is to last that long. Instead, such a statement is deemed only to set the employee's frequency of pay while the employment continues.

3) Agreement for "Permanent" Employment

Even agreements for a "permanent" job or employment "for life" or employment "for so long as the employee chooses" are usually interpreted to be *terminable at the will of either party*. [35 A.L.R. 1432; **Ruinello v. Murray,** 36 Cal. 2d 687 (1951)]

a) Note

There are cases in which an agreement for "permanent" employment (or any other indefinite period) will be interpreted literally. These are usually cases in which either (i) the agreement *specifically limits* the employer's power to fire the employee (*e.g.*, "permanent employment except in case of improper performance by employee") or (ii) the *circumstances clearly indicate* that the parties really did have permanent employment in mind (*e.g.*, the employee takes a very low salary in early years with the promise of a significant share of the profits in later years if the business is successful, or the employee releases a claim against the employer in exchange for the promise of permanent employment). [**Drzewiecki v. H & R Block, Inc.,** 24 Cal. App. 3d 695 (1972)]

4) Employee Handbooks

Large employers often issue employee handbooks that include material on employment security. For example, a handbook may provide that employees will not be discharged without good cause or will discharged only if they previously have been reprimanded or if certain grievance procedures have been followed. The *majority rule* is that statements of this sort in employee handbooks are *enforceable* promises and therefore overcome the presumption that employment is at will in the absence of a contract for a specific term. [*See, e.g.*, **Pine River State Bank v. Mettille,** 333 N.W.2d 622 (Minn. 1983)] However, courts in some states have held that employee handbooks will not be accorded this kind of contractual status. [*See, e.g.*, **Heideck v. Kent General Hospital, Inc.,** 446 A.2d 1095 (Del. 1982)]

5) Other Factors

Even in the absence of an employee handbook, the doctrine that employment is at will in the absence of a contract for a specific term can be overcome by evidence of contrary intent. This evidence may take the form of an *express* oral promise by the employer (*e.g.*, an express promise that employment will be terminated only for cause). Alternatively, the at will doctrine may be overcome by *implication* from other factors, including the personnel policies or practices of the employer, the employee's longevity of service, actions or communications by the employer reflecting assurances of continued employment, and the practices of the industry in which the employee is engaged. [**Foley v. Interactive Data Corp.,** 47 Cal. 3d 654 (1988)]

a) Comment

Because the at will doctrine is relatively entrenched, not all courts may be ready to find that the doctrine is overcome by an implied, as opposed to an express, promise. Indeed, as pointed out above, traditionally agreements that expressly provided that employment would be "permanent" or "for life" or the like were usually interpreted to be terminable at will.

(b) Distributorship and Franchise Contracts

When the duration of a distributorship or franchise contract is left open (*e.g.*, Manufacturer *A* appoints *B* to be its exclusive sales representative, but no period of time is specified or indicated), the law implies that the contract will last a *"reasonable"* time, which is often interpreted to be the time it will take for the distributor to recover their investment. [**Allied Equipment Co. v. Weber Engineered Products,** 237 F.2d 879 (4th Cir. 1956)]

3. U.C.C. Provisions

In contracts for the sale of goods, the U.C.C. contains rules that enforce contracts even when they are characterized by a significant amount of indefiniteness. The U.C.C. also includes a number of "gap filler" provisions. To begin with, U.C.C. section 2–204(3) provides that "even though one or more terms are left open, a contract for [the sale of goods] does not fail for indefiniteness if the parties have intended to make a contract and there is a reasonably certain basis for giving an appropriate remedy."

a. Gap Fillers

Other sections of the U.C.C. fill gaps by providing designated terms that govern if there is a certain type of gap, or by providing how a certain kind of gap should be filled. *Note:* The U.C.C. does *not* contain a gap filler on the *quantity* of goods to be sold.

(1) Price

Under U.C.C. section 2–305(1), if the parties *so intend* they can conclude a contract for sale even though the price is not settled. In such a case, the price is a *reasonable price at the time for delivery* if: (i) nothing has been said as to price, (ii) the price is left to be agreed upon by the parties and they fail to agree, *or* (iii) the price is to be fixed in terms of some standard set by a third person or agency (such as a market), and it is not so set.

(a) Note

If the parties *intend not to be bound* unless the price is fixed or agreed upon, and the price is not fixed or agreed upon, then there is no contract. In such cases: (i) the buyer must return any goods already received or, if unable to do so, must pay the reasonable value of the goods at the time of delivery, and (ii) the seller must return any portion of the price paid on account. [U.C.C. § 2–305(4)]

Example: Joe agrees to buy from Marilyn a rare sculpture of ancient Greek origin, with Arturo, the preeminent expert on ancient Greek sculptures, to set the price. Arturo refuses to do so. The parties probably intended to be bound only if Arturo fixed the price. Therefore, there is no contract after Arturo's refusal.

(2) Place of Delivery

Under U.C.C. section 2–308, if the place of delivery for goods is not specified, the place of delivery is the *seller's place of business*. (However, in the case of identified goods that the parties know are in some other place, that other place is the place of delivery.)

(3) Time for Shipment or Delivery

Under U.C.C. section 2–309, if the time for shipment or delivery is not specified, delivery is due in a *reasonable time*.

(4) Time for Payment

Under U.C.C. section 2–310, if the time for payment is not specified, payment is due at the time and place at which the buyer is to *receive* the goods.

(5) Duration of Contract

Under U.C.C. section 2–309, if a contract provides for successive performances but is indefinite in duration, the contract is valid for a **reasonable time,** but either party may terminate the contract at any time unless otherwise agreed.

(6) Effect of Gap Filler Provisions

In summary, under the U.C.C., in theory a bargain may be enforceable even though it omits the price, the place of delivery, the time for shipment or delivery, the time for payment, and the duration of the contract. Remember, however, that the U.C.C. gap filler provisions are applicable only "if the parties have intended to make a contract and there is a reasonably certain basis for giving an appropriate remedy" (*supra*, p. 139). If too many terms are missing, the court may conclude that the parties did **not** intend to make a contract but rather that they were engaged only in preliminary negotiations.

U.C.C. GAP FILLERS — GILBERT

A CONTRACT GOVERNED BY THE U.C.C. WILL NOT FAIL FOR INDEFINITENESS IF THE PARTIES *INTENDED* TO MAKE A CONTRACT AND THERE IS A REASONABLE BASIS FOR GIVING AN APPROPRIATE *REMEDY*. THE CONTRACT *MUST SPECIFY THE QUANTITY* OF GOODS INVOLVED, BUT THE U.C.C. PROVIDES THE FOLLOWING "GAP FILLER" PROVISIONS FOR OTHER CONTRACT TERMS:

PRICE	Reasonable price at the time of delivery
PLACE OF DELIVERY	Delivery at the seller's place of business (or the place where identified goods known to be in another place are located)
TIME FOR SHIPMENT OR DELIVERY	Shipment or delivery within a reasonable time
TIME AND PLACE FOR PAYMENT	Due at the time and place where the buyer is to receive the goods

DURATION OF CONTRACT REQUIRING SUCCESSIVE PERFORMANCES	Contract is valid for a reasonable time (but the parties may terminate the contract at any time unless otherwise agreed)

4. Modern Trend Toward Increased Enforcement of Indefinite Contracts

Modern authorities are beginning to apply the U.C.C. approach, above, to contracts generally (rather than only to contracts for the sale of goods). Under this trend, courts that believe the parties intended to make a contract are generally more willing to supply reasonable terms to fill the gaps than they were in the past. The trend is reflected in Restatement Second, which provides: "As a standard of reasonable certainty, it is enough if the terms provide a basis for determining the existence of a breach and for giving an appropriate remedy." [Rest. 2d § 33]

EXAM TIP

Watch out for agreements missing more than one material term (*e.g.*, a contract lacking a price term, the duration of performance, and the location of performance). Although under both the common law and the U.C.C. the court can fill some contract gaps through implication, an agreement must contain enough terms to show that the parties *intended to make a contract.*

5. Indefiniteness Cured by Part Performance

An agreement that would otherwise not be enforced because it is too indefinite may be enforced if the parties have *begun performance*. [**Bettancourt v. Gilroy Theatre Co.,** 120 Cal. App. 2d 364 (1953)]

Example: An agreement between Seller and Buyer that Seller will sell Buyer 500 bushels of beans per month at $2 a bushel for 12 months may be fatally indefinite if Seller has many types of beans for sale, because there is no indication of grade, type, and quality. But if Seller subsequently sends, and Buyer accepts, several deliveries of No. 4 red pinto beans, this part performance identifies the subject matter of the contract and therefore supplies the requisite degree of certainty. [*See* **Brown-Crummer Investment Co. v. Arkansas City,** 266 P. 60 (Kan. 1928)]

a. Rationale

Enforcement of indefinite agreements on the basis of part performance generally rests on one or more of the following theories:

(1) Part performance pursuant to the agreement shows that the parties believed they had completed a contract and were not still in preliminary negotiations;

(2) The greater the extent to which performance has already occurred, the more unjust it is to let one of the parties off the hook, and therefore the more ready the court will be to supply missing terms; and

(3) Performance may fill a gap left in the contract by showing what the parties believed the relevant term was.

6. Bargains Capable of Being Made Certain

In some cases, the parties do not fix a material term in the contract, but they do set a method for fixing the term. Such a bargain is enforceable if it makes reference to an ***objective standard*** that is to be used to fix the missing term.

a. Standards for Determining Price

For example, bargains in which *A* agrees to sell to *B* at a price "as then quoted on the grain exchange" or "the same as that in the Ajax Co. contract" are enforceable. [**Kladivo v. Melberg,** 227 N.W. 833 (Iowa 1930)]

b. Output and Requirements Contracts

A bargain in which *A* agrees to supply *B* with "all your requirements of coal" or to sell *B* "the entire output of my plant" is sufficiently certain. Both "requirements" and "output" may be objectively determined. [**Twin City Pipe Line Co. v. Harding Glass Co.,** 283 U.S. 353 (1931)]

(1) Caveat

See supra, p. 22, concerning the interpretation of such a contract.

c. Custom or Usage

Terms may also be rendered certain by reference to local custom or usage. For example, an offer to execute a conveyance "in the usual form" is sufficiently certain. In such a case, the standard is the type of conveyance that is usual in the community. [**Bondy v. Harvey,** 62 F.2d 521 (2d Cir. 1933)]

7. "Agreements to Agree"

Frequently, parties make an agreement in which they explicitly reserve some essential term to be determined in the future, not by reference to an objective standard, but by their future agreement. Such an agreement is known as "an agreement to agree." If the term involved is material, the traditional rule is that the agreement is unenforceable; *i.e.*, such an agreement does not give rise to a legal obligation unless and until the parties actually reach agreement on the relevant term. [**Joseph Martin, Jr., Delicatessen, Inc. v. Schumacher,** 52 N.Y.2d 105 (1981)]

a. Rationale—the Courts Will Not Make a Contract for the Parties

The rationale of the traditional rule is that the courts can neither force the parties to agree nor determine what they would agree upon. Furthermore, in such cases it is said that there is no room to supply a "reasonable" term because the parties have not simply left a gap but have provided a specific gap-filling mechanism (their future agreement), which has failed.

b. Complete Omission vs. "Agreement to Agree"

The result under the traditional rule is that if the parties make no provision at all for a material term, such as price, the courts might supply a reasonable term and uphold the contract (*supra*, p. 139). However, if the parties provide that the term is "to be agreed upon," under the traditional rule the agreement usually will not be enforced.

c. Minor Terms Reserved

If the term "to be agreed upon" is a *minor* one, the contract generally will not be rendered unenforceable. For example, a construction contract for a large office building that is otherwise sufficiently certain as to its terms will not be rendered fatally indefinite because some relatively minor architectural detail is "to be agreed upon." [Rest. 2d § 33]

d. U.C.C. Provision

As in cases where the parties simply leave a gap, the U.C.C. is much more inclined to enforce agreements to agree than is the traditional rule. Under U.C.C. section 2–305, in a contract for the sale of goods an agreement to agree on price does not render a bargain unenforceable, provided the court finds that the parties intended to conclude a contract. In such a case, if the parties fail to reach an agreement as to price, then the price is *"a reasonable price at the time of delivery."*

e. Future Trend

The Restatement takes the same position as the U.C.C. regarding enforcement of agreements to agree on price [*see* Rest. 2d § 33, ill. 8], and so do some modern courts [*see, e.g.,* **Drees Farming Association v. Thompson,** 246 N.W.2d 883 (N.D. 1976)]. The trend among modern courts will probably be to continue to erode the traditional rule and enforce a contract that leaves a material term to future agreement, provided the parties have manifested an intent to conclude a contract. [*E.g.,* **Fischer v. CTMI, L.L.C.,** 479 S.W.3d 231 (Tex. 2016)]

8. Bargains Subject to Power of One Party Concerning Performance

Questions frequently arise as to whether a bargain is sufficiently definite if one party has reserved some power concerning performance.

a. Unrestricted Option

(1) Common Law

At common law, if either party retains an unlimited power to decide the nature or extent of their performance, their promise is considered "illusory" and thus fails as adequate consideration for a counterpromise. (*See supra*, p. 11.)

Example: *A* makes an employment agreement with *B* under which *A* will pay *B* "such wages as I wish" [**Gulf Colorado & San Francisco Railway v. Winton,** 7 Tex. Civ. App. 57 (1894)], or *A* agrees to buy services from *B* at a price "solely within our discretion" [**Davis v. General Foods Corp.,** 21 F. Supp. 445 (S.D.N.Y. 1937)]. Under the traditional rule, these contracts would be unenforceable as illusory.

(2) U.C.C. Position

Under the U.C.C., if it appears that the parties intended to be bound, an agreement for the sale of goods at a price to be fixed by the seller or by the buyer *is enforceable.* [U.C.C. § 2–305; *supra,* p. 20] The U.C.C. provides that the party who is to fix the price does not have unlimited discretion; the price must be fixed in *good faith.* Otherwise, the other party can either cancel the contract or set a reasonable price themselves. Furthermore, if the parties leave the price to be fixed otherwise than by their agreement (*e.g.,* by a third party who will decide the price) and no price is set as a result of one of the parties' *fault,* the other party may either cancel the contract or set a reasonable price themselves.

> **Example:** Seller sells 10 tons of coal to Buyer for delivery next winter, the price to be fixed by a third party. Seller convinces the third party not to fix a price. Under the U.C.C., Buyer can cancel the contract or enforce the contract at a reasonable price.

(3) Future Trend

As in the case of agreements to agree, the Restatement takes the same position as the U.C.C. on a power to set a term [Rest. 2d § 34], and it is likely that some modern courts will hold that an apparently unrestricted power to set a price does not amount to an illusory promise, because the power is limited by the general obligation to perform contracts in good faith.

b. Details of Performance

A bargain that is otherwise sufficiently definite is enforceable if it leaves details of performance to be determined later by one of the parties. The party that has the power to specify such future details must do so in good faith. [Rest. 2d § 34, comments a–b; U.C.C. § 2–311(1)]

c. Alternative Promises

Generally, a bargain is not too indefinite merely because it reserves to one party the right to choose which of two or more performances will be rendered, provided that *each* performance would constitute consideration when taken alone (*supra*, pp. 17–18).

(1) Promisor's Option

Thus, a bargain in which *A* agrees to sell "my horse or my cow, whichever *I* choose, for $100" is enforceable. If the seller refuses to deliver either, the buyer is entitled to damages based on the less valuable animal. [Rest. 2d § 34] However, if the promisor has an option to take an action that would ***not*** constitute consideration, the contract is unenforceable. Thus if *A* agrees that if *B* pays $100, *A* will either sell *B* a horse or serve on a jury the next time *A* is called, the contract is unenforceable. Because service on a jury is simply performance of a legal obligation, it does not constitute consideration under the legal duty rule, and a bargain that reserves in the promisor the right to perform alternatives is not enforceable unless *each* of the alternatives constitutes consideration. (*See supra*, p. 17.)

(2) Promisee's Option

A bargain in which *A* agrees to sell *B* "my horse or my cow, whichever *you* choose, for $100" is also enforceable. However, unlike an alternative promise at the promisor's option, an alternative promise at the promisee's option is enforceable even if only *one* of the alternatives is supported by consideration. Therefore, if *A* agrees with *B* for $100 either to sell *B* a horse or to serve when called on a jury, and *B* has the power to choose between these two alternatives, the contract is enforceable because *one* choice is supported by consideration. (*See supra*, p. 18.)

d. Promise Dependent on Ability to Perform

A bargain in which one party agrees to pay another "as soon as I am *able*" is enforceable because the party's financial ability to pay is capable of objective determination. [**Van Buskirk v. Kuhns,** 164 Cal. 472 (1913)]

9. Agreements Contemplating Future Written Contracts

A special problem that is related to indefiniteness occurs where parties enter into an agreement on the understanding that a formal written contract will be executed, and that does not occur. The question then arises, what was the parties' intent in providing for the written instrument?

a. Writing as Evidentiary Memorial

If it appears that the parties intended the future writing only as an *evidentiary memorial* of the terms of their agreement, and that the agreement, although not yet formally memorialized, is complete, then the agreement is enforceable. [**Saunders v. Pottlitzer Bros. Fruit Co.,** 144 N.Y. 209 (1894); **Goad v. Rogers,** 103 Cal. App. 2d 294 (1951)]

b. Writing as Consummation of Agreement

If, however, it appears that the parties intended not to be bound unless and until a writing was executed (*i.e.*, if it appears that the writing was intended to be the *consummation* of the negotiations), then the agreement is *not* enforceable unless and until the formal written contract is executed. [**Stanton v. Dennis,** *supra*, p. 136; Rest. 2d § 27; 165 A.L.R. 752]

c. Determining Intent

In determining whether the parties intended the written contract to be a memorial of their agreement or a consummation of their negotiations, important factors to consider are: (i) whether the contract is of a type usually put in writing; (ii) whether there are few or many details; (iii) whether the amount involved is large or small; and (iv) whether a formal writing is necessary for full expression of the type of agreement in question. [**Mississippi & Dominion Steamship Co. v. Swift,** 29 A. 1063 (Me. 1894); Rest. 2d § 27]

(1) Note

Sometimes there are special circumstances indicating that the primary intention was simply to memorialize the bargain—*e.g.*, the negotiations may have consisted of a series of letters, and the purpose of the proposed writing appeared to be simply to collect all the terms together in one instrument.

10. Preliminary Agreements

Another problem related to indefiniteness occurs when parties reach a *preliminary* agreement in contemplation of a future final contract. The question arises whether the parties intended this preliminary agreement to be binding, and if so, the extent to which the parties intended to be bound. In a leading case, **Teachers Insurance & Annuity Association of America v. Tribune Co.,** 670 F. Supp. 491 (S.D.N.Y. 1987), the court distinguished between two kinds of preliminary agreements:

a. Agreement Contemplating Formalization

The first kind of preliminary agreement is one in which the parties have reached agreement on the issues that they determined to require negotiation, but they have expressed an intention to *formalize* the agreement as an evidentiary memorial. This type of preliminary agreement is ***binding as a contract*** at the time it is made. It is "preliminary" only in the sense that it remains to be formalized in the way the parties contemplated. (*See supra*, p. 145.)

b. Agreement Contemplating Further Good Faith Negotiations

The second kind of preliminary agreement is one that expresses a mutual commitment to a contract on agreed major terms while recognizing the existence of *open terms* that will be negotiated in good faith in the future. The most common (although not the only) case in which this type of agreement arises is that in which the parties have signed a "letter of intent" or commitment containing general terms and providing that the parties intend to negotiate toward a final contract. Although the existence of explicitly open terms in the preliminary agreement generally suggests that a binding agreement has not been reached, that is not necessarily so. Within the last several decades, courts have begun to recognize that parties can bind themselves to a concededly incomplete agreement in the sense that they accept a mutual commitment to *negotiate* together in *good faith* in an effort to reach a final agreement (within the scope of the terms that have been settled in the preliminary, concededly incomplete agreement).

(1) Express Preliminary Agreement to Negotiate in Good Faith

Under the modern cases, an express agreement between *A* and *B* to negotiate in good faith is enforceable, as is an agreement by *A* that for a designated period they will not negotiate with anyone other than *B* about the subject of a proposed contract with *B*. [**Channel Home Centers v. Grossman,** 795 F.2d 291 (3d Cir. 1986)]

(2) Implied Agreement to Negotiate in Good Faith

Even *without* an express agreement to negotiate in good faith, there is an *implication* in many preliminary agreements that the parties are mutually committed to negotiate in good faith on those terms that have not been covered in the preliminary agreement so that a final agreement can be executed.

(3) Content of Obligation to Negotiate in Good Faith

The obligation to negotiate in good faith generally has been described as preventing a party from: (i) renouncing the agreed upon terms of a deal without trying to negotiate the unresolved terms, (ii) abandoning the negotiations without having made a good faith effort to consummate them, or (iii) insisting on terms that are either inconsistent with or do not carry out the intent of those terms that have been agreed upon. [**A/S Apothekernes Laboratorium for Specialpraeparater v. I.M.C. Chemical Group, Inc.,** 873 F.2d 155 (7th Cir. 1989)]

EXAM TIP — GILBERT

If two parties are involved in preliminary negotiations and one party backs out, remember that although preliminary agreements are often unenforceable because they are too indefinite to form a contract, an *express or implied* agreement to *negotiate in good faith is enforceable*. Therefore, although the injured party will not be able to enforce agreements made during preliminary negotiations, they may be able to prevent the other party from backing out of the deal in bad faith.

---

11. Reliance on Indefinite Contracts

In the well-known case of **Hoffman v. Red Owl Stores, Inc.,** 133 N.W.2d 267 (Wis. 1965), an agent of Red Owl Stores, Inc., promised Joseph Hoffman and his wife that he would sell the Hoffmans a supermarket franchise for $18,000. This price was later raised to $26,000. The Hoffmans made several expenditures and sold their bakery in reliance on this promise.

However, the agent later required Mrs. Hoffman's father to sign an agreement stating that his $13,000 loan to his son-in-law and daughter for the purchase of the franchise was in fact a gift, and the price of the franchise was again increased to $34,000. Negotiations failed and the Hoffmans sued Red Owl. The court held that although the agreement was too indefinite to enforce, the Hoffmans' reliance on the agreement entitled them to **reliance damages** because the conditions for promissory estoppel were satisfied (*i.e.*, the agreement was one on which Red Owl should have realized the Hoffmans would rely, the agreement induced such reliance, the Hoffmans suffered a loss, and injustice could be avoided only by compensating the Hoffmans for their loss). The court said that section 90 of Restatement First, which embodies the reliance principle (*i.e.*, the principle of promissory estoppel; *see supra*, p. 46 *et seq.*) "does not impose the requirement that the promise giving rise to the cause of action must be so comprehensive in scope as to meet the requirements of an offer that would ripen into a contract if accepted by the promisee."

a. Part Performance as Alternative

Reliance on an indefinite contract often takes the form of part performance. In such cases, the traditional rule that part performance may make an otherwise indefinite contract enforceable may make it ***unnecessary*** to resort to a reliance analysis. Accordingly, the *Red Owl* doctrine is most likely to be invoked when one party to an indefinite agreement has relied by ***preparing*** to perform rather than by beginning to perform.

(1) Note

If ***part performance*** makes an otherwise indefinite contract enforceable, the party who partly performs may be able to bring suit for ***expectation*** damages (not merely reliance damages, which is normally the limit under the *Red Owl* doctrine). (*See supra*, p. 47.)

b. Duty of Good Faith Negotiation as Alternative

Red Owl was decided at a time when the duty to negotiate in good faith had not yet been fully developed. That duty may be a better fit for a given fact situation than the reliance approach of *Red Owl*.

c. Application of *Red Owl* Doctrine

As a practical matter, therefore, the *Red Owl* doctrine is most readily applied when the parties have not entered into a preliminary written agreement or begun performance but one party has nevertheless begun preparing to perform. In *Red Owl* itself, the defendant seems to have led the plaintiffs on by constantly dangling the prospect of a final contract before them, knowing or having reason to know that they would rely on that prospect. Although the *Red Owl* opinion did not explicitly turn on the defendant's leading-on, conduct of this kind presents the strongest case for applying the *Red Owl* doctrine.

B. Mistake

1. In General

Doctrines addressing mistake in contract law fall into five categories: "mutual mistake," "unilateral mistake," "mistake in transcription," "misunderstanding," and "mistake in transmission." These names are sometimes incomplete or slightly misleading.

2. Mutual Mistake

In ordinary language, the term "mutual mistake" means a shared mistake made by both of the parties to a contract. As used in contract law, however, the term normally refers to a special kind of mutual mistake, namely, a mistaken *assumption* shared by both parties as to the *conditions of the outside world*.

a. Older Test

At one time, courts held that the test for whether mutual mistake constituted a defense was whether the mistake concerned the "substance" or "identity" of the contract's subject matter (in which case the contract would be voidable), or only its "accidents" or "collateral attributes" (in which case the contract would ***not*** be voidable). [*See, e.g.,* **Sherwood v. Walker**, 33 N.W. 919 (Mich. 1887)] Such distinctions were neither very illuminating nor easily workable, and few if any courts would now use this test.

> **Example:** Walker contracted to sell Sherwood a cow that both parties believed was barren. Before delivery of the cow, Walker discovered the cow was pregnant, and thus more valuable. Under the older test, the contract could be rescinded because the parties made a mutual mistake as to the substance of the contract's subject matter (*i.e.,* the cow was a breeding cow rather than a barren cow). [**Sherwood v. Walker,** *supra*]

b. Modern Rule

The modern rule is that when parties enter into a contract under a mutual mistake concerning a *basic assumption of fact* on which the contract was made, the contract is voidable by the adversely affected party if the mistake had a material effect on the agreed exchange and the adversely affected party did not bear the risk that the assumption was mistaken. [Rest. 2d § 152]

> **Example:** On May 5, April contracts to sell her famous racehorse, Apex, to Mae. Unbeknownst to either party, Apex had died on the night of May 4. The contract is voidable by Mae, because both parties were mistaken as to a basic assumption on which the contract was made (*i.e.,* that Apex was alive), the mistake is material, and the mistaken assumption was not one as to which Mae, the adversely affected party, bore the risk of mistake.

> **Example:** Liz leases Silverlake to a band, "The Lads," for one day for the purpose of conducting a rock concert on the property. Unbeknownst to either party, a municipal ordinance had just been enacted that prevents such use of Silverlake. The lease is voidable by The Lads because both parties were mistaken as to a basic assumption on which the contract was made (*i.e.,* that concerts could be held on Silverlake), the mistake is material, and the assumption was not one as to which The Lads, the adversely affected party, bore the risk of mistake.

c. When a Party Bears Risk of Mistake

Under the modern rule, mutual mistake is not a defense when the adversely affected party *bore the risk* that the assumption in question might be mistaken. [Rest. 2d § 154] A common instance of this type of case occurs when the parties knew that the relevant assumption was *doubtful*. According to Restatement First, "where the parties know that there is doubt in regard to a certain matter and contract on that assumption, the contract is not rendered voidable because one is disappointed in the hope that the facts accord with the wishes. The risk of the doubtful fact is then assumed as one of the elements of the bargain." [Rest. 1st § 502, comment]

Example: Buyer agrees to buy from Seller a tract of land situated in a remote desert area. Seller states that she believes, but is not positive that, she has good title to the land. She makes no representation that she has good title, and the contract provides only that Seller will convey such title as she has. Buyer believes that Seller has good title to the land, and Buyer makes no title search, as Seller knows. It turns out that Seller does not have good title. Buyer does not have a defense of mutual mistake, because he knew that there was an element of doubt concerning the assumption that Seller owned the land. [Rest. 2d § 154, ill. 1]

d. Mistake in Judgment No Defense

Similarly, a contract is not voidable on the ground of mutual mistake if the mistake concerns *prediction* or *judgment*—for example, if both parties erroneously think the market price of potatoes will go down, or that a horse one is buying from the other is not fast enough to race successfully.

3. Unilateral Mistake

A different type of mistake in contract law is *unilateral mistake*. In ordinary language, the term "unilateral mistake" means a mistake made by one, rather than both, of the parties to a contract. As used in contract law, however, the term normally refers to a special kind of unilateral mistake, namely, a *mechanical* error of computation, perception, or the like concerning a basic assumption on which the contract was made. For example, where one party submits a bid to the other based on an error in addition, so that the bid is unintentionally low, there has been a mechanical error in computation. Similarly, if A says, "I will buy that box for $16," and B accepts thinking A has offered $60, there has been a mechanical error in perception. Most unilateral mistake cases concern errors in computation (mental or by computer), typing, or printing.

a. Nonmistaken Party Aware of Error

If the nonmistaken party either *knew or should have known* of the other party's mechanical mistake, the mistake is said to be a *"palpable"* unilateral mistake. A palpable unilateral mistake makes the contract *voidable* by the mistaken party. "One cannot snap up an offer or bid knowing that it was made in mistake." [**Tyra v. Cheney,** 152 N.W. 835 (Minn. 1915); *and see* **Peerless Glass Co. v. Pacific Crockery & Tinware Co.,** 121 Cal. 641 (1898)]

(1) Actual Knowledge Not Necessary

It is sufficient that the nonmistaken party *should have known* of the mistake, as where one bid is substantially and inexplicably lower than all others.

Example: Contractor bids $700,000 on a construction project. The next lowest bid is $1,700,000. This substantial difference in price is sufficient to charge the nonmistaken party with knowledge that Contractor's bid reflected an error in computation. Therefore, the contract is voidable by Contractor. [*See* **M.F. Kemper Construction Co. v. City of Los Angeles,** 37 Cal. 2d 696 (1951)]

(2) Analysis

The rule that a palpable unilateral mistake of computation or the like prevents contract formation is often said to be an exception to the objective theory of contracts, because the mistake is subjective. However, the purpose of the objective theory is to protect the promisee's reasonable expectations. If the promisee knew or should have known that the promisor made a unilateral mistake of computation or the like, then either (i) the promisee has no expectation that the promisor intended to form a contract or (ii) such an expectation is not reasonable.

(3) Errors in Judgment

The rule concerning palpable unilateral mistake applies only to mechanical errors, such as errors in computation or the like. It does not apply to *errors in judgment* as to the value or quality of the work done or goods contracted for, or as to the likelihood of future conditions.

Example: Seller offers to sell her car to Buyer for $500, and Buyer accepts. Buyer knows that Seller's car has a market value of $1,500 and that this fact is unknown to Seller. The contract is enforceable.

Example: Artist sells a painting to Collector for $100, believing the work is unlikely to be regarded as significant. Collector, a prominent art expert, is confident that the painting will eventually be worth several orders of magnitude more than $100. Collector's judgment proves to be correct. The contract is enforceable.

Compare: Artist intends to offer a painting for $20,000 to Collector by email. In the email, Artist mistakenly types "$200.00" instead of "$20000." Collector accepts Artist's offer. The error is a palpable unilateral mistake and the contract is voidable by Artist.

b. Nonmistaken Party Reasonably Unaware of Error

If the nonmistaken party neither knew nor had reason to know of the other party's unilateral mistake, the traditional rule is that there is a ***binding contract.***

(1) Damages

Under this rule, if the mistaken party discovers the mistake and refuses to perform, the nonmistaken party is entitled to expectation damages (*see infra*, p. 251). [**Crenshaw County Hospital Board v. St. Paul Fire & Marine Insurance Co.,** 411 F.2d 213 (5th Cir. 1969)]

(2) Modern Trend

However, a number of modern cases hold that if the mistaken party notifies the other party of a unilateral mistake before the nonmistaken party has changed their position in reliance, the mistaken party can *rescind* the contract. [**St. Nicholas Church v. Kropp,** 160 N.W. 500 (Minn. 1916)] Furthermore, some of the modern cases hold that even if the nonmistaken party *has* changed their position, their recovery will be limited to damages required to compensate them for their *reliance.* Although these cases are in the minority, they appear to represent the trend of decision.

4. Mistranscription

Mistranscription occurs when the parties make an oral agreement which they reduce to a signed writing, but through some clerical (*i.e.*, mechanical) mistake the writing does not correctly embody the oral agreement. In such cases, the aggrieved party is entitled to the equitable remedy of *reformation.* Under this remedy, the writing is reformed by the court so that it corresponds to the oral agreement. However, to obtain reformation the aggrieved party must prove their case not merely by the usual "preponderance of the evidence" but by a higher standard—usually "clear and convincing" evidence. [**Goode v. Riley,** 28 N.E. 228 (Mass.

1891); *and see* Remedies Summary] Also, because reformation is an equitable remedy, such cases are tried by a judge rather than by a jury.

5. Misunderstanding

A principle of contract interpretation discussed in Chapter 2 (*see supra*, p. 114) is also commonly treated as a type of mistake. Namely, when the two parties subjectively intend for an expression (words or conduct) to have different meanings, and those meanings are *equally* reasonable, the case is classified as a *misunderstanding*. In such a case, *no contract* is formed. Note that this rule is inapplicable when one party's interpretation is *more reasonable* than the other's. Then, the fact that the two parties subjectively intend two different meanings does not prevent contract formation. Instead, a contract is formed, and the meaning of the disputed expression is the meaning intended by the party whose interpretation is more reasonable.

6. Mistake in Transmission by Intermediary

The fifth kind of mistake concerns cases in which an offeror uses an intermediary—such as an interpreter or (in the past) a telegraph company—to transmit a communication and the intermediary makes a mistake in transmitting the communication. Normally this type of mistake involves a mistransmitted offer.

a. Offeree Aware of Mistake

As in the case of a unilateral mistake, if the offeree knew or should have known of the mistake—for example, because of the magnitude of the discrepancy between an offered price and the market price—they cannot "snap up" what they know to be an erroneous price. Accordingly, if the offeree attempts to accept, a contract will not be formed. [**Germain Fruit Co. v. Western Union,** 137 Cal. 598 (1902)]

b. Offeree Unaware of Mistake

In cases where the offeree neither knows nor should know of the mistake, there is a split of authority:

(1) Majority View

The majority view is that a contract is formed on the terms conveyed to the offeree by the *intermediary.* Some courts rationalize this result on the theory that the intermediary acts as the agent of the offeror, and the offeror is liable for the acts of its agent. [**Des Arc Oil Mill v. Western Union Telegraph Co.,** 201 S.W. 273 (Ark. 1918)] The problem with this rationale is that the intermediary is usually not an agent under the law of agency. Other courts adopt the rationale that the offeror chose the intermediary who caused the error; where one of two innocent parties must suffer, the one who caused the loss should bear the burden thereof; and that by choosing the intermediary, the offeror caused the loss. [**Ayer v. Western Union,** 10 A. 495 (Me. 1887)] This rationale, however, breaks down if the offeror was not the first of the parties to use the intermediary (*e.g.*, suppose the offeree first used the same intermediary to send an inquiry to the offeror). Besides, using a particular intermediary is often a reasonable thing to do.

(2) Minority View

Under the minority view, no contract results where there is an error in transmission, on the ground that the parties have neither objectively nor subjectively reached an agreement. [**Strong v. Western Union,** 109 P. 910 (Idaho 1910)]

APPROACH TO "MISTAKE" CASES IN CONTRACT LAW

Type of Mistake	Number of Parties Making the Mistake	
	1	2
Mechanical error (*e.g.*, typo, calculation error)	Unilateral Mistake	Mistranscription (when mistake affects written document that both parties endorse as memorandum of their deal)
Basic mistake about factual assumption (*e.g.*, item for sale is topaz, not diamond)	Not a "mistake" case: Nondisclosure *or* Misrepresentation	Mutual Mistake
Interpretive error (*i.e.*, misunderstanding what a word means)	Not a "mistake" case: the more reasonable interpretation ordinarily prevails	Misunderstanding

An additional type of mistake case is "**Mistake in Transmission by Intermediary**," in which an intermediary conveys a communication incorrectly. That doctrine is of sharply diminished importance today, because it mainly arose in cases involving telegrams.

RESULTS OF DIFFERENT TYPES OF MISTAKE

TYPE	DEFINITION	RESULT
MUTUAL MISTAKE	A mistake by *both* parties to a contract concerning a *basic assumption of fact* on which the contract was based.	The contract is voidable by the adversely affected party if the mistake has a *material effect* on the contract and the adversely affected party *did not bear the risk* that the assumption was mistaken.
UNILATERAL MISTAKE	A mistake by *one party* to a contract concerning a *basic assumption* on which the contract was based, usually involving a *mechanical kind of error*.	If the nonmistaken party *knew or should have known* about the mistake, the contract is *voidable* if the mistake has a *material effect* on the contract and the adversely affected party *did not bear the risk* that the assumption was mistaken. Otherwise, the contract is

		enforceable (usually be expectation damages, but under a modern trend perhaps by reliance damages only).
MISTRANSCRIPTION	A mistake in ***writing out the terms*** of an oral agreement.	The writing is ***reformed*** to conform with the oral agreement.
MISUNDERSTANDING	A mistake in which both parties to a contract have ***different but equally reasonable interpretations*** of expressions used in attempting to form the contract.	***No contract*** is formed.
MISTAKE IN TRANSMISSION BY INTERMEDIARY	A mistake by an ***intermediary in transmitting*** the terms of an offer to the offeree.	If the offeree ***knew or should have known*** of the mistake, ***no contract*** is formed. Otherwise, under the majority view, a contract based on the ***intermediary's terms*** is formed.

c. Practical Significance

The practical significance of mistakes in transmission by an intermediary has been much reduced by changes in modes of communication. Most of the intermediary cases involve telegrams that are incorrectly typed by the telegraph company. With the advent of the internet, the use of telegraph companies and other intermediaries who must type out a message has drastically declined. Most mistakes in transmission today are therefore likely to involve either clerical errors by the offeror or a failure of the offeror's or offeree's equipment (*e.g.*, autocorrect). The rules concerning such errors have not yet fully emerged, but such cases are more likely to be treated under the doctrine of ***unilateral mistake*** today. Cases involving similar facts to mistakes in transmission by an intermediary today may arise if a broadcaster edits a recorded interview in which an offeror makes a contractual offer intended for broadcast but viewers are unaware that the broadcast was edited. [*Cf.* **Kolodziej v. Mason,** 774 F.3d 736, 738 (11th Cir. 2014)]

C. Contracts Induced by Misrepresentation, Nondisclosure, Duress, or Undue Influence

1. Misrepresentation

A misrepresentation is a statement that is not in accord with the facts. [Rest. 2d § 159]

a. Fraudulent Misrepresentation

In contract law, a misrepresentation is *fraudulent* if the misrepresenting party *intends* an assertion to induce another party to enter an agreement *and* the misrepresenting party either: (i) knows or believes the assertion is untrue, (ii) lacks confidence in the truth of the assertion but presents it as fact, *or* (iii) says or implies that there is a basis for the assertion, such as personal knowledge or investigation, when in fact such a basis does not exist. [Rest. 2d § 162] If one party justifiably relies on a fraudulent misrepresentation made by another and enters a contract as a result of that misrepresentation, the contract is *voidable* by the innocent party. [Rest. 2d § 164]

Example: Buyer asks Salesman if he sells any waterproof shoes. Salesman tells Buyer that a certain pair of shoes is waterproof. Salesman actually does not know whether the shoes are waterproof, and the shoes in fact are not waterproof. Buyer buys the shoes because she thinks they are waterproof. The sale is voidable by Buyer.

b. Material Misrepresentation

In contract law, a misrepresentation is *material* if (i) the assertion probably will induce a *reasonable* person to agree or (ii) the misrepresenting party knows the assertion probably will make a *particular* person agree. [Rest. 2d § 162] A contract that results from a *material* misrepresentation (even if it is not fraudulent) is *voidable* by a party who justifiably relies on it and agrees to a contract as a result of it. [Rest. 2d § 164]

Example: Same facts as in the example above, except Salesman truly believes the shoes are waterproof. Although Salesman's misrepresentation is no longer fraudulent, it is still material because the assertion that the shoes were waterproof would probably induce a reasonable person in Buyer's position to buy the shoes. Therefore, the sale is voidable by Buyer.

2. Nondisclosure

a. General Rule

The general rule is that contracting parties do not have an obligation to disclose facts concerning the subject matter of the contract to each other. [Rest. 2d § 161] Contracts are voidable if they result from fraudulent or material misrepresentation, or from an affirmative attempt to *conceal* material facts [Rest. 2d § 160], but it is often stated that one party to a contract has no general duty to disclose information or to take steps to correct the other party's mistakes of fact.

Example: In a store, Salesman overhears Buyer express a belief to Buyer's friend that the shoes that Buyer are about to buy are waterproof. Salesman knows the shoes are not waterproof, but he says nothing and takes no steps to correct Buyer's misapprehension. Buyer buys the shoes. The sale is *not* voidable.

b. Exceptions

In several circumstances, however, one party to a contract does have a duty to disclose facts to the other party. In such circumstances, a failure to disclose a fact may amount to a *misrepresentation* and thus render a contract voidable under the rule above concerning fraudulent and material misrepresentations. [Rest. 2d § 161]

(1) Misleading Half-Truths

If a party chooses to reveal some facts, doing so in a misleading way can constitute misrepresentation (*see supra*, p. 154) even if the stated facts are not themselves untrue. [Rest. 2d § 159, comment b] For example, a party might state half-truths—*e.g.*, might make a true statement but strategically omit qualifications or elaborations that render the statement an effective misrepresentation.

Example: The dean of Law School states to Applicant that Law School is accredited by the American Bar Association. At the time the dean makes this statement, it is technically true, but as the dean knows, the American Bar Association is planning to revoke the school's accreditation later that day. Failing to disclose that fact, given the dean's assertion about accreditation, amounts to a misrepresentation.

(2) Failure to Correct a Previous Statement

Similarly, nondisclosure may amount to misrepresentation if a party fails to correct a previous statement in light of new or newly discovered information. [Rest. 2d § 161(a)]

Example: Same facts as above, except that the dean learns of the ABA's decision three days later, to her great surprise. The dean's statement was not a misrepresentation at the time it was made, but if the dean does not take new steps to correct it and Applicant enrolls, the contract with Law School is voidable.

(3) Relationships of Trust or Confidence

Nondisclosure of material facts is required if the prospective parties are in a fiduciary relationship or another relationship of trust or confidence. [Rest. 2d § 161(d)]

(4) Disclosure to Correct Mistakes About Writings

Disclosure is also required to correct the other party's known mistake about the meaning or content of a writing. [Rest. 2d § 161(c)] This rule has a similar rationale to those of the doctrine of mistranscription (*supra*, p. 150) and the rule of interpretation governing situations in which one party knows that another party is assigning an unreasonable meaning to an expression (*supra*, p. 115).

(5) General Possible Exception

Disclosure may also be required, even if none of the other exceptions apply, if a material fact is known to one party by virtue of their special position and could not be readily determined by the other party in the exercise of normal diligence. This exception has commonly been applied to cases of the sale of residential homes. For example, if a seller of a house, by virtue of their special position and experience as owner of the house, knows of a nonapparent termite infestation, in many states the seller may be obliged to disclose the infestation to a prospective buyer, especially if the parties reside in an area in which buyers normally do not commission termite inspections before purchasing homes. [**Hill v. Jones,** 725 P.2d 1115 (Ariz. Ct. App. 1986)]

(a) Broad Possibilities for Exception

Restatement Second states an even broader possible general exception, requiring disclosure necessary to "correct a mistake of the other party as to a basic assumption on which that party is making the contract . . . if non-disclosure of the fact amounts to a *failure to act in good faith and in accordance with reasonable standards of fair dealing*" (emphasis added). [Rest. 2d § 161(b)]

3. Duress

A contract is voidable on the ground of duress where consent was induced by ***wrongful*** or ***improper*** threats. [Rest. 1st §§ 492–495; Rest. 2d §§ 175–176] A contract is also commonly said to be "void"—*i.e.*, not formed at all—in the unusual event that apparent assent results from physical compulsion (*e.g.*, a bidder at an auction raises their hand only because it was physically raised by someone else against the bidder's will). [Rest. 2d § 174]

a. Wrongful or Improper Threat

Threats are clearly wrongful when they threaten crimes, torts, criminal prosecution, or bad-faith civil process (*e.g.*, threatening to "tie someone up with lawsuits forever" with no basis). [Rest. 2d § 176(1)] Threats to take economic actions like breach of contract may be improper if (i) made in bad faith and (ii) used to extract unfair terms. [Rest. 2d § 176(2); s*ee also supra*, p. 31]

b. Economic Duress

A threat to withhold something another party badly needs or wants is not in itself duress, because it is not wrongful to refuse to contract or to agree to contract only on very favorable terms. But economic duress is a defense to the enforcement of a contract when:

(i) One party commits or ***threatens to commit a wrongful act,*** potentially including a breach of contract, that would place the other in a position that would seriously threaten their property or finances unless the other party enters into a contract; *and*

(ii) ***No adequate means are available to avoid or prevent the threatened loss,*** other than entering into the contract.

Example: Client engages Attorney as tax counsel to resist a large tax deficiency assessed against him by the Internal Revenue Service (I.R.S.). Attorney waits until just before the deadline for filing a reply with the I.R.S., then forces Client to sign a very high contingency-fee agreement by threatening that unless Client agrees to the fee, Attorney will not file the necessary papers, and Client would thus be liable for the full tax assessment. At this point, it is too late for Client to find another lawyer who would make a timely filing. The agreement is unenforceable on the ground of economic duress. [**Thompson Crane & Trucking Co. v. Eyman,** 123 Cal. App. 2d 904 (1954)]

EXAM TIP

The issue of economic duress often comes up in cases of contract **modification**, because one party may be explicitly or implicitly threatening breach if the modification is not made. (*See supra*, p. 31.) However, threatening breach of contract does not itself amount to economic duress because (i) the "threatened" party may have reasonable alternatives to contract modification (such as suing for breach of the original contract) and because (ii) it is not always wrongful to threaten breach of contract.

4. Undue Influence

Undue influence is unfair persuasion of a party, A, who is under the domination of the person exercising the persuasion, B, or who by virtue of the relation between them is justified in assuming that B will not act in a manner inconsistent with A's welfare. If a party's assent is induced by the other party's undue influence, the contract is voidable by the victim.

Example: Elderly Aunt is cared for by Nephew. Nephew pressures Aunt to sell him some of her personal property at an unfairly low price. An undue influence defense will likely succeed here, because by virtue of the relationship Aunt was justified in assuming that Nephew would not act in a manner inconsistent with her welfare.

D. Unconscionability

1. Introduction

The principle of unconscionability is a very important doctrine whose precise scope has remained somewhat uncertain.

2. Development of Doctrine—U.C.C.

Although traces of a doctrine of unconscionability can be found at early common law, the doctrine in its modern form was introduced into contract law by U.C.C. section 2–302.

a. U.C.C. Section 2–302

U.C.C. section 2–302 provides that "[i]f the court as a matter of law finds the contract or any clause of the contract to have been unconscionable at the time it was made the court may refuse to enforce the contract, or it may enforce the remainder of the contract without the unconscionable clause, or it may so limit the application of any unconscionable clause as to avoid any unconscionable result." Note that under section 2–302 it is normally up to the trial judge, rather than the jury, to decide whether a contract or provision is unconscionable. Note also that though the U.C.C. applies the concept of unconscionability in section 2–302, it does not *define* the term.

b. Extension

Strictly speaking, U.C.C. section 2–302 applies only to contracts for the sale of goods. However, since the original promulgation of the U.C.C., courts have generally held that the principle of unconscionability is applicable to all contracts, and the principle is now also embodied in Restatement Second section 208.

3. Meaning and Scope of Doctrine

Despite the general acceptance of the principle of unconscionability, its meaning and scope are still uncertain. Many commentators draw a distinction between "procedural" unconscionability (*i.e.,* an unconscionable *bargaining process*) and "substantive" unconscionability (*i.e.,* contract *terms* that are unconscionable without regard to the process by which those terms were reached, because they are lopsided). [113 U. Pa. L. Rev. 435 (1965)]

a. Procedural Unconscionability—Unfair Surprise

Many (and perhaps most) cases of unconscionability involve ***"unfair surprise."*** Unfair surprise occurs when the party who drafts a contract includes a term in the contract having reason to know that the term does not accord with the other party's fair expectations and that the other party will not notice the term. This is an example of procedural unconscionability, because inclusion of such a term without calling it to the other party's attention involves an unfair bargaining process. [U.C.C. § 2–302, comment]

(1) Adhesion Contracts

Unfair surprise is particularly likely in form adhesion contracts—*i.e.,* contracts in which the parties occupy substantially unequal bargaining positions and the party in the inferior bargaining position is forced to "adhere" to the terms in the other's form on a "take it or leave it" basis, rather than having terms dickered out. [**Wheeler v. St. Joseph Hospital,** 63 Gal. App. 3d 345 (1977); 16 Kans. L. Rev. 303 (1968)] Traditional examples of form adhesion contracts include life insurance policies, consumer loan agreements, and residential leases. Unfair surprise may result because a given term in a form is contrary to reasonable expectations as to what provisions a form of its general *type* would include and the term is not pointed out, not explained, or written in obscure language.

(2) Party's Lack of Knowledge of Provisions in Contract

(a) Traditional View

The traditional rule was that each party to a contract was charged with knowledge of its provisions; *i.e.,* each was bound by what they signed, whether or not they read, understood, or even knew of the provisions in question. Under this rule, there was no doctrine of unfair surprise. This rule was known as the "duty to read."

(b) Modern Rule

Modern cases, however, tend to hold that, at least when a form adhesion contract is involved, a contracting party is bound only by those provisions that are not unfairly surprising. [**California State Auto Association v. Barrett Garages, Inc.,** 257 Cal. App. 2d 71 (1967)] As Restatement Second puts it, "Where the [form drafter] has reason to believe that the party manifesting . . . assent would not do so if he knew that the writing contained a particular term, the term is not part of the agreement." [Rest. 2d § 211(2)]

e.g. Example: Sonnenberg, the owner of a department store, requests Travelers Insurance Company to issue a liability insurance policy covering Sonnenberg's premises. Travelers agrees to do so. The policy, as issued, includes a provision that excludes liability arising out of the use of elevators, even though Travelers knows that Sonnenberg's store has elevators. A reasonable person in Sonnenberg's position would expect a premises liability policy to include liability for all accidents on the premises, including elevator accidents. Travelers does not call Sonnenberg's attention to the exclusion. The exclusion is unconscionable as unfairly surprising and will not be enforced. [**Portella v. Sonnenberg,** 181 A.2d 385 (N.J. 1962)]

> **Example:** Burns Insurance Company insures Homer's residential property, including homeowner's liability. A provision of the policy excludes liability to domestic employees, but the wording of the provision is so obscure that its effect would not be understood by a reasonable person in Homer's position and is not in fact understood by Homer. The exclusion is unconscionable as unfairly surprising and will not be enforced.

(c) Comment—Protection of Weaker Party

The harsher or more one-sided the provision in question, the more scrupulous the courts usually are in requiring that the weaker party had actual knowledge of the provisions.

b. Substantive Unconscionability

The extent to which the courts will invalidate a contract or its terms solely because of substantive unconscionability—*i.e.*, lopsided or oppressive terms—without regard to defects in the bargaining process is still unresolved.

(1) U.C.C.

The Comment to U.C.C. section 2–302 states that "[t]he principle [of unconscionability] is one of prevention of oppression and unfair surprise . . . and not of disturbance of allocation of risks because of superior bargaining power."

(2) Restatement Second

The Comment to Restatement Second section 208 takes the position that it *is* possible for a contract to be oppressive taken as a whole, despite the fact that there is no weakness in the bargaining process, but it adds that unconscionability ordinarily involves other factors as well as overall imbalance. [Rest. 2d § 208, comment]

(3) Cases

Although most unconscionability cases have involved an unfair bargaining *process,* some cases have invalidated the terms of a contract on the basis that the *price* charged was unconscionable—*i.e.*, that the buyers were being charged far more for goods than the goods were actually worth. [**Maxwell v. Fid. Fin. Servs.,** 907 P.2d 51 (Ariz. 1995); **American Home Improvement, Inc. v. MacIver,** 201 A.2d 886 (N.H. 1964)]

> **Example:** A contract for encyclopedias sold door-to-door (with sales largely directed toward consumers of limited education and economic means) was held unconscionable where it was shown that the price charged was roughly two and one-half times the reasonable market price of the books. [**Kugler v. Romain,** 279 A.2d 640 (N.J. 1971)]

EXAM TIP

When deciding whether a contract is unconscionable, remember that unconscionability must exist ***at the time the contract was made.*** Therefore, an event occurring ***after*** contract formation that makes the terms lopsided (*e.g.*, a drought causing the price of oranges to quadruple) cannot result in unconscionability, although it may sometimes provide a basis for relief under the doctrine of unexpected circumstances (*see infra*, p. 241 *et seq.*).

(4) Substantive Unconscionability as Evidence of Procedural Unconscionability

Substantive unconscionability may also provide evidence of procedural unconscionability. That is, the existence of sharply unfair terms may lend credence to one party's claim that the bargaining process was defective or involved unfair surprise.

4. Types of Unconscionable Provisions

The following types of provisions have been attacked as unconscionable in various settings:

a. Exculpatory Clauses

An exculpatory clause is a clause releasing a party from liability for injury caused by their actions. Such clauses often raise problems of unconscionability.

(1) Intentional Wrongs

An exculpatory clause relieving a party from liability for their own intentional wrongs is usually held violative of public policy and hence illegal. [*See, e.g.*, Cal. Civ. Code § 1688]

(2) Negligence

Provisions relieving a party from liability for their own negligence raise greater difficulty.

(a) Injuries to the Person

In theory, a disclaimer of liability for harm to the person caused by negligence is enforceable ***unless*** it is unconscionable. In practice, however, such disclaimers are commonly, although not invariably, held to be unconscionable—either because the disclaimer is contained in a form contract of adhesion and is unreasonably surprising or because the agreement that contains the disclaimer affects the public interest and the injured party is a member of a protected class. [*See, e.g.*, **Tunkl v. Regents of the University of California,** 60 Cal. 2d 92 (1963)] Nevertheless, some cases do enforce disclaimers of liability for harm to the person caused by negligence, especially if the contract concerns activities that are known to be hazardous. [**Garretson v. United States,** 456 F.2d 1017 (9th Cir. 1972)—experienced ski-jumper signed entry blank for a ski-jumping tournament that contained a clear and prominent clause releasing sponsors of the tournament from liability for injuries the ski-jumper might sustain]

(b) Injuries to Property

Provisions that relieve a party from liability for lost profits or injury to property caused by that party's negligence are frequently upheld, provided the injured party had some choice and no unfair surprise was involved (*see infra*, p. 161). [**Mayfair Fabrics v. Henley,** 222 A.2d 602 (N.J. 1967); **Sweeney Gasoline & Oil Co. v. Toledo, Peoria & Western Railroad,** 247 N.E.2d 603 (Ill. 1969)]

b. Disclaimers and Limitations of Warranty Liability

There is in every contract for the sale of goods a warranty that the seller has good title to the goods. [U.C.C. § 2–312] In addition, a *merchant* seller *impliedly warrants* that goods sold are *merchantable* (*i.e.*, the goods meet certain basic standards, including suitability for their ordinary purposes). [U.C.C. § 2–314] Furthermore, any seller who has reason to know that the buyer intends to use the goods purchased for a particular purpose and that the buyer is relying on the seller's skill or judgment in selection of suitable goods *impliedly warrants* that the goods are *fit for the particular purpose.* [U.C.C. § 2–315] A seller may try to limit implied warranty liability in two different ways, and such limitations are not necessarily unconscionable.

(1) Disclaimers

First, the seller may attempt to disclaim (*i.e.*, negate) the warranty altogether. U.C.C. section 2–316 provides that to exclude or modify the implied warranty of merchantability, the *language must mention merchantability* and, in the case of a writing, the disclaimer must be conspicuous. To exclude the implied warranty of fitness for a particular purpose, the language *must be in in writing and conspicuous.* However, the U.C.C. also provides that *all* implied warranties may be excluded by expressions calling the buyer's attention to the exclusion of warranties and making it clear that implied warranties are excluded (*e.g.*, "as is" or "with all faults").

(2) Limitation of Remedies

U.C.C. section 2–719(1)(a) provides that agreements for the sale of goods may limit the buyer's remedies. Thus, instead of disclaiming a certain warranty, the seller may limit liability for breach of that warranty. For example, agreements often may limit the buyer's remedies for breach of warranty to repair and replacement of defective goods. U.C.C. section 2–719(1)(a) is subject to two major exceptions:

(a) Limitation Disallowed—Exclusive Remedy Fails of Its Purpose

First, U.C.C. section 2–719(2) provides that "where circumstances cause an exclusive or limited remedy to fail of its essential purpose, remedy may be had as provided in this Act." This provision is most commonly invoked when the contract specifies that a buyer's only remedy is repair or replacement of the goods, and the seller neither repairs nor replaces within a reasonable period of time.

(b) Limitation Disallowed—Personal Injury

Second, U.C.C. section 2–719(3) provides that consequential damages may be limited or excluded unless the limitation or exclusion is unconscionable, but that "limitation of consequential damages for injury *to the person* [resulting from] consumer goods is prima facie unconscionable." (U.C.C. section 2–719(3) adds that limitation of damages where the loss is *commercial* is not prima facie unconscionable.)

1) Application

Although U.C.C. section 2–719(3) provides that a limitation on consequential damages for injury to the person resulting from consumer goods is only "prima facie" unconscionable, in practice such a limitation is almost invariably viewed as unconscionable by the courts. [*See, e.g.*, **Collins v. Uniroyal, Inc.,** 315 A.2d 30 (N.J. 1974)]

E. Statute of Frauds

1. In General

Absent a statute that provides otherwise, oral contracts are enforceable. However, a universal statute called the Statute of Frauds requires *certain types* of contracts to be memorialized in a writing signed by "the party to be charged" (*i.e.*, the party against whom enforcement of the contract is sought). This universal statute stems from the English Statute of Frauds of 1677. If an oral contract falls within one of the specific categories of contracts that must be memorialized in a writing under the Statute of Frauds, the contract is said to be "within the Statute"—*i.e.*, the Statute of Frauds is a defense to enforcement of the contract **unless some exception** (*e.g.*, part performance) to the Statute applies. If an exception *does* apply, it is said that the contract is "taken out of the Statute"—*i.e.*, the Statute is then not a defense for the promisor. In short, if a contract is "within the Statute" it is unenforceable against a party who has not signed a writing containing the contract's material terms—unless some exception takes the contract "out of the Statute," in which case the contract *is* enforceable.

2. Purpose

The basic purpose of the Statute of Frauds is to prevent fraudulent lawsuits by plaintiffs who might falsely claim that a contract was made when it was not. Courts have often opposed or limited the Statute of Frauds, however, noting that it is as likely to cause fraud as to prevent it. Accordingly, the Statute has developed many exceptions and limitations over the years.

3. Types of Contracts That Must Be Memorialized in Writing

Following the original English Statute of Frauds, modern American Statutes of Frauds commonly require at least five categories of contracts to be memorialized in a writing: (i) contracts for the sale of an interest in land; (ii) contracts for the sale of goods (now covered by the U.C.C.); (iii) contracts in consideration of marriage; (iv) contracts not to be performed within one year from the time they are made; and (v) contracts of suretyship.

Note: Some states add other types of contracts to their specific Statutes of Frauds. For example, New York's statute includes agreements to pay finder's fees in business deals (fees for "negotiating the purchase [or] sale . . . of any real estate[,] business opportunity, [or] business" or for "procuring an introduction to a party to the transaction or assisting in the negotiation or consummation of the transaction" [N.Y. General Obligation Law § 5–701(a)(10)]). California's statute applies to some loans over $100,000 and to various other financial transactions. [Cal Civ. Code § 1624] The statutes in Florida and Texas cover guarantees by some healthcare providers about the results of medical procedures. [Fla. Stat. § 725.01; Tex. Bus. & Com. Code § 26.01]

a. Contracts for Sale of Interest in Land

The Statute of Frauds applies to contracts for the sale of land or of any interest therein.

(1) Leases

Leases are covered by the sale-of-an-interest-in-land provision of the Statute unless explicitly excepted. However, many Statutes of Frauds do exclude leases for one year or less, meaning that such leases do not need to be memorialized in a signed writing. [*E.g.*, Cal. Civ. Code § 1624]

(2) What Constitutes "Interest in Land"?

It is often difficult to determine just what constitutes an "interest in land" within the meaning of the Statute of Frauds. In general, what constitutes an interest in land is determined by property law. For example, a lease (subject to the exception above) is often included because property law treats leasehold interests as a type of real-estate interest, but a hotel booking is ordinary not considered a property *interest* in land because property law treats it simply as a license to *use* the land.

(a) Note

A contract to *share the profits* or proceeds from the purchase or sale of land is *not* within the Statute because it is not a contract for sale and does not promise to convey an interest in land.

(3) Part Performance Doctrine

Part performance of an oral contract for the sale of an interest in land operates somewhat differently on sellers and purchasers.

(a) Sellers

A seller who has performed their side of an oral contract for the sale of an interest in land by conveying the interest to the buyer can recover the purchase price even if there is no signed writing.

(b) Purchasers

Part performance by the purchaser of an interest in land may take a contract out of the Statute for purposes of an action *in equity*—i.e., a suit for specific performance (which seeks an order from a court to a party to perform under a contract). However, the traditional part performance exception to the Statute of Frauds does *not* apply to an action against the seller *at law*—i.e., an action for damages.

1) Requirements Under Traditional Rule

Under the traditional rule, the exception to the sale-of-land provision for part performance by a purchaser applies only if the purchaser, with the consent of the seller, either (i) made a *valuable improvement* on the land or (ii) took or retained *possession* and *paid a part of the purchase price.*

a) Note

Under some cases, taking possession, even without part payment, suffices.

2) Reliance Doctrine

Under modern law, with the development of the reliance principle in the Statute of Frauds (*see infra*, pp. 171–172), part performance that does not meet the traditional test but that constitutes reliance may be sufficient to estop the other party from pleading the Statute of Frauds. On this theory, part performance may be relevant even if the action is at law (*i.e.*, for damages).

b. Contracts for the Sale of Goods—U.C.C. Section 2–201

The modern Statute of Frauds provision applicable to sales of goods is set forth in U.C.C. section 2–201. Under section 2–201, a contract for the sale of any goods for the price of *$500 or more* is within the Statute of Frauds.

(1) "Goods" Defined

"Goods" includes all tangible movable property. It does not include intangible securities or services.

(2) Exceptions

U.C.C. section 2–201 recognizes several exceptions. Under these exceptions, an oral contract for the sale of goods for $500 or more *will* be enforced under the following circumstances:

(a) Receipt and Acceptance of Goods

The buyer receives and accepts all or part of the goods (in which case the contract becomes enforceable as to the goods *accepted and received*) [U.C.C. § 2–201(3)(c)];

(b) Part Payment

The buyer makes part payment for the goods (in which case the contract is enforceable as to the goods for which *payment has been made*) [U.C.C. § 2–201(3)(c)];

(c) Special Manufacture

The contract calls for the manufacture of special goods for the buyer not suitable for sale to others in the ordinary course of the seller's business, and the seller makes either a *"substantial beginning"* in the manufacture of the goods or *commitments* for their procurement [U.C.C. § 2–201(3)(a)];

(d) No Objection to Confirmation

(i) The contract is *between merchants;* within a reasonable time a *written confirmation,* which satisfies the Statute of Frauds as to the sender, is sent; and the recipient does not dispatch a written objection thereto within 10 days [U.C.C. § 2–201(2)]; or

(e) Admission

The contract is admitted by the party against whom enforcement is sought "in his *pleadings* or *testimony* in court" [U.C.C. § 2–201(3)(b)].

EXAM TIP

An acronym for remembering when a writing signed by the party to be charged is *not required* for a sale of goods, even if for $500 or more, is SWAP: *Specially* made goods, *Written confirmation* by a merchant, *Admission* in court, or *Performance* through receipt and acceptance of goods or part payment. These elements take the contract out of the Statute of Frauds.

(3) Modifications

A modification of a contract for the sale of goods is within the Statute of Frauds if the *new agreement* that results from putting together the original contract and the modification is within the Statute.

Example: Seller orally agrees to sell Buyer two used cars for $900. Before the time for delivery, Seller and Buyer orally modify the contract so that Seller will sell only one of the cars for $450. The modification is not within the Statute of Frauds because, under the new agreement, the price of the goods is less than $500.

Compare: In the example above, if the original contract had been to sell one car for $450, and the contract was then orally modified to cover two cars for $900, the modification would be within the Statute of Frauds.

(4) Contracts for Both Goods and Services

Often a contract requires both supplying goods and rendering services. [*E.g.*, **Pittsley v. Houser,** 875 P.2d 232 (Idaho Ct. App. 1994)—sale and installation of carpet] These contracts might or might not be governed by the U.C.C. (and therefore its Statute of Frauds provision). A contract does not come within the U.C.C. Statute of Frauds merely because it involves an incidental supply of goods, like a contract to repair a television set in which the repairer also furnishes parts. Conversely, a contract does not fall outside the U.C.C. Statute of Frauds merely because it requires an incidental furnishing of services, like a contract to sell a dining-room set in which the seller also delivers the table and unpacks the chairs. In borderline cases, the *"predominant factor"* of the contract determines whether it is a contract for goods or for services.

(a) Minority Rule—Contract Separated into Component Parts

An alternative, minority approach is to separate the contract into its component parts. For example, a court could break apart a contract to install an air-conditioning system into (i) a contract to sell the air-conditioning system and (ii) a contract to provide installation services. Under this approach, the U.C.C. would apply to the one part of the contract (sale of goods) but not to the other part of the contract (rendering of services).

c. Contracts in Consideration of Marriage

Contracts in consideration of marriage are within the Statute of Frauds. This provision of the Statute is interpreted to refer to marriage settlement contracts and prenuptial contracts that include financial provisions. The provision is *not* interpreted to apply to simple mutual promises between prospective spouses to marry. These contracts are (somewhat arbitrarily) considered to be "contracts to marry" rather than "contracts in consideration of marriage." (Note, however, that in many or most states suit can no longer be brought by one prospective spouse against another for breach of a promise to marry.)

Example: Mother orally promises Son that if Son marries Jon, she will give the couple $10,000 after the wedding. Son and Jon marry. The promise is not enforceable under the Statute of Frauds because it was not in writing.

Compare: Annie and Alvin orally agree to marry. The agreement is not within the Statute of Frauds because each promise to marry is deemed to be in consideration of the other promise to marry, not in consideration of marriage itself. (This is just a contract to marry, not a "contract in consideration of marriage.")

cf. **Compare:** The father of one prospective spouse and the mother of the other prospective spouse orally agree that if the marriage takes place they will each give $5,000 to the couple. The agreement is not within the Statute of Frauds because each promise is deemed to be given in consideration of the *other promise*, not in consideration of marriage.

d. Contracts That Cannot Be Performed Within One Year of Making

Under the "one-year provision" of the Statute of Frauds, contracts that *by their terms cannot be performed within one year* from the making thereof must be memorialized in a writing. The one-year period begins at the date the contract is *made*, not when performance is promised. [4 Corbin on Contracts § 19.1 (2019)]

(1) Statute Not Applicable if Performance Within One Year Is Possible Although Unlikely

A contract that will probably take more than one year to perform, or that seems to envision performance over more than one year, may nonetheless be *capable* of being fully performed within one year. Such a contract is not within the Statute and is therefore enforceable even though oral.

Example: The following oral contracts would not be within the one-year provision because they are capable of being performed in one year, even if such performance is unlikely:

- A promise to take care of another person until they die.

- A promise to pay a pension until death. [**Leonard v. Rose,** 65 Cal. 2d 589 (1967)]

- A promise to service and maintain equipment "as long as you need it." [**Warner v. Texas Railway,** 164 U.S. 418 (1896)]

- A promise of "lifetime" employment. *Caveat:* Some statutes require "lifetime" contracts to be in writing. [*See, e.g.*, N.Y. Gen. Oblig. Law § 5–701]

- A promise to perform complex construction services that were envisioned to take three to ten years but which could be completed within a year without violating the terms of the agreement. [**C. R. Klewin, Inc. v. Flagship Props., Inc.,** 600 A.2d 772 (Conn. 1991)]

EXAM TIP

A contract is not within the Statute of Frauds just because it *actually* takes more than a year to perform it, nor is it within the Statute of Frauds because a *lawsuit* is brought more than a year after the contract was made. Only contracts that *cannot* be performed within a year, under their terms, are within the Statute of Frauds. To decide whether this rule applies, look for *explicit* terms in the contract that require performance to take more than a year.

(a) Performance Distinguished from Excuse

Contracts that can (even theoretically) be *performed* within a year are outside the Statute of Frauds (and therefore don't require a writing), but a contract is not outside the Statute of Frauds only because it might terminate within a year as a result of excuse or subsequent agreement. [Rest. 2d § 130, comment b]

 Example: Company hires Employee for a two-year term under an oral contract. This contract is within the Statute of Frauds, and therefore requires a signed writing to be enforced, even though Employee might die (and thereby end the contract) during the first year. This result is true even if Employee is very ill and unlikely to live for more than a year at the time the contract is made.

(2) Exception for Performance

Even if a contract cannot be performed within one year, the great weight of authority holds that once the contract has been *fully performed on one side,* it will be enforceable even though it was oral. [Rest. 2d § 130(2)]

Example: In an oral agreement, Landscaper promises to maintain Owner's property for two years, and Owner promises to pay Landscaper $5,000 at the end of that time. Landscaper fully performs. Owner's promise to pay $5,000 can be enforced.

(a) Rationale

Even if the contract was not enforceable, the party who performed could sue in restitution for the benefit conferred. (*See infra*, p. 171.) Allowing suit on the contract itself avoids the difficulty of measuring the value of the benefit conferred.

(3) Exception for Securities—U.C.C.

U.C.C. section 8–113 provides that oral contracts for the sale of securities are enforceable, even if the one-year rule would otherwise apply. [U.C.C. § 8–113]

e. Suretyship Contracts

Under the suretyship provision of the Statute of Frauds, promises made to a creditor of a debtor to "answer for" (*i.e.*, to be responsible for or guarantee) the debtor's obligation must be memorialized in a writing. The original English Statute of Frauds also provided that promises by an executor or administrator of an estate to pay the decedent's debts out of their own funds must be memorialized in a writing. However, this requirement falls within the suretyship provision, so the same rules apply. The suretyship provision is subject to some important *exceptions:*

(1) Promise to Debtor

If the promise is made to *the debtor* (*e.g.*, "I promise to pay your obligation to your creditor"), the promise does not fall within the suretyship section of the Statute of Frauds. Such a promise is therefore enforceable even if it is oral, assuming there is consideration. [Rest. 2d § 123]

(2) Promisor Is Primary Obligor

The Statute of Frauds also does not apply to a contract in which the promisor promises to be *primarily* liable for a third person's obligation (*e.g.*, "Send a vacuum cleaner to Jo and bill it to me"). It applies only to contracts in which the promisor promises to be secondarily liable (*e.g.*, "I will pay for the vacuum Taylor is buying from you if Taylor doesn't pay for it").

(3) Main-Purpose Rule

A suretyship promise is enforceable, even though oral, if it appears that the promisor's *main purpose* in guaranteeing the obligation of another was to secure an advantage or pecuniary benefit *for themselves.* [Rest. 2d § 116]

Example: Subcontractor refuses to furnish further labor and materials in the construction of Owner's house because the credit of Owner's principal contractor, General, is bad. To get her house completed, Owner orally guarantees Subcontractor that she will pay all amounts owed by General to Subcontractor if Principal does not pay. Owner's promise is enforceable. Her main purpose was not to aid Subcontractor but to get her own house completed. [**Kampman v. Pittsburgh Contracting & Engineering Co.,** 175 A. 396 (Pa. 1934)]

CONTRACTS REQUIRING A WRITING — GILBERT

TO ENFORCE THE FOLLOWING CONTRACTS, THERE MUST BE A WRITTEN MEMORANDUM SIGNED BY THE PARTY AGAINST WHOM ENFORCEMENT IS SOUGHT:

- ☑ Contracts for the sale of an interest in *land*
- ☑ Contracts in consideration of *marriage*
- ☑ Contracts that *cannot be performed within one year* of formation (except for contracts to sell securities)
- ☑ *Suretyship* contracts (*i.e.*, contracts where the promisor guarantees a third party's obligation to the third party's creditor)
- ☑ Contracts for the *sale of goods for $500 or more*, as long as the U.C.C. exceptions (*e.g.*, contracts for specially manufactured goods in which the seller has made a substantial beginning of performance; receipt and acceptance of goods by the buyer) do not apply

---

4. Type of Writing Required

The Statute of Frauds does not ordinarily require that *the contract* between the parties be in writing (although individual state statutes may sometimes require this). Normally, there need only be *a writing* that is *signed* by the "party to be charged"—normally the defendant in a breach-of-contract lawsuit. This writing may be an informal "memorandum" of the agreement, as long as it contains the deal's *essential terms*. "Writings" need not be written with pen and paper; electronic communications and signatures count under the Statute of Frauds.

a. Essential Terms

To satisfy the Statute, a memorandum normally must include:

(1) The identity of the *contracting parties;*

(2) A description of the *subject matter* of the contract; and

(3) The *terms and conditions* of the agreement.

b. Recital of Consideration

Many states provide that a writing will not satisfy the Statute of Frauds unless it states "the consideration." Normally this requirement has little meaning, because a writing that fails to state what each party was to do would probably be insufficient to satisfy the Statute of Frauds in any event. The major application of this requirement is to contracts of suretyship, where the writing often states the surety's promise without stating the consideration for that promise.

c. U.C.C. Provisions

In contracts for the sale of goods, which are governed by the U.C.C., a writing can satisfy the Statute of Frauds even though it is less complete than is usually required. Under the

U.C.C., there need only be "some writing sufficient to indicate that a contract for sale has been made" and specifying the *quantity* term. Such a writing will suffice even though it omits or incorrectly states the price, time and place of payment, and quality of the goods. Even if it states the quantity term incorrectly, a writing will satisfy the Statute of Frauds, but the contract will not be enforceable beyond the quantity of goods specified in the writing. [U.C.C. § 2–201; *and see* Sale & Lease of Goods Summary]

(1) Written Confirmations

The U.C.C. also provides that if one merchant sends a written confirmation of a contract to another merchant in a form sufficient to bind the sender, the recipient is bound unless they object within 10 days following receipt—even though the recipient merchant never signed anything. [U.C.C. § 2–201(2); *see supra*, p. 158 *et seq.*]

d. Electronic Records

Electronic records—*e.g.*, emails, PDFs, voicemails, text messages—count just like traditional written documents for the purposes of the Statute of Frauds. [U.E.T.A. § 7] That is, an email or PDF file satisfies the Statute of Frauds if it is otherwise sufficient under the Statute's requirements.

e. Signature

The signature on a requisite writing need not be handwritten to satisfy the Statute of Frauds; it can be typed, printed, or electronically made. A party's initials or any other mark may be a sufficient signature if so intended. The main test is whether the party made the "signature" with the intent to authenticate the writing—*i.e.*, to demonstrate that it was they who "signed" the writing. [U.C.C. § 1–201(b)(37); U.E.T.A. § 2(8)]

(1) Broad interpretation

Courts and statutes have adopted a very broad definition of "signature." For example, in an advertisement that constitutes an offer, the inclusion of the company's name in the advertisement is a signature for the purposes of the Statute of Frauds. [**Donovan v. Rrl Corp.,** 109 Cal. Rptr. 2d 807, 27 P.3d 702 (2001); Rest. 2d § 131, ill. 2] In an email, the "From:" header can be sufficient to count as a signature on its own, even if a signature is not present in the body of an email. [**Khoury v. Tomlinson,** 518 S.W.3d 568 (Tex. App. 2017)] The Comment to U.E.T.A. suggests that saying "It's me" in a voicemail message can be a signature if that is the speaker's intent, as can clicking a button on a website that says "I agree." [U.E.T.A. § 2(8), comment]

(2) Agents' Signature

The original Statute of Frauds expressly provided that a memorandum was sufficient if signed by an authorized agent of the party to be charged. It was not required that the agent's authority to sign also be in writing. Thus, if *P* orally authorized *A* to buy land on their behalf, and *A* signed a land purchase contract, "*P*, by their agent *A*," *A* was bound.

(a) Equal Dignity Statutes

However, some states have "equal dignity" statutes. Under such statutes, if a contract is required by law to be in writing under the Statute of Frauds, a principal is bound to a contract signed by the agent only if the *agent's authority is also in writing*. [*See, e.g.*, Cal. Civ. Code § 2309]

(3) Party to Be Charged Must Sign

Only the party to be charged (*i.e.*, sought to be held liable under the contract) must have signed a writing. The fact that the party seeking to enforce the contract has not signed a writing is immaterial, even if that means that one party can enforce a contract while the other cannot.

Example: Vendor and Purchaser make an oral agreement for the sale of land. Purchaser sends the following email to Vender: "I'm very happy with our deal and looking forward to seeing it through. Please let me know if you have any questions. Signed, Purchaser." Vendor can enforce the contract, but Purchaser cannot.

(4) Location of Signature

Normally, the signature (however made) can appear anywhere on the relevant instrument. However, a few statutes say that the writing must be "subscribed." Some courts applying such statutes have required a signature at the bottom of the writing.

f. Consolidation of Several Documents

The required writing need not appear in a single document. Instead, several documents (signed and unsigned, as long as one is signed) may be "pieced together" to form the required writing. This is easiest when the documents clearly refer to each other, but some courts have permitted the use of extrinsic evidence to explain how apparently unrelated writings are in fact related. [Rest. 2d § 132]

g. Sales at Auction

Sales at auction are usually oral. However, the auctioneer's written memorandum of the terms of a sale is held to be a sufficient writing against both the buyer and the seller, on the theory that in making the memorandum the auctioneer is the agent of both the buyer and the seller. [Rest. 2d § 135]

EXAM TIP **GILBERT**

To be sufficient under the Statute of Frauds, something *in writing* must contain the contract terms. Recall that the writing need not be a full-fledged contract; it need not even be in a single document. Thus, several pieces of correspondence between the parties could be a sufficient memorandum of the agreement; a text message or a memo written on a napkin also could suffice. The key is that there is something in writing "signed" by the party to be charged.

---

5. Effect of Noncompliance with the Statute of Frauds

a. Majority View—Contract Unenforceable but Not Void

In most states, failure to comply with the Statute of Frauds renders a contract *voidable*—*i.e.*, unenforceable against a party who has not signed the requisite writing—but not void. [U.C.C. § 2–201; Rest. 2d § 138; **Walter H. Leimert Co. v. Woodson,** 125 Cal. App. 2d 186 (1954)]

(1) Effect

Under this view, although a suit cannot be brought on an oral contract that is within the Statute of Frauds, the contract is valid for all other purposes. For example, if the oral contract is confirmed in a later memorandum, the contract becomes enforceable against a party who signed the later memorandum even though no new consideration is given (*supra*, p. 37). Similarly, once a contract that falls within the Statute of Frauds has been performed on both sides, neither party is entitled to recover back what they have given (as if there had been no contract). [Rest. 2d § 145]

(2) Third Party Cannot Raise Defense of Statute of Frauds

The Statute of Frauds normally may be asserted only by a party to the contract, not by a third person. Thus, if Seller orally promises to convey Blackacre to Buyer and gives Buyer immediate possession of the property, including the right to rents payable from Tenant, Tenant cannot refuse to pay the rent to Buyer on the ground that Buyer's contract was oral.

b. Minority View—Contract Void

In a few states, the Statute provides that failure to comply with the Statute renders a contract *void.* Under this view, the Statute of Frauds might be a defense to the formation, not merely the enforcement, of a contract. [**Ward v. Ward,** 30 P.2d 853 (Colo. 1934)] In general, however, the courts have not put much weight on whether a given Statute of Frauds provides that contracts that fail to comply with the Statute are "void."

6. Recovery in Restitution

Normally, a party who has conferred a benefit pursuant to a contract that falls within the Statute of Frauds can recover in restitution for the value of the benefit, even if they cannot enforce the contract.

a. Rationale

A suit to recover the benefit is not technically within the Statute of Frauds. The Statute says that no action shall lie to enforce contracts that fall within it. A suit to recover the value of a benefit is technically not an action to enforce the contract but an action in restitution or quasi-contract. Moreover, it would be unjust to permit a party to retain benefits received under the contract without paying for them.

b. Distinguish Part Performance Exceptions

In certain cases, part performance (or full performance on one side) creates an exception to the Statute of Frauds and makes a contract enforceable—either in full, as in sale-of-land cases (*see supra*, p. 163) or in part, as in sale-of-goods cases (*see supra*, p. 164). As just pointed out, even if the law did not recognize these part performance exceptions, a party who had rendered performance could recover the value of the benefit conferred in restitution. The significance of the part performance exceptions is that when such an exception is applicable, it allows the performing party to sue ***on the contract*** for expectation damages, rather than merely in restitution or quasi-contract for the value of the benefit conferred.

(1) Caveat

Remember that only certain kinds of part performance result in the enforceability of a contract that falls within the Statute (*see supra*, pp. 163, 164). If part performance does not make a contract enforceable, the remedy remains a suit in restitution for the value of the benefit conferred.

7. Reliance on Contracts Within the Statute of Frauds

a. Reliance on the Contract

The traditional rule was that reliance on a contract that is within the Statute of Frauds does not create an exception to the Statute—*i.e.*, reliance does not take a contract out of the Statute—except insofar as the reliance involved part performance of the kind that takes a contract out of the Statute. However, a growing number of modern cases hold that reliance by one party may estop (preclude) the other from asserting the Statute of Frauds as a defense, even if the reliance does not consist of part performance of a kind that satisfies the Statute.

Example: Buyer orally agrees to buy a group of used cars from Seller, and Seller transports the cars across the country to deliver them to Buyer. Buyer then refuses to proceed with the purchase. In the meantime, the used car market has fallen sharply. Buyer is estopped to rely on the Statute as a defense, because if the contract is not enforced, Seller would suffer an unconscionable loss as a result of his reliance. [**Goldstein v. McNeil,** 122 Cal. App. 2d 608 (1954)]

b. Restatement in Accord

Restatement Second adopts the position that one party's reliance on a contract that is within the Statute of Frauds may estop the other party from pleading the Statute as a defense. In particular, Restatement Second section 139 provides that when a contract is within the Statute of Frauds, but the promisor has induced action or forbearance by the promisee so that "injustice can be avoided only by enforcement of the promise," the promise is enforceable. [Rest. 2d § 139] Under the Restatement rule, whether a promise that falls within the Statute of Frauds should be enforced because of reliance depends upon the availability and adequacy of other remedies, particularly restitution; the extent to which the promisee's detrimental reliance was substantial, reasonable, and foreseeable; and the extent to which the oral agreement is corroborated by the reliance or other evidence.

F. Lack of Contractual Capacity

1. Minors

A contract made by a minor (an "infant"—in most states, a person younger than 18) is ***voidable*** at the minor's option, although the minor may enforce the contract against the adult.

a. Restitution

In general, a minor is not even liable for the value of benefits they have received under the contract, although if they disaffirm the contract they must return anything that they received under the contract and still retain at the time of disaffirmance. However, a minor ***is*** liable in restitution for the reasonable value of ***necessaries*** furnished to them.

(1) "Necessaries"

"Necessaries" includes food, clothing, shelter, and whatever else is needed for the minor's subsistence, health, comfort, or education, taking into consideration the minor's age, status, and condition in life.

(a) **Note**

In some states, a minor is liable for the reasonable value of necessaries furnished to or purchased by them only if they are emancipated from their parents or if their parents are unable to provide the necessaries. [*See, e.g.*, Cal. Civ. Code § 36]

2. Mental Incapacity

a. Traditional Rule

The traditional rule is that a person lacks the mental capacity to contract *only if* their mental processes are so deficient that they lack understanding of the nature, purpose, and effect of the transaction. [95 A.L.R. 1442] This is sometimes referred to as the "cognitive test." Under this test, which is the majority rule, psychological or emotional problems that affect a party's judgment or reason do not in themselves constitute mental incapacity for the purposes of contract law. Rather, the psychological condition must actually deprive the party of an understanding of what they are doing. [**Smalley v. Baker,** 262 Cal. App. 2d 824 (1968)—person with bipolar disorder held competent]

b. Restatement Rule

Restatement Second adopts a rule that expands the doctrine of mental incapacity: a party lacks capacity if "he is *unable to act in a reasonable manner* . . . and the other party has *reason to know* of his condition." [Rest. 2d § 15] This is sometimes referred to as the "affective test."

c. Effect of Incapacity

A contract entered into by a person lacking mental capacity is *voidable* by that person (or a guardian acting on their behalf), but not by the other contracting party.

(1) Note

In many states, contracts made by people who have been *adjudicated* insane or mentally incompetent are void, rather than merely voidable. [*See, e.g.*, Cal. Civ. Code § 40]

d. Restitutional Liability for Necessaries

A person who lacks mental capacity (or their estate) is liable in restitution for the value of any necessaries furnished to them.

3. Drunken or Drugged Persons

Drunkenness and drugs raise problems of *temporary* incapacity. Each case must be judged on its own facts. The test, however, remains the same—whether the person was so intoxicated or drugged as to be unable to understand the nature, purpose, and effect of what they were doing. [**Backus v. Sessions,** 17 Cal. 2d 380 (1941)]

a. Restatement Second Rule

Restatement Second's rule, not widely adopted, is that contracts with people who are so drunk that they cannot *reasonably* act in relation to the transaction (or reasonably understand its nature and effects) are voidable, but only if the other party has *reason to know* of the drunkenness. [Rest. 2d § 16]

G. Illegal Contracts

1. In General

If a proposed contract is legal at the time an offer is made but becomes illegal before acceptance of the offer, the intervening illegality terminates the offer as a matter of law. If a contract is made, and is legal when made, but becomes illegal thereafter, the contract is discharged (*see infra*, p. 241).

2. What Constitutes Illegality?

A contract is illegal if either the consideration or the object of the contract is illegal. Some contracts are illegal because they are expressly prohibited by statute (*e.g.*, gambling contracts and contracts in restraint of trade). Other contracts are illegal because they violate public policy (*e.g.*, contracts to defraud or injure third parties).

a. Indirect Aid in Accomplishment of an Illegal Act

An otherwise valid contract is not illegal merely because its performance will indirectly aid in the accomplishment of an illegal act, provided the illegal act does not involve a serious crime or great moral turpitude. For example, a seller can recover the price of furniture even though they know the buyer was purchasing the furniture for an illegal gambling casino, provided the seller does nothing in furtherance of the unlawful design. Similarly, a lender can recover money loaned even though they knew the borrower intended to use the money for illegal gambling, provided the lender takes no part in the gambling.

3. Effects of Illegality

An illegal contract is ***void***, and the general rule is that if a contract is illegal the courts ***will not intercede*** to aid either party. Therefore, if the contract is executory, neither party can enforce it. If the contract is partly performed, neither party can recover in restitution for benefits conferred. The rationale is that the public importance of discouraging such transactions outweighs considerations of possible injustice between the private parties. [Rest. 1st § 598] However, there are some important exceptions to these rules:

a. Severable Portion May Be Enforced

First, if the agreement is "severable" into legal and illegal portions, and the illegal portion does not go to the "essence of the bargain," the legal portion may be enforced. [Rest. 1st § 606] An agreement is severable for these purposes only if it expressly requires performance in distinct installments or portions and a separable consideration is provided for each such portion (*see infra*, p. 234 *et seq.*).

b. "Locus Penitentiae" Doctrine

Second, some decisions hold that if one party to an illegal contract repents and repudiates the contract before any part of the illegal purpose is carried out, that party may obtain restitutionary recovery for the value of what they gave in performance prior to repenting and repudiating. [Rest. 1st § 605; **Wasserman v. Sloss,** 117 Cal. 425 (1897)]

c. Not "in Pari Delicto"

Third, a party who has conferred a benefit under an illegal contract may be entitled to bring suit in restitution for the value of the benefit conferred if that party is not guilty of serious moral turpitude and is not as blameworthy as the other party. In such cases, the relatively innocent party is said not to be "in pari delicto" (Latin for "in equal fault"). This exception is *inapplicable* if the contract is *malum in se* ("evil in itself"—such as a contract for murder). [**Smith v. Bach,** 183 Cal. 259 (1920)]

(1) Where One Party Is Member of Protected Class

If one party to a contract that is illegal by reason of statute is a member of the class for whose benefit the statute was enacted, that party is usually not considered in pari delicto. Thus, an employee who works a greater number of hours than permitted by statute is not in pari delicto with their employer and can recover for their extra services. Similarly, an investor who purchases stock that is issued in violation of the "blue sky law" (*i.e.*, state securities statutes, which are designed to protect investors) is not in pari delicto with the corporation and may recover the purchase price paid for the stock. [**Randal v. Beber,** 107 Cal. App. 2d 692 (1951); *cf.* Rest. 3d Restitution & Unjust Enrichment § 32(1)—restitution is available whenever it "is required by the policy of the underlying prohibition"]

d. Contract Only Malum Prohibitum

Restitutionary recovery may also be available if the contract is only *malum prohibitum* (against some statute or regulation but not *malum in se*—*i.e.*, not bad on its own, apart from the statute or regulation). In such cases, the courts will not enforce the illegal contract, but they may permit a party to obtain restitution for benefits conferred. [Rest. 1st § 604]

Example: Television Station hires Fireman to do part-time work as a television baseball game announcer, knowing that Fireman is a city employee and that a city ordinance prohibits city employees from accepting part-time jobs. Fireman may recover from Television Station in restitution for the value of his services because violation of the ordinance does not involve an affront to public morals. [**Vick v. Patterson,** 158 Cal. App. 2d 414 (1958)]

Example: A usurious contract is also only malum prohibitum. The lender therefore can usually recover the principal sum loaned, but not the usurious interest. [**Haines v. Commercial Mortgage Co.,** 200 Cal. 609 (1927)]

e. Licensing Requirements

Statutes frequently require people to obtain a license or permit from an appropriate governmental authority in order to engage in a specified business or occupation (such as doctor, attorney, construction contractor, or stockbroker). If an unlicensed person contracts to perform services, whether the contract is enforceable depends upon the purpose of the licensing statute.

(1) License for Protection of Public

If the purpose of the licensing requirement is to protect the public from unqualified persons (*i.e.*, to assure that license holders have certain minimum qualifications), a contract negotiated by an unlicensed person relating to the business is usually held illegal, and the unlicensed person will be denied recovery in restitution for the value of the services.

(a) Note

Even in this kind of case, if a party has *substantially complied* with the licensing laws, that compliance may be held sufficient. Some courts do not allow the other party to the contract to avoid obligations under the contract merely because of technical violations (*e.g.*, late renewal of permit), as long as the public has received substantially the protection contemplated by the licensing law. [**Alaska Prot. Servs. v. Frontier Colorcable,** 680 P.2d 1119 (Alaska 1984)]

(2) License for Fiscal Regulation or Taxation

In contrast, if a licensing requirement is imposed primarily for purposes of fiscal regulation or taxation, rather than to protect the public from unqualified persons, contracts entered into by the unlicensed person are usually held enforceable notwithstanding the lack of a license.

Example: Cities usually require that businesses operating in the city obtain a business license, but such licensing is normally for revenue-raising purposes, and the cities do not make judgments about the qualifications of the licensees. Failure to obtain such a license is generally held not to render contracts entered into by the unlicensed person unenforceable.

Chapter Four
Third-Party Rights and Obligations

CONTENTS	PAGE
Chapter Approach	178
A. Third-Party Beneficiaries	178
B. Assignment of Rights and Delegation of Duties	191

Chapter Approach

Once you have established that an enforceable contract has been formed, you should next consider whether any third parties (*i.e.*, persons *not parties to the contract*) have any rights or duties under the contract. The types of third parties who may have rights or duties under a contract are third-party beneficiaries, assignees of contractual rights, and persons to whom contractual duties have been delegated.

1. **Third-Party Beneficiaries**

    If a question sets out a contract that provides for performance to be rendered to someone or to benefit someone who is *not a party*, you have a third-party beneficiary situation. To decide whether this third party has the right to enforce the contract, you must:

    — *Classify the third party* as an "incidental" or an "intended" beneficiary (or, under the older terminology, as an "incidental," "donee," or "creditor" beneficiary);

    — Consider whether any *defenses* may be available to the promisor; and

    — If the promisor and the promisee have attempted to *modify* the contract, determine whether, if the third party has a right to enforce the contract, the rights of the third party have *vested*.

2. **Assignment/Delegation**

    If a question sets out a situation where one of the original parties to the contract has transferred rights or delegated duties under the contract to a third person, you have an assignments problem. In that case, consider:

    — *Whether the rights may be assigned* or the duties delegated; and

    — *The effect* of the assignment or delegation on the various parties.

A. Third-Party Beneficiaries

1. In General

The question often arises whether a person who was not a party to the bargain, and who gave no consideration, can enforce the contract if they would have benefited from the contract's performance. This type of person is called a "third-party beneficiary."

e.g. **Example:** Peter contracts to paint Penny's building for $10,000, using paint sold by Theo. Can Theo enforce Peter's promise? (Under the conventional terminology used in such cases, ***Penny*** is the ***promisee, Peter*** is the ***promisor***, and ***Theo*** is the ***third-party beneficiary.***)

a. Original Common Law Rule—Promise Unenforceable by Third-Party Beneficiary

The original common law rule was that in order to maintain an action on a contract, a person must have given consideration to, and be in privity of contract with, the party against whom they are seeking to enforce the contract. Hence, a third-party beneficiary could not enforce a contract.

b. **Modern Law**

Under modern law, a third-party beneficiary may sue and recover in appropriate cases. [**Lawrence v. Fox,** 20 N.Y. 268 (1859); 81 A.L.R. 1289] The question is, what kinds of cases are appropriate?

2. Traditional Modern Law Test—Third Party Must Be Creditor Beneficiary or Donee Beneficiary

Even under modern law, not every person who would benefit from performance of a contract can bring suit on it as a third-party beneficiary. Under the traditional test, popularized by Restatement First, third-party beneficiaries are divided into three classes: (i) creditor beneficiaries, (ii) donee beneficiaries, and (iii) incidental beneficiaries. Creditor and donee beneficiaries can bring suit under the contract; incidental beneficiaries cannot.

a. Creditor Beneficiary

A third party is a "creditor beneficiary," and can enforce the contract, if the promisee's primary intent was to discharge an obligation they owed to the third party. [Rest. 2d § 302]

Example: Holly owes $300 to Lawrence. Holly then makes a contract with Fox. Under this contract, Holly loans Fox $300, and in exchange Fox (the promisor) promises to pay Lawrence (the third-party beneficiary) the $300 owed by Holly (the promisee) to Lawrence. Lawrence is a creditor beneficiary and can bring suit against Fox if Fox fails to pay him the $300. [**Lawrence v. Fox,** *supra*]

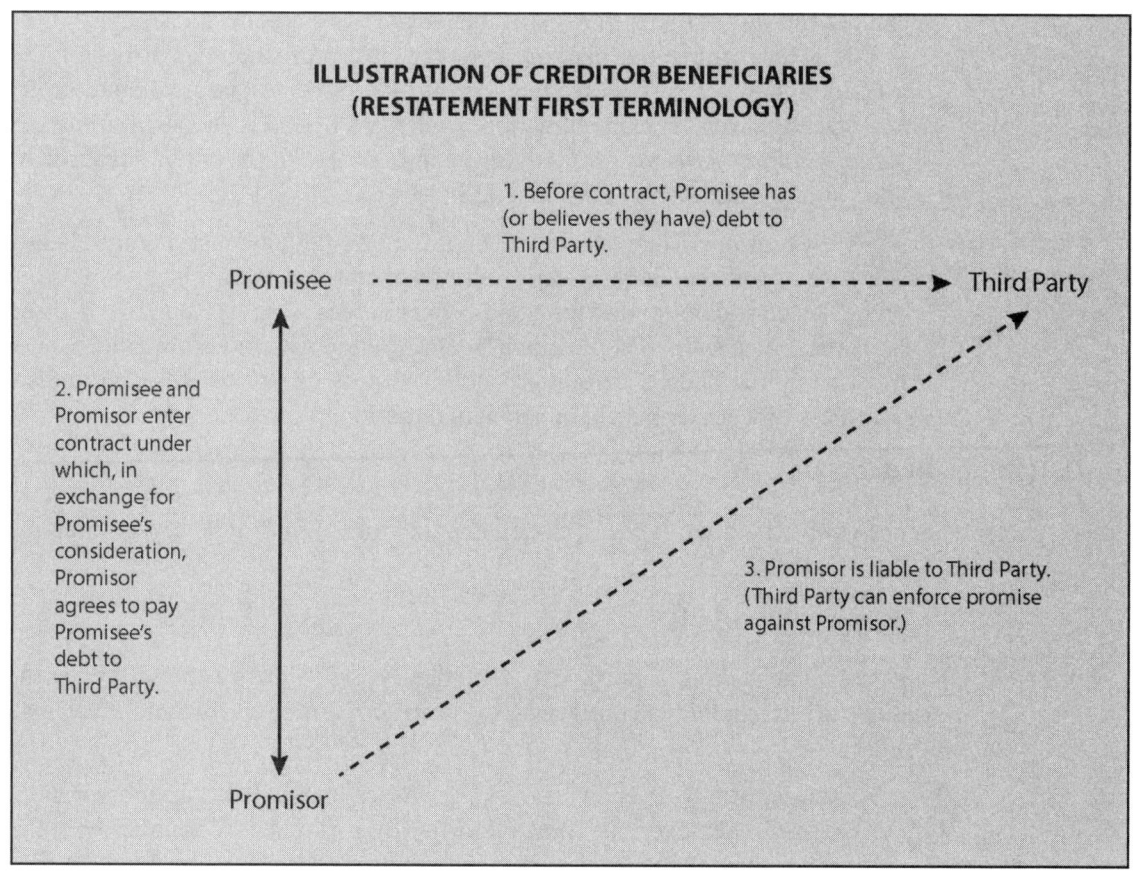

(1) Rationale

Permitting a creditor beneficiary to enforce a contract is justified for two reasons:

(a) Prevents Unjust Enrichment

Permitting a creditor beneficiary to enforce the contract prevents unjust enrichment of the promisor. The promisor has received consideration for their promise to perform for the benefit of the third party, and they should not be permitted to retain the consideration and not perform.

(b) Prevents Excessive Litigation

Permitting a creditor beneficiary to sue also saves unnecessary litigation. Even if a creditor beneficiary could not sue the promisor, they could still sue the promisee on the promisee's obligation to them. The promisee could then turn around and sue the promisor for not discharging the promisee's promise to the creditor beneficiary. Allowing the creditor beneficiary to sue the promisor directly therefore collapses two suits into one.

(2) Must There Be an Actual Obligation Owed to the Third Party?

Is it necessary, to establish creditor beneficiary status, that the promisee owed an *actual* obligation to the third party, or is it sufficient that the promisee *believed* they owed such an obligation?

(a) General Rule—Promisee's Intent Determinative

The general rule is that a third-party beneficiary is a creditor beneficiary if the promisee, in making the bargain with the promisor, intended to satisfy an obligation they *believed* they owed the third-party beneficiary, whether or not they actually owed such an obligation. Under this rule, it is sufficient if there is a *supposed* or *asserted* obligation owing to the third party. [**Hamill v. Maryland Casualty Co.**, 209 F.2d 338 (10th Cir. 1954)]

Example: Theo asserts a claim of $1,000 against Penny. Penny believes the claim is valid. Shortly thereafter, Peter buys goods from Penny. As consideration for the goods, Peter agrees to pay $1,000 to Theo. As the parties later learn, Theo's claim against Penny was in fact invalid. Under the general rule, Theo is a creditor beneficiary and can enforce Peter's promise, regardless of whether his claim had actual merit.

b. Donee Beneficiary

Restatement First defined two types of donee beneficiaries. Either type can enforce the contract.

(1) Intent to Confer a Gift

Under Restatement First, a third-party beneficiary is a "donee beneficiary" if the promisee's primary intent in contracting is to *confer a gift* on the beneficiary. [Rest. 1st § 133]

Example: Mrs. Beman, who is dying, wishes to give her house to her niece Marion. To achieve this objective, Mrs. Beman makes a contract with her husband, Judge Beman. By the terms of the contract, Mrs. Beman agrees not to change her will, under which her husband is the principal legatee and will inherit a life estate in the house. In exchange, Judge Beman agrees that on his death he will leave the value of the house to Marion. Marion is a donee beneficiary, and she can enforce the contract against Judge Beman. [**Seaver v. Ransom,** 224 N.Y. 233 (1918)]

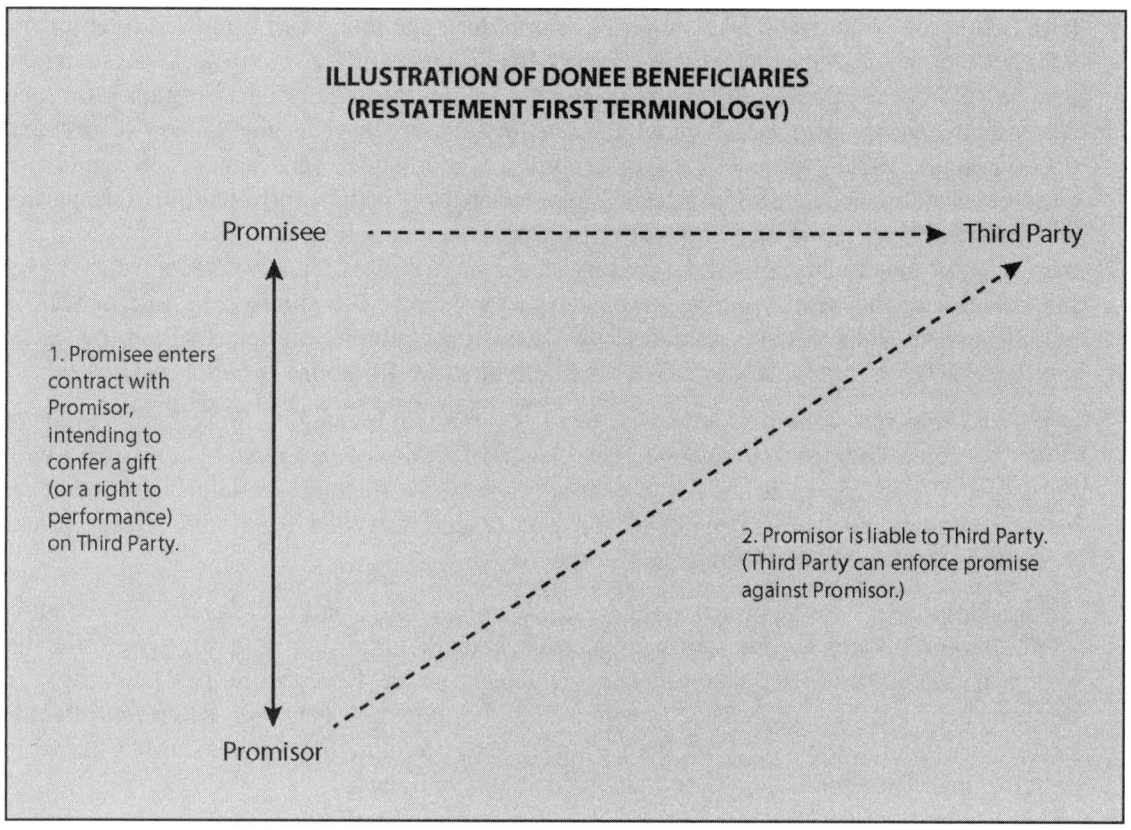

(2) Intent to Confer a Right to Performance

A third-party beneficiary is also a donee beneficiary under Restatement First if the promisee intended to confer on the beneficiary a *right against the promisor to some performance, other than as a gift.*

Example: Dealer contracts with Insurance Company that Insurance Company will indemnify anyone who purchases an auto from Dealer for loss due to fire or theft within one year after the purchase. Buyer purchases a car from Dealer on Dealer's assurance that Buyer is insured by Insurance Company. Buyer is a donee beneficiary, because Dealer intended to confer on Buyer a right against Insurance Company (even though it was not a gift).

c. Incidental Beneficiary

Under the Restatement First terminology, a third party who would benefit from the performance of a contract, but who is neither a creditor beneficiary nor a donee beneficiary, is an "incidental" beneficiary and cannot bring suit under the contract.

Example: Peter contracts with Penny to build a house on Penny's land. Construction will greatly enhance the value of neighboring property owned by Theo. If Peter breaches the contract and Theo brings suit against Peter, Theo will lose because he is only an incidental beneficiary. Peter was not discharging a debt to Theo, and it was clearly not Penny's intent to confer a gift on Theo or a right against Peter.

3. Restatement Second Terminology

Restatement Second substitutes the term *"intended beneficiary"* for the terms "creditor" and "donee" beneficiary, and it retains the term "incidental beneficiary." Thus, under the terminology of Restatement First, a ***donee*** or ***creditor*** beneficiary can bring suit to enforce a contract but an ***incidental*** beneficiary cannot, while under the terminology of Restatement Second, an ***intended*** beneficiary can bring suit but an ***incidental*** beneficiary cannot. However, although the ***terminology*** has changed, the ***tests*** remain largely the same. Under Restatement Second section 302(1), "a beneficiary of a promise is an intended beneficiary if recognition of a right to performance in the beneficiary is appropriate to effectuate the intention of the parties and either (a) the performance of the promise will satisfy an obligation of the promisee to pay money to the beneficiary; or (b) the circumstances indicate that the promisee intends to give the beneficiary the benefit of the promised performance." Essentially, the test in section 302(*l*)(a) is equivalent to the Restatement First test for creditor beneficiaries, and the test in section 302(*l*)(b) is equivalent to the Restatement First test for donee beneficiaries.

Example: Testator employs Attorney to draft a will leaving all of Testator's estate to Legatee. Legatee is an intended beneficiary of Attorney's promise to draft such a will, because allowing Legatee to sue Attorney is appropriate to effectuate Testator's intent that her estate (or its value) end up in Legatee's hands and Testator intended to benefit Legatee. [**Lucas v. Hamm,** 56 Cal. 2d 583 (1961)]

Compare: Peter contracts with Penny to build a house on Penny's land. The contract requires Peter to use roofing materials manufactured and sold by Theo. If Peter breaches the contract, Theo cannot bring suit against Peter. Recognition of Theo's right to performance was not necessary to effectuate the contract between Peter and Penny, performance would not satisfy an obligation of Peter to Penny, and Peter did not intend to benefit Theo. Therefore, Theo is only an incidental beneficiary.

a. **Problem**

It is easy to see why creditor beneficiaries and true gift beneficiaries (*i.e.*, beneficiaries toward whom the promisee had a donative intent) should be able to sue on the contract. The hard cases are those that do not fall into these two categories. Restatement First dealt with this problem by allowing a third party who was neither a creditor beneficiary nor a true gift beneficiary to bring suit as a "donee beneficiary" *if the promisee intended* to confer upon the beneficiary a right against the promisor to some performance, other than as a gift. However, this formulation was not very helpful in solving the hard cases, because the promisee's intent in these cases is seldom clear. The introductory part of Restatement Second section 302(1) adopts a more useful test to deal with the noncreditor, nongift cases—*i.e.*, whether recognition of a right in the beneficiary is appropriate to effectuate the intention of the parties. However, section 302(1)(b) then adds to that test a requirement that the circumstances indicate that the promisee intended to give the beneficiary the benefit of the required performance. The Restatement Second therefore also uses an intent test in such cases, despite the fact that intent in the noncreditor, nongift cases is seldom clear.

(1) **Comment**

A better principle to deal with the noncreditor, nongift cases is as follows: A third-party beneficiary should have power to enforce a contract if (i) allowing the beneficiary to enforce the contract is a necessary or important means of effecting the contracting parties' performance objectives, as manifested in the contract read in the light of surrounding circumstances, or (ii) allowing the beneficiary to enforce the contract is supported by reasons of policy or morality independent of contract law and would not conflict with the parties' performance objectives. This principle is comparable to the general, introductory part of the Restatement Second principle—whether recognition of a right is appropriate to effectuate the intention of the parties—but does not include, as does the Restatement Second, a requirement that the promisee *intended* to give the beneficiary the benefit of the promised performance, because intent in such cases is difficult to determine.

4. Recurring Third-Party Beneficiary Cases

Many third-party beneficiary cases fall into recurring patterns. Four of these will be discussed here: assumption agreements, agreements between testators and attorneys that would benefit would-be legatees, government contracts, and surety bonds.

a. Assumption of a Mortgage

In an assumption agreement, one person (the promisor) assumes (*i.e.*, undertakes to perform) the obligations already owed by another (the promisee) to a third party. The third party in an assumption agreement is a creditor beneficiary because, by definition, the promisor has assumed an obligation that the promisee owed to the third party. A common type of assumption agreement involves mortgages. A mortgage is an interest in real property (*e.g.*, a house) that secures a debt owed by the mortgagor (the debtor) to the mortgagee (the creditor). A person who sells property that is subject to a mortgage often requires the purchaser to assume the mortgage debt.

(1) Purchaser "Assumes" Mortgage Debt

Suppose a purchaser of real estate *"assumes"* (*i.e.*, agrees to pay) an existing mortgage on the real estate as part of the purchase transaction. In that case, the mortgagee is a creditor beneficiary of the purchaser's promise. Therefore, in the event of default, both the assuming purchaser and the original mortgagor are personally liable for the full mortgage debt. The mortgagee may be able to foreclose its lien on the property and, in most states, sue the *mortgagor and/or the purchaser* for any deficiency owing after the property is sold. [**Corning v. Burton**, 62 N.W. 1040 (Mich. 1894)]

(2) Purchaser Takes "Subject to" Mortgage

In some cases, a purchaser of mortgaged property merely takes the property *"subject to"* the mortgage, rather than assuming the mortgage. In such cases, there is no assumption agreement, and the mortgagee therefore has no action against the purchaser for payment of the mortgage debt. In the event of default, *only the mortgagor* is personally liable for the full mortgage debt. The mortgagee can foreclose its lien on the property and, depending on applicable state law, the mortgagee may be able to sue the *mortgagor* for any deficiency owing after the property is sold.

"ASSUMING" VS. PURCHASING "SUBJECT TO" MORTGAGE		**GILBERT**
	"ASSUMPTION" OF MORTGAGE	PURCHASE "SUBJECT TO" MORTGAGE
EXAMPLE	The purchaser of a house agrees to assume the seller's mortgage debt	The purchaser of a house agrees to buy the seller's house subject to the mortgage debt but does not assume the seller's mortgage debt
STATUS OF THE MORTGAGEE (CREDITOR)	Mortgagee is a creditor beneficiary of the assumption agreement	Mortgagee does not have creditor beneficiary status
CAN THE MORTGAGEE SUE THE PURCHASER?	Yes	No
CAN THE MORTGAGEE FORECLOSE ON THE MORTGAGE LIEN AND SELL THE PROPERTY?	Yes	Yes

(3) Purchaser Assumes a Mortgage from Seller Who Only Took Subject to the Mortgage

Suppose *A* owns mortgaged real property and sells it to *B* in a contract under which *B* buys **subject to** the mortgage rather than *assuming* the mortgage. *B* then sells the property to *P*, who **assumes** the mortgage. Is *P* liable to the mortgagee?

(a) Majority View

The majority view is that *P* is **not** liable, on the ground that *B* did not intend to confer an unconditional right on the mortgagee, but either acted under the mistaken impression that *B* was liable or intended to make *P* liable only if *B* was liable.

(b) Minority View

There is, however, a minority view that holds *P* liable in such a case. The theory is that *B* must at least have **supposed** *B* owed a duty to the mortgagee, or *B* would not have gotten *P* to assume the mortgage. This supposed duty is sufficient to make the mortgagee a creditor beneficiary because a person is a creditor beneficiary if the promisor agrees to pay either an actual **or** an asserted or supposed obligation of the promisee (*supra*, p. 180).

b. Would-Be Legatees

Another recurring kind of third-party beneficiary case is one where a client retains an attorney to draft a will that would benefit a third party. The attorney fails to draft the will in accordance with the client's wishes or fails to draft the will properly. The client dies, and the third party does not receive anything from the client's estate because of the attorney's failure. Most modern courts hold that the third party has a right against the attorney as an intended third-party beneficiary of the contract between the client (the promisee) and the attorney (the promisor). [*See, e.g.*, **Guy v. Liederbach,** 459 A.2d 744

(Pa. 1983)] This makes sense because unless the third party is given the right to sue the attorney, an important objective of the contract between the client and the attorney—making the third party a beneficiary of the client's estate—will not be fulfilled.

(1) Negligence

Some courts reach pretty much the same result by allowing the client to sue the attorney in tort for negligence. [*See, e.g.*, **Heyer v. Flaig,** 70 Cal. 2d 223 (1969)] Both theories were adopted in **Hale v. Groce,** 744 P.2d 1289 (Or. 1987).

c. Government Contracts

Contracts with the government often benefit either the public generally or a specific class of members of the public. The general rule is that a member of the public who would benefit from a promise to render a performance to a federal, state, or local government is not deemed an intended beneficiary of the promise and cannot bring suit to enforce the promise, even if the performance was to be rendered directly to that member or similar members of the public.

Example: Rensselaer Water Co. contracted with a city to, among other things, supply the city with fire hydrant water. Moch, whose property was destroyed by fire because the hydrants did not have sufficient water pressure, could not recover damages from Rensselaer. [**Moch v. Rensselaer Water Co.,** 247 N.Y. 160 (1928)]

(1) Restatement First Exception

Under Restatement First, the general rule is subject to an exception where an intention is manifested in the contract, as interpreted in the light of the circumstances surrounding its formation, that the promisor will compensate members of the public for injurious consequences arising from breach. [Rest. 1st § 133]

Example: City enters a contract with Builder in which Builder promises to build a subway for City and pay damages to anyone who is injured by the construction work. Homeowner's house is damaged when the land settles beneath it as a result of the subway construction. Homeowner can sue Builder under the Restatement First because Builder's intention to compensate members of the public was manifested in the contract.

(2) Restatement Second Exceptions

Under Restatement Second, the general rule is subject to an exception where either (i) the terms of the contract provide for liability to the members of the public in question or (ii) the government is subject to liability to the members of the public for the damages they suffer because the performance was not rendered, and a direct action against the promisor is consistent with the terms of the contract and with the policy of the law authorizing the contract and prescribing remedies for its breach. [Rest. 2d § 313]

Example: Same facts as in the above example. Homeowner can sue Builder under Restatement Second because the terms of the contract provide for liability to members of the public injured by the construction work. [Rest. 2d § 313, ill. 3]

Example: Municipality owes a duty to the public to keep its streets in repair. Construction Company contracts with Municipality to repair certain streets. However, one street is not repaired and Citizen, a member of the public, is injured. Citizen can sue Construction Company for damages under Restatement Second because the government is liable to Citizen for her injuries, and a direct action against Construction Company is consistent with the terms of the contract and the policy of the law authorizing the contract and prescribing remedies for its breach. [Rest. 2d § 313, ill. 5]

(3) Comment

As a practical matter, it is often very difficult to determine whether a government contract falls within the general rule or within an exception. Members of the public are much more likely to be deemed intended beneficiaries if (i) they are part of a small and relatively well defined group (*e.g.*, a small group of home buyers or tenants) who would benefit by the performance of contracts entered into specifically to protect their interests and (ii) the government suffers no compensable damages from the breach, so that if the members of the public are not allowed to bring suit, there is no practicable sanction for nonperformance.

Example: Contractor breached a contract with the government under which it agreed to build homes with certain specifications for veterans. The court held that 12 veterans who purchased homes that did not meet the specifications could, as intended beneficiaries, sue Contractor. [**Shell v. Schmidt**, 126 Cal. App. 2d 279 (1954)]

Example: Developer breached a contract with the government under which it agreed not to charge more than specified rents. Tenants of an apartment building to which the contract applies can sue Developer as intended beneficiaries. [**Zigas v. Superior Court**, 120 Cal. App. 3d 827 (1981)]

d. Suits by Subcontractors Against Sureties of General Contractors

In the typical construction setting, a private or public entity—an owner—makes a contract with a general contractor who agrees to perform specified construction. The general contractor, in turn, contracts with various subcontractors, who agree to perform portions of the construction. Because contractors are typically thinly capitalized, an owner often requires a general contractor to provide either a *performance bond*, under which a surety guarantees the owner that the contractor will perform its contract with the owner; a *payment bond*, under which the surety specifically guarantees the owner that the claims of subcontractors will be paid; or both. Can an unpaid subcontractor sue the surety as a third-party beneficiary under a payment bond or a performance bond between the surety and the owner?

(1) Payment Bonds—Traditional Analysis

Traditionally, the courts distinguished between payment bonds running to public owners and payment bonds running to private owners. Subcontractors were allowed to recover under payment bonds running to public owners but not under payment bonds running to private owners. The distinction rested on an application of the intent-to-benefit test found in Restatement Second section 302 (*see supra*, p. 182) to the assumed motivations of public and private owners in requiring the general contractor's payment obligations to be bonded. The analysis was as follows:

(a) Private Owners

A subcontractor usually has a right to file a lien on a private owner's property for the value of the work it has performed. As a result, if the general contractor fails to pay a subcontractor, a private owner may be required either to pay the subcontractor itself or to bear the impact of a foreclosure under the lien.

Accordingly, the courts reasoned, when a private owner requires a general contractor to bond its payment obligation to subcontractors, the private owner's intent must not be to benefit the subcontractors, but rather to benefit *itself by* ensuring that it will not suffer economic injury as a result of liens filed by unpaid subcontractors. Under the intent-to-benefit test, therefore, the subcontractors *could not sue* the surety in a private construction case because the owner did not intend to benefit them.

(b) Public Owners

On the other hand, the lien laws typically do not extend to public construction. Therefore, a public owner will typically suffer no economic injury if subcontractors are not paid. Accordingly, if a public owner requires a general contractor to bond its payment obligation, the owner's intent must be to benefit not itself but the *subcontractors*, and under the intent-to-benefit test the subcontractors *could sue* the surety in a public construction case.

(2) Payment Bonds—Modern Analysis

The modern tendency is to allow subcontractors to recover against the sureties of payment bonds in *both* private and public cases. Modern courts recognize that both public and private owners have self-regarding objectives that are best effectuated by allowing subcontractors to sue a surety on a payment bond.

(a) Rationale—Public Owners

Public owners may reasonably believe that the cost of construction will be lower if subcontractors are afforded assurance of payment. Subcontractors will make lower bids to general contractors if they need not impound the risk of nonpayment into their costs, and if subcontractors' bids are lower, general contractors' bids will also be lower.

(b) Rationale—Private Owners

Essentially the same analysis applies to private construction. It is true that in the case of private construction, unpaid subcontractors often will not lose out completely, because they will be protected under the lien laws. Despite the lien laws, however, some risk will remain: The lien laws are not always easy to comply with, enforcing a lien can be complex and expensive, and the private owner's equity may be less than the total claims of lienholders. Even in the case of private construction, therefore, a subcontractor who is not afforded assurance of payment is likely to bid more than it otherwise would. A private owner may also want to afford subcontractors assurance of payment to avoid the transaction costs involved when liens are filed.

(3) Performance Bonds

If an owner requires a *performance bond*, but not a payment bond, an unpaid subcontractor should not be able to enforce the contract against the surety as a third-party beneficiary. Unlike a payment bond, a performance bond does not explicitly provide that subcontractors will be paid. Given the wide availability and frequent use of payment bonds, the decision of an owner to obtain only a performance bond reveals that the contracting parties' performance objectives do not include affording subcontractors assurance of payment, so subcontractors should not be allowed to enforce a performance bond.

5. Defenses That Can Be Asserted by Promisor Against Beneficiary

Assuming that a third-party beneficiary can bring suit under a contract, the question arises, what kinds of defenses can the promisor assert against the third-party beneficiary?

a. Defenses That Promisor Could Have Asserted Against Promisee

The promisor can assert against a third-party beneficiary any defense that the promisor could have asserted against the promisee concerning *formation or performance* of the contract. [**Williams v. Paxson Coal Co.,** 31 A.2d 69 (Pa. 1943)]

Example: Penny agrees to paint Peter's house in exchange for Peter's promise to pay $5,000 to Theo to satisfy a claim that Theo has against Penny. Theo is a creditor beneficiary and can bring suit against Peter. However, if in entering into the contract Penny was guilty of fraud, or failed to paint Peter's house, Peter could assert these matters as a defense in an action by Theo against Peter for nonpayment.

b. Defenses That Promisee Could Have Asserted Against Beneficiary

Suppose the *promisee* could have had a defense against the third-party beneficiary. For example, suppose that in the last example Penny could have asserted a defense against Theo if he had sued her on his preexisting claim against her. Can the *promisor* assert such a defense against the third-party beneficiary?

(1) Creditor Beneficiary Cases

As a practical matter, the issue of whether the promisor can assert a defense that the *promisee* has against the beneficiary is likely to arise only in a creditor beneficiary context, like the last example. Unless there was a preexisting relationship between the promisee and the beneficiary, such that the promisee owed or appeared to owe an obligation to the beneficiary, there is not much likelihood that the promisee would have a defense against the beneficiary. The concept of a defense implies that there is a claim against which the defense can be asserted. Only in the creditor beneficiary context will the beneficiary normally have a claim against the promisee prior to the contract at issue.

(2) Problem of Interpretation

The issue whether the promisor can raise a defense of the promisee against the beneficiary is to some extent a problem of interpretation. If the promisor's promise is interpreted as a promise to *pay whatever liability that the promisee was under to the beneficiary,* then the promisor could raise any defense the promisee could raise. If, however, the promisor's promise is interpreted as a promise to *pay a given amount of money to the beneficiary,* then the promisor cannot raise such a defense. The courts normally tend to give the latter interpretation, and therefore they generally do not allow a promisor to raise a defense against a beneficiary even if the promisee could have raised the same defense against the beneficiary. [*See* **Rouse v. United States,** 215 F.2d 872 (D.C. Cir. 1953)]

c. **Rights of Beneficiary Against Promisee; Rights of Promisee Against Promisor**

   (1) **Donee Beneficiary Contracts**

   If a third-party beneficiary is a *donee beneficiary,* then by definition the promisee did not owe the beneficiary a preexisting obligation. Accordingly, if the promisor fails to perform, the beneficiary cannot sue the *promisee,* because the promisee owed the beneficiary no obligation. Correspondingly, the *promisee* cannot recover *damages* against the promisor for failure to perform, because the promisee has suffered no loss: the performance of the contract would have benefited the beneficiary, not the promisee. However, under the modern trend of authority, the promisee *can seek specific performance* of the promisor's promise for the very reason that the legal remedy is inadequate. [**Croker v. New York Trust Co.,** 245 N.Y. 17 (1927); *see infra,* p. 256]

   Example: Peter and Penny contract with each other to share the costs of supporting their aged uncle, Theo. If Peter refuses to pay his share, Penny cannot recover damages from Peter but may seek specific performance of Peter's promise.

   (2) **Creditor Beneficiary Contracts**

   If a third-party beneficiary is a *creditor* beneficiary, then by definition the promisee owed the third party a preexisting obligation. Therefore, if the promisor fails to pay the beneficiary, the beneficiary can sue the promisee on the original (preexisting) obligation. Correspondingly, the promisee can sue the promisor for a failure to perform because as a result of such a failure, the promisee's obligation to the beneficiary, which the promisor agreed to discharge, instead remains outstanding.

THIRD-PARTY BENEFICIARY CONTRACTS—RIGHTS AND DUTIES			GILBERT
	INTENDED/DONEE BENEFICIARY	**INTENDED/CREDITOR BENEFICIARY**	**INCIDENTAL BENEFICIARY**
EXAMPLE	Amy wants to give John a gift. Amy later promises to paint Lulu's portrait, and in return, Lulu promises to pay the $500 portrait fee to John instead of Amy. John is an intended (or donee) beneficiary of the contract between Amy and Lulu.	Amy owes a $500 debt to John. Amy later promises to paint Lulu's portrait, and in return, Lulu promises to pay the $500 portrait fee to John instead of Amy. John is an intended (or creditor) beneficiary of the contract between Amy and Lulu.	Amy promises to paint Lulu's porch for $500. The freshly painted porch will increase the value of Neighbor's property. Neighbor is an incidental beneficiary of the contract between Amy and Lulu.
CAN THE BENEFICIARY SUE THE PROMISOR?	Yes	Yes	

CAN THE BENEFICIARY SUE THE PROMISEE?	No	Yes (on the preexisting obligation)	
CAN THE PROMISOR ASSERT AGAINST THE BENEFICIARY THE DEFENSES THAT THE PROMISOR COULD HAVE ASSERTED AGAINST THE PROMISEE?	Yes (defenses to formation or performance of the contract)	Yes (defenses to formation or performance of the contract)	
CAN THE PROMISOR ASSERT AGAINST THE BENEFICIARY THE DEFENSES THAT THE PROMISEE COULD HAVE ASSERTED AGAINST THE BENEFICIARY?	No (a donee beneficiary normally has no claim against the promisee against which the promisee would have a defense)	A matter of interpretation; generally not	

6. Termination or Variation of Third-Party Beneficiary's Rights—Vesting

Even though a third-party beneficiary is a donee or creditor—or, under the modern terminology, *intended*—beneficiary, until the beneficiary's rights *vest* they can be cut off or varied by a modification of the contract entered into by the promisor and the promisee. On the other hand, once a third-party beneficiary's rights vest, an agreement between the contracting parties cannot impair or vary the beneficiary's rights under the contract. There are several different approaches to the issue of when vesting occurs.

a. Restatement First View

Under one approach, adopted in Restatement First, the law draws a distinction between creditor and donee beneficiaries. Under this approach, a *donee beneficiary's* rights vest upon the making of the contract. [Rest. 1st §§ 142, 135, comment a] In contrast, a *creditor beneficiary's* rights vest only when the beneficiary detrimentally relies or brings suit on the contract. [Rest. 1st § 143]

b. Restatement Second View

Under a second approach, adopted in Restatement Second, the rights of *any* intended beneficiary, whether creditor or donee, vest only when the beneficiary either: (i) *manifests assent* to the promise in a manner invited or requested by the parties; (ii) *brings suit* to enforce the promise; or (iii) *materially changes position* in justifiable reliance on the promise. [Rest. 2d § 311] Most modern courts would probably go along with this approach.

e.g. **Example:** Harry contracts to purchase Lydia's painting for $200,000, and it is agreed that Harry will pay the $200,000 to Lydia's favorite Niece, Sara, rather than to Lydia. Lydia tells Sara of the arrangement, and Sara then signs a contract to purchase a house with the money she will receive from Harry. Lydia later decides that she no longer likes Sara, and Lydia and Harry modify their contract so that Harry will pay Lydia instead of Sara. Sara can enforce the original contract; under Restatement Second, her rights vested because she materially changed her position in justifiable reliance on the contract.

EXAM TIP   **GILBERT**

It is important not to overemphasize the concept of vesting in the law of third-party beneficiaries. Unlike property law, where vesting is very important, in the law of third-party beneficiaries vesting is relatively unimportant. The issue of vesting is significant to only one very limited question: Can the promisor and the promisee modify a contract that the third party could have enforced in the absence of the modification? If the third-party beneficiary's rights have vested, the answer to that question is no. If the third-party beneficiary's rights have not vested, the answer to that question is yes. But in any event, you normally do **not need to consider whether vesting has occurred unless** the promisor and the promisee have attempted to *modify* the contract **and** the third-party beneficiary could have enforced the contract in the absence of the modification. So, for example, vesting is normally irrelevant in determining whether a third-party beneficiary can enforce a contract, and whether, if they can enforce the contract, there are defenses against them other than modification.

B. Assignment of Rights and Delegation of Duties

1. In General

This section deals with problems that arise when a party to a contract seeks either to *assign* (transfer) a right arising under the contract to a third party or to *delegate* a duty imposed under the contract to a third party.

a. Nature of an Assignment

In general, an assignment is the transfer of an intangible right. In particular, in contract law an assignment is a transfer of a contract right.

(1) Terminology

In the law of assignments, the transferor of rights under an original contract is known as the *assignor;* the other (nonassigning) party to the original contract is known as the *obligor;* and the transferee of the rights is known as the *assignee.*

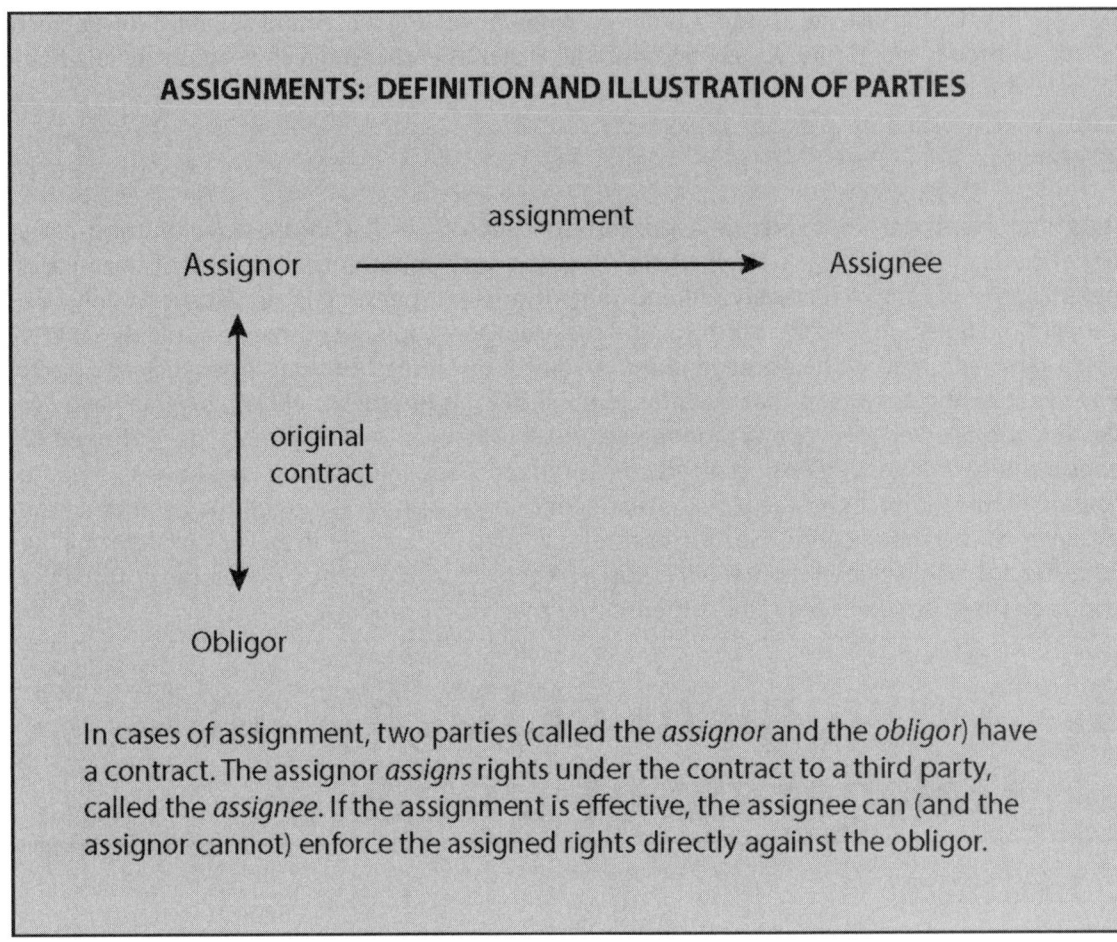

ASSIGNMENTS: DEFINITION AND ILLUSTRATION OF PARTIES

In cases of assignment, two parties (called the *assignor* and the *obligor*) have a contract. The assignor *assigns* rights under the contract to a third party, called the *assignee*. If the assignment is effective, the assignee can (and the assignor cannot) enforce the assigned rights directly against the obligor.

(2) Effect of Assignment

An assignment of a contractual right operates to **extinguish** the right in the assignor and set the right up exclusively in the assignee. [Rest. 2d § 317] Thus, as a result of an assignment, the assignee has a direct right against the obligor. Under modern law, all jurisdictions recognize that an assignee is the real owner of the transferred right and that the assignee alone may enforce the assigned right against the obligor. The assignee is the "real party in interest," insofar as that right is concerned, and may sue directly on the contract in their own name without joining the assignor.

(3) Governing Law—U.C.C. Article 9

Today, Article 9 of the U.C.C. is the most important source of law governing assignments. Article 9 covers almost all assignments, subject to specific exceptions. Article 9 applies (subject to the exceptions) to any transaction that is intended to create a security interest in personal property—*i.e.*, *secured transactions*. **Sales** of certain types of claims, including accounts and chattel paper (as opposed to the creation of security interests in such claims) are brought within Article 9 to avoid difficult problems of distinguishing between those transactions that are intended for security and those that are not so intended. Accordingly, under Article 9 persons who purchase most types of claims are treated the same way as persons who take such claims as security for a debt.

(a) Definitions

Among the key terms used in U.C.C. Article 9 are "account," "chattel paper," "general intangibles," and "account debtor."

1) Account

An "account" is a right to payment of a monetary obligation for such things as property or services—whether or not the right has yet been earned by performance—that is not evidenced by chattel paper or an instrument. The term covers most types of choses in action (*i.e.*, claims or rights to receive payments that can be enforced at law).

2) Chattel Paper

The term "chattel paper" means a record or records that evidence both a monetary obligation and a security interest in specific goods. A "record" is information that is inscribed on a tangible medium or stored electronically or in some other medium and is retrievable in perceivable form.

3) General Intangibles

The term "general intangibles" covers miscellaneous types of contractual rights and other personal property other than chattel paper, instruments, and certain other items. Examples are goodwill (*i.e.*, the favor a business wins from the public), literary rights, and rights to performance.

4) Account Debtor

An "account debtor" is the person who is obligated on an account, chattel paper, or general intangible.

(b) Exclusions

1) Types of Claims

Article 9 of the U.C.C. does not apply to certain types of *claims,* such as wage claims, nonagricultural liens created by state statute or other law for services or materials (*e.g.*, mechanic's liens), and most insurance benefits.

2) Types of Assignments

Article 9 also does not apply to certain types of *assignments,* such as:

a) Assignments of accounts or contract rights *as part of the sale of the business* out of which the accounts or contract rights arose;

b) Assignments of a right to payment under a contract *to a person who is also to render performance* under the contract (*i.e.*, to a delegee; *see infra*, p. 207);

c) Assignments for *collection purposes only*;

d) *Donative assignments*;

e) A transfer of a *single account* to an assignee in whole or partial satisfaction of an *existing indebtedness.*

(4) Governing Law—Common Law

Many of the common law rules governing the assignment of contract rights have been drastically altered by Article 9 of the U.C.C. However, the common law rules are still important, partly as a background to understand the U.C.C. provisions and partly because the common law rules still generally govern assignments that are expressly excluded from Article 9.

EXAM TIP   **GILBERT**

If an exam question concerns the assignment of a right, check to see ***what type of right*** is being assigned before beginning your answer. If the right concerns personal property, Article 9 applies. If the right concerns real property, or the assignment is excluded from Article 9 for other reasons, only the common law applies.

---

2. Rules Governing the Assignability of Rights

a. General Rule

The general rule is that all contract rights are assignable.

b. Exceptions—Nonassignable Rights

A right may not be assigned if an assignment would "***materially change the duty*** of the obligor, or ***materially increase the burden or risk*** imposed on him by his contract, or ***materially impair his chance of obtaining return performance*** or ***materially reduce its value*** to him." [Rest. 2d § 317; *and see* similar provision in U.C.C. § 2–210(2)—applicable to assignments of contracts for the sale of goods]

(1) Rights Whose Assignment Would Materially Change the Obligor's Duty

(a) Personal Service Contracts

Rights may not be assigned if the effect would be to require the obligor to perform *personal services* to the assignee. [**Davis v. Basalt Rock Co.**, 107 Cal. App. 2d 436 (1951)]

Example: Aria employs Omar to paint her portrait. Later, Aria (the assignor) attempts to assign her rights under the contract to her aunt Avery (the assignee). Avery may not compel Omar (the obligor) to paint her portrait.

1) Rationale

The performance of personal services for anyone other than the original obligee could materially change the nature of the obligor's duties. Whenever such services are involved, the law implies that the personal relationship between the obligor and the obligee is important. Therefore, the obligee cannot transfer their rights to another person.

2) What Constitutes Personal Services?

The test of what constitutes personal services, for these purposes, is whether the performance so involves the personality or personal characteristics of the obligor that it would be unfair to require the obligor to render the performance to a third person.

> **Example:** Examples of contracts for personal services, under which rights cannot be assigned, include contracts for the services of a portrait painter, a lawyer, a physician, an architect, or the like. On the other hand, repair or construction contracts usually are ***not*** interpreted as involving personal services. Therefore, a construction contractor normally can be required to render their performance to an assignee of the person for whom the contractor originally agreed to perform the work.

(b) "Requirements" and "Output" Contracts

A contract in which one party, *A*, has the right to compel the other party, *B*, to buy all the goods *A* can produce (*i.e.*, an "output" contract) or to provide all the goods *A* needs in its business (*i.e.*, a "requirements" contract) is generally not assignable by *A*. Because the assignee might have far different output or far different requirements from *A*, the assignment could materially change the duty of *B*. [34 A.L.R. 1184]

(2) Rights Whose Assignment Would Materially Increase the Burden or Risk of the Obligor

Rights under a contract cannot be assigned if the assignment would materially increase the burden or risk of the obligor.

(a) Insurance

The most obvious application of this principle is to insurance policies. Such policies are contracts predicated on a designated risk assumed by the insurer in connection with a named insured. Because the risk assumed in insuring one person differs from the risk assumed in insuring another person, the right to be insured under a specific policy is generally not assignable. This is true not only as to life insurance but also as to liability and casualty insurance. The risks created by one person's conduct, or ownership of property or a business, are different from another's.

1) Right to Insurance Proceeds

While the right to be ***insured*** may not be assignable, the right to ***benefits*** under an insurance contract—*i.e.*, the right to payment of money on the occurrence of the contingency that is insured against (such as the death of the insured or the destruction of insured property)—generally ***can*** be assigned. Requiring the payment of money to an assignee, rather than to the named insured, does not materially increase the insurer's burden or risk.

(b) Credit

When personal credit is involved, a substitution of debtors may materially increase the obligor's risk. Therefore, a right to the extension of credit generally cannot be assigned.

> **Example:** Oliver agrees to loan money to Bella in a month, the loan to be secured by Bella's promissory note. Betty decides she does not want the loan, and she attempts to assign Oliver's promise to make the loan to her needy friend, Claire. Claire cannot compel Oliver to take her promissory note in place of Bella's, because Claire's credit may not be as good as Bella's.

| **EXAM TIP** | **GILBERT** |

If an exam question puts in issue the ability of contracting parties to assign their rights, make sure you analyze the ***rights and duties of each party separately,*** because one party may be able to assign their rights while the other may not. Therefore, in the above example, although Bella may not assign her right to receive the loan, Oliver may assign his right to receive Bella's payment of the loan obligation because payment to a different creditor is ordinarily deemed not to change a debtor's duty, burden, or risk. [Rest. 2d § 317, comment d]

1) Purchase Money Mortgages

The same principle applies when a seller of real estate has agreed to accept a mortgage on the property as part of the purchase price and the buyer attempts to assign their rights under the contract of sale.

Example: Liam agrees to sell Blackacre to Mia for $50,000, payable $20,000 in cash and the balance in installments that will be secured by a mortgage on Blackacre executed by Mia. Prior to the closing, Mia attempts to assign all of her rights under the contract to Carter. Most authorities would hold that the assignment is ineffective, on the ground that Carter's credit is not the same as Mia's. Although the property that is to serve as security for the debt remains unchanged, the personal obligation of Carter on a mortgage note is different from the personal obligation of Mia. [**American Lithographic Co. v. Ziegler,** 103 N.E. 909 (Mass. 1914)] (Of course, Mia could go through with the purchase, execute the mortgage herself, and then transfer title to Carter. However, in that event, Mia would remain subject to personal liability to Liam.)

(3) Assignment That Would Materially Change Contract Terms

Even if rights under the contract are assignable—because an assignment won't materially change the duties of the obligor, materially increase the burden or risk imposed on them by the contract, materially impair their chance of obtaining return performance, or materially reduce the value of that performance to them—an assignment will not be allowed to alter the material terms of the contract.

Example: Diana contracts to deliver goods to Luna at Luna's place of business. Luna assigns her rights under the contract to Cindy, whose place of business is across town. The assignment is not effective to change the place of delivery. If Cindy wants the goods, she must accept delivery at Luna's place of business.

3. Partial Assignments

Assignable rights under a contract may be transferred to one assignee or divided up among several assignees. Alternatively, the assignor may assign only some rights and retain the balance.

a. Early Rule

At early common law, a partial assignment was held to be ineffective, on the theory that it increased the burden on the obligor because they would have several persons to pay instead of one and would face the possibility of increased litigation. However, a partial assignment was enforceable *in equity* if the partial assignee joined, in their suit, all other partial assignees (and the assignor, if the assignor retained any rights under the contract).

b. Present Rule

Today, partial assignments are generally enforced even at law. However, it is still usually necessary to join all the other partial assignees as parties (and also to join the assignor if the assignor retained any rights under the contract), unless joinder is not feasible and it is otherwise equitable to proceed without joinder. [Rest. 2d § 326; *see* Civil Procedure Summary]

4. General Requirements for an Effective Assignment

Any manifested intention by a contractual party to make a *present* transfer of rights (*i.e.*, a transfer of rights that does not require further action) under the contract to another person will constitute an assignment. [Rest. 2d § 324] A manifested intention by a party to make a *future* transfer of rights to another person is not an assignment, but it may form a *contract to assign.* (Note, however, that an assignor may make a present transfer of a right that is to *arise* in the future; *see infra*, p. 199.) The right that is assigned must be adequately described and *present words of assignment must be used.*

a. Test

The test for whether "present words of assignment" are used is whether the language manifests an intent by the assignor to divest themselves completely and immediately of the right in question and transfer the right to the assignee. The word "assign" need not be used. Words such as "sell," "transfer," "convey," and "give" will usually suffice.

b. Consideration

Consideration is *not required* for an assignment; a gratuitous assignment is effective.

c. Gratuitous Assignments Generally Revocable

Although consideration is not required for an assignment to be effective, a gratuitous assignment is *revocable* subject to the following exceptions:

(1) Delivery of Tangible Token

If a *chose* (*i.e.*, a claim or a right) is represented by a "tangible token," delivery of the tangible token makes even a gratuitous assignment irrevocable.

(a) Traditional Approach

Under the traditional approach, a right is represented by a tangible token if the right normally can be enforced only by surrender, or proof of possession, of a document that represents the right (*e.g.*, a savings-account passbook, a negotiable instrument, or a stock certificate).

(b) Restatement Approach

Under the Restatement, a tangible token is defined more broadly to include any document or thing "of a type customarily accepted as a symbol or as evidence of the right assigned." [Rest. 2d § 332]

(2) Writing

The general rule is that a gratuitous assignment is also irrevocable if the assignment is made in a writing that is *delivered* to the assignee.

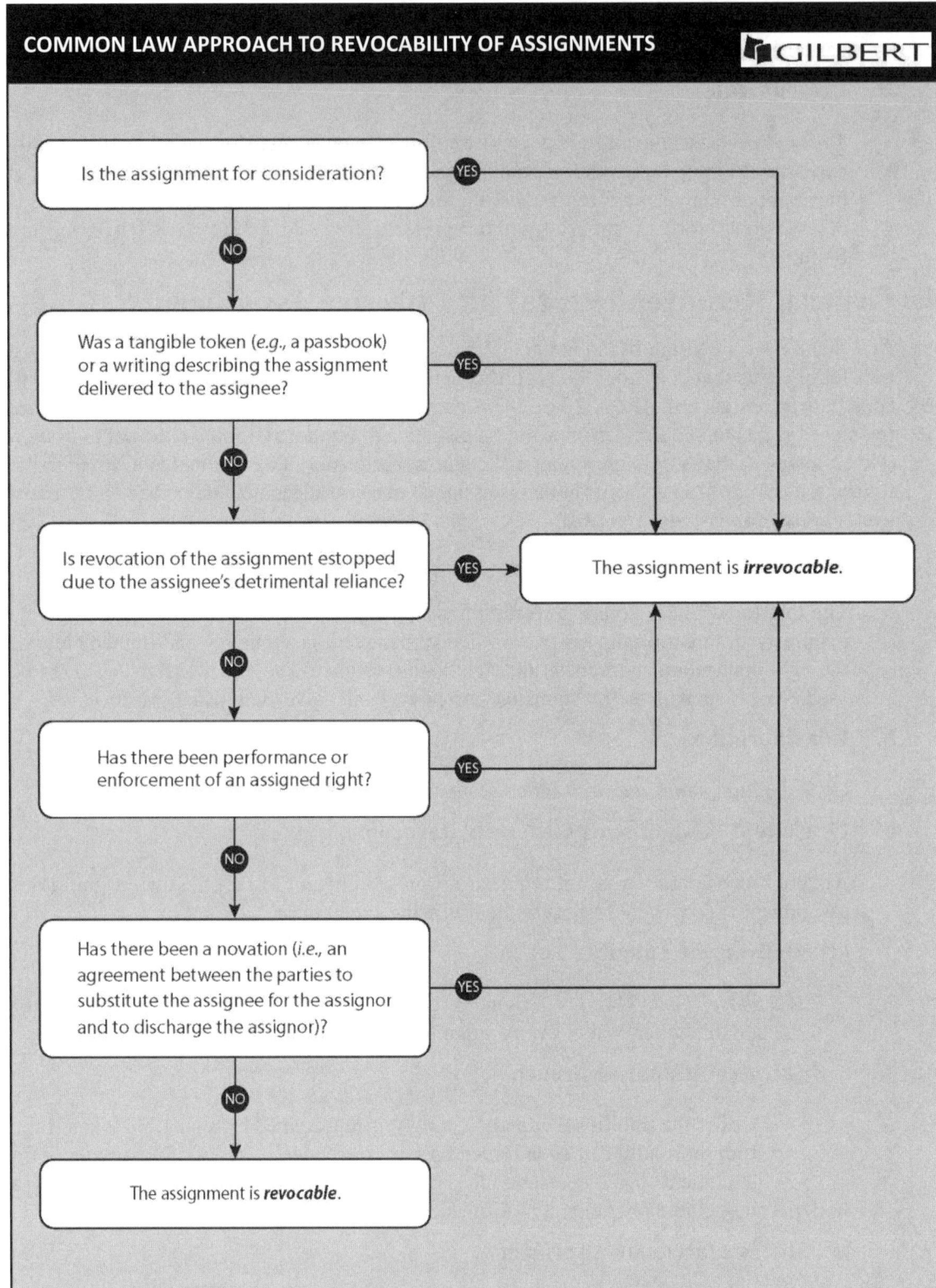

(3) Estoppel

If the assignee of a gratuitous assignment ***detrimentally relies*** on the assignment, the assignor may be estopped to revoke the assignment.

(4) Performance

A gratuitous assignment becomes irrevocable if, prior to revocation, the assignee receives payment or performance from the obligor, or obtains a judgment against the obligor by enforcing the assigned right.

(5) Novation

An assignment is irrevocable if the assignee, the assignor, and the obligor *all mutually agree* that the assignor should be substituted for the assignee, so that the assignor's rights and duties under the contract are discharged. Such a three-way agreement is known as a "novation."

d. How Revoked

A gratuitous assignment that has not been made irrevocable by delivery of a tangible token, a writing, estoppel, performance, or novation is effectively revoked by any of the following:

(1) A *notice of revocation* given by the assignor to either the assignee or the obligor;

(2) The assignor's *later assignment of the same right* to another;

(3) The *death of the assignor*;

(4) The *bankruptcy of the assignor*; or

(5) An *acceptance by the assignor of payment or performance directly from the obligor*.

e. Requirements for Effective Assignment Under U.C.C.

U.C.C. section 9–203 provides that, with certain exceptions, a security interest is not enforceable against the debtor or third parties unless either the debtor has signed or otherwise authenticated a security agreement describing the assigned collateral, or the assigned collateral is already in the assignee's possession (*e.g.*, the collateral consists of a claim embodied in a negotiable instrument that has been transferred to the assignee).

5. Effectiveness of Assignments of Future Rights

As used in the law of assignments, "future rights" refers to rights that are *expected* to arise under either (i) an *existing* contract or a continuing business relationship or (ii) a *future* contract or business relationship. At common law, there is a marked difference in the assignability of these two types of future rights.

a. Future Rights Under an *Existing* Contract

At common law, rights expected to arise in the future under an *existing contract* are generally freely assignable, even though the right is conditional on such matters as the assignor's performance under the contract. [Rest. 2d § 320]

b. Future Rights Under a *Continuing* Business Relationship

Furthermore, some authorities at common law allow the assignment of a right to payments that are expected to arise out of a *continuing business relationship*, even though there is no contractual obligation for the payments to be made or the relationship to continue.

 Example: Farmer assigns to Creditor payments that Farmer expects to receive for Farmer's crop at the end of the year from Distributor, with which Farmer currently has an at-will contractual relationship that could be terminated at any time and under which Distributor is not bound to accept Farmer's crop. Under the Restatement this is likely a valid assignment. [Rest. 2d § 321]

c. Future Rights Under a *Future* Contract or Business Relationship

At common law, rights under a *future* contract or a *future* business relationship are ***not*** assignable. The theory is that an assignment is a transfer, and a person cannot transfer something that they do not have. [**Herbert v. Bronson,** 125 Mass. 475 (1878)]

(1) Equitable Relief Possible

Even at common law, however, although an attempted assignment of rights under a future contract or a future business relationship is ineffective as an assignment, if it is given for consideration the attempted assignment is treated as a ***contract to assign*** the right if and when it does arise. Therefore, if the right does arise, equity may grant specific performance of the promise to assign by compelling the assignment to be made at that point. [**Holt v. American Woolen Co.,** 150 A. 382 (Me. 1930)] However, because such an assignment is enforceable only in equity, equitable considerations govern. Thus the assignment will not be enforced if a subsequent bona fide purchaser acquired the right after it came into existence, provided the purchaser took without notice of the prior assignment. Nor will such an assignment be enforced against creditors of the assignor who attach the assigned rights without having notice of the prior attempted assignment. [**Stokely Bros. v. Conklin,** 26 A.2d 147 (N.J. 1942)]

d. U.C.C.

For the most part, the common law rules concerning the assignment of future rights have been changed by the U.C.C. Article 9 explicitly recognizes the validity of an assignment of future rights and gives the assignee of such rights priority over most competing claimants, provided a financing statement describing the assignment is properly filed. [U.C.C. § 9–204; *see infra*, p. 207] Recall, however, that Article 9 does not apply to all assignments. (*See supra*, p. 193.)

6. Effect of Contractual Provisions Prohibiting Assignment

a. Traditional View

At common law, a contractual provision prohibiting the assignment of rights under a contract is valid, both as to the parties and as to any assignee with notice thereof. [Rest. 2d § 319; *and see* Rest. 2d § 317] However, such provisions are not favored, because they interfere with free alienability of rights. Accordingly, although the general common law principle is that such provisions are valid, the courts have adopted a number of rules that effectively reduce the force of the common law principle.

(1) Prohibitions on Assignments Are Construed as Promissory in Nature

If a contract contains only a ***promise*** not to assign the contract (*e.g.,* a provision that "No assignment hereof shall be made" or that "*A* agrees not to assign this contract without the prior consent of *B*"), the promise is said to destroy the ***right,*** but not the ***power,*** to make an assignment. Accordingly, although the obligor (the nonassigning party) will have an action against the ***assignor*** for breach of the contractual provision prohibiting assignment, the assignment will be valid as between the ***assignee*** and the obligor. Furthermore, unless the assignment causes special injury to the obligor, the obligor normally can recover only nominal damages in a suit against the assignor.

(2) Contractual Prohibitions in the Form of a Condition

However, if a prohibition against assignment is phrased as a condition rather than as a promise (*e.g.*, "any assignment hereof shall be void" or "in the event of an assignment, this contract shall terminate"), at common law the provision is generally given full force and effect. Such a provision is said to destroy not only the obligee's right but also their ***power*** to assign, so that an assignment in violation of the provision is unenforceable.

b. Restatement Approach

The Restatement nominally retains the principle that contractual prohibitions on assignment are enforceable but adopts strong rules of construction against such provisions, as follows [Rest. 2d § 322]:

(1) Contract Term That Prohibits Assignment of "the Contract"

A contractual provision that prohibits an assignment of "the contract" is to be construed to bar only the ***delegation*** by the assignor of their duties or conditions, not an assignment of rights under the contract (*see infra*, p. 207 *et seq.*, for discussion of delegation).

(2) Contract Term That Prohibits Assignment of Rights Under the Contract

A contractual provision that prohibits an assignment of rights under the contract (as opposed to prohibiting an assignment of "the contract") is to be interpreted:

(a) To give the obligor a ***right to damages*** in the event of a prohibited assignment, but *not* to render the assignment ineffective;

(b) ***Not to forbid the assignment of a right to damages for breach*** of the whole contract or the assignment of a right arising out of the assignor's due performance of their entire obligation; and

(c) To be ***for the benefit of the obligor*** and not to prevent the assignee from acquiring rights against the assignor, nor to prevent the obligor from rendering performance to the assignee as if there were no such prohibition.

c. U.C.C. Approach

(1) Contractual Prohibition Ineffective

U.C.C. section 9–406(d), which is applicable to most commercial assignments, provides that a term in any contract between an account debtor and an assignor is ineffective if it prohibits, restricts, or requires the account debtor's consent to the assignment or transfer of, or the creation of a security interest in, an ***account, chattel paper, payment intangible*** (*i.e.*, a general intangible under which the debtor's principal obligation is a monetary obligation), or ***promissory note.*** (*Note:* This section does not apply to the ***sale*** of a payment intangible or a promissory note. [U.C.C. § 9–406(e)]) Broadly speaking, therefore, U.C.C. section 9–406(d) denies the enforceability of contractual prohibitions and restrictions of, and requirements for the debtor's consent to, the assignment of most types of rights to payment if Article 9 is applicable to the assignment.

(2) Right to Damages Assignable

Similarly, U.C.C. section 2–210(2) provides that the right to *damages* for breach of a *sales* contract is assignable, even in the face of an express contractual prohibition on assignment thereof.

7. Wage Assignments

An assignment of wages to be earned in the future under an existing contract of employment is effective, under the principle that future rights expected to arise under an existing contract are assignable. (*See supra*, p. 199.) [**McDonald v. Hudspeth,** 129 F.2d 196 (10th Cir. 1942)]

a. Employment Terminable at Will

This is true even where the existing employment contract is terminable at will by the employer or employee, so that there is no assurance that assigned wages will be earned under the contract. [**Duluth S.S. & A. Railway v. Wilson,** 167 N.W. 55 (Mich. 1918); Rest. 2d § 321(1)]

b. Statutory Restrictions

However, many states have statutory restrictions on the assignability of future wages. For example, California Labor Code section 300 permits such an assignment only if a separate written instrument containing the consent of the employee's spouse (if the employee is married) or the employee's parent (if the employee is a minor) has been filed with the employer. Even then, under the statute an assignment of wages not yet earned is valid only to cover "necessities of life" furnished to the employee by the assignee.

c. Constitutional Issue

Wages are usually assigned as security for a loan. If the debtor-employee fails to repay the loan, the creditor can go directly to the employer and force the employer to pay the assigned wages to the creditor rather than to the employee. In effect, therefore, the wage assignment is a substitute for suing the employee and garnishing their wages if they fail to pay a judgment, but without the protection of a judicial hearing. A constitutional question has arisen whether such a practice constitutes a "taking" of the employee's property (their wages) without due process of law in violation of the Fourteenth Amendment—*i.e.*, whether the employee must be afforded some sort of notice and judicial hearing before the creditor is permitted to enforce the wage assignment. [*See* **Sniadach v. Family Finance Corp.,** 395 U.S. 337 (1969)—notice and hearing required before *garnishment* of an employee's wages] To date, the courts have upheld private enforcement of wage assignments, on the ground that no "state action" is involved, and the procedural safeguards of the Fourteenth Amendment therefore do not apply. [**Bond v. Dentzer,** 494 F.2d 302 (2d Cir. 1974)]

8. Rights, Liabilities, and Defenses After Effective Assignment

An effective assignment extinguishes the assigned right in the assignor and sets it up in the assignee. Thereafter, only the assignee is entitled to performance from the obligor (*supra*, p. 192).

a. Rights of the Assignee Against the Obligor

(1) Right of Direct Action

An assignee can enforce the assigned rights by a direct action against the obligor. The assignee may bring a lawsuit in their own name.

(2) Effect of Notice to Obligor

Once the obligor has knowledge of the assignment, they must render performance to or pay the assignee. If the obligor renders performance to or pays the assignor, they do so at their own risk. [**Nelson v. Fernando Nelson & Sons,** 5 Cal. 2d 511 (1936)]

b. Defenses Available to the Obligor Against the Assignee

(1) General Rule

The general rule concerning defenses that the obligor may assert against an assignee is set out in U.C.C. section 9–404, which for the most part reflects the common law. Under section 9–404, a defense can be asserted by the obligor against the assignee, whether the defense arises before or after notice of the assignment is given, if (i) the defense asserts that the contract under which rights were assigned was not validly formed (*e.g.*, a defense that the original contract lacked consideration) or (ii) the defense arises **under** the contract or the transaction that gave rise to the contract (*e.g.*, a claim that the assignor or the assignee has performed defectively).

(2) Holder in Due Course and Waiver of Defenses

The general rule that an obligor can assert contract-related defenses against the assignee is modified if (i) the assigned claim is represented by a negotiable instrument and the assignee is a "holder in due course," or (ii) the assigned claim arose under a contract in which the obligor waived the right to assert, against an assignee, defenses they might have against the assignor.

(a) Holder in Due Course

If a claim is embodied in a negotiable instrument, the claim is assigned by assigning or transferring the instrument. A *negotiable instrument* is one that, among other things, contains an unconditional promise or order to pay a sum certain in money and no other promise, order, obligation, or power. The most common examples of negotiable instruments are promissory notes and checks. An assignment or transfer of a negotiable instrument to a holder in due course is called a "negotiation." A holder in due course is an assignee who takes the claim for value, in good faith, and without notice of any defense. If a negotiable instrument is negotiated (*i.e.*, transferred) to an assignee who is a holder in due course, the obligor cannot assert even contract-related defenses against the holder, except for certain limited defenses relating to contract formation, such as incapacity and duress.

(b) Waiver-of-Defense Clauses

A similar result can be achieved, even in an assignment of a claim that is not embodied in a negotiable instrument, by a waiver-of-defense clause—*i.e.*, a clause (in the contract that was assigned) under which the obligor agrees that they will not assert any defenses against an assignee that they may have against the assignor.

(c) F.T.C. Rule

A Federal Trade Commission rule now effectively limits both the holder-in-due-course doctrine and waiver-of-defense clauses in consumer credit sales. Under this rule, a person who sells consumer goods or services on credit must include a ***notice*** in any consumer credit contract or note that any assignee (including any holder) of the contract takes subject to all claims and defenses that the consumer-debtor could assert against the seller. The language of this notice deprives the instrument of its negotiability by rendering it conditional. The rule also makes it unlawful for such a seller to accept, as payment from a consumer, the proceeds of a loan made to the consumer by a creditor to whom the seller referred the consumer (or who is affiliated with the seller through a contract, business arrangement, or common control), unless an equivalent notice is contained in the contract or note given by the consumer to the creditor. The language becomes part of the contract between the creditor and the consumer-debtor and thereby grants the defenses to the consumer-debtor. [16 C.F.R. §§ 433.1, 433.2]

1) Rationale

The purpose of the F.T.C. rule is to reallocate the burden of any loss resulting from seller misconduct in the consumer market from the innocent consumer-purchaser to the seller or to a creditor/lender that finances the transaction by purchasing the consumer's note or lending on the security of such a note. Such a creditor/lender is likely to be in a better position than the consumer to police the seller.

(d) Consumer Protection Statutes

Some statutes governing retail installment contracts provide that an assignee of such a contract takes subject to all "equities or defenses" of the buyer against the seller-assignor—even defenses that did not exist at the time of the assignment. [*See, e.g.*, Cal. Civ. Code § 1804.2]

(e) Modification After Notice of Assignment

Suppose an assignor assigns certain rights under the contract, such as a right to one or more payments, but otherwise continues to perform the contract. After the assignment has been made, and after the obligor has been given notice of the assignment, the assignor and the obligor modify the contract in good faith. Does the modification affect the rights of the assignee?

1) Traditional View

The traditional view is that the modification does not affect the assignee's rights, because an obligor who has received notice of an assignment deals with the assignor at their own peril (*see supra*, p. 203).

2) Modern Trend

However, U.C.C. section 9–405, recognizing commercial realities, provides that in the case of commercial assignments a modification of or a substitution for a right to payment that ***has not yet been fully earned by performance*** is effective against the assignee if made in ***good faith***. [*See also* Rest. 2d § 338] A modification of or a substitution for a right to payment that ***has*** been fully earned by performance is effective against the assignee if made in good faith ***and*** if ***no notice*** of the assignment was given to the obligor. [U.C.C. § 9–405]

(3) Unrelated Defenses

Unlike contract-related defenses, defenses that are unrelated to the contract under which the rights were assigned (*e.g.*, a claim by the obligor against the assignor under a ***different*** contract) can be asserted against the assignee if, but only if, the defense accrued ***before*** the assignee gave the obligor notice of the assignment.

(a) Definition of "Accrue"

The term "accrue," in this context, is ambiguous. A claim might be deemed to accrue, for this purpose, either when the obligation that gives rise to the claim is incurred or when the obligation is actually due and payable. One court has held that a claim does not accrue, for this purpose, until it is actually due and payable. [**Bank of Kansas v. Hutchison Health Services, Inc.,** 785 P.2d 1349 (Kan. 1990)]

c. Rights of Assignee Against Assignor—Warranties of Assignor

In every assignment for consideration the assignor impliedly makes the following warranties to the assignee:

(i) That the ***assigned right actually exists*** and is subject to no limitations or defenses other than those stated or apparent at the time of assignment;

(ii) That any ***document or paper with regard to the assignment is genuine*** and what it purports to be;

(iii) That the assignor has ***the right to assign*** the assigned right—*i.e.*, that they have made no prior assignment of the same right; and

(iv) That the assignor will do nothing in the future to defeat the assigned right—*i.e.*, they will ***not attempt a subsequent assignment*** of the same right.

[Rest. 2d § 333]

9. Priority of Competing Assignees

Suppose an assignor assigns the same right to two or more assignees. In a contest between the prior and the subsequent assignee, which assignee prevails?

a. Common Law

The common law is relatively well-settled in two kinds of cases—those in which the prior assignment is revocable and those in which the assigned claim is embodied in a tangible token.

(1) If Prior Assignment Revocable

Under common law, if the prior assignment is revocable (*see supra*, p. 197 *et seq.*), a subsequent assignment revokes the prior assignment, and the subsequent assignee therefore prevails over the prior assignee. [Rest. 2d § 342]

(2) Tangible Token

The subsequent assignment also prevails under common law if the assigned claim is represented by a tangible token [*cf. supra*, p. 197] and the prior assignee left the token in the assignor's possession—at least if the subsequent assignee gave value and took possession of the token. The rationale of this rule is that an assignee who leaves a tangible token in the assignor's possession should be estopped from claiming priority over a subsequent assignee, because by leaving the token in the assignor's hands the prior assignee allowed the impression to be created that the assignor still owned the claim.

(3) Other Cases

If the first assignment is not revocable and the claim is not represented by a tangible token left in the assignor's hands, there are three competing rules at common law: the "New York rule," the "English rule," and the "Massachusetts rule."

(a) "New York Rule"

Under the New York rule, as between successive assignees of the same right, the first in time (*i.e.*, the prior assignee) prevails. The rationale of the New York rule is that once an irrevocable assignment is made, the assignor has no further interest left to assign. The subsequent assignee therefore gets nothing, because there is nothing to get. [**Salem Trust Co. v. Manufacturers' Finance Co.,** 264 U.S. 182 (1923)]

(b) "English Rule"

Under the English rule, as between successive assignees of the same right, the first assignee to give notice to the obligor prevails—provided that the assignee who first gave notice to the obligor paid value and did not have notice of the prior assignment. [**Haupt v. Charlie's Kosher Market,** 17 Cal. 2d 843 (1941); 110 A.L.R. 774]

1) Rationale

The rationale of the English rule is that it is easy for an assignee to give notice to the obligor, and if the prior assignee does give such notice, a person who is offered an assignment of the same claim has an opportunity to find out that the claim has already been assigned by checking with the obligor, who in effect functions as a sort of private recording office. In the absence of an official recording system, unless an assignee gives such notice to the obligor, a subsequent assignee will have no way of finding out that the claim was already assigned. (A dishonest assignor who wants to assign the same claim twice is not likely to advise the subsequent assignee that the claim has already been assigned.) The English rule provides an incentive to give such a notice.

(c) "Massachusetts Rule"

Under the Massachusetts rule, if the prior assignment is not revocable, the prior assignee prevails unless the subsequent assignee acquires the assignment in good faith and for value, and either:

1) Takes from the assignor a tangible token representing the claim;

2) Collects the claim from the obligor;

3) Obtains a judgment against the obligor; or

4) Secures a novation from the obligor.

b. U.C.C.

Article 9 of the U.C.C. has radically changed the rules on priority between competing assignees of contract rights within its scope. Under Article 9, most assignments are protected in order of their filing or perfection. [U.C.C. § 9–322] To achieve that result, Article 9 employs two basic concepts: ***attachment*** and ***perfection***.

(1) Transactions Covered

The U.C.C. provisions apply both to outright sales of claims such as ***accounts*** and ***chattel paper*** (*see supra*, p. 193) and to assignments of such property for security purposes—*i.e.*, as collateral for a loan. However, recall that Article 9 does not apply to certain types of claims or certain types of transactions. (*See supra*, p. 193.) If there are successive assignments of a claim that is not covered by Article 9, priority between the successive assignees continues to be governed by the common law.

(2) Attachment

A security interest under Article 9 normally ***attaches*** when the creditor enters into a security agreement with the debtor that gives the creditor a security interest in collateral, and (i) the debtor has rights in the collateral or the power to transfer rights in the collateral to a secured party; (ii) the creditor gives value; and (iii) either the debtor signs or otherwise authenticates a security agreement describing the collateral or the creditor has or takes possession of the collateral pursuant to the agreement. [U.C.C. § 9–203] When the security interest attaches, it becomes enforceable against the debtor. [U.C.C. §§ 9–201(a), 9–203(a), (b)] In theory, it is also enforceable against third parties, such as competing assignees, but in practice it is often or even typically enforceable against third parties only if it is "perfected."

(3) Perfection

In most cases, an Article 9 security interest that has attached is ***perfected*** only by filing, in a designated state office, a financing statement that describes the collateral and sets forth the parties' names and addresses. A very few types of security interests are perfected "automatically" upon attachment (*i.e.*, upon creation of the security agreement in the manner specified by Article 9). For example, purchase-money security interests in most consumer goods are perfected in this way. [U.C.C. § 9–309(1)] In addition, filing is not required to perfect an assignment of accounts or payment intangibles that does not alone or in conjunction with other assignments to the same assignee transfer a significant part of the outstanding accounts or payment intangibles of the assignor. [U.C.C. 9–309(2)] Furthermore, in certain cases, a secured party can perfect a security interest without filing by taking ***possession*** of the collateral. [U.C.C. §§ 9–310, 9–313]

(a) First to File or Perfect

Among competing assignees, the first assignee to file or perfect prevails, even if that assignee's security interest was created ***after*** the security interest of another assignee, and even if that assignee ***knew*** of the other assignee's security interest when they filed or perfected. [U.C.C. § 9–322(a)]

10. Delegation of Duties

a. Nature of a Delegation

A delegation of a contractual duty is an appointment by a contractual party of another person to perform that party's contractual duties.

(1) Terminology

The party who delegates a duty is called the *"obligor"* or the *"delegor."* The other original party to the original contract, to whom the delegated duty is owed, is called the *"obligee."* The party to whom the duty is delegated is called the *"delegee."* [Rest. 2d § 318]

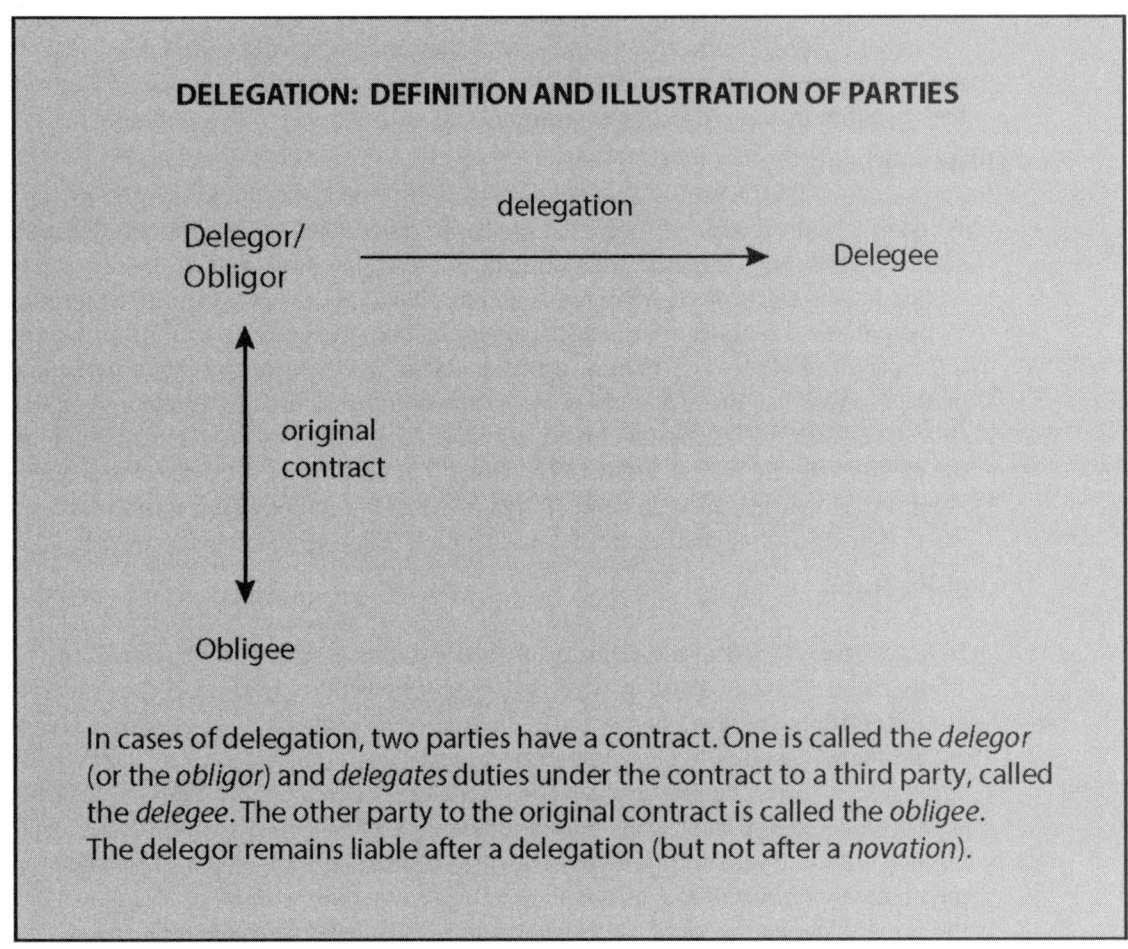

DELEGATION: DEFINITION AND ILLUSTRATION OF PARTIES

In cases of delegation, two parties have a contract. One is called the *delegor* (or the *obligor*) and *delegates* duties under the contract to a third party, called the *delegee*. The other party to the original contract is called the *obligee*. The delegor remains liable after a delegation (but not after a *novation*).

(2) Novation

A ***delegation*** differs from a ***novation***. A novation is a three-party agreement under which the obligee agrees to completely discharge the original obligor and accept another in the obligor's place. Thus, a novation is a substitution of parties to the contract. A delegation does not have this substitutional effect. The original obligor remains liable for the performance of all obligations, but the delegee is also liable—both to the obligor, with whom the delegee has directly contracted, and to the obligee, who is a creditor beneficiary (*see supra*, p. 179) of the delegee's promise to perform the obligor's duty under the original contract.

Example: Emily contracts with Sophia to mow her lawn once a week. Emily later delegates her duty to mow Sophia's lawn to Milo. Emily (the delegor) is still liable to Sophia (the obligee) if the contract is breached by Milo (the delegee). Milo is liable both to Emily under the delegation contract and to Sophia as a creditor beneficiary of the delegation contract.

Compare: Same facts as in the above example, except that rather than delegating her duty to Milo, Emily agreed with Milo and Sophia that Milo should be substituted for Emily in the original contract and Emily's duty should be discharged. In this case, Emily is no longer liable to Sophia under the original contract, and only Milo is liable to Sophia under the new novation contract.

b. What Duties Are Delegable

In the absence of an agreement otherwise, any contractual duty can be delegated unless the obligee has a substantial interest in having the original obligor perform the duty personally. Thus, except when performance by a delegee would vary materially from the performance promised by the obligor, a contractual duty may be performed by a delegee without constituting a breach of contract. [Rest. 2d § 318; U.C.C. § 2–210(1)]

(1) Application

(a) Personal Services

The principal example of a nondelegable duty is a duty to perform *personal* services. If the contract requires performance by, for example, a portrait painter, an author, a teacher, or a lawyer, the duty to render this performance cannot be delegated to another—no matter how competent—without the obligee's consent.

(b) Other Contracts

Most other contractual duties are delegable. For example, most duties to manufacture or deliver goods or to construct or repair buildings are delegable.

(2) Effect of Contractual Restriction on Delegation

Provisions in a contract that limit either party's right to delegate duties are normally enforced. Such provisions evidence the parties' intent that the services involved are personal or otherwise not meant to be delegated. Unlike restrictions on assignment, restrictions on delegation of duties do not clash with the policy in favor of free alienability of *rights*.

c. Effect of Valid Delegation of Duties

A valid delegation of duties does not excuse the delegor from their duty to perform. However, as between the delegor and the delegee, the delegation places the primary responsibility to perform on the delegee. The delegor becomes *secondarily liable*—as surety—for performance of the duty. [**Crane Ice Cream Co. v. Terminal Freezing & Heating Co.,** 128 A. 280 (Md. 1925)]

(1) Distinguish—Assignment of Rights

Contrast this rule with the effect of a valid assignment of rights, which operates to extinguish the rights of the assignor and set those rights up entirely in the assignee.

(2) U.C.C.—Right of Obligee to Demand Assurance

In contracts for the sale of goods, a delegation of performance entitles the obligee to demand assurances of performance from the delegee. [U.C.C. § 2–210(5); *and see* Sale & Lease of Goods Summary]

d. Effect of Attempt to Delegate Nondelegable Duty

An *attempt* to delegate a nondelegable duty is not a breach of contract, because the original obligor (the delegor) remains liable for performance in any event. However, if in such a case the original obligor indicates to the obligee that the obligor will not perform personally, that may be a sufficient repudiation of the obligor's duties under the contract to constitute an anticipatory breach of contract (*see infra*, p. 238 *et seq.*).

e. **Rights of the Obligee Against the Delegee**

(1) **Promise to Assume Duties**

Usually, as part of a delegation of duties, the delegee expressly or impliedly promises the delegor that the delegee will perform the duties owed by the obligor/delegor to the obligee. Such a promise constitutes an assumption agreement (*cf. supra*, p. 183) in which the obligee is a creditor beneficiary of the delegee's promise and therefore may sue the delegee for nonperformance.

(2) **Implied Assumption of Duties**

In some cases, one party to a contract simply "assigns" the contract to another, who does not expressly agree to perform the assignor's duties under the contract. The question then arises whether the courts should imply a promise by the assignee of the contract to perform the assignor's duties from the fact that the assignee has accepted benefits under the contract.

(a) **Traditional View**

The traditional view, associated with **Langel v. Betz**, 250 N.Y. 159 (1928), which involved the assignment of a contract for the sale of land, was that the mere acceptance by an assignee of the assignor's rights under the assigned contract was not sufficient to imply a promise by the assignee that the assignee would perform the assignor's duties under the contract.

(b) **Modern View**

The trend of modern authority is the reverse. A growing number of courts and the Restatement hold that if a contract that is wholly or partially executory on both sides is assigned, the assignment is normally to be construed as a delegation, and acceptance of the assignment is normally to be construed as acceptance of the delegation—*i.e.*, as an assumption of duties under the contract. The result is the same, therefore, as if the assignee had expressly assumed the duties—*i.e.*, the assignee is liable to both the assignor and the obligee in the event of nonperformance.

1) **Rationale**

Absent evidence to the contrary, it is the probable intent of the assignor and assignee in such cases that the assignee bear the burdens, as well as receive the benefits, of the contract. [Rest. 2d § 328; **Imperial Refining Co. v. Kanotex Refining Co.**, 29 F.2d 193 (8th Cir. 1928)]

a) **Note**

In deference to **Langel v. Betz**, *supra*, Restatement Second provides that the A.L.I. expresses no opinion as to whether the general rule Restatement Second adopts (that an assignee of a contract who accepts the assignment impliedly promises to perform the duties thereunder) applies to land-sale contracts. [Rest. 2d § 328]

2) **U.C.C.**

For contracts for the sale of goods, the modern view is adopted in the U.C.C. Section 2–210(4) provides that an assignment of "the contract," or of "all my rights under the contract," or an assignment in similar general terms, is an assignment of rights and, unless the language or the circumstances indicate the contrary—as where the assignment is for security—is also a delegation of performance of the duties of the assignor. Section 2–210(4) also provides that acceptance of such an assignment by the assignee constitutes a promise by the assignee to perform those duties. This promise is enforceable either by the obligee under the original contract or by the assignor.

(3) Effect of Tender by Delegee

If a duty is delegable, and a delegee makes a satisfactory tender of performance to the obligee, the latter must accept the tender or the duty is discharged.

ASSIGNMENT VS. DELEGATION		GILBERT
	ASSIGNMENT	**DELEGATION**
EXAMPLE	Manuco contracts to manufacture widgets for Buyer. Manuco later assigns its right to receive payment from Buyer to Lender, a creditor of Manuco. Manuco is the assignor, Buyer is the obligor, and Lender is the assignee.	Manuco contracts to manufacture widgets for Buyer. Manuco later delegates its duty to manufacture widgets to Widgetco. Manuco is the delegor/obligor, Buyer is the obligee, and Widgetco is the delegee.
WHEN INVALID	Assignments that: (i) *materially change the duty* of the obligor (*e.g.*, assignment of personal services contract), (ii) *materially increase the burden or risk* imposed by the contract (*e.g.*, assignment of insurance policy), or (iii) *materially impair the chance of or the value of a return performance* are invalid.	Delegations in which *performance by the delegee varies materially* from performance promised by the delegor (*e.g.*, delegation of personal services contract) are invalid.
WHO MAY ENFORCE	The assignee can enforce against the obligor.	The obligee can enforce against the delegor and the delegee. The delegor can enforce against the delegee.

Chapter Five

Performance and Breach

CONTENTS	PAGE
Chapter Approach	214
A. Obligation to Perform in Good Faith	214
B. Express Conditions	216
C. Implied Conditions	226
D. Order of Performance	227
E. Doctrine of Substantial Performance	231
F. Divisible Contracts	234
G. Material vs. Minor Breach	235
H. Anticipatory Breach	238
I. Changed Circumstances—Impossibility, Impracticability, and Frustration	241
J. Discharge	245

Chapter Approach

If a contract has been formed and there are no defenses to formation, you should ask:

1. Did a party fail to *perform in good faith*, even if they did not violate the literal terms of the contract?
2. If one party failed to perform, was there an *express condition* to that party's performance? If so, was the condition fulfilled or was fulfillment of the condition excused?
3. If one party failed to perform, was there an *implied condition* to that party's performance? In particular, was the other party required to have rendered performance, or to have made a tender of performance, before the nonperforming party came under a duty to perform?
4. If a party who was required to perform first did not perform *perfectly*, did they nevertheless perform substantially? If so, they may be able to sue on the contract.
5. If a party to the contract who was required to perform first did not perform substantially, was the contract *divisible*? If so, performance of part of the contract may allow recovery as to that part.
6. If *both* parties failed to perform, was one party's failure to perform justified because the other party had committed a *material breach*?
7. Did a party *repudiate* the contract, even though the time for that party's performance had not yet arrived? If so, the other party might be able to bring suit under the doctrine of anticipatory breach.
8. Did it appear that a party would be *unable* to perform, even though the time for performance had not arrived and that party had not repudiated? If so, the other party might be entitled to assurances that performance would occur.
9. Was a failure to perform excused by doctrines covering changed circumstances, like *impossibility* or *frustration*?
10. Was the contract *discharged* by a mutual rescission, a release, an accord and satisfaction, or acceptance of a full-payment check?

A. Obligation to Perform in Good Faith

1. In General

Under modern contract law, each party has an obligation to perform in good faith. For example, U.C.C. section 1–304 provides: "Every contract or duty within the Uniform Commercial Code imposes an obligation of good faith in its performance and enforcement." This concept permeates the entire U.C.C. Similarly, Restatement Second section 205 provides: "Every contract imposes upon each party a duty of good faith and fair dealing in its performance and its enforcement." Under the obligation to perform in good faith, even a party who does not breach any *explicit* provision of an agreement may nevertheless have breached the duty of good faith.

2. What Constitutes Good Faith?

Exactly what constitutes good faith is not always clear. U.C.C. Article 1 ("General Provisions"), section 1–201(b)(20), defines good faith as "honesty in fact and the observance of reasonable commercial standards of fair dealing." The Comment to Restatement Second section 205 describes good faith as "faithfulness to an agreed common purpose and consistency with the justified expectations of the other party." The Comment also excludes "bad faith" conduct violating community standards of decency, fairness, or reasonableness from its definition of good faith. Courts have found bad faith to include "evasion of the spirit of the bargain, lack of diligence and slacking off, willful rendering of imperfect performance, abuse of power to specify terms, and interference with or failure to cooperate in the other party's performance." [Rest. 2d § 205, comment]

Example: Seller agreed to sell four houses to Buyer for $800,000. As Buyer knew, Seller did not own the houses, but instead intended to purchase them at a foreclosure sale. Buyer then attended the foreclosure sale herself and outbid Seller for the houses, acquiring them for $780,000. By entering into the contract with Seller to purchase property that Buyer knew Seller would need to purchase at the foreclosure sale, Buyer impliedly agreed that Buyer would do nothing to prevent Seller from acquiring the property at the sale. Presumably, if Buyer had not interfered, Seller could have purchased the houses for (at most) the same price that Buyer paid. Seller would then have been able to sell the houses to Buyer under the contract. Buyer has not acted in good faith, and Seller is entitled to damages of $20,000, representing the difference between the contract price and the amount Buyer paid at the foreclosure sale, which is the amount Seller would presumptively have paid if Buyer had not outbid Seller.

Compare: Wilkoff promises to sell 2,600 tons of iron rail to Iron Trade Products, delivery to be made on a later date. Wilkoff contemplates obtaining the rails on the open market. During the interim, Iron Trade Products buys large amounts of rails from other sources. Iron Trade Products's large purchases drive up the market price and make it difficult for Wilkoff to obtain the 2,600 tons ordered. Iron Trade Products has not acted in bad faith, because it is reasonably to be anticipated that a purchaser of standard goods will buy from various sources of supply. [**Iron Trade Products Co. v. Wilkoff Co.,** 116 A. 150 (Pa. 1922)]

a. Comment

The Comment to Restatement Second section 205 described above reflects the *"excluder" theory*, a leading theory of the meaning of good faith. Under this theory, good faith is understood as the absence of bad faith; *i.e.*, the inquiry is not whether a performance was in good faith, but rather whether it was in bad faith. The theory is known as the "excluder" theory because under the theory good faith has no meaning of its own but instead excludes, as impermissible, various forms of conduct that constitute bad faith. Under a second theory, good faith limits a party's discretion when performing under a contract by preventing the party from using that discretion to recapture opportunities that they had forgone by making the contract. Under a third theory, good faith simply serves as a way for the court to supply missing contract terms through the process of implication.

B. Express Conditions

1. In General

A contract may expressly provide that a party does not have a duty to perform unless some condition is fulfilled. In such a case, the party's failure to perform will normally be *justified* if the condition was not fulfilled.

2. Definitions

a. Condition

To understand conditions, it is important to understand that there is a difference between (i) whether a party is bound under a contract and (ii) whether a party who is bound under a contract has come under a duty to perform. A party is bound under a contract if the contract has consideration and is not subject to any defense (*e.g.*, fraud). However, a party who is bound under a contract may not come under a duty to perform unless and until some specified event or state of the world occurs. An event or state of the world that must occur before a party to a contract has a duty to perform is known as a *condition*. More accurately, for contract-law purposes the term "condition" normally means *either*.

(i) An event or state of the world that must occur or fail to occur *before* a party has a duty to perform under a contract; or

(ii) An event or state of the world the occurrence or nonoccurrence of which *releases* a party from its duty to perform under a contract.

> **e.g. Example:** A contract between James and Emma provides that James will employ Emma, on specified terms, as manager of an auto dealership if James is awarded the dealership, and that Emma will accept such employment. Both parties are bound under the contract, but neither party comes under a duty to perform unless and until James is awarded the dealership. James's being awarded the dealership is a *condition*.

b. Express Condition

The term "express condition" normally refers to an *explicit contractual provision* which in substance provides that either (i) a described event or state of the world must occur or fail to occur *before* a party has a duty to perform or (ii) if a described event or state of the world occurs or fails to occur, a party will be *released* from a duty to perform. To put this differently, an express condition is an express statement in the contract that provides that either (i) a party to the contract does not have a duty to perform unless some event or state of the world occurs or fails to occur or (ii) if some event or state of the world occurs or fails to occur, the obligation of a party to perform one or more of their duties under the contract is suspended or terminated.

c. Strict Usage

In strict usage, the term "condition" refers only to events and states of the world, and the term "express condition" refers to contractual provisions. In general legal usage, however, the term "condition" is often used to refer to contractual provisions as well as states of the world, and this latter usage is followed in this book.

3. Conditions and Promises Distinguished

a. In General

A *promise* is an undertaking to perform or refrain from performing some designated act. A *condition* or *express condition* is a provision the fulfillment of which creates or extinguishes a duty to perform under a contract.

b. Differences in Legal Effect of Promises and Conditions

(1) Breach and Liability

An unexcused failure to perform a *promise* in a contract is always a breach of contract and always gives rise to liability, however minimal. On the other hand, nonfulfillment of a *condition* is *not* a breach of contract and does not give rise to liability.

(a) Comment

In a few cases a provision in a contract is **both** a promise and a condition. (*See infra*, p. 220.) And in a few other cases, a promise can be *implied* from a condition. (*See infra*, p. 220.) However, these cases do not represent a departure from the basic principle that nonfulfillment of a condition is not a breach of contract and does not give rise to liability. What gives rise to breach and liability in such cases is that the provision either is a promise as well as a condition or gives rise to a promise by implication. In its role as a condition, the provision does not give rise to either breach or liability.

(2) Excuse of Performance

Breach of a *promise* by one party may or may not excuse the other party's duty to perform under the contract. Nonfulfillment of a *condition* normally will excuse a duty to perform if the duty was subject to the condition.

(3) Interrelation of Conditions and Promises

If a party's *promise* to perform is subject to a condition, there can be no breach of contract by that party until the condition has been fulfilled.

Example: Anne contracts to loan Bob $50,000 on June 1 if the market value of Bob's gold-mine stock is at least $100,000 on that date. The attainment by the stock of a market value of $100,000 on June 1 is a condition to Anne's duty to loan the money. If the state of affairs specified in the condition occurs (*i.e.*, if the stock has a market value of at least $100,000 on June 1), Anne's duty to perform comes due, so that if Anne fails to loan the money, she will be liable for breach. If the state of affairs specified in the condition does not occur, Anne's duty to perform does not come due and will never arise; *i.e.*, unless the gold-mine stock has a market value of at least $100,000 on June 1, Anne is under no duty to loan Bob any money. But because the provision concerning the value of Bob's stock was a condition and not a promise, the failure of Bob's stock to have a market value of $100,000 on June 1 is not a breach of contract and does not give rise to liability.

	PROMISE VS. CONDITION	
	PROMISE	**CONDITION**
DEFINITION	An undertaking to perform or refrain from performing a certain act	A provision the fulfillment of which creates or extinguishes a duty to perform under a contract
EXAMPLE	"I *agree to sell* you my car for $10,000"	"I agree to mow your lawn once a week for a year *if I continue to live in this town*"
RESULT IF PROMISED PERFORMANCE/ CONDITION DOES NOT OCCUR	Nonperforming party breaches contract and incurs liability. Other party's performance may be excused.	Party not fulfilling condition does not breach contract or incur liability. Duties subject to the condition are excused.

4. Reasons for Using Express Conditions

Why would parties use an express condition rather than a promise? In some cases, it is because the relevant party is not willing to promise that the state of events in question will occur. For example, in the last example, neither Anne nor Bob may be willing to promise that the stock will have a value of at least $100,000 on June 1. Another reason for using express conditions rather than promises is to avoid the doctrine of substantial performance. (*See infra*, pp. 231–234.) Under that doctrine, if Josh promises some performance to Kiara, Josh can sue Kiara even if Josh has performed his promise only ***substantially*** (rather than perfectly). A slight deviation from the promise renders Josh liable to Kiara for damages, but it might not prevent Josh from insisting on Kiara's performance. On the other hand, if the contract states expressly that Kiara shall incur no obligation to Josh unless Josh's performance is perfect or meets some other stated criterion, then Kiara will not be liable under the contract if Josh performs only substantially, unless the condition is excused. (*See infra*, pp. 223–225.)

5. Interpretation of a Provision as Condition or Promise

The determination whether a particular contractual provision is a condition or a promise—or both—is of far-reaching importance. Such a determination may control whether one of the parties is in breach of contract, and it will establish the rights and duties of the parties under the contract.

a. Parties' Intent Controls

Ordinarily, it is not difficult to determine whether a particular provision is a promise or a condition. The issue depends on the parties' intent, and the ***words*** used by the parties will typically indicate that intent. However, cases may arise where the contract language is ***ambiguous*** and the court must interpret a provision to determine whether the parties intended a specified state of affairs in the contract to be (i) a state of affairs that one party undertakes to bring about, so that the provision is a promise, or (ii) a state of affairs that must exist before some other provisions of the agreement (which are clearly promises) give rise to a duty of performance, so that the provision is a condition.

Example: Buyer enters into a contract to buy Seller's car. The contract provides, "it being understood that the car must be capable of a speed of 125 miles per hour." Seller's car cannot attain that speed. The parties' intent will control the court's interpretation of this ambiguous provision. If the speed term is interpreted to be a condition, the failure of the car to reach 125 miles per hour discharges Buyer's duty to buy the car but does not give rise to any cause of action against Seller. If the speed term is interpreted to be a promise by Seller, the failure of the car to reach 125 miles per hour affords Buyer an action against Seller for breach of contract.

b. **Where Parties' Intent Unclear**

There is no stock formula to resolve ambiguities concerning whether a given provision is a promise or a condition. The ultimate test is the intention of the contracting parties, and each case therefore must be decided on its own facts. However, the following factors may be relevant:

(1) Words Used

Words like "provided," "if," and "when" usually indicate that the parties intended an express condition rather than a promise. Words like "promise" and "agree" usually indicate a promise.

(a) **Note**

Words by themselves might not be determinative.

Example: Suppose Acme Insurance Company issues a policy to Owen, insuring Owen's house against fire, and one of the policy provisions reads: "Insured *agrees* not to keep gasoline on the premises." Although phrased in terms of a promise, the provision is really a *condition* of the insurance. Acme would have no cause of action against Owen for breach of contract because Owen kept gasoline on the premises. But Owen's doing so would excuse Acme's duty to pay in the event of a loss by fire attributable to the gasoline.

Compare: Conversely, a contract provision that "all obligations hereunder are conditional upon submitting the matter to arbitration in the event of a dispute" might be interpreted as an enforceable promise by each party to arbitrate. [*See* **Hamilton v. Home Insurance Co.,** 137 U.S. 370 (1890)]

(2) In Case of Doubt, Construe Provisions as Promises

In case of doubt, contractual provisions will ordinarily be *construed to be promises* rather than conditions. Such a construction generally operates to give effect to the *parties' expectations.* First, failure to perform a promise will entitle the other party to damages, while failure to fulfill a condition imposes no liability. Second, failure to fulfill a condition normally excuses performance by the party whose performance is subject to the condition and therefore effectively terminates the contract, which is a relatively drastic outcome. In other words, if a contractual provision is a condition, one party may lose their right to an agreed exchange after they have relied substantially on the expectation of that exchange by preparation or performance. In contrast, breach of a promise may give rise only to an action for damages without terminating the obligation to perform. [**Green County v. Quinlan,** 211 U.S. 582 (1909)] When it is doubtful whether an agreement makes an event a condition of an promisor's duty, an interpretation that will reduce the risk of forfeiture is preferred. Interpreting a contractual provision as a promise decreases the risk of forfeiture; interpreting a contractual provision as a condition increases the risk of forfeiture.

Example: In the car-sale example *supra*, p. 218 ("it being understood that the car must be capable of a speed of 125 miles per hour"), the provision would probably be interpreted as a promise rather than as a condition. Therefore, if

Seller fails to deliver a car that is capable of 125 miles per hour, Buyer would be entitled to sue for breach of contract.

Example: On May 29, Jasmine contracts with Trucker to transport certain merchandise. Jasmine agrees to pay Trucker $1,000 "provided Trucker leaves Los Angeles with the goods immediately and delivers the goods to Jasmine's agent in New Orleans on June 1." Trucker delays leaving Los Angeles but is still able to deliver the goods to Jasmine's agent in New Orleans on June 1. Is Jasmine's obligation to pay the freight to Trucker conditional on Trucker's having left immediately on May 29? Unless it was shown that Trucker's leaving "immediately" had some special importance to Jasmine, the provision would probably be construed as a promise, the nonperformance of which would entitle Jasmine to damages (if any) but would not excuse Jasmine's duty to pay the freight. A contrary interpretation might be appropriate if it appeared that Trucker's leaving immediately had some special significance to Jasmine.

6. Implication of a Promise from a Condition

In some cases, a contractual term that operates as a condition also gives rise, *by implication*, to a promise relating to the condition.

Example: On June 1, Robert agrees to assign his lease on government-owned land to Vita for a $13,000 payment from her, payable that day. The assignment is "subject to approval by the Secretary of Interior." Robert promises to return the $13,000 if the Secretary does not give Vita approval by December 31. The Secretary does not approve the assignment by that date, but Vita did not seek such approval. Vita sues for return of the $13,000 she paid to Robert. Vita is not entitled to the $13,000. Although the Secretary's approval is a condition, the condition also gives rise, by implication, to a promise by Vita that she will seek the Secretary's approval in good faith.

7. Provision Both Promise and Express Condition

In some cases, a provision may be both a promise and a condition—*i.e.*, a party may commit (promise) to bring about a given state of events, and the contract containing that commitment may also expressly state that the other party's duty to perform under the contract is conditioned on the occurrence of the state of events.

Example: Trucker promises to get Jasmine's goods to New Orleans by June 1, and the contract expressly provides that Jasmine will have no duty to pay Trucker unless the goods arrive by that time. Getting the goods to New Orleans by June 1 is both a promise by Trucker and a condition to Jasmine's liability.

8. Conditions Precedent and Conditions Subsequent

a. Conditions Precedent

A "condition precedent" is a condition under which some state of affairs must occur *before* a party has a *duty to render performance* under a contract.

b. Conditions Subsequent

A "condition subsequent" is a condition under which occurrence or nonoccurrence of a state of affairs *extinguishes or terminates a duty to perform* that had previously arisen. For example, assume Fran agrees to work for Pizza Barn for a specified period unless Fran is admitted to law school during that period. Fran's duty to remain in Pizza Barn's employ is subject to the condition subsequent that she not be admitted to law school. [*See* **Hartman v. San Pedro Commercial Co.**, 66 Cal. App. 2d 935 (1944)]

c. **True Conditions Subsequent vs. Conditions Subsequent in Form Only**

True conditions subsequent are rare. Many provisions are *worded* as conditions subsequent *in form* but are conditions precedent in *substance*.

Example: Insurance Company insures Customer against loss by fire. The policy provides, "any liability of the insurer under this policy is discharged if either (i) proof of loss is not submitted within 30 days after the accident or (ii) suit is not brought against the insurer for the claimed loss within 12 months from the date of accident." The first provision (the proof-of-loss provision) is a condition subsequent in form, but in substance it is a condition precedent to the insurer's duty to pay because that duty does not arise unless and until a proof of loss is filed within 30 days after the accident. In contrast, the second provision, requiring suit within 12 months, is a true condition subsequent. This condition has the effect of a private statute of limitations. The insurer's duty to pay arises when the proof of loss is submitted, but if the suit is not brought within 12 months from the date of the accident, the duty is effectively discharged. [**Brandyce v. Globe & Rutgers Fire Insurance Co.,** 252 N.Y. 69 (1929)]

d. **Procedural Effect of Condition Subsequent**

In a lawsuit for breach of contract, the plaintiff is normally required to allege in the complaint, and to prove, that all conditions precedent to the defendant's duties have occurred or that there is some excuse for the nonoccurrence of such conditions. That is, the burden of pleading and burden of proof of the occurrence of conditions *precedent* is generally on the plaintiff. In contrast, the burden of pleading and the burden of proof of the occurrence of conditions *subsequent* is generally on the defendant.

(1) **Note**

Statutes in many jurisdictions provide that in *pleading* the occurrence of conditions precedent, it is sufficient to allege generally that all such conditions have occurred. The defendant then has the burden of denying, specifically and with particularity, any condition precedent that they allege has *not* occurred. [*See, e.g.*, Fed. R. Civ. P. 9(c)]

9. Conditions of Satisfaction

a. **Performance to Satisfaction of Promisor as Condition Precedent to Promisor's Duty to Perform**

Assume Painter promises to paint Owner's house, and Owner promises to pay Painter $1,000 provided Owner is "satisfied with the work done." Because Owner's satisfaction is a condition, Owner is not under a duty to pay unless satisfied. The problem is how Owner's satisfaction is to be evaluated. In particular, the problem is whether the performance must meet with Owner's *actual personal* satisfaction or must only be a performance that would meet with the satisfaction of a *reasonable person*. The modern trend is to construe a provision requiring the promisor's satisfaction according to the *subject matter* of the contract.

(1) **Subject Matter Involves Mechanical Fitness, Utility, or Marketability**

In contracts involving mechanical fitness, utility, or marketability (*e.g.*, construction or manufacturing contracts), a condition of satisfaction is interpreted to be fulfilled by a performance that would satisfy a *reasonable person*. It is therefore immaterial that the promisor was not personally satisfied if a reasonable person would have accepted and approved the performance tendered. [**Duplex Safety Boiler Co. v. Garden,** 101 N.Y. 387 (1886)]

(2) Subject Matter Involves Personal Taste or Judgment

On the other hand, if the contract involves personal taste or personal judgment, a condition of satisfaction is interpreted to be fulfilled only if the promisor is ***personally satisfied.*** For example, contracts for portraits, for dental work, or for tailoring all require the promisor's personal satisfaction. [**Mattei v. Hopper,** 51 Cal. 2d 119 (1958)]

(a) Lack of Satisfaction Must Be Honest and in Good Faith

Even if a condition requires personal satisfaction, the condition will fail to be fulfilled only if the promisor's lack of satisfaction is honest and in good faith. Therefore, if the promisor refused to examine the promisee's performance or otherwise rejected the performance in bad faith, the condition of satisfaction will be ***excused.*** [**Williams v. Hirshorn,** 103 A. 989 (N.J. 1918)]

1) Comment

Although technically the reasonableness, as opposed to the honesty, of the promisor's dissatisfaction is irrelevant if the subject matter of the contract involves personal taste or judgment, a lack of reasonableness is ***evidence*** that the promisor's dissatisfaction was not in good faith. [**Mattei v. Hopper,** *supra*]

b. Performance to the Satisfaction of a Third Person

In many contracts, an express condition requires the satisfaction of a third person rather than a party to the contract. In particular, construction contracts often include a condition requiring the satisfaction of the owner's architect or engineer. When the satisfaction of a third person is a condition, most courts take the position that the condition requires the ***actual personal satisfaction*** of the third person. As in the case where a party's personal satisfaction is required, however, a condition that requires a third person's personal satisfaction will be excused if the third person's dissatisfaction is not ***honest and in good faith.*** [**Thompson-Starrett Co. v. La Belle Iron Works,** 17 F.2d 536 (2d Cir. 1927)] Moreover, under a minority view, such a condition is excused if the third person acted under a ***gross mistake.*** [Rest. 2d § 227]

10. Conditions Relating to Time of Payment

Frequently a contract provides that payment is to be made upon the occurrence of a certain event. For example, Contractor agrees to pay Subcontractor for Subcontractor's work "five days after Owner shall have paid Contractor therefor." This kind of provision appears on its face to make the occurrence of the designated event (in the example, payment by Owner) a condition to payment by the promisor. However, the courts distinguish, in such cases, between (i) provisions that should be interpreted as a promise to pay that is enforceable ***only if*** the condition has occurred and (ii) provisions that should be interpreted as an unconditional promise to pay, with payment ***postponed*** until occurrence of the event designating the time of payment. If the second interpretation is given, the courts hold that if the event designating the time of payment does not occur, payment must nevertheless be made within a reasonable time.

Example: Contractor agrees to pay Subcontractor "as funds are received by Contractor from Owner." Most courts hold that such a provision falls into the second category above, so that Contractor must pay Subcontractor even if Owner becomes insolvent. [*See, e.g.,*

J. Dyer Co. v. Bishop International Engineering Co., 303 F.2d 655 (6th Cir. 1962); *but see* **Mascioni v. Miller, Inc.,** 261 N.Y. 1 (1933)—contra] The rationale for this outcome is that in the absence of a special contractual provision, the insolvency of an owner would not be a defense to a claim by a subcontractor against a contractor. The parties can change that result by contract, but the court will not construe a contractual provision to change the result unless the provision does so very explicitly.

11. Excuse of Conditions

Normally, there is no obligation to perform a contractual duty unless all its applicable conditions have been fulfilled. In some cases, however, a condition may be *excused*, so that a duty must be performed even though the condition has not been fulfilled.

a. Excuse of Condition by Prevention or Hindrance

A condition will be excused if the party favored by the condition wrongfully prevents or hinders the fulfillment of the condition. A party to a contract *cannot take advantage of their own wrongful conduct* to escape liability under the contract.

Example: Contractor contracts to build a house for Owner, and Owner promises to pay Contractor $100,000 for the house "on presentation of a certificate of completion from my architect, Alfonse." Presentation of the certificate is a condition to Owner's duty to pay. Contractor finishes the house, but Owner improperly bribes Alfonse not to give the certificate of completion. The condition is excused.

Example: Seller has given Buyer an option. It is a condition to the exercise of the option that Buyer "tender the purchase price to Seller at Seller's office during business hours on January 15." If Seller goes into hiding or otherwise refuses to see Buyer on the date set, the condition is excused. [**Unatin 7-Up Co. v. Solomon,** 39 A.2d 835 (Pa. 1944)]

(1) Element of Wrongfulness

To excuse a condition, the prevention or hindrance must be wrongful. This does *not* require a showing of bad faith or malice. Rather, it essentially means that in light of the terms of the contract, the objective of the contract, and the circumstances, the other party *would not have reasonably anticipated* the type of prevention or hindrance that occurred.

Example: In the option example above, even if Seller merely forgot about the option and was not in the office on January 15, the condition is excused because Buyer would not have reasonably anticipated that Seller would be out of the office on January 15.

(2) Termination of a Business

Many contracts are conditioned on the continued operation of a business. In such a case, whether closing down the business constitutes wrongful prevention, and therefore excuses the condition, depends on the type of contract involved and the reason for the closing.

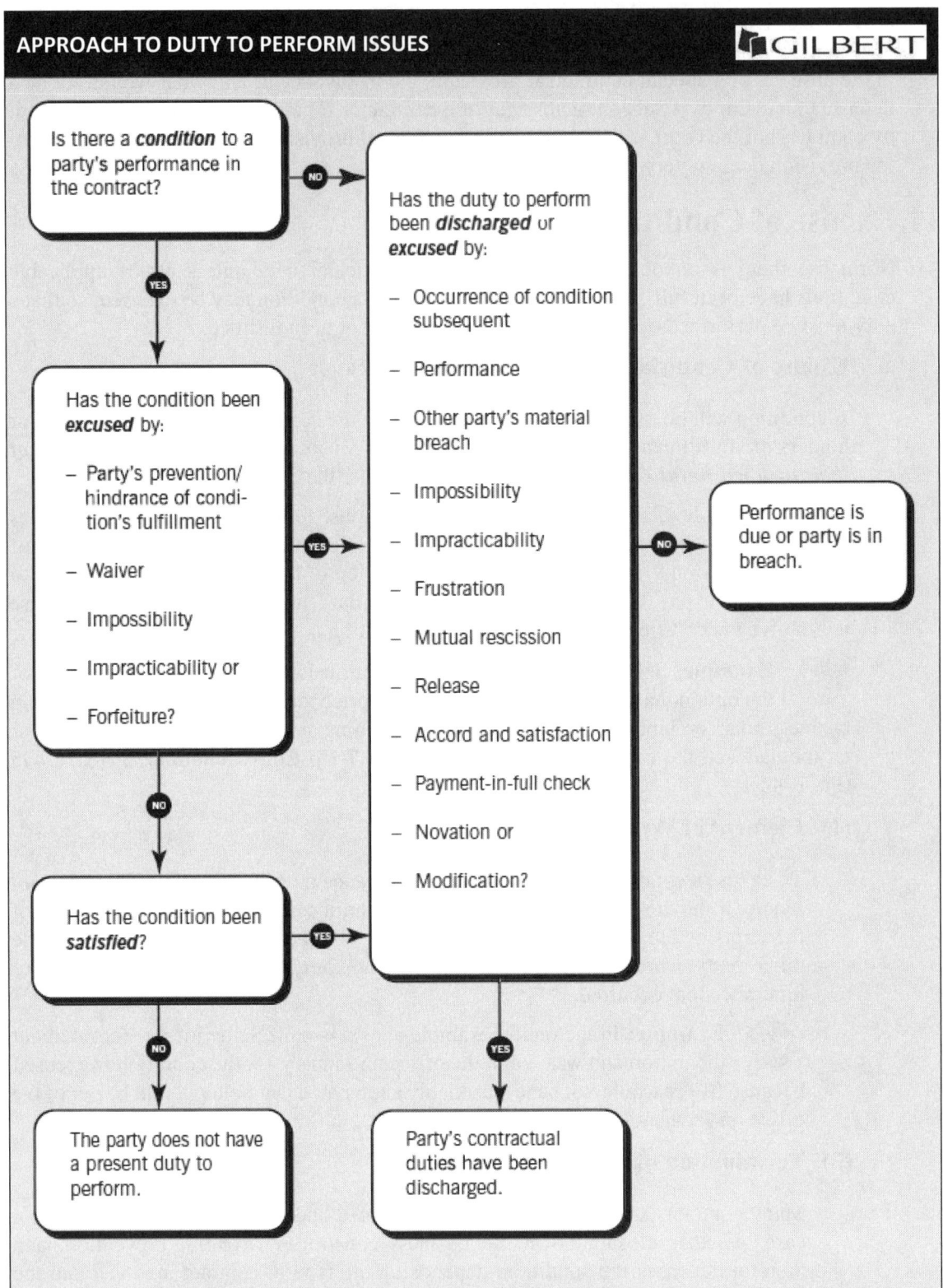

(a) **Requirements and Output Contracts**

Assume that Seller contracts to sell the output of its furniture factory to Buyer for the next five years. It is then a condition to Seller's duty to perform that the factory *has* output. Suppose that one year after the contract is made, Seller closes down the factory. Is the condition that Seller's factory have output excused, so that Buyer can sue Seller for failure to deliver any furniture, despite the nonoccurrence of the condition? Most courts hold that the answer depends on whether Seller had valid economic reasons for the closing *other than* losses resulting from the contract with Buyer. [**Neofotistos v. Harvard Brewing Co.,** 171 N.E.2d 865 (Mass. 1961)] The Comment to U.C.C. section 2–306 states, "A shut-down by a requirements buyer for lack of orders might be permissible when a shut-down merely to curtail losses would not." (*See also supra*, p. 22.)

(b) Agreements Conditioned on "Profits"

Similarly, if a contract between two parties requires one party to pay the other a designated share of the profits from a business, the *existence* of profits from the business is a condition to the party's obligation. What if the party sells the business?

Example: Seller sells factory to Buyer for $100,000 plus an additional $25,000 if Buyer makes any profit from the business in the first year of operation. Prior to the expiration of one year, Buyer sells the business. The condition of having made a profit during the year is excused, so that Seller can sue Buyer despite the nonoccurrence of the condition. Buyer is liable for the additional $25,000 if Seller can show that the value of the business was $25,000 greater than the amount Buyer paid for it. [**Du Pont de Nemours Powder Co. v. Schlottman,** 218 F. 353 (2d Cir. 1914)]

b. Waiver

A party by ***words or conduct*** may waive a right to insist on the fulfillment of a condition upon which their duty of performance depends. This subject is discussed *supra*, p. 42.

c. Impossibility

Impossibility or impracticability excuses the fulfillment of a condition if fulfillment of the condition is not a material part of the agreed exchange and forfeiture would otherwise result. (For further discussion of the doctrine of impossibility/impracticability, *see infra*, pp. 241–244.)

Example: Insurance Company issues Roger an accidental injury insurance policy, which provides that notice within 14 days of an accident is a condition of Insurance Company's duty. Roger is injured as a result of an accident covered by the policy but is in a coma as a result of the accident and is unable to give notice for 20 days. Roger gives notice as soon as he is able. Since the giving of notice within 14 days was impossible and was not a material part of the agreed exchange, and forfeiture would result if the condition is not excused, the nonoccurrence of the condition is excused, and Roger has a claim against Insurance Company under the policy. [Rest. 2d § 271, ill. 2]

d. Forfeiture

If the nonfulfillment of a condition would cause a disproportionate forfeiture, fulfillment of the condition may be excused ***unless*** the fulfillment of the condition was a material part of the agreed exchange.

Example: Hudson Lines, an ocean carrier, carries Widgetco's goods under a contract providing that it is a condition of Hudson Lines's liability for damages to cargo that "written notice of claim for loss or damage must be given within 10 days after removal of goods." Widgetco's cargo is damaged during carriage, and Hudson Lines knows of this. On removal of the goods, Widgetco notes in writing on the delivery record that the cargo is damaged. Five days later, Widgetco informs Hudson Lines over the telephone of a claim for that damage and invites Hudson Lines to participate in an inspection within the 10-day period. Hudson Lines inspects the goods within the period, but Widgetco does not give written notice of its claim until 25 days after removal of the goods. Because the purpose of requiring the condition of written notice is to alert the carrier and enable it to make a prompt investigation, and because this purpose had been served by the written notice of damage and the oral notice of claim, the court may excuse the nonoccurrence of the condition to the extent required to allow recovery by Widgetco. [Rest. 2d § 229, ill. 2]

EXAM TIP   GILBERT

Even if you find that a duty to perform is subject to a condition, check to make sure the condition has not been *excused*. A condition can be excused if: (i) a party **prevents or hinders** fulfillment of the condition, (ii) a party **waives** the condition, (iii) the condition cannot be performed due to *impossibility*, or (iv) fulfillment of the condition would cause a disproportionate *forfeiture*.

C. Implied Conditions

1. In General

Recall that for contract law purposes, a "condition" means either (i) an event or state of the world that must occur or fail to occur before a party's performance under a contract comes due or (ii) an event or state of the world the occurrence or nonoccurrence of which releases a party from its duty to render performance under a contract. The term "express condition" normally refers to an *explicit contractual provision* providing that a described event or state of the world must occur or fail to occur before a party's performance under a contract comes due, or an explicit contractual provision providing that if a described event or state of the world occurs or fails to occur, a party will be released from its duty to render performance under a contract. Often, however, it can be *implied* that the duty to render performance under a contract is conditional upon the occurrence of some event or state of the world, even though the contract does not explicitly state this. If so, there is said to be an "implied" or "constructive" condition that the relevant event or state of the world must occur before the performance of one or both parties comes due.

2. Implied Conditions of Performance

By far the most important and common type of implied condition to the duty of each party to a contract to render performance is that the *other party* has either rendered *its* performance or made a tender of its performance. For example, suppose Steve and Jim make a contract under which Jim will paint Steve's house by May 30, and Steve will pay Jim $3,000 on June 1. It is then an implied condition to Steve's duty to pay $3,000 that Jim will have painted the house.

a. Dual Effect

Note the dual legal effect of Jim's failure to paint Steve's house by June 1: (i) the failure is a breach of contract for which *Jim* will be liable in damages, and (ii) the failure is nonfulfillment of an implied condition to *Steve's* duty to pay on June 1, so that Steve does not come under that duty.

3. Implied Conditions of Cooperation and Notice

Implied conditions of cooperation and notice are also common.

a. Implied Condition of Cooperation

Under an implied condition of cooperation, the obligation of one party to render performance is impliedly conditioned on the other party's cooperation in that performance.

> **Example:** Seller promises to deliver certain goods to the "No. 2 loading dock" of Buyer's factory. It is an implied condition to Seller's duty to deliver the goods that such a loading dock exists, that the dock is reasonably accessible for making a delivery, and that Buyer permits Seller to make the delivery at the dock.

b. Implied Condition of Notice

Often, it is a condition to one party's performance of a duty under a contract that the other party give *notice* that the performance is due. A condition of notice is most commonly applied when a party could not reasonably be expected to know a fact that triggered the duty to perform unless such notice was given.

> **Example:** Jennifer leases a building to David and promises to maintain and repair the interior of the building as necessary. It is an implied condition to Jennifer's promise to repair that David will give her reasonable notification of the need for repairs and will permit her to enter to make the repairs. David therefore cannot sue Jennifer for failure to make a needed repair unless he has first notified Jennifer that the repair is required and given Jennifer an opportunity to make the repair.

D. Order of Performance

1. Introduction

As pointed out above, in many cases one party to a contract is not obliged to perform unless and until the other party has completed or tendered performance. This leaves open the question, "In what order are the parties to perform?" Sometimes, a contract explicitly provides for the order, or sequence, of the parties' performances, so that it is clear which party's performance is an implied condition to the other's performance. Often, however, a contract does not explicitly provide for the order in which the performances are to occur. Contract law has developed a number of rules governing the issue of order of performance when a contract is not explicit on the subject. These rules are phrased in the language of conditions because they address the issue: under what circumstance is the duty of performance of one party *impliedly conditional* on the actual performance or tender of performance by the other party?

2. Performance That Takes Time Is a Condition to Performance That Will Not Take Time

If one party's performance will take some period of time, whereas the other's performance can be accomplished in a moment of time, it is implied that the *performance that takes time must occur first*. Accordingly, completion of the performance that will take time is an *implied condition* to the duty to render the performance that will not take time.

> **Example:** Tiffany promises to paint Bob's house in consideration for Bob's promise to pay $3,000. The completion of Tiffany's performance (which will take time) is an implied condition to Bob's duty to pay (which will not take time).

> **Example:** Pat promises to serve as Jane's assistant. Jane promises to pay $2,000 a month for Pat's services. The completion of Pat's performance each month is an implied condition to Jane's duty to pay Pat each month.

3. Earlier Performance Is Condition to Later Performance

If one party promises to perform at a date *prior* to that on which the other party promises to perform, the first party's performance is an implied condition to the other party's duty to perform.

Example: Joe promises to deliver a horse to Lucy on March 1, in return for Lucy's promise to pay Joe $1,000 on April 1. Joe's delivery of the horse is an implied condition to Lucy's duty to pay.

4. Performances to Occur Simultaneously at Fixed Time—Conditions Concurrent

If both performances can be rendered simultaneously or nearly simultaneously and the contract sets the *same time* for both performances, tender of performance by each party is an implied condition to the other party's duty to perform; *i.e.*, neither party is obliged to perform unless and until the other party tenders performance. In such cases, each party's performance is said to be an *implied condition concurrent* to performance by the other.

Example: Vikki contracts to sell her car to Jake for $10,000. The contract states that both the purchase price and the car are to be exchanged on July 1. Tender of performance by each party is an implied condition concurrent to the other party's obligation to perform. If Jake fails to tender the purchase price on July 1, Vikki's duty to deliver the car does not arise. If Vikki fails to tender the car on July 1, Jake's duty to pay does not arise.

a. Effect

The legal effect of conditions concurrent is much the same as that of other implied conditions. If the condition concurrent is *fulfilled* (*i.e.*, if tender is made by one party) the other party's duty to perform *arises*. If the condition concurrent is *not fulfilled* (*i.e.*, if tender is not made) the other party's duty *does not arise*. Accordingly, in a sales contract that does not involve a credit term, there is ordinarily no breach of contract by the seller until the buyer tenders payment, and no breach of contract by the buyer until the seller tenders delivery. Tender by either party is sufficient to make the other party's duty to perform absolute; lack of tender means that the other party's duty does not arise.

5. No Time Set for Either Performance and Performances Can Occur Simultaneously

The same rule applies if no time is set for performance of either promise and the promises are capable of being performed simultaneously or nearly simultaneously. In such a case, tender of performance by each party is an *implied condition concurrent* to the other party's duty to perform.

Example: Ava contracts to sell her car to Milo for $10,000. No time is specified. Payment and delivery are conditions concurrent to each other.

6. Time Set for One Performance but Not Other

The *same rule* also applies if both promises can be rendered simultaneously or nearly simultaneously and a time is set for one party's performance but not for the other's.

Example: On May 15, Debbie promises to sell her car to Stacy for delivery on June 1 in consideration of Stacy's promise to pay $2,000 for the car. No time is set for Stacy's performance. Payment and delivery on June 1 are implied conditions concurrent to each other.

7. Anticipatory Repudiation

A performance or tender that would normally be an implied condition to the other party's performance or tender will be *excused* if the other party repudiates the contract prior to the time when performance was to occur.

a. Rationale

One purpose of this rule is to avoid forcing the innocent party to remain futilely in readiness to perform, and to tender performance, on the date set in the contract.

b. Ability to Perform

Although a party who is the victim of a repudiation does not have to make a tender or hold themselves ready to make a tender, they may be required to show that, but for the repudiation, they had the *ability* to perform.

> **Example:** Carla agrees to sell stock to Darryl, delivery on July 1. On June 1, Carla repudiates. Darryl can sue Carla without making a tender of payment, but Darryl may be required to show that he had the financial ability to tender payment.

c. Anticipatory Repudiation as a Breach

In addition to excusing the nonrepudiating party from holding themselves ready to perform and from tendering performance, the repudiating party may be liable for breach of contract even if the time for performance has not yet arrived. This aspect of the doctrine of anticipatory repudiation (or "anticipatory breach"), as well as further details of the doctrine, are discussed *infra*, pp. 238–241.

8. Prospective Inability to Perform

Sometimes it becomes apparent prior to the scheduled time of performance that one party to a contract will be unable to perform when the time comes for their performance. This is known as "prospective inability to perform" or "prospective failure of performance." The prospective inability to perform of one party *excuses* the other party from holding themselves ready to perform, rendering performance, or tendering performance, as an implied condition to the first party's duty to perform. (If a party's prospective inability to perform is caused by their *voluntary conduct,* it may also constitute an anticipatory breach with an attendant immediate right of action for the party. *See infra*, p. 238.)

> **Example:** Louisa enters into a contract to sell Blackacre to Richard on June 1 for $100,000. On May 25, Louisa conveys the property to Stan. By her conduct in conveying Blackacre to Stan, Louisa has made it appear that she will be unable to perform her promise to convey Blackacre to Richard on June 1. Louisa's prospective inability to perform excuses the condition that Richard, in order to put Louisa in breach of contract, hold himself ready to perform or make an actual tender on June 1.

a. Facts Constituting Prospective Inability to Perform

The following recurring fact patterns are illustrative of a prospective inability to perform.

(1) Vendor's Conveyance or Encumbrance of Contracted-for Property

After contracting to sell land or specific goods to one party, the vendor conveys or mortgages the property to another party, retaining no apparent right to reacquire the property before the date set for conveyance. The vendor's conduct constitutes a prospective inability to perform. [Rest. 2d § 264; **James v. Burchell,** 82 N.Y. 108 (1880)]

(2) Promisor's Making of an Inconsistent Contract with Another

The same result follows if the promisor makes a contract with another that is inconsistent with their contractual obligation to the promisee. [Rest. 1st § 318(c)]

Example: On June 1, Mary hires Sam as a sales representative, and Sam agrees to report to work on July 1. However, on June 2, Sam goes to work for another company under a one-year contract. By accepting such employment, Sam has made it appear that he will be unable to work for Mary. Sam's prospective inability to perform excuses Mary from holding herself ready to employ him.

(a) Contracts Not inconsistent

If it is possible to render service to *both the promisee and another,* the fact that the promisor has entered into a contract with another is not a prospective inability to perform their contract with the promisee.

(3) Insolvency

Insolvency or bankruptcy of a party to whom credit is to be extended under a contract does not constitute prospective inability to perform so as to excuse the solvent party's duty of performance. However, insolvency or bankruptcy may justify the solvent party in *suspending performance* until they have received either the remaining performance or an adequate assurance that the remaining performance will occur.

Example: Craig promises to paint Jennifer's house on August 1, and Jennifer promises to pay Craig $1,000 on September 1. On July 15, Craig discovers that Jennifer is insolvent. Craig's duty to paint Jennifer's house on August 1 is not discharged, but Craig has the right to insist on either payment in cash on the date of performance or an adequate bond securing payment on September 1. [**Hanna v. Florence Iron Co.,** 222 N.Y. 290 (1918)]

(a) Goods

The U.C.C. specifically provides that in contracts for the sale of goods, insolvency of either party gives the other the right to *demand assurances of performance* before proceeding further with their own performance under the contract. [U.C.C. § 2–609; *see* below]

(4) U.C.C.

Under the U.C.C., either party to a contract for the sale of goods has the right to demand *"adequate assurance of performance"* from the other party if reasonable grounds exist for believing the other party's performance may not be tendered. Until such assurance is given, the first party has the right to suspend its *own* performance. An unjustified failure to comply with a reasonable demand for assurance within 30 days constitutes a *repudiation* of the contract as a matter of law. [U.C.C. § 2–609]

(a) Restatement

The Restatement takes the position that a comparable principle should apply to all contracts, not just contracts for the sale of goods. [Rest. 2d § 251]

E. Doctrine of Substantial Performance

1. Introduction

As shown above, normally performance or tender by one of the parties to a contract, or by each party in the case of conditions concurrent, is an implied condition to the other party's duty to render performance. In other words, if A's performance is to come first, B does not come under a duty to perform until A has performed; if A and B are to perform simultaneously, neither A nor B comes under a duty to perform until the other tenders. However, ***substantial*** performance, as opposed to *perfect* performance, is usually sufficient to satisfy an implied condition of prior or simultaneous performance. In other words, if A's performance is an implied condition to B's performance, the condition will usually be satisfied by A's ***substantial*** performance. If A has substantially performed, B will come under a duty to perform even though A's performance is not perfect, unless perfect performance either is an *express* condition (*see supra*, p. 216) or is required by some exception to the substantial performance doctrine. (Note also that if A has substantially but not perfectly performed, B can sue A for the damages that result from the flaws in A's performance. *See infra*, p. 233.)

2. Significance

The significance of the substantial performance doctrine is that when the doctrine applies, a party can ***bring suit*** on the contract as a plaintiff—for expectation damages (*see infra*, p. 251)—even though that party has breached the contract by not rendering a perfect performance. (Of course, to be successful in such a suit, that party would need to show that the other party breached the contract too.)

a. Offset

However, if a plaintiff sues for breach but has performed less than perfectly themselves, the defendant is entitled to offset any remedy awarded against the defendant by the amount of damages the defendant incurred as a result of the plaintiff's breach.

3. Rationale

If Builder promises to build a house for Owner and Owner promises to pay $100,000 for the house, the law implies that Builder's performance is a condition to Owner's duty to pay the contract price. But if Builder has done everything except to install three doorknobs or one light switch, it seems unfair—and not a necessary implication—to deny Builder contractual recovery, subject to an offset for damages from the less-than-perfect performance.

4. What Constitutes "Substantial" Performance?

Whether a less-than-perfect performance is nevertheless "substantial," within the meaning of the substantial performance doctrine, is a question of fact to be governed by the circumstances of each case. The test is whether the performance meets the ***essential purpose*** of the contract. [**Plante v. Jacobs,** 103 N.W.2d 296 (Wis. 1960)] Among the factors to be considered are the extent of the contracted-for benefits that the innocent party has received, the extent to which damages will be an adequate compensation for the breach, the extent to which a forfeiture will occur if the doctrine is not applied, and the extent to which the breach was wrongful or in bad faith.

a. Willfulness

At one time, it was often stated that the doctrine of substantial performance was inapplicable if the plaintiff was guilty of a willful or intentional breach of contract. The modern view, however, is that even a conscious and intentional departure from the contract may constitute substantial performance. Rather, willfulness is to be considered as *one of several factors* involved in deciding whether there has been substantial performance.

5. Application

a. Construction Contracts

The doctrine of substantial performance has been applied primarily in cases involving construction contracts, where it would be unjust to allow an owner to retain the value of a building free of charge just because the contractor made some small deviation from the agreed specifications.

b. Contracts for the Sale of Goods—U.C.C.

In theory, the U.C.C. adopts a *"perfect tender" rule,* rather than the substantial performance doctrine, in cases involving contracts for the sale of goods. Under the perfect tender rule, substantial performance is insufficient for a seller of goods. Instead, under this rule, the seller must make a tender of goods that conform "perfectly," rather than merely substantially, to the contract specifications in order to put the buyer under an obligation to take and pay for the goods. [U.C.C. § 2–601]

(1) Exceptions

However, the U.C.C. makes a number of exceptions to the perfect tender rule—so many, in fact, that when all is said and done there is little left to the rule.

(a) Time for Performance Not Yet Expired

Under U.C.C. section 2–508(1), if a tender of goods is rejected because the goods do not conform to the contract and the time for performance has *not yet expired,* the seller has the right to notify the buyer of an intention to cure and then has the right to make a conforming delivery within the contract time.

Example: Seller contracts to deliver 500 Brand X widgets to Buyer for $500 on July 1. Seller delivers Brand Y widgets on June 15 and Buyer rejects them as nonconforming. Even though Seller has not made a perfect tender, Seller has the right to notify Buyer of Seller's intention to cure and to deliver Brand X widgets by July 1.

(b) Installment Contracts

Under U.C.C. section 2–612, if a contract for the sale of goods is an installment contract (*i.e.*, a contract calling for periodic deliveries and payments), the buyer cannot reject an installment, even though the installment does not conform to the contract, if (i) the nonconformity of the installment *does not substantially impair* the value of the whole contract; (ii) the nonconformity can be *cured;* and (iii) the seller gives *adequate assurance* of cure.

Example: Seller contracts to deliver 500 Brand X widgets in installments of 100 widgets per month for $500. If Seller delivers 85 Brand X widgets and 15 Brand Y widgets in the third installment, Buyer cannot reject the installment if the nonconformity does not impair the value of the whole contract, the nonconformity can be cured by delivery of 15 Brand X widgets, and Seller gives Buyer adequate notice of cure.

(c) Reasonable Grounds for Believing Tender Conforms

Under U.C.C. section 2–508(2), even if the defect in goods cannot be cured within the contract time and the contract is not an installment contract, the perfect tender rule is not applicable if the seller had *reasonable grounds* to believe the tender would be acceptable, despite the defect, with or without a money allowance. In such a case, the buyer can reject a nonconforming tender, but the seller can then notify the buyer of their intention to cure the defect, and if the seller retenders a conforming delivery within a reasonable time, the buyer must accept it.

Example: Seller contracts to deliver 500 Brand X widgets to Buyer for $500 on July 1. In the past, Buyer has accepted Brand Y widgets in place of Brand X widgets. Seller delivers 500 Brand Y widgets on July 1 and Buyer rejects them as nonconforming. Because Seller had reasonable grounds to believe the Brand Y widgets would be acceptable, Seller can cure by notifying Buyer of Seller's intention to cure and delivering Brand X widgets within a reasonable time after the July 1 due date.

EXAM TIP   **GILBERT**

When determining whether a party has a duty to perform after the other party renders *defective or incomplete performance,* first check to see whether the contract is governed by common law or U.C.C. Article 2. If the contract is governed by common law, use the doctrine of *substantial performance.* If the contract is governed by Article 2, apply the *perfect tender rule* and its exceptions.

---

6. Damages

As noted above, under the substantial performance doctrine, a party who has substantially performed is entitled to enforce the contract—that is, to sue for *expectation damages* (*see infra,* p. 251). However, the other party is entitled to an *offset* for damages resulting from the fact that the performance was not perfect. [**Plante v. Jacobs,** *supra,* p. 231]

a. Cost of Completion

Normally, the measure of damages for the failure to perform perfectly is the amount it would cost to *repair the deficiency* in the performance or to make the work *conform to the contract.* This measure is known as "cost of completion" damages. [23 A.L.R. 1436]

b. Diminution in Value

However, if repair or reconstruction would involve *"substantial economic waste"* or if cost-of-completion damages would be *disproportionate* to the end to be served, the measure of damages will usually be the amount by which the deficiency in the performance diminishes the value of the performance. (*See infra,* p. 264.)

Example: Builder and Owner make a contract under which Builder will construct a house for Owner for $350,000. One of the specifications of the contract is that Builder will use Acme plumbing pipes. Instead, Builder uses Baker plumbing pipes, which are functionally identical to Acme pipes. The problem does not come to light until construction is completed. The cost of completion (*i.e.*, the cost to remedy the defect) would be $200,000: $50,000 to tear apart the house to get at the pipes and $150,000 to replace the pipes and repair the house. That measure of damage will not be awarded. Instead, damages will be the amount by which the use of Baker pipe diminishes the value of the building as compared to its value if Acme pipe had been used. [**Jacob & Youngs, Inc. v. Kent,** 230 N.Y. 239 (1921)]

7. Remedy in Restitution

Even if the breaching party has *not* rendered substantial performance, they may have a right to recover in restitution for the value of performance rendered to and retained by the innocent party. In theory, the recovery in restitution is measured by the benefit conferred, minus an offset for damages. In practice, however, the measure of restitutionary recovery when performance is incomplete but readily remedial is usually the *unpaid contract price less the cost of completion,* up to the value of the benefit actually received by the defendant. This formula may often result in the same recovery as would be granted if there *had* been substantial performance.

F. Divisible Contracts

1. General Rule

A contract is said to be divisible if it is possible to *apportion* the parties' performances into *matching or corresponding pairs* that the parties treat as equivalents.

> **Example:** Contractor promises to build a garage for Owner for $10,000, a pool for $18,000, and a tennis court for $7,000, for a total price of $35,000. Unless circumstances indicate otherwise, the contract is divisible into three pairs of matched parts: building the garage and paying $10,000; building the pool and paying $18,000; and building the tennis court and paying $7,000.

2. Significance

If a contract is divisible, a party who has performed one or more parts is entitled to collect the contract price for those parts, even if they breach the other parts.

a. Note

Because there is still one contract (even though it is divisible), the right to collect the contract price for the parts performed is subject to an offset for damages resulting from breach of the other parts.

3. "Entire" Contract

A contract that is not divisible is said to be "entire." To say that a contract is "entire" means only that the need to show substantial performance of the *whole* contract is a condition to bringing suit on the contract and cannot be avoided by bringing suit on individual parts of the contract.

4. Employment Contracts

If an employment contract or a statute requires periodic salary payments (*e.g.*, $3,000 per month), courts usually hold the contract to be *divisible* into different time periods. Therefore, if an employee breaches the contract, they may nevertheless recover wages for each period they have completed, minus an offset for damages (if any) resulting from their breach. [**Clark-Rice Corp. v. Waltham Bleachery & Dye Works,** 166 N.E. 867 (Mass. 1929)]

G. Material vs. Minor Breach

1. Introduction

An actual breach of contract, at the time performance is due, always gives rise to an immediate cause of action for **damages**. However, not every breach also **excuses the other party's duty of performance**. For example, if Contractor has contracted to build a $100 million commercial building for Owner, and Contractor puts the wrong doorknobs on some doors, Contractor will be liable for damages, but Owner will not be excused from performing. Whether a breach by one party excuses the other party's duty of performance depends on whether the breach is *"material" or "minor."*

2. Distinguishing Material from Minor Breach

There is no hard-and-fast line between what constitutes a material breach and what constitutes only a minor breach. Every case must be decided on its own facts.

a. Relevant Factors

The following six factors are normally relevant to determining whether a breach is material or minor:

(1) *The extent to which the breaching party has already performed.* A breach at the outset ("in limine") is more likely to be considered a material breach.

(2) *Whether the breach was willful, negligent, or the result of purely innocent behavior.* A willful breach is much more likely to be held material.

(3) *The extent of uncertainty* that the breaching party will perform the remainder of the contract.

(4) *The extent to which, despite the breach, the nonbreaching party will obtain (or has obtained) the substantial benefit they bargained for.*

(5) *The extent to which the nonbreaching party can be adequately compensated* for the defective or incomplete performance by means of damages.

(6) *The degree of hardship* that would be imposed on the breaching party if it were held that the breach was material and that they therefore had no further rights under the contract.

b. Repudiation

A repudiation consists of words or conduct by a party to a contract that a reasonable person would interpret as an expression of refusal to render *any further performance.* An act that would otherwise constitute only a minor breach will be treated as a material breach if accompanied by a repudiation. For example, if Painter is under a contractual duty to paint Owner's factory for eight hours a day for 10 days, and Painter paints only for 7.5 hours on the third day, that would probably in itself be only a minor breach. However, if Painter's actions were coupled with an express repudiation of the balance of the contract, it would be treated as a material breach.

c. Effect of Parties' Agreement

The contract itself may expressly or impliedly make the time, manner, or other detail of performance a matter of *bargained-for importance* as to one party or the other. If so, deviations from the agreed performance that otherwise would be regarded as only minor breaches will instead be considered *material*.

Example: Owner promises to pay Painter $10,000 to paint Owner's house by June 1, it being understood that Owner has planned a wedding in the house for June 8. Under these circumstances, any delay past June 1 could be considered a material breach.

(1) "Time Is of the Essence" Provision

Traditionally, the courts held that if a contract contains a provision that "time is of the essence," even a slight delay in performance would constitute a *material breach*.

(a) More Lenient Modern Trend

Today, to avoid forfeitures some courts hold that if the overall circumstances indicate that the date set for performance was not of great importance to the parties, a *minor delay will not* constitute a material breach even though the contract contains a provision that time is of the essence, at least in the absence of more explicit language concerning the effect of a delay. [**Katemis v. Westerlind,** 120 Cal. App. 2d 537 (1953)]

3. Effect of Material Breach

A material breach has two effects. First, it gives rise to an *immediate* cause of action for breach of the entire contract. Second, it *excuses* further performance by the innocent party.

4. Effect of a Minor Breach

A minor breach of contract also gives rise to an immediate cause of action for whatever damages were caused by the breach. However, a minor breach does *not* give rise to a cause of action on the entire contract. A minor breach may *suspend, but it does not excuse,* the other party's duty of further performance. Therefore, if a breach is minor, the breaching party is still entitled to enforce the contract, subject to an offset for whatever damages resulted from the minor breach.

Example: Painter agrees to paint Owner's factory for eight hours a day for 10 days. On the third day, Painter only paints for 7.5 hours but does not repudiate the contract. Painter would be liable for whatever damages Owner sustained as a result of the breach, but the breach would not give Owner the right to sue for breach of the entire contract or to terminate the contract, nor would it excuse Owner's duty to pay Painter (subject to an offset for damages resulting from the breach).

5. Response to Breach

Suppose that *A* and *B* have an ongoing contract. In the midst of the contract, *B* commits a breach but does not repudiate; on the contrary, *B* wants to continue performing. How may *A* respond?

a. Material Breach

If *B*'s breach is material, *A* may (i) *sue B for damages* resulting from the breach but let the contract continue or (ii) *terminate* the contract and sue *B* for breach of the whole contract ("total breach").

b. Minor Breach

If *B*'s breach is not material, *A* can sue *B* for damages resulting from the breach. However, *A **cannot terminate*** the contract. In fact, if *A* terminates the contract, *A* will be in total breach themselves, and ***B can sue A***. Therefore, a decision by *A* as to whether a breach by *B* is material or minor is fraught with danger, because if *A* guesses wrongly that the breach is material and terminates the contract, *A* may end up owing substantial damages to *B*.

6. Material Breach vs. Substantial Performance

The doctrine of material breach bears an obvious relationship to the doctrine of substantial performance. Both doctrines ordinarily distinguish between what could colloquially be called "major" or "very important" breaches (on one hand) and "minor" or "less important" breaches (on the other). It is sometimes said that material breach and substantial performance are ***mirror-image doctrines:*** if a party has substantially performed, then any breach they may have committed is not material; if a party has committed a material breach, then their performance cannot be substantial. Although the view of material breach and substantial performance as mirror-image doctrines may hold true in many cases, it is not true in all cases, and it masks an important difference between the two concepts. This difference can be seen in the following example:

> **Example:** Luke and Laura are parties to a contract that Luke has breached in some way. If Luke has largely, but not perfectly, completed his performance and Laura refuses to pay the contract price on the ground that Luke has committed some breach, Luke would try to invoke the doctrine of substantial performance. Luke's purpose in invoking the doctrine would be to enable him to sue Laura on the contract for the contract price (minus damages resulting from his breach), rather than being limited to a suit based on the benefit he conferred. In contrast, suppose that while Luke is still attempting to perform after committing some breach, Laura orders Luke to stop performing and terminates the contract on the ground of Luke's breach. Luke may then argue that although he breached, the breach was not sufficiently serious to justify Laura's response (*i.e.*, the breach was not material). As a corollary, Luke would argue that because his breach was minor, Laura herself has committed material breach in terminating the contract. Laura, of course, would argue just the opposite: that Luke's breach was material and allowed Laura not only to terminate the contract but to sue Luke for total breach.

a. Summary

In short, the doctrine of ***substantial performance*** is usually invoked by a promisor who has ***breached*** the contract in some way but nevertheless wants to ***sue*** for the contract price—subject to an offset for damages—despite their own breach. In contrast, the concept of ***material breach*** is usually invoked when the promisee has terminated on the ground of the promisor's breach, and the promisor argues that the promisee had ***no right to terminate*** (and that the promisee is therefore in breach, themselves, for terminating). Of course, in such cases the promisee will argue that they did have a right to terminate (and furthermore that they can sue for total breach).

(1) Substantial Performance

To put this more generally, the doctrine of substantial performance concerns the question: When can a party who has breached a contract nevertheless bring suit under the contract to recover ***damages*** for nonpayment for the work performed, and when are they limited to an action based on the other party's ***unjust enrichment*** instead?

(2) Material Breach

In comparison, the concept of material breach concerns the questions: Can the victim of a given breach (i) invoke the sanction of terminating the contract and (ii) bring suit for damages for ***breach of the whole contract*** ("total breach")? Or is the victim of breach (i) not permitted to invoke the sanction of termination, (ii) limited to an action for damages for *"partial breach,"* and (iii) ***themselves in breach*** if they try to terminate the contract?

(3) Significance

As a consequence of the difference between substantial performance and material breach, the concept of material breach may arise in cases where the doctrine of substantial performance would not. For example, suppose a party commits a breach very early in their performance. If the other party terminates the contract, the breaching party could not invoke the doctrine of substantial performance because they hardly have performed at all. However, they may be able to invoke the concept of material breach and claim that their breach was insufficiently material to justify the other party's response of terminating the contract. Accordingly, a breach may be immaterial even if there is no substantial performance.

H. Anticipatory Breach

1. In General

As described above, if either party to a contract, in advance of the time set for performance, ***repudiates*** the contract, the repudiation excuses the other party from holding themselves ready to perform, rendering performance, or tendering performance. In addition, the innocent party may generally treat anticipatory repudiation as a ***present material breach*** of contract (*i.e.*, an *"anticipatory breach"*) and bring an immediate action for the entire value of the promised performance. [U.C.C. § 2–610]

2. Acts Sufficient

The repudiation need not be by ***words***. A voluntary act that disables the promisor from performing will also constitute a repudiation (for example, the promisor's making inconsistent contracts with another; *see supra*, p. 230).

3. Insistence on Terms Not Part of the Contract

Insistence upon terms that are not contained in a contract constitutes an anticipatory breach. Similarly, there is an anticipatory breach if a party to a contract demands a performance to which they have no right under the contract and states that unless their demand is complied with they will not render their promised performance.

4. Requirement of Unequivocal Repudiation

Only an express or implied ***unconditional refusal*** to perform as promised in the contract will constitute an anticipatory repudiation. A mere expression by the promisor of "doubt" that they will be able to perform is not sufficient to constitute a repudiation. However, such an expression may constitute a prospective inability to perform, which would permit the other party to suspend performance (*see supra*, pp. 229–230) and to demand adequate assurance of performance (*see infra*, p. 240).

Example: Buyer is under a contractual duty to buy 100 tons of coal per week from Seller for one year, beginning June 1. In August, Buyer says to Seller, "Unless the demand for steel increases, I may stop buying coal under our contract after October." This is not a sufficient repudiation to constitute an anticipatory breach.

5. Exception Where Nonrepudiating Party Has Completed Performance

The doctrine of anticipatory breach does not apply in cases where, at the time of repudiation, the *only remaining duty of performance* is the duty of the repudiating party. These are referred to as cases in which only a *unilateral obligation* remains. In such cases, an anticipatory repudiation does not give rise to an immediate cause of action for breach, and the innocent party must wait to sue until there is an *actual breach* at the time set for the other party's performance.

Example: Tammy offers to pay Josef $1,000 in three installments, beginning on December 1, if Josef can increase Tammy's sales 50% by June 1. Josef does so. On September 1, Tammy says, "I'm not going to pay you under that contract." Josef has no immediate cause of action against Tammy; he must wait until the installments become due.

Example: Sonja promises to pay Stacy $1,000 on July 1 in consideration of Stacy's promise to paint Sonja's house by June 15. Stacy promises and completes the painting on time, but Sonja repudiates on June 17. Stacy has no cause of action until the payment is due.

Compare: Richard agrees to convey title to Blackacre to Rudy on November 1, and Rudy agrees to pay $5,000 upon receipt of the deed. On October 1, Rudy repudiates. Here, Richard has an immediate cause of action for damages because, at the time of the repudiation, duties were owed by Richard as well as by Rudy.

a. Exception Usually Applies to Unperformed Duty to Pay Money in Installments

As a practical matter, this exception mainly arises in contracts where the only unperformed duty is to pay money in installments. In many (though by no means all) of these cases, even though the promisee has no *duties* left to perform, the promisor's continuing duty remains subject to some *condition* or *contingency*. For example, the promise may be to make fixed payments to the plaintiff during the plaintiff's life or while the plaintiff's physical disability persists. In such cases, the exception can be explained on the ground that it may not be possible to know, at the time of the repudiation, how many installments must eventually be paid, because the duration of the relevant condition is unclear. An obvious problem with the exception is that the plaintiff may end up having to bring a series of lawsuits. In most cases, however, the defendant will probably conform its conduct to the court's initial decision and thereafter make payments voluntarily. If the defendant does continue to withhold installments even after an adverse judgment on the earlier installments, the courts are unlikely to require the plaintiff to keep bringing suits. For example, in such a case the court could issue a decree for specific performance ordering future installments to be paid as they fall due.

6. Retraction

The general rule is that a repudiating party may retract its repudiation at any time prior to the date set for its performance, unless the innocent party has either *accepted* the repudiation or has *changed its position* in detrimental reliance thereon. [U.C.C. § 2–611(2); **Clavan v. Herman,** 131 A. 705 (Pa. 1926)]

e.g. Example: Allie repudiates her executory land sale contract with Ling. In reliance thereon, Ling sells the property to John. Allie cannot subsequently retract her repudiation and sue Ling for damages for nonperformance, because Ling's reliance bars the retraction. [**Rayburn v. Comstock,** 45 N.W. 378 (Mich. 1890)]

7. Determining Damages

a. Mitigation [§ 839, 841]

The general rule in cases of anticipatory repudiation is that the injured party must act promptly to *mitigate* damages after learning of the repudiation, although there is some law, mostly old, to the contrary. When there is a duty to mitigate, a party that fails to do so is not entitled to recover the damages they could have avoided if they had mitigated. If the innocent party is in the midst of rendering performance when the other party repudiates, the innocent party must stop unless doing so would involve greater damages than completing the performance (as where leaving goods half manufactured would result in total waste). If the innocent party is supposed to receive performance, they must look elsewhere for the performance that was due under the contract if failing to do so would increase their damages.

b. U.C.C.

In the case of contracts for the sale of goods, which are governed by the U.C.C., there is some ambiguity as to how damages are measured for anticipatory breach. Under U.C.C. section 2–708, the measure of damages for repudiation by the *buyer* is the difference between the contract price and "the market price *at the time and place for tender."* (Emphasis added.) In the case of breach by the *seller,* the buyer may either *"cover"* (*i.e.*, make a good faith purchase of, or a contract to purchase, replacement goods within a reasonable time) or recover *damages* equal to "the difference between the market price *at the time the buyer learned of the breach* and the contract price." [U.C.C. §§ 2–712(1), 2–713(1)] Although there is some support for a rule that the buyer learns of the breach when performance is *due,* most cases adopt the rule that the buyer learns of the breach when they learn of the *repudiation* or, at most, within a *reasonable time* thereafter. A "reasonable time," in this context, would be the time required for the buyer to find an alternative source of supply in the market. In a rapidly changing market, this might be almost the same time as the buyer learns of the repudiation.

8. Prospective Inability to Perform

If one party's prospective inability to perform (*see supra*, pp. 229–230) is caused by their *voluntary conduct,* it may constitute an anticipatory breach, with an attendant immediate right of action for the other party.

a. U.C.C.

Under the U.C.C., either party to a contract for the sale of goods has the right to demand *"adequate assurance of performance"* from the other party if reasonable grounds exist for believing the other party's performance might not be tendered. This rule applies even when the prospective inability to perform is *not* the result of the promisor's voluntary act (for example, if a buyer learns that the seller's source of supply is on strike). Until such assurance is given, the promisee has the right to suspend its own performance. Accordingly, in the coal example (*supra*, p. 238) where Buyer says, "Unless the demand for steel increases, I may stop buying coal under our contract after October," even though Buyer's statement is not an anticipatory breach, it may give Seller grounds for suspending performance and demanding assurance. An unjustified failure to provide adequate assurances within 30 days after the demand constitutes a repudiation of the contract as a matter of law. [U.C.C. § 2–609]

b. Restatement

The Restatement takes the position that comparable rules should apply to all contracts, not just contracts for the sale of goods. [Rest. 2d § 251]

I. Changed Circumstances—Impossibility, Impracticability, and Frustration

1. General Rule—Impossibility and Impracticability

Performance of a contract will normally be excused if the performance has been made "impossible"—more accurately, impracticable—by the occurrence of an event whose nonoccurrence was a ***basic assumption*** on which the contract was made, ***unless*** the adversely affected party has explicitly or implicitly ***assumed the risk*** that the contingency might occur.

a. What Constitutes "Impossibility"?

At one time, it was commonly said that for a performance to be excused by changed circumstances the change had to be such as to render the performance "impossible." In practice, however, the courts have normally only required that the performance be rendered ***impracticable*** (and that the other elements of the general rule be fulfilled). The U.C.C. has explicitly adopted the impracticability test for contracts for the sale of goods [U.C.C. § 2–615], and modern cases now tend to adopt that approach. Therefore, the term ***"impossibility,"*** for purposes of contract law, ***includes impracticability*** and should be so understood. Remember, however, that not every type of impossibility/impracticability is an excuse for nonperformance. The impracticability must involve the occurrence of an event whose nonoccurrence was a ***basic assumption on which the contract was made,*** and the adversely affected party ***must not have assumed the risk*** of that event occurring.

2. Recurring Types of Impracticability Cases

a. Supervening Illegality or Act of Government

A promisor's performance is excused if performance has become illegal because of a supervening change in the law after the time of contracting or because of some other act of government. [Rest. 1st § 458]

> **e.g. Example:** Examples of such supervening changes include new zoning ordinances or building laws [**Cordes v. Miller,** 39 Mich. 581 (1878)] and new governmental embargoes on exports [**Millar & Co. Ltd. v. Taylor & Co. Ltd.,** [1916] 1 K.B. 402].

b. Supervening Destruction or Nonexistence of Subject Matter

A promisor's duty to perform is excused if the subject matter of the contract or the specified means for performance is destroyed or becomes nonexistent after the contract is entered into, ***without fault*** of the promisor. [Rest. 1st § 460; *and see* U.C.C. §§ 2–613, 2–614]

> **Example:** A contract to use an auditorium for entertainment purposes is discharged by the destruction of the auditorium. [**Taylor v. Caldwell,** [1863] 3 Best & S. 826] A contract to drive logs downstream is discharged if the river is too low to drive logs on. [**Clarksville Land Co. v. Harriman,** 44 A. 527 (N.H. 1895)]

c. **Specific Source of Supply Contemplated**

A seller's duty to furnish goods under a contract of sale may be excused by the ***failure*** of a particular source of supply that was contemplated or specified by both parties to the contract.

> **Example:** A contract to sell potatoes to be grown on specified land is discharged by failure of the crop. [**Anderson v. May,** 52 N.W. 530 (Minn. 1892)]

> **Compare:** If, in a contract for the sale of potatoes, no particular land was either specified or contemplated by the parties, the promisor's duty to supply potatoes would not be excused by one particular crop's failure, even if the promisor subjectively intended to fulfill the contract from the crop that failed. [**Anderson v. May,** *supra*]

(1) **Where Seller Is a Middleman**

Failure of a middleman's source of supply will ***not*** typically be a defense, because ordinarily no particular source of supply is contemplated by ***both*** the middleman and the buyer. That is, the middleman may be counting on a particular source of supply, but the middleman's buyer usually will count on the middleman only. However, failure of a middleman's source of supply may excuse the middleman *if* (i) the source of supply is shown to have been contemplated or assumed by the parties at the time of contracting as the exclusive source of supply, *and* (ii) the middleman has taken all due measures to assure that the supply will not fail. [U.C.C. § 2–615, comment 5; **Canadian Industrial Alcohol Co. v. Dunbar Molasses Co.,** 258 N.Y. 194 (1932)]

> **Example:** Alcohol Co. contracted with Dunbar, a middleman, to purchase 1.5 million gallons of molasses in several shipments from National Sugar Refinery. Dunbar did not make a contract with the refinery assuring the necessary supply of molasses. During the course of the contract, the refinery was unable to supply enough molasses to fill Alcohol Co.'s needs. Dunbar cannot claim a discharge due to impracticability because, although the parties contemplated a certain source of supply, Dunbar did not take all due measures to assure himself the supply would not fail. [**Canadian Industrial Alcohol Co. v. Dunbar Molasses Co.,** *supra*]

d. **Construction Contracts—Destruction of Work in Process**

Suppose a property owner engages a contractor to build a house on their property at a designated location, and after the contractor has performed most of the work, the building is accidentally destroyed by fire due to the fault of neither party. The general rule is that the contractor's duty to construct a building is ***not*** excused by destruction of the work in progress. Construction is not rendered impracticable, because the contractor can still rebuild. If the contractor fails to rebuild, they will therefore be in ***breach*** of contract. Furthermore, they will not be permitted any recovery in restitution for the work that was destroyed, because that work conferred no benefit on the property owner. [**School District v. Dauchy,** 25 Conn. 530 (1857)]

(1) Note

The duty of the contractor to perform *on time* may be excused by destruction of the building. Thus, for example, a provision requiring the contractor to pay liquidated damages for delay (*see infra*, pp. 265–266) may be inoperative for whatever period is reasonably required to rebuild. **[U.S. Fidelity & Guaranty Co. v. Parson,** 112 So. 469 (Miss. 1927)]

e. Contracts to Repair—Destruction of the Premises to Be Repaired

The result is different when a contractor is hired to renovate or repair an *existing* building rather than to build a new one. In such cases, if the building is destroyed by fire or other calamity, the contractor's duty to continue performance is excused, and to the extent that the contractor has already performed, they are allowed to recover in restitution for the reasonable value of the work done prior to the destruction of the building. [28 A.L.R.3d 788]

f. Land Sale Contracts—Destruction of Improvements

Under property law, a purchaser of real property is deemed to be the equitable owner of the property from the time the contract to sell the property is executed, even before the closing and passage of title. Under the *traditional rule* of contract law, the *purchaser* was deemed to bear the risk of damage to or destruction of improvements on the real property between the time of the contract's execution and the time of the closing, on the theory that the purchaser is the equitable owner during that period. Under this rule, such damage or destruction does not excuse the purchaser's obligation to pay the full contract price for the property at the closing. However, a number of *modern jurisdictions* have changed the rule, so that the risk of such loss is on the *seller* until the closing or until passage of title. In these jurisdictions, material damage to or destruction of the improvements prior to closing or passage of title excuses performance.

g. Sale of Goods—Destruction of the Goods

Under the U.C.C., if a contract involves goods that were *identified when the contract was made*, then if the goods are destroyed without fault of either party and before the risk of loss passed, the contract is avoided. [U.C.C. § 2–613] If goods are to be shipped to the buyer, the risk of loss passes to the buyer when the seller duly delivers the goods to the carrier, *unless* the contract requires the seller to deliver the goods at a particular destination, in which case the risk of loss passes when the goods are tendered to the buyer at that destination. If no shipment is involved, the risk of loss passes upon the buyer's receipt of the goods if the seller is a merchant; otherwise, the risk of loss passes to the buyer upon tender of delivery. [U.C.C. § 2–509]

h. Death or Illness in Personal Service Contracts

Under a contract to render or receive personal services, death or incapacitating illness of the person who was to render or receive the personal services *excuses* both parties from the duty to perform. For example, if one party promises to paint another party's portrait, either party's incapacitating illness would excuse both parties.

(1) What Constitutes "Personal Services"?

The best test for whether services are "personal," within the meaning of this rule, is whether the right to receive the services could be validly *assigned* or the duty to perform the services could be validly *delegated*. (*See supra*, p. 209.)

3. Temporary Impracticability

Impracticability that is temporary rather than permanent merely *suspends* (rather than excuses) the promisor's duty while the impracticability continues. After the impracticability ceases, the duty reattaches *only* if performance thereafter would not substantially increase the burden on either party or make the performance different from what was promised.

Example: The leading case on this point is **Autry v. Republic Productions,** 30 Cal. 2d 144 (1947). Here the court first held that the drafting of an actor into the Army to serve from 1942 to 1945 rendered the actor's performance of a motion-picture contract, which was to expire in 1943, temporarily impossible to perform. The court then concluded that the actor's duty to perform did not reattach upon his discharge from the Army, because in the interim there had been substantial changes in the value of the dollar and in tax laws, which would have imposed a material detriment on the actor that was not contemplated by either party when the contract was signed in 1938.

4. Partial Impracticability

If (i) only part of the promisor's performance is rendered impracticable, (ii) the remainder of performance is not made materially more difficult or disadvantageous thereby, and (iii) the promisor is still able to render substantial performance, the *promisor remains bound* to render the performance as so *modified*, and the *promisee remains bound* to accept it with an appropriate *offset*.

Example: Contractor agrees to build a house for Owner using, among many other materials, Acme pipe. After the contract is made, Acme Pipe Company goes out of business, and Acme pipe therefore cannot be obtained. The contractor's duty to use Acme pipe is excused, but the contractor remains under a duty to construct the house and use substituted pipe, and the owner is under a duty to pay for the house, subject to an offset for the change in pipe.

a. U.C.C.

The U.C.C. adopts a counterpart of this principle in section 2–614(1): "Where without fault of either party the agreed berthing, loading, or unloading facilities fail or an agreed type of carrier becomes unavailable or the agreed manner of delivery otherwise becomes commercially impracticable but a commercially reasonable substitute is available, such substitute performance must be tendered and accepted."

5. Recovery in Restitution for Part Performance

If either party has rendered part performance prior to the circumstances that excuse completion of performance, that party may recover in *restitution* for the reasonable value of the part performance. [**McGillicuddy v. Los Verjels Land & Water Co.,** 213 Cal. 145 (1913)]

a. Reliance

A few cases suggest that if two parties have a contract and one party's performance is excused by impracticability, the other party can recover the value of their *reliance*, even though the reliance did not result in a benefit to the original party, if justice so requires. [*See, e.g.,* **Albre Marble & Tile Co. v. John Bowen Co.,** 155 N.E.2d 437 (Mass. 1959)]

6. Frustration

Even if performance of a contract is not made impracticable by changed circumstances, performance may be excused under the doctrine of *frustration* if the *purpose* or *value* of the contract has been destroyed by a supervening event that was not reasonably foreseeable at the time the contract was entered into. This doctrine arose from the famous **Coronation Case** [**Krell v. Henry,** [1903] 2 K.B. 720] in which the English court held that performance of a contract for licensing rooms to view a coronation procession was excused by the unexpected cancellation of the procession. Clearly, the parties' performances were not impracticable—the rooms could still be licensed and paid for—but the whole value of the contract had been destroyed by cancellation of the coronation.

Example: Jackie promises to pay Dennis a certain sum for advertising Jackie's hotel in a souvenir program, and Dennis promises to print and sell the program as a souvenir of a yachting race. The outbreak of war forces indefinite postponement of the race, but Dennis nevertheless publishes the program. Jackie's duty to pay is excused by the doctrine of frustration, because cancellation of the race totally destroyed the value of advertising in the program. [**Alfred Marks Realty Co. v. Hotel Hermitage Co.,** 156 N.Y.S. 179 (App. Div. 2nd Dept. 1915)]

Example: Hotel Co. promises to pay a monthly sum to Golf Club for permitting hotel guests to play on Golf Club's course. The hotel then burns down. Hotel Co.'s duty to pay is excused under the doctrine of frustration. [**LaCumbre Golf & Country Club v. Santa Barbara Hotel Co.,** 205 Cal. 422 (1928)]

Compare: Tenant leases a building in which to sell cars. Due to a war, new cars are no longer available. Tenant's duty to pay is not excused by the doctrine of frustration. The value of the lease is *not totally destroyed*, because the tenant can either sell used cars or sublet the building to someone else to use for a different purpose. [**Lloyd v. Murphy,** 25 Cal. 2d 48 (1944)]

EXAM TIP   GILBERT

Be sure to differentiate between the doctrines of impracticability and frustration. *Impracticability* involves changed circumstances that make it extremely difficult or impossible for a party to perform but that *do not destroy the purpose* for which the contract was created. However, *frustration* involves changed circumstances that *destroy the purpose* for which the contract was created but that do not make it more difficult or impossible for a party to perform. For example, suppose Buyer contracts with Seller to buy 1,000 tons of iron to repair a ship. Subsequently, a war causes the price of iron to rise astronomically. The contract is impracticable because it is extremely difficult for Buyer to perform, although the purpose of the contract (*i.e.*, ship repair) still exists. If, on the other hand, there is no war but the ship is instead destroyed by fire, the purpose of the contract is frustrated because Buyer no longer has any need for the iron, but it is still possible for Buyer to pay for the iron and for Seller to deliver it.

J. Discharge

1. Introduction

This section considers problems that may arise under certain methods by which contracts can be discharged—in particular, mutual rescission, release, accord and satisfaction, and full-payment checks.

2. Discharge by Mutual Rescission

If a contract is still executory (*i.e.*, performance is not completed) on both sides, it can be discharged by an *express agreement between the parties* to rescind or "call off" the contract.

Such an agreement is itself a binding contract that is adequately supported by consideration because each party surrenders its right to require performance by the other.

a. Executory Duties on Both Sides

A contract can be discharged by mutual rescission only if the duties are executory on *both* sides. If one of the parties has completed performance, a mutual rescission is no longer possible because the other party has already received what it was promised, so it has no right to any further performance that it can give up. (However, in such cases, the contract still might be discharged by other means.)

b. Modification

A mutual rescission should be distinguished from a *modification.* In a mutual rescission, each party gives up the right to require further performance by the other. In a modification, either the contract continues with modified duties on one or both sides, or only one party gives up a right. The latter case often raises a problem of consideration under the legal duty rule, but that rule has been limited by statute and caselaw. (*See supra*, pp. 24–37.)

c. Formalities

A mutual rescission need not be in writing unless the agreement to rescind would effect a retransfer or reconveyance of an interest in land or a sale of goods within the Statute of Frauds. For example, an agreement to rescind a contract for the sale of land, where title has already passed, would operate as a sale of the land and therefore would need to be in writing under the "interest in land" provision of the Statute of Frauds. (*See supra*, p. 162.)

d. Third-Party Beneficiary Contracts

Recall that if a third-party beneficiary's rights have "vested," a mutual rescission is not effective to vary the obligation to the third party. (*See supra*, p. 190.)

3. Release

A contract may be discharged by the execution and delivery of a release in which the maker expresses their intention to extinguish existing contractual rights in their favor, provided the release is supported by *adequate consideration.*

a. Some Statutes Abolish Consideration Requirement if Release Is in Writing

By statute in a number of states, a written release is effective to discharge a contract even without new consideration. The writing is accepted as a *substitute* for consideration. [*See, e.g.*, Cal. Civ. Code § 1541]

(1) U.C.C.

U.C.C. section 1–306 provides that any claim arising out of an alleged breach of contract for the sale of goods (or any other contract falling within the U.C.C.) is effectively *discharged* "by agreement of the aggrieved party in an authenticated record"—*e.g.*, a signed writing or email—even without consideration.

4. Accord and Satisfaction

A contract can be discharged by an accord and satisfaction or a substituted contract. (*See supra*, pp. 38–41.) Recall, however, that an executory (unexecuted) accord gives rise to special problems.

5. Payment-in-Full Check

A contract may be discharged by a check that is marked "payment in full" or the like, ***even though*** the check is for less than the amount claimed to be due, if the check is cashed by the party to whom the check is sent and certain other conditions are met. The law of full-payment checks is discussed *supra*, pp. 36–37.

Chapter Six
Remedies

CONTENTS	PAGE
Chapter Approach	250
A. Introduction	251
B. Basic Measures of Damages	251
C. Expectation Damages—General Limitations	252
D. Specific Performance—General Principles	256
E. Expectation Damages and Specific Performance—Applied to Factual Contexts	256
F. Nominal Damages	265
G. Liquidated Damages	265
H. Punitive Damages	267
I. Damages for Emotional Distress	267
J. Restitutionary Damages	268

Chapter Approach

If you have determined that there is a breach of a valid and enforceable contract, you need to consider the appropriate remedies for that breach. If you have determined that a valid and enforceable contract does *not* exist, you need to consider whether a party has conferred a benefit for which they should be compensated. There are two basic types of remedies: damages (an award of money) and specific performance (an order from a court to a party to perform as promised).

1. **Damages**

    There are three basic measures for damages:

    — *Expectation damages:* This measure is the usual means of compensating the victim of a breached ***bargain.*** Expectation damages give the victim enough money to put them in the position they would have been in if the promise had been ***performed***. Expectation damages are limited to ***reasonably foreseeable*** damages, so that not all consequential damages will necessarily be recoverable. They also must be ***reasonably certain*** in order to be awarded. Expectation damages often are measured by the cost for a promisee to purchase a ***reasonable substitute*** (*e.g.*, "cover") for performance.

    — *Reliance damages:* This measure is generally used when a promise is enforceable only because of reliance, as in the case of a relied-upon donative promise. Reliance damages give the breach victim their ***costs***, so that they are put back into the position they would have been in had the promise ***not been made.***

    — *Restitutionary (or quasi-contract) damages:* This measure is usually awarded when a party has conferred a benefit on another under circumstances where the other is ***not contractually liable*** for the benefit (*e.g.*, where the benefit has been conferred by mistake). However, under certain conditions this measure can be used against a party who has ***breached*** a contract, as an alternative to expectation damages. When the contract is a ***losing contract*** for the victim (*i.e.*, one in which the innocent party would have lost money if the other party had performed instead of breached), the restitution measure may be better for the innocent party than the expectation measure.

    The best general approach to damages problems is to recognize that each type of damages restores the plaintiff to a different ***baseline***. Expectation damages aim to put the promisee where they would have been if the promise had been ***performed***. Reliance damages aim to put the promisee where they would have been if the promise had ***never been made*** (and thus ordinarily cover the promisee's ***costs*** that resulted from the other party's promise). Under Restatement Second, restitution restores a ***benefit*** (like a payment) that one party has conferred on another.

    Once you have identified the baseline, you can compare it to the current state of affairs in a fact pattern in order to determine how much money needs to be awarded. For example, in computing expectation damages, you need to determine how much money is needed to put the promisee in an equivalent position to one in which the promise had been performed (*e.g.*, how much money is needed for the promisee to purchase a substitute for performance in the market?). You also need to account for any limitations on damages, like the duty to ***mitigate*** or the requirement of ***reasonable foreseeability***.

2. **Specific Performance**

    Specific performance is available only when the ***remedy at law is inadequate.*** This includes cases where the subject matter is unique, including contracts for interests in land and contracts for the sale of unique goods. Specific performance will not be awarded to force someone to work under an employment contract, even if the employee's services are unique and damages are inadequate, but some courts might issue an injunction against the breaching party to prevent them from working for others.

A. Introduction

1. Types of Remedies

There are two basic types of remedies in contracts: *damages* (*i.e.*, an award of money) and *specific performance* (*i.e.*, an order from a court to a contracting party to perform as promised).

B. Basic Measures of Damages

1. Damage Measures

There are three basic types of damage measures:

a. Expectation Damages

Expectation damages have the purpose of placing the victim of a breach in the position they would have been in if the promise had been *performed*. Expectation damages give the injured party the **benefit of the bargain** and are usually used when the broken promise is enforceable because it was part of a bargain (*see supra*, p. 5).

(1) Incidental Damages

Incidental damages include expenses such as the cost of shipping goods to and from a buyer who has wrongfully rejected the goods, the costs of storing and insuring goods pending resale after a buyer wrongfully rejects them, and the cost of going to the market to purchase substitute goods or of advertising a resale. If the injured party incurs such incidental damages, they are normally **added** to their expectation damages.

b. Reliance Damages

Reliance damages are based on the nonbreaching party's *costs* (including opportunity costs) that result from another party's promise. Reliance damages have the purpose of putting the nonbreaching party in the position they would have been in had the promise **not been made**. This measure usually is used where the promise is enforceable because (and only because) it was relied upon, as in the case of a **relied-upon donative promise** (*see supra*, pp. 46–47).

c. Restitutionary (or Quasi-Contract) Damages

Restitutionary damages (sometimes referred to as "quasi-contract damages") are based on the reasonable value of a **benefit conferred**. Restitutionary damages are often associated with the law of restitution, rather than the law of contract, and are therefore sometimes not thought of as "contract damages." In a contract setting, the restitution measure of damages is most commonly used in three situations:

(1) Where a party has **conferred a benefit under a contract that turns out to be unenforceable** because of some defense (*e.g.*, because the contract is within the Statute of Frauds and is not in writing);

(2) Where there was an enforceable contract and a breach, but the *contract was a losing one* for the innocent party, and that party is better off with restitution damages than with expectation damages (*see infra*, p. 269); and

(3) Where *no contract was formed, but a benefit was conferred in a precontractual stage* when the parties believed they had concluded or would conclude a contract (as where a benefit was conferred during, and as part of, an agreement to agree or preliminary negotiations that eventually broke down).

C. Expectation Damages— General Limitations

Most contracts (and most contracts questions) involve bargains, and expectation damages are the normal remedy for breach of a bargain. Many contracts problems raise questions involving general limitations on expectation damages—mainly foreseeability, certainty, and mitigation. This section considers those limitations.

1. The Principle of Hadley v. Baxendale

In **Hadley v. Baxendale,** 156 Eng. Rep. 145 (Ex. Ch. 1854), a mill's crank shaft broke, and the owners of the mill had to send the broken crank shaft by carrier to the manufacturer as a pattern for a new crank shaft. The mill and the carrier then entered a contract of carriage in which the carrier promised to deliver the crank shaft to the manufacturer by the next day. However, the carrier delivered the crank shaft several days late. The court held that the mill could not recover the lost profits from the days it could not operate because of the carrier's delay. The decision was based on the following rules: A party injured by a breach of contract can recover only those damages that (i) should "reasonably be considered [as] arising naturally, *i.e.*, according to the usual course of things," from the breach or (ii) might "reasonably be supposed to have been in the contemplation of both parties, at the time the contract was made, as the probable result of the breach of it." The two branches of the court's holding are known as the first and second rules of **Hadley v. Baxendale.**

a. General and Consequential Damages

On the basis of the two *Hadley* rules, contract law has conventionally distinguished between general or direct damages (on one hand) and special or consequential damages (on the other hand).

(1) General Damages

General or direct damages are the damages that flow from a given type of breach without regard to the particular circumstances of the victim of the breach. General damages are never barred by the principle of *Hadley*, because by their very definition such damages should "reasonably be considered [as] arising naturally, *i.e.*, according to the usual course of things" from the breach. For example, if a seller breaches a contract for the sale of goods, it follows naturally that the buyer suffers damages equal to the difference between the contract price and the market price or cost of cover (*i.e.*, the cost of buying substitute goods). This difference can normally be recovered as general damages.

(2) Consequential Damages

Special or consequential damages are the damages, above and beyond general damages, that flow from a breach as a result of the buyer's particular circumstances. Typically, consequential damages consist of lost profits (although other kinds of consequential damages may occur). For example, suppose a seller breaches a contract for the sale of a die press that the buyer plans to use rather than resell. The buyer's consequential damages are the difference between (i) the profits the buyer actually earned after the breach and (ii) the profits they would have earned if the die press had been furnished as promised.

(a) Reasonable Foreseeability

Today the principle of *Hadley* is normally restated to mean that consequential damages can be recovered only if, at the time the contract was made, the ***defendant had reason to foresee the damages as a probable result of the breach.***

Example: Seller contracts with Buyer to sell Buyer a steam boiler, delivery to be made in 10 days. Buyer is a commercial laundry and needs the boiler to meet rapidly expanding demand. No comparable boiler is then available on the market. Seller breaches. If Seller knew or should have known of the special circumstances concerning Buyer's needs and inability to buy a substitute boiler promptly, so that the buyer's loss of profit if the boiler is not delivered is reasonably foreseeable, Buyer can recover the lost profits as consequential damages. If Seller neither knew nor should have known of the special circumstances, Seller is liable only for Buyer's general damages (the difference between the contract price of the boiler and its market price).

1) "Significant Likelihood" May Suffice

Despite the use of the term "probable" in the standard formulation, the formulation would normally be interpreted to allow consequential damages to be recovered if, at the time the contract was made, there was a ***significant likelihood*** that they would result from breach, even though the likelihood was less than 50%.

2. Certainty

Damages can be recovered only if their amount is ***reasonably certain*** of computation. Damages that are not reasonably certain of computation are referred to as ***"speculative."***

a. Application to Profits

The certainty limitation is encountered frequently when the damages in question are ***lost profits.*** Courts often differentiate between lost profits for a new business and lost profits for an existing business.

(1) Existing Business

Profits for an existing business generally are not treated as speculative and are recoverable, because future profits can usually be estimated from past profits.

(2) New Business Rule

If the result of a breach is to prevent the nonbreaching party from setting up a new business (*e.g.*, a breach by a landlord of a lease of commercial space to a new retail business), the courts in the past were reluctant to award lost profits, on the theory that the profits of a new business are inherently speculative. Today, however, the tendency is to examine each case on its own merits and to allow recovery of lost profits even in the case of a new business if the profits can be determined with reasonable certainty—for example, by comparison with similar businesses in the vicinity.

b. Modern Trend

In general, the modern trend is not to cut off damages on the ground of uncertainty unless the uncertainty is fairly severe. For example, the U.C.C. provides that "the remedies provided by [the U.C.C.] must be liberally administered . . . ." [U.C.C. § 1–305]

EXAM TIP   GILBERT

If an exam question involves recovery of lost profits, be conscious of potential ***Hadley v. Baxendale*** and certainty issues. However, don't be too quick to deny relief. You should mention that there is a possibility a court will deny recovery of lost profits, but today more is regarded as foreseeable and certain than in the past. You should look for details in the fact pattern on which to base a determination of foreseeability and certainty of damages. (For example, is there evidence of profits from a similar business to aid in the determination of certainty? Is there a prior relationship between the parties that would lead lost profits to be foreseeable?)

---

c. Reliance as a Surrogate for Expectation Damages When Expectation Damages Are Uncertain

A party may choose to seek reliance damages as a remedy for breach of contract, in order to recover their *costs*, as an alternative to expectation damages. This rule may be particularly helpful to a promisee whose profits are too uncertain to be awarded. [Rest. 2d § 349; **Security Stove & Manufacturing Co. v. American Railways Express Co.,** 51 S.W.2d 572 (Mo. Ct. App. 1932)]

e.g. **Example:** Manufacturer develops a prototype for a product that it wishes to demonstrate at a convention in order to find a distributor for the product. It contracts with a delivery service to deliver the prototype to the convention, but the delivery is delayed in breach of contract. If Manufacturer's expected profits from exhibiting the prototype at the convention are uncertain, Manufacturer may seek reliance damages as an alternative to expectation damages in order to recover its costs (*e.g.*, the shipping fee, the fee to register at the convention, travel costs of employees to the convention). [**Security Stove,** *supra*]

(1) Rationale

The justification for this type of recovery is that even though the promisee's ***profits*** are uncertain, their reliance damages—*i.e.*, the costs they incurred—***are*** certain and were incurred with the expectation of profit. Thus, the promisee's costs represent a component of their expected profits that can be awarded even though their total profits are too uncertain to be the basis for recovery.

(2) Limitation

Because reliance damages are used, in cases like this, to ***measure*** a certain-enough component of the promisee's lost profits from breach, courts have given the promisor a chance to show that, in fact, the promisee would have had no profits from breach (or lesser profits from breach than their full costs), because the contract was a losing or unproductive contract. If the promisor can make such a showing, then the promisee's damages will be reduced so that they do not exceed what the promisee's profits would have been if the contract had been performed. [**L. Albert & Son v. Armstrong Rubber Co.,** 178 F.2d 182 (2d Cir. 1949)]

> **Example:** Same facts in the example above. Suppose Manufacturer's costs in reliance on the contract are $20,000 in total but that the delivery service can prove that even if the delivery had been on time, it is extremely unlikely that Manufacturer would have earned more than $15,000 from any distribution contracts it could have picked up at the convention. Manufacturer's damages may be limited to $15,000 instead of $20,000. (If the delivery service can prove that Manufacturer would have earned ***nothing*** even if the delivery contract had been performed, Manufacturer will not be able to recover its reliance damages under this rule.)

3. Duty to Mitigate

An injured party is not permitted to recover damages that could have been avoided by reasonable efforts. This principle is often referred to as the duty to mitigate damages. The application of this principle varies according to the type of contract involved.

a. Contracts for the Sale of Goods

Under the U.C.C., if the seller fails to deliver, the buyer has a right to cover (*i.e.*, buy substitute goods and recover damages; *see infra*, p. 257). If the buyer fails to cover, they will be barred from recovering any consequential damages that they could have prevented by covering. [U.C.C. § 2–715(2)] Similarly, if the buyer repudiates the contract prior to delivery, the seller cannot run up the damages by incurring freight charges for packing, delivery, and so forth. If the goods are still in the process of manufacture at the time of repudiation, the seller must stop production unless completion would facilitate resale and thereby reduce the damages for which the buyer is liable. [U.C.C. § 2–704(2)]

b. Employment Contracts

If an employer wrongfully terminates the employment, the employee is under a duty to mitigate by looking for a comparable job. (*See infra*, p. 262.)

c. Construction Contracts

(1) In General

A contractor is under a duty to not add to the owner's damages by continuing to work after the owner breaches the contract. In particular, a contractor cannot recover for expenses in continuing construction after the owner repudiates the contract. [**Rockingham v. Luten Bridge Co.,** 35 F.2d 301 (4th Cir. 1929)]

(2) Replacement Job

A contractor is usually not under a duty to secure an alternative construction job during the period in which it would have been working on a canceled contract, because it is not required to take additional business risks as a result of the owner's breach. Even if the contractor does take on another job during that period, its profits on that job would normally not reduce its damages, because it probably could have taken on the other job even if the owner had not breached (by hiring extra workers). However, if the owner can show that the contractor would not have been able to take on the new job but for the owner's breach, the profits on the new job should reduce the contractor's damages.

d. Expenses Incurred in Mitigating Damages Are Recoverable

Expenses incurred by the nonbreaching party in a reasonable effort to mitigate damages are recoverable as incidental damages, whether or not the effort was successful.

e.g. Example: The fees paid to an employment agency by a wrongfully discharged employee seeking a new job are added to the employee's damages, whether or not the job search was successful.

D. Specific Performance—General Principles

1. Definition

Specific performance is a remedy in which the court orders a breaching party to perform. If a party disobeys an order for specific performance by refusing to perform, they may be in "contempt of court" and threatened with jail as a means to compel their performance.

2. Origin and General Rule

Specific performance is an equitable remedy, which means it arose originally in a system of courts historically known as *equity*. For historical reasons, courts use their powers of equity only when there is no *adequate* remedy at law. Therefore, specific performance is available only when damages (the standard "legal," versus "equitable," remedy for breach of contract) are not an adequate remedy. There are a number of cases where damages are not an adequate remedy—in particular, where the contract concerns a unique subject matter or where damages cannot be measured with reasonable certainty. Special rules concerning when specific performance (or an equivalent remedy) will or will not be granted are discussed below in connection with recurring types of cases.

3. Discretion

Because of their history as an equitable remedy, courts retain discretion as to whether to issue an order for specific performance. For example, courts may take into account the general public interest before choosing to issue an order of specific performance. Moreover, courts are not bound by the parties' agreement that specific performance should apply to their case. [**Ed Bertholet & Assocs. v. Stefanko,** 690 N.E.2d 361 (Ind. Ct. App. 1998)] A trial court's decision to issue (or decline to issue) specific performance is normally reviewed, on appeal, only for abuse of discretion.

E. Expectation Damages and Specific Performance—Applied to Factual Contexts

1. Contracts for the Sale of Goods

Article 2 of the U.C.C., which governs contracts for the sale of goods, provides a number of remedies for breach of contract. The nature of these remedies depends on whether it is the seller or the buyer who has breached.

a. **Breach by Seller**

In the case of a breach of contract for the sale of goods by the seller, the buyer's remedies fall into two major categories. One category consists of the buyer's remedies when the buyer has accepted goods that are defective, and the buyer cannot or does not want to rightfully revoke acceptance. Typically, an action in this category is for breach of *warranty*. The second category consists of the buyer's remedies when the seller fails to deliver the goods or the buyer either properly rejects the goods or properly revokes acceptance.

(1) **General Damages for Breach as to Accepted Goods**

If the buyer has accepted goods that do not conform to the contract, the seller has committed a *breach of warranty*. For breach of warranty, the buyer may recover the loss resulting in the ordinary course of events from the seller's breach as determined in any reasonable manner. [U.C.C. § 2–714] Unless special circumstances show proximate damages of a different amount, the usual measure of damages for breach of warranty is the value that the goods **would have had if they had been as warranted** minus the value of the goods **accepted**. This difference may be measured either directly, by determining the value of the goods as they are and the value of the goods as they were warranted to be, or indirectly, by determining the cost of repairing or otherwise modifying the goods so that they are in their warranted state.

e.g. **Example:** Buyer and Seller have a contract under which Seller will sell construction equipment to Buyer for $50,000. The equipment that Seller delivers to Buyer is defective, in breach of an express promise (warranty) about the quality of the equipment. The cost to Buyer to repair the equipment so that it would conform to the warranty is $100,000. Buyer may recover $100,000 in damages from Seller. [**Cont'l Sand & Gravel, Inc. v. K & K Sand & Gravel, Inc.,** 755 F.2d 87 (7th Cir. 1985)]

(2) **General Damages if Seller Fails to Deliver or Buyer Rightfully Rejects or Revokes Acceptance**

(a) **Difference Between Contract Price and Market Price**

In a contract for the sale of goods, one formula to measure damages for breach by the seller when the seller has failed to deliver or where the buyer has rightfully rejected or revoked acceptance is (i) the *market price* of the goods at the time the buyer learned of the breach minus (ii) the *contract price*. [U.C.C. § 2–713]

(b) **Cover**

Alternatively, the buyer can "cover"—*i.e.*, purchase substitute goods from other sources. If the buyer covers in good faith and in a commercially reasonable manner, they can recover (i) the *cost of cover* (*i.e.*, the cost of the substitute goods) minus (ii) the *contract price*. [U.C.C. § 2–712]

(3) **Specific Performance and Replevin**

What if a buyer of goods is not satisfied with damages remedies and seeks specific performance instead? The traditional test for determining whether specific performance was available for the buyer of goods was whether the goods were "unique." Today, contracts for the sale of goods are governed by the U.C.C., which has expanded the traditional rule.

(a) U.C.C. Provisions

U.C.C. section 2–716(1) gives the buyer a right to specific performance "where the goods are unique *or in other proper circumstances*." In addition, section 2–716(3) gives a buyer a right comparable to the remedy of replevin (*i.e.*, an action to be awarded possession of goods) "if after reasonable effort he is unable to effect cover for the goods or the circumstances reasonably indicate that such an effort will be unavailing," and the goods either were in existence when the contract was made or were later identified to the contract.

1) Comment

The Official Comment to U.C.C. section 2–716 states that Article 2 "seeks to further a more liberal attitude than some courts have shown in connection with specific performance of contracts of sale."

Example: Laclede contracts with Amoco to provide a long-term supply of propane so that Laclede can furnish it to residential customers over the next decade or so. The good itself—propane—is clearly not "unique," and other suppliers of propane over the short term are available. Nonetheless, specific performance is permitted under the U.C.C. because Laclede cannot readily find a substitute for Amoco's long-term supply. [**Laclede Gas Co. v. Amoco Oil Co.,** 522 F.2d 33 (8th Cir. 1975)]

(4) Buyer's Incidental and Consequential Damages

In a proper case, the buyer may also be able to recover incidental and consequential damages. [U.C.C. § 2–715]

(a) Incidental Damages

Incidental damages resulting from the seller's breach include: (i) expenses reasonably incurred in inspection, receipt, transportation, and care and custody of goods that the buyer rightfully rejects; (ii) any commercially reasonable charges, expenses, or commissions in connection with effecting cover; and (iii) any other reasonable expense incident to the delay or other breach. [U.C.C. § 2–715(1)]

(b) Consequential Damages

Consequential damages resulting from the seller's breach may include any loss resulting from general or particular requirements and needs of which the seller at the time of contracting had reason to know and which could not reasonably be prevented by cover or otherwise. Consequential damages also may include bodily injury or property damage to the buyer that proximately results from any breach of warranty. [U.C.C. § 2–715(2)]

1) Unconscionable to Waive for Personal Injury in Consumer Cases

Recall that a contract provision that purports to waive consequential damages for bodily injury in cases of consumer contracts is "prima facie unconscionable." [U.C.C. § 2–719(3); *see supra*, p. 161] Accordingly, if such damages are otherwise available to a buyer of goods, a contract provision that purports to limit them is unlikely to be effective. Otherwise, a contract is ordinarily permitted to reduce or eliminate the availability of consequential damages, and it is commonplace for contracts to do so.

(5) Damages for Late Performance

If the seller breaches by *late* performance, the goods were to be resold by the buyer, and the seller knew or had reason to know that the goods would be resold, the buyer can recover damages for reduction in the market value of the goods between the time performance was due and the time performance was rendered.

b. Breach by Buyer

(1) General Damages Measures

(a) Market Damages

If a buyer refuses to purchase the goods it has contracted for, the seller can recover from the buyer (i) the ***contract price*** of the goods minus (ii) the ***market price*** at the time and place for tender under the contract. [U.C.C. § 2–708(1)]

(b) Lost Profits

If the market price/contract price formula is inadequate to put the seller in as good a position as performance would have (*e.g.*, if the contract price is equal to or less than the market price), then the measure of damages is the profit (including reasonable overhead) that the seller would have made from full performance by the buyer. This is called the "lost profits" or "lost volume" measure. [U.C.C. § 2–708(2)]

1) "Profits"

If the seller is a ***dealer***, "profits" under the above formula means contract price minus the seller's cost of purchasing the goods. If the seller is a ***manufacturer***, "profits" under the above formula means contract price minus manufacturing costs.

2) Application

The lost profits or lost volume measure normally is available for a seller only if the goods are relatively homogeneous and in relatively deep supply.

Example: Seller is a boat retailer who purchases standard model boats from Manufacturer for resale. Seller pays Manufacturer $9,000 for each boat. Buyer 1 agrees to purchase a boat from Seller for $13,000. The boat is on Seller's showroom floor. Later, Buyer 1 refuses to take delivery. Seller then sells the same boat to Buyer 2 for $13,000. Seller can recover $4,000 from Buyer 1—the $13,000 contract price minus Seller's $9,000 cost. *Rationale:* If Buyer 1 had gone through with the contract, Seller would still have sold a boat to Buyer 2, because Seller's boats are identical. Seller would then have had two $4,000 profits—one from Buyer 1 and one from Buyer 2. Thus, to put Seller in as good a position as it would have been in if Buyer 1 had not defaulted, Seller needs to recover $4,000. [**Neri v. Retail Marine Corp.**, 285 N.E.2d 311 (N.Y. 1972)]

(c) Resale

Alternatively, the seller can resell the goods in good faith and in a commercially reasonable manner and then recover from the buyer (i) the *contract price* minus (ii) the *resale price*. [U.C.C. § 2–706]

(2) Action for the Price

The seller's counterpart to a suit for specific performance is an action for the price of the goods (as opposed to damages). A seller can maintain an action for the price if (i) the buyer has breached by refusing to purchase goods that have already been *"identified to the contract"* and (ii) the seller is *unable to resell* after reasonable efforts, or such efforts would be unavailing. [U.C.C. § 2–709]

e.g. Example: Buyer orders calendars imprinted with Buyer's name. Seller manufactures the calendars, but before they can be shipped, Buyer repudiates the contract. If (as is likely) Seller is unable to resell calendars with Buyer's name on them, Seller can bring an action for the full contract price.

(a) "Identified to the Contract"

If the relevant goods are in existence when the contract is made, they are "identified to the contract" when they are set aside as the goods to which the contract refers. If the relevant goods are not in existence when the contract is made, then identification to the contract occurs when the seller ships, marks, or otherwise designates the goods as the goods covered by the contract. [U.C.C. § 2–501]

(3) Incidental Damages

In a proper case, the seller can recover incidental damages resulting from the buyer's breach. These include any commercially reasonable charges, expenses, or commissions incurred by the seller in the transportation, care, and custody of the goods after the buyer's breach in connection with the return or resale of the goods. [U.C.C. § 7–210]

SUMMARY OF ARTICLE 2 REMEDIES	BUYER BREACH (NONPAYMENT)	SELLER BREACH (BREACH OF WARRANTY)
BUYER ACCEPTS AND RETAINS GOODS	Seller recovers *contract price* PLUS *incidental* damages	Buyer recovers value goods *would have had* if they had been as warranted minus value of goods *accepted* PLUS *incidental* and *consequential* damages

	BUYER BREACH (WRONGFUL REFUSAL OF GOODS)	**SELLER BREACH (WRONGFUL FAILURE TO TENDER GOODS)**
BUYER DOES NOT ACCEPT AND RETAIN GOODS OR SELLER DOES NOT TENDER GOODS	Seller recovers *contract price* minus *market price* at time and place for tender *or* *contract price* minus *resale* price *or* *lost profits* (if unlimited supply) *or* *contract price* (if goods have been identified to contract and seller is unable to resell them) **PLUS** *incidental* damages	Buyer recovers *market price* at time buyer learned of breach minus *contract price* *or* recovers *cost of "cover"* (i.e., cost of substitute goods) minus *contract price* *or* is entitled to *specific performance* if appropriate (*e.g.*, if goods are unique) *or* is entitled to *possession* if buyer is unable to cover and goods were either in existence when contract was made or were later identified to the contract **PLUS** *incidental* and *consequential* damages

2. Contracts for the Sale of Realty

a. Breach by Seller

(1) Damages

Many states hold that if the seller breaches a contract for the sale of realty by refusing to convey, the purchaser's damages are limited to out-of-pocket costs, such as payments made so far toward the purchase price and expenses incurred in connection with the purchase (*e.g.*, title charges and escrow fees), **unless** the seller's refusal to convey was in bad faith. That is, in many states, without a showing of the seller's bad faith, the purchaser is **not** entitled to recover a general measure of expectation damages (such as the market value minus the contract price).

(a) "Bad Faith"

As used in this context, "bad faith" frequently includes sellers who (i) knew at the time they made the contract that they did not have good title or (ii) *deliberately* refuse to perform, as opposed to being unable to convey good title due to some unknown easement or other defect in title. [*E.g.*, **Key v. Alexander,** 108 So. 883 (Fla. 1926)]

(b) Effect

If the seller's breach was in bad faith, the buyer can recover the *market price* minus the *contract price,* even in states that ordinarily restrict the buyer to recovery of out-of-pocket costs.

(2) Specific Performance

Specific performance is routinely available to real-estate buyers (assuming the seller has the capacity to convey title), in the form of a decree ordering the seller to execute a deed in the buyer's favor. Damages are considered an inadequate remedy because every piece of land is *unique* to some extent and because (for that reason) the value of land is always to some extent conjectural.

b. Breach by Buyer

(1) Damages

If a contract for the sale of real estate is breached by the buyer, the seller is entitled to recover the *contract price* minus the *fair market value* of the land in question. [68 A.L.R. 137]

(2) Specific Performance

Alternatively, the seller can get specific performance in the form of a decree ordering the buyer to take title to the land and pay the agreed price. The seller's right to specific performance is based on mutuality of remedy and the need for a formal termination of the buyer's interest in the land by foreclosure.

(a) Effect

The seller's remedy of specific performance is normally not intended to actually make the buyer specifically perform by paying the purchase price. Rather, it is a mechanism to clear the seller's title by cutting off the buyer's rights and also to establish the seller's damages through a resale of the property. To achieve these objectives, a decree of specific performance against a buyer of property will normally provide that if the purchase price is not paid by a given date, the right of the buyer to "redeem" the property by paying the price is cut off or "foreclosed." Usually, once the foreclosure date passes the seller can resell the property and claim damages against the buyer for the deficiency, *i.e.*, the original contract price minus the price at which the property was sold at the foreclosure sale.

3. Employment Contracts

a. Breach by Employer

If an employer discharges an employee in breach of an employment contract or otherwise commits a material breach, the employee is entitled to recover the *remainder of their wages* minus either (i) the *wages the employee actually received* in a substitute employment or (ii) the wages they *would have received* had they properly attempted to mitigate damages.

(1) Mitigation

If the employer wrongfully terminates an employment contract, the employee is under a duty to exercise reasonable efforts to locate a position *of the same rank and*

type of work in the same locale. The burden usually is on the *employer* to show that such other positions were available. [**Copper v. Strange & Warner Co.,** 126 N.W. 541 (Minn. 1910)]

> **Example:** An actress hired for the female lead in a musical to be filmed in Los Angeles is ***not*** required to accept substitute employment as the lead in a dramatic western to be produced in Australia; the latter role is not comparable to the former role. [**Parker v. 20th Century Fox,** 3 Cal. 3d 176 (1970)]

b. Breach by Employee

If an employee quits in breach of contract or otherwise commits a material breach, the employer is entitled to recover (i) the ***wages the employer must pay to a replacement for the employee*** minus (ii) the ***employee's wages.***

> **Example:** Sal contracts to work for Maria for one year at $2,000 per month but quits after one month to take a better job. Maria has to pay $2,500 per month to get a qualified replacement. Maria's damages are $500 per month times 11 months, or $5,500.

c. Specific Performance

Employment contracts are not specifically enforceable by either the employee or the employer. The objection to specific performance is that it is unwise, inappropriate, and potentially oppressive to extract from an unwilling party a performance involving personal relations.

(1) Injunction

Although courts will not order an employee to work for the employer, in some cases courts will enjoin an employee from working for a competitor of the employer. Often such an injunction would be tantamount to ordering specific performance, because the employee may be unable to get a good job except with a competitor. Accordingly, Restatement Second adopts the rule that a "promise to render personal service exclusively for one employer will not be enforced by an injunction against serving another if its probable result will be to compel a performance involving personal relations the enforced continuance of which is undesirable or will be to leave the employee without other reasonable means of making a living." [Rest. 2d § 367(2)]

4. Construction Contracts and Other Contracts for Services

a. Terminology

The most common type of service contract is a construction contract, in which a contractor provides services to an owner.

b. Breach by Owner

If the owner commits a material beach of a construction contract, the contractor is entitled to recover (i) the ***contract price,*** minus (ii) the ***out-of-pocket costs*** remaining to be incurred by the contractor at the time of breach, with (iii) an ***offset for amounts already paid*** by the owner.

(1) Alternative Formula

Under an alternative formula, the contractor is entitled to recover (i) its ***lost profits*** on the contract, plus (ii) its ***out-of-pocket costs*** prior to breach, again with (iii) an *offset for amounts already paid* by the owner. Normally, the two formulas, although they look very different, produce the same result, unless the contractor has made a losing contract.

(2) Rationale and Analysis

The first formula can be understood as awarding the contractor (i) the price that they *lost* by not being paid by the owner minus (ii) the costs that they *saved* because of the owner's breach (given that, as a result of the breach, the contractor could stop construction early). If the contractor has fully performed and the owner has not paid anything, the contractor's damages would simply be the full contract price. The second formula can be understood as giving the owner what they contracted for: money sufficient to cover their costs and to give them an expected profit. If the contractor has incurred no costs on the contract at the time of breach, the contractor's damages would simply be their lost expected profits under the contract.

Example: Owner contracts with Contractor to build a swimming pool for $20,000. Under the contract, Contractor's total costs will be $17,000 (so that its profit will be $3,000—*i.e.*, the $20,000 price minus the $17,000 in costs). Owner breaches (*e.g.*, by indicating without justification that they will refuse to pay) after Contractor has spent $5,000 building part of the pool. Owner has paid no part of the contract price so far. On these facts, Contractor's damages are $8,000. Under the first formula above, this figure can be understood as $20,000 (contract price) minus $12,000 (Contractor's remaining costs under the contract—*i.e.*, costs that Contractor saved because of the breach). Equivalently, under the second formula above, the damages can be understood as $5,000 (the Contractor's incurred costs so far) plus $3,000 (what the Contractor's profit would have been under the completed contract).

Example: Same facts as above, but Owner had already paid $2,000 toward the contract price at the time of breach. Under both formulas, this $2,000 payment would simply reduce the damages Owner must pay by $2,000. Contractor's damages would therefore be $6,000 under both formulas.

c. Breach by Contractor

(1) Cost of Completion

When the contractor breaches by failing to complete construction or performing an inadequate job, the owner can usually recover damages based on the difference between the contract price and the *cost of completing the contract* by contracting with a substitute contractor. [125 A.L.R. 1242]

(2) Diminished Value Damages

However, if completion would lead to substantial economic waste or the cost-of-completion measure would be unreasonably disproportionate to the value to be gained by the owner, the courts will sometimes measure the owner's damages by a *diminution in value* measure—the *value of what the owner would have received* if the contractor had performed the contract in full minus the *value of what the owner actually received*. (*See supra*, p. 233.) [**Peevyhouse v. Garland Coal & Mining Co.**, 382 P.2d 109 (Okla. 1962)—a widely questioned application of this rule]

(a) Comment

There is no mechanical way to apply the tests involving waste and disproportion. It is routine for owners to pay contractors much more for work than the amount by which the work increases a property's market value—*e.g.*, most kitchen remodels or swimming pools cost more money than they add to the market value of a house. Some owners pay large amounts because of their individual goals and would require damages under the cost-of-completion measure in order to achieve those goals; by contrast, if an owner holds a property only as an investment, the diminution-in-value measure may suffice. [*See* **Advanced, Inc. v. Wilks,** 711 P.2d 524 (Alaska 1985)]

d. Specific Performance

The general rule is that a contract for construction will not be specifically enforced, mainly because damages are usually an adequate remedy. However, courts can grant specific performance of construction contracts if they believe damages are not an adequate remedy. Courts sometimes say that specific performance is unavailable in construction contracts because of the incapacity of the courts to superintend a contractor's performance, but this principle has not been consistently applied, and it is questionable because "superintending" compliance with an order for specific performance normally involves the same sort of determinations that courts routinely make in deciding whether a party has breached a contract in the first place.

5. Contracts for Carriage

If a contract for carriage (transportation) is breached by *late performance* by the carrier, the subject matter of the contract involves goods that were to be sold by the shipper, and it was reasonably foreseeable to the carrier that the goods were to be sold, the shipper can recover damages for reduction in the market value of the subject matter between the time performance was due and the time it was rendered. Otherwise, the damages for late performance by a carrier are often measured by the reasonable daily rental value of the shipped goods multiplied by the number of days of delay—or, if that is not easily determined, by the prevailing rate of interest on the value of the shipped goods. [**Wood v. Joliet Gaslight Co.,** 111 F. 463 (7th Cir. 1901)]

F. Nominal Damages

1. General Rule

Any breach of contract, no matter how slight, normally entitles the aggrieved party to *some* damages. If the party cannot prove any loss, the court will award "nominal" or "token" damages—normally, $1.

G. Liquidated Damages

1. In General

A liquidated damages provision is a provision in a contract that *fixes the amount of damages* that will be recoverable in the event of a breach. ("Liquid" here simply means "clear," and lawyers use the term "liquidated sum" to mean a certain amount rather than one whose value is in dispute.) The enforceability of such a provision depends on whether the court finds it to be a valid liquidated damages provision or a "penalty." If the court determines that the provision is a penalty, it is not enforceable, and the promisee is limited to whatever actual damages they can prove.

2. Contract Terminology Not Controlling

The name the parties give such a provision is not controlling. A provision calling for "$10,000 as liquidated damages in the event of breach" may be shown to be a penalty and therefore may not be enforceable.

3. Requirements for Valid Liquidated Damages Provision

Courts have used two factors to decide whether a clause is for liquidated damages or a penalty:

a. Damages Difficult to Estimate

The harder it is to measure damages at the time the contract was made, the more likely a clause will be held to be a liquidated damages clause (and thus enforceable) rather than a penalty clause (and thus unenforceable).

b. Reasonable Estimate

For a clause to be enforceable, it must be a *reasonable estimate* of the regular expectation damages that would result from a breach.

Example: Contractor promises to pay Owner $300 per day for any delay in completing a building contract. It is clear that when completed, the rental value of the building will be only $300 per week and that delays will lead Owner to suffer no other costs. The contractual provision is an unenforceable penalty, because it is not a reasonable forecast of the damages that will result from breach.

(1) "Second Look" at Events After Contract Formation

The traditional rule was that whether a clause was a reasonable estimate of damages (and thus enforceable) was to be determined based only on information that was available at the time the contract was made. The modern rule, adopted in many states, is that a court can also evaluate events subsequent to contract formation to determine the reasonableness of a clause's estimate of damages (and thus its enforceability). Under this rule, as both Restatement Second and the U.C.C. put it, a damages clause is enforceable if its measure is "reasonable in the light of the *anticipated* or *actual*" loss caused by the breach. [Rest. 2d § 356; U.C.C. § 2–718 (emphasis added)]

4. Deposits

A deposit may serve the same function as a liquidated damage provision if the contract purports to allow the promisee to retain the deposit even though the deposit exceeds the promisee's actual damages. On the recovery of deposits in such cases, *see infra*, pp. 269–270.

a. U.C.C. Rules

In contracts for the sale of goods, if the seller justifiably refuses to deliver goods because of the buyer's breach, the buyer is entitled to restitution of any amount by which the sum of the buyer's prior payments (including a deposit) *exceeds* (i) the amount set in a valid liquidated damages provision, or (ii) if there is no such provision, 20% of the value of the performance, or $500, whichever is smaller. This right to restitution is subject to an offset to the extent that the seller establishes damages other than liquidated damages. [U.C.C. § 2–718]

H. Punitive Damages

1. General Rule

It is widely said that punitive damages are **not available** for breach of contract, partly on the theory that "the mere availability of such a remedy would seriously jeopardize the stability and predictability of commercial transactions, so vital to the smooth and efficient operation of the modern economy." [**General Motors Corp. v. Piskor,** 281 Md. 627 (1977)] However, many states do allow punitive damages for breach of contract in egregious cases or subject to particular rules.

2. Availability

a. Tort

Punitive damages are available if the conduct constituting the breach is independently a tort, such as fraud.

b. Extremely Blameworthy Conduct

In some states, breach of contract can lead to punitive damages if the promisor's conduct is reprehensible. States adopt varying ways to describe this principle, sometimes allowing punitive damages for conduct that is "outrageous," "malicious," "oppressive," "wanton," "spiteful," or the like. [*E.g.*, **Delta Rice Mill, Inc. v. Gen. Foods Corp.,** 583 F. Supp. 564 (E.D. Ark. 1984)—"willful or malicious conduct in relation to the contract"]

c. Breach of the Duty of Good Faith—Insurance Contracts[§ 951]

Punitive damages may be available for a breach of the duty of good faith. The most well-established line of cases in which punitive damages have been awarded for breach of contract on the ground of bad faith consists of cases involving breaches by insurance companies—in particular, (i) a bad faith failure to settle with a third party who brought a claim against the insured or (ii) a bad faith denial of liability to the insured under the policy. Although there have been occasional cases in which the court imposed punitive damages for bad faith breach of contract in noninsurance contexts, the bad faith exception generally has been limited to the insurance context.

I. Damages for Emotional Distress

1. General Rule

Damages for emotional distress are **not allowed** in ordinary contract cases, even if emotional harms are foreseeable under the *Hadley* principle (*see supra*, p. 252). However, if either the subject matter of the contract or the nature of the breach make emotional harms **particularly likely** to result from breach, damages for emotional harm may be available. [Rest. 2d § 353]

2. Applications to Specific Factual Contexts

a. Bodily Injury

Damages for emotional distress arising from breach of contract may be awarded if the breach causes bodily injury.

b. Personal Interests

Damages may also be awarded for emotional distress if the contract was of a type that involved *personal,* as opposed to strictly commercial or financial, interests, so that emotional distress was a particularly likely result. Common examples of such cases are contracts to care for children [**Lane v. Kindercare Learning Ctrs., Inc.,** 588 N.W.2d 715 (Mich. Ct. App. 1998)], contracts between innkeepers and guests, contracts for the carriage and proper disposition of dead bodies, and contracts for the delivery of messages concerning death.

Example: Builder contracts to construct a house for Owner. Builder knows when the contract is made that Owner is in delicate health and that proper completion of the house is of great importance to Owner. Because of delays and departures from specifications, Owner suffers nervousness and emotional distress. In an action by Owner against Builder for breach of contract, the element of emotional distress will *not* be included as a loss for which damages may be awarded because the contract does not concern a personal interest. [Rest. 2d § 353, ill. 1; *but see* **B & M Homes v. Hogan,** 376 So. 2d 667 (Ala. 1979)]

Compare: Travel Company sells Tourist a holiday travel package at a hotel in Switzerland. The hotel is not at all as Travel Company described, and Tourist's vacation is ruined. Tourist may be able to recover for his emotional distress because the contract concerned a personal interest.

J. Restitutionary Damages

1. Unenforceable Contracts

Restitutionary damages are available to recover the value of a benefit conferred on another if the benefit was conferred under a contract that is unenforceable because of the Statute of Frauds, the doctrine of impossibility, or other comparable excuses, such as mutual mistake.

Example: Frank pays Liza $500 for Liza's promise to sing at Frank's wedding. Liza develops laryngitis and cannot sing at the wedding. Liza will be discharged from the contract under the doctrine of impossibility (*see supra*, p. 243), but Frank can recover the $500 in restitution.

2. Restitution in Favor of Promisee

Like reliance damages (*see supra*, p. 254), restitutionary damages may also be awarded as an alternative to expectation damages for breach of contract. In particular, restitutionary damages may be available against a promisor who has *materially* (or "totally") breached a contract, even if the promisee has no expectation damages under the contract because it is a "losing" contract for the promisee. [Rest. 2d § 373]

Example: Owner contracts with Contractor to build a structure for $200,000. Costs of materials and labor subsequently fall sharply, making the contract a very attractive one for Contractor and an unappealing one for Owner. Nonetheless, Contractor breaches before doing any work. Owner makes a substitute contract for $120,000 to build the same structure. Owner has no expectation damages, because the breach has saved Owner money, given that Owner's total cost to build the structure is now $120,000 instead of $200,000. [**Louise Caroline Nursing Home, Inc. v. Dix Constr. Corp.,** 285 N.E.2d 904 (Mass. 1972)] But if Owner had paid $15,000 to Contractor toward the contract price, Owner may recover the $15,000 in restitution.

a. Calculation

When the promisee seeks to recover restitution for services it has provided to the promisor under a contract, restitutionary damages normally will be measured by the *market value* of the promisee's performance, rather than by the actual enrichment of the promisor. This is known as *quantum meruit*, a Latin phrase that means "how much they earned."

(1) Contract Price as Possible Limit

Under the traditional rule, the contract price does not generally set a limit on the restitutionary damages of a promisor, although it may be evidence of the market value of a promisor's services. However, a modern trend, exemplified by section 38(2)(b) of the Restatement (Third) of Restitution & Unjust Enrichment, would impose such a limit.

Example: Programmer agrees to develop a website for Company for a fee of $20,000. Company breaches after Programmer has developed and delivered 95% of the website to Company. Under the traditional rule, Programmer may recover for the reasonable value of their services "off the contract"—*i.e.*, not limited by the contract price, although the contract for $20,000 may be evidence of the market value of Programmer's services. [Rest. 2d § 373] Under the Restatement (Third) of Restitution & Unjust Enrichment, Programmer may not recover more than the "the price of . . . performance as determined by reference to the parties' agreement" in restitution. [Rest. 3d Restatement & Unjust Enrichment § 38(2)(b)]

(2) Exception for Full Performance

Even under the traditional rule, the promisee is limited to the contract price if it has *fully*, rather than partially, performed.

Example: Same facts as above, but Programmer has completed and delivered 100% of the website to Company. Programmer's recovery is limited to $20,000, regardless of any question about the abstract value of Programmer's services in the marketplace.

b. Return of What Has Been Received

Ordinarily, the value of what the promisee received from the promisor under the contract (including the market value of services) will be deducted from the plaintiff's recovery in restitution.

3. Restitution in Favor of Breaching Promisor

Under modern law, even a promisor who is in material breach, and therefore could not sue on the contract, may be able to bring an action to recover the value of the benefits they have conferred on the promisee, subject to an offset for the promisee's damages. Such cases are known as "plaintiff in default" cases, because the plaintiff is allowed to bring a suit even though they are in material breach of contract.

a. Application

This kind of recovery can apply to a deposit that was made by the breaching party, to the extent that the deposit exceeds the innocent party's damages and to the extent that the deposit was not also agreed upon as a valid liquidated damages provision (*see supra*, p. 266).

b. Significance

Recall that a party who has *substantially* performed a contract can bring suit *on the contract* even though they have not performed perfectly, subject to an offset for their breach. Therefore, a party who has substantially performed does not need to bring an action for restitutionary damages as a plaintiff in default. However, if the plaintiff's default is not minor but is so significant that they have not even rendered substantial performance, a suit for restitutionary damages as a plaintiff in default would be appropriate.

c. Willful Breach

At one time, the majority view was that if a breach was willful, the breaching party could not recover restitutionary damages for the benefit conferred. Modern courts are increasingly inclined to allow even a willfully breaching plaintiff to recover.

EXAM TIP

Always keep restitutionary remedies in the back of your mind. Look first for a valid contract allowing the plaintiff relief. But *if there is no valid contract*, an action in quasi-contract may provide restitutionary damages if the plaintiff has *conferred a benefit*.

4. Disgorgement

In some cases, a promisee may be able to recover the *promisor's gains from breach*, a remedy known as disgorgement. Section 39 of the Restatement (Third) of Restitution & Unjust Enrichment would allow this remedy when (i) the expectation measure "affords inadequate protection to the promisee's contractual entitlement" and (ii) the promisor's breach is "deliberate." Disgorgement has long been recognized as a remedy in cases of conversion of property or breach of fiduciary duty, but there is a modern trend for courts to hold that it is available independently for breach of contract in appropriate cases.

Example: A former CIA employee writes a book about his time at the CIA in breach of a term in his employment agreement. Expectation damages for the United States are impossible to measure or prove under the circumstances. To provide an adequate remedy for breach of the employment agreement, the United States may recover the former employee's profits from his book. [**Snepp v. United States,** 444 U.S. 507 (1980)]

Exam Questions and Answers

QUESTION I

Alfred Ohner and Ted Kwik had been friends for a number of years. They had served in the Army together during the Gulf War, and Kwik had saved Ohner's life on one occasion by shooting a sniper who had drawn a bead on Ohner. Both lived in Denver, Colorado. In October 2007, Ohner finished construction of a new 100-unit apartment house in Denver called *The Crescent*. Ohner and Kwik then entered into a written contract under which Kwik rented *The Crescent* from Ohner for 10 years, at a rental of $100,000 per year, beginning January 1, 2008. The parties contemplated that Kwik would take on management of *The Crescent* as his full-time business and would pay all operating expenses, making a profit on the difference between rentals and expenses.

The Crescent was scheduled to be opened in January 2008. Based on projected expenses an annual rental of at least $2,000 per unit was necessary just to break even. The initial annual rental was set at $2,300 per unit, giving Kwik a projected profit of approximately $30,000 per year. All the units were quickly rented by January 1 under standard two-year leases for a term beginning January 1, 2008, and ending December 31, 2009.

By the time the 2008–2009 leases were about to expire, annual operating costs for *The Crescent* had risen so high that in order to maintain a $30,000 profit, annual rents for 2010 and 2011 would have to be set at $2,600. However, by late 2009, several other luxury singles apartment houses had been built in the same area of Denver and were charging lower rents. It therefore proved extremely difficult to re-rent *The Crescent*'s units for $2,600. In February 2010, Ohner told Kwik that it was obvious that Kwik was going to go broke unless he could lower his rents to that of his competitors. To keep Kwik from going broke, Ohner told Kwik he was lowering the rent he charged Kwik from $100,000 to $70,000/year for the next two years, which would enable Kwik to make a $30,000 annual profit by renting *The Crescent*'s units at $2,300/year. Kwik thanked Ohner profusely and then began offering the vacant units at a $2,300/year rental on standard two-year leases ending in early 2012. Within a short time all the vacant units were leased.

In July 2010, Ohner and Kwik had a falling-out over a game of poker. Kwik accused Ohner of cheating. Ohner was enraged and demanded that Kwik retract the statement. Kwik refused. Ohner then said, "That's it for us; our friendship is over. What I did for you on *The Crescent* is off, too. From now on, you pay me the regular rent."

What are Kwik's rights?

QUESTION II

On September 21, Prentice Farm Supplies Co. received from Dayview Seed & Grain Company an envelope containing clover seeds. On the face of the envelope was written, "No. 1 Red Clover seed, 5,000 lbs. in stock, like sample. We are asking 24 cents per pound." No letter accompanied the envelope.

On September 23, Prentice wrote to acknowledge receipt of the sample. In its letter Prentice advised Dayview that it had accumulated quite a stock of clover seed and preferred to wait a while "before operating further," but stated that it might nevertheless be interested if Dayview could come down somewhat on the price.

On October 4, Dayview emailed Prentice's operations manager: "In reply to your note, we still have available the 5,000 lbs. of No. 1 Red Clover seed from which your sample was taken. We want 23 cents per pound. We have been made an offer of 22 and 3/4 cents per pound."

On October 15, Prentice's operations manager sent a reply to the email: "We accept this offer." At the time of this email the market price of No. 1 Red Clover seed was 25 cents per pound. Dayview immediately emailed back, "No, your reply was too late—sorry." Prentice then purchased 5,000 lbs. of No. 1 Red Clover seed on the market at 25 cents per pound.

Prentice now brings an action against Dayview based on the above facts. Discuss.

QUESTION III

On August 15, Cheshire University requested bids from Bildgood, Inc., a large construction firm, and seven other contractors for the construction of a new dormitory for Cheshire's medical school. Under the terms of the bidding, the bids were to be submitted on October 5, and Cheshire had two days to award a contract. On October 4, Bildgood computed its total bid, which came to $1.55 million. The bid was submitted on October 5; it proved to be the low bid, and Bildgood was awarded the contract, which was signed on October 6. The other bids were $1.8, $1.9, $2.0, $2.1, $2.2, and $2.3 million, respectively.

In computing and organizing its bid, Bildgood had used Addup Cloud Bid Manager, an online service for construction contractors, to which Bildgood began subscribing on October 2. On October 7, Addup notified Bildgood that it had discovered a defect in the software and asked Bildgood to check its bid data in a certain manner. Upon running this check, Bildgood discovered that its data inside Addup's system had been corrupted. It promptly reran the raw data for the Cheshire bid manually and got a (correct) result of $1.95 million. On October 8, Bildgood notified Cheshire that its $1.55 million bid had been erroneous because of defective software; that the correct bid should have been $1.95 million; and that it would perform at this price but not for less. Cheshire insisted on performance at the contract price; Bildgood categorically refused. On October 9, Cheshire approached Alpha Construction, the contractor that had bid $1.8 million, but Alpha declined to take on the job, stating that in the interim it had taken on another major commitment. Three days later, Cheshire entered into a contract with Deutron Sisters, which had entered a bid of $1.9 million—the third-lowest bid. Cheshire then brought suit against Bildgood.

Discuss.

QUESTION IV

Assume the same facts as in Question III, above, except (1) that Bildgood sues Addup and (2) that Addup had sold a specialized physical calculator to Bildgood rather than cloud software. At the trial, Bildgood shows that before purchasing the calculator, Bildgood acquainted Addup with its commercial situation.

What result?

QUESTION V

Nigel, from England, books a hotel room at the Lakeshore Hotel in the U.S. for "11/12/19" on the hotel's website. By convention, in England "11/12" refers to December 11 (*i.e.*, the 11th day of the 12th month), whereas in the U.S. it refers to November 12 (*i.e.*, the 12th day of the 11th month). Nigel intends to book the room for December 11, but Sheraton's website records a booking for November 12.

As Nigel is making the reservation, the website lists it as a "prepaid" booking for $400, and the website says the following near the button that confirms the sale: "This is a nonrefundable room rate. To receive this rate, you must prepay at the time of booking. If you do not show up for a prepaid booking, you will lose the prepayment." Nigel does not read this text, but he chooses this rate because it's cheaper than a $480 rate labeled "refundable rate." He offers his credit card for the booking on a webpage that indicates that he will be charged $400. His card is charged immediately.

Nigel shows up to the hotel on December 11, 2019, but the hotel is full that day, and they do not give him a room. Nor do they offer him a refund, explaining that he missed his booking for November 12 and that the booking is nonrefundable.

Discuss Nigel's rights against the Lakeshore Hotel, assuming U.S. contract law governs.

QUESTION VI

Frances Fee owned a summer home in the mountains known as "Lakerest." Lakerest was a pleasant house surrounded by attractive scenery, but its chief attraction was that it fronted the eastern side of Blue Heron Lake. This was a small artificial lake, ideal for swimming and boating during the summer months, which had been created by construction of a dam that retained the waters of Blue Heron Stream. The lake had been built as a reservoir and was owned by the state. Theoretically it was open to the public, but as a practical matter it was used almost exclusively by the owners of the houses fronting the lake, because it was almost completely surrounded by private property and was relatively inaccessible.

On October 1, Fee agreed to sell Lakerest to Alice Aqua for $250,000. Section 5 of the contract of sale provided as follows:

> 5. Vendor acknowledges that purchaser has paid her a deposit of $10,000 on the property at the time of the execution of this agreement. The balance of the purchase price, $240,000, shall be payable at the closing, which shall take place on December 1. If the vendor is unable to convey good and marketable title at the closing, or if the improvements on said property shall be destroyed or materially damaged prior to the closing, said deposit shall be returned to purchaser, on her demand, and neither vendor nor purchaser shall be liable for any damages. If the purchaser fails to pay the balance of the purchase price at the closing for any other reason, said deposit shall not be refunded.

On November 15, an earthquake tremor occurred near Lakerest. Although the tremor did no damage to any of the lakefront houses, it destroyed the dam that had retained Blue Heron Lake's waters. As a result, the lake's waters emptied out into the old bed of Blue Heron Stream, and the lake was destroyed. There was no prospect that a new dam would be built in the immediate future, and the stream that took its place was much too shallow for either boating or swimming.

When Aqua learned what had happened, she called Fee to tell her that she would not consider going through with the deal. Fee instituted an action against Aqua for breach of contract. Aqua counterclaimed for return of her $10,000.

On May 1, Fee sold Lakerest to David Dry for $115,000.

Discuss.

QUESTION VII

Reflex Studios, Inc. entered into a contract with Alan Grume under which Reflex agreed to take photographs of Grume's wedding for $2000, with a deposit of $200. Through the negligence of Reflex, no photographer showed up at the wedding, and no pictures were taken. You are Grume's lawyer. He asks you what are his rights. You quickly conclude Reflex is in breach. To what damages may Grume be entitled?

QUESTION VIII

Same facts as above, but Reflex intentionally breached their contract with Grume because, just before Grume's wedding, they received an offer from a wealthier couple to take photos of their wedding for $6000. Do any of Grume's rights change?

QUESTION IX

Albert Penn was a professional writer, specializing in American politics. Penn had a regular three-times-a-week newspaper column and also wrote magazine articles and books.

Talia Tawker was a state senator. In late 2017, Tawker decided to seek a seat in the United States Senate in the 2020 election. Tawker assembled a small campaign staff, and in August 2018, she approached Penn and asked him to do a "campaign" (*i.e.*, favorable) biography, running about 300 pages, for $15,000. Penn declined. Tawker then raised the price to $20,000, but Penn still declined, stating that he had a lot of irons in the fire and did not want to commit himself to a single major project. Tawker then stated, "I really want to get you for this biography. I will tell you what. If you deliver a completed manuscript to me by April 1, 2019, I will pay you $30,000." Penn replied, "Right."

Soon after, Penn began work on the Tawker biography. By October 1, 2018, Penn had done most of a rough draft of the book, representing about half the total needed for a completed manuscript. On October 2, Tawker withdrew from the race, and emailed Penn, "Don't begin the manuscript, as it's no longer needed."

What are Penn's rights?

QUESTION X

Wolf Chemical Company was a major chemical producer. Through its Raremetals Division, Wolf was engaged in the business of processing certain kinds of ores, including rutile, which contains the metal titanium. Wolf's Raremetals Division accounted for approximately 5% of its business.

Andrews Mines, Inc. was the owner of a rutile mine. The process of refining rutile to extract the maximum amount of titanium at the cheapest possible price is a highly skilled and very expensive one. Since Andrews had no processing facilities, it approached Wolf as a possible purchaser of its ore. On its part, Wolf was eager to acquire a long-term assured source of rutile, which was then in short supply and promised to remain so for a considerable period of time.

On April 5, 2017, Andrews and Wolf entered into a contract under which Andrews agreed to sell to Wolf, and Wolf agreed to purchase, Andrews' entire rutile output through April 15, 2022. The price of rutile is figured per pound of unrefined titanium contained in the rutile. Prices are quoted and paid for unrefined titanium, not for rutile. Usually the purchase price of a batch of rutile is fixed by an assay (that is, by a scientific estimate) of the amount of unrefined titanium it contains. However, the agreement between Wolf and Andrews provided that promptly on delivery of rutile by Andrews, Wolf would refine the rutile to extract the titanium, certify the amount of titanium it had extracted, and pay for that amount a price equal to 97% of the market price for unrefined titanium on the date of the certificate. Wolf's certificate would be conclusive as to the amount of titanium it had extracted, but any dispute concerning the market price of unrefined titanium on the date of the certificate would be submitted to arbitration.

On January 15, 2020, Wolf entered into a contract with Xavier, Inc., providing for the sale to Xavier of Wolf's Raremetals Division for $2 million. Xavier was a major tobacco company that was attempting to diversify its operations.

Xavier promptly notified Andrews that the Andrews-Wolf contract had been assigned to it in connection with its acquisition of Wolf's Raremetals Division, and it directed Andrews to address all further shipments to it (Xavier) at the former Wolf plant. Andrews promptly wrote to Wolf (with a copy to Xavier) that it did not recognize the validity of the assignment. Xavier replied that Wolf would continue to accept shipment of rutile from Andrews in its own name, and while such ore would be accepted on Xavier's behalf, Wolf would agree to be responsible for payment of the purchase price.

Andrews replied that it would not deliver any ore to Wolf or Xavier under such arrangements and began selling its ore on the market.

What are Xavier's rights against Andrews?

ANSWER TO QUESTION I

1. **Was There Consideration for Ohner's Modification of Kwik's Lease?** In February 2010, Ohner in effect agreed to modify the lease by promising to accept $70,000/year in full discharge of Kwik's obligation to pay $100,000/year. The first issue is whether this modification is enforceable.

    a. **Legal duty rule; donative promise:** Under the legal duty rule, a promise to accept less than one is legally entitled to in satisfaction of the full obligation is not legally enforceable, on the ground that such a promise lacks consideration. (*See, e.g.*, *Foakes v. Beer*.) Absent duress or unconscionability, it seems questionable whether this rule is sound, because in the usual case the promise is given as the price for at least an implied counterpromise, so that consideration is apparently present in the form of a bargain. In this case, however, it is arguable that Ohner's promise lacks consideration even if the legal duty rule is not applied, on the theory that the promise was *donative* in nature. The general rule is that a donative promise lacks consideration—*i.e.*, such a promise is unenforceable. (It may be that there was in fact a bargain here—that Ohner had an economic interest in keeping *The Crescent* fully rented, and that in exchange for Ohner's modification Kwik impliedly promised to lower rentals to $2,300/year, which he was not legally obliged to do. This construction, however, seems strained.)

    b. **Moral obligation:** Assuming the promise was donative, it may have been based on ***past consideration***. Although the usual rule is that moral or past consideration is insufficient to support a promise, modern caselaw has increasingly enforced a promise based on a moral obligation arising out of a past material benefit conferred on the promisor, or, perhaps, a past output by the promisee, at least to the extent of the benefit conferred or the output. Here Kwik had undoubtedly conferred a substantial benefit on Ohner—he had saved Ohner's life. On the other hand, it is not completely clear that Ohner was under a moral obligation to Kwik. Kwik's action was performed in the course of Kwik's own duties as a soldier, and at no apparent risk to himself. There is a difference between gratitude and moral obligation. Moreover, Ohner's rent concession does not seem to have been intended as a "repayment" to Kwik for a specific benefit provided, rather than a gift to a friend.

    c. **Reliance:** Reliance is viewed as either a substitute for consideration (bargain theory) or as consideration itself. The term "promissory estoppel" remains in wide use as a description of the principle that reliance may make a donative promise enforceable. Even if Ohner's promise was donative, under the principle of promissory estoppel it would be *legally enforceable* if relied upon in a reasonable, foreseeable way, at least to the extent of the reliance. Certainly it was foreseeable that Kwik would lower the rentals on vacant apartments to $2,300/year. Ohner's promise should therefore be enforced at least as to those apartments rented at $2,300 in reliance on the promise.

    d. **Waiver:** It might be argued that rather than making a promise, in effect Ohner "waived" payment of $30,000. However, that should not make a difference in the result; any transaction involving the legal duty rule can be verbalized in the form of a waiver. Additionally, without reliance or consideration as independent factors, a waiver in a case like this could probably be retracted.

    e. **Modification without more:** Partly in recognition of the unsoundness of the legal duty rule, the tendency of the law may be to uphold any modification of an executory contract without the requirement of fresh consideration. Thus U.C.C. section 2–209(1) provides that "An agreement modifying a contract within this Article needs no consideration to be binding." Section 2–209 is inapplicable to Kwik and Ohner, because their transaction does not involve a sale of goods (although it might be utilized by analogy as persuasive authority). However, Restatement Second section 89(a) provides that "A promise modifying a duty under a contract not fully performed on either side is binding . . . if the modification is fair and equitable in view of circumstances not anticipated when the contract was made." To the extent this section represents the law, it might be applicable to this case, on the premise that construction of the other singles apartments constituted "circumstances not anticipated when the contract was made." However, while Kwik and Ohner may not have specifically thought about the possibility of such construction, it was certainly a foreseeable circumstance.

 f. **Completed gift:** Where the legal duty rule is applicable, there is a split of authority in contracts involving an ongoing performance by both sides as to whether an agreement to accept a lesser payment than due is enforceable to the extent that is executed. Insofar as Ohner's intention was donative, it is arguable that a completed gift has been made as to that portion of the rent actually forgiven prior to the retraction.

2. **Is There a Statute of Frauds Defense?** In addition to the defense of no consideration, Ohner may have a Statute of Frauds defense, because his promise to modify the lease terms was oral and involved a term of more than two years; it could not be completed within one year from the making of the promise. Although there was part performance here, part performance does not take a contract out of the one-year provision unless performance is completed on one side. Some types of part performance may take a contract out of the interest-in-land provision, but mere payment is usually insufficient. Additionally, an action for damages may not lie, as the part performance exception to the Statute of Frauds does not traditionally apply to actions at law insofar as interests in land are concerned. Kwik's reliance, however, might take the transaction out of the Statute to the extent of the reliance.

ANSWER TO QUESTION II

1. Formation of a contract requires an offer, an acceptance, and consideration. The envelope received on September 21 appears to have been an ***invitation to bid,*** rather than an offer, because the envelope was apparently unsolicited and suggested a quantity of stock but not a quantity being offered to Prentice specifically. In other words, Prentice probably would reasonably have imagined others could have received similar envelopes. Moreover, the words "we are asking" indicate preliminary negotiations as well.

2. The letter of September 23 was also an ***invitation to bid,*** insofar as it indicated Prentice might be interested if Dayview came down on the price. It was not specific enough to be an offer.

3. The email of October 4 might be deemed still another invitation (*i.e.,* an offering circular), but it is better interpreted as an ***offer.*** The communication seems individualized, and it is in response to an invitation (*i.e.,* the letter of September 23). To be legally sufficient as an offer, a statement must meet two criteria: (i) ***intent*** to make a bargain; and (ii) ***definiteness*** of terms. Generally speaking, a statement will not be considered an offer unless it makes clear: (i) the subject matter of the proposed bargain; (ii) the price; and (iii) the quantity involved. It is not absolutely clear that the entire 5,000 lbs. is being offered, but in light of the circumstances that seems to be a reasonable inference, despite the fact that the quote is per pound. The email does not state terms of payment or delivery, but that does not seem fatal since reasonable terms could easily be implied. And of course offers can certainly be made by email. The reference to another offer might be construed to indicate that Dayview was only soliciting offers, but it seems at least equally reasonable to construe the reference to mean, "Because we already have an offer for 22 and 3/4 cents, our offer at 23 cents is a reasonable price, and in any event is not negotiable, so please do not bother to try to get us down in price again."

4. If the offer does not state a period of time during which it will remain open, the offeree's power of acceptance lapses after the expiration of a reasonable time. Thus, under the circumstances, even assuming the October 4 wire was an offer, the answering wire of October 15 was not effective as an acceptance because it was not dispatched within a reasonable time,

considering (i) the offer was by email, the sender can assume it was received quickly (especially when set in the context of the original solicitation, which was by mail); (ii) Dayview apparently had an offer in hand, which it would not want to delay acting on for too long; and (iii) the market price of clover seed was apparently subject to serious fluctuations over short periods of time. Therefore, no contract was formed between Prentice and Dayview.

ANSWER TO QUESTION III

1. **Expectation Damages:** Cheshire will undoubtedly claim damages for breach of contract measured by its expectation—$.35 million, the difference between $1.55 million (its contract price with Bildgood), and $1.9 million (its contract price with Deutron). Should this claim succeed?

    a. **Palpable mistake:** Bildgood's mistake was of the kind normally called "unilateral"—that is, a mistake arising out of the calculations of one of the parties, rather than a mistake in the assumptions shared by both. Such a mistake is generally a defense when it is "palpable"—that is, when the nonmistaken party knew or should have realized that the mistake had been made—because in such a case the nonmistaken party's expectation is not worthy of much protection. On the other hand, if the mistake is "impalpable"—if the nonmistaken party neither knew nor should have known of its existence—the cases are split on whether the mistaken party has a defense in an action for expectation damages. The majority of the cases hold that there is no such defense, but a minority, particularly the more recent cases, hold that there is.

    The first question therefore is whether the mistake was palpable. The fact that Bildgood, itself a contractor, did not realize the bid was unusually low speaks against this. But it is arguable that Cheshire was in a better position than Bildgood to realize that Bildgood had made a mistake because Cheshire could see the extent to which Bildgood's bid differed from all the others. How significant was this difference? The seven bids put in by the other contractors ranged from $1.8 million to $2.3 million, mostly at intervals of $.1 million. Bildgood's bid was $1.55 million, $.25 million less than the second lowest bid. On balance, this does not seem to be enough in itself to put Cheshire on notice. By hypothesis the winning bid will always be the lowest, so some interval between Bildgood's bid and the second lowest bid must be expected. The interval was admittedly substantial—but it was much less than the interval between the second lowest and the highest bids ($.5 million). Of course, a difference on the low side is frequently more striking than a difference on the high side, because costs set a lower limit, whereas nothing sets an upper limit. Nevertheless, in the absence of other evidence the range of the bids would not in itself seem enough to have put Cheshire on notice that a mistake had been made.

    b. **Impalpable mistake:** Assuming the mistake was impalpable, should it nevertheless serve as a defense to an action for expectation damages? Under the majority view, the answer is no, but there is a modern trend that where the defendant has entered into a contract only by reason of a mechanical mistake it should be sufficient if they reimburse plaintiff for actual reliance. The rationale behind the cases rejecting this position is two-fold: (1) the courts should not defeat the legitimate expectation formed by the nonmistaken party as a result of the defendant's fault; and (2) unilateral mistakes are normally difficult or impossible to prove objectively—that is, because they normally occur in the defendant's own mental processes, they can normally be established only through proof of the defendant's subjective intent, and the courts have been noticeably reluctant in contract cases to let a party get out of a contract on the basis of such proof.

    Cheshire v. Bildgood, however, is distinguishable from the usual unilateral mistake case. First, the mistake did not occur in Bildgood's subjective mental processes. It occurred in the objective world of software and presumably is susceptible of completely objective proof. Second, Bildgood was not at fault in the making of the mistake: Rather, Addup had erred. In light of these factors, and because the trend of authority is in favor of limiting damages in such cases to reliance, Bildgood's mistake should serve as a defense to a suit by Cheshire for expectation damages.

2. **Reliance Damages:** If Cheshire cannot recover expectation damages, what damages, if any, can Cheshire collect from Bildgood? The cases are agreed that even if unilateral mistake will serve as a defense to a suit for expectation damages, the nonmistaken party is entitled to reimbursement for reliance. (Of course, usually the mistaken party is at fault, whereas Bildgood was not; nevertheless, to the extent Cheshire relied on Bildgood's promise, it seems more appropriate to cast any resulting loss on Bildgood than on Cheshire.)

Cheshire appears to have relied on Bildgood's promise by accepting Bildgood's bid rather than another. If Bildgood had not made its incorrect bid, Cheshire would presumably have accepted the second-lowest bid, which was $1.8 million, and because bids are normally deemed offers, Alpha would have had to enter into the contract if its bid had been accepted within the two-day period. Therefore, Cheshire should be entitled to receive $.1 million, representing the difference between the contract price with Deutron ($1.9 million) and the price Cheshire would have had from Alpha ($1.8 million) but for Bildgood's mistake.

ANSWER TO QUESTION IV

1. **General Damages:** When Addup sold Bildgood the calculator there was an implied warranty of merchantability. Under U.C.C. Article 2 (which applies here because the calculator is a good), a merchant seller impliedly warrants that goods sold are merchantable—that is, the goods are fit for their ordinary purposes. [U.C.C. § 2–314] A calculator that cannot add properly is not fit for its ordinary purpose of performing mathematical calculations, and thus Addup breached its implied warranty of merchantability. Therefore, Bildgood should be able to return the machine, or to collect damages equal to the difference between the value of the calculator as it is and the value it would have if it met the implied warranty of fitness (which might be measured by the cost of repairs necessary to correct the defect).

2. **Special Damages:** In addition, Bildgood may be able to collect from Addup the amount of damages, if any, that Bildgood must pay to Cheshire. Unless Bildgood was guilty of contributory negligence (which seems rather unlikely), such amounts would be proximately caused by Addup's breach of implied warranty. The only question, therefore, would be whether such damages were foreseeable within *Hadley v. Baxendale* (which has not been changed by the U.C.C.). Today the principle of *Hadley v. Baxendale* is normally restated to mean that consequential damages can be recovered if, at the time the contract was made, the seller had reason to foresee that the consequential damages were the probable result of the breach. Since Bildgood had acquainted Addup with its situation, it was foreseeable when the contract was made that if the calculator was defective Bildgood might enter an incorrect bid. Further, *Hadley v. Baxendale* is primarily used by the courts to limit damages by cutting off claims for lost profits. A claim by Bildgood against Addup based on the damages (if any) Bildgood must pay to Cheshire would not be a claim for lost profits but instead for out-of-pocket expenses, and it would likely be treated sympathetically.

ANSWER TO QUESTION V

1. **Meaning of the Agreement.** There's no problem forming a contract on a website, but here there's a misunderstanding or, similarly, an interpretive question as to what the parties agreed to. Nigel has one meaning in mind because of the English convention; the hotel had another in displaying dates using the U.S. convention. This is similar to the *Peerless* case in that both sides have a potentially reasonable understanding, but their understandings do not match. If the interpretations are equally reasonable—which could arguably be the case because those who set up the website knew it would be accessible all over the world—there is no contract,

and Nigel is entitled to a refund as a matter of restitution. But Lakeshore Hotel's meaning is probably more reasonable overall, given that it was following local conventions, as hotel websites tend to do; for example, hotels normally list check-in times in local time, not Greenwich Mean Time. Accordingly, the hotel's meaning (a booking on November 12) would likely prevail.

2. **Form Terms.** The terms on the website bind Nigel in this case even though he didn't read them. There is a split of authority on how to handle terms that are unreasonable, unconscionable, etc., but here the term is fairly standard for a hotel website. That is, reasonable consumers understand that they can save money on prepaid, nonrefundable rates, and Nigel here specifically chose the prepaid rate over the "refundable" rate. Moreover, the relevant terms were displayed prominently and amounted essentially to dickered terms, given the choice the website offered. So Nigel is bound to the nonrefundable rate even if he didn't read or understand the details. The result could be different if the term were surprising or oppressive.

Even if the hotel's right to keep $400 from Nigel is construed as a liquidated damages clause, $400 is a reasonable forecast of the hotel's damages from a missed booking for a room that goes at approximately that rate. That is, it's reasonable for the hotel's managers at the time of booking to think that a room cancellation could cost them about one night's room charge.

Accordingly, Nigel is unlikely to have any legal remedy against the hotel.

ANSWER TO QUESTION VI

1. **Fee's Claim**

    a. **Amount of damages:** A preliminary question in Fee's suit is the amount of her damages. If Fee is successful, she would be entitled to contract price ($250,000) minus market value at the time of breach. This is a general damages measure. While the question does not state what the market value was at the time of breach, the sale to Dry at $115,000 only two and a half months later is very strong, almost conclusive, evidence of such value. In other words, if successful, Fee's damages would probably be $135,000 ($250,000 minus $115,000), minus the $10,000 she already has.

    b. **Aqua's defenses:** This raises the question of whether Aqua has any defenses.

    (1) Aqua might claim that section 5 is a liquidated damages provision that applies to Aqua as well as to Fee, thereby limiting Fee's damages to the $10,000 deposit. However, the provision does not purport to limit Fee's remedy, and it is unlikely to be construed to do so.

    (2) A second and stronger defense is that of frustration. ("Impossibility" would not be applicable, because the performances of both parties are literally possible.) The doctrine of frustration arose from the *Coronation Case, Krell v. Henry,* which held that performance is excused if the purpose or value of the contract has been destroyed by a supervening event that was not reasonably foreseeable at the time the contract was entered into. As in *Krell v. Henry,* where the plaintiff was buying not just a room but a room with a view, so here Aqua was buying not simply a house but a lakeside summer house. Even the name—Lakerest—indicates the integral significance of the lake. While opinions about frustration can differ in a given case, Aqua should probably be excused under the defense of frustration. The assignment of risks in the contract itself suggests this result too; while the provision doesn't literally apply to what happened (because the lake isn't an improvement on the property itself), it shows that the parties did not want to be governed by the traditional rule that the buyer bears all risks of damage to or destruction of improvements to real property until title passes—a questionable rule in any event.

2. **Aqua's Counterclaim:** Frustration should also lead Aqua to get her $10,000 back. Fee might argue that some courts have distinguished between money paid before the frustrating event and money remaining to be paid at that point. However, this distinction seems unsound. A stronger argument in Fee's favor is that the contract specifies that the deposit shall be returned under only two conditions (material destruction of improvements on the property or failure to make good title), neither of which has occurred, and that it goes on to provide that if the named "purchaser . . . fails to pay the balance of the purchase price at the closing for any *other reason,* said deposit will not be refunded." However, the purpose of that clause seems pretty clearly to give the vendor a right to keep the deposit only if the purchaser *unjustifiably* fails to complete payment. For instance, suppose the improvements on the property had *not* been destroyed, but a fissure had opened up cutting the property in half; would the fact that such a condition was not specifically mentioned in the provision be a defense to a claim for return of the down payment? Frustration and impossibility problems arise precisely because the parties did not specifically foresee specific kinds of events; hence, without strong proof to the contrary, a general clause like this should not shift the risk of all unforeseen events on to the purchaser.

ANSWER TO QUESTION VII

Because this was a contract for services, the normal measure of damages would be the reasonable cost of completion minus the unpaid portion of the price. However, completion now seems impossible—although perhaps damages could be measured by the cost of restaging the wedding and photographing the restaged version. (It is assumed that Grume could not have mitigated by hiring a substitute photographer in time or by getting a friend to take pictures.)

Where cost of completion is inappropriate, damages can usually be measured by the difference between the value of what the injured party ended up with and the value of what they would have ended up with had the contract been performed. In this case, however, most of the value of the promised pictures would have been largely sentimental, and contract law normally protects only economic interests. Nevertheless, exceptions are sometimes made, particularly when the subject matter of the contract is a personal interest. Because that is the case here, sentimental or subjective value might be taken into account in a diminished value measure.

Grume might also seek damages for mental anguish. Again, such damages normally are not permitted for breach of contract. But because this case specifically deals with a personal interest, and because the mental anguish was particularly foreseeable under the circumstances, such damages might be appropriate in this case.

In any event, Grume is of course entitled to restitution of his $200.

ANSWER TO QUESTION VIII

Because Reflex has now made a profit from its breach—and under some authorities (like the Restatement (Third) of Restitution and Unjust Enrichment), because the breach was deliberate—disgorgement of that profit may now be a possibility. That is, Grume may be able to recover Reflex's profit from the breach—here, the difference between $6000 and $2000, at least assuming Reflex's costs to photograph the two weddings would have been roughly the same. Particularly if a jurisdiction doesn't recognize as compensable Grume's subjective harms in lost wedding photos or emotional distress during the wedding, Grume would have no other remedy for this breach (apart from getting his deposit back), strengthening the case for disgorgement.

Punitive damages, however, wouldn't be unavailable just because the breach was intentional and opportunistic.

ANSWER TO QUESTION IX

1. **Bilateral vs. Unilateral Contract:** The initial question is whether Tawker and Penn entered into a bilateral contract or whether Tawker merely made an offer to enter into a unilateral

contract—that is, an offer that could be accepted only by performance of an act. If the parties had made a bilateral contract, Tawker's revocation is clearly ineffective. If Tawker's offer was for a unilateral contract, however, greater difficulties are presented.

Tawker's words, at least, seem to call for an act—delivery of the completed manuscript by April 1, 2019. The words, however, are not necessarily decisive: some offers that seem to call for acts can be interpreted as calling for promises—*e.g.*, "I will give you $500 to paint my house."

Restatement Second section 32 says that if an offer is ambiguous as to whether it calls for a promise or an act, either method of acceptance should suffice. This leaves open (i) whether the offer was ambiguous, and (ii) whether Penn made a promise. The answer to both questions seems to be "no." In response to Tawker's second offer, Penn had indicated that he did not want to be committed to a single major project—*i.e.*, did *not* want to make a promise. Tawker seems to have been responding to this reaction by setting up the transaction so that the money would serve as a lure, thus insuring performance through incentive rather than through commitment. It is true that Penn said, "Right," which might evidence an exchange of promises, but the word is equally consistent with Penn saying, in effect, "Understood. Structuring the transaction in this way, so that I am not committed but will get $30,000 if I perform, is fine with me."

2. **Consequences If the Transaction Is Deemed to Be an Offer for a Unilateral Contract:** If the offer is for a unilateral contract, an initial problem is whether Penn was required to give notice that he had begun performance. Probably not. Tawker indicated that she would pay $30,000 if the manuscript was completed by April 1, and a reasonable person in Penn's position probably would not have felt obliged to give any notice, on the theory that he would either produce the manuscript by April 1 and get the $30,000, or not. Also, Penn's statement, "Right," might be taken to put Tawker on notice that Penn was at least seriously interested.

   A second problem is whether the offer was revocable. In classical theory, an offer for a unilateral contract was revocable at any time prior to completion of the act required. Thus, if the Tawker-Penn transaction is deemed an offer for a unilateral contract, under classical theory Tawker would have no obligation to Penn because the revocation occurred prior to completion of the act. However, it is now widely acknowledged that an offer for a unilateral contract generally *cannot be withdrawn once performance has begun,* as was the case here, because of the offeree's *reliance* on the offeror's implied promise to hold the offer open. Thus, Tawker's countermand would be wrongful.

3. **Changed Circumstances:** Tawker might argue that she was excused by virtue of changed circumstances—specifically, her withdrawal from the race. This is not a case of impossibility—Penn could still finish the biography and Tawker could still pay for it. If Tawker has an excuse at all, therefore, it is under the doctrine of frustration—the book can no longer serve its intended purpose. However, it is unlikely that the frustration doctrine would be applied to this case. First, the book would still have some value to Tawker, even under the changed circumstances. Second, the changed circumstance was a result of Tawker's own decision and does not seem to be the kind of risk Penn should bear.

4. **Statute of Frauds:** The Statute of Frauds does not present a problem. The transaction involves services rather than goods, and performance could take place within one year.

ANSWER TO QUESTION X

Rights are normally assignable unless the assignment would materially vary the other party's corresponding rights, or, to use the U.C.C. terminology, the obligor has a substantial interest in the obligee's identity. Was that the case here?

If the Andrews-Wolf contract had merely called for the purchase and sale of rutile at a price keyed into the market, so that Wolf's only duty was to make payment, Wolf's rights certainly would have been assignable. However, here there was more: Wolf also had to **_refine_** the rutile to extract the titanium it contained, and had to certify how much titanium it had extracted. This certificate was to be conclusive. That in itself indicates that Wolf's rights were not assignable, because clearly the identity of the person making such a certificate would be highly important to Andrews. Of course, despite the language of the contract, the certificate might not really be "conclusive" in the ordinary sense of the term, because it probably would be open to Andrews to show that the certificate were fraudulent or issued in bad faith. On the other hand, it would not be easy for Andrews to know how much titanium had actually been extracted, let alone prove it; in other words, Andrews had to place a fair amount of trust and confidence in Wolf, which it would not necessarily have in Wolf's assignee.

Furthermore, we are told that "the process of refining rutile to extract the maximum amount of titanium is a highly skilled and very expensive one." Since Andrews' payment depended on the amount of rutile extracted, it is clear that this also gave it a substantial interest in the identity of the refiner; refinement by a less skilled refiner would mean less payment for Andrews. Furthermore, one refiner might be willing to spend extra money to extract the maximum amount of titanium, whereas another might not. These considerations have particular force in this case, because Wolf was a major chemical company, experienced in the business, whereas Xavier was a newcomer.

Xavier might argue that since Wolf's **_entire_** Raremetals Division was being bought, as a practical matter the same organization probably would continue to run the refining operation. Nevertheless, on balance, Andrews appears to have a substantial interest in having the contract performed by Wolf, so that the contract would not be assignable without Andrews' consent.

Wolf's offer to accept shipment of the rutile is of no real significance, nor is its offer to be ultimately responsible for the purchase price, because it would be liable in any event under ordinary principles of contract law.

All this being so, Andrews is within its rights in declining to make further shipments under the contract.

Review Questions and Answers

Review Questions

CONSIDERATION

		FILL IN ANSWER

1. Chandler executes a written guaranty to Ross of a debt then due from Joey. The guaranty is stated to be in "consideration of $1 paid to me by Ross, receipt of which is hereby acknowledged." Is Chandler's guaranty binding if the dollar is never paid? _____

2. Fred and Barney were involved in a traffic accident in which Barney sustained serious personal injuries. Fred has agreed to pay Barney $5,000 for Barney's promise not to sue him.

   a. Assume that Barney had been advised by his attorney that he had no valid claim against Fred, but he nevertheless still honestly believed that he could win in front of a sympathetic jury. Could Barney enforce Fred's promise to pay $5,000? _____

   b. Assume that Barney realized he had no valid claim against Fred, but that Fred was still willing to pay him $5,000 for a written release. If Barney executes the release, can he enforce Fred's promise to pay $5,000? _____

3. Manufacturer orally agrees to sell Retailer as many Frisbees for $1 each as Retailer may choose to order within the next 30 days.

   a. Manufacturer cancels before Retailer places an order. Is Manufacturer liable? _____

   b. Assume that the contract provided that Manufacturer was to sell Retailer "as many Frisbees as she needed for her retail store" (instead of as many as she "chose" to order). Would Manufacturer be liable for canceling? _____

4. *A* places an order with *B* for all of *A*'s IT service needs. *B*'s order form specifies "all orders subject to cancellation by *B* without notice at any time."

   a. The next day *A* wishes to get out of the deal. Is there a contract binding *A*? _____

   b. Suppose the order form said "All orders are subject to cancellation on 30 days' written notice by *B*." Is there a contract binding *A*? _____

   c. Assume that the contract was otherwise enforceable, but that it contained the following provision: "*A* shall have the right to terminate all obligations hereunder if the services are not performed efficiently, as determined by *A* in his sole and absolute discretion." In light of this provision, is there a binding contract? _____

5. Dealer contracts to sell a car to Oliver, a minor, for $1,000. Later, Dealer realizes that Oliver is a minor and refuses to go through with the sale on the ground that a minor's promise is not sufficient consideration. Can Oliver enforce the contract? _____

6. *A* promises to assign to *B* a patent owned by *A*, in exchange for *B*'s promise to pay *A* $10,000. *B*'s obligation is conditioned on the favorable termination _____

of pending litigation concerning the patent's validity. Is *B*'s promise valid consideration for *A*'s promise?

7. Homeowner signs an agreement with Broker under which Broker is given the exclusive right to sell Homeowner's house during the next three months, for a specified commission. The next day Homeowner seeks to cancel, asserting that Broker did not give any consideration, and therefore there is no contract. Can Homeowner cancel? _____

8. The First Bank of Nowhere is robbed. It posts a reward offer of $10,000 for information leading to the arrest of the robber. Officer Williams captures the robber. May she recover the reward? _____

9. Andre promises to design and build a sunroom for Mario for $20,000. Andre has almost completed performance when he realizes that the contract is a losing proposition and tells Mario that he cannot complete the sunroom unless Mario pays him an additional $6,000. Mario promises to pay the $6,000. Is his promise enforceable? _____

10. Builder contracts to build a house for Owner, to be completed by June 1. Builder subcontracts the electrical work to Sparks, to be completed by May 15. Owner fears delay by Sparks and promises them a $500 bonus to make sure the job is finished on May 15. If Sparks finishes on time, can they enforce Owner's promise? _____

11. *A* has borrowed $1,000 from *B* and executed a 6% interest-bearing promissory note due on June 1. On May 15, *A* tells *B* that *A* will not be able to pay back the $1,000 and offers to satisfy the debt by delivering shares worth $700. *B* accepts and takes delivery of the shares. *B* then sues *A* for $300. Can *B* recover? _____

12. Able, a carpenter, told his friend and neighbor, Clutz, that he would be happy to give Clutz some help in building his new garage. When the garage was completed with Able's help, Clutz said to Able, "I really appreciate your help. I'll help you paint your house in return." However, Clutz later changed his mind.

    a. Can Able enforce Clutz's promise? _____

    b. Assume that Clutz made his promise just after Able began helping. Would the promise then be enforceable? _____

13. Minister was employed by Church for 40 years. On Minister's retirement, there was no adequate pension plan. Therefore, two months after Minister's retirement, wealthy Parishioner promised to pay Minister $500 per month for life.

    a. Is Parishioner's promise enforceable as a contract? _____

    b. Would it make any difference whether Parishioner's promise was oral or in writing? _____

    c. Assume that in reliance on Parishioner's promise, Minister contracted to purchase a home in a retirement village which Minister would otherwise have been unable to afford. Is Parishioner's promise enforceable? _____

    d. Assume that Parishioner's promise to pay Minister $500 per month for life was conditioned on Minister's continuing to write sermons for _____

Church "if requested by Church." Church never made any such request. Is Parishioner's promise enforceable as a contract?

14. Debtor owes Friend a $1,000 debt that is barred by the statute of limitations.

   a. Assume Debtor telephoned Friend and promised to pay the $1,000. Can Friend enforce this promise?

   b. Assume Debtor wrote to Friend, "I know I owe you $1,000, but I won't pay it." Does Debtor's written acknowledgment of the debt make it now enforceable?

   c. Assume Debtor wrote to Friend, "I will pay you $700 of what I owe you, when I sell my car." Can Friend now enforce the $1,000 debt?

   d. Would the answer to any of the above be different if Debtor's promise was to pay a debt that had been discharged in bankruptcy (rather than barred by the statute of limitations)?

15. Sherry purchases Keir's car and promises to pay $3,000 for it. Shortly thereafter, Sherry discovers that Keir fraudulently misrepresented the mileage and condition of the car. Even so, Sherry likes the car and tells Keir that she will pay him for the car. Is this new promise enforceable?

16. Nia becomes ill while driving across country. She stops at a farmhouse and seeks aid. Farmer takes Nia in and nurses her back to health. On leaving, Nia promises to send Farmer $5,000 for his efforts. Is Nia's promise enforceable as a contract?

17. James loaned money to Will on a promissory note. Will died penniless and without repaying the loan. Will's father, however, agreed to repay Will's debt "in order to clear my son's good name." Is the father's promise enforceable?

MUTUAL ASSENT—OFFER AND ACCEPTANCE

18. In the course of a television interview, actress Amy stated, "I'm always having problems with my weight . . . I'd give a thousand dollars for the secret of staying thin!" Buford wrote Amy a letter stating, "The secret of staying thin is to eat less and exercise more. You owe me $1,000." Is Buford entitled to the $1,000?

19. Is there an enforceable contract in the following cases?

   a. Alice telephoned the Elite Grocery Co., with whom she maintained an account, and ordered 50 pounds of prime beef for a dinner party. No mention was made of price. Elite billed Alice $5 per pound ($250), which was the regular posted price of such beef at the store. Alice refuses to pay claiming that she could have purchased the same quality meat elsewhere for $200. Is she contractually bound to pay the full $250?

   b. Jon contracted to furnish janitorial services to Ben's offices for one year at a set price. At the end of the one-year period, he continued his services for three more years. Ben paid the contract price for the first two years but now refuses to pay for the last year. Is Ben bound to pay the contract price?

c. Ivy was seriously injured in a traffic accident. While she was unconscious, bystanders summoned Dr. Dudley, who performed a delicate operation on Ivy and later sent her a bill for $68,500. Is Ivy contractually bound to pay this amount?

20. Has a contract been formed if—

   a. Desperate writes Buyer, "I am eager to sell my house. I would consider $20,000 cash." Buyer promptly replies, "You've got a deal!"

   b. Clothing Store advertises a well-known brand of suits "regularly priced at $220, today only $150." Customer comes to the store in response to the ad, selects a suit, and tenders $150.

   c. Builder sends Owner a "letter agreement" for certain construction work which states "formal contract to follow." Owner writes "accepted" across the "letter agreement," signs it and returns it to Builder.

   d. Merchant *A* writes to Merchant *B*, "Dear *B*, I can quote you flour at $20 a barrel in carload lots for immediate acceptance." *B* writes, "Send three carloads."

21. Sam advertises in the newspaper that he will be auctioning off all of his household goods at a specified time and place.

   a. Is Sam bound to proceed with the auction?

   b. If, during the course of the auction, Sam feels that the bids are too low, can he withdraw the goods?

   c. Assume that the auction is announced to be "without reserve." Benita makes a bid, but immediately changes her mind and yells "I revoke" before the fall of the hammer. Is Benita bound by her bid?

22. On March 1, *A* wrote to *B* offering to sell *A*'s house for $140,000. The letter stated that the offer would remain in effect for only five days.

   a. Assume *B* received the letter on March 3 and sent an acceptance letter on March 7. Has a contract been formed?

   b. Assume that the house was destroyed by fire on March 6, and *B* sent her acceptance letter the next day unaware of this. Is there a contract?

   c. Assume *A* telephoned *B* on March 5, saying "I revoke my offer." *B* replied, "You can't revoke because you promised that the offer would remain in effect for five days." If *B* immediately then delivers a written acceptance, is there a contract?

   d. Assume that on March 5, *A* and *B* signed a memo in which *A* agreed to keep the offer open until March 10, for which *B* was to pay $100. On March 8, *A* emailed *B* revoking the offer. Can *B* accept the offer on March 9?

   e. Assume that on March 4, with *A*'s knowledge and approval, *B* had an expensive engineer's report made on *A*'s house. Can *A* still revoke the offer?

23. Sellars offers to sell to Byers a parcel of land for $5,000.

    a. Assume Byers replies, "I will pay you $4,800 for the parcel." Later that day, Byers says, "OK, I'll pay the $5,000," but Sellars now refuses to sell. Is there a contract? _____

    b. Assume Byers's first reply was, "Will you accept $4,800?" Would her subsequent "acceptance" of the $5,000 offer form a contract? _____

    c. Assume that Byers mailed a rejection to Sellars, but later the same day changed their mind and email an acceptance to Sellars. The acceptance was in fact received by Sellars prior to the rejection. Is there a contract? _____

    d. Suppose Byers had mailed an acceptance to Sellars, but later that day changed their mind and emailed a rejection, and the rejection was received by Sellars *prior* to the acceptance. Is there a contract? _____

24. Blue, Inc. mails an order to Gates for certain computer services. Gates replies: "Order acknowledged; will receive our attention and advise shortly."

    a. Is there a contract? _____

    b. Two days later, Gates writes Blue, Inc. "accepting" the order, but stating that services cannot be provided for six weeks. Is there a contract? _____

25. Father writes to Daughter, who is living away from home, as follows: "I am old and lonely and miss you terribly. If you'll come back home and take care of me for the rest of my life, I'll make you the sole beneficiary of my will. You don't need to promise—in fact, you can terminate the arrangement at any time if it doesn't suit you. Just come."

    a. If Daughter gives up her career and moves back home and starts to take care of Father, can Father later revoke his offer? _____

    b. Assume Father does not revoke, but after a few years Daughter tires of the arrangement and moves out and leaves Father alone. Can Father sue Daughter for breach of contract? _____

    c. Assume Daughter returns home in response to Father's letter, but mainly because she wanted to do so out of love and concern for Father and not because she was interested at the time about being the sole beneficiary of his will. If Daughter cares for Father for the rest of his life, can she enforce his promise against his estate? _____

26. *A* makes a written application for life insurance through an agent for *B* Insurance Company, pays the first premium, and is given a receipt stating that the insurance "shall take effect on approval of the application" at *B*'s home office. *B*'s home office approves the next day, but the day after, before notice of approval has been sent, *A* dies. Was *A* covered by the insurance policy? _____

27. Frasier posts a $100 reward for the return of his dog. Roz reads the reward offer, searches for and finds the dog, and returns it. Can Roz collect the $100 even though she never notified Frasier that she was going to accept the reward offer? _____

28. Rich writes to Lender stating, "If you will lend my brother, *B*, $1,000, I will guaranty repayment." On receipt of this letter, Lender loans the money to *B*. If Lender fails to notify Rich that it has done so within a reasonable time, can Lender enforce Rich's guaranty? _____

29. Frasier posts a $100 reward for return of his lost dog. In the meantime, Roz has found the dog and returns it to Frasier, unaware of the reward offer. If she later finds out about the reward, can Roz collect the $100? _____

30. Which, if any, of the following offers can be accepted *only* by performance? _____

    (A) *A* orders goods from *B* on specified terms and further states, "Ship at once."

    (B) *A* offers a reward of $100 for a lost diamond bracelet.

    (C) *A* says to *B*, "I'll pay you $15 to mow my lawn this afternoon."

    (D) *A* says to *B*, "If you finish that table you are making and deliver it to my house today, I'll give you $100 for it."

31. *A* sends an order for 1,000 12-inch Frisbees to *B* Manufacturing Co., with instructions to ship immediately.

    a. Suppose that *B* immediately ships the goods by common carrier. The next day, and before receipt of the Frisbees, *A* wires a revocation of his order. Is there a contract? _____

    b. Suppose *B* was out of 12-inch Frisbees and therefore shipped 11.5-inch Frisbees instead. Is there a contract at the time of shipment? _____

32. Brendan has been renting Anita's house for many years, and he has offered to buy it on several occasions but Anita has refused. Finally, Anita sends Brendan a letter stating, "I'm now ready to sell the house at the price we have been discussing over the past several years. Knowing that you want the house, I'll consider that we have a deal, unless I hear from you otherwise." Brendan makes no reply to this letter but does *not* wish to purchase the house at this time. Is there a contract? _____

33. *A* mails *B* an offer to lease *B*'s house for $1,000 per month; the offer states "reply immediately."

    a. *B* immediately mails acceptance, but the envelope is lost and never received by *A*. Is there a contract? _____

    b. Assume that *B* had accidentally misaddressed the envelope to *A*, and as a result it ended up in another city. However, the postmaster in the other city happened to know *A* personally and forwarded the letter to *A*, who received the letter several days later. Is there a contract? _____

34. Art mails Bob an offer to sell him a restored Model T Ford for $2,000. Ignorant of Art's offer, Bob mails Art an offer to buy the same car for the same amount. On receiving Bob's letter, Art decides the car is worth more and notifies Bob he will not sell. Is there a contract? _____

35. Ajax Oil Co. leases one of its service stations to Don. The lease provides it is "terminable at will of Ajax." Prior to signing the lease, Don questioned Ajax about this clause and was assured that it would not be exercised so long as Don's sales exceeded 50,000 gallons per month. Ajax later attempts to terminate the lease, even though Don's sales are in excess of the figure stated.

    a. Is evidence of Ajax's oral promise admissible under the parol evidence rule? _____

    b. Assume that the lease provided that Ajax could terminate only "for good cause." Would Ajax's oral promise to Don be admissible? _____

DEFENSES

36. Builder offers to build a house for Owner at a specified price. Owner accepts.

    a. If Builder does not state a completion date for the house, is there a contract? _____

    b. Suppose Builder hires Foreman at a monthly salary of $1200, payable weekly, but two days later Builder fires Foreman without cause. Was Builder legally obligated to employ Foreman for a reasonable length of time? _____

    c. If Builder's offer included no plans or specifications, is there a contract? _____

    d. Assume that Builder's offer does contain plans and specifications except as to paint and wallpaper, which are to be "selected at a later date." Has a contract been formed? _____

37. Armour agrees to sell to Carnegie "whatever amount of coal you will need to run your factory this winter," at $100 per ton. Is this agreement sufficiently definite to constitute a contract? _____

38. Ebeneezer agrees to employ Bob for one year as a sales manager. Under traditional contract law rules, is there an enforceable contract in the following cases, assuming that Ebeneezer breaches before Bob begins to work?

    a. Ebeneezer promises to pay Bob "a salary to be settled between us at the end of each month." _____

    b. Ebeneezer promises to pay Bob "a fair share of the profits derived from your services." _____

    c. Ebeneezer promises to pay Bob "half the profits on any increased sales after you come to work." _____

    d. Ebeneezer promises to pay Bob a salary of $1,500 per month "provided my sales volume is sufficient to enable me to pay this amount." _____

    e. No provision is made for salary. _____

39. Benny is a large retailer of toys. He anticipates a seasonal rush on Frisbees and therefore contracts with Ajax, a Frisbee manufacturer, to purchase "as many Frisbees as you can produce within the next 30 days, at a price to be determined by you."

    a. Is the contract sufficiently certain as to quantity? _____

    b. Is the contract sufficiently certain as to price? _____

40. *A* offers to sell to *B* a packet of diamonds for $50,000. *B* agrees to buy.

    a. Assume that *A* had misjudged the quality of the stones, that their fair market value was really $100,000, and that *B* was aware of *A*'s error. Is there a contract? _____

    b. Assume that *A* had miscounted the number and weight of the stones in the packet and that *B* was aware of *A*'s error. Is there a contract? _____

41. Bess owns two cars of equal value—a Ford and a Chevrolet. Bess offers to sell "my car" to Abe for $2,500. Abe accepts with the intent of purchasing the Chevrolet and later demands delivery of that car. Bess refuses on the ground that she honestly intended to sell only the Ford. Is there a contract? _____

42. Ryder is injured when the bus on which he is riding crashes because of the negligence of the driver. The ticket purchased by Ryder contains a provision in large print stating that the carrier shall not be liable for injuries caused by its agents and employees. Is Ryder bound by this provision? _____

43. Retailer *S* sells a vacuum cleaner to customer *B* at more than three times the price at which *B* could have purchased the same vacuum cleaner from other stores in the same community. Does *B* have any defense? _____

44. Landlord orally agrees to lease a large factory building to Tenant for one year. The building is worth several million dollars, and the rent is $10,000 per month. Is the oral lease enforceable? _____

45. *A* and *B* orally agree to work together in the development of a tract of real estate that *A* owns and to split whatever profits are obtained. After the property is fully developed, it is sold at a big profit, but *A* refuses to give *B* any share. Is the oral agreement enforceable? _____

46. Ajax, a Frisbee manufacturer, orally agrees to sell 1,000 Frisbees to Benny for the price of $1,000.

    a. Assume that the Frisbees are to be shipped in two shipments and that after sending the first shipment, Ajax changes its mind and refuses to send the balance of the Frisbees. Can Benny enforce the oral agreement against Ajax for the balance of the goods? _____

    b. Assume that Benny had made a down payment of $200 but Ajax has not shipped anything. Can Benny enforce Ajax's promise to sell him the 1,000 Frisbees? _____

    c. Assume that the Frisbees were to be specially manufactured by Ajax with Benny's name and advertising slogan permanently imprinted thereon and that after Ajax had completed production, but before shipment, Benny canceled his order. Can Ajax enforce the oral agreement against Benny? _____

47. Which, if any, of the following types of oral agreements fall within the Statute of Frauds provisions applicable to contracts not to be performed within one year? _____

    (A) A lifetime employment contract.

    (B) A lease of personal property terminable at will.

    (C) A five-year option to purchase personal property.

48. Carla is an employee of Aerospace Co., and she has recently been transferred to a new city. Carla wishes to lease a house in the new city from Lessor. Lessor telephones Aerospace for a reference on Carla.

    a. Assume that Aerospace tells Lessor, "Don't worry about Carla's credit. If she doesn't pay the rent, we will." Lessor then rents to Carla. If Carla defaults, can Lessor recover from Aerospace? _____

    b. Assume that Aerospace had told Carla to negotiate her own lease with Lessor and orally assured Carla that Aerospace would pay whatever rent was charged by Lessor. Can Aerospace refuse to pay on the ground that its promise was oral? _____

49. Do the following writings satisfy the Statute of Frauds?

    a. S and B orally agree on the sale of S's 100-acre farm for $1,500 per acre. They date and sign the following memorandum: "Agreement this date re sale of S's farm to B. $1,000 paid on purchase price; balance due when deed delivered. (signed)" _____

    b. An oral agreement for the sale of goods is followed by the following signed memorandum:
    "Jan. 15. Received $100 down on purchase price of 500 Frisbees. Balance due on delivery within 10 days. (signed)" _____

    c. An otherwise sufficient memorandum of an oral agreement for the sale of Blackacre is signed by X "as agent of Seller." X has authorization from S, the owner of Blackacre, to sell it on S's behalf, but X's authority is only oral. _____

50. If a contract fails to comply with the Statute of Frauds, may the seller recover in restitution for any benefits conferred thereunder? May the buyer? _____

51. Ajax orally promised to pay Bob a salary of $40,000 per year for five years and his moving expenses, if Bob would quit his present job and come to work for Ajax in another city. Bob agreed to do so but requested a written contract. Ajax assured him that the company attorney would prepare such a contract as soon as possible, but Ajax needed Bob to start at once. Accordingly, Bob sold his house, moved his family, and commenced to work for Ajax. He was fired without cause two months later. Can Bob enforce Ajax's oral promise even though no written contract was ever executed? _____

52. Tom, a 15-year-old, has run out of money while on a trip away from home. Polly gives him food, a place to sleep, and his bus fare home, in exchange for Tom's promise in writing to pay Polly $200 to cover these costs. Is Tom's promise enforceable? _____

53. Distraught with loneliness, wealthy and eccentric Donald engages Lulu as a traveling companion and promises to pay Lulu $2,500 per month for such companionship. Donald has a long history of emotional instability. Can Lulu enforce Donald's promise? _____

54. Slicker sells a chemical apparatus to Leroy knowing that Leroy intends to use the apparatus to make moonshine in violation of the law. Can Slicker recover the contract price for the apparatus from Leroy? _____

55. A local statute requires all chiropractors to be licensed. C, who is not licensed, contracts with and performs chiropractic services for B for a specified fee. B refuses to pay.

    a. Can C recover the contract fee? _____

    b. Can C recover the reasonable value of the services in restitution? _____

THIRD-PARTY RIGHTS AND OBLIGATIONS

56. Laura claims that her neighbor, Bob, owes her $200. Bob has always disputed Laura's claim. Even so, in order to avoid further embarrassment in the neighborhood, Bob agrees to do some yardwork for Teresa and Teresa agrees to pay Laura instead of Bob $200 for this work. If Teresa fails to make this payment, can Laura enforce Teresa's promise? _____

57. A consumer advocacy group enters into an agreement in which a company promises to refund the price of a widget to any purchaser who bought a defective widget within a specified time. Can Ralph, who bought a widget during that time, enforce the promise? _____

58. Jewell contracts to purchase Dominic's grocery store, and as part of the purchase price agrees to pay off the bills owing to Dominic's suppliers, one of whom is Sam.

    a. Assume that Sam learns of the sale of Dominic's business and informs Jewell and Dominic of his assent but takes no action because Jewell has a good reputation and he expects that she will pay off Dominic's bill as agreed. However, Jewell and Dominic revise their contract so that Jewell is no longer obligated thereunder to pay off Sam. Does Sam have a valid claim against Jewell? _____

    b. Assume that Jewell failed to pay off supplier Sam and that there is no defense to enforcement of the Jewell-Dominic contract. Sam now demands payment from Dominic, the original debtor. Can Dominic sue Jewell *without first paying off Sam*? _____

59. Jewell contracts to purchase Dominic's grocery store, and as part of the purchase price, she agrees to give Dominic's parents a 10% discount on any groceries purchased by them from the store during the forthcoming year.

    a. Assume that later, in order to resolve a dispute between themselves, Jewell and Dominic change their agreement so as to cut out any discount to the parents. Still later, Dominic's parents find out about the discount deal in the original contract. Do Dominic's parents have any valid claim against Jewell? _____

    b. Assume that Dominic's parents' rights had vested in time. Assume further that when Jewell took over the grocery store, she found considerably less inventory than Dominic had represented. If Dominic's parents now sue Jewell for their discount, can Jewell assert the inventory shortage as a defense to their suit? _____

60. Are the following enforceable as third-party beneficiary contracts?

    a. Father promises Son that he will not sell the family home, in exchange for Son's promise to pay Daughter's college tuition. Daughter sues to enforce Son's promise. _____

    b. Bank agrees to loan money to A, so that A can pay off a debt A owes to B. B sues to enforce Bank's promise. _____

61. A owns a house on which there is a $70,000 mortgage owing to Bank. A sells the house to B.

    a. If B is aware of the mortgage and expressly takes "subject to" it, does B become *personally* liable to Bank in the event of default? _____

    b. Assume that B later resold the house to C, and that C expressly "assumed" the mortgage debt. In the event of default on the mortgage, is C personally liable to Bank? _____

    c. Assume that Bank fails to recover from either B or C and therefore sues A (original owner). Can it recover? _____

62. Are the following assignments effective?

   a. Ava is about to undergo a serious operation. She mails the following letter to her friend, Bruce:

   > Dear Bruce: I want you to have the debt owed me by Cooper and will write him a letter telling him so. (signed)

   Ava dies shortly after Bruce receives this letter and before Ava had a chance to write to Cooper. Can Bruce enforce the assignment? _____

   b. To settle a bona fide dispute with Bruce, Ava orally assigns to him a half interest in a $1,000 negotiable promissory note payable to Ava that Ava retains in her possession. Later, Ava refuses to share the payments with Bruce. Can Bruce enforce the assignment? _____

63. Which, if any, of the following contract rights are assignable?

   a. Amy is employed as a sales representative for Homecare Products. She receives a salary, but her employment is terminable at will. Can Amy make an effective assignment of her *future wages*? _____

   b. Amy is employed as a real estate salesperson by Ajax Realtors. She receives no salary but, instead, a share of each commission obtained by Ajax on sales she procures. Can Amy make an effective assignment of her share of *future commissions*? _____

   c. Amy is writing a book of her memoirs, which several publishers are eager to publish. Can Amy make an effective assignment of the royalties she will receive on this book before signing with a publisher? _____

   d. Amy is planning to marry and hires Claude to design an original wedding gown for her, for which she pays $1,000 in advance. Shortly thereafter, she breaks her engagement. Can Amy make an effective assignment of her right to have Claude design a gown to her friend Bella, who is also planning to marry? _____

   e. Amy has contracted with Shea Grower to supply her with as much shea butter as she needs for her cosmetic manufacturing business, at $100 per quart. Can Amy make an effective assignment to Henry, who is also a cosmetics manufacturer, of her contract with Shea Grower? _____

   f. Amy owns a cosmetics manufacturing plant on which she carries a fire insurance policy. If Amy sells the plant to Emma, can she make an effective assignment of the fire insurance policy to Emma without the insurance company's consent? _____

   g. Bank has agreed to loan Amy $100,000 for use in her cosmetics business. If Amy sells the business to Emma before the loan is consummated, can Amy make an effective assignment to Emma of her right to the bank loan? _____

64. Aaron is a plumbing contractor. He contracts to furnish labor and material for the plumbing in a large office building being constructed by Baker, for the sum of $100,000.

   a. Assume that the contract contains a provision stating "neither party shall assign this contract without the other's consent." If Baker sells the building to Cooper during the course of construction, can Baker make _____ an effective assignment of her rights to Aaron's services without Aaron's consent?

    b. Assume that the contract provision stated that "any assignment of any right hereunder without the other party's consent shall be null and void." Can Aaron, after finishing the job, make an effective assignment of his right to the $100,000?

    c. Assume that the contract provision stated "no assignment of this contract shall be made." Can Aaron *delegate* to another plumber, Potter, the duties to perform his contract with Baker?

65. Ann signed a contract under which she is obligated to pay $5,000 to Ben for dancing lessons. Ben immediately assigned the monies due under this contract to Chester, who immediately notified Ann of the assignment. Chester is now suing Ann to enforce payment. Would the following be valid defenses for Ann to assert against Chester?

    a. Ann was unaware that she was signing a contract: she reasonably thought it was a contest entry form.

    b. Ben gave her only half the dancing lessons promised.

66. Alice buys a vacuum cleaner from retailer Ben. She promises to pay for it in six monthly installments of $50 each. Ben assigns the contract to First Finance Co., who paid value and took without notice of any defense. First Finance Co. sues Alice for nonpayment. Is it a valid defense for Alice that, before she was aware of the assignment, Ben promised to refund her the price of a defective refrigerator purchased in another transaction?

67. By way of a gift, Amos tells Bob, "I hereby assign to you the $10,000 debt owed to me by *X*." Later, however, Amos makes a written assignment of the same debt to Chris. As between Bob and Chris, who is entitled to collect the debt?

68. Employee borrows money from Bank and assigns as security his wages then due from Employer. The next day, Employee makes a similar loan from and assignment to Finance Co. (which has no knowledge of Bank's interest). Finance Co. notifies Employer of its assignment before Bank does. Assume there are no restrictions on wage assignments.

    a. As between Bank and Finance Co., which is entitled to priority?

    b. Is the question of priority here affected by the U.C.C.?

    c. Suppose that Employer actually *paid* Employee's wages to Finance Co., in response to Finance Co.'s notice of assignment. Would Bank have a valid claim against Finance Co. for a share of the wages?

69. After Actor had contracted to star in Producer's new play, he received a better offer to appear in a film. Therefore, he assigned all his rights and duties under his contract with Producer to Standby.

    a. Standby is ready and willing to perform. Is Producer obligated to accept Standby's performance?

    b. Assume that Producer is willing to allow Standby to perform instead of Actor. If Standby walks off the job halfway through the contract, can Producer sue *Actor* for damages?

70. Archer contracts to purchase Baker's farm for $50,000. With Baker's consent, Archer "sells, transfers, and assigns" to Childs his contract with Baker. Can Baker sue Childs for performance? _____

PERFORMANCE AND BREACH

71. Able signs a contract to buy Baker's house for $267,500 "if I am able to obtain a mortgage loan for $260,000, at 7% interest, payable over 20 years." Assume that Able tries but is unable to obtain the described loan, and therefore refuses to proceed with the purchase. Is Able in breach of contract? _____

72. Broker procures a buyer for Owner's house. Owner promises to pay Broker a commission of $1,500 "on close of escrow." If thereafter the buyer refuses to proceed with the sale (and hence escrow never closes), is Owner under any duty to pay the $1,500 to Broker? _____

73. Borrower borrows money from Friend, promising to repay "as soon as I am able." If Borrower thereafter refuses to seek employment, and therefore has no money, is he under any duty to repay the loan? _____

74. Club charters an airplane from Airline for "flight from San Francisco to depart 10:00 a.m., June 1, to arrive in Papeete, Tahiti, 6:00 p.m., June 2." Due to mechanical delays the flight is 10 hours late in departure. Assume no statutes are applicable.

    a. Is Club obligated to pay the charter fee? _____

    b. Is Airline liable to Club for breach of contract? _____

75. Buyer orders 1,000 Frisbees from Seller at a price of $1 each. No credit term is agreed on but Buyer reserves the right to return any or all of the Frisbees within 30 days after delivery.

    a. Is Buyer obligated to pay for the Frisbees during the 30-day period? _____

    b. If Seller sues Buyer for the price, does Seller have to *prove* that it made complete delivery of the goods? _____

    c. If Seller sues Buyer for the price, does Seller have to *prove* that Buyer made no return of any of the goods during the 30-day period? _____

    d. Assume Buyer intended to sell the Frisbees at the County Fair and that its order therefore stated: "Buyer reserves right to cancel this order if County Fair is not held this year." If Seller sues Buyer for the price, does Seller have to *prove* that the County Fair was held? _____

76. Farmer engages Digger to dig a new water well on Farmer's property. Farmer agrees to pay Digger $2,000 "provided the well water is fit for human consumption as determined by the State Water Board." Digger brings in a new well, but the State Water Board finds the water unfit for human consumption.

    a. If Digger can prove that the State Water Board has applied *unreasonably* strict standards in testing the water, can it collect from Farmer? _____

    b. Assume that Farmer's promise to pay was "provided that the well water is of a quality *satisfactory* to me" (Farmer) and Farmer now says that the quality is unsatisfactory. If Digger can prove that Farmer is acting *unreasonably*, can it enforce Farmer's promise to pay the $2,000? _____

77. Owner gives Broker a written listing to find a buyer for Owner's house. Nothing is said about Broker having the right to show the inside of the house to prospective purchasers. If Owner refuses to allow Broker to show the inside of the house (and Broker is therefore unable to obtain a purchaser), can Broker collect the commission provided in the listing agreement? _____

78. Owner contracts to sell his house to Purchaser for $100,000 and to repair a broken toilet therein prior to the date set for closing. On the date set for closing, Owner tenders a deed but has still not fixed the toilet. If Purchaser refuses to proceed with the purchase, can Owner enforce the contract? _____

79. Owner agrees to sell their house to Buyer for $100,000. The contract provides that the purchase price is to be paid by Buyer, and the deed is to be delivered by Owner, on June 1. On that date, nothing happens.

   a. On June 2, can Owner sue Buyer for breach? _____

   b. On June 2, can Buyer sue Owner for breach? _____

80. Bertha advertises a car for sale. Andy offers to purchase the car for $2,000, payable $200 per month for the next 10 months. Bertha says, "I accept." In the absence of any other understanding, is Bertha entitled to hold onto the car until she receives the full purchase price? _____

81. Artist agrees to paint a portrait for Lawyer, in exchange for which Lawyer agrees to draft a will for Artist. Artist gets very busy and puts off Lawyer's portrait, and Lawyer therefore never draws a will for Artist, although she clearly had time to do so. Can Artist recover damages from Lawyer for breach of contract? _____

82. Arthur promises to move in and care for his wealthy Uncle for the rest of his life, in exchange for which Uncle promises to pay Arthur $500 per month and also to name him sole beneficiary of his estate.

   a. If Uncle later, *without cause*, refuses Arthur's care and orders him to leave, can Arthur enforce Uncle's promise to name him as sole beneficiary? _____

   b. Assume that Uncle never ordered Arthur to leave but became increasingly disagreeable as he grew older, making if far more difficult for Arthur to care for him. Would Arthur be excused from his duty to care for Uncle for the rest of his life? _____

83. Owner signs a written listing authorizing Broker to sell Owner's house and requiring Owner to pay Broker a commission "on closing of the sale." Thereafter, Broker interests Purchaser in the property, and Purchaser signs a written agreement to buy Owner's house on the terms of the listing. Prior to closing, however, Purchaser wrongfully refuses to perform. Owner could, but does not, file legal action against Purchaser, and hence the sale never "closes." Can Broker recover any commission from Owner? _____

84. Owner hires Manager to collect rents and manage Owner's apartment house for a period of five years, for which Manager is to be paid 5% of the gross rentals received by Owner. At the end of the first year, Owner sells the apartment house, and the purchaser does his own managing. Can Manager now sue for damages? _____

85. Owner contracts to sell his house to Purchaser, the purchase price to be paid and the deed to be delivered on June 1.

   a. Assume that on May 1, Owner tells Purchaser that she is involved in divorce litigation and that her wife will not release her interest in the property, thereby making Owner unable to convey it. Purchaser therefore does not tender payment on June 1. If Owner tenders clear title on June 1 (Owner's wife having released her interest by then), is Purchaser in breach? _____

   b. Assume the same facts as in the previous paragraph, but assume further that Purchaser told Owner on May 1 that in view of Owner's pending divorce litigation, Purchaser would look elsewhere for a house. If Owner thereafter clears the title and gives Purchaser notice thereof ***before*** June 1, can Owner enforce the contract? _____

86. Sam agrees to sell his car to his friend, Bob, for $18,000, the price to be paid and the car transferred within 10 days.

   a. The next day, Sam receives a better offer from Fred and accepts Fred's offer (still not delivering the car, however). Bob learns of this and buys himself another car. If the deal with Fred falls through, can Sam enforce Bob's promise to buy the car? _____

   b. Would the answer be the same if Sam was a new car dealer and the car sold to Bob was part of his stock? _____

   c. Suppose that the day after the agreement was made, Bob declared bankruptcy. Relying on this, Sam sold the car to someone else. On the tenth day, Bob tenders the $18,000. Is Sam in breach? _____

87. Owner leases a vacant lot to Promoter for 10 years. Promoter agrees to erect a carwash thereon and to pay Owner as rent "one-third of the profits received from operation of the car wash."

   a. If Promoter never gets the car wash built because she is unable to obtain financing, can Owner enforce the lease? _____

   b. If Promoter in fact erects the car wash but hires her family and friends at such exorbitant salaries that there are ***no*** profits, can Owner recover any rent from Promoter? _____

   c. If after operating the car wash for a while, Promoter determines that it cannot be operated profitably and hence closes it down, can Owner recover future rent from Promoter? _____

88. To settle divorce litigation, Wife releases her marital rights in certain property, and Husband agrees to pay Wife $10,000 a year for five years. After the first installment is paid, Husband informs Wife that he will make no further payments to her. Can Wife bring suit immediately for the remaining four installments? _____

89. Ace contracts to manufacture and deliver 10,000 spark plugs to Beta on April 1. Beta needs them on that date to keep its assembly line running. On February 1, Ace advises Beta, "I'm having trouble locating the raw materials I need to fill your order and may not be able to deliver on time." Beta immediately notifies Ace that it will purchase its spark plugs elsewhere. If _____

Ace ends up in fact able to manufacture spark plugs on time and tenders delivery on April 1, is Beta in breach if it refuses to accept delivery?

90. In January, Amos contracted to sell his house to Beulah for $170,000, the purchase price to be paid and deed to be delivered on June 1.

   a. On March 1, Beulah writes Amos, "I've had second thoughts about buying your home. I won't pay you that amount of money unless you repaint the house and fix up the yard." Could Amos sue Beulah for breach of contract upon *receipt* of this letter? _____

   b. On April 1, Beulah writes Amos, "I'm no longer concerned about the paint and yard work. However, my attorney has just advised me that your title is defective and not to proceed with the purchase. Of course, I have to follow his advice. Sorry." If in fact Amos has a clear and perfect title, can he sue Beulah for breach of contract *on receipt* of this letter? _____

   c. Assume that, notwithstanding her letters to Amos, Beulah tenders the full purchase price on June 1. Can Beulah still enforce the contract? _____

   d. Assume that after receipt of Beulah's letters, Amos had replied, "You have no valid excuse for breaking our contract. I expect you to pay the full purchase price on June 1, as agreed." However, not hearing anything further from Beulah, Amos decided not to wait until June 1 and resold the properly to another. If Beulah shows up with the full purchase price on June 1, is Amos in breach? _____

91. Developer contracts with Builder to install sewers in a large housing tract for a price of $600,000, construction to start in six months. Before Builder has done anything, Developer writes him a letter stating, "I have decided to have another company install the sewers instead of you. Send me a bill for whatever expenses you have incurred."

   a. If, instead, Builder goes ahead and procures the supplies, equipment, and labor that they will need to perform the contract and shows up on the job site ready to perform, can they enforce the contract for the full $600,000? _____

   b. Assume that it was Builder who repudiated the contract before any performance. Developer waits until the end of the six-month period to see if Builder will change their mind and then hires another contractor. Consequently, Developer then has to pay $60,000 more because costs of construction have increased in the interim. Can Developer recover the $60,000 from Builder? _____

92. Owner contracts to sell his house to Purchaser for $100,000, and June 1 is the date set for closing. The contract requires Purchaser to pay the purchase price in five equal installments of $20,000 each, due January 1, February 1, March 1, April 1, and May 1. Purchaser makes the first four payments but is unable to raise the final $20,000.

   a. Can Purchaser enforce the contract against Owner on June 1? _____

   b. Can Owner enforce the contract against purchaser on June 1 *without first tendering a deed* to the property? _____

93. Don orders 1,000 cases of spaghetti from Giovanni, to be delivered in five equal monthly shipments (200 cases each). A total purchase price of $5,000 is specified, but the time for payment is not mentioned.

   a. Assume that Giovanni delivers the first shipment and demands payment of $1,000 (200 cases at $5 each), but Don refuses to pay until the balance of the order is received. Can Giovanni sue and recover for the 200 cases delivered? _____

   b. Assume that Giovanni had delivered the first two shipments (totaling 400 cases), but then received a better offer from one of Don's competitors and therefore cut off any further shipments to Don. Under such circumstances, could Giovanni sue and recover for the 400 cases delivered? _____

   c. Assume that the contract stated: "This contract is indivisible, and Don shall pay nothing whatsoever unless and until full and complete delivery is made." If Giovanni had delivered 800 cases and then his plant was shut down by a strike, so that he was unable to make the final delivery, could he recover anything for the 800 cases delivered? _____

94. On March 15, Andrew contracts to buy Bianca's house, closing to occur on April 30. However, on April 15, Bianca requests a 60-day extension because she has not yet found a place to move, and Andrew good-naturedly agrees.

   a. Assume that on April 30, Andrew changes his mind and tenders payment and requests a conveyance, and Bianca refuses. Is Bianca in breach of contract on that date? _____

   b. Assume that on April 29, Andrew notified Bianca that he was unwilling to stick by his promise to extend closing for 60 days and demanded a conveyance not later than May 15. Could Andrew enforce the contract by proper tender on May 15? _____

   c. Assume that the sale closed on May 15 as demanded by Andrew. Is Andrew entitled to recover anything from Bianca for Bianca's use of the property during the two-week period? _____

95. Owner engages Contractor to build a house. The contract calls for Owner to make progress payments upon completion of various portions of the construction, as evidenced by a certificate signed by Architect. Owner makes the first three progress payments to Contractor without the certificate. Has Owner waived the right to insist on the Architect's certificate before making future progress payments? _____

96. Alpha engages Builder to remodel his kitchen and to install therein new Frigi-Queen built-in appliances. Because Frigi-Queens are in short supply, Builder installs another brand of appliances which has a reputation as good as Frigi-Queen.

   a. Alpha refuses to pay Builder for the remodeling because of the unauthorized substitute of brands. Can Builder collect the contract price from Alpha? _____

   b. Assume that the reason for the substitution of brands was simply that Builder was unable to get as good a discount on Frigi-Queen appliances as he could on the brand he installed. Can Builder collect the contract price from Alpha? _____

c. Assume that Alpha's contract with Builder provided "any deviation or substitution without Alpha's consent shall render this contract void, and Alpha shall be under no obligation to pay Builder anything." Can Builder collect the contract price from Alpha? _____

d. Assume that in addition to substituting appliances without Alpha's consent, Builder also failed to install the proper electrical wiring, so that the appliances installed are constantly shorting out. Could Builder recover anything from Alpha—on the contract or in restitution? _____

97. Alpha goes to XYZ Department Store and orders new Frigi-Queen built-in appliances, to be delivered to her home on May 1. She and her roommate plan to install the appliances themselves. XYZ is short of Frigi-Queens and therefore delivers on May 1 another brand that has as good a reputation and costs the same. Alpha refuses to accept delivery of the appliances. Can XYZ collect from Alpha for its loss of profit on the sale? _____

98. Don orders 1,000 cases of spaghetti from Giovanni, 200 cases to be shipped "immediately" and 200 cases on the first of each month thereafter. The agreement requires Don to pay $5 per case—*i.e.*, $1,000, on receipt of each shipment.

    a. If Giovanni delays the first shipment to Don for more than two weeks, is Don justified in canceling the contract and rejecting any later shipments from Giovanni? _____

    b. If Don was more than two weeks late in paying Giovanni for the first shipment, is Giovanni justified in canceling the contract and refusing further shipments to Don? _____

    c. Assume that the order form signed by Don contained a "time is of the essence" clause. If Don was only one day late in making the first payment, would Giovanni be justified in canceling the contract and refusing any further shipments? _____

    d. Assume that the final shipment by Giovanni was timely but contains only 150 cases. Must Don accept and pay for this short shipment? _____

99. Alpha contracts with Builder to build her a new house on a lot she owns. Builder had almost completed the house when it was struck by lightning and destroyed. Builder sues Alpha for the contract price less cost of completion. Will he recover? _____

100. Alpha contracts with Builder to build her a new house on a lot she owns.

    a. During the course of construction, Builder encounters rapidly rising prices of labor and materials. It turns out that it will cost Builder **double** the amount he estimated when contracting with Alpha. Is he in breach if he refuses to complete the job? _____

    b. Builder is injured while on the job site and suffers a broken leg. Because of this, he is unable to return to the job within the period specified in the contract. Is he in breach if he fails to complete the house on time? _____

c. Assume the contract required Builder to construct Alpha's house "in accordance with City Building Code" standards. If the City thereafter changes its Building Code, so as to make performance of the contract by Builder more expensive, is he excused from performing for the same price? _____

101. Aria leases to Camilla for 99 years a large tract of undeveloped land at a rental of $5,000 per month, upon which Camilla is to erect a large shopping center (as per agreed plans). Shortly thereafter, a zoning ordinance is enacted that restricts development of the property to single-family residences.

    a. Is Camilla's obligation to erect the shopping center discharged? _____

    b. Is Camilla entitled to cancel the lease (*i.e.*, is her obligation to pay the rent discharged)? _____

102. Wanda agrees to sell her prize-winning poodle to Brenda for $1,500 and to ship the poodle cross-country to Brenda by air carrier the next day.

    a. If, unknown to either party, the poodle had died the night before they contracted, could Brenda sue Wanda for damages for nondelivery? _____

    b. Assume that Wanda delivered the poodle to the air carrier, but the poodle was killed in a crash of the plane. Could Wanda sue Brenda for the $1,500 purchase price? _____

    c. Assume that all air carriers were grounded by bad weather, and Wanda shipped the poodle to Brenda by truck instead. If Brenda refused to accept the poodle because of the delay, could Wanda enforce the contract? _____

103. Lew executes a written lease to Ted for 99 years covering a large tract of undeveloped land, which Ted planned to develop as a shopping center. Later, the land is zoned to prevent this use, and the parties agree in writing to cancel the lease.

    a. If Lew later changes his mind and sues to enforce the lease, is he bound by the agreement to cancel? _____

    b. Would the answer be the same if the agreement to cancel was oral? _____

104. Theo signs a contract to purchase a tractor from Lucas for $10,000, payable within 30 days following delivery. Upon delivery, Theo complains of various defects in the tractor. Although Lucas does not regard Theo's complaints as reasonable or justified, Lucas and Theo agree in writing to reduce the purchase price by $500.

    a. If Lucas later changes his mind and sues to collect the full purchase price, is he bound by his agreement to reduce the price? _____

    b. Would the answer be the same if the agreement was oral? _____

105. Sandy owes Pete $1,500 on a personal loan, which she finds difficult to repay. Sandy offers to pay off the loan by painting Pete's house, and Pete gladly agrees to this because he was planning to have his house painted anyway, and the cheapest bid he got was $1,800.

    a. If Sandy later changes her mind and refuses to paint Pete's house, can Pete sue Sandy (1) for the original $1,500 debt *and* (2) for the extra $300 it cost him to get his house painted? _____

b. If Sandy actually painted Pete's house but did a poor job, could Pete later sue Sandy for the $1,500 original debt? _____

c. Suppose that it cost Pete $500 to correct and complete the paint work that Sandy was supposed to do. If Sandy gave Pete a check for $100 marked "in settlement of all claims re my paint job" and Pete cashed this check, can Pete thereafter recover from Sandy for the balance of the damages? _____

REMEDIES

106. If a seller intentionally and in "bad faith" refuses to perform a contract for the sale of goods, is an award of punitive damages proper? _____

107. Duke orders 10,000 Frisbees to be manufactured by Easy according to Duke's specifications and carrying Duke's brand name and advertising. If Easy tenders delivery and Duke wrongfully refuses to accept, can Easy thereafter recover the full purchase price? _____

108. Alpha contracts with Builder to remodel her kitchen.

   a. Before Builder starts to work, Alpha's house is accidentally destroyed by fire. Builder tenders performance. Can he recover from Alpha his loss of profits on the remodeling job? _____

   b. Assume that the fire had taken place *after* Builder had started the job. Can he recover anything from Alpha? _____

109. Martha agrees to sell her house to John for $170,000. The fair market value of the house is $172,000. Martha's title proves defective so that she cannot convey marketable title. Can John recover $2,000 damages? _____

110. Producer hires Designer to design and create the costumes for a new Broadway show, for the sum of $50,000. The contract requires that all costumes be completed one week prior to the opening date.

   a. If Designer is one day late in completing the gowns but this delay causes no postponement of the show or other loss to Producer, can Producer recover anything from Designer? _____

   b. If Designer is two weeks late in completing the gowns, and the delay results in a loss of over $200,000 to Producer—extra salaries to cast, theater rental, etc.—can Producer recover this entire amount from Designer (less, of course, the $50,000 contract price)? _____

   c. If Designer fails to complete the costumes at all, and as a direct result Producer has to cancel the show entirely, can Producer recover the ***profits*** that it claims it would have made had the show opened on time? _____

111. Tom Johns, a singer, contracts to perform for one week in the floor show at the Starburst Hotel, for the sum of $25,000.

   a. Assume Starburst management notifies Johns well in advance of his starting date that it has changed its mind and has hired someone else for the week in question. Can Johns recover the full $25,000 from Starburst? _____

   b. In a suit brought by Johns against Starburst, is the burden on Johns to prove that he could not find other suitable employment during the week in question? _____

c. Assume that Johns had started to perform as agreed, but the third night he showed up drunk, got in a fight with the management, walked off the job, and refused to return. Starburst rushed in Danny Davis, Jr., as a replacement. Can Johns recover anything from Starburst for the two nights he worked? _____

d. Would the answer to the preceding question be the same if (instead of walking off the job) Johns had become seriously ill and was unable to perform for the balance of the week? _____

112. Alpha hires Builder to remodel her kitchen, as per agreed plans, for a total price of $14,000, due on completion, and which (after deducting the cost of labor and materials) will result in a net profit of $2,000 to Builder.

    a. If, before Builder starts the job or incurs any costs, Alpha notifies Builder that she has changed her mind and does not wish to proceed, can Builder still recover his lost profits ($2,000)? _____

    b. Would the answer to the preceding question be the same if Alpha proved that Builder had free time as a result of not having to remodel her kitchen and made no effort to seek other jobs during this period? _____

    c. Assume that Alpha had insisted on the following provision in the contract: "In event Builder fails to complete the work by (agreed date), he must pay Alpha $500 for each day's delay thereafter." If there is a delay in completion which is Builder's fault, can Alpha recover $500 per day in addition to her other damages? _____

113. Acme orders 1,000 Frisbees from Baker and pays a premium price of $1.50 each (regular price is $1 each) in consideration of Baker's promise to deliver no later than July 1. The contract also provides that if Baker is late in delivery, he must pay Acme $500 as a "penalty." If Baker is two weeks late in delivery, but Acme suffers *no* actual damage because of the delay, can it recover the $500? _____

Answers to Review Questions

1.	**YES**	A guaranty of an *existing* debt must be supported by consideration to be enforceable. However, most courts will enforce a written guaranty which *recites consideration* (even though the consideration has *not* in fact been paid). [pp. 7, 8]
2.a.	**YES (modern view)**	Modern courts hold that forbearance to sue is a valid consideration if the claimant *honestly* believes they have a valid claim *regardless of the reasonableness* of their belief. [p. 9]
b.	**PROBABLY**	Some authorities (including the Restatement) take the view that a *written release constitutes consideration* even if there is neither a reasonable basis for the claim released nor a good faith belief in its validity. [p. 10]
3.a.	**NO**	Retailer gave no consideration because her promise to purchase as many as she "chooses" was an illusory promise. *Note:* Manufacturer's agreement also cannot be enforced as a "firm offer" because it was oral. "Firm offers" between merchants must be signed and in *writing*. [U.C.C. § 2–205] [pp. 11–12, 82, 84–85]
b.	**YES**	This would be a *"requirements" contract*, and thus Retailer's promise would not be illusory. [pp. 21–22]
4.a.	**NO**	At least under the doctrinal rule, a provision giving one side the right to cancel *at will and without notice* renders that promise illusory; hence it is not consideration and there is no contract, so the other party is not bound. [p. 14] Depending on the facts, courts may be motivated to find a way around this rule if possible (*e.g.*, to locate some consideration, however small, in *B*'s promise).
b.	**YES**	*B* has made a real promise, since it *must supply* *A*'s service requirements for a minimum of 30 days. [pp. 14, 16] Therefore, *B*'s promise constitutes consideration, and the parties have a contract, so *A* is bound.
c.	**YES (modern view)**	Even though the term "absolute discretion" is used, the modern (and U.C.C.) interpretation requires the exercise of *good faith*; hence there is no power to terminate at will, and the promise therefore is not illusory. [pp. 17, 19]
5.	**YES**	Even though a minor's promise is voidable, it is *sufficient consideration* to support a counterpromise. Thus, a minor can enforce a contract even though it cannot be enforced against the minor. [p. 16]
6.	**YES**	A *conditional* promise is sufficient consideration provided the condition does not give the promisor the alternative of canceling the obligation. Here, *B* had no such right, and hence its promise is good consideration. [p. 17]
7.	**NO**	Even if Broker did not expressly promise to do anything, there was at least an *implied promise* to use *reasonable or best efforts* to find a buyer, because this was a contract for exclusive dealing. This implied

		promise is sufficient consideration to support Homeowner's promise to pay a commission. [p. 20]
8.	NO	It would be against public policy to allow a public officer to claim a reward for performing an act which is within the scope of her duties per the legal duty rule. In this case, the officer had a *public* duty to capture the robber. Thus, she is not entitled to recover the reward. (*Compare:* If the acts required to obtain the reward were *not within the scope* of the officer's preexisting duty, the officer would be able to claim the reward.) [pp. 24–25]
9.	PROBABLY NOT	At least under the traditional rule, courts would *refuse* to enforce the promise on the ground that Andre was already under a contractual duty to perform, and his continued performance therefore imposes no "legal detriment" under the legal duty rule. A modern trend is to enforce the promise *without consideration* if the unforeseeable difficulties render the demand for additional compensation *fair* and equitable in light of the circumstances. (The U.C.C. permits modification of a contract for the sale of goods without consideration, but the contract here is one for services rather than for the sale of goods.) [pp. 26, 29]
10.	SPLIT OF AUTHORITY	Yes under the majority rule, although not under the minority view. *Note:* This is a case where the preexisting duty is owed to a *third person* (Builder), rather than the promisor (Owner). [p. 28]
11.a.	NO	Under the legal duty rule, payment of a lesser sum in exchange for discharge of the preexisting debt is not sufficient consideration on its own for the discharge. But payment *before maturity* or in a *different medium* are two of the many changes to the original transaction that can constitute consideration. [p. 32]
12.a.	NO	A promise based on *"moral consideration" or "past consideration,"* because of gratitude or a prior favor, is not enforceable in most jurisdictions. Although some courts hold that a promise based on a moral obligation is enforceable to the extent the promisor was enriched by the promisee's action, in this case it is not clear that Clutz ever came under a moral obligation. [pp. 43, 48, 50]
b.	YES	Under these circumstances, the promise would have tended to *induce* Able to help in the completion of the garage. Hence, there would be bargained-for consideration for Clutz's promise, and it would be enforceable. [p. 5]
13.a.	NO	Minister did not *bargain* for Parishioner's promise. (It relates to Minister's prior services and hence would be a case of "past consideration.") [pp. 5, 48, 50–51]
b.	NO	The fact that a promise is in writing does not make it enforceable. By statute in some states a writing may raise a *presumption* that there is an adequate consideration, but that presumption is rebuttable by proof of the real consideration (or lack thereof) for the promise. [p. 44]
c.	DEPENDS	On whether such reliance could have been reasonably expected. Under the doctrine of "promissory estoppel," courts will enforce a *relied-upon* promise if the reliance was *reasonably expected* by Parishioner. (However, under modern law, the promise may be enforced only to the extent of the reliance.) [pp. 46–47]

d.	**YES**	This appears to be a bargain; Minister has bound themselves to perform services on a condition beyond their control. The fact that Minister's promise may have little tangible value is immaterial *if* the promise is really bargained-for, as is the fact that Church, rather than Parishioner, receives the "benefit" of Minister's promise. (But note that if the promise is put in merely for show, as a mere recital of consideration, it may be deemed merely nominal consideration, and Parishioner's promise might therefore be unenforceable.) [pp. 5, 7, 17]
14.a.	**NO (majority)**	Most states require that the promise or acknowledgment of a debt barred by the statute of limitations be in *writing* or that the debtor make part payment of the barred debt. Thus, Debtor's oral promise would not be enforceable. [p. 49]
b.	**NO**	The courts may imply a promise to pay from an *acknowledgment* of the debt, but a promise cannot be implied from a *refusal* to pay the barred debt. [p. 49]
c.	**NO**	But Friend can enforce the promise on the terms contained therein—*i.e.*, $700 when Debtor sells the car—because it is the *new promise* and not the old debt that is enforceable. [p. 48]
d.	**MAYBE**	In "a.," Friend might be able to enforce the *oral* promise. *Reason:* In most states there is *no* requirement that a promise to pay a debt discharged by bankruptcy be in writing. However, under the Bankruptcy Code, a promise to pay a debt discharged in bankruptcy is enforceable only if several stringent requirements are met, and not enough information is given here to determine whether, under the Code, this agreement is enforceable. [p. 50]
15.	**YES**	Sherry's preexisting duty (to pay $3,000) was *voidable* because of the fraud. She had the option of rescinding or ratifying the sale. Her new promise is enforceable *without new consideration* and is not subject to the fraud defense. [p. 49]
16.	**SPLIT OF AUTHORITY**	Farmer's services were apparently rendered *without* expectation of payment and are therefore regarded as mere "moral" or "past" consideration for Nia's promise; hence, unenforceable in most states. However, the trend of authority is to enforce such a promise to the extent of the benefit conferred. [pp. 48, 50–51]
17.	**PROBABLY NOT**	The promise to discharge the son's debt is apparently based only on moral or past consideration and is not binding on the promisor. Even under the modern view, a promise based on a moral obligation will normally not be enforced where the promisor *did not receive a direct economic benefit*, although in principle a court could determine that Will's father received a "benefit" of some kind from the loan to Will. [p. 51]
18.	**NO**	Whether a person intends to be contractually bound is measured by an *objective* standard. Thus, if a *reasonable* person would have realized that Amy's offer was made in jest (no true bargaining intent), there is no contract—even if Buford took her seriously. [p. 55]
19.a.	**YES**	A contract may be "implied in fact" from the *conduct of the parties.* Here, the fact that Alice maintained an account with Elite indicates that she had done business there before. Hence, she should have known that

they would bill her the regular store prices, and by telephoning an order without mentioning price she *impliedly agreed* to pay that price, unless it is manifestly unreasonable. [p. 57]

b. **YES** Again, a contract may be implied from the *conduct of the parties.* John's continuing performance was an implied offer to extend their contract each year, and Ben's acceptance is implied from his conduct in permitting John to continue and by paying the contract rate for the first two years. [p. 57]

c. **NO** Because Ivy was unconscious, she did not expressly or impliedly agree to anything. However, Dudley can still recover from Ivy through an implied-in-law contract in order to prevent unjust enrichment (and in cases such as this, to encourage rendering services in an emergency). As a matter of policy, the law will fictionally imply a request by Ivy for Dudley's services. However, in implied-in-law contracts a party may recover only the *reasonable value* of their services, which might be less than the $68,500 billed by Dudley. [p. 58]

20.a. **NO** An offer must evidence a *present* contractual intent. Desperate's words suggest an *invitation* to Buyer to make an offer. Buyer's purported "acceptance" is at most an offer, which Desperate would then be free to accept or reject. [p. 59]

b. **NO** Advertisements to the public are generally held to be mere *invitations* for an offer, on the ground that the advertiser has not committed itself to an unlimited quantity of the goods. [p. 60]

c. **DEPENDS** On the *parties' intent* as to the effect of the letter agreement. If both parties intend to be bound only by the written contract, the "letter agreement" would be deemed preliminary only. Otherwise, it will be enforceable. (This assumes that the letter of intent would be sufficiently definite to enforce but for the addition of the words "formal contract to follow.") [p. 145]

d. **PROBABLY** "Quoting" of prices is commonly understood as only *inviting* an offer. But here, because it was directed to a specific person (*B*), and *A* added the words "for immediate acceptance," most authorities would hold this manifests an intent to make a binding offer. [p. 61]

21.a. **NO** The advertisement of an auction is an *invitation* for offers and is not in itself an offer. [p. 62]

b. **YES** Unless the property is *explicitly* put up for sale "without reserve," the auction is deemed to be "with reserve," which permits the seller to withdraw the goods at any time before the fall of the hammer (acceptance). [pp. 62–63]

c. **NO** Even though the *seller* is bound to sell the goods at an auction without reserve, this does not prevent a bidder from revoking their "acceptance" prior to the fall of the hammer. [p. 62]

22.a. **YES** An offer terminates by operation of law after expiration of the period of time specified in the offer. The period commences to run on the date of actual *receipt* of the offer or on the date it would normally be received. Because the offer was received on March 3 and there does not appear to be an unreasonable delay in the transmission, the five-day acceptance period would start to run on March 3. As the

		acceptance was dispatched within five days, a contract was formed. [pp. 65, 104]
b.	NO	Destruction of the subject matter prior to acceptance terminates the offer. [p. 89]
c.	NO	The general rule is that offers are revocable even though there may be an express promise not to revoke. And a written offer can be revoked orally. The revocation must be communicated to the offeree and becomes effective on *receipt*. Since A learned of the revocation prior to A's attempt to accept, no contract was formed. [pp. 80, 82]
d.	YES	*If* the offeror receives *consideration* to keep the offer open, they cannot revoke it during the stated period because an *option* will be created. *Compare:* Under the U.C.C., a written offer by a merchant, containing words of firmness, cannot be revoked for the time stated or a reasonable time (but in no event more than three months) even absent consideration. [pp. 83, 84]
e.	NO	The trend of authority is that an offeror may be estopped to revoke if the offeree has *foreseeably and reasonably* relied to their detriment on a promise to keep the offer open. [p. 83]
23.a.	NO	Byers's $4,800 counteroffer *terminated* their power of acceptance. Byers's purported acceptance thereafter did not form a contract. [p. 67]
b.	YES	The question is neither a rejection nor a counteroffer, but an *inquiry.* Sellars's offer would therefore still be open, and Byers's acceptance would create a contract. [p. 67]
c.	YES	Generally, an acceptance is effective on dispatch unless there has been a *previous* rejection. In such event, acceptance is effective only on *receipt.* However, since Sellars in fact received the acceptance prior to the rejection, a contract was formed. (But if Sellars regards the later-arriving rejection as a repudiation of the acceptance, and relies on it, Byers will be estopped from enforcing the contract.) [p. 112]
d.	YES	Under the mailbox rule, the contract was formed on dispatch of the acceptance, even though Sellars *learned* of the rejection first. (If, however, Sellars *relied* on the earlier-received rejection and contracted to sell the property to a different buyer, Byers should be *estopped* from enforcing the contract.) [p. 111]
24.a.	NO	To be effective, an acceptance must be *unequivocal* (here, Gates has apparently put off a decision and acknowledged only the receipt of the offer). [pp. 67, 68]
b.	DEPENDS	Ordinarily, an acceptance must be a *mirror image* of an offer (except if U.C.C. Article 2 applies). Because Blue, Inc.'s order did not specify time for provision of services, the law will imply a term of "reasonableness" based on the nature of the contract, custom and usage in the community, and prior dealings between the parties. If six weeks is reasonable, the variance in the "acceptance" would not prevent formation of a contract. [pp. 69, 137]
25.a.	NO	Father's offer is for a unilateral contract. (He is bargaining for Daughter's lifetime care, not for a mere promise.) Since the performance will take time to complete and the offeree has *started*

		performance, the offer *cannot* be revoked under the principle of Restatement Second section 45. [p. 86]
b.	**NO**	Father specifically did *not* bind Daughter to anything. Her caring for Father was merely the start of her acceptance of his offer for a unilateral contract. [p. 97]
c.	**YES**	The offeree's knowledge of an offer for a unilateral contract is sufficient for their act to count as an acceptance if it meets the terms of the offer. The offeree need not be motivated by the offer for a there to be a unilateral contract. [p. 96]
26.	**YES**	In a bilateral contract situation, the offeree must use "reasonable efforts" to communicate the return promise *unless* the offer expressly *dispenses* with notice (which seems to be the case here). [p. 93]
27.	**YES**	Ordinarily the offeree of a *unilateral* contract need not notify the offeror that they intend to perform or are performing the act. [p. 94]
28.	**NO**	While the offeree ordinarily does not need to give notice that performance has begun, they usually do have to give notice within a *reasonable time* after performance is completed, unless the offeror has waived notice or the performance itself would come to the offeror's attention in reasonable course. If the offeree does not give such notice, the offeror's obligation is discharged. [pp. 94–95]
29.	**NO (majority rule)**	Even though Roz performed the act bargained for, she did not do so with *knowledge* of the offer. Hence, no contract. [p. 96]
30.	**(B)**	Where it is clear from the circumstances that the offeror is not interested in a return promise, the offer is for a *unilateral* contract and can be accepted only by performance. In (A), (C), and (D) it is not clear whether the offer can be accepted only by performance or whether a promise to perform would be sufficient. In such cases, Restatement Second construes the offers as inviting acceptance *either* by performance or by a *promise* to perform (*i.e.*, bilateral contract). [p. 98]
31.a.	**YES**	Under U.C.C. section 2–206(1)(b), an offer to buy goods for prompt or current shipment can be accepted *either* by notice (promising to ship) *or by actual shipment.* Note that when an offeree chooses to accept by shipment, they must also *notify* the offeror that shipment has been made "within a reasonable time"; otherwise, the offeror could treat the offer as having lapsed before acceptance. [U.C.C. § 2–207] Here, however, *B* had no opportunity to notify *A* of shipment; *A*'s revocation therefore was too late. [p. 98]
b.	**YES**	Shipment is an acceptance under section 2–206(*1*)(b), above, even if the goods shipped are *nonconforming.* However, the shipment of such goods is also a *breach* of the contract formed by the shipment, so that the buyer can either reject the goods or take delivery and sue the seller for any damages. (The seller can avoid this by notifying the buyer that the shipment is offered only as an *accommodation.*) [p. 99]
32.	**NO**	Anita's letter cannot be regarded as an "acceptance" of any outstanding offer by Brendan. Rather, it is itself an offer. The mere fact that an offeror states that silence will constitute an acceptance does not deprive the offeree of the right to remain silent *without* acceptance.

			(*Compare:* If Brendan had remained silent *with the intent* of accepting, silence would constitute an acceptance.) [pp. 99–101]
33.	a.	**YES**	Under the mailbox rule, an acceptance of an offer is effective upon proper dispatch (mailing), even if received late or not received at all. [p. 104 *et seq.*]
	b.	**NO**	If an acceptance is misaddressed or sent by unauthorized means, it is effective as an acceptance only if it arrives on time. Here *A*'s offer requested an *"immediate"* reply, whereas *B*'s reply was in fact received several days beyond the normal time for mail delivery. Hence it would be concluded that *A*'s offer had in fact lapsed before *B*'s purported acceptance was received. [p. 107]
34.		**NO**	An offer must be *communicated* to the offeree in order to create a power of acceptance. Bob's offer to Art was therefore *not* an acceptance of Art's offer but rather was a crossed offer. [p. 113]
35.	a.	**NO (traditional view)**	If the lease appeared on its face to be the *final and complete integration* of the parties' agreement, the parol evidence rule would bar evidence of prior inconsistent agreements—unless there is a showing of *fraud* or another exception applies. [pp. 118–120, 124]
	b.	**YES**	To explain or interpret the term "good cause." Parol evidence is always admissible in the process of *interpreting* terms used in a written agreement. (While some courts might let in the evidence in "a." above on similar grounds, most courts would say either that the term "at will" needs no explanation or that the evidence would *contradict* rather than explain the term.) [p. 125]
36.	a.	**YES**	If the offer is silent as to the time for performance, the courts will generally imply that the contract is to be performed within a *reasonable* time. (*Compare* 38.e., below. Here the term is less essential and more susceptible of objective determination.) [p. 137]
	b.	**NO**	When the *duration* of the contract is omitted from the offer, the law normally implies that the contract will last for a reasonable time. But *employment agreements* are treated differently; they are normally deemed terminable *at will* by either party regardless of how the salary is to be paid, unless the employer has specifically limited its right to terminate the employee. [pp. 137–138]
	c.	**NO**	If there is a complete gap as to the *subject matter* of the offer, there can be no contract. (No basis for implication of "reasonable" terms here.) [p. 136]
	d.	**YES**	If the term that the parties have left open is an *essential* term of the contract, the offer is deemed too uncertain and there is no legal obligation until future agreement. But selection of paint and wallpaper would seem to be only a *minor* term, hence the agreement will be deemed enforceable. If subsequently the parties cannot agree on the term, the "reasonable" test will be applied. [p. 142]
37.		**YES**	This is a typical "requirements" contract. Even though the exact quantity is not stated, it can be supplied by an *objective standard* (Carnegie's requirements). [p. 142]

38.a.	**NO**	"Agreements to agree" are too indefinite to enforce where, as here, the value of the subject matter (Bob's services) is not readily ascertainable. (Also, there is no room for implication of a promise to pay the "reasonable" value of such services, because this is *not* what the parties agreed.) [p. 142]
b.	**NO**	A promise to pay a "fair" share is *too indefinite* to enforce (same as "a.," above). [p. 137]
c.	**YES**	Here, the amount due would be ascertainable by computation (sales increase and profits therefrom); hence the agreement is sufficiently definite. The key is that the method of computation must make reference to an *objective standard* to be used. [p. 142]
d.	**YES**	Most courts would agree that whether Ebeneezer *is* "able" to pay this amount *is* capable of objective determination (*e.g.*, by evidence as to normal accounting standards and business practices). [p. 144]
e.	**NO**	The court could find that a "reasonable" salary was implied but would be *unlikely* to do so where *performance had not begun*, since there is no clear standard as to what a reasonable salary would be for such a position, and the omitted term is essential. [p. 136]
39.a.	**YES**	For the same reason as in answer 37 (except this is an "output" rather than a "requirements" contract). [p. 142]
b.	**YES**	At common law, if one party had the unlimited right or choice to set the price, the promise was deemed too indefinite and illusory. However, under section 2–305 of the U.C.C., a contract for the sale of goods in which one party sets the price is enforceable, as long as it appears the parties intended to be bound; however, Ajax must set the price in *good faith*. [p. 143]
40.a.	**YES**	The rule concerning palpable unilateral mistake applies only to mechanical errors. Unless there is a fiduciary relationship between the parties, *A*'s error in judgment as to *value* or quality—*even if known to B*—does *not* affect *B*'s rights under the contract. [p. 150]
b.	**NO**	The result is different where the mistake is a mere *mechanical* miscalculation, known to the other party. Such an offer cannot be "snapped up" by the offeree. [p. 149]
41.	**DEPENDS**	Bess is charged with knowledge that her offer was ambiguous because she owned two cars. If Abe was *also aware* that Bess owned two cars, there is a *misunderstanding*, both meanings are equally reasonable, and the contract will not be enforced if each party subjectively intended a different car. However, if Abe was not aware that Bess owned two cars, there is a binding contract on what Abe subjectively intended (the Chevrolet). [p. 114, 151]
42.	**NO**	Although provisions excusing a party from liability for ordinary negligence (but not willful misconduct) may be enforceable where the parties have equal bargaining power, here the parties do *not* have equal bargaining power. Moreover, there is a public interest in a carrier's performance. Therefore, exculpatory clauses in contracts with common carriers that exculpate the carrier from liability for bodily

			injuries caused by its negligence are generally held unenforceable as contrary to public policy. [p. 160]

43. **DOUBTFUL** — No such defense was allowed at common law. However, the U.C.C. now authorizes courts to refuse enforcement of "unconscionable" terms in contracts for the sale of goods; a *few* courts, at least, have held that *gross overcharging* by a retail seller may constitute "price unconscionability," at least in consumer transactions. The consumer would have an easier time challenging oppressive *terms* in fine print. [p. 159]

44. **YES (most states)** — A lease of land (regardless of its value or the amount of rent) for *one year or less* does *not* fall within the Statute of Frauds in most states. [p. 162]

45. **YES** — The Statute of Frauds applies to the transfer of any *interest* in real property, but an agreement to share profits or income from land *does not* constitute an "interest" in the land itself. Hence, it is not within the Statute and can be enforced even though it is oral. [p. 163]

46. a. **NO** — An oral contract for the sale of goods priced at *$500 or more* is unenforceable under the Statute of Frauds, except to the extent that it has already been performed. [p. 164]

   b. **NO** — Prior to enactment of the U.C.C., many courts held that a down payment made the entire contract enforceable. But under the U.C.C., the contract is enforceable only *proportionately* (to the extent of "goods for which payment has been made and accepted"). Here, Benny can recover his $200 or enforce Ajax's promise as to 200 Frisbees only. [p. 164]

   c. **YES** — A contract to manufacture special goods for the buyer that are *not suitable for resale to others* (as here, with *B*'s own advertisements thereon) is enforceable once the seller has made a "substantial beginning" in their manufacture. [U.C.C. § 2–201] [p. 164]

47. **NONE** — The relevant part of the Statute of Frauds covers only contracts that *cannot possibly* be performed within one year from the making of the contract. [p. 166]

   (A) The lifetime employee may die within one year. (But note that some states have statutes that explicitly require lifetime contracts to be in writing.) [p. 166]

   (B) The lease may be terminated within one year.

   (C) The option may be exercised within one year.

48. a. **NO** — Under its *suretyship provision*, the Statute of Frauds requires a promise to answer for the debt of another to be memorialized in writing. [p. 167]

   b. **NO** — The Statute of Frauds does not apply where the promise is made directly *to the debtor.* Such a promise is enforceable even though oral, assuming there is consideration. [p. 167]

49. a. **NO** — The memorandum omitted one essential term—the *price*. [p. 168]

   b. **YES** — Under the U.C.C., *less completeness is required;* even though the writing omits an important term (here, price) it will be sufficient if it

c.	**YES**	indicates that a contract for sale has been made and it indicates the quantity term. [p. 168]
		At common law. But note that some states have "equal dignity" statutes that provide that if a contract is required to be in writing under the Statute of Frauds, ***the agent's authority*** to execute such a contract ***must also be in writing.*** [p. 169]
50.	**YES (as to both parties)**	Whether the contract is deemed ***voidable*** (unenforceable) or ***void*** (no contract at all), ***either*** party may still obtain restitution, in order to avoid an unjust result, for ***benefits*** conferred even though there is no recovery under the contract. [p. 171]
51.	**PROBABLY YES**	Many courts hold that if a party represents that they will cause the agreement to be formalized in writing, they will be estopped from asserting the Statute of Frauds as a defense. Furthermore, there is a modern trend to enforce promises that are within the Statute but have been relied on. [p. 172]
52.	**NOT AS A CONTRACT**	A minor's promise (even for necessaries) cannot be enforced as a contract. ***However,*** the other party (Polly) may recover the reasonable value of necessaries furnished to a minor in restitution, and the written promise is evidence of the value. [p. 172]
53.	**YES**	Emotional instability does not mean a person lacks contractual capacity. A promise is enforceable unless the promisor was so deficient as to ***lack understanding*** of what they were doing. (*Compare:* Result would be different if promisor had ***previously been adjudged*** incompetent.) [p. 173]
54.	**YES (most courts)**	A valid contract is not made illegal by knowledge that the subject matter will be used for an illegal purpose that does not involve great moral turpitude. *Compare:* If Slicker somehow ***facilitates*** the illegality—*e.g.*, sets up the apparatus for Leroy at a hidden location—Slicker will not be permitted to recover. [p. 174]
55.a.	**NO**	When a license or permit is required for the purpose of ***protecting*** the public from unqualified persons, a contract for services entered into by an unlicensed person is generally held illegal and unenforceable. [p. 175]
b.	**NO**	When a license is required for protective purposes, the courts have refused to permit ***any recovery*** by the unlicensed person. [p. 175]
56.	**YES**	Under the general rule, Laura qualifies as a creditor beneficiary. A ***supposed*** or ***asserted*** duty to a third party is sufficient to create creditor beneficiary status. [pp. 179–180]
57.	**YES**	A third-party beneficiary need not be individually named in the agreement. It is sufficient if the ***class*** of persons of which they are a member and for whose benefit the contract was made is sufficiently identified. [p. 181]
58.a.	**SPLIT OF AUTHORITY**	The issue here is whether Sam's rights have so ***"vested"*** as to prevent the contracting parties from changing their agreement. Under the modern Restatement Second view, a creditor beneficiary's rights vest when they assent to the contract, bring suit, or detrimentally rely thereon. Under this view, Sam would have a valid claim. The

		Restatement First view is that a creditor beneficiary's rights vest only if the beneficiary has brought suit or detrimentally relied. Under this view, Sam would not have a claim. (However, detrimental reliance might be found here, for example, if Sam failed to take some action to enforce his claim that he otherwise would have taken but for Jewell's promise—*e.g.*, filing suit to attach Dominic's assets or to garnish the funds payable on the sale of Dominic's business. If so, Sam would have a claim even under the Restatement First view.) [p. 190]
	b. **YES**	As between Jewell and Dominic, Jewell is now the primary obligor on the debt to Sam (Jewell having assumed the debt as part of the purchase); Dominic is *surety* for Jewell's performance. And, the surety can sue in equity for specific performance without first paying off the debt themselves. [p. 189]
59.a.	**SPLIT OF AUTHORITY**	Most courts would say *"no"* applying the same rules as above; *i.e.*, a third-party beneficiary's rights vest only when they learn of and assent to the deal, file suit, or otherwise detrimentally rely thereon. Here, the donee beneficiaries (the parents) did not find out about the discount until *after* the promise had been rescinded. A few authorities, however, take the view that a *donee* beneficiary's right vests automatically on the making of the contract (knowledge and assent not required). Under this view, the parents would prevail even though Jewell and Dominic later agreed to eliminate the provision in question. [p. 190]
	b. **YES**	The promisor can always assert against a third-party beneficiary whatever defenses she could have asserted against the *promisee* (Dominic) in connection with formation and performance of the contract. Here, the defense of fraud or material breach could have been asserted against the seller (Dominic) and therefore also can be asserted against the third-party beneficiaries. [p. 188]
60.a.	**YES**	The primary purpose of the contract is determined by the *promisee's* (Father's) *intent*. It would appear from these facts that Father agreed to forbear from selling *in order to obtain a benefit* for Daughter. She would therefore have the right to enforce the contract against Son. [p. 182]
	b. **NO**	The primary purpose of the agreement is to benefit *A*, rather than *A*'s creditor, *B*. [p. 182]
61.a.	**NO**	One who only purchases *"subject to"* a mortgage has made no agreement to pay it. Hence, no third-party beneficiary contract exists upon which any claim of personal liability could be based. [p. 183]
	b. **SPLIT OF AUTHORITY**	One view is that *C* is not liable because no actual duty to Bank was owed by *B* (*see* previous answer) and therefore there was no liability to "assume." The other view is that *C* is liable: *B*'s apparent purpose was to guard against *B*'s *supposed* liability, and that is enough to create a creditor beneficiary contract. [p. 184]
	c. **YES**	The original obligor remains liable (as surety) notwithstanding another's assumption of the mortgage debt. [p. 183]
62.a.	**YES**	A gratuitous assignment is irrevocable if made in a *signed writing* that is *delivered* to the assignee. [p. 197]

b.	**YES**	An assignment given for ***consideration*** is irrevocable, whether oral or in writing. [p. 197]
63.a.	**YES**	Future rights under an existing contract are assignable even though the right is conditional. Hence, even though Amy's wages will be paid only if she remains employed by Homecare Products, the assignment is valid. (*But note:* There are often ***statutory restrictions*** on wage assignments.) [pp. 199, 202202]
b.	**YES**	Even though Amy's commissions will be entirely dependent on her selling property, a ***continuing business relationship*** exists between her and Ajax, and her "business expectancies" are held assignable by most (not all) courts. [p. 199]
c.	**NO**	Because there is as yet no existing royalty contract. Rights under a contract ***not yet in existence*** are not assignable. (However, if she does make a purported assignment thereof for a consideration, it will be treated as a contract *to* assign, and equity will grant specific performance if she ever finds a publisher.) [p. 200]
d.	**DEPENDS**	On whether Claude's designing for Amy so intimately involves her own personality or appearance that it would be ***unreasonable*** to require Claude to design for someone else (Bella). [p. 194]
e.	**NO**	This is a "requirements" contract. Henry's "requirements" might vary significantly from Amy's and thus ***materially vary*** Shea Grower's duties under the contract. [p. 195]
f.	**NO**	Because it might ***materially increase the burden or risk*** assumed by the insurance company (Emma's operations might not be as safe as Amy's). If assignment of a right would increase the burden or risk in any material way, the right is nonassignable. [p. 195]
g.	**NO**	When personal credit is involved, any substitution of debtors would ***materially vary*** the risk. Hence, the right to borrow money from another is a nonassignable right. [p. 195]
64.a.	**YES**	Because of a policy favoring free assignability, the provision would probably be construed as preventing only delegation of the performance of duties. Such a provision destroys the ***right,*** not the ***power***, to make an assignment, despite the fact that the obligor will have an action for breach of the contractual provision. [p. 200]
b.	**YES**	Even though this provision is broad enough to affect Aaron's power as well as his right to assign, under the U.C.C. such restraints are normally unenforceable where the only right involved is to the ***receipt of money*** (here, an account). [p. 201]
c.	**NO**	A contract for plumbing installation is probably not a personal service contract. Even so, the provision against assignment of "the contract" is generally held ***effective*** to bar any delegation of duties. [p. 201]
65.a.	**YES**	Lack of contractual intent is a defense to contract ***formation*** that can be asserted by an obligor against any assignee. [p. 203]
b.	**YES**	An assignee takes subject to all defenses against the assignor ***arising under the contract***, even when the defense accrues after notification

		of the assignment (*except* where negotiable instruments are involved). [p. 203]
66.	**YES**	An assignee takes *subject to* defenses arising both before and after the obligor receives notice of the assignment. [p. 203]
67.	**CHRIS**	Because the assignment to Bob was gratuitous and oral, it was revocable and was *revoked* by the subsequent assignment to Chris. [p. 205]
68.a.	**SPLIT OF AUTHORITY**	The "New York rule" is first in time (Bank); the "English rule" is first to give notice (Finance Co.); the "Massachusetts rule" is first in time subject to certain exceptions that are inapplicable here (Bank). [p. 206]
b.	**NO**	The U.C.C. provisions for filing of financing statements do not apply to wage claims. [p. 207]
c.	**NO**	Under either the New York, English, or Massachusetts rule, an assignee who obtains payment is deemed to have a stronger equity and therefore prevails. [p. 206]
69.a.	**NO**	A duty to perform personal services is *nondelegable.* Indeed, Actor's attempt to delegate his duties may be regarded as an anticipatory breach of contract. [p. 209]
b.	**PROBABLY NOT**	A mere delegation of duties does not excuse the delegating party from their duty to perform. They *remain secondarily liable* in the event the delegee fails to perform. However, the result is different if there is a *novation*—i.e., if Producer was willing to discharge Actor from his contract and to make a *new contract* with Standby. Under the circumstances of this case, there was probably an implied novation, because once Producer accepts Standby, it is unrealistic to say that Producer continues to look to Actor as secondarily responsible for full performance. [pp. 207, 209]
70.	**PROBABLY NOT**	The issue here is whether any *promise* by Childs to perform can be implied from their mere acceptance of the assignment. The traditional view was that it could *not*. While the modern trend is to imply a promise if consistent with the *parties' probable intent*—i.e., if Childs was to receive the benefits, they probably were also intended to bear the burdens—Restatement Second "expresses no opinion as to whether" this modern view applies (as here) to *sales of land.* [p. 210]
71.	**NO**	A cause of action for breach of contract lies only where the defendant has failed to perform an *unconditional* duty to perform. The issue here is whether the quoted phrase *conditioned* Able's promise to purchase Baker's house or was a *promise* binding Able to obtain the financing (so that he is in breach by failing to obtain it). In determining this, courts look to the *intent of the parties* as evidenced by the words used, custom and usage, and all the surrounding circumstances. Here, the word "if" suggests a condition, as does the fact that the event (obtaining financing) was not something subject to Able's absolute control; as a matter of practical usage, most purchasers of real estate would regard the purchase as being conditional on obtaining satisfactory financing. Able may have implicitly promised to use reasonable efforts to insure that the condition was fulfilled, but he apparently did use such efforts. [pp. 216, 218–219]

72.	**NO**	The quoted phrase would be construed as an express *condition* on Owner's duty to pay a commission because this is consistent with parties' probable intent (no sale, no commission due). The fact that a third party is to perform supports construction as a condition. [p. 218]
73.	**YES**	Either on the theory that the quoted phrase was *not* a condition at all but only a *promise* as to the approximate time for repayment, or on the theory that Borrower implicitly promised to use reasonable efforts to become able to repay the loan. [pp. 218–220]
74.a.	**PROBABLY**	Time is ordinarily *not* of the essence unless expressly made so. Moreover, the preferred construction of a doubtful provision is that it is a promise rather than a condition of Club's obligation to pay. [pp. 219, 222]
b.	**YES**	Failure to perform a promise constitutes a *breach* for which at least *nominal damages* (*infra*) would be available. [p. 217]
75.a.	**YES**	Unless otherwise agreed (by credit terms), payment is due on *delivery* of goods. [U.C.C.§ 2–310] [p. 140]
b.	**YES**	The delivery of the goods was an implied condition *precedent* to Buyer's duty to pay. The burden of proof as to the occurrence of a condition precedent is always on the *plaintiff* (here, Seller). [p. 220, 221]
c.	**NO**	The right of return would probably be regarded as a *true condition subsequent* (*i.e.*, it would cut off Buyer's otherwise absolute duty to pay for the goods received). The burden of proof as to the occurrence of such a condition is a matter of *defense*—in this case, on Buyer. [pp. 220, 221]
d.	**NO**	Buyer's duty to pay is conditioned on the Fair's being held. Although *worded* as a condition subsequent (Buyer reserving right to "cancel"), it is really a condition precedent in effect—*i.e.*, no Fair, no duty to pay ever arises! But because it is *worded* as a condition subsequent, most courts would still impose the *burden of proof* on the defendant-promisor (Buyer). [p. 221]
76.a.	**NO**	Most courts hold that where the approval or satisfaction of a third person (here, Water Board) is a condition, strict literal compliance is required—*i.e.*, it is *immaterial* whether the third person or agency was "reasonable" in withholding its approval. Dissatisfaction must be *honest and in good faith,* and although *reasonableness* is irrelevant here, a lack of it can be *evidence* that the promisor's dissatisfaction was not in good faith. [p. 222]
b.	**NO**	As long as Farmer was acting *honestly* and in *good faith* in finding the water unsatisfactory. A condition of satisfaction is given literal effect where the object is a matter of personal taste (and water quality would seem to fit in this category). [p. 222]
77.	**YES**	On the theory that conditions "necessary" to the performance are *"implied in fact"* conditions to the contract. The test is simply whether the parties, as reasonable persons, would have agreed on the condition had they thought about it. (Here, the right to show the inside of the house would seem "necessary" to procure a purchaser for the house.)

		Failure of such a "necessary" condition excuses any duty of counterperformance—*i.e.*, Owner's refusal to allow Broker to show the house excuses the condition that Broker obtain a purchaser for the house, and it renders Owner's duty to pay absolute. [p. 226]
78.	**PROBABLY**	Owner's performance (to deliver the deed and to repair the toilet) was an implied condition precedent to Buyer's duty to pay. However, an ***implied condition can be excused by substantial performance*** (*infra*), and here the value of what has been tendered (title to the house) would probably be considered "substantial performance." Failure to repair the toilet would be an "immaterial breach" (*infra*) for which Buyer would be entitled to an ***offset*** of money damages. *Caution:* The result would be opposite if the parties made repair of the toilet an express condition (*e.g.*, "Buyer to pay *only when* title passes and toilet fixed"). In such a case, most courts would hold Buyer under *no* duty to perform. [pp. 227, 231]
79.a.	**NO**	Payment by a Buyer is a promise to perform, as is delivery of deed by Owner. But each party's performance is also an ***implied condition concurrent*** to the other party's performance. The result is that until Owner delivers (or tenders) the deed, Buyer's ***duty to pay does not arise***, and vice versa. [p. 228]
b.	**NO**	For the same reasons. [p. 228]
80.	**YES**	Unless the parties otherwise agree, payment of the *full* purchase price is an ***implied condition precedent*** to the seller's duty to deliver goods. [p. 227]
81.	**NO**	Where no time is fixed for the performance of either promise, each is an ***implied condition concurrent*** to the other. Neither can place the other in breach without tendering their own performance, and neither need proceed with performance unless the other is proceeding apace. [p. 228]
82.a.	**YES**	Under the doctrine of ***prevention.*** If Arthur has tendered the care for which Uncle was bargaining and Uncle has refused it, the condition (Arthur's performance) is excused, and Uncle's duty to perform is absolute. (*Note:* The ***remedy*** here would probably be to impose a constructive trust against Uncle's estate at time of his death—"quasi-specific performance"; *see* Remedies Summary.) [p. 223]
b.	**PROBABLY NOT**	This is the kind of risk one ***assumes*** in a contract of this type. There is not sufficient "wrongfulness" to constitute prevention. Wrongfulness does not require a showing of bad faith or malice. Rather, it essentially means that in light of the terms of the contract, the objective of the contract, and the circumstances, the other party would not have reasonably anticipated such conduct. [p. 223]
83.	**NO**	The doctrine of prevention does *not* apply here. Courts generally hold that prevention exists only when a party has done something affirmative to hinder occurrence of a condition (here, "closing of sale"). ***Mere inaction is not enough.*** Although every contract implies a promise of cooperation, passiveness is not deemed a breach of covenant. [p. 223]

84.	**YES**	Owner's sale of the property prevented Manager from rendering the services contracted for by Owner. Thus, Manager's further performance was *excused.* The majority view is that a cause of action arises immediately (Manager need not wait five years). Manager is entitled to recover 5% of the rentals likely to be received during the next four years, less whatever he earns by reason of being excused from performing such services. (*See* discussion of mitigation, *infra.*) [pp. 223, 240]
85.a.	**NO**	Under the doctrine of *prospective inability to perform,* if it *reasonably* appeared that Owner would be unable to deliver clear title, Purchaser would be entitled to rely thereon in *suspending* his own performance until it appeared that Owner could perform, meaning that Purchaser would have a reasonable period after June 1 within which to pay. [p. 229]
b.	**SPLIT OF AUTHORITY**	Some courts hold Purchaser is *justified* in canceling in light of Owner's prospective inability to perform. Other courts assert that there must be *detrimental reliance* on the prospective inability to perform (*e.g.,* Purchaser actually buying another house, etc.) before Purchaser is excused. [239]
86.a.	**NO**	Again, under the doctrine of prospective inability to perform (the seller having contracted to convey the same property to another), the purchaser is justified in changing his position in reliance; having done so, Bob is discharged from the contract. [p. 230]
b.	**NO**	If it reasonably appeared that Sam could obtain another car like the one in question within the 10-day period, there is no prospective inability to perform. [230]
c.	**YES**	Insolvency or bankruptcy of the other party may be relevant if credit was to be extended, but it is immaterial where (as here) a *cash sale* is involved. (*Note:* Under U.C.C. section 2–609, Sam would have been entitled to demand assurances of performance from Bob upon learning of his bankruptcy.) [p. 230]
87.a.	**YES**	Inability to obtain financing does *not* constitute impossibility of performance; hence Promoter's erecting and operating the car wash was not excused. However, the rent provision is probably too speculative to enforce because the profits from the new carwash are too uncertain (at least without more specific evidence). Owner would probably be limited to the reasonable value of the use of the property. [p. 241, 253]
b.	**YES**	The condition that there be "profits" is excused under the doctrine of prevention. Promoter's acts show breach of her *implied promise* to act reasonably in computation of "profits." Owner should recover a third of whatever profits *would have been* realized but for the excessive salaries charged (*i.e.,* using normal accounting and business practices). [p. 225]
c.	**DEPENDS**	On whether Promoter acted *reasonably* in closing down the car wash. If in fact it reasonably appeared no "profits" could be earned, Promoter was *not* obligated to remain in business at a loss. (*Compare:* If the lease required rent payments based on a percentage of *sales or gross*

		receipts—rather than net profits—the result would differ; *i.e.*, courts would find an implied promise to remain in business throughout the lease, whether run profitably or not.) [p. 223]
88.	**NO**	A party to a contract cannot claim breach until the other party's performance is due. The one exception is the doctrine of repudiation (anticipatory breach). However, this doctrine does not apply unless there are executory duties on ***both*** sides. Here, Wife has fully performed her side; only Husband's duties are executory. Hence, Wife cannot sue until the due date of each installment. [p. 239]
89.	**YES**	Mere expression by the manufacturer of ***doubt*** as to ability to perform is not a repudiation (which requires words that are positive and unequivocal). Beta therefore was ***not*** justified in canceling the contract and hence is in breach. *Note:* Under the U.C.C., Beta's remedy was to ***demand adequate assurances of performance*** by Ace. If Ace had failed to provide adequate assurances within a "commercially reasonable" period of time, ***then*** the failure would be treated as a repudiation of the contract by Ace. [U.C.C. § 2–609(4)] [pp. 230, 238]
90.a.	**YES**	Beulah's letter demands performance of conditions that were not part of the sale and to which she is not entitled. She is, therefore, refusing to perform as originally agreed, and this is sufficient repudiation. Under the doctrine of repudiation, the nonbreaching party is entitled to sue ***immediately*** for breach. [p. 238]
b.	**YES**	A repudiation is a repudiation. The repudiator's good faith (here, reliance on advice of counsel) does not detract from the fact that she *is* repudiating. [p. 238]
c.	**YES**	A repudiator ***can retract*** the repudiation—***unless*** in the interim the other party notified the repudiator that they accepted the repudiation (in which case the contract would be discharged by rescission) or they changed their position in reliance thereon (*e.g.*, by selling to another; *see* below). Note, however, that the retraction must be made ***in sufficient time*** to enable the other party to perform. Here, if Beulah did not notify Amos that she was going ahead with the purchase until June 1, Amos would not be expected to stand by with a deed in his hand. Consequently, Amos would have a ***reasonable time after*** June 1 within which to tender delivery of the deed. [p. 239]
d.	**NO**	The weight of authority is that the innocent party's demand that the contract be honored does not affect their right to rely on the repudiation. Here, because Amos relied on the repudiation, Beulah can no longer retract it and demand performance. [p. 239]
91.a.	**NO**	The innocent party owes a ***duty not to enhance*** damages. Ordering the supplies, equipment, and labor after the repudiation only enhanced the damages. Builder would be limited to whatever their ***profits*** would have been had they completed the job (*i.e.*, $600,000 minus their costs of performance). [p. 240]
b.	**DEPENDS**	On whether Developer's delay in securing another contractor was "commercially reasonable." If it was ***not***, then Developer owed a duty to mitigate damages and cannot recover damages resulting from their failure to do so. [p. 240]

92. a. **NO** Payment of the *full* purchase price is an *implied condition precedent* to Owner's duty to convey. (Nothing less can be considered "substantial" performance.) Stated differently, a default in 20% of the purchase price is a "material" breach by Purchaser, which *excuses* any duty of performance by Owner. (*But note:* Purchaser probably would be entitled to recover their payments from Owner in *restitution,* at least to the extent that such payments exceeded any damage suffered by Owner as the result of Purchaser's breach.) [pp. 231–234]

b. **YES** Normally, tender and payment are implied conditions concurrent, meaning that neither party can place the other in breach until he first tenders full performance himself. [p. 228] However, here there is a "material" breach by Purchaser on May 1, prior to the date Owner's performance is due. The "material" breach on May 1 *excuses* Owner's duty of counterperformance on June 1. Hence, Owner is entitled to sue Purchaser for breach without tendering the deed. [p. 235]

93. a. **YES** This contract is divisible because the value of each case can be ascertained by dividing the total purchase price by number of cases, and each appears to have some proportionate value to Don. Under such circumstances the seller *can demand a proportionate part* of the purchase price. [p. 234]

b. **YES** As long as the contract *is* divisible, the breaching party can recover for the part performed, *even though the breach is willful* or in bad faith (here, to pursue an overbid from the buyer's competitor). [p. 234]

c. **YES** But only in restitution. In view of the express condition, no recovery on the contract would be allowed (full delivery was an express condition precedent to his duty to pay). But since the breach was nonwillful, relief in restitution would be proper for the reasonable value of the spaghetti delivered (which might be *less* than the contract price, however). [p. 234]

94. a. **NO** Having agreed to the extension, Andrew is *estopped* from asserting the original closing date to the extent that Bianca has relied thereon. Here, Bianca has apparently not prepared her title for closing on April 30 in reliance on the extension agreement and hence is not in breach on that date. [p. 225]

b. **PROBABLY** A gratuitous waiver of a condition *can* be retracted provided the other party has not relied to their detriment thereon. (Nothing here shows any reliance by Bianca on Andrew's promise to extend for 60 days.) The only requirement is that the other party be given a *reasonable* period of time within which to perform; here, the two-week period (April 30 to May 15) would seem reasonable. [p. 43]

c. **NO** In the absence of some agreement to this effect, the condition (time for closing) is waived, and hence there is no breach of contract and no right to damages. The party waiving the condition assumes the risk of such loss or damages. [p. 225]

95. **NO** Repeated waivers of a condition do *not* by themselves bar a party from asserting it in the *future.* (The result *might* be different if elements of detrimental reliance or hardship were involved.) [p. 42]

96.a. **YES** — On the theory of substantial performance. Although Builder's performance (including installation of Frigi-Queen appliances) was an *implied* condition precedent to Alpha's duty to pay, and although there has been a partial breach in Builder's performance (hence, the condition has *not* been performed), still the forfeiture would be too great, and thus the courts will enforce the contract on the theory that the condition has been "substantially performed." Alpha will have a right to offset any damages he can prove by virtue of the unauthorized substitution. [p. 231]

b. **PROBABLY NOT** — Because in such a case his breach would be regarded as *willful* and in *bad faith*. Under the modern view, willfulness and bad faith are factors used in deciding whether there has been substantial performance (here, there probably is no substantial performance because of the presence of both factors). [p. 232] *Note:* The tough issue is whether courts would allow restitutional recovery in such a case. Normally, restitutionary relief is not allowed to a willful wrongdoer. But where, as here, there would be tremendous unjust enrichment, courts may treat the breach as "trivial" and grant restitutionary recovery (the reasonable value of Builder's performance) notwithstanding. [pp. 231, 232, 234]

c. **NO** — Because the doctrine of substantial performance does not apply where Builder's complete performance is (as here) made an *express* condition precedent to Alpha's duty to pay. But again, *restitutionary relief might still be available* (see above). [pp. 234, 236]

d. **DEPENDS** — On whether Builder's performance falls short of being "substantial." The test is whether the performance meets the *essential purpose* of the contract. If it is *not* substantial (and facts here suggest this), Builder certainly cannot recover on the contract. Furthermore, most courts will also *deny Builder any relief in restitution* even though there clearly could be an element of forfeiture in such cases. [pp. 231, 234]

97. **NO** — The doctrine of substantial performance has no application to contracts for the sale of goods. Instead, the U.C.C. adopts the *"perfect tender" rule*. Alpha is free to reject any variation from what she ordered. The possibility of forfeiture, which is the basis for the doctrine of substantial performance, is not present here. [p. 232]

98.a. **DEPENDS** — On whether the delay in first shipment "substantially impaired the value of the contract." [U.C.C. § 2–612(3)] *Compare:* If this were *not* an installment contract, the delay in delivery would probably be held a "material" breach. U.C.C. section 2–601 provides that if the delivery *fails in any respect to conform* to the contract the buyer may reject the whole. [p. 232]

b. **NO** — Delay in payment of money normally is *not* regarded as a "material" breach because the delay normally can be compensated for in damages. But the delay *would suspend* Giovanni's duty to make further shipments until payment is received. [p. 235]

c. **YES** — At least under the traditional rule, if the parties have *expressly* made time of the essence, the courts generally give it literal effect. [p. 236]

d.	**PROBABLY**	On the theory that the breach is minor and the contract is ***divisible***—*i.e.*, the value of each case can be ascertained ($5 per case) and each apparently has the same value to Don. Under these circumstances, unless Don can prove that the 50-case shortage "substantially impairs" the value of that installment to him, he must accept and pay for the 150 cases (offsetting any damages caused to him by the shortage). [U.C.C. § 6–612(2)] [p. 234]
99.	**NO**	Here, the contract *is not* rendered impracticable to perform. The subject matter was a house ***to be built*** (not an existing house). Builder can rebuild, and hence the contract is *not* impracticable to perform, although the time for completion would be extended accordingly. Builder suffers the cost of loss (no recovery in restitution for destroyed work either). [p. 242]
100.a.	**YES**	Courts will excuse a party's performance if it is ***impracticable***, but here, the cost of performance would have to be more extreme to be impracticable. [p. 241]
b.	**YES**	The services to be rendered by Builder would appear to be delegable by him to another. Hence, his personal inability to perform does not discharge his duty under the contract. (***Compare:*** If a ***personal service*** contract was involved, death or disability of the person to render such services ***would*** discharge the contract. But a construction contract is not generally so regarded.) [p. 243]
c.	**PROBABLY NOT**	This is ***not*** a case where his performance would be illegal by reason of a supervening act of government. This is simply a case where his performance will be more expensive. Most courts would hold Builder ***assumes the risk*** of such changes. *Compare:* If the change was totally unforeseeable and the added costs were tremendous, rescission on the ground of changed circumstances might be possible. [p. 241]
101.a.	**YES**	If performance of a contract has become ***illegal*** due to change in law enacted after the contract was entered into, the duty to perform is excused. [p. 241]
b.	**DEPENDS**	On whether doctrine of frustration applies. Camilla would have to show two things here: (i) that the enactment of this zoning restriction was ***not reasonably foreseeable*** at time of contracting; and (ii) that the restriction ***totally or nearly destroys*** the purpose or value of the contract. The second element here is doubtful, because the holder of a 99-year lease might still be able to develop the property into residential tracts (although some buyers might decline to purchase because she could not convey the fee.) [p. 244]
102.a.	**NO**	The death or destruction of the subject matter of the contract ***at the time the contract was entered into*** prevents the contract from arising. Hence, neither party could enforce. [p. 241]
b.	**YES**	In contracts for sale of goods that involve shipment by carrier, the risk of loss is transferred to buyer at time goods are ***delivered*** to carrier (unless otherwise agreed). [U.C.C. § 2–509] [p. 243]
c.	**DEPENDS**	On whether her shipping by truck was a "commercially reasonable" decision under the circumstances. [U.C.C. § 2–614] (If it was ***not***, the inability to ship by air ***would*** excuse performance.) [p. 241]

103.a. **YES**   The issue is whether the agreement to cancel (rescind) is itself enforceable. It is if supported by *consideration* on both sides. Here, there clearly is consideration—each party gave up the executory obligations of the other. (Lew gave up future rent, and Ted gave up the right to future use of the property.) [p. 245]

b. **NO**   Where the contract itself is required to be in writing under the Statute of Frauds (here, 99-year lease), most courts hold that any rescission thereof *must also be in writing* to be effective. [p. 246]

104.a. **YES**   There probably is consideration here (resolving a bona fide dispute). However, even if there were not, an agreement to modify a *contract for the sale of goods* is enforceable *without* consideration. [U.C.C. § 2–209] [p. 29]

b. **NO**   A written contract for the sale of goods can be modified orally *except* when the contract as modified falls within the Statute of Frauds, and contracts for goods priced at $9,500 fall within the Statute. [p. 165]

105.a. **YES**   The agreement to pay off the loan by having Sandy paint the house was an *"accord"*—supported by consideration, and effective itself as a contract. Hence, Sandy's repudiation is a breach for which she is liable in damages. [p. 246]

b. **DEPENDS**   On how "poor" a job Sandy did. If it was *"substantial" performance,* it would be sufficient to satisfy and discharge the original debt; Pete's remedy would be to sue Sandy for whatever it cost to repair or complete the job. If *not "substantial,"* then the painting would not constitute a satisfaction of either the original debt or the accord agreement. [pp. 38, 231]

c. **NO**   *If* there is a *bona fide dispute* as to the amount due or the right to collect a debt, the creditor's cashing of a check conspicuously marked "payment in full" generally is deemed an accord and satisfaction discharging any claim for a greater amount if the check is tendered in good faith. [U.C.C. § 3–311] [pp. 36–37, 247]

106. **NO**   Punitive damages normally are *not* recoverable in an action for breach of contract, even for intentional breach. (*Compare:* There may be exceptions where the breach also constitutes *tortious* conduct or, in some states, is unusually and extremely reprehensible in some way.) [p. 267]

107. **YES**   The normal measure of damages for breach of a contract for sale of goods is the market price at the time and place for delivery minus the contract price. *However,* where, as here, the goods are manufactured to the buyer's specifications and are not resalable (bearing Duke's brand name and advertising) the seller can recover the *full contract price.* [p. 260]

108.a. **NO**   Destruction of the house *excuses* performance. Here, the existence of a kitchen to "remodel" was the contemplated subject matter of the contract. Since it has been destroyed through the fault of neither party, *both* parties' duties of performance are excused. [p. 243]

b. **YES**   He can recover the reasonable value of his performance (but *not* his loss of profits on the job). If performance is excused after performance

		has commenced, the performing party is entitled to ***recovery in restitution*** for the value of his performance. Even though his performance has not resulted in any real "benefit" to Alpha, Builder is entitled to recover the costs of his labor and materials. [p. 244]
109.	**SPLIT OF AUTHORITY**	The ordinary remedy for breach of a bargain contract is expectation damages (here, market price minus contract price), but many jurisdictions provide more limited remedies in real-estate contracts that the seller breaches without "bad faith." In those jurisdictions, the purchaser is often limited to recovery of some or all of their ***"out of pocket" losses*** (down payment, title charges, etc.) unless "bad faith" is shown. [p. 261]
110.a.	**YES**	For each breach of contract, ***at least nominal damages*** of $1 can be recovered. [p. 265]
b.	**YES**	If such damages were ***reasonably foreseeable*** to both parties at the time of contracting. Under the doctrine of ***consequential damages,*** the promisor is liable to the promisee for all damages that the promisor had reason to foresee would be the probable result of the breach. Here, it would seem that a designer would be aware of the kind of damages Producer would suffer by reason of the delay, and hence should be liable therefor—even though they far exceeded the contract price. [p. 253]
c.	**PROBABLY NOT**	Because there is ***not sufficient certainty*** that there would be any profits, or how much. There may be no satisfactory way of knowing whether a new Broadway show would operate at a profit or a loss. However, under modern law economic models based on sufficiently similar shows or other evidence (*e.g.*, advance ticket sales) could be persuasive. [pp. 253–254]
111.a.	**DEPENDS**	On whether Johns made a bona fide effort to mitigate damages by finding other comparable jobs during the week in question. Even though the employer is clearly in breach, the employee is under a ***duty to mitigate*** damages. [p. 255]
b.	**NO**	Failure to mitigate damages is a matter of defense, meaning the burden would be on Starburst to prove that such employment ***was*** available. [pp. 255, 262]
c.	**YES (modern view)**	The modern trend, at least, is to allow recovery in ***restitution*** for the reasonable value of services provided, even where the employee is clearly in breach and their breach is ***willful.*** Such recovery would be offset, however, by any loss or expense the employer suffers by reason of the breach (*e.g.*, losses in canceling the show, costs incurred in hiring a replacement above what would have been payable under the contract). [pp. 269–270]
d.	**NO**	The answer would be different, because illness on the part of a person who is to render personal services makes performance impossible and thus ***excuses*** the duty to perform the balance of the contract. *Result:* Johns could recover in restitution for the reasonable value of the nights he worked, ***without any offset*** for the cost of replacing him. [p. 268]

112.a. **YES**   Where the owner breaches a construction contract *before* any work is done, the contractor's *lost profits* is the proper measure of damages. [p. 263]

b. **YES**   A contractor is *not* under any duty to mitigate damages resulting from the owner's breach. The theory is that every construction job involves its own peculiar business risks and the contractor should not be required to assume new or different risks because of the owner's breach. [p. 255]

c. **DOUBTFUL**   To be enforceable as a valid liquidated damages clause, the amount stipulated must be a *reasonable forecast* of whatever damages are likely to result. Here, it is doubtful that the $500 per day figure is a reasonable forecast of actual damages—*i.e.*, it does not appear to be tied into the costs of eating out as opposed to cooking at home, or loss of use of that space in the house. Therefore, it is probably unenforceable as a penalty. [pp. 265–266]

113. **PROBABLY**   The U.C.C. would allow recovery if the $500 was a reasonable forecast of *actual or anticipated* damages. [U.C.C. § 2–718(1)] The fact that the provision was labeled a "penalty" does *not* by itself make it unenforceable. A strong argument here for enforceability is that Baker was paid a $500 premium for prompt delivery, and it would be unjust to allow him to breach and still retain the premium. Hence, the $500 "penalty" would appear to be a reasonable *forecast* of damages. [p. 266]

Table of Cases

1464-Eight, Ltd. v. Joppich, 8
A/S Apothekernes Laboratorium for Specialpraeparater v. I.M.C. Chemical Group, Inc., 146
Aceros Prefabricados, S.A. v. TradeArbed, Inc., 77
Adams v. Lindsell, 104
Advanced, Inc. v. Wilks, 265
Air Products & Chemicals, Inc. v. Fairbanks Morse, Inc., 79
Alaska Northern Development, Inc. v. Alyeska Pipeline Service Co., 123
Alaska Prot. Servs. v. Frontier Colorcable, 176
Albre Marble & Tile Co. v. John Bowen Co., 244
Alfred Marks Realty Co. v. Hotel Hermitage Co., 245
Allied Equipment Co. v. Weber Engineered Products, 139
American Home Improvement, Inc. v. MacIver, 159
American Lithographic Co. v. Ziegler, 196
Ammons v. Wilson & Co., 101
Anderson v. May, 242
Angel v. Murray, 29
Asinof v. Freudenthal, 113
Atchison, Topeka & Santa Fe Railway v. Andrews, 137
Atwell v. Jenkins, 16
Austin Instrument v. Loral Corp., 31
Automatic Sprinkler Co. v. Sherman, 137
Automatic Vending Co. v. Wisdom, 19
Autry v. Republic Productions, 244
Ayer v. Western Union, 151
B & M Homes v. Hogan, 268
Backus v. Sessions, 173
Bank of Kansas v. Hutchison Health Services, Inc., 205
Batsakis v. Demotsis, 5
Bendalin v. Delgado, 136
Bernstein v. W.B. Manufacturing Co., 14
Bettancourt v. Gilroy Theatre Co., 141
Bishop v. Eaton, 94, 95
Bond v. Dentzer, 202
Bondy v. Harvey, 142
Brackenbury v. Hodgkin, 86
Bradbury, In re, 52
Brandyce v. Globe & Rutgers Fire Insurance Co., 221
Brant v. California Dairies, Inc., 56
Brightwater Paper Co. v. Monadnock Paper Mills, 22
Broadnax v. Ledbetter, 96
Brown v. Hebb, 48
Brown-Crummer Investment Co. v. Arkansas City, 141
Buescher v. Lastar, 49
C. R. Klewin, Inc. v. Flagship Props., Inc., 166
Caldwell v. Cline, 65
California State Auto Association v. Barrett Garages, Inc., 158
Canadian Industrial Alcohol Co. v. Dunbar Molasses Co., 242
Channel Home Centers v. Grossman, 146
Choice v. Dallas, 96
Cities Service Oil Co. v. National Shawmut Bank, 105
City Stores Co. v. Ammerman, 136

Clark-Rice Corp. v. Waltham Bleachery & Dye Works, 235
Clarksville Land Co. v. Harriman, 242
Clavan v. Herman, 239
Cole-McIntyre-Norfleet Co. v. Holloway, 101
Collins v. Uniroyal, Inc., 161
Columbia Hyundai, Inc. v. Carll Hyundai, Inc., 71
Columbia Nitrogen Corp. v. Royster Co., 126
Conant v. Evans, 52
Continental Sand & Gravel, Inc. v. K & K Sand & Gravel, Inc., 257
Copper v. Strange & Warner Co., 263
Cordes v. Miller, 241
Corning v. Burton, 183
Craft v. Elder & Johnston Co., 60
Crane Ice Cream Co. v. Terminal Freezing & Heating Co., 209
Crenshaw County Hospital Board v. St. Paul Fire & Marine Insurance Co., 150
Croker v. New York Trust Co., 189
Culton v. Gilchrist, 68
Dale R. Horning Co. v. Falconer Glass Indus., Inc., 77
Davis v. Basalt Rock Co., 194
Davis v. General Foods Corp., 143
Davis v. Jacoby, 98
Dawkins v. Sappington, 96
Day v. Caton, 103
De Cicco v. Schweizer, 28
Delta Rice Mill, Inc. v. Gen. Foods Corp., 267
Denney v. Reppert, 25
Des Arc Oil Mill v. Western Union Telegraph Co., 151
Diamond Fruit Growers, Inc. v. Krack Corp., 73
Dick v. United States, 113
Dickinson v. Dodds, 81
Dobias v. White, 42
Donovan v. Rrl Corp., 169
Dorton v. Colins & Aikman Corp., 73
Doughboy Industries, Inc., In re, 71
Drees Farming Association v. Thompson, 143
Drennan v. Star Paving Co., 63
Drzewiecki v. H & R Block, Inc., 138
Du Pont de Nemours Powder Co. v. Schlottman, 225
Duluth S.S. & A. Railway v. Wilson, 202
Duncan v. Black, 10
Duplex Safety Boiler Co. v. Garden, 222
Dyer v. National By-Products, Inc., 9
Ed Bertholet & Assocs. v. Stefanko, 256
Elkhorn-Hazard Coal Co. v. Kentucky River Corp., 59
Embry v. Hargadine-McKittrick Dry Goods Co., 114
Fairmount Glass Works v. Grunden-Martin Woodenware Co., 62
Falconer v. Mazess, 105
Feinberg v. Pfeiffer Co., 46, 47
Fischer v. CTMI, L.L.C., 143
Flambeau Products Corp. v. Honeywell Information Systems, Inc., 33
Foakes v. Beer, 32
Foley v. Interactive Data Corp., 138
G.C. Casebolt Co. v. United States, 113
Gaines & Sea v. R.J. Reynolds Tobacco Co., 137

Contracts | 331

Gardner Zemke Co. v. Dunham Bush, Inc., 73, 78
Garretson v. United States, 160
General Motors Corp. v. Piskor, 267
Germain Fruit Co. v. Western Union, 151
Getty Terminals Corp. v. Coastal Oil New England, Inc., 128
Gianni v. R. Russel & Co., 119
Goad v. Rogers, 145
Goldstein v. McNeil, 172
Goode v. Riley, 150
Goodwin v. Hidalgo County Water Control & Improvement District No. 1, 66
Gray v. Martino, 25
Green County v. Quinlan, 219
Gulf Colorado & San Francisco Railway v. Winton, 143
Gurfein v. Werbelovsky, 16
Guy v. Liederbach, 184
Haas v. Myers, 110
Hadley v. Baxendale, 252
Haines v. Commercial Mortgage Co., 175
Hale v. Groce, 185
Hamer v. Sidway, 3
Hamill v. Maryland Casualty Co., 180
Hamilton v. Home Insurance Co., 219
Hanna v. Florence Iron Co., 230
Harris v. More, 25
Hartman v. San Pedro Commercial Co., 220
Hatten, Estate of, 52
Haupt v. Charlie's Kosher Market, 206
Hayden v. Hoadley, 118
Heideck v. Kent General Hospital, Inc., 138
Helle v. Landmark, Inc., 12
Henthorn v. Fraser, 106
Herbert v. Bronson, 200
Heyer v. Flaig, 185
Hicks v. Bush, 124
Hill v. Corbett, 44
Hill v. Gateway, 129
Hill v. Jones, 156
Hobbs v. Massasoit Whip Co., 100
Hoffman v. Red Owl Stores, Inc., 146
Holt v. American Woolen Co., 200
Hotchkiss v. Nat'l City Bank, 56
Humble Oil & Refining Co. v. Westside Investment Corp., 68, 83
Hunt Foods and Industries, Inc. v. Doliner, 122
Hurst v. W. J. Lake & Co., 117
Imperial Refining Co. v. Kanotex Refining Co., 210
Indiana Manufacturing Co. v. Hayes, 102
Interform Co. v. Mitchell, 119
International Filter Co. v. Conroe Gin, Ice & Light Co., 93
Iron Trade Products Co. v. Wilkoff Co., 215
J. Dyer Co. v. Bishop International Engineering Co., 223
Jacob & Youngs, Inc. v. Kent, 234
Jaffray v. Davis, 33
James Baird Co. v. Gimbel Bros., 84
James v. Burchell, 229
Jenkins Towel Service, Inc. v. Fidelity-Philadelphia Trust Co., 63
Johnson v. Federal Union Surety Co., 69
Joseph Lande & Sons, Inc. v. Wellsco Realty, Inc., 28
Joseph Martin, Jr., Delicatessen, Inc. v. Schumacher, 142
Julian v. Gold, 35
Kampman v. Pittsburgh Contracting & Engineering Co., 168
Katemis v. Westerlind, 236
Keller v. Holderman, 115
Key v. Alexander, 261
Khoury v. Tomlinson, 169
Kirksey v. Kirksey, 46
Kladivo v. Melberg, 142
Klockner v. Green, 96
Kolodziej v. Mason, 153
Kossick v. United Fruit Co., 9
Kugler v. Romain, 159
Kukuska v. Home Mutual Hail-Tornado Insurance Co., 101
L. Albert & Son v. Armstrong Rubber Co., 255
Laclede Gas Co. v. Amoco Oil Co., 258
LaCumbre Golf & Country Club v. Santa Barbara Hotel Co., 245
Lane v. Kindercare Learning Ctrs., Inc., 268
Langel v. Betz, 210
Lawrence v. Fox, 179
Lefkowitz v. Great Minneapolis Surplus Store, 60, 61
Leo F. Piazza Paving Co. v. Bebek & Brkich, 63
Leonard v. Rose, 166
Levine v. Blumenthal, 35
Lewis v. Browning, 110
Lindner v. Mid-Continent Oil Corp., 16
Lingenfelder v. Wainwright Brewery Co., 27
Livingston v. Evans, 67
Lloyd v. Murphy, 245
Loring v. City of Boston, 65
Louise Caroline Nursing Home, Inc. v. Dix Constr. Corp., 269
Louisville Tin & Stove Co. v. Lay, 102
Lucas v. Hamm, 182
Lucy v. Zehmer, 56
M.F. Kemper Construction Co. v. City of Los Angeles, 149
Mascioni v. Miller, Inc., 223
Massey v. Del-Valley Corp., 34
Masterson v. Sine, 119, 121
Mattei v. Hopper, 23, 222
Maxwell v. Fid. Fin. Servs., 159
Mayfair Fabrics v. Henley, 160
McDonald v. Hudspeth, 202
McGillicuddy v. Los Verjels Land & Water Co., 244
McGlone v. Lacey, 99
McMichael v. Price, 21
Melroy v. Kemmerer, 34
Miami Coca-Cola Bottling Co. v. Orange Crush Co., 14, 15
Midland National Bank v. Security Elevator Co., 95
Millar & Co. Ltd. v. Taylor & Co. Ltd., 241
Mills v. Wyman, 48
Minneapolis & St. Louis Railway v. Columbus Rolling-Mill, 68
Mississippi & Dominion Steamship Co. v. Swift, 145
Mitchill v. Lath, 121
Moch v. Rensselaer Water Co., 185
Moore v. Shell Oil Co., 19
Morrison v. Thoelke, 112
Moulton v. Kershaw, 62
Mullen v. Hawkins, 10
Nanakuli Paving & Rock Co. v. Shell Oil Co., 126
National Union Fire Insurance Co. v. Ehrlich, 100
Nelson v. Fernando Nelson & Sons, 203
Neofotistos v. Harvard Brewing Co., 225
Neri v. Retail Marine Corp., 259
Nguyen v. Barnes & Noble Inc., 131
Norcia v. Samsung Telecommunications America, LLC, 129
Office Pavilion S. Florida, Inc. v. ASAL Prods., Inc., 13
Old American Life Insurance Co. v. Biggers, 51, 52
Oswald v. Allen, 114

Pacific Gas & Electric Co. v. G.W. Thomas Drayage & Rigging Co., 116
Palo Alto Town & Country Village v. BBTC Co., 105
Parker v. 20th Century Fox, 263
Payne v. Cave, 62
Peerless Glass Co. v. Pacific Crockery & Tinware Co., 149
Peevyhouse v. Garland Coal & Mining Co., 264
Pessin v. Fox Head Waukesha Corp., 21
Petterson v. Pattberg, 86
Phillips v. Moor, 103
Pine River State Bank v. Mettille, 138
Pittsley v. Houser, 165
Plante v. Jacobs, 231, 233
Poel v. Brunswick-Balke-Collender Co., 69
Polaroid Corp. v. Rollins Envtl. Servs., 92
Portella v. Sonnenberg, 159
Price v. Okla. Coll. of Osteopathic Med. & Surgery, 69
ProCD, Inc. v. Zeidenberg, 129
Pym v. Campbell, 124
Raffles v. Wichelhaus, 114
Randal v. Beber, 175
Rayburn v. Comstock, 240
Real Estate Co. of Pittsburgh v. Rudolph, 8
Rockingham v. Luten Bridge Co., 255
Rouse v. United States, 188
Rowe v. Chesapeake Mineral Co., 115
Ruinello v. Murray, 138
Ryder v. Wescoat, 66
Salem Trust Co. v. Manufacturers' Finance Co., 206
Saunders v. Pottlitzer Bros. Fruit Co., 145
Schnell v. Nell, 43
School District v. Dauchy, 242
Schwartzreich v. Bauman-Basch, Inc., 30
Scott v. Moragues Lumber Co., 14, 17
Scott-Burr Stores Corp. v. Wilcox, 105
Seaver v. Ransom, 181
Security Stove & Manufacturing Co. v. American Railways Express Co., 254
Shell v. Schmidt, 186
Sherwood v. Walker, 148
Shubert Theatrical Co. v. Rath, 105, 106
Shuey v. United States, 81
Smalley v. Baker, 173
Smith v. Bach, 175
Snepp v. United States, 270
Sniadach v. Family Finance Corp., 202
Southern California Acoustics Co. v. C.V. Holder, Inc., 97
Southern Concrete Services, Inc. v. Mableton Contractors, Inc., 126
Specht v. Netscape Communications Corp., 131
Springstead v. Nees, 9
St. Nicholas Church v. Kropp, 150
Stanton v. Dennis, 136
State Dep't of Transp. v. Providence & Worcester R.R., 69
Steiner v. Mobil Oil Corp., 78
Stevenson, Jaques & Co. v. McLean, 67
Stokely Bros. v. Conklin, 200
Strong v. Sheffield, 11
Strong v. Western Union, 151
Sweeney Gasoline & Oil Co. v. Toledo, Peoria & Western Railroad, 160
Taylor v. Caldwell, 242
Taylor v. Merchant's Fire Insurance Co., 110
Teachers Insurance & Annuity Association of America v. Tribune Co., 145
Teer v. George A. Fuller Co., 127
Thompson Crane & Trucking Co. v. Eyman, 156

Thompson-Starrett Co. v. La Belle Iron Works, 222
Tinn v. Hoffman, 113
Tunkl v. Regents of the University of California, 160
Twin City Pipe Line Co. v. Harding Glass Co., 142
Tyra v. Cheney, 149
U.S. Fidelity & Guaranty Co. v. Parson, 243
Unatin 7-Up Co. v. Solomon, 223
Union Central Life Insurance Co. v. Imsland, 42
Van Boskerck v. Aronson, 26
Van Buskirk v. Kuhns, 144
Vick v. Patterson, 175
Vitacost.com, Inc. v. McCants, 132
Vitty v. Eley, 96
Walker v. Keith, 137
Walter H. Leimert Co. v. Woodson, 170
Ward v. Ward, 171
Warner v. Texas Railway, 166
Washington Chocolate Co. v. Canterbury Candy Makers, 18
Wasserman v. Sloss, 174
Watkins & Son v. Carrig, 30
Webb v. McGowin, 51
Western Homes, Inc. v. Herbert Ketell, Inc., 137
Wheeler v. St. Joseph Hospital, 158
White v. Corlies, 90
Wickham & Burton Coal Co. v. Farmers' Lumber Co., 22
Williams v. Favret, 97
Williams v. Hirshorn, 222
Williams v. Paxson Coal Co., 188
Wisconsin Knife Works v. National Metal Crafters, 128
Wood v. Joliet Gaslight Co., 265
Wood v. Lucy, Lady Duff-Gordon, 20
Zabella v. Pakel, 50
Zigas v. Superior Court, 186

Table of U.C.C. Sections

U.C.C. Article 1 215
U.C.C. Article 2 .... 233, 279, 311
U.C.C. Article 9 .... 192, 193, 200
U.C.C. § 1–201(b)(3) 117, 126, 169
U.C.C. § 1–303(a) 116, 117, 126
U.C.C. § 1–304 .... 19, 20, 30, 214
U.C.C. § 1–305 254
U.C.C. § 1–306 246
U.C.C. § 2–104(1) 76
U.C.C. § 2–201 .... 164, 169, 170, 315
U.C.C. § 2–202, comment 3 122
U.C.C. § 2–204(3) 139
U.C.C. § 2–205 .... 8, 9, 84, 85, 307
U.C.C. § 2–206(2) 95, 98, 99, 106, 312
U.C.C. § 2–207 .... 54, 69, 71, 72, 73, 74, 75, 76, 77, 78, 79, 92, 100, 312
U.C.C. § 2–209(1) 29, 30, 127, 128, 276, 327
U.C.C. § 2–210(2) 194, 202, 209, 211
U.C.C. § 2–302 .... 157, 159
U.C.C. § 2–302, comment 158
U.C.C. § 2–305(1) 20, 137, 139, 143, 314
U.C.C. § 2–306(2) 20, 22, 23, 225
U.C.C. § 2–308 140
U.C.C. § 2–309 .... 15, 140
U.C.C. § 2–310 .... 140, 320
U.C.C. § 2–311(1) 144
U.C.C. § 2–312 161
U.C.C. § 2–314 .... 161, 279
U.C.C. § 2–315 161
U.C.C. § 2–316 161
U.C.C. § 2–328(3) 62, 63
U.C.C. § 2–501 260
U.C.C. § 2–508(1) 232, 233
U.C.C. § 2–509 .... 243, 326
U.C.C. § 2–601 .... 232, 325
U.C.C. § 2–609 .... 230, 241, 322, 323
U.C.C. § 2–610 238
U.C.C. § 2–611(2) 239
U.C.C. § 2–612 .... 232, 325
U.C.C. § 2–613 .... 242, 243
U.C.C. § 2–614 242
U.C.C. § 2–615 .... 241, 242
U.C.C. § 2–704(2) 255
U.C.C. § 2–706 260
U.C.C. § 2–708 .... 240, 259
U.C.C. § 2–709 260
U.C.C. § 2–712(1) 240, 257
U.C.C. § 2–713 257
U.C.C. § 2–713(1) 240
U.C.C. § 2–714 257
U.C.C. § 2–715(2) 255, 258
U.C.C. § 2–716(1) 258
U.C.C. § 2–718 .... 266, 329
U.C.C. § 2–719(1)(a) 161, 258
U.C.C. § 3–311 37
U.C.C. § 6–612(2) 326
U.C.C. § 7–210 260
U.C.C. § 8–113 167
U.C.C. § 9–201(a) 207
U.C.C. § 9–203 .... 199, 207
U.C.C. § 9–203(a) 207
U.C.C. § 9–203(b) 207
U.C.C. § 9–204 200
U.C.C. § 9–309(1) 207
U.C.C. § 9–310 207
U.C.C. § 9–313 207
U.C.C. § 9–322 207
U.C.C. § 9–404 203
U.C.C. § 9–405 204
U.C.C. § 9–406(d) 201

Table of Restatements

Reference	Page
Rest. 1st § 133	180, 185
Rest. 1st § 135, comment a	190
Rest. 1st § 142	190
Rest. 1st § 143	190
Rest. 1st § 239	123
Rest. 1st § 240	120
Rest. 1st § 241	124
Rest. 1st § 318(c)	230
Rest. 1st § 458	241
Rest. 1st § 460	242
Rest. 1st §§ 492–495	156
Rest. 1st § 502, comment	148
Rest. 1st § 598	174
Rest. 1st § 604	175
Rest. 1st § 605	174
Rest. 1st § 606	174
Rest. 2d § 4	57
Rest. 2d § 15	173
Rest. 2d § 16	173
Rest. 2d § 18	56
Rest. 2d § 19	56
Rest. 2d § 20	114
Rest. 2d § 24	58
Rest. 2d § 27	145
Rest. 2d § 30	106
Rest. 2d § 33	141, 143
Rest. 2d § 33, ill. 1	60
Rest. 2d § 33, ill. 8	143
Rest. 2d § 34	144
Rest. 2d § 34, comments a–b	144
Rest. 2d § 37	89
Rest. 2d § 39	67
Rest. 2d § 40	111
Rest. 2d § 41	65, 66
Rest. 2d § 42	81
Rest. 2d § 43	81
Rest. 2d § 48	88
Rest. 2d § 49	65
Rest. 2d § 50	90
Rest. 2d § 53(1)	90
Rest. 2d § 54	95
Rest. 2d § 56	93
Rest. 2d § 59	69
Rest. 2d § 60	108
Rest. 2d § 62	90, 91
Rest. 2d § 63	105, 110, 111, 112, 113
Rest. 2d § 65	107
Rest. 2d § 66	106
Rest. 2d § 67	108
Rest. 2d § 68	104
Rest. 2d § 69(1)(a)	102
Rest. 2d § 69(1)(b)	101
Rest. 2d § 69(1)(c)	100
Rest. 2d § 69(2)	102
Rest. 2d § 70	103
Rest. 2d § 71	5, 8
Rest. 2d § 72	5
Rest. 2d § 73	24, 25, 33
Rest. 2d § 73, comment b	26
Rest. 2d § 74	10, 28, 33, 34
Rest. 2d § 75	16
Rest. 2d § 78	16
Rest. 2d § 79	5
Rest. 2d § 82	48, 49
Rest. 2d § 83	50
Rest. 2d § 84(1)	42
Rest. 2d § 84(2)	43
Rest. 2d § 85	49, 50
Rest. 2d § 86	44, 51
Rest. 2d § 87	8, 84
Rest. 2d § 87(1)(a)	83
Rest. 2d § 88	9
Rest. 2d § 89	29
Rest. 2d § 90	47, 97
Rest. 2d § 90(2)	44
Rest. 2d § 116	167
Rest. 2d § 123	167
Rest. 2d § 130(2)	167
Rest. 2d § 130, comment b	166
Rest. 2d § 132	170
Rest. 2d § 135	170
Rest. 2d § 138	170
Rest. 2d § 139	172
Rest. 2d § 145	171
Rest. 2d § 152	148
Rest. 2d § 154	148
Rest. 2d § 154, ill. 1	149
Rest. 2d § 159	154
Rest. 2d § 159, comment b	155
Rest. 2d § 160	154
Rest. 2d § 161	154, 155
Rest. 2d § 161(a)	155
Rest. 2d § 161(b)	156
Rest. 2d § 161(c)	155
Rest. 2d § 161(d)	155
Rest. 2d § 162	154
Rest. 2d § 164	154
Rest. 2d § 174	156
Rest. 2d §§ 175–176	156
Rest. 2d § 176(1)	156
Rest. 2d § 176(2)	156
Rest. 2d § 201	56, 114, 115
Rest. 2d § 201(1)	115
Rest. 2d § 201(2)	115
Rest. 2d § 201(2)(b)	55
Rest. 2d § 202	116
Rest. 2d § 202(5)	117
Rest. 2d § 203(b)	117
Rest. 2d § 205, comment	215
Rest. 2d § 208, comment	159
Rest. 2d § 209	119
Rest. 2d § 210	123
Rest. 2d § 211(2)	158
Rest. 2d § 211, comment d	131
Rest. 2d § 213	123
Rest. 2d § 213, comment c	123
Rest. 2d § 216	120, 123
Rest. 2d § 217, comment b	124
Rest. 2d §§ 219–221	116
Rest. 2d § 222	117

Rest. 2d § 223	116
Rest. 2d § 227	222
Rest. 2d § 229, ill. 2	226
Rest. 2d § 251	230, 241
Rest. 2d § 264	229
Rest. 2d § 271, ill. 2	225
Rest. 2d § 281	40
Rest. 2d § 281, comment c	40
Rest. 2d § 281, comment e	39
Rest. 2d § 302	179
Rest. 2d § 311	190
Rest. 2d § 313	185
Rest. 2d § 313, ill. 3	185
Rest. 2d § 313, ill. 5	186
Rest. 2d § 317	192, 194, 200
Rest. 2d § 317, comment d	196
Rest. 2d § 318	209
Rest. 2d § 319	200
Rest. 2d § 320	199
Rest. 2d § 321	200
Rest. 2d § 321(1)	202
Rest. 2d § 322	201
Rest. 2d § 324	197
Rest. 2d § 326	197
Rest. 2d § 328	210
Rest. 2d § 332	197
Rest. 2d § 333	205
Rest. 2d § 338	204
Rest. 2d § 342	205
Rest. 2d § 349	254
Rest. 2d § 353	267
Rest. 2d § 353, ill. 1	268
Rest. 2d § 356	266
Rest. 2d § 367(2)	263
Rest. 2d § 373	268, 269
Rest. 3d R&UE § 32(1)	175
Rest. 3d R&UE § 38(2)(b)	269

Index

ACCEPTANCE
See Offer and Acceptance

ACCORD AND SATISFACTION
Accord defined, 38
Discharge of contractual duty by, 246
Executory accord
    Defined, 38
    Effect, 38–42
Satisfaction
    Defined, 38
    Effect, 38

ANTICIPATORY BREACH
See Breach of Contract

ANTICIPATORY REPUDIATION, 229
See also Breach of Contract; Anticipatory breach

ASSIGNMENT
Assignee rights
    Against assignor, 205
    Against obligor, 202–203
Assumption of duties by assignee, 183–184, 210–211
Attachment of security interest, 207
Change in burden or risk assumed by obligor, 195–196
Change in duty of obligor, 194–195
Change in material term of contract, 196
Defenses against assignee
    Consumer protection statutes, impact of on obligor's defenses, 204
    Contract related defenses, 203
    In general, 203–205
    Modification of contract by assignor and obligor, 204
Delegation of duties. See Delegation of Duties
Direct action by assignee against obligor, 202
Donative assignments, 180–181, 197
Future rights, 199–200
    In future wages, 202
    In nonexisting future contract, 200
    Under existing contracts and business relationships, 199–200
General requirements, 197
Holders in due course, 203
In general, 191–194
Insurance, 195
Mortgages, 196
Notice to obligor, effect of, 203
Novation, compared with, 208–209
Output contracts, 195
Partial assignments, 196–197
Perfection of security interest, 207
Personal service contracts, 194–195
Priority among assignees, 205–207
    English rule, 206
    Massachusetts rule, 206
    New York rule, 206
Prohibition of assignment, 200–202
Real party in interest, 192
Requirements contract, 195
Revocability of assignments, 197–199
Security interest, assignment as creating, 192–193, 200
Substitution of debtors, 195–196
Token chose, 197, 205–206
Wage assignments, 202
Waiver of defense, 203
Warranties, implied, 205

AUCTIONS, 62–63

BARGAIN PROMISES
See Consideration

BILATERAL CONTRACTS
Acceptance of offer for, 90–94
Unilateral contracts, distinguished from, 11–12, 15–16

BREACH OF CONTRACT
    See also Damages; Specific performance
Anticipatory breach, 238–241
    Determining damages, 240
    Duty to mitigate damages, 240
    Immediate cause of action for, 238
    Retraction of repudiation, 239–240
    What constitutes, 238–239
Excuse of condition, 223–225
Material vs. minor breach, 235–238
    Parties' agreement as determining, 236
Pleading and proof, burden of, 221
Repudiation, what constitutes, 235, 238
Responses to breach, 236–237

BROWSEWRAP CONTRACTS
See Electronic Contracts

CAPACITY TO CONTRACT
Intoxicated persons, 173
Mental incapacity, 173
Minors, 172–173
    Quasi-contractual liability for necessaries, 172–173

CLICKWRAP CONTRACTS
See Electronic Contracts

CONDITIONS
    See also Excuse of Conditions
Conditions concurrent, 228
Conditions precedent, 220
Conditions subsequent, 220–221
Defined, 216
Distinguished from promises, 217–218
Excuse
    By prevention or hindrance, 223–225
    Forfeiture, 225–226
    Impossibility, 225
    Waiver, 225
Express conditions
    Defined, 216
    In general, 216
Implied conditions, 226–227
Implying promise, 225–226
Interpretation as condition or promise, 218–220

Order of performance, 227–230
    Anticipatory repudiation, 229
    Prospective inability to perform, 229–230
Performance to satisfaction of promisor, 221–222
Performance to satisfaction of third person, 222
Pleading and proof, burden of, 221
Relating to time of payment, 222–223
Substantial performance, 231–234. *See also* Substantial Performance

CONSIDERATION
See also Promissory Estoppel
Accord and satisfaction, 38–42. *See also* Accord and Satisfaction
Agreements allowing one party to supply material term. *See also* Indefiniteness; Interpretation and implication, 18–20
Alternative promises, 17–18
"Bargain" approach, 3–4
Bargain as consideration, 5
Bargain promises, 5–37
"Benefit/detriment" approach, 3
Conditional promises, 17, 45–46
Donative promises
    Conditional, 45–46
    Relied upon. *See also* Promissory estoppel, 46–47
    Unrelied upon
        In general, 43–44
        Nominal consideration, effect of, 44–45
        Seal, effect of, 44
        Writing, effect of, 44
"Enforceable factor" approach, 4
Exclusive dealing contracts, 20–21
Forbearance on legal claim, 9–11
Guaranties, 8–9
Illusory promises, 11–24
Implied promises, 20–21
Moral consideration. *See also* past consideration, below, 48–52
Mutuality of obligation, 11–12
Nominal consideration, 7–9, 83
Options, 8
Output contracts, 21–24
Past consideration, promises based on
    In general, 48–52
    Promise based on expense incurred by promisee, 51–52
    Promise to pay debt barred by statute of limitations, 48–49
    Promise to pay debt discharged in bankruptcy, 50
    Promise to pay fixed amount in liquidation of legal obligation, 52
    Promise to pay moral obligation arising out of past economic benefit to promisor, 50–52
    Promise to perform a voidable obligation, 49–50
Preexisting legal duty
    Contractual duties, 26–38
    Duty owed to third person, 28
    In general, 24–38
    Modification, 29–30
        Waiver, compared with, 30
    Payment of lesser sum in discharge of greater, 32–38
    Performance in exchange for promise of increased payment, 27–32
    Public duties, 25–26
    Rescission of contract under which duty owed, 30
    Unliquidated obligations, 33–34
Writing
    As substitute for consideration, 30
Release, 35
Requirements contracts, 21–24
Seal, effect of, 44
Surrender of claim, 9–11
Void promises, 16–17
Voidable promises, 16, 49–50
Waivers, 30, 42–43. *See also* Waiver

CONSTRUCTION CONTRACTS
Damages, 255
Impossibility of performance, 242–243
Substantial performance, 232

CONSUMER PROTECTION
Defenses against holders of commercial paper, 203
Retail installment contracts, 203–204
Unconscionability, 157–161
Waiver-of-defense clauses, 203

CONTRACTORS AND SUBCONTRACTORS
See Subcontractor Bids

CONTRACTS CONCLUDED BY CORRESPONDENCE
See Offer and Acceptance

CONTRACTS FOR SALE OF GOODS
See Sale of Goods Contracts

CONTRACTS FOR SALE OF LAND
See Land Sale Contracts

CONTRACTS IMPLIED IN FACT
See Implied in Fact Contracts

CONTRACTS IMPLIED IN LAW
See Implied in Law Contracts

DAMAGES
See also Quasi-Contractual Recovery Certainty Requirement, 253–255
Consequential damages, 253
Construction contracts
    Breach by builder, 264–265
    Breach by owner, 263–264
    Duty to mitigate damages, 255
Cost-of-completion measure, 264
Diminution in value measure, 264–265
Disgorgement, 270
Divisible contracts, 234–235
Emotional distress, 267–268
Employment contracts
    Breach by employee, 263
    Breach by employer, 262–263
    Duty to mitigate damages, 255, 262–263
Expectation measure, 251
General damages, 252
Hadley v. Baxendale, 252–253
In general, 251–270
Incidental damages, 251
Land sale contracts, 261–262
Liquidated damages, 265–266
Mitigation of damages, 240, 255–256
Nominal damages, 265
Penalty clauses, 265–266
Punitive damages, 267
Reliance damages, 251
Restitutionary damages, 251–252, 268–270
Revocation of unilateral offer after performance begun, 86

Sale of goods contracts
    Breach by buyer, 259–261
    Breach by seller, 257–259
    Duty to mitigate damages, 255
    In general, 256–261
    Profits, 259
Specific performance, 256–258, 262–263, 265
Speculative damage limitation, 253–255
    Profits, application to, 253–254
Substantial performance, 233–234

DEFENSES RELATING TO FORMATION OF CONTRACT
Duress, 156–157. *See also* Duress
Illegal contracts, 174–176. *See also* Illegality
Indefiniteness, 135–147. *See also* Indefiniteness
Lack of contractual capacity, 172–173. *See also* Capacity to Contract
Misrepresentation, 154. *See also* Misrepresentation
Mistake, 147–153. *See also* Mistake
Nondisclosure, 154–156. *See also* Nondisclosure
Statute of Frauds, 162–172. *See also* Statute of Frauds
Unconscionability, 157–161. *See also* Unconscionability
Undue influence, 157. *See also* Undue Influence

DELEGATION OF DUTIES
    See also Assignment
Conjoined with assignment, 210–211
Delegability of duties, 209
Express assumption of duties, 210
In general, 207–211
Nondelegable duty, effect of attempt to assign, 209–210
Novation distinguished, 208–209
Restriction on delegation, 209
Rights of obligee against delegee, 210–211
Tender of performance by delegee, 211

DISCHARGE OF CONTRACTUAL DUTIES, 245–247
See also Accord and Satisfaction; Conditions; Frustration of Purpose; Impossibility and Impracticability; Modification; Novation; Releases; Rescission; Statute of Limitations

DISCLOSURE
See Nondisclosure

DIVISIBLE CONTRACTS
Employment contracts, 234–235
"Entire" contract, 234
Illegal contracts, 174
In general, 234–235

DURESS
Defense to enforcement of contract, 156–157
Exception to parol evidence rule, 124

ELECTRONIC CONTRACTS
Browsewrap terms, 131
Clickwrap terms, 130–131
In general, 104, 130
U.E.T.A., 104, 130

EMPLOYMENT CONTRACTS
Assignment of wages, 202
Damages, 255, 262–263
Divisible contracts, 234–235

EQUAL DIGNITY STATUTES, 169–170

EXCLUSIVE DEALING CONTRACTS, 20–21
See also Output Contracts; Conditions, Excuse; Requirements Contracts

EXCUSE OF CONDITIONS, 223–225
See also Breach of Contract; Conditions, Excuse; Divisible Contracts; Impossibility and Impracticability; Prevention of Condition of Other Party's Performance; Repudiation; Substantial Performance; Waiver

EXECUTORY ACCORD
See Accord and Satisfaction

FIRM OFFERS
See Offer and Acceptance

FORM CONTRACTS
    See also Unconscionability
Contract formation, problems of, 69–79
Exculpatory clauses, 160
Last shot rule, 69–70

FRAUD
See Misrepresentation

FRUSTRATION OF PURPOSE, 244–245
See also Impossibility

FULL-PAYMENT CHECKS, 36–38

GAP FILLERS, 139–141

GOOD FAITH
See Requirements Contracts; Sale of Goods Contracts

GUARANTIES
See Suretyship, Contracts of

ILLEGALITY
In general, 174–176
In pari delicto, 174–175
Indirect aid of illegal objective, 174
Licensing requirements, 175–176
Locus penitentiae, 174
Malum in se, 174–175
Malum prohibitum, 175
Severable contracts, 174
Supervening illegality as excuse for nonperformance, 241

ILLUSORY PROMISES, 11–24
See also Consideration

IMPLICATION
See Interpretation and Implication

IMPLIED-IN-FACT CONTRACTS, 57–58, 99–100

IMPLIED-IN-LAW CONTRACTS, 58

IMPOSSIBILITY AND IMPRACTICABILITY
    See also Frustration of Purpose
Construction contracts, 242–243
Death or illness in personal service contracts, 243
Destruction
    Of source of supply, 242
    Of subject matter, 241–243
Discharge of duty as result of, 241
Excuse of condition as result of, 225
Frustration of purpose distinguished, 244–245
Impossibility includes impracticability, 241
In general, 241–244
Land sale contracts, 243
Partial impracticability, 244
Personal service contracts, 243
Repair contracts, 243
Sale of goods contracts, 243
Supervening illegality, 241
Temporary impracticability, 244

INDEFINITENESS
See also Interpretation and Implication
"Agreements to agree," 142–143
Alternative promises, 17–18, 144
Certainty of terms required, 135–136
Distributorship contracts, 139
Employment contracts, 137–139
In general, 135–147
Intent to contract, 136–137
Objective standard of implication, 19, 142
Option re performance reserved to one party, 143–144
Part performance as cure, 141
Preliminary agreements, 145–146
Price omission of, 136–137
Reliance on indefinite contract, 146–147
Time for performance, omission of, 137–139
U.C.C. provisions, 139–141, 143–144
Written contract contemplated, 145

INFANCY
See Capacity to Contract

INJUNCTIVE RELIEF
See Specific Performance

INSOLVENCY, 230

INSURANCE CONTRACTS
Assignment of, 195
Silence as acceptance, 101

INTERPRETATION AND IMPLICATION
See also Rules of Construction
Course of dealing, 116
Course of performance, 116
Doubtful provision, interpretation as promise or condition, 218–220
Extrinsic evidence, 115–116
Good faith, general obligation of, 19–20
Implication
    Of promise, 20, 23–24
    Of terms, 136–139
Objective theory of interpretation, 55
    Exceptions to, 114–115
Parol evidence rule, exception to, 120–129
Peerless rule, 114–115
Standards of interpretation, 114–117
Trade usage. *See* Usage of trade
Usage, 116–117
Usage of trade, 117

LAND SALE CONTRACTS
Assumption of mortgage, 183–184, 196
Damages, 261–262
Destruction of premises, risk of, 243
Impossibility of performance, 243
Writing, requirement of. *See* Statute of Frauds

LIMITATION OF LIABILITY
See Unconscionability; Exculpatory clauses

LIQUIDATED DAMAGES
See Damages

LIQUIDATED OBLIGATIONS
Payment of lesser amount as discharge of, 32–37, 247

MAILBOX RULE, 104–110
See also Offer and Acceptance; Correspondence as means of

MAILING OF UNORDERED MERCHANDISE, 102–103

MATERIAL BREACH
Distinguished from minor breach, 235
    Parties' agreement, 236
        "time is of essence" provision, 236
    Repudiation, 235
Effect of breach, 236
Relation to substantial performance, 237–238

MENTAL INCAPACITY
See Capacity to Contract

MIRROR IMAGE RULE, 69–79
See also Offer and Acceptance

MISREPRESENTATION
Defense to enforcement of contract, 154
Exception to parol evidence rule, 124
Voidable obligation, promise to perform, 49–50

MISTAKE
Assumption of risk, 148–149
In general, 147–153
Judgment errors, 149, 150
Mistranscription of contract, 150–151
Misunderstanding, 151
Mutual mistake, 148–149
Parol evidence rule, exception to, 124
Transmission by intermediary, 151–153
Unilateral mistake, 149–150

MODIFICATION OF CONTRACT
Assigned contract, 204
In general, 29–30
No-oral-modification clause, 127–128
Statute of Frauds, 165
Writing, requirement of, 127–128

MORAL OR PAST CONSIDERATION, 48–52
See also Consideration

MORTGAGES
See Land Sale Contracts, Assumption of Mortgage; Third-Party Beneficiary Contracts, Recurring Third-Party Beneficiary Cases, Assumption of Mortgage

MUTUAL ASSENT
Express contracts, 57
Implied contracts
    Implied in fact, 57–58
    Implied in law, 58
Objective theory, 55–57

MUTUALITY OF OBLIGATION, 11–24

NONDISCLOSURE, 154–156

NO-ORAL-MODIFICATION CLAUSE
See Modification of Contract

NOVATION, 199, 208–209

OFFER AND ACCEPTANCE
Advertisements, 60–61
Auctions, 62–63
Bids by contractors and subcontractors, 63–64, 97
Conditional acceptance, effect of, 68–74
Conduct, contracts implied from
    Implied-in-fact contracts, 57–58
    Implied-in-law contracts, 58
Correspondence
    As means of offer and acceptance
        Medium of communication of, 106–109

Misdelivered, 110
Timely dispatch of, 105–106
Time period stated in offer, interpretation of, 65, 105
Under option, 105, 106
Waiver of notice of, 93–94
When effective, 91, 104–105
Withdrawal or repudiation of dispatched acceptance, effect of, 112–113
Crossed offers, 113
In general, 104–113
"Mailbox rule," 93, 104–110
Rejection, when effective, 111–112
Revocation, when effective, 110
Counteroffer, effect of, 67–68
Crossed acceptance and revocation, 110
Crossed offers, 113
Death of offeror, effect of, 88–89
Email
When received, 104
Firm offers, 8, 82–84
Lapse of time
No time for acceptance fixed in offer, 65–66
Time for acceptance fixed in offer, 65
Late acceptance, effect of, 103, 106
"Mailbox rule." See Correspondence, As means of offer and acceptance, above
Mailing of unordered merchandise, 102–103
Mirror-image rule, 69–79
Modes of acceptance. See also Conduct, Contracts implied from, above; Silence as acceptance, below
Act, 94–97
Act substituted for promise, 93
Ambiguity as to whether offer requires act or promise, 98–99
Promise, 90–94
Silence, 99–103
Tender of performance where offer requires acceptance by promise, 91
Use of subcontractor's bid, 97
Mutual assent
Express contracts, 57
Implied contracts, 57–58
Objective theory of contracts, 55–57
Notice of acceptance
Act required by offer, 94–95
Promise required by offer, 93–94
Offer
Advertisements, 60–61
Legal significance of, 58
Offering circulars, 61–62
What constitutes, 58–60
Preliminary negotiations, distinguished from offers, 59
Qualified acceptance. See Conditional acceptance, above
Rejection, Effect of, 66–67
Reliance on offer for bilateral contract, effect of, 46–47
Repudiation of acceptance, 112–113
Revocation. See also Correspondence, As means of offer and acceptance, above; Revocation; Unilateral Contracts, Revocation of offer after performance begun
Assignments, 195
Communication, requirement of, 81–82
Firm offers, 8, 82–84
In general, 80–88
Options, 83
Sale of goods contracts, 84–85
Rewards, as motivation for act constituting acceptance, 96
Shrinkwrap terms, 129–130

Silence as acceptance
Exercise of dominion, 102
In general, 99–103
Insurance cases, 101
Late acceptance, 103
Mailing of unordered merchandise, 102
Previous dealings, effect of, 100
Solicitation by offeree, 100–101
Termination of offeree's power of acceptance
Changed circumstances, 89
Conditional or qualified acceptance, 68–73
Counteroffer, 67–68
Death of offeror, 88–89
In general, 64–89
Inquiry as to terms of offer, 67
Lapse of time, 65–66
Options, 66–68
Rejection, 66–67
Revocation. See Revocation above
U.E.T.A., 104, 130
Unilateral contracts. See Unilateral Contracts
Withdrawal of acceptance, 113

ONLINE CONTRACTS
See Electronic Contracts

OPTIONS
Acceptance of, when effective, 105
Consideration, requirement of, 8–9
Counteroffer, effect of, 67–68
Death or incapacity of offeror, effect of, 89
Revocability of, 83

OUTPUT CONTRACTS, 21–24
See also Requirements Contracts

PAROL EVIDENCE RULE
Any relevant evidence test, 119
Exceptions to rule
Collateral terms, 120
Conditions precedent, 124–125
Interpretation of contract, 125–127
Lack of consideration, 124
"Naturally omitted" terms, 120–122
Separate consideration, 120
Face of instrument test, 119
Fraud, use of parol to show, 124
Integration, what constitutes, 118–119
Modifications, 127–129
Partial integration, 123
Plain meaning rule, 125
Statement of rule, 118

PAST CONSIDERATION
See Consideration

PENALTY CLAUSES
See Damages

PREEXISTING LEGAL DUTY, 24–38
See also Consideration

PRELIMINARY NEGOTIATIONS
See Indefiniteness; Offer and acceptance

PREVENTION OF CONDITION OF OTHER PARTY'S PERFORMANCE
Closing down business as, 223–225
In general, 223
Wrongfulness, requirement of, 223

PROMISSORY ESTOPPEL
    See also Unilateral Contracts, Revocation of offer after performance begun
Consideration, compared with, 47
Donative promises, reliance on, 46–47
Former rule, 46
Modern rule, 46–47
Substantial reliance not required, 47

PROSPECTIVE INABILITY TO PERFORM, 229–230, 240–241
    See also Conditions, Order of performance

QUANTUM MERUIT
    See Quasi-Contractual Recovery

QUASI-CONTRACT
    See Quasi-Contractual Recovery

QUASI-CONTRACTUAL RECOVERY
    See also Restitution
Benefits conferred
    Under contract within Statute of Frauds, 171–172
Breach of contract, remedy for, 268–269
Implied-in-law contracts, 58, 103
Impossibility of performance, 244
In general, 58, 103

REAL PARTY IN INTEREST IN ASSIGNMENTS, 192

REJECTION, 66–67
When effective, 111–112

RELEASES
Consideration, 10–11, 246
Discharge of contractual duty by use of, 246

RELIANCE
See Promissory Estoppel; Unilateral contracts, Revocation of offer after performance begun

REMEDIES
See Breach of contract; Damages; Quasi-contractual recovery; Specific performance

REPUDIATION, 235
See also Breach of contract, Anticipatory breach

REQUIREMENTS CONTRACTS
Assignment of, 195
Consideration, 21–24
Going out of business
    As excuse by prevention, 223–225
    Implied promise to stay in business, 22–24
Good faith obligation, 22
Quantity limitations, 22

RESCISSION
By mutual agreement, 30, 245–246
Contracts for benefit of third person, 190–191, 246
Writing, requirement of, 246

RESTITUTION
    See also Quasi-Contractual Recovery
Basis for, 103
Disgorgement, 270
Liability of minor for value of necessaries, 172–173
Liability of person lacking mental capacity for value of necessaries, 173
Measure of damages, 251–252, 268–270
Part performance prior to circumstances of impracticability, 244
Relative to substantial performance, 234

Where contract falls within Statute of Frauds, 171–172

REVOCATION
    See also Offer and Acceptance
Communication of, 81
Firm offers, 82–85
In general, 80–88
Offers for unilateral contracts, 85–88
When effective, 81, 110

REWARDS
See Offer and Acceptance

RULES OF CONSTRUCTION
Course of dealing, 116
Course of performance, 116
Trade usage, 117

SALE OF GOODS CONTRACTS
Acceptance stating additional or different terms, 69, 71–79
    Knockout rule, 77–78
Adequate assurance of performance, 230, 240–241
Assignment, 211
Duty to mitigate damages, 255
Firm offer, 8, 84–85
Full-payment checks, 36–38
General obligation of good faith, 19–20, 214–215
Implied promise to use best efforts, 20–21
Impossibility of performance, 241–244
Indefiniteness, 139–141
Modification, 29–30, 127–129
Notice of acceptance of offer for unilateral contract, 95
Offer calling for acceptance by either promise or act, 98–99
Parol evidence rule, 122–123
Perfect tender rule, 232–233
Price to be fixed, 139
Reasonable notification of termination, 15
Release, 246
Remedies for breach, 256–261
Requirements and output contracts, 22–24
Retraction of repudiation, 239–240
Statute of Frauds, 164–165
Unconscionability, 157, 159, 161

SALE OF LAND
See Land Sale Contracts

SEAL, CONTRACTS UNDER, 44

SEVERABLE CONTRACTS
See Divisible Contracts

SHRINKWRAP CONTRACTS
See Offer and Acceptance

SILENCE AS ACCEPTANCE
See Offer and acceptance

SPECIFIC PERFORMANCE
    See also Damages, Specific performance
Assignment of future rights, 202
Consideration, adequacy of, 5
Part performance of land sale contracts, 163

STATUTE OF FRAUDS
Auctions, 170
Electronic records, as satisfying, 169
Estoppel to plead, 163, 171
Guaranty contracts. *See* Suretyship provision, below
Investment securities, 167
Land sale contracts, 162–163
    Part performance of, 163

Main purpose rule, 167–168
Marriage provision, 165–166
Memorandum, requirement of, 168–170
Modification of contract within Statute, 127, 165
Noncompliance with, effect of, 170–171
One-year provision, 166–167
    Part performance, 167
Part performance
    Land provision, 163
    One-year provision, 167
    Sale of goods, 164
Promise to pay debt barred by statute of limitations, 49
Promise to pay debt discharged by bankruptcy, 50
Purpose of Statute, 162
Reliance, effect of, 172
Rescission of contract within Statute, 246
Restitution of benefits conferred, 171–172
Sale of goods contracts
    Admissions, 164
    Goods made specially to order, 164
    In general, 164–168
    Part payment, 164
    Written confirmation, receipt of, 164
Suretyship provision, 167–168

STATUTE OF LIMITATIONS
Promise to pay debt barred by statute, 48–49

SUBCONTRACTOR BIDS
Status as offers, 63–64
Use of as acceptance thereof, 97

SUBSTANTIAL PERFORMANCE
Construction contracts, 232
In general, 231
Measure of damages, 233–234
Recovery in restitution, 234
Relation to material breach, 237–238
What constitutes, 231–232

SURETYSHIP, CONTRACTS OF
Consideration requirement, 8–9
Writing requirement. *See* Statute of Frauds, Suretyship provision

TENDER OF PERFORMANCE
By offeree where offer for bilateral contract, 91

TERMINATION OF CONTRACT
At will without notice, 14–15

THIRD-PARTY BENEFICIARY CONTRACTS
Beneficiary's rights
    Against promisee, 189–190
    Against promisor, 178–181
Creditor beneficiaries, 179–180
Defenses available to promisor, 188
Donee beneficiaries, 180–181
Examples
    Assumption of mortgage, 183–184
    Government contracts, 185–186
    Surety bonds, 186–187
    Would-be legatees, 184–185
Incidental beneficiaries, 181
In general, 178–179
Intended beneficiaries, 182–183
Promisee's rights against promisor, 189–190
Termination of beneficiary's rights, 190–191

UNCONSCIONABILITY
    See also Consumer Protection
Adhesion contracts, 158
Disclaimers and limitation of remedies, 161
Disparity in value, 5
Exculpatory clauses, 160
Substantive unconscionability, 159–160
Unfair surprise, 158–159

UNDUE INFLUENCE, 157

UNILATERAL CONTRACTS
Bilateral contracts distinguished from, 15, 85
Notice of acceptance, requirement of, 94–95
Obligation of offeree, 97
Offers for
    Ambiguity as to whether acceptance requires act or promise, 98–99
Performance
    Not motivated by offer, 96
    Preparation, compared to, 87–88
Revocation of offer after performance begun, 86–88

UNJUST ENRICHMENT
See Quasi-Contractual Recovery

UNLIQUIDATED OBLIGATIONS
Payment of some amount as discharge of, 33–34

WAIVER
Consideration for, 30, 42–43
Definition of, 42
Enforceability, 42–43
Excuse of condition by, 225
Modification distinguished, 30
Of notice of acceptance, 93–94
Retraction of, 43
Waiver-of-defense clauses, 203

WARRANTIES
In assignments for consideration, 205
Sale of goods contracts, 161
    Disclaimers, 161
    Limitations, 161

WRITING, REQUIREMENT OF
In contract. *See* Modification of Contract, Writing, Requirement of; Statute of Frauds